Mattley

Contemporary Sociological Theory

CONSULTING EDITOR: Charles Page, UNIVERSITY OF MASSACHUSETTS

Contemporary Sociological Theory

Edited by Fred E. Katz STATE UNIVERSITY OF NEW YORK AT BUFFALO

Random House **New York**

ISBN: 0–394–30332–6

Library of Congress Catalog Card Number: 70–121972

Manufactured in the United States of America by The Kingsport Press, Inc.,
Kingsport, Tenn.

First Edition
987654321

Dedicated to the memory of **Max, Jenny,** and **Ludwig Katz**

Contents

Introduction

There exists a passion for comprehension . . . ALBERT EINSTEIN

This book has its origin in a sense of unease about the planless and aimless nature of the training of sociological theorists. Many sociologists appear to accept the stereotype of theorists as people who deal in esoterica and who must have most unusual talent. This is an unsociological perspective toward one whose activities are carried out as a social role in a social context. The role of theorist has specific components and can be learned. The components include mastery over a body of social knowledge and, perhaps, some useful areas of ignorance. Also included is a distinctive posture toward reality. That posture consists of skepticism toward things as they appear, passionate commitment to a search for order (and faith in the existence of order, somewhere, somehow), and venturesomeness in inventing and testing abstract schemes. The posture includes the ability to engage in playfulness as well as in deadly earnest quests; and it includes detachment and hard commitments.

For anyone learning sociological theory there exist the challenges of getting acquainted with theories of the present and the past and getting some kind of overview and synthesis of the major approaches.[1] A crucial additional challenge lies in trying to learn to do theoretical work—here *doing* theory is the issue. The problem of how to do theory has, of course, received a great deal of attention. The most active efforts in the past twenty years have been those of philosophers of science and certain sociologists, notably Gross and Zetterberg, who have focused on the analysis of the structure of theory.[2] The work in this area has aroused considerable attention. However, it emphasizes mainly the dissection and analysis of theory, rather than the invention of new theory. Therefore, it has a rather indirect bearing on the specific problem of how to train theorists. At best, it develops some necessary skepticism about existing theories.

The theorist is essentially an artisan who must learn his trade by doing. He differs from the scholar, who is in the business of appreciation rather than the sacrilegious business of reformulating existing thought patterns or developing new explanatory principles. Ideally, there should be training programs for theorists, just as there are now programs that train persons to be good empirical field researchers, with emphasis on data gathering and data analysis.

To learn the role of theorist, one must do theory. One way of doing theory is to serve an apprenticeship under a practitioner—studying and working under the tutelage of a person who is an active theorist. This is probably the way in which most theorists are actually trained. What is learned in such a situation is not so much a set of particular theories as an orientation and stance toward phenomena. Another way of learning to do theory is by carrying out exercises in theory-formation. For this purpose, one can conceive of workbooks that give guidance for doing exercises in various kinds of theories.[3] The present book of readings is a second alternative. It offers a sampling of existing theories. The readings illustrate that while the function of a theory is to explain concrete events, the function of the theorist is to create analytic devices, conceptual schemes, and models. The theorist must have considerable freedom to try out various perspectives and must be willing to accept three fundamental facts: Theory deals only with *aspects* of concrete reality. Theoretical schemes inherently involve arbitrary decisions about what is relevant and what is irrelevant. And, finally, the schemes and models, though arbitrarily created, must be applied and pursued doggedly, with fervor for and immersion in the particular scheme. This emphasis is reiterated in the introductions to the three parts of the book. The aim here is not to include the complete field of theoretical exposition. The book neither surveys all approaches nor explores any one approach to its fullest extent. It is hoped that enough material is offered to illustrate the power of various major approaches as they are used to carry out explanations. But the real objective is to show the regimen under which the sociological theorist operates, what sort of options are available to him and, even more importantly, what kind of discipline governs his work.

It will be evident that work with theory has a dual nature. One aspect of this duality involves theorizing, or doing theory—that is, revising, reformulating, and replacing established theories and formulating new ones. The other aspect involves sufficient, occasionally even dogmatic, adherence to particular theoretical perspectives to enable these perspectives to be thoroughly explored. The selected readings in this book tend to focus on the second aspect; the editorial introductions try to do justice to the first.

The choice of the selections was dictated by the conviction that a book on theory should present a specific point of view. Sheer eclecticism and "complete" surveys of fields[4] tend to create confusion. A person who has had a full exposure to one orientation will be in a stronger position after the exposure. Not only will he have a firm grounding in his orientation, but he will also be more qualified to reject some or all parts of that orientation. His rejection, if it comes, will be made on an informed basis rather than on the basis of hearsay and secondary acquaintance.

This book emphasizes structural sociology. This approach does not imply a static conception of sociology. Indeed, if other sciences can be a guide, structural formulations can provide the best tools for understanding dynamics. Thus, the calculus in mathematics is a structural conception of rates of change, and the DNA principle in biology and the periodic table in chemistry are structural formulations that help to specify the direction and form of change in these fields. In all these, the critical ingredients are the identification of some sort of fundamental units and the formulation of precisely stated rules for combination and transformation of these units. This also applies to cybernetic systems, where the fundamental units are items of information that are processed and utilized. What are the fundamental units of sociology? The answers depend on the conceptual system one chooses to use and the problems one wishes to solve. A social behaviorist, because of his emphasis on the individual's involvement in person-to-person interactions, might agree with Don Martindale that they are "the self-conscious actions of individuals."[5] Structural sociologists, on the other hand, regard roles and institutions as the basic units. They are sometimes misunderstood because the individual person is not the fundamental unit.

As the selections will show, structuralists work with a great variety of schemes and concepts. Structuralists share the assumptions that orderly processes exist and that some sort of fundamental units, and their properties, can be discovered. But aside from sharing these assumptions, they do a variety of different forms of theorizing. This book tries to illustrate this variety and to demonstrate that all of these forms of theorizing are approaches in the continuing work of creating theories.

Does structural sociology address itself to the problems of the real world—to creating a lasting peace, to social injustice, to the present revolution that demands an expansion of the quality of life beyond making a living and toward creative participation in one's personal destiny and in one's society? These problems call for the redesigning of societies. Since the time of Comte and Saint-Simon there have been sociologists who have, indeed, tried to design better societies.

Structural sociology has a two-part approach to the pressing problems of the world. One part consists of trying to understand and improve the process of doing sociological work. Here the focus is on the very process of harnessing sociological knowledge and bringing this knowledge to bear on specific concrete problems. This is discussed more fully in the introduction to Part III, "Concerning Concreteness." The main point is that it seems to be just as important to clarify the process of harnessing knowledge as it is to focus on the actual theories about the social problems of our day. From a theoretical point of view it is assumed that knowledge harnessing is itself a social process whose properties and structure can be understood.

The second part of the approach to social problems is more indirect. It consists of deliberate development of valid abstract systems of knowledge. The main assumption is that the power of a theory—its capacity to offer accurate explanations and predictions—depends on its having been formulated in such a way that it has the generalized character of stating something significant about *many* situations. This is not apt to lead to theories of poverty among Mexican Americans in the Southwest but to theories of intergroup and intercultural relations. It will not lead to theories about black and white conflict but to theories of dominance and submission, social integration and social differentiation, and so forth.

In the heat of an ongoing social movement, there is great temptation to accept the layman's formulation of what constitutes "the problem." What is real in commonsense terms may, in fact, be an intellectual dead end. There is a paradox here. The theorist must be prepared to maintain considerable detachment from the pressures of his surroundings if he is to make a significant contribution to the world—to the world of sociological knowledge and to the immediate world where sociological knowledge is needed. In this book, several selections in Part III, "Concerning Concreteness," implicitly cope with the task of improving human societies. In addition, Amitai Etzioni's essay in Part II deals with this problem rather explicitly.

The book is divided into three parts. "Concerning Frameworks," "Concerning Models," and "Concerning Concreteness." This forms a sequence from the more abstract to the more concrete. Efforts to map out the fundamental boundaries of the sociological realm are included under "Concerning Frameworks."

Here, as in the rest of the book, the selections do not make up a complete version of one framework but, instead, show a number of different approaches to the process of creating a framework.

Part II, "Concerning Models," is perhaps the most explicitly theoretical portion of the book. It includes a number of separate and fairly specialized theories. Each commands attention because it is intrinsically relevant and interesting sociologically. Each requires further empirical verification and further theoretical development.

Part III, "Concerning Concreteness," illustrates efforts to apply sociological theories to the concrete social world. It includes efforts to explain specific historical occurrences and to help produce strategies for creating a planned future. In short, it aims to understand concrete social events and also to forge tools for controlling such events. Here, as in the other parts, the selections are rather short; the objective is to whet the appetite rather than to satisfy.

Finally, all three parts are subdivided into macro- and micro- units. In the first decades of the present century, microsociology dominated Western sociology, especially in the United States. Now, however, large-scale phenomena are receiving renewed attention. This is necessary in a world that is becoming increasingly capable of transcending community and even national barriers to communication. Conceptually, it may not be important to separate macro- and microsociology. It seems worth preserving the distinction, however, since it represents a continuing division of labor among practicing sociologists.

Notes

1. There are various published works that codify areas of sociological work. See Bruce J. Biddle and Edwin J. Thomas, eds., *Role Theory: Concepts and Research*, New York: Wiley, 1966, especially Parts I–III. See also Robert M. Marsh, *Comparative Sociology: A Codification of Cross-Societal Analysis*, New York: Harcourt, Brace & World, 1967. Implicitly, most readers are efforts at codification. For a recent attempt to codify the whole of present-day sociological theory, see Walter L. Wallace, ed., *Sociological Theory, An Introduction*, Chicago: Aldine, 1969, especially Part I.
2. See, for example, Llewellyn Gross, ed., *Symposium on Sociological Theory*, New York: Harper & Row, 1959. A similar, although more synthetic effort can be found in Hans L. Zetterberg, *On Theory and Verification in Sociology*, Totowa, N. J.: Bedminster Press, 1963.
3. Arthur Stinchcombe's excellent book would serve this purpose. See Arthur Stinchcombe, *Constructing Social Theory*, New York: Harcourt, Brace & World, 1968.
4. Books that claim to be surveys of entire fields frequently do, in fact, have a distinct point of view. Perhaps it is a matter of explicitly facing up to and acknowledging one's blinders. Yet even with the best of intentions, an author is frequently unable to place himself accurately. After all, Marx claimed that he was not a Marxist, and Radcliffe-Brown believed that he was not a functionalist.
5. Don Martindale, *Institutions, Organizations and Mass Society*, Boston: Houghton Mifflin, 1966, p. 110.

Part One | Concerning Frameworks

Frameworks are conceptual devices intended to help bring about some sort of order in a field. They provide categories in which to place discrete items of information into useful contexts. They also help to define criteria for judging the relevance of current scientific activities to previous work. They can, in short, be of help in the sifting and sorting process that is required in attempting to cope with the flood of existing research activity. But more important, frameworks can define the basic intellectual guidelines of a discipline. They do so by formalizing the main assumptions into some kind of orderly scheme that, in turn, acts as the starting point for specific theorems and predictions. However, frameworks also present a potential danger. They can lead to a modern version of scholasticism; they can become logical exercises in building classification upon classification, whose relevance to anything in the real world becomes increasingly remote. There are no absolute guidelines for judging when frameworks have ceased to be fruitful and have become burdens to progress. Frameworks, like other scientific formulations, serve their purpose best when they produce their own obsolescence—when they produce levels of knowledge that require new frameworks.

It is fashionable to carry out interdisciplinary research and to be eclectic in the kinds of theoretical concepts used. Doubtless, many old boundaries of discipline are no longer fruitful. The political scientist studies and theorizes about social stratification; the sociologist studies political relations among nations, and so forth. When one deals with concrete problems, eclecticism is absolutely necessary. A concrete problem, be it a war between two countries or a riot in a city, typically involves the convergence of a variety of different forces. To say that such problems are basically sociological, political, psychological, or economic is simply wrong. All of these dimensions, and others, are involved. The problem is to determine how to harness all knowledge that is relevant to the concrete problem at hand. The need for eclecticism with respect to concrete problems will be taken up in Part III of this book.

Frameworks are addressed to a different set of problems. They constitute a strategy for developing coherent *analytic theory*, not explanations of concrete events. To be sure, a theory that has no conceivable bearing on concrete reality is of little use. But there is a crucial difference between these two strategies. The science of analytics deals with *aspects* of reality and develops these into orderly schemes. The result of this is generalization; one can say *something* that applies to *many* situations. In contrast, concreteness is devoted to saying *many* things about *one* situation. Thus the analytic formulations about gravitational force apply to many concrete situations. But they do not fully explain the fall of a particular apple from a particular tree at a particular time: they do not explain the swaying of the tree's limbs that led to the fall of the apple, the actions of the boy who shook the limbs and caused them to sway, or the behavior of the girl who challenged the boy to shake the limbs. Such concrete situations require the use of eclectic knowledge. In contrast, in a strategy for developing analytic theory, a framework must, first and foremost, have recognizable internal coherence. The analytic concepts that are used must have some common base, and they must be interrelated in a way that does not do violence to that base.   For example, a framework might describe social organizations in terms of social positions.   It would emphasize systems of interrelated positions, where each position has relatively specific boundaries and where the expected behavior for the occupant of the position is built into the specifications of the position.   Such a framework omits psychological characteristics of the occupants of the positions.   One may work out a scheme showing how personality characteristics of the participants in the organization can be linked to the positional framework. This would be a legitimate procedure, but it would not necessarily be relevant to the position-focused framework.   A complete positional scheme of organizational structure and processes is possible without reference to the personality characteristics of the participating persons.

The analytic process of building a framework requires willingness to stick to a few concepts and carry these as far as possible while resisting the temptation to add concepts that will assure greater "completeness" in the concrete sense.   Some scholars use the term "framework" for any kind of topical outline.   It is probably wise to restrict the term to analytically integrated schemes. Analytic integration implies using a few variables consistently and systematically and developing them into a scheme.   In this framework building the self-conscious restraint, the deliberate use of only *some* variables, is the basic source of strength.   All this is the very antithesis of eclecticism, which necessarily prevails in any attempt to explain concrete phenomena.

There are various frameworks in contemporary sociology.   These are often presented as though they were polarities—conflict theory versus functionalism, radical versus establishment sociology, and behavioral versus normative-prescriptive sociology.   All these distinctions contain some measure of truth, and also a good deal of oversimplification and confusion.   Yet taken together, they suggest a degree of vitality in the field of sociology.   There are various efforts to create syntheses among existing factions.[1]   Still, distinctly different approaches to creating frameworks remain.

The present part, indeed the whole book, is based on the conviction that, although a formal description of various approaches may seem to meet the criteria of scholarship, it is not very useful to the student who actually wants to learn sociology.   It is best to see frameworks in action, to see them being used to explain phenomena rather than presented in formal terms.   This does more justice to the actual learning process and to the present state of sophistication of sociology.   But showing frameworks in action creates problems: One must necessarily be arbitrary in the choice of illustrative material: the illustrations may divert attention from the frameworks because they dwell on substantive empirical material; each illustration necessarily offers an incomplete exposition of each total framework.   The matter of incompleteness is an unsolvable problem.   The motivated and curious student can, of course, go to the original source and get more information.   The objective here is to present enough material to convey the distinctive character of various approaches to the process of creating frameworks.   This presentation must include scaffolding of assumptions, hypotheses, and so on. It must convey some sense of the cogency of the frameworks. The cogency of frameworks is a complicated matter. There are frameworks that have become tainted without having been scientifically refuted. And there are frameworks that remain cogent after scientific refutations have taken place. Both patterns are affected by the intrusion of external social forces into fields of science. Examples of the first, the easy tainting of frameworks, are the attacks against Einsteinian "Jewish" physics in Nazi Germany and attacks against Darwinian evolutionary theory in the American Bible Belt. Examples of the second, the stubborn persistence of "disproven" frameworks, are the persistence of the Lysenko interpretation of evolutionary theory in Communist Russia and the reemergence of evolutionary theory in anthropology, under Leslie White, after a generation of scholars had done their best to debunk the evolutionary theories of Morgan, Tyler, and Spencer. In social theory, Marxism remains cogent after the thorough refutation of Marxism by Max Weber. Doubtless Marxism is kept alive by its continuing political utilization in various societies rather than its scientific merits as an explanatory and predictive theory.

The fate of frameworks leaves the young scholar with problems. He does not want to begin his professional life wedded to a discarded framework. Why have a lifelong courtship with death? Yet, he must be aware that frameworks have a very uncertain death, as well as an uncertain life. The student's task is to learn to trust his informed intuition about frameworks, to assess which orientation best brings forth his own potentials. The present book tries to help the student by giving him a strong exposure to a very broadly conceived from of structural sociology, where innovativeness is encouraged by seeing the diversity that can coexist under an overarching framework.

Frameworks (and models, discussed in Part II) involve arbitrary sets of inter-dependent assumptions. They inevitably leave out much, but this may be helpful in tackling particular problems. Thus, Max Gluckman writes about psychologists' criticisms of economists and anthropologists for their "crude assumptions about human motivation." But Gluckman suggests that these economists and anthropologists may make "these neglectful assumptions knowingly and deliberately . . . [The] issue is not whether the assumptions are crude, but rather whether they materially affect the analysis and conclusions."[2]

The following selections lean toward functionalist positions as opposed to other existing frameworks. Other orientations, such as cybernetics and syntheses of various perspectives, are presented in Parts II and III of the book. The reason for giving such emphasis to functionalism at this point is that proponents of this position have developed seemingly viable frameworks most effectively; indeed, they are specialists in framework-building. This description of structural sociology, rather than surveys of diverse frameworks, presents the position that offers the strongest examples of frameworks.

MACROSCALE FRAMEWORKS

The selection from Talcott Parsons and Neil J. Smelser's *Economy and Society*, "Some Congruences Between Economic and Sociological Theory," sets forth the main features of a scheme that Professor Parsons developed over a number of years. The details of this scheme have tended to change with each publication, but the main points remain intact. Basically, Parsons has constructed a distinctively sociological framework.[3] The components of the framework include entities that are fairly closely identifiable in concrete terms, such as groups, associations, and organizations. But more important, they include social processes and structures as entities that are identifiable only by considering the part they play in a context.

Professor Parsons has repeatedly emphasized the idea that sociology, like other sciences, owes its power to its ability to develop distinctive abstractions and bring them into action. He has attempted to develop a distinctive set of sociological abstractions into a rather complete framework. Many features of the framework are illustrated in the Parsons and Smelser selection. Perhaps the most crucial feature is the way in which it offers a delineation of functional systems and shows how they create facilities for solving problems. Four fundamental types of problems are emphasized: (1) maintenance of value patterns and control of tensions; (2) integration, or solidarity, among parts of the system; (3) attainment of goals; (4) adaptation to the environment.

The authors make the case that many economic concepts find logical equivalents in other social processes and that economics can be regarded as a subsystem of society, both in its relation to other sectors of the society and internally as a social system in its own right. The framework can be (and has been) applied to other sectors of social life, such as politics and religion.

Robert N. Bellah's selection, "The Value System," is taken from a book that outlines the interdependence of religion and other social structures in Japan during the Tokugawa period, 1600–1868. The selection focuses on the ways in which values are incorporated into various social structures. It does so by utilizing many concepts from the Parsonian scheme, particularly the functional basis of delineating major social processes and the use of pattern variables for categorizing values.

The two selections by S. N. Eisenstadt illustrate that a distinctly structural approach to sociology can help to explain social change. In "Institutionalization and Change," the theme is that "the institutionalization of any system creates in its wake the possibilities for change." Basically, the framework concentrates on macroscopic institutions. Such institutions are similar to what anthropologists used to call culture complexes. Specifically, they consist of the patterns of interrelated values and the related, relatively organized behavior patterns that are embedded in the social order of a society. The principal institutions of a society use a considerable proportion of its resources and form the society's most conspicuous structural features. Thus, modern societies tend to institutionalize large-scale industrial production and centralized political administration. Eisenstadt's thesis is that the very process of institutionalization—the way the value patterns and the related behavior come to be included in an existing social order—involves compromises and stresses. The nature of this process and the internal structure of institutions themselves create the necessary conditions for social change.   Indeed, Eisenstadt holds that one can predict the direction that change will take if one understands a society's institutions.

Eisenstadt also dwells on the sequences and transformations in the process of grafting new patterns onto an existing social order.   This type of historical analysis can make prediction difficult, and it threatens to become overwhelmingly detailed and discursive.   However, Eisenstadt guards against this by coming back again and again to the sociological concepts that explain the structure of institutions and the process whereby they come to be incorporated into a social order.

The second selection by Eisenstadt, "Transformation of Social, Political, and Cultural Orders in Modernization," focuses on conditions that are conducive to the development of "modernized" societies.   The thesis is that modernization requires certain institutional structures that have some measure of autonomy and, most important, a capacity to adapt to continuously changing conditions.   He uses the cases of China, Japan, India, and the Islamic countries to show how institutional structures that have such characteristics may emerge.   Eisenstadt then considers whether, once emerged, they are adequate for dealing with modern conditions.   He pays particular attention to existing value patterns and group affiliations in relation to political structures.   However, the institutional structure is seen as only one of several major factors in the modernization process. It creates the necessary flexibility "under which more active groups and elites could attempt to institute new principles of cultural direction and social integration.   But the mere existence of structural flexibility neither assured that such groups would appear nor indicated the type of integrative orientation they would develop."

The Eisenstadt selections use a framework that centers on institutions as the basic structures and institutionalization as the basic process.   There are two additional features of the framework: collectivities—such as families, social classes, castes—and overarching value patterns.

The empirical focus on historical events introduces sequential processes that depend on unique occurrences, and idiosyncratic blendings and developments. This kind of "concreteness" suggests that the selections could have been placed in Part III, under "Concerning Concreteness."   They are placed under "Concerning Frameworks" because of their distinctive focus on a theory of inter- and intra-institutional processes.

Claude Lévi-Strauss, as Robert Zimmerman explains in "Lévi-Strauss and the Primitive," attempts to delineate the structural features of man's thought about social reality.   He proposes that there are fundamental modes of thought to be discovered that have been employed by all mankind, from primitive to modern man.   The nature of the "logic" involved in these modes of thought might easily baffle the person who has been brought up on Aristotelian logic.   The thought patterns are not above man's natural world but, instead, correspond to his actual involvement and participation in the world.   They include connections among apparently disconnected items.   Professor Zimmerman's essay provides a good overview of Lévi-Strauss's work.   Toward the end of the essay there is a critique of the structural approach such as Lévi-Strauss uses.   The approach is criticized for its remoteness from reality and from passion, for "its trivialization of our deepest instincts."   A structuralist might reply that one can enjoy sugar even if one knows its chemical formula, that is, its structure.   However, the critique is cogently stated and, in fact, summarizes a point of view that is frequently heard.

The selection from *The Savage Mind*, "Totem and Caste," illustrates Lévi-Strauss's conception of the relation between groups.   This includes a discussion of exchange processes and affiliations and separations, and the varying degrees of complexity with which these can be expressed.   He pays particular attention in the latter part of the selection to the fragmentation of groups and the implications of this occurrence.

MICROSCALE FRAMEWORKS

Probably the most complete structural-functional framework for studying societies has been developed by Marion J. Levy, Jr.[4]   He carries his framework through with awesome perseverence, lucidity, and precision.   For theorists his work is useful not merely as a functional scheme addressed to the questions: which problems must every society solve and how are the solutions institutionalized?   It is useful for its commitment to the isolation of social structures amid the ongoing flux of human behavior.   It is strictly sociologistic sociology; it does not incorporate psychology or other adjacent disciplines.[5]   Levy also makes a very explicit distinction between concrete and analytic structures.   Finally, although his work is committed to scientific explanations, it does not dwell on the rituals of science.   For instance, data-gathering techniques, indeed, the entire technology of handling data, receive scant attention.   But attention is paid to clear, orderly thinking that is attuned to empirical reality.   There is also open admission of the arbitrariness of scientific constructs.

The selection from Levy, "Aspects of any Relationship," is included in the micro-category because it deals with a limited feature in the hierarchy of social structures, namely, the ways interactions between two or more actors are defined. The selection is taken from a book that develops a comprehensive comparison between the social structure of modernized and nonmodernized societies. Levy's "aspects" refer to analytic structure.   A chair is a concrete entity; its aspects include mass, color, shape, and so on.   The following value aspects of social relationships are postulated and used for making systematic comparisons among different structures: rational-traditional, universalistic-particularistic, functionally specific-functionally diffuse, avoidant-intimate, individualistic-responsible, and hierarchical-nonhierarchical.   They are an elaboration of Parsons' pattern variables.   A number of generalizations and predictions are offered.

The selection by Siegfried F. Nadel, "On Social Systems," offers another approach to structural frameworks.   It is a morphological point of view, that regards roles as social positions and social structures as systems of interrelated positions.

Without being overly abstruse, the author develops a calculus to add considerable precision to the analysis of social structures. And, like Levy, he shows the possibility of deriving theorems and predictions from a structural perspective. Nadel's scheme, however, is probably somewhat closer to being in a workable mathematical form than is Levy's formulation.

"Regulation of Want Conversion: Structural Mechanisms," by David Easton, a political scientist, presents a portion of a framework that portrays political processes in terms of a flow of action. From an environment come influences upon the system; within the system various transformations occur; the system produces an output to the environment; the environment, in turn, produces feedback in the form of new inputs to the system. This selection presents one segment of this framework, namely, the process of converting wants to demands upon the system. This conversion occurs in the very early stages of the environmental impact. Although the focus is on political systems, the framework can clearly be applied to other social systems.

Notes

1. See, for example, Ralf Dahrendorf, *Class and Class Conflict in Industrial Society*, Stanford, Calif.: Stanford University Press, 1965; Gerhard Lenski, *Power and Privilege*, New York: McGraw-Hill, 1966.
   Perhaps the most far-reaching efforts at synthesis exist in the work on general-systems theory. For a convenient survey, see Walter Buckley, ed., *Modern Systems Research for the Behavioral Scientist*, Chicago: Aldine, 1968. In the present book, the selections by Etzioni and Maruyama are in the general-systems vein.
2. Max Gluckman, ed., *Closed Systems and Open Minds*, Chicago: Aldine, 1964, p. 8.
3. There are many commentaries on Parsons' work. One of the most careful and insightful is by W. J. H. Sprott. See his "Principia Sociologica," *British Journal of Sociology*, 3, September 1952, 203–221; and "Principia Sociologica, II," *British Journal of Sociology*, 14, December 1963, 307–320. See also, Percy S. Cohen, *Modern Social Theory*, London: Heinemann, 1968, especially chap. 5.
4. See Marion J. Levy, Jr., *The Structure of Society*, Princeton, N. J.: Princeton University Press, 1952; and *Modernization and the Structure of Societies*, Princeton, N. J.: Princeton University Press, 1966.
5. Some other functionalists do concern themselves with the "boundary" problems between social structures and other sectors. Neil J. Smelser, for example, has worked on boundary processes between social structures and personality. See his *Theory of Collective Behavior*, New York: Free Press, 1963.

Macroscale Frameworks

1 . Some Congruences Between Economic and Sociological Theory . **Talcott Parsons and Neil J. Smelser**

A. BETWEEN CATEGORIES

A social system is the system generated by any process of *interaction*, on the socio-cultural level, between two or more "actors." The actor is either a concrete human individual (a person) or a collectivity of which a plurality of persons are members. A person or a collectivity participates in a given system of interaction not usually with its whole individual or collective "nature" or set of motives or interests, but only with that sector relevant to this specific interaction system. Sociologically we call such a sector a *role*. Typical examples of sociological roles are those of husband, businessman, voter, etc.; an individual may be an incumbent of all these roles at once.

A society is the theoretically limiting case of the social system which, in its sub-systems, comprises *all* the important roles of the persons and collectivities composing its population. This is a limiting concept, only approximated, for example, by a modern national society. A society in the theoretical or the empirical sense is a network of differentiated sub-systems in very complex relation to each other.

Reprinted with permission of The Macmillan Company and Routledge & Kegan Paul Ltd. from *Economy and Society, A Study in the Integration of Economic and Social Theory* by Talcott Parsons and Neil J. Smelser. First published in the United States of America by The Free Press, a Corporation 1956.

Social interaction is the process by which the "behaviour" or change of state of members in a social system influences (a) the state of the system and (b) each other's states and relations. Every concrete act thus originates in a unit (member) and has effects on the state of the system and its other component units. Hence these units constitute a system in the scientific sense that a change of state of any one will effect changes in the states of one or more others and thus of the system as a whole.

We may now note a first case of matching between the general paradigm of a social system and the frame of reference of economic theory. In the process of interaction, an act analysed in terms of its direct meaning for the functioning of the system, as a "contribution" to its maintenance or task performance, is called a *performance*.[1] On the other hand, an act analysed in terms of its effect on the state of the actor toward whom it is oriented (and thus only indirectly, through his probable future action, on the state of the system) is called a *sanction*. This is an analytical distinction. Every *concrete* act has both a performance aspect and a sanction aspect. But in the analysis of any particular process in a system the distinction—in terms of the relative primacy of one of these two aspects—is of the first importance.

We wish to suggest that the economists' distinction between short-term supply and demand is a special case of this distinction between performance and sanction in the general theory of social interaction. Supply is the "production" of utility or economic value; each act of the supplier is interpreted by the economist in terms of its contribution to the functioning of the economy or one of its subsystems, e.g., the production of a particular class of goods or services. Demand is the disposition to "pay," in a process of market exchange, for the availability of such goods and services. The economist interprets the *significance* of any given state of demand in terms of its bearing on the disposition of the relevant supplying agencies to produce in the future. Thus only indirectly does the state of demand bear on the performance of function in the economy.

The respects in which supply and demand constitute a special case of the performance-sanction schema will be investigated presently in the light of terms such as "production of income" or "economic value" as the criteria of contribution to the functioning of the economy. In the meantime we might point to a further fit between the supply-demand and performance-sanction frames of reference. The economist formulates conditions of supply and conditions of demand in terms of schedules which represent functional relations between quantity and price. Perhaps the most fundamental theorems of economic analysis are those governing the slopes of supply and demand curves: a theoretical supply curve must always slope upward, i.e., the greater the amount supplied, the higher the price; and a demand curve must always slope downward, i.e., the greater the amount demanded, the lower the price offered.[2]

The same logic applies to the performance-sanction relationship in all social interaction. The *amount* of performance contribution is a function of the expectation (and in the long run, receipt) of sanction, or as psychologists would put it, of "reward." Conversely, amount of sanction or reward is a function of amount of performance contribution. The conceptual structure is identical. The difference lies only in the specific types of performance and sanction which are economically significant, namely of "production" and "money returns," or in this general sense, of "profit."[3]

A second parallel between the schema of interaction and economic usage concerns the classification of objects. The familiar economic distinction between "goods," "services," and a less precise third category concerning "technique," "knowledge," "the arts," etc., is a resultant of two fundamental crosscutting distinctions in the general theory of social interaction. The first of these distinctions is among physical, social and cultural objects; the second is between quality and performance.

All action takes place in a situation which consists in (a) "physical" objects, which do not interact reciprocally with the actor; (b) "social" objects, or other actors to which the actor orients his action and with whom he interacts reciprocally; and (c) "cultural" objects, or "information," which is a special kind of generalization of the meaning of physical and social objects. Only interacting actors constitute a social system. Physical objects, either in their "intrinsic" significance, or as symbols which control access to and use of information, are always part of the situation of particular actors and of social systems.[4]

The economic classification of commodities as either "goods" or "services" is a special case of the general distinction between physical and social objects. A "good" in the economic sense is a physical object which is demanded because it is held to be want-satisfying. A "service" is a performance by one or more actors, also having economic value; there is no intervention of physical objects on other than symbolic levels. The third category—"cultural objects"—also appears in economic theory, especially in connection with the significance of information in economic processes and in connection with such concepts as the "state of the arts." On the whole, however, there has been a lack of clarity in dealing with this class of objects both in economics and in the general theory of action.

The gross classification of goods as a special case of physical objects and services as a special case of social objects is, however, not sufficiently precise for many purposes. In certain cases, e.g., slavery, social objects may up to a point be treated as goods. To account for such cases, we introduce the distinction between performance and quality, which is an assessment of the significance of objects and events according to "whether or not the object . . . is considered to be a performance of a social object, or significant as the consequence of a performance and hence as an expression of the intentions of the actor concerned."[5] If this condition is fulfilled, then the significance of the object is as performance; if not, its significance is as quality. An actor's age is a quality, his achievement on an examination a performance.

Applied to the goods-services distinction, a good is an object or event of economic value which is significant as quality; a service is an object or event of economic value which is significant as performance. Of course, this distinction overlaps with that between physical and social objects, since only social objects can perform and have intentions. Yet it differs in so far as it permits the assessment of those aspects of social objects defined as goods or qualities. Thus, in the slavery example, the significance of buying and selling slaves in the market is as "goods," i.e., independent of their performance; on the other hand, the working contribution of slaves on a plantation is still a "service," i.e., performance in its economic significance. Conversely, economists often speak of physical goods as performing "services" over time. This usage is acceptable in calling attention to the fact that such goods are not utilized all at once but are the source of a "flow" of utility. In the sense in which we have spoken of services as pertaining to social objects above, however, physical goods do not perform services since their utilization is not part of a reciprocal interplay on the action level between *actors*. It is this interactive interplay which makes process in the economy that of a *social* system.

We might merely mention a third point of matching between economics and the general theory. In any balancing of performances and sanctions, there is a "something" which each party values and which depends upon the action of the other. This parallels the economic frame of reference in the discussion of the phenomenon of exchange. Supply and demand makes empirical sense because each party supplies some wanted, desired, or valued thing to the other. In Professor Knight's terms,[6] there is "mutual advantage" in exchange. In the typical economic case the supplier offers and the consumer receives goods and services and the consumer offers and the supplier receives money income. We will discuss the mechanisms which regulate exchange relations in Chapter III [of *Economy and Society: A Study in the Integration of Economic and Social Theory*]. For the present we merely point out that the conceptual structure in economics which defines the elements involved in an exchange transaction can be generalized to all cases of performance-sanction balancing.

B. BETWEEN SYSTEM TYPES

So far we have treated parallels between economic and sociological theory only on the elementary level of logically equivalent concepts. To push the parallels further, we must develop the concept of a *system* of interacting units. Most economists' statements of the scope of economics explicitly include the notion of system. A classical illustration is Marshall's delineation of economics as concerned with those aspects of men's attitudes and activities which are subject to measurement in terms of money. A more recent authoritative statement is Harrod's: "The method of procedure is to take certain elements of the situation as given—namely the preference lists of individuals[7] for goods and services, the terms on which they are willing to contribute their assistance in production and the current state of technology—and to take other elements as unknown, namely the prices of all commodities which will be produced and of factors which will be employed, and the precise methods of production among the variety of those technically possible which will be used. If the elements taken as known were in fact known, it would be possible to write down a number of equations expressing some of the unknowns as functions of the others.   The object of this procedure would be to provide means of showing how changes in the fundamental data, desires, etc., will govern the course of events."[8]

Harrod, like Marshall, is referring to a conceptual scheme's scope of relevance. At the same time he is isolating the particular type of empirical system analysable in terms of this scheme.   This system, the economy, is the set of relations of units of social interaction *in so far as*—within the limits of the "givens"—their interaction determines prices, quantities, and methods of production.

To elucidate the meaning of this conception it will be necessary to elucidate certain fundamental conceptions of the theory of social systems.   The whole society is in one sense part of the economy, in that all of its units, individual and collective, *participate in* the economy.   Thus households, universities, hospitals, units of government, churches, etc., are *in* the economy.   But *no* concrete unit participates *only* in the economy.   Hence no concrete unit is "purely economic." This fact is clear in the case of persons who, as family members, for example, are involved in many non-economic activities and functions.   But it is equally true of collectivities such as the business firm.   Economic considerations may be primary for the firm, but the latter clearly has, for example, "political" aspects as well.

In interpreting the above propositions the critical problem concerns the relations between the most general concepts of *social system* and the more specific concept of a *collectivity*.   A social system, we have said, is *any* system generated by the interaction of two or more behaving units.   The basic criterion for establishing the existence of such a system is the existence of meaningful interdependence between the actions of the units (interaction).   Thus the consequences of actions by any one unit can be traced through the system; ultimately these consequences "feed back" to the units initiating the change.   All this is implied by the notion of interdependence.   In this most general sense we propose to treat the economy as a social system.

A collectivity, on the other hand, is a *special type* of social system which is characterized by the capacity for "action in concert."   This implies the mobilization of the collectivity's resources to attain specific and usually explicit goals; it also implies the formalization of decision-making processes on behalf of the collectivity as a whole.   This explicitness applies both to the legitimation of the rights of specific units to make such decisions and the obligations of other units to accept and act upon the implications of these decisions.   The formal organization (e.g., a bureaucracy in the widest sense) is the prototype of such a system.

It follows that the economy as we conceive it is *not* a collectivity, even though every concrete social system has an economic aspect. For reasons we will set forth in the next chapter [of *Economy and Society: A Study in the Integration of Economic and Social Theory*], it is, in its "developed" sense, a sub-system of the total society.[9]   As a social sub-system, the economy is differentiated on the basis of *functions* in the society.   As such it consists of modes of orientation of actors and their relation to the orientations of other actors through a process of mutually oriented decision. A collectivity, on the other hand, is never unifunctional but always multifunctional. For this reason the economy cannot be a collectivity. Certain concrete acts and certain collectivities (e.g., the business firm) may have *primarily* economic functions, to be sure. But a collectivity's primary function never exhausts its functional significance in the larger system in which it is a concrete unit.

The concept of the functional differentiation of a social system and the concept of a collectivity thus *in principle* cut across each other. Both are types of organization in terms of social sub-systems, but they must not be identified with each other. In considering the relation of the economy to the total society—hence the empirical applicability of economic theory—we must investigate *both* the "pure theory" of an economy *and* the ways in which the economy is involved in the structure of collectivities in the society.

Societies differ from each other in the degree to which the collectivities of which they are composed are differentiated in terms of functional primacy. For instance, in our society the bulk (but not all) of economic production is carried on in the functionally specialized organizations we call firms, which are sharply differentiated from the households of which "workers" in the firms are members. In classical peasant agriculture, on the other hand, the household and the productive unit are a single undifferentiated collectivity. Further, societies will differ in the degree of elaboration of the system of economically differentiated units and in the mode of relation of these units to other functional exigencies of the society. We shall have occasion to illustrate and expand these ranges of variation below.

In the light of these considerations we must now turn to two general questions concerning the relation between the conceptual status of a social system and that of the economy.

What are the most important features of a social system by means of which we may define the cognate features of an economy? In what respects is an economy, considered as a differentiated sub-system of a society, differentiated from other cognate (i.e., functional) sub-systems of the same society?

According to the general theory, process in any social system is subject to four independent functional imperatives or "problems" which must be met adequately if equilibrium and/or continuing existence of the system is to be maintained.[10]

A social system is always characterized by an institutionalized value system. The social system's first functional imperative is to maintain the integrity of that value system and its institutionalization. This process of maintenance means stabilization against pressures to change the value system, pressures which spring from two primary sources: (1) Cultural sources of change. Certain imperatives of cultural consistency may mean that cultural changes taking place *outside* the value system relevant to the social system in question (e.g., changes in the belief system) may generate pressures to change important values *within* the social system. The tendency to stabilize the system in the face of pressures to change institutionalized values through cultural channels may be called the "pattern maintenance" function. (2) Motivational sources of change. Motivational "tensions," arising from "strains" in any part of the social situation or from organic or other intra-personal sources, may threaten individual motivation to conformity with institutionalized role expectations. Stabilization against this potential source of change may be called "tension management." The first functional imperative, therefore, is "pattern maintenance and tension management" relative to the stability of the institutionalized value system.

Every social system functions in a situation defined as external to it. The processes of interchange between system and situation are the foci of the second and third major functional imperatives of the system.

The first interchange concerns the situation's significance as a source of consummatory goal gratification or attainment. A goal state, for an individual actor or for a social system, is a *relation* between the system of reference and one or more situational objects which (given the value system and its institutionalization) maximizes the stability of the system. Other things equal, such a state, once present, tends to be maintained, and if absent, tends to be "sought" by the action of one or more units of the system. The latter case is necessary because only in limiting cases are processes in the situation closely "synchronized" with processes in the system of action; hence the system must "seek" goal states by controlling elements of the situation.[11] Goal states may be negative, i.e., noxious situational conditions, or positive, i.e., a maximization of favourable or "gratifying" conditions.

The second interchange deals with the problem of controlling the environment for purposes of attaining goal states. Since relations to the situation are problematical, there arises a *generalized* interest in establishing and improving control over the situation in various respects. Of course the pursuit of particular goal states involves such control. A different order of problem is involved, however, in the generalization of facilities for a variety of system and sub-system goals, and in activity specialized to produce such facilities. When a social system has only a simply defined goal, the provision of facilities or the "adaptive" functions is simply an undifferentiated aspect of the process of goal attainment. But in complex systems with a plurality of goals and sub-goals the differentiation between goal attainment and adaptive processes is often very clear.

Whatever the interacting units in a system process—motivational units of personality (need dispositions), roles of individual persons in a social system, or roles of collectivities in a more macroscopic social system—the actions of the units may be mutually supportive and hence beneficial to the functioning of the system; but also they may be mutually obstructive and conflictful. The fourth functional imperative for a social system is to "maintain solidarity" in the relations between the units in the interest of effective functioning; this is the imperative of system integration.

The four fundamental system problems under which a system of action, in particular a social system, operates are thus (latent) pattern maintenance (including tension management), goal attainment, adaptation, and integration. Their gross relations to each other are schematically represented in Figure 1.

Any system of action can be described and its processes analysed in terms of these four fundamental categories. The aim of analysing a system is to assess the effects of changes in the data of the system, the situation and the properties of its units, on changes in the state of the system and the states of its component units; statements about the effects on the system and its units are framed in terms of these four dimensions. For instance, we say a system "adapts" to certain situational disturbances. Furthermore, if these categories formulate "directions" in which process can move, certain constraints prevent processes from moving equally in all directions at once, at least unless very specific conditions are fulfilled. Indeed, the idea of system itself implies such constraints.

A	G
Adaptive Instrumental Object Manipulation	Instrumental-Expressive Consummatory Performance and Gratification
L	I
Latent-Receptive Meaning Integration and Energy Regulation Tension build-up and drain-off	Integrative-Expressive Sign Manipulation

KEY

1. **A**–Adaptation
2. **G**–Goal Gratification
3. **I**–Integration
4. **L**–Latent-Pattern Maintenance and Tension Management

Figure 1. The Functional Imperatives of a System of Action*

* Adapted from Figure 2, p. 182, in *Working Papers, op. cit.* The above figure deals with the "functional imperatives" aspect of the system of action; that in the *Working Papers* deals with the "phase movement" aspect. Cf. Chap. IV, pp. 242–45.

Now we may specify the relations between this conceptual scheme and some fundamental economic concepts on a level where the economy, is treated as a system. We will deal first with the concepts of production and utility, then with the factors of production and shares of income, and finally with the concept of cost. Throughout this discussion we will be using the above outline of a social system *to refer to two different system levels.* The first system reference is that to an *economy* as such; thus we will ask what is meant by the goal orientation of an economy as a system, by its adaptive imperatives, by its integration and its value pattern. The second system reference is to the *society*, of which the economy is a differentiated *sub*-system. The basic categories—goal attainment, adaptation, integration, and pattern maintenance—are, of course, the same as for the economy, but their specific references (empirical content) are different.

We wish to suggest that the two systems in question, the society and the economy, articulate in the following way: the economy is that sub-system of a society which is differentiated with primary reference to the *adaptive* function of the society as a whole. This proposition is very important indeed; we will return to it again and again. It is what we mean by the assertion that an economy is a *functional* sub-system of a society.

Economists seem to agree that the paramount goal of economic activity—and hence of an economy as a system—is best defined as "production." But what is meant by production? Production of what? For a long time it seemed plausible to define production in physical terms: production of commodities and services, of numbers of automobiles, of tons of coal, of woman-hours of domestic service. This idea has proved to be entirely inadequate. On two grounds economists have been forced to seek a reference different from physical products. First, physical units must be given a "meaning" or "economic significance"; and second, qualitatively different physical units, such as tons and hours, must be rendered quantitatively comparable. The agreed reference for economists has been, in the first instance, to "consumers' wants." A good or service has economic value or significance in so far as it is a means to "want satisfaction." In this sense it has utility and added utility (i.e., income) constitutes an addition to the "wealth" of the community.

Maximizing utility or the economic value of the total available means to want satisfaction therefore defines the system goal of an economy. A goal state has been defined above as a satisfactory *relation* between the state of a system and relevant objects in the external situation. For the economy this relation is some optimum between the state of the economy, in the sense of the productive achievements of its members, and the individual and collective members of society, *in their roles as consumers.* Though largely the same concrete persons occupy consumers' roles and producers' roles respectively, these roles belong in different systems. We define the former as outside the economy, the latter as inside.[12]

To summarize: the concept of production defines the goal orientation of the economy as a sub-system of the society. Production is of utility, or of goods and services in so far as they satisfy wants. Wealth is defined as the aggregate economic value of such goods and services at any given time. Income is defined as the flow of command over such values per unit of time.

If this is acceptable, then what is the significance of "want satisfaction" from the standpoint of the society as a total social system? According to the general theory, the goal of a differentiated sub-system "contributes" to the functioning of its larger system. We have defined the economy's contribution as specialization in the solution[13] of the adaptive problem of the larger system. This adaptive function now may be more closely defined. Negatively it implies the minimization of subjection to control by the exigencies of the external situation (e.g., floods, famines, shortages, etc.). Positively it implies the possession of a maximum of fluid disposable resources as means to attain *any* goals valued by the system or its sub-units. The general concept for these disposable resources is wealth from a static point of view and income from the point of view of rate of flow.

In defining production, utility, wealth and income, the focal point of reference is for us the *society* as a system. The role of producer is *internal* to the economy as a sub-system of the society; that of consumer is *external* to the economy in the sense that it pertains to one or more *other* sub-systems of the society. But the functional *significance* of these concepts is evaluated in terms of the *institutionalized value system* of the total society, and only as mediated through this, in terms of its sub-systems including individual personalities. From our point of view, therefore, utility or the satisfaction of wants should not be defined in relation to "the individual" but in relation to the society. Its significance for the individual is a function of the kind of society in question and the place of individuals in it. There is no reason, moreover, to assume that this function is the same for all societies.

We repeat: the goal of the economy is not simply the production of income for the utility of an aggregate of individuals. It is the maximization of production relative to the whole complex of institutionalized value-systems and functions of the society and its sub-systems. As a matter of fact, if we view the goal of the economy as defined strictly by socially structured goals, it becomes inappropriate even to refer to utility at this level in terms of individual preference lists or indifference curves. This view of utility also means that, in formulating concepts of social utility or utility in a social context, it is not necessary even to consider the time-honoured economic problems of the interpersonal comparability of utility, the cardinal and/or ordinal measurement of utility, etc. Since the individual is not the defining unit for the maximization of utility, it is inappropriate to refer to the measurability of utility *among* individuals. Therefore, it is correct to speak, with only apparent paradox, of the "maximization of utility" in a social context without at the same time making *any* statements about the interpersonal measurability of utility. The theoretical occasion for drawing such comparisons in the traditional sense does not arise at all, since the categories of wealth, utility, and income are states or properties of social systems and their units and do not apply to the personality of the individual except *through* the social system.

Utility, then, is the *economic value* of physical, social or cultural objects in accord with their *significance as facilities* for solving the adaptive problems of social systems. Wealth is the aggregate of this value for a given social system at a given time (Adam Smith was correct to speak of the *wealth of nations* rather than their individual members). Income is the *rate* of production or reception of such value for a period of time.

Economic valuation is a mechanism by which particularized significances of specific resources for individuals and collectivities are *generalized* in terms of their significance to the system as a whole. This generalized reference is not a "result of" certain properties of individuals' wealth or income but is the central defining characteristic of income or wealth. To be sure, individuals have wealth or income as "shares" of societal wealth or income, but it does not follow that the wealth of a society is an aggregate of the *independently given* wealth of its members.

The relation between this social aspect of income and wealth on the one hand and individual motivation on the other can be analysed adequately in terms of modern personality theory, most of which has developed since economic theory became crystallized along these lines. The essence of this personality theory is that economic values, which form the basis of the meaning of wealth and income to the individual, are internalized in the process of socialization. They are social values which become part of the personality in its development, not "propensities" of the individual which determine social processes. We will treat this problem in detail in Chapter III [of *Economy and Society: A Study in the Integration of Economic and Social Theory*].

We realize that this position runs counter to what is probably the dominant strand of at least the English-speaking tradition of economics.[14] We feel that the prominence of this "individualistic" strain in the treatment of want-satisfaction and utility is a relic of the historical association of economic theory with utilitarian philosophy and psychology. If pushed to its extreme, it leads to a type of psychological and sociological atomism: this position has been set forth perhaps most conspicuously by Robbins.[15] But in more moderate form it permeates the work of such authors as Pareto,[16], Hicks,[17] and certain welfare economists.[18]

Our view accords with that of Marshall (in his treatment of the relation of wants and activities) as it links directly with that of Weber and Durkheim. In addition to its other merits, Marshall's contribution seems altogether to avoid what many economists conclude to be an insoluble problem: the comparison of individual preference lists *assumed in advance* to be independent of each other. We will try to show that for purposes of the theory of the economy of a social system this assumption is both unnecessary and contrary to fact.

Finally, our emphasis is associated with a shift in perspective in the definition of wealth. The earlier emphasis was on physical consumers' goods and their "hedonistic" consumption values. The later emerging emphasis has been on the *generalizing* of wealth as purchasing power, hence on its relation to productivity and to the control of behaviour. Wealth is not so much an inventory of commodities as an instrumentality for achieving goals and inducing the co-operation of actors in that achievement. This shift of emphasis in our opinion prepares the way for a genuine integration of economic and sociological theory which has been blocked by the remnants of utilitarianism.

To return to our main analysis: we regard the transition from production to consumption as a "boundary process" between the economy and other parts of the society. When the process of production is completed the economy has "done its job." The product is put at the disposal of other sub-systems for whatever uses may be relevant. Consumption in the broadest sense is thus *any* use to which economically valuable goods and services are put, other than as means of production in the economic sense.

The lines along which we might push this conception of boundary process further are suggested by the consequence of the fact that the economy is confronted by all the essential functional problems of any social system. So far we have dealt only with the boundary process which involves the economy's primary output of or production of consumable goods and services (the attainment of its goal as a system).

But the economy has adaptive needs of its own. In order to produce, it must acquire disposable resources for productive purposes. If wealth is the stock and income the flow of resources at the disposal of the society, there should be a corresponding body of disposable resources available to the economy for its own specialized uses. We suggest that the concept of capital as ordinarily used by economists constitutes precisely this stock or flow of resources available for production.[19]

In essential respects the resources available for economically productive and non-productive uses are interchangeable. For the economy the functional problem is the process of determination of the proportion of the society's resources to be made available for economic production. There is a boundary process concerned with the determination of this share. More particularly, there is an input of capital into the economy and a return to those who decide to relinquish resources they control from alternative uses. This boundary involves the adaptive processes of the economy itself; it concerns the capital market and the relations between capital, interest and related phenomena.

Another boundary of the economy concerns disposable resources, the supply of which is not contingent on short-term economic sanctions. This boundary is of a different order from the two mentioned above. The inputs include "physical" resources in the traditional economic sense of land factors; it also includes two other categories. The first is "cultural" objects, in so far as they are available for economic production without specific cost. This would include "the state of the arts," commonly held technology, intuitive knowledge of market conditions and "business experience," etc. The second involves human services for productive purposes in so far as there is an underlying commitment to work independent of current economic sanctions. Examples of this category are both an underlying commitment to work and differentials in ability which give rise to the "rent of ability."[20] These three factors within limits, therefore, behave like land in the physical sense; hence it is legitimate to group them together as "land" for economic analysis.

According to the general theory of social systems, the "land" elements are *governed* by an institutionalized system of values; hence they are most closely associated with the pattern-maintenance sub-system of the economy. Such values will, within limits, be acted upon wherever appropriate, independent of cost. Their availability marks a third boundary process of the economy.

A fourth boundary concerns the integration of the economy. Integration refers to the way in which available resources are combined in the productive process. The conception of organization as a factor of production by Marshall is appropriate; this is the locus of the entrepreneurial function as developed by Schumpeter and his followers.[21] In its economic context integration refers to the long-term apportioning of men and machines, in accordance with production opportunities.

We have omitted the input of labour into the economy, that factor most directly related to the output of goods and services for consumption. This is the contribution of the worker which is sensitive to short-term economic sanctions (payment of wages, etc.). There are thus two distinct components in human services. The first is the underlying willingness to work; the second the response to the specific rate of remuneration and conditions of employment.

In the next chapter [of *Economy and Society: A Study in the Integration of Economic and Social Theory*] we will carry the analysis of these boundary processes of the economy and their input-output relations further than we have been able to in this introductory discussion. At the present stage, however, we suggest an important conclusion. If the view of the economy as a differentiated sub-system of the total society is accepted as a point of departure, then such a sub-system is subject to *particular and determinate* types of boundary interchange with the rest of society and with the physical environment. The economic categories—factors of production on the one hand and shares of income on the other—can be identified as the appropriate inputs and outputs, respectively, over these boundaries.

In interpreting this conclusion, we do not identify the boundaries of the economy with any particular "organizational" features of any particular society. In very highly differentiated cases, some of the boundaries may coincide approximately with specific concrete markets such as the market for consumers' goods and the labour market in our society. In a peasant society, on the other hand, the boundary between production and consumption lies to a large extent within the same household, regarded as a collectivity. This view is, of course, not new; economists have long been aware that the factors of production cannot be identified with concrete organizations or groups in any simple way and that organizational arrangements vary from one society to another.

Assuming these qualifications, we treat *labour* (as a factor) as the input of human service into the economy in so far as it is contingent on short-term economic sanctions. This is balanced by *wages*, or "consumers' income" (not goods and services). *Capital* is treated as the input of fluid resources into the economy: this input is contingent on decisions between productive and consumption uses. It is balanced by a category of income which traditionally has been called *interest*.[22] The third input are those factors available for production, but not contingent on immediate economic remuneration. These factors fall into three sub-classes—physical resources, cultural resources and social resources—which we group under *land*. These are balanced by various kinds of *rents*. Finally, there is the factor of *organization* balanced by *profit* in the technical sense.[23]

Among the input-output items in the "rent" category are certain human factors. We think it is legitimate to identify these, at least in part, with what Marshall discussed under the heading of "activities" as distinguished from "wants" as the subject-matter of economics. As is well known, Marshall insisted that the "science of wants" could only be half of economics; the other half is the "science of activities." With respect to the orientation of human behaviour, it is clear that he referred to those respects in which men were devoted to productive functions without specific relation to short-term economic reward; because "work, in its best sense, the healthy energetic exercise of faculties is the aim of life, is life itself." We agree that this is true, in so far as work is not in the usual sense "economically motivated" but is an expression of internalized values. Thus Marshall's theory of activities falls naturally into place, instead of being an anomalous "foreign body" in the corpus of economic theory.[24]

The striking fact, in sum, is the correspondence—category for category—between the established economic classifications of the factors of production and the shares of income and a classification of the input-output categories of social systems which was arrived at in work on the level of general theory independently, without the economic categories in mind at all. Whether this correspondence is genuine or spurious can best be evaluated only after we have used it to interpret various substantive propositions of economic theory and to explore the relations between the economy and the rest of society more thoroughly.

Notes

1. Cf. Parsons, T., Bales, R. F., and Shils, E. A., *Working Papers in the Theory of Action*, 1953, Chap. V, Sec. V.
2. Cf. Schumpeter, J. A., "The Instability of Capitalism," *Economic Journal*, Sept. 1928, reprinted in *Readings in Economic Analysis*, ed. R. V. Clemence, 1950. Schumpeter points out that the alleged "exceptions" to these generalizations must be referred to empirical discontinuities in the data of an economic system. They have empirical consequences, but they are not reasons for altering the fundamental theory. They concern, in our terminology, noneconomic factors.
3. The economic generalization about the slopes of supply and demand curves (the only significant meaning of the expression "the law of supply and demand") and what psychologists call the "law of effect" are two different special cases of the same fundamental generalization about action, namely, the "law of equivalence of action and reaction" (cf. *Working Papers*, Chap. III). It should be noted that our remarks are limited to short-term supply and demand curves. Long-term supply curves can be horizontal or they may even slope downward. This qualification, however, has its parallel in the other social sciences. In psychology, for instance, the "law of effect" depends strictly upon timing, and cannot be said to be the only significant principle of learning. Furthermore, in the general theory of action, the "law of equivalence of action and reaction" is not the only principle governing the relationship bteween performance and sanction. Indeed, it often is not strictly applicable to longer-term processes.
4. Cf. Parsons and Shils, eds., *Toward A General Theory of Action*, 1951, pp. 64–67.
5. Parsons, Bales, and Shils, *Working Papers in the Theory of Action*, p. 81.
6. Knight, Frank H., "Ethics of Competition," Chap. II in the volume of essays under that title, 1935.
7. (Can we not say "actors," individual or collective?—Authors.)
8. Cf. Marshall, Alfred, *Principles of Economics*, Book I, Chap. II, p. 15 (8th ed., 1925); Harrod, R. F., "Scope and Method of Economics," *Economic Journal*, Sept. 1938, reprinted in Clemence, ed., *Readings in Economic Analysis, op. cit.*
9. Cf. Parsons and Shils, "Values, Motives and Systems of Action," Chap. III of Part II of *Toward a General Theory of Action*. Where, however, economic goals are explicitly paramount in the action (as distinguished from values—cf. below, pp. 20–29 and 175–87 [of *Economy and*

Society: A Study in the Integration of Economic and Social Theory]) of a total society, we conceive the economy to be subordinated to the political or some other non-economic aspect of that society. The modern theory of a "free enterprise" economy in which the economy is subject to controls but not to any centralized "direction" is, with certain qualifications, in accord with our conception of the economy as a sub-system highly differentiated from other cognate sub-systems of the society.

10. Cf. *Working Papers in the Theory of Action, op. cit.*, Chaps. III and V.

11. The supply of oxygen in accordance with the biological need for air is an example of high synchronization between system process and situation; the supply of food is an example of a situational process relatively unsynchronized with organic needs.

12. This duality (in this respect) of system membership for the same concrete individuals illustrates the central point that a social system does not comprise the *total* action of concrete persons and collectivities, but only their actions *in specific roles*. The precise sense in which we consider consumers external to the economy is outlined in Chap. II, pp. 53–55 and 70–72 [of *Economy and Society: A Study in the Integration of Economic and Social Theory*].

13. This is always only relatively satisfactory.

14. This, incidentally, seems to be the only critical point in this chapter at which we are forced to enter directly into the internal controversies of economics.

15. Robbins, L., *The Nature and Significance of Economic Science* (2nd ed., 1948). Robbins refuses to admit that even the individual has an integrated system of goals or wants—he is motivated by an unorganized plurality of "conflicting psychological pulls" (p. 34). Taking this position precludes recognizing any higher order social integration of goals or values. Cf. Parsons, "Some Reflections on 'The Nature and Significance of Economics,'" *Quarterly Journal of Economics*, May 1934.

16. Cf. *The Mind and Society, op. cit.*, Vol. IV, Chap. XIII, Secs. 2111–2146. Pareto distinguishes between several types of utility to individuals and several types to collectivities. Furthermore, he distinguishes between ophelimity *of* a collectivity (which does not exist because individual ophelimities cannot be compared) and ophelimity *for* a collectivity (which is determined independently of the comparison between ophelimities of different individuals). While Pareto's subtle discussion of these distinctions shows that he was aware of the significance of several system-levels as reference-points for discussion of welfare and utility, we feel our conception of utility goes well beyond Pareto in so far as we *exclude* (not merely consider impossible to solve) the problem of interpersonal comparison of individual ophelimities.

17. Hicks, J. R., *Value and Capital* (2nd ed., 1946). While Hicks and other indifference curve analysts do not necessarily subscribe to such a doctrinaire atomistic position as Robbins', their starting-point is individual preference lists, and few systematic attempts are made to tie this set of schedules to the social system.

18. Cf. for example, Pigou, A. C., *The Economics of Welfare* (4th ed., 1952). Cf. below, pp. 30–32 [of *Economy and Society: A Study in the Integration of Economic and Social Theory*].

19. The definition of capital as "producers' wealth" as opposed to "consumers' wealth" definitely implies this distinction. In another context, the fact that "capital" as a term is applied both to liquid funds and to "physical stock" refers to the fact that commitment of resources to actual production may vary in degree. For discussion of the various levels of commitment of capital resources, cf. Chaps. III and IV below [in *Economy and Society: A Study in the Integration of Economic and Social Theory*].

20. This rent is often referred to as one sort of quasi-rent. Marshall, *Principles, op. cit.*, pp. 425 ff.

21. Cf. *Principles, op. cit.*, Book IV, pp. 138–139; *The Theory of Economic Development, op. cit.*, Chap. II.

22. Certain questions about this category are raised in Chapter II of *Economy and Society: A Study in the Integration of Economic and Social Theory*.

23. These identifications deal only with the monetary rewards for the factors of production. The relations between money income and real income will be discussed in Chap. II, pp. 70 ff. [of *Economy and Society: A Study in the Integration of Economic and Social Theory*].

24. Cf. Pigou, A. C., ed., *Memorials of Alfred Marshall*, 1925, p. 115, and Parsons, *Structure of Social Action*, Chap. IV. This, it will be noted, is a revision of the view put forward in the senior author's earlier study of Marshall. May we again call attention to the resemblance between Marshall's empirical views in this field and those of Max Weber in connection with his study of the relation between Protestantism and capitalism—despite all the difference of perspective of these two writers. In view of the interpretation of the place of economic rationality as the "value system" of the economy (Chaps. III and V [of *Economy and Society: A Study in the Integration of Economic and Social Theory*]), this coincidence will take on special significance.

2 . The Value System . **Robert N. Bellah**

. . . We have already maintained [in *Tokugawa Religion*] that the Japanese value system is characterized by the primacy of "political" values. These may be defined by the combination of the pattern variables of particularism and performance, or as those values appropriate to the goal-attainment dimension of the social system; these being merely two ways of saying the same thing.[1] When we say that the primary concern is for the system goal, we imply the value of particularism. It is the particular system or collectivity of which one is a member which counts, whether it be family, *han*[2] or Japan as a whole. Commitment to these tends to take precedence over universalistic commitments, such as commitment to truth or justice. There was of course universalism and universalistic commitment in Tokugawa Japan. All we maintain is that particularism held primacy. The importance of the collectivity and of one's particularistic relation to it, is indicated by the enormous symbolic importance of the head of the collectivity, whether this be family head, feudal lord or emperor. This tended to be a representative role—the head stood for the collectivity—and very often not an executive role, actual executive functions being left to the chief clerk, or a leading retainer, etc. Thus one's particularistic tie to one's collectivity is symbolized as loyalty to its head. The enormous importance of loyalty in Japan is, then, a concrete expression of the values for which we are postulating primacy. It is important to note that this loyalty is loyalty to the head of one's collectivity, whoever that person may be. It is loyalty to a status rather than to a person, as such. There may be and often was a deep personal attachment to the head, but this was not a prerequisite for loyalty. This is important in connection with political rationalization. It implies the possibility of a deep loyalty to a person (e.g. the emperor or *shōgun*) with whom the individual has no personal relation at all, and thus of a powerful political influence far beyond the sphere of mere personal influence. This generalized particularism, then, may serve in certain ways as a functional equivalent for universalism in the process of the rationalization and extension of power.

Similarly, when we say that the primary concern is for the system goal, we imply the value of performance. The concern is primarily with system *goal* rather than system *maintenance*, and a goal must be attained. Thus performance or achievement becomes a primary value. The great importance of status in Japan had previously led me to postulate a primacy of quality or ascription in the value system. There is indeed no doubt of the very great importance which this value has. Perhaps, however, the primacy of performance will become clearer if one considers that status itself does not validate. Only performance in the service of the system goal is really validating. Even those in the very important representative roles, the heads of collectivities, are in a larger context subordinates engaged in laboring for the attainment of goals in the superordinate system. Even the emperor is responsible to his ancestors for his behaviour and must account to them. There tends not to be at any level in Japanese life a status style of life which, once attained, is its own validation (as against, say, the status style of life of the Chinese gentry). The importance of performance values is further illustrated in the family, where ascription normally holds primacy. Very intensive levels of performance were apparently demanded from children, with at least the threat of disinheritance for inadequacy or waywardness.[3] Conversely, masters in the arts and crafts not infrequently adopted especially gifted pupils as their heirs and successors. Loyalty in Japan implied not mere passive devotion but active service and performance. It should be noted that a high valuation of performance implies comparisons of relative achievement, and the standards by which such comparisons are made must be universalistic. This consideration together with the pseudo-universalism implied in the generalization of particularism discussed above, lead to the inference that universalism may be found to have a considerable if secondary importance.

It must be noted that though goal-attainment is of primary concern in the value system, the content of the goals to be obtained is relatively variable. Naturally the goals chosen will, or it is thought that they will, increase the power and prestige of the collectivity. But the power and prestige of the collectivity may be increased through internal peace and prosperity, through victory in war, through imperialistic expansion, through becoming a model for other nations in peacefulness and a high level of culture, etc. The primacy of goal-attainment values, "political" values in the present sense, is not, then, dependent on the specific content of the goals chosen. Therefore even a radical and sudden shift in the content of the goal cannot be expected to have any seriously disruptive effect on the central value system.[4]

The central values, which, as has been shown above, give primacy to the goal-attainment dimension, naturally have important implications for values with respect to the other three dimensions.[5] With respect to the adaptive problem, those behaviours which are adaptive in the pursuit of the collective goals are most highly valued. The military is, in terms of the present conceptual scheme, exactly the adaptive arm of the polity. It is therefore not at all surprising that the military should have very high prestige in Japan. It displays the type case of adaptive action which is entirely subordinated to the system goal. Economic behaviour tends to be suspect because it may not be subordinated to the system goal but rather to some sub-system goal; it may be "selfish." But to the degree that economic behaviour can be seen as furthering the system goal, it is perfectly legitimate. In general, work itself is not a value, but rather work as an expression of selfless devotion to the collective goal is valued. The motivation to work, however, may be just as strong in such a society as in one in which work is valued for its own sake.

Integrative values are strong but tend to be subordinated to the goal-attainment values. Harmony must be maintained in the collectivity because conflicts between the members would not only be disloyal to the head but would disrupt the smooth attainment of collective goals. Thus harmony, willingness to compromise, unaggressiveness, etc. are highly valued, whereas disputatiousness, contentiousness, overweening ambition or other disruptive behaviour is strongly disvalued. In order to avoid friction a great deal of everyday life is formalized. Close conformity to a multiplicity of detailed prescriptions for behaviour tends to reduce all conflict to a minimum and ensure the smooth functioning of collective life. The emphasis on harmony, on the maintenance of the collectivity seemingly for its own sake is so great that it is likely that at some periods and for some groups the integrative values had primacy over the goal-attainment values.[6] It would seem, though, that the dominant pattern exhibited the primacy of goal values. Appeals to loyalty to the head of the collectivity and to pre-eminent system goals could override concern for harmony and motivate the breaking through of old social forms, the disruption of old collectivities, and the abandonment of old forms of prescribed behaviour. This potentiality contributed to the dynamism and ability for fairly rapid social change without disruption of the central values which differentiates Japan from societies in which system-maintenance-integrative values have primacy and are ends in themselves.

Finally, the sphere of "cultural" values seems to contain two distinct clusters of values. One of these is closely subordinated to the primary values already discussed, while the other seems to define an area sharply separated from that of the central values though in certain respects complementary to it.

The first group may be illustrated by the strong value on learning, study or scholarship (*gakumon*). This value which relates to the regard for the written word, for books, and for teachers and education in general, is not an end in itself. Rather it is valued because of its results in action. Learning for its own sake . . . tends to be despised. The merely erudite man is not worthy of respect. Rather learning should eventuate in practice. A truly learned man will be a truly loyal and filial man. The same considerations hold with respect to religion. It is, of course, impossible to deprive religion entirely of the character of being an end in itself, but there is a tendency in this direction.   Or else there is a tendency to fuse the religious end and the secular end, religious values and the secular goal-attainment values.   We shall have more to say on this in the sections on religion [in *Tokugawa Religion*].   An example of the tendency to value religion for its results in action rather than for its own sake would be the attachment of the warrior class to Zen Buddhism in certain periods.   It was seen almost as a system of training which aided in the self-abnegating performance of actions expressing loyalty to one's lord.   The latter remains the central value and religion is subordinated to it (or subsumed in it).   This general tendency to value cultural phenomena as means to action rather than as ends in themselves can probably be seen as inhibiting any very strong emphasis on theory as opposed to practice. The pursuit of theory whether in philosophy or in science does not seem strongly developed in traditional Japan.   On the other hand, the strong regard for cultural phenomena which had visible results in action perhaps helps to explain the relatively strong attraction of the Japanese to Western science, even at periods when their access to it was difficult and even dangerous.   It is interesting that the first subject to be studied was medicine.   The 18th century Japanese physicians who studied Dutch medical textbooks were impressed by the accuracy of the information and its practical application more than by its theoretical sophistication.

The second cluster of "cultural" values which can be discriminated may be called the aesthetic-emotional values.   As opposed to the values discussed above these tend to be ends in themselves rather than subordinate to the central values. They are, however, allowed expression only in certain rather sharply segregated contexts and under rather rigidly defined conditions.[7]   It would be a mistake, however, to underestimate the importance of these values.   For many individuals and even groups they have at some periods probably held primacy, and their existence probably always poses a certain threat to the central value system. These values center not on collective goals but on private experience.   They define an area of individual expression and enjoyment.   This may be in the aesthetic appreciation of nature or art, in the delicate ritual of the tea ceremony, in the vicarious thrills of the theater, in the refined eroticism of the gay quarters, or in sentimental and effusive human relationships of love or friendship.   Such behaviour is legitimate and indeed very highly valued in Japanese culture.   But there is always the possibility of its shading over into a sumptuous if sensitive hedonism, especially among those classes which can afford to gratify their tastes. In such a situation individual goal-gratification displaces collective goal-gratification as the central value and thus the strongest sentiments must be mobilized against it.   Such a hedonism is the essence of "selfishness" which is the greatest vice, just as loyalty is the greatest virtue.   In order to guard against such a consequence, aesthetic-emotional values are restricted to rather well defined areas and an almost ascetic austerity is highly valued in the area of consumption.   The strength of the hedonistic tendency, however, is illustrated in the development of a refined, sensitive and often very expensive austerity, which serves rather to express than destroy its opposite, among certain circles.

So far we have had almost nothing to say about the family, which is so important in traditional Japanese life. This is because, in our view, the family is the polity writ small. Practically all that was said above about the value system of the total Japanese society can be applied to the family. Instead of loyalty the highest value is filial-piety (*kō*) but its function is the same. It implies the same attitude toward the head of the collectivity and the same central concern for the collective goal. In using the term family we mean to include lineage as well as nuclear family. The Japanese family is conceived as continuously handed down from the ancestors of old. Reverence for parents is subsumed in a larger concept of reverence for ancestors. The structural features of the Japanese family will be discussed briefly later on in this chapter [of *Tokugawa Religion*], but we may point out here that lineages are related to each other in terms of main and branch houses, the main house being the line of direct inheritance and the branch being cadet houses. On the broadest level family and nation are one, the imperial family being the main house of which all Japanese families are branches. It is however the household, composed ideal typically of the parents, the eldest son, who will inherit the house, and his wife and children, which is the primary focus of the value of filial piety. It is very important to stress that in the dominant value system filial piety is subordinate to loyalty; polity overrides family; and in case of conflict of loyalty the first duty is to one's lord rather than to one's family. This is in clear contrast to China where the reverse holds true. These values are not seen, however, to be contradictory. Rather they are felt to be mutually re-inforcing. The filial son will make a loyal minister; the family is the training ground for social virtues. Further, the family tends to be the unit of society rather than the individual. The status of family head is both internally central and externally the lowest "official" role in the polity. The family does not stand over against the polity but is integrated into it and to an extent penetrated by it. It does not serve as a locus for a different value system, but rather for a virtually identical one.

Above we have considered those values which are important at the social system level in that their institutionalization in a sense defines the social structure. We have not been concerned with the "metaphysical" underpinnings of these values nor with general orientations to time, nature and man. A discussion of these is reserved for the next chapter [of *Tokugawa Religion*] when their relation both to the social values discussed above and to the religious system can be analyzed.

The values discussed in this section were largely constant throughout the Tokugawa Period. If anything, they became more intense and more widely propagated as the period progressed, if we are to credit the influence of the many religious, ethical and educational movements which arose. The *samurai* class best typifies these values, at least in ideal, but they became quite general among all classes by the end of the Tokuwaga Period. On the other hand, there is no doubt that hedonistic values made considerable headway in the cities among both *samurai* and *chōnin*.[8] They were not, however, able to attain any semblance of legitimacy, and were constantly under attack from the moralists of all classes. There is a real sense in which the Meiji Period (1868–1911) was a culmination and intensification of the central values rather than a rejection of them, and they have remained strong throughout modern times. A discussion of the strains involved in the partial disintegration of these values in modern times and of the attempts to revive them lies outside the scope of this study.

Notes

1. The reader is advised to refer to figure 1 [on page 10 of *Tokugawa Religion*] as an aid to clarifying the relations between these terms.
2. *Han* is the Japanese word for "fief." This term is often translated "clan" but as it is a territorial unit under a feudal lord and in no way a kinship unit this term seems unadvisable.
3. This point may be illustrated by a story told about one of Ninomiya Sontoku's most prominent pupils, Tomita Kokei. When starting off from his home village early one morning to attend the Confucian school in Edo, he heard footsteps and turned around to see his mother running after him. He asked what was the matter and she replied, "If you do not succeed, you need not return home." (Armstrong: *Just Before the Dawn*, p. 153.)
4. This point has been made by Ruth Benedict in *The Chrysanthemum and the Sword*.
5. The approach to the analysis of values used here is configurational. The values we are discussing are not primarily a matter of presence or absence. All societies have, in the broad sense in which we use the term, political values. But not all societies give primacy to these values as the Japanese seem to have done. Values which other societies hold primary are not necessarily absent in Japan, but are of secondary importance and usually strongly influenced by the primary political value cluster. [The four dimensions of systems upon which values may focus are goal attainment, adaptation, integration, and cultural values—Ed.]
6. Professor Parsons has suggested that this may be a matter of phase alternation. The four dimensions of figure 1 [on page 10 of *Tokugawa Religion*] when viewed temporally may be considered as four phases. There may be inherent strains in a basic commitment to goal-attainment values which require a periodic shift of emphasis to integrative values. The same kind of shift can, I think, be seen in China, but there the primary emphasis is on integrative values and the shift to goal-attainment values seems to be the more temporary.
7. This point is made by Ruth Benedict in *The Chrysanthemum and the Sword*.
8. *Chōnin* means "townsman." This term was used to cover the merchant and artisan classes and was often used as a synonym for *shōnin*, or merchant.

3 . Institutionalization and Change
Shmuel N. Eisenstadt

This paper illustrates the combination of systematic institutional analysis with the analysis of change, showing that the explication of change is inherent in the systematic analysis of concrete societies or parts thereof.

Claims have long been made that structural or "structural-functional" analysis, with its stress on systems, equilibrium, common values and boundary-maintenance, not only neglects problems of change, but is analytically incapable of dealing with them.   In response, many sociologists have recently asserted that not only is there no necessary contradiction between structural analysis and the analysis of change, but that on the contrary the two are basically compatible.

As formulated, for instance, by Moore, the argument is that every society (or social system) is inherently predisposed to change because of basic problems to which there is no overall continuous solution.[1]   These problems include uncertainties of socialization, perennial scarcity of resources relative to individual aspirations, and contrasting types of social orientation or principles of social organization (e.g., *Gemeinschaft* vs. *Gesellschaft*) within the society.   While this general view has been accepted to some extent, it has given rise to the contrary claim that it is couched in terms too general to explain the specific directions of change in any concrete society, that such specificity is beyond the province of "structural" analysis, and that such analysis can explain any concrete change only by reference either to very general and hence inadequate causes, or to forces external to the system.[2]

These difficulties can be at least partially overcome by recognizing that the general "predilections" to change inherent in any social system become "concretized" or "specified" through the process of institutionalization.   Our major point is that the institutionalization of any social system—be it political, economic or a system of social stratification or of any collectivity or role—creates in its wake the possibilities for change.   The process of institutionalization is the organization of a societally prescribed system of differentiated behavior oriented to the solution of certain problems inherent in a major area of social life.[3]

The organization of such systems of behavior involves the creation and definition of norms to regulate the major units of social behavior and organization, criteria according to which the flow of resources is regulated between such units,

From *The American Sociological Review*, Vol. 29, No. 2, 1964, pp. 235–247, by permission of the American Sociological Association.   This paper was written in 1962/3 when the author was Carnegie Visiting Professor of Political Science at M.I.T.   I am indebted to Professor R. N. Bellah for detailed comments on earlier versions of this paper.   Parts of this paper were presented at the Fifth International Congress of Sociology, Washington, D.C., in September 1962.

and sanctions to ensure that such norms are upheld.   All these involve the maintenance of the specific boundaries of the system, i.e., the maintenance of the units
that constitute it, of its relations with outside systems, and of the norms that
delineate its specific characteristics.

And yet the very attempt to institutionalize any such system creates in its wake
the possibility for change.   These are possibilities not only for general, unspecified change but for more specific changes, which develop not randomly but in
relatively specific directions, to a large extent set by the very process of institutionalization.   Hence a systematic structural analysis is a prerequisite for an
adequate analysis of change.[4]

II

We shall illustrate this general point by analyzing the process of institutionalization in one type of political and one type of religious system, drawing on recent
work on the social and political structure of the historical centralized bureaucratic
Empires, i.e., the Sassanid, Roman, Byzantine, Chinese, Caliphate and Ottoman
Empires and the European states in the period of absolutism,[5] and on the development of religious institutions within them.[6]

The majority of these Empires developed from (a) patrimonial empires such as
Egypt or the Sassanid Empire; (b) dualistic nomadic-sedentary empires (necessarily sharing many characteristics with the patrimonial ones); (c) feudal systems, such
as the European absolutist states; or (d) city-states (the Roman and Hellenistic Empires).   Despite the great variety in historical and cultural settings, we may designate some common features in the first stages of establishment of such polities.

The Empires were first established through interaction between the political
goals of the rulers who established them, and the broader conditions prevailing
in their respective social structures.   The initiative for the establishment of these
polities came, in all cases, from the rulers—emperors, kings or members of a
patrician ruling elite (like the more active and dynamic element of the patrician
elite in Republican Rome).   These rulers came, in most cases, from established
patrician, patrimonial, tribal or feudal families.   Some were usurpers, coming
from lower-class families, who attempted to establish new dynasties or to conquer
new territories, and some were conquerors who attempted to establish their rule
over various territories.

In most cases such rulers arose in periods of strife and turmoil during dis-
memberment of the existing political system or during acute strife within it.   Usually their aim was to reestablish peace and order.   They did not, however, attempt
to restore the old order in its entirety, although for propagandist reasons they
sometimes upheld such restoration as political ideology or slogan.   They sought
to establish a more centralized, unified polity in which they could monopolize
and set the political goals, without being bound by traditional aristocratic, tribal
or patrician groups.   Even the conquerors—as in the Roman, Islamic or Spanish
American Empires—had some vision of distinctly political goals and attempted to

transmit it to at least part of the conquered population. These aims were very often oriented against, and opposed by, various social and political groups. However great the turmoil, unrest and internal strife, some groups always either benefited from it (or hoped to do so) or aimed to reestablish the "old" order in which they held positions of power and influence.

To implement their aims against aristocratic patrician forces, the rulers found allies, active or passive, among the strata whose interests were opposed to those of the aristocratic groups and who could benefit from weakening the aristocracy and establishing a more unified polity. These allies were, basically, of two kinds. The first were the more active (mostly urban) economic, cultural and professional groups who, by origin or by social interest and orientation, or both, were opposed to the traditional aristocratic groups. The second were the larger, politically and socially more passive strata, including especially peasants and also lower urban groups who could benefit, even if indirectly, by the weakening of the aristocratic forces.

To implement their aims the Emperors attempted to establish a relatively centralized administration and to mobilize the resources needed for the neutralization, weakening or destruction of their enemies.

III

The successful institutionalization of the organizations through which the rulers could realize their aims was thus dependent first on the emergence of political entrepreneurs, the Emperors and their immediate entourage, who had the vision and ability to create new political entities.

Second, it depended on the existence, within the broader society, of certain specific conditions. Briefly, the most important of these conditions was the development, in all major institutional spheres, of a certain level of differentiation, i.e., the development of specific collectivities and roles in the major institutional spheres, such that the activities and resources of large parts of the population were freed from ascriptive (kinship, lineage, aristocratic) commitments and thus could be made available to the rulers.

These different social groups were willing to provide resources and support mostly because they perceived these Emperors as the best available choice among the various existing possibilities (as compared to more traditional aristocratic pretenders or to a state of continuous disorder). They may have identified themselves to various degrees with the goals and symbols of the Emperors; they may have hoped that the Emperors would help them attain some of their own goals, and in maintaining their values, establish norms and organizations to help regulate some of their internal problems, or they may have seen these Emperors as the least evil among the available choices.

To the degree that both sets of conditions developed in a given society, the possibility that a new imperial political system would be institutionalized was relatively great.

These conditions developed, for instance, though in varying degrees, in China from the beginning of the Han dynasty, in Byzantium and the Roman Empire in their formative stages, and in the Caliphates at the initial stages of their development.

In the Greek City States, on the other hand, while the broader social conditions did develop, there arose no group of leaders or entrepreneurs capable of forging a new polity. In other historical cases—e.g., those of Charlemagne or Genghis Khan—such leaders did arise but the broader social conditions were lacking.[7]

IV

But even when such conditions were propitious, and the new political leaders could obtain enough support, such support was of varying quality and intensity.

Several basic attitudes of the major strata toward the premises of the political systems of these Empires and toward the rulers' primary aims can be distinguished. The first attitude, evinced chiefly by the aristocracy, was one of opposition to the premises of the political systems. The second, passivity, was manifested mainly by the peasantry and sometimes also by other groups interested only in maintaining their limited local autonomy and their immediate economic interests.

The third attitude, found mostly in the bureaucracy, in some urban groups and in part of the professional and cultural elite, consisted of basic identification with the premises of the political system and willingness to fight for their interests within the framework of existing political institutions. The fourth attitude, developed mainly by the more differentiated urban groups and by the professional and intellectual elite, favored changes in the scope of the political system.

These attitudes often overlapped in concrete instances, and the attitudes of each group and stratum varied in different societies and periods. Moreover, the attitudes of any one group were never homogeneous and stable, and they could change according to the conditions or the demands made by the rulers. The concrete constellations of these various political attitudes of the major social groups greatly influenced the extent of their political participation.

V

Out of the interaction between these goals of the rulers on the one hand, and the broader social conditions and the varied attitudes of the various social strata on the other, the specific characteristics of these Empires became institutionalized.

Whatever the differences between the aims of various rulers and whatever the attitudes of the various groups, once the major contours of the Empires were institutionalized, various organizations developed within them—mostly through the efforts of the rulers—to implement policies designed to maintain the specific external and internal boundaries of the system, that is, its specific institutional contours and characteristics.

The most important characteristic of these Empires was the coexistence, within the same political institutions, of traditional, undifferentiated political activities, orientations and organizations with more differentiated, specifically *political* goals. Or in more general terms, the autonomy of the political as a distinct institutional sphere was limited. Autonomy of the political sphere was manifest first in the tendency toward political centralization, second, in the development by the rulers of autonomous political goals and third, in the relatively high organizational autonomy of executive and administrative organs and activities.

But the differentiation of political activities, organizations and goals was, in these political systems, limited by several important factors. First, the rulers were usually legitimated in terms of basically traditional-religious values, even where they stressed their own ultimate monopoly of such values. Second, the subject's political role was not fully distinguished from other basic societal roles—such as, for instance, membership in local communities; it was often embedded in local groups, and the citizen or subject did not exercise any direct political rights through a system of voting or franchise. Third, many traditional ascriptive units, such as aristocratic lineages or territorial communities, performed crucial political functions and served as units of political representation. As a consequence, the scope of political activity and participation was far narrower than in most contemporary political systems.

Let us briefly analyze the policies of the rulers. First, they were interested in the limited promotion of free resources and in freeing them from commitments to traditional aristocratic groups. Second, the rulers wished to control these resources, to commit them, as it were, to their own use. Third, they tended to pursue various goals—e.g., military expansion—that could, in themselves, have exhausted many of the available free resources.

Perhaps the most interesting example of these policies is the rulers' attempts to create and maintain an independent free peasantry with small-holdings and to restrict the big landowners' enchroachments on these small-holdings, in order to assure both the peasants' independence and the provision of resources to the rulers.

Of special importance too was the establishment of colonies and settlements of peasant soldiers, to make certain that the state would have sufficient military manpower. These colonies were not necessarily state-owned: they were closely associated with more complicated economic measures and policies, like various types of taxation. The policy of establishing such colonies evolved particularly in societies whose problems of frontier defense were of paramount importance. In Byzantium one purpose of the famous system of themes, supposedly evolved by the Emperor Heraclius (A.D. 610–641), was to provide adequate manpower for frontier garrisons. This was achieved by starting colonies of free peasants from which soldiers were involuntarily recruited. A similar pattern was established in the Sassanid Empire by Khousru the Great. The T'ang Emperors of China also organized the peasant militia on similar lines.[8]

VI

But the initial institutionalization of these political systems did not, in itself, assure their continuity. The very process of institutionalizing these Empires created new problems—mainly because maintaining the conditions necessary for these institutions became a more or less continuous concern of the rulers, so that special policies, activities and organizations had to be set up to ensure their perpetuation. Because the rulers had to pursue continuously certain policies oriented against some social groups and in favor of others, the contradictions among their various goals and in the attitudes of various groups to the basic premises of the system were evoked, and the negative orientations of certain groups were intensified. Though not always consciously grasped by the rulers, these contradictions were nevertheless implicit in their structural positions, in the problems and exigencies with which they dealt, and in the concrete policies they employed to solve these problems.

These internal contradictions developed in almost all the major institutional spheres, but perhaps especially in the sphere of legitimation and stratification. As we have seen, the rulers often attempted to limit the aristocracy's power and to create new status groups such as the free peasantry, a nonaristocratic official-dom, and so on. But these attempts faced several obstacles. Regardless of the number of new titles created or of the degree to which new or lower strata were encouraged, the symbols of status used by the rulers were usually very similar to those borne by the landed, hereditary aristocracy or by some religious elites. To create an entirely new secular and "rational" legitimation based on universalistic social principles was either beyond their capacities or against their basic political interest, or both. To do so would necessarily have enlarged the sphere of political participation and consequently increased the influence of various strata in the political institutions. The rulers therefore were usually unable to transcend the symbols of stratification and legitimation represented by the very strata whose influence they wanted to limit.

Thus the ability of the rulers to appeal to the lower strata of the population was obviously limited. Even more important, because of the emphasis on the superiority and worth of aristocratic symbols and values, many middle or new strata and groups tended to identify with them and consequently to "aristocra-tize" themselves.

Contradictions in the rulers' policies and goals developed in another direction as well. However tradition-bound the ruling elite may have been, its policies required the creation and propagation of more flexible "free" resources in various institutional fields, and the propagation of free resources gave rise to or promoted many religious, intellectual and legal groups whose value orientations differed from the traditional ones. Although in many societies all these groups were weak and succumbed to the influence of more conservative groups, in other cases —as in Europe—they developed into relatively independent centers of power, whose opposition to the rulers was only stimulated by the latter's conservative policies.

Similar contradictions also existed in the military, economic, and cultural spheres. Thus, for example, the growing needs of the Sassanid and Byzantine Empires in the last centuries of their respective Empires, for military manpower and economic resources, caused them to weaken the independent peasantry through mobilization and taxation, and to increase the power of the landed aristocracy. These policies undermined the very bases of their Empires.[9]

VII

But contradictions in the activities of the rulers and in the attitudes of the various strata did not constitute the only important foci of potential change in these political systems. Of no less importance was the possibility that the very organs created to implement the goals and policies of the rulers could develop goals and activities opposed to the basic premises of these political systems. The most important problem of this kind arose from the tendency of members of the bureaucratic administration to develop autonomous political orientations and activities.

First, the power that these bureaucracies acquired in societies in which there were usually but few "constitutional" limits on power and in which access to power was relatively limited, put the members of the bureaucracy in an especially privileged position. Second, the great emphasis, in these societies, on ascriptive symbols of status, necessarily "tempted" the members of the bureaucracy to use their power to acquire such symbols or to convert their positions into ascriptive, often hereditary status symbols. Third, the relatively low level of economic development and social differentiation permitted only limited development of special professional roles and only inadequate remuneration for them. The fact that in most of these societies the sale of offices was a very common expedient fully attests to this.

As a result of these conditions, members of the bureaucracies often tended to distort many of the customary or explicit rules and to divert many services to their own benefit or to that of some social groups with whom they were identified, and they tended to be both alienated from other groups in the society and oppressive toward them. In other words, they displaced the goal of service to the rulers and the various social strata, emphasizing goals of self-interest and aggrandizement instead.

On the other hand, the relative weakness of many political groups, and the great dependence of the bureaucracy on the rulers, often weakened and undermined the relative autonomy of the bureaucracy and brought about its total subjugation to the rulers. The latter could divert all the activities of the bureaucracy to their own exclusive use and prevent it from upholding any general rules for providing services to other strata in the society.

Thus the bureaucratic administration in these societies could, potentially, develop political orientations which were to some extent opposed to the basic premises of these polities and which generated changes that could not be contained within the institutional framework of the polity.

VIII

In these ways the very process of institutionalizing the political systems of these Empires created the possibility of change—change that could be absorbed within the institutional structures as well as change that undermined them.

The concrete reasons for these changes were usually series of events closely related to the various contradictions described above, the impingement of external events (such as wars, invasions, or fluctuations of trade routes), or interaction between internal and external processes.

In more concrete terms, the main factors generating processes of change in these Empires were (a) the continuous needs of the rulers for different types of resources and especially their great dependence on various "flexible" resources; (b) the rulers' attempts to maintain their own positions of control, in terms of both traditional legitimation and effective political control over the more flexible forces in the society; (c) the development in most of these societies, of what has been called *Primat der Aussenpolitik*[10] and the consequent great sensitivity of the internal structure of these societies to various external pressures and to international political and economic developments; (d) the development of various autonomous orientations and goals among the major strata and their respective demands on the rulers. These changes were more intensive so far as the rulers emphasized very "expensive" goals that exhausted the available economic and manpower resources, or different strata developed strong, autonomous political orientations.

In such situations, the rulers' tendency to maintain strong control over the more differentiated strata could become predominant, thus increasing the power of traditional forces and orientations and sharpening the conflicts between the traditional and the more flexible, differentiated strata, so that the latter were destroyed or alienated from the rulers. The excessive demands of the rulers in such situations, the growing public expenditures and the consequent increase of taxation and inflation, if not checked, often struck hardest at those groups whose economic organization was based on more flexible resources.

At such times, a continuous flux of foreign elements—mercenaries, hirelings and personal helpers of the rulers—often invaded the centers of the realms. With the depletion of the native strata and the growing external and internal exigencies, they succeeded in infiltrating some of the most important political posts (such as those of eunuchs, military commandments and viziers) and finally in totally usurping the ultimate power. Foreign merchants sometimes played a similar role, as in Byzantium or the Ottoman Empire, where they gradually succeeded in monopolizing all the tradeposts abandoned by the depleted indigenous merchants.

Where, as in Europe, these economically and socially more active strata were not depleted, they became alienated from the rulers, their policies and the political institutions of the society, becoming hotbeds of revolt and change.

Such developments usually intensified the great sensitivity of the rulers and the society to various external economic and political changes (in trade routes or in international price movements, or through the intrusion of foreign elements). Usually, some combination of external and internal pressures and exigencies precipitated changes in the political systems of these Empires. Hence, the greater the intensity of these internal contradictions and the greater the pressure of external exigencies that could not be dealt with by internal forces, the more quickly changes accumulated in these societies.[11]

IX

Some salient features of these changes were: First, interaction between internal and external events was greatly dependent on the special systemic characteristics of these political systems. While naturally enough many external events, such as invasions, were entirely beyond the control of any given Empire, each polity constituted part of a relatively "international" environment. Because of its basically expansionist goals and its great dependence on free economic resources, each Empire was especially sensitive to various specific developments in its broader environment. Moreover, external events and influences could very easily become closely interwoven with many of the internal problems of these Empires.

Second, while some such exigencies and problems are common to all political systems, their *specific* nature depends on the structure of the institutional system. Thus, the special sensitivity of the centralized bureaucratic Empires to such exigencies and pressures and to international economic fluctuations was rooted first, in their rulers' great emphasis on military and expansionist goals and second, in their need for various "free" resources, the availability of which depended on the international economic situation.

Similarly, while all political systems are influenced by and dependent on the efficiency and political loyalty of their administrative personnel, these Empires were especially sensitive to the possibility that the bureaucracy might become "aristocratized," "parasitic," and inflated. This sensitivity was due first to the fact that the bureaucracy was the ruler's main instrument for implementing his goals and overcoming his political opponents, and second, to the constant danger that the free resources so necessary for the implementation of his goals might be depleted by the encroachments of various aristocratic or traditional groups and by the aristocratic tendencies of the bureaucracy.

These specific sensitivities also determined the location of the foci from which the impetus to change developed. Such foci tended to develop, in these political systems, mainly though certainly not only, in two basic spheres. One was that of economic and social organization. The level of differentiation of this sphere and the nature of its internal, autonomous organization was crucial to the development of different levels of resources on the one hand and different levels of political demand on the other.

The other sphere was that of values, or "culture." This sphere encompassed the legitimation of the system and of the ruler and, because the active cultural elites regulated many aspects of communication in the society, it greatly influenced the level of demands made on the central political institutions. While in many cases cultural values kept the level of such demands within the confines of the system, in other cases, as in the Islamic or European countries, values became a very important focus of charismatic innovations that might easily have undermined the existing system and created entirely new perceptions of the political sphere among many social groups.

Both economic organization and special cultural values strongly influenced the specific sensibilities of these systems and the generation of change within them. And when the two developed simultaneously, in the direction of either increasing or diminishing differentiation, their impact on the destiny of these political systems was of crucial importance.

Finally, the directions of change and the outcomes of the processes of change were to a very large extent set by the nature of the institutional systems of these Empires and by their internal problems. The range of political systems that arose on the ruins, as it were, of these Empires was relatively limited. Short of total disorganization, they could either "recede" into some type of relatively uncentralized patrimonial or feudal system (but not, for instance, into a city-state or a primitive system) or become a relatively more differentiated oligarchic modern system (but not a mass democracy or a "canton-democracy").

X

The preceding analysis has drawn on illustrations only from the political sphere. But the same problems of institutionalization are found in any other major social sphere. We shall briefly illustrate this by analyzing the problems of institutionalization of religions and religious organizations in the Empires analyzed above.[12]

The religions that developed within the confines of these Empires were among the major world religious systems: the Mazdean religion in Iran, Confucianism, Taoism and Buddhism in China and India, Islam, Eastern Christianity in Byzantium, Catholicism in Europe and Spanish America and, later in Europe, Protestantism. These religions were usually developed through the activities of great religious innovators—either outstanding individuals or small groups of intense religious devotees—who attempted to create new cults and doctrines, and to spread and establish them in their respective societies.

Despite the great variety among these religions, they share important characteristics in some aspects of their value orientations, especially in their orientations to social reality.

The first such aspect is the breadth of the "group referent" of these religions; in most cases it was wider than any ascriptive or territorial group in these Empires.

The basic religious group referents were the total society as the bearer of religious values, the specific religious community, and such wider potential religious collectivities as "all believers" or "all mankind."

The second major characteristic of these religious value orientations is their emphasis on individual moral or religious activism, stressing the devotee's commitment to certain religiously prescribed tenets and lines of action and to the endeavor to implement them in social life.

Third, each of these value systems developed relatively independent ideological systems, attempting to organize and evaluate, in terms of ultimate values, the social reality in which they grew up, to shape the world in terms of religious values and purposes, and to convert others to the same endeavor. The commitments imposed by these ideological systems were not simply embedded in ritual and religious acts but implied the development of more specific social or political activities.

All of these orientations denote the detachment of religious orientations from basic ascriptive symbols and communities. They were developed mainly in the centers of religious activity by the more active religious leaders and innovators. Among the broader strata the differentiation of religious activities and organizations was much more limited. Nevertheless these orientations did develop to some extent, constituting the basis for the potential willingness of these groups to join the new religions and for the possibility of their institutionalization.

From the interaction of the major religious orientations with the religious leaders' concrete goals and with the broader social and religious conditions prevalent in the society, as well as from the more specific relations with the rulers and other groups, developed the specific institutional characteristics of these religions, their organization into churches, orders and sects or the more diffuse organizational patterns characteristic of China.

But in all these Empires, the distinctiveness of the religious sphere was limited. On the one hand, there were many specialized religious organizations, such as temples, religious "foundations," priestly associations, sects, churches, and monastic orders, many of which were organized in a bureaucratic manner, and, in conjunction with these, many specialized religious roles—priests, preachers, monks, and occupants of different positions in ecclesiastical organizations and hierarchies. On the other hand, however, the worshipping community was, to a very large extent, either identical with local groups or closely related to them. Only within the various sects and monastic orders did a special type of religious community develop.

Neither the institutionalization nor the continuity of these religious systems was assured. The religious leaders who aimed to establish and institutionalize them within their respective societies faced several basic problems. The most general problem stemmed from the existence of relatively free-floating cultural and religious orientations and activities which were not embedded in ascriptive units. To maintain their place in the cultural order, religious organizations had to shape and direct these resources. They not only had to ensure the loyalty and adherence of their members, but they also had to compete for economic resources, manpower, allegiance and support, both with other religious groups and with other social spheres, especially the political and economic ones.

Thus, the leaders of these religions were faced with the internal problems of formulating and formalizing their creeds and traditions so as to articulate and organize them on a relatively differentiated cultural level, and also with the necessity of regulating and channelling the diverse dynamic orientations and elements that could develop within them.

In connection with these internal problems several policies and patterns of activity were developed by the religious elites and organizations in these societies. Perhaps the most important of these was the very extensive formalization and codification of religious traditions, as manifested in the codification of sacred books, in the development of schools devoted to interpretation of the texts, in the growth of special educational organizations for the spread of religious knowledge and in the elaboration of comprehensive ideologies.

The religious leaders also faced more concrete organizational and external problems. Becuase they depended, in all their endeavors, on both the rulers and the broader strata in the society, they developed several basic aims. The first was to gain full official recognition and protection from the State as the established religion or, at least as a secondary but recognized and protected one. The second aim was to maintain independence and autonomy in the performance of the major religious functions, especially in internal government, organization of activities, and recruitment of members. This meant relative autonomy in the propagation of the creed and the maintenance of shrines, temples, and educational institutions, as well as independent determination and transmission of the major religious values and dogma. The demands for autonomy were directed mainly against the rulers and the bureaucracy who, as we have seen earlier, usually aspired to control the activities of the religious elite and to incorporate them into the general framework of their administrative activities.

The third major political objective of the religious elite, closely related to the first, was to preserve and extend the material bases (i.e., property) of the religious groups and institutions and to enhance their general social positions. A fourth objective, at least for some members of the religious elite, was to obtain positions of political and administrative influence.

XI

Whatever the success of the religious leaders in achieving these aims, the very institutionalization of these religions within the framework of their respective societies and polities could create continuous tension and give rise to several new problems.

The religious organizations needed the protection and help of the political institutions to establish and maintain their positions, organizations, and property, just as the political institutions needed the basic legitimation and support that could be provided only by the religious elite. This mutual dependence of relatively autonomous spheres could easily create many tensions, since each aimed to control the structural positions of the other and thus provide for its own needs. But whatever the scope of such conflicts and tensions, some *modus vivendi* was usually established, constituting a basic aspect of the institutionalization of these religions.

Thus in all of the societies studied, the religious elite upheld both the traditional legitimation of the rulers and supported, in principle, at least some of their political orientations and policies, despite the numerous conflicts over concrete issues arising between themselves and the political elite. Moreover, in most of the societies studied, the political participation of religious groups was, at least for certain periods of time, contained well within the basic framework of bureaucratic policy and institutions. In such cases these groups furthered the development of legitimate political struggle and contributed in this way to the continuity of the regime. The Mazdean Church in Persia, the Byzantine Church, and especially the Confucians and Buddhists in the Chinese Empire actively participated in politics and cooperated with the rulers. Thus they contributed, directly or indirectly, to the continuity of these systems. At the same time, the State provided important protection for the religious organizations.

But whatever the concrete *modus vivendi* between the rulers and any given religious elite or organization, in almost none of these societies—with the partial exception of Confucianism in China—did such mutual accommodation persist throughout the life of the Empire or of the religious organizations.

The very institutionalization of any such *modus vivendi* created the possibility for change both within the religions themselves and in their relations with other institutional spheres. The process of institutionalizing these religions and the necessity for continuous maintenance through varied policies and accommodations could easily enhance the contradictions inherent in the orientations of the religious leaders.

These contradictions were of several, often overlapping, kinds. One was between a "conservative" orientation that accepted the existing social order and the place of religion within it, on the one hand, and, on the other hand, a more radical orientation aiming to extend the autonomy of religious orientations and activities. Another was between an "other-worldly" emphasis stressing the perfection of purely religious attitudes and activities, and a more active, this-worldly orientation aiming at the transformation of the world.

Such contradictions were rooted in the relative autonomy and independent historical origins of the religious sphere, in its continuous interaction with the political sphere and in the nature of its value orientations. All these characteristics could serve as foci of crystallization for new religious groups—sects, groups of devotees, or "free-lance" religious intellectuals upholding one or another of these orientations in its purity as against the more "compromise-ridden" activities of the established religious leaders and organizations. The religious elites, in the course of working out and implementing their various *modi vivendi* with the rulers, and in attempting to maintain their own interests, tended to alienate some of the religiously active elements as well as some of the broader strata.

Moreover, the relatively complex organizations of these religions, and the great importance of a formal written tradition and its exegesis, were fertile ground for the rise of various sectarian movements and orders. The possibility of sectarian development was also enhanced by the fact that in many of these societies several religious bodies and organizations competed with one another for pre-dominance.

Hence within all these religions there developed many processes of change, which created new forms of religious organization. Some of these could be contained within the established religious framework, while others completely undermined it.

The same factors frequently also predisposed some of the religious groups and elites to develop more extreme political orientations and to participate—as in China, Persia, or Byzantium—in radical political and social movements, such as peasant uprisings, urban movements, and conspiracies. Cooperation between popular movements and leaders of religious secret societies was a common characteristic of rebellions in China and to some extent Byzantium and of peasant uprisings in France.

In still other cases—or in the same societies under changing circumstances—these religious organizations could also influence processes of change in the political system by instigating or furthering the withdrawal of active social and political support from the ruling elites. In this way they undermined the political frameworks of the Empires and indirectly also the bases of the *modus vivendi* between political and religious institutions.

The exact strength and direction of these processes of change depended greatly on the basic value orientations and institutional characteristics of the religions and on the nature of their struggles and accommodations with the rulers and other centers of power in the society.

But the direction of these changes was not random, nor were these changes limitless. Organizationally, religious institutions could either undergo what might be called the "ossification" and "indrawing" of existing churches, as in the case of the Eastern Church after the fall of the Byzantine Empire, or, through the development of various sects and more independent religious activities, be trans-formed into less homogeneous and monolithic, more differentiated structures, as was the case in Western Christianity, especially in Protestantism, and to a lesser extent in early and "middle" Islam. The effect of these changes on religious orientations is either to enhance the tendency towards "other-worldliness," social passivity, wthdrawal and mysticism, or to encourage more active and differentiated this-worldly activity.[13]

XII

The preceding analysis of the processes of change in the centralized Empires and in the major religions that developed within them is intended to illustrate the ways in which the institutionalization of a political, a religious, or any other social system in itself creates the potentialities and directions of change.[14]

The institutionalization of any social system means that certain norms, sanctions and organizations must be set up, and that policies through which these norms can be upheld and applied to a relatively large and complex variety of social situations must be implemented. These things are done by people who are placed in or attempt to achieve strategic positions and who aspire to certain goals. The new norms regulate the provision of various resources from other parts of the society to these power positions and to the new organizations, some of the relations among the different groups in the society, and the obligations of the occupants of these positions toward various groups in the society.

While the occupants of these positions naturally attempt to set up norms in accord with their own values, goals and interests, they also define certain norms shared by a number of groups. Very often they legitimize these norms by values that are purportedly shared, to some extent, by a large part of the society and symbolized by themselves. Hence, such values tend to be binding on the rulers themselves.

But whatever the success of such attempts to establish common norms and legitimize them in terms of common values and symbols, these norms are probably never fully accepted by the entire society. Most groups within any society or collectivity tend to exhibit some autonomy in terms of their attitudes toward any such institutionalization, and they vary greatly in the extent of their willingness or ability to provide the resources demanded by the system. While for very long periods of time a great majority of the members of a given society may be to some degree identified with the values and norms of the system and willing to provide it with the resources it needs, other tendencies also develop. Some groups—like the aristocracy in the case of the Empires discussed above—may be greatly opposed to the very premises of the institutionalization of a given system, may share its values only to a very small extent, and may accept these norms only as the least among evils and as binding on them only in a very limited sense.

Others may share these values and accept the norms to a greater degree but, like the cultural and economic elites or sects, may look on themselves as the more appropriate repositories of these same values, may oppose the concrete level at which the norms are institutionalized by the elite in power, and may attempt to interpret them in different ways. Others again may develop new interpretations of existing values and strive for a change in the very basis of the institutional order. Hence any institutional system is never fully "homogeneous," that is, fully accepted or accepted to the same degree by all those participating in it, and these different orientations all may become foci of conflict and of potential institutional change.

Even more important, from the point of view of our analysis, is that whatever the initial attitudes of any given group to the basic premises of the institutional system, these may greatly change after the initial institutionalization of the system. Any institutionalization necessarily entails efforts to maintain the boundaries of the system, through continuous attempts to mobilize resources from different groups and individuals, and to maintain the legitimacy of the values, symbols and norms of the system. But continuous implementation of these policies may affect the positions of different groups in the society, giving rise to continuous shifts in the balance of power among them and in their orientations to the existing institutional system and its values.

Moreover, the institutionalization of any system usually creates new collectivities and organizations, such as the bureaucratic organizations in the centralized Empires. These organizations necessarily develop needs, interests, and orientations of their own which may impinge on various other groups and institutional spheres.

Similarly, changes in the balance of forces within the system also facilitate the development and "maturation" of certain inherent tendencies in the structure and orientation of key groups and elites, as in the tendencies of some religious groups to develop and establish wider universalistic orientations and membership units, which may then develop beyond the basic premises of the system.

These processes may be intensified by the systemic relations between any given institutional framework or sphere and other spheres within the society. Whatever the degree of integration of the "total" society, systemic relations between, e.g., the political and the economic, or the political and the kinship systems, are inherent in any on-going society. But as has been so often pointed out, the basic or predominant orientations and norms regulating each of these institutions differ to some extent. For example, family and kinship units tend to emphasize particularistic, diffuse, and ascriptive orientations while economic units emphasize universalism and achievement.[15]

These different institutional spheres, represented by the structurally patterned activities of occupants of the major positions within them, attempt to maintain their autonomy and tend to make contradictory demands on different groups to provide them with the necessary resources. Each may look for support from different groups in the society, thus exacerbating potential conflicts among the various groups, changing their relative strengths and possibly undermining the premises of a given institutional system.

These contradictions, conflicts and shifts in the balance of power may lead to the depletion of the resources needed to maintain a given system or give rise to the crystallization of new foci of resources and orientations which may in turn seek to create a new institutional system.

Events leading to different processes of change, as has been pointed out before, also affect the relations between any given institutional system and its external environment. Each institutional system is especially sensitive, in terms of dependence on resources and maintenance of its own boundaries, to certain aspects of its relations with its environment.

XIII

Thus we conclude that the institutionalization of a system creates the possibility that "anti-systems," or groups with negative orientations toward its premises, will develop within it. While the nature and strength of such anti-systems may vary, as between different institutional (i.e., religious, political) systems and between different types within each, and while they may often remain latent for very long periods of time, they also constitute important foci of change, under propitious conditions.

The existence of such contradictions or conflicts among the different institutional spheres and among different groups does not, of course, preclude the possibility that the system will maintain its boundaries more or less continuously, through a hierarchy of norms and accommodation or partial insulation of different subsystems, and that a definite order and stable relations among the system's parts will persist. But the possibility of conflict and potential change is always present, rooted in the very process of institutionalization, and the direction and occurrence of change depend heavily on the nature of this process.

Just as the predilection for change is necessarily built into any institutional system, so the direction and scope of change are not random but depend, as we have shown in discussing the processes of change in the Empires and in the great religions, on the nature of the system generating the change, on its values, norms and organizations, on the various internal forces operating within it and on the external forces to which it is especially sensitive because of its systemic properties. These various forces naturally differ between religious and political institutions and among different societies, but sensitivity to these forces and the tendency to change are inherent in all of them.

The analysis presented above does not pretend to solve all the problems in analyzing social change; we have not discussed the mechanisms of change, nor the relations between changes at different institutional levels of a given society. But at least we have indicated that for conceptual tools adequate to the analysis of change we need not necessarily go beyond systematic sociological analysis; rather, a full explication of systematic sociological concepts can provide a fruitful initial step for the analysis of change.

Notes

1. See Wilbert E. Moore, "A Reconsideration of Theories of Social Change," *American Sociological Review*, 25 (December, 1960), pp. 810–818, and Kingsley Davis, "The Myth of Functional Analysis as a Special Method in Sociology and Anthropology," *American Sociological Review*, 26 (December, 1959), pp. 752–772.
2. See, for instance, Ronald Philip Dore, "Function and Cause," *American Sociological Review*, 26 (December, 1961), pp. 843–853; Kenneth E. Bock, "Evolution, Function and Change," *American Sociological Review*, 28 (April, 1963), pp. 229–237.
3. Following Alvin W. Gouldner and Helen P. Gouldner, *Modern Sociology, An Introduction to the Study of Human Interaction*, New York: Harcourt, Brace, 1963, p. 484; see also Harry M. Johnson, *Sociology, A Systematic Introduction*, New York: Harcourt, Brace, 1960, ch. 2; Talcott Parsons, *The Social System*, Glencoe, Ill.: The Free Press, 1951, chs. 2 and 5.
4. Some parallel indications can be found in Thomas F. O'Dea, "Sociological Dilemmas, Five Paradoxes of Institutionalization," in Eduard A. Tiryakian (ed.), *Sociological Theory, Values and Sociocultural Change, Essays in Honor of Pitirim A. Sorokin*, New York: The Free Press of

Glencoe, 1963, pp. 71–91; see also Neil J. Smelser, *Theory of Collective Behavior*, New York: The Free Press of Glencoe, 1963, esp. chs. 2 and 3.

5. See Shmuel N. Eisenstadt, *The Political Systems of Empires*, New York: The Free Press of Glencoe, 1963, and "The Causes of Disintegration and Fall of Empires—Sociological and Historical Analyses," *Diogenes*, 34 (Summer, 1961), pp. 82–158.

6. See Shmuel N. Eisenstadt, "Religious Organizations and Political Process in Centralized Empires," *The Journal of Asian Studies*, 21 (May 1962), pp. 271–294, and *The Political Systems of Empires, op. cit.*

7. For a fuller exposition of this statement, see Eisenstadt, *The Political Systems of Empires*.

8. *Ibid.*, ch. 7.

9. *Ibid.*, ch. 12.

10. This term has been often used by F. Altheim in his studies of Roman and Sassanid History; see for instance, F. Altheim, *Gesicht von Abend und Morgen*, Frankfurt: Fischer Verlag, 1955, *passim*.

11. See Eisenstadt, *The Political Systems of Empires*, chs. 7 and 10.

12. See Eisenstadt, "Religious Organizations and Political Process," *op. cit.*

13. *Ibid.*

14. The same basic considerations are applied to role analysis in Shmuel N. Eisenstadt, Dov Weintraub and Nina Toren, "Analysis of Role Change," Jerusalem: The Hebrew University, Department of Sociology, Technical Note No. 7, Contract No. AFGI (052)–480 (mimeo.), 1963.

15. See Alvin W. Gouldner, "Reciprocity and Autonomy in Functional Theory," in Llewellyn Gross (ed.), *Symposium on Sociological Theory*, Evanston, Ill.: Row Peterson, 1959, pp. 241–271, and Gideon Sjoberg, "Contradictory Functional Requirements and Social Systems," *The Journal of Conflict Resolution*, 4 (June, 1960), pp. 198–258.

4 . Transformation of Social, Political, and Cultural Orders in Modernization
Shmuel N. Eisenstadt

The institutionalization of change, or the development and crystallization of new institutional settings requires the internal transformation of the societies or groups within which it occurs.   The capacity for such internal transformation is manifest in structural frameworks or cultural symbols that enable some groups to mobilize

From *The American Sociological Review*, Vol. 30, No. 5, October 1965, pp. 659–673, by permission of the American Sociological Association.   The 1964 MacIver Award lecture, delivered at the Presidential session of the Eastern Sociological Society, April 1965, in New York.   A preliminary version of the first part of this lecture was given at the University of New Delhi, January 1965.   The research reported in this document was sponsored partly by the Air Force Office of Scientific Research through the European Office of Aerospace Research (OAR), U.S. Air Force.

new forces and resources without necessarily destroying the existing structure.[1] In modernizing societies, internal transformation is especially critical because modernization requires not only a relatively stable new structure but one capable of adapting to continuously changing conditions and problems.[2]

Modernization, of course, does not imply a "smooth" process of "balanced" or "equilibrated" growth. It has always been a revolutionary process of undermining and changing the existing institutional structure. But the possibility of successful institutionalization of an innovating or revolutionary process is never inherent in the revolutionary act itself. It depends on other conditions, primarily the society's capacity for internal transformation.

A society can be forced to modernize under the impact of external forces, and indeed 19th- and 20th-century modernization has meant, to a very large extent, the impingement of Western European institutions on new countries in the Americas, in Eastern and Southern Europe, and in Asia and Africa. Some of these societies have never—or not yet—gone beyond adaptation to these external impingements. Lacking a high degree of internal adaptability, many become stagnant after having started on the road to modernity, or their modern frameworks have tended to break down.[3] Moreover, different societies necessarily develop different institutional patterns, so that the spread of modernization has entailed a great deal of structural diversity.

Modernization, however, is associated with some definite structural characteristics. Among these the most important are a high level of structural differentiation, and of so-called "social mobilization," and a relatively large-scale, unified and centralized institutional framework. Beyond this basic core, the aforementioned structural diversity may develop. These structural characteristics are not to be regarded as simple indices of successful modernization, and their development does not necessarily assure successful modernization. Rather they are necessary but not sufficient conditions for the development and continuity of a modern institutional structure sufficiently capable of dealing with continuously changing problems to assure sustained growth.[4]

Among these conditions, of special importance is the establishment of viable, flexible and yet effective symbolic and organizational centers, responsive to the continuous problems of modernization and able to regulate them. At the same time, a more flexible orientation with new goals and a commitment to the new centers and their needs must be developed among the more active social groups. Here some aspects of the pre-modern structure of modernizing societies are especially important. With the exception of the African and to some extent the Latin American ones, most pre-industrial societies began modernizing, or were pushed into it, with a relatively complex, differentiated institutional structure. Within the great historical and Imperial civilizations for example, centralized and differentiated structures and organizations already existed, together with *relatively* autonomous basic institutional spheres—political, religious or ideological, and social organization and stratification.[5]

The centralized frameworks and the relatively autnomous institutional spheres were crucial to the transformative capacities of these societies, for they facilitated the initial modernization and helped make the new modern centers and frameworks work efficiently. Different constellations of these characteristics, however, greatly influence transformative capacity in general, as well as the particular institutional form that modernization may take in a given case.

In the following analysis I shall point out some of the constellations that facilitate—or impede—modernization, focusing on three aspects of the relations among the various institutional spheres in pre-modern societies. The first of these aspects is the relation between the dominant value-system and political institutions; the second is the place of the political system in the stratification system; and the third is the degree of internal cohesion and social autonomy in the major social groups and strata within these societies. I shall attempt to test the fruitfulness of this approach first by analyzing the major Asian societies—China, Japan and India—coming only later to a brief analysis of modern European societies.

CHINA[6]

China has had a long tradition of centralization, and a degree of social, political, and cultural continuity probably unparalleled in the history of mankind. Under the Imperial system Chinese society could absorb many changes brought about by conquests, changes of dynasties and rebellions, yet this great civilization was relatively unable to modernize itself from within, either through reformation of the Imperial system or through the initial revolution that developed against it. True, many reform movements did develop within the Chinese Imperial system, ranging from relatively "conservative," "traditional" attempts to preserve the Confucian ethic and its cultural primacy, to the more radical movements attempting to transform dominant value orientations and to establish a system independent of Confucian orientations and symbols. But as Levenson and others[7] have shown, these reforms were not very successful either in changing the ideology and institutions of the Imperial system or in creating new, viable frameworks.

Similarly, the first modern revolution against the Imperial system did not establish a viable, modern political system. Many external factors no doubt contributed to this failure, but it is still worthwhile to analyze the influence of some internal factors.

The first such factor is the nature of the legitimation of the Imperial system— the relation between Imperial political institutions and the major cultural centers, ideology and symbols.   Here we find, among the great historic Imperial civilizations, the closest interweaving, almost identity, of cultural with political centers. Although in principle many universalistic ethical elements in the dominant Confucian ideology transcended any given territory or community, in actuality this ideology was very closely tied to the specific political framework of the Chinese Empire.   The Empire was legitimized by the Confucian symbols but the Confucian symbols and Confucian ethical orientation found their "natural" place and framework, their major "referrent," within the Empire.[8]

This, of course, was also related to the fact that no church or cultural organization in China existed independently of the state. The Confucian elite was a relatively cohesive group, sharing a cultural background which was enhanced by the examination system and by adherence to Confucian rituals and classics. But its organization was almost identical with that of the state bureaucracy, and except for some schools and academies it had no organization of its own. Moreover, political activity within the Imperial-bureaucratic framework was a basic referent of the Confucian ethical orientation, which was strongly particularistic and confined to the existing cultural-political setting.[9]

The relation between Chinese political and cultural orders is parallel to that between the political system and social stratification. The most interesting point here is that the total societal system of stratification was entirely focused on the political center. The Imperial center, with its strong Confucian orientation and legitimation, was the sole distributor of prestige and honor. Various social groups or strata did not develop autonomous, independent, status orientations, except on the purely local level; the major, almost the only wider orientations were bound to this monolithic political-religious center. Of crucial importance here is the structure of the major stratum linking the Imperial center to the broader society—the literati. This stratum was a source of recruitment to the bureaucracy and also maintained close relations with the gentry. Their double status orientation enabled the literati to fulfil certain crucial integrative functions in the Imperial system.[10] Their special position enabled them to influence the political activities of the rulers and of the leading strata of the population. But they exerted this influence by upholding the ideal of a hierarchical social-political-cultural order binding on the rulers and these strata. The very existence of the literati as an elite group was contingent on the persistence of the ideal of a unified Empire.

These characteristics of the literati were among the most important stabilizing mechanisms in the Imperial system, helping it to regulate and absorb changes throughout its long history. But these same characteristics have also severely inhibited development of a reformative or transformative capacity in China's culturally and politically most articulate groups.

Capacity for reform or transformation in the broader groups of Chinese society is also affected by their strong "familism"—the basis of their internal cohesion and self-identity. Familism has often been designated as one cause of China's relatively unsuccessful modernization. But as Levy has shown in his later analysis, it is not the familism as such that was important but rather the nature of the family's internal cohesion and its links with other institutional spheres.[11] The family was a relatively autonomous, self-enclosed group, with but few broader criteria or orientations. Beyond the commitment to the bureaucracy of those who attained positions within it, the primary duty of individuals was to increase family strength and resources, not to represent the family's worth according to external goals and commitments.

In combination, these various aspects of Chinese social structure go far toward explaining the weakness of the initial stages of China's modernization. The identity between the cultural and the political orders and the specific characteristics of the literati tended to maintain the dominance of a stagnative neo-traditionalism, that continuously reinforced the non-transformative orientations in Chinese culture.

Under the first impact of modernization, Chinese intellectuals and bureaucrats faced certain problems stemming from the fact that their basic cultural symbols were embedded in the existing political structure. Any political revolution or reformation necessarily entailed rejecting or destroying the cultural order. Similarly, the strong ideological emphasis on upholding the social-political status quo inhibited the emergence of new symbols to legitimize new social institutions relatively independently of the preceding order.[12] Hence there developed little capacity for viable, flexible institution building, especially in the legal, legislative or administrative fields. Many such institutions were formally initiated, but they lacked both "pre-contractual" bases of legitimation and the broader societal conditions and resources for effective functioning.[13]

But this weakness of initial reform and revolutionary movements in Imperial and post-Imperial China was only partly due to the ideological identity between the cultural and the political orders. No less important were the relations between political institutions and the system of social stratification. In the social sphere as in the ideological or cultural sphere, there were few points of internal strength, cohesion and self-identity on which new institutional frameworks could be founded or which could support institutional changes.

This weakness was reinforced by the limited reformative capacities of the family. When the Empire crumbled and processes of change swept over it, disorganizing and dislocating the traditional structure, and especially the major links to the center—the literati and the bureaucracy—family groups were largely dissociated from the center, but they lacked the strength to create new autonomous links. These family groups tended also to develop neo-traditional orientations, but because they were "closed" groups they could not regulate such demands effectively. In the more modern setting, they became highly politicized, making demands on the new, and for them not fully legitimate center, which sapped the resources available for internal redistribution and thus undermined the new institutional frameworks.

ISLAM

Throughout its history Islam has emphasized the identity between the religious and political communities, seeking to fuse these two institutional spheres in a manner almost unique in the history of the great universalistic religions.[14] This identity between political and religious communities represents a very important similarity between the Chinese and Islamic societies, though its religious or ideological bases are very different.

The Islamic states, especially the early Caliphates, developed out of a conquest in which a new universal religion was created and borne by conquering tribes.

This identity between tribe and religion became weaker in later stages when the more centralized-bureaucratic empires (the Abbasides and Fatimides) developed and ethnically heterogeneous elements were welded together through a common religion and a new political framework, but political and the religious communities were united throughout the history of Islamic states.[15]   Moreover, political issues (e.g., succession, and the scope of the political community) initially constituted the main theological problems of Islam.[16]

This political-religious unity had specific ideological and structural consequences.   Within the Caliphate there developed, on the one hand, a very strong universalistic-missionary orientation and a strong emphasis on the state as the framework of the religious community but subordinate to it.   On the other hand, religious functionaries and groups did not develop an overall, independent, and cohesive organization.   This combination limited political participation mostly to court cliques and the bureaucracy, but it also gave rise to extreme sectarian movements, some seeking to destroy the existing regime and establish a new, religiously pure and true one, others politically passive.   Thus, strong reform movements based on universalistic and transcendental orientations did develop under Islam.[17]   But it is very significant that these movements were successful only so far as they were not politically oriented and did not have to establish new central political institutions within the framework of Islamic tradition.

Islam reform movements were more successful in colonial situations, as in Indonesia or in Malaysia, where there were active minorities or where their political objective was to attain independence, and in cultural, educational and economic activities, than they were in the independent Muslim states where they had to try to establish a new Islamic polity.   Islamic reform movements in India in the early 20th century, for instance, evinced a relatively strong emphasis on educational and cultural innovation.   Subsequently, these movements were transformed into more populist, political ones during the immediate pre-partition period and especially in Pakistan after independence.[18]

Close identity between the political and the religious communities inhibited Islamic reform movements in ways somewhat similar to, but not identical with those in China.   In the Islamic states as in China the identity between cultural and political institutions severely limited possibilities for the innovations necessary to develop viable modern legislative and juridical institutions;[19] nor did traditional Islamic prescriptions for appropriate political behavior facilitate legal innovations.[20]

Attempts to build modern nation-states on an Islamic base faced tremendous obstacles.   The Islamic tradition was challenged by various new secular-national symbols [that] challenged the Islamic traditions, and efforts to legitimize national identities in terms of Islamic tradition intensified conflicts among various units.[21]   The history of the attempt to establish an Islamic polity in Pakistan, for example, and similar experiences in various Middle Eastern countries, illustrate some of these difficulties.[22]   Among the older Muslim states, only Tunisia—through a variety of circumstances I cannot go into here—seems to have succeeded, to some extent at least, in overcoming them.[23]   (In Turkey—at the very core of the older

Ottoman Empire—new institution building was attempted only through the complete negation of the Islamic tradition at the central political and symbolic level.[24])

With regard to the relations between political institutions and social stratification, Islamic patterns are less similar to the Chinese. The system of stratification in many Islamic societies was not focused to the same extent on the state, though in some extreme cases, as in the core of the Ottoman Empire, similar tendencies did develop. But on the whole, various social and cultural groups—e.g., the religious groups, the ulemas—evinced a higher degree of organizational and social autonomy. True, these same groups often became centers of reaction and traditionalism, but their autonomy did create possibilities for intellectual ferment and social change.

Moreover, in many Islamic societies a tradition of local, especially urban, community autonomy existed, even if it was only latent. Although the martial Ottoman rule weakened this tradition, on the whole, it persisted at the peripheries of the Empire, enhancing receptivity to modern intellectual and organizational trends and facilitating the concomitant development of various professional, entrepreneurial, administrative and intellectual groups.[25] But the inability of these groups to develop new, more effective links with the center, or to develop adequate self-regulative mechanisms, gave rise here also to a relatively high degree of politicization. Nevertheless, the major potential for reform and modernization must be sought within these groups.

JAPAN

The Japanese case is at a different pole of comparison with the Chinese one: here the importance of structural differences exceeds that of ideological or value orientations.

On the purely ideological level one may, at first sight, perceive a strong similarity between the Japanese and Chinese experiences. Indeed, an even more closed, particularistic orientation and collective identity existed in Japan. The identity between cultural and political orders was even closer, and universalistic elements or orientations beyond the existing political and national framework weaker,[26] so that emphasis on the Confucian ethic (though mixed with Buddhist and Shinto elements) created an even stronger identification with the particular polity than in China.

But paradoxically enough these elements did not greatly impede the internal transformation and modernization of Japanese society, although they influenced the directions and limits of modernization. On the value-orientation level, as well as on that of the structural location of the central symbols of the society, several points of flexibility developed. First the structure of the center in the Tokugawa period differed in several crucial and important aspects from the Chinese or any other centralized Imperial system. The Japanese centralization took place under a special form of feudalism, and although the various autonomous feudal traditions were weakened or frozen they did not entirely lose their vitality.[27] Even more important, the arrangement of Tokugawa political institutions was such that the center was less monolithic than the strong ideological identity between cultural and the political orders might suggest.

The dissociation between the symbolic center, represented by the politically ineffective Emperor, and the politically effective center of the Shogunate obviated several of the potential consequences of a close identity between the polity and the cultural order.[28]   In some ways this organizational duality was equivalent to a dissociation—on the substantive level—between the cultural and the political orders.   This has facilitated a political revolution anchored in the ancient Imperial political symbolism and created an almost uniquely successful initial modernization based on neo-traditional orientations and symbols.[29]   (Some of the traditional Kingdoms like Morocco, Buganda, or Ethiopia, may also attempt to modernize in this way, though they are handicapped by the absence of a similar dissociation between the traditional symbols and the effective political centers. But Professor Inkeles has drawn my attention to the fact that a development very similar to the Japanese one has lately been taking place in Nepal.)

The revival of the older symbolic center greatly facilitated and supported the overthrow, by an oligarchic revolution, of the political center of the Shogunate. This continuity of the Imperial tradition was not purely "decorative," but constituted the major focus of the new value orientations and the new national identity, and it greatly helped to mobilize the loyalties of the broader strata.[30]   Such a transformation could not have been so easily attained in China or the Islamic states, where overthrow of the political center would undermine the cultural order, and the mobilization of older traditional loyalties would diminish possibilities for developing a modern, effective political center.

Several aspects of Japanese religion enhanced the transformation.   First, the syncretic nature of Japanese religion, and the relative lack of rigid orthodoxy, facilitated the absorption of new contents.   Second, strong transcendental orientations, evinced in different ways in some Buddhist and Confucian circles, became more pronounced in the late Tokugawa period, which facilitated the development of independent standards under which various groups or individuals formulated legitimate collective goals.[31]   The combination of religious syncretism with this transcendental emphasis facilitated both the redefinition of collective goals according to the more modern orientation of the Meiji oligarchs and the mobilization of wider loyalties in their implementation.

Other aspects of Japanese feudalism were also of great importance in the relatively successful initial modernization of the society.   The hierarchically interlocked groups comprising the feudal system of stratification were strongly committed to collective obligations.[32]   In their criteria of status and self-identity these groups evinced a relatively high degree of autonomy, but unlike the Chinese groups, these were not closed.   Their identity, and the mutual obligations it entailed, were not entirely dependent on the political center.   Nor were there homogeneous high-status political-cultural groups like the literati to monopolize the central political and elite positions. The major strata were much more dispersed and heterogeneous: there were clusters of feudal landlords, merchant and intellectual groups, each with some autonomy. Moreover, these groups were structurally linked to each other and to the center. All of these characteristics facilitated either self-transformation or a high degree of adaptability to any changes initiated by the center.

This structural aspect of the status system was reinforced by the transcendental elements of the religious orientation, permitting the transfer of loyalties from the old feudal-Shogunate-centered hierarchy to the new center.[33]

Certain aspects of Japanese family structure were also important here.[34] Although the family was a basic focus of solidarity and loyalty in Japan as in China, its place depended to a large extent on its ability to further collective interests. Hence family units could develop semi-autonomous mechanisms to regulate their own activities and problems, minimizing initial demands on the center and conferring upon it the loyalties and resources of family groups.[35]

Because the older political and feudal regimes contained these seeds of autonomy and self-transformation, Japanese modernization proceeded rapidly. Industrialization, promulgated from the center, mobilized broad groups and strata. A new system of stratification emerged, as the Meiji oligarchs, themselves stemming from secondary aristocratic groups, abolished not only the political power of the older aristocracy but also its status symbols and economic (agrarian) bases. The Meiji monopolized the symbolic and political center, but they often used renovated traditional Imperial symbols to legitimize a much greater status flexibility. Although the status symbols and hierarchy they developed were close to the political center and to the oligarchs in power, emphasizing bureaucratic positions, the monolithic political forms that developed in China did not appear. In rural as well as urban sectors of Japanese society, the Meiji created more flexible, relatively autonomous new criteria for status, making it possible for new groups to crystallize their status.[36]

Some of the more specific structural characteristics of Japanese modernization can also be related to specific points of flexibility in the Tokugawa period. Among these the most important was the combination of universalistic and particularistic criteria regulating and channelling social mobility and mobilization. In the educational system, and on the "entry" to occupational statuses, universalistic criteria were applied, especially in the various periods or stages of examinations. But beyond this entrance stage, on almost all levels of the social and occupational structure, various particularistic units, such as school cliques, company and bureaucratic cliques and groups, small labor groups, etc., tended to crystallize. Within these units many traditional forms and attitudes persisted, and little mobility occurred between them. At the same time, however, the extent of overlapping between different particularistic units was relatively small, with few ecological crystallizations of such overlapping, so that particularistic developments did not impede and may even have facilitated status flexibility and recrystallization in certain social groups.[37]

This flexibility enabled Japan to deal with many of the problems of modernization, though not with all of them.   She could not avoid various breakdowns, the most important of which took place in the late 1920's and early 1930's.[38]   During that period various new elites—the more modern and independent middle classes, professional, and intellectual groups, as well as some workers' organizations—attempted to enlarge the scope of their political participation.   Failing to absorb these new elements, the modern system broke down and this gave rise to the militarist regimes of the thirties.   This development was mostly due to the rulers' attempt to stifle new demands, and to control these new groups and their demands through bureaucratic and military factions under the aegis of Imperial symbols. The initial incorporation of new demands in the early Meiji period was also done through such factions, but because the system was not fully institutionalized it could not cope with the growing dissociation among the modern business and intellectual elites and working-class leaders on the one hand, and the more traditional and oligarchic elites on the other.

Here several weaknesses in the process of Japanese modernization stand out. The first was in the nature of the symbolic transformation of the center.   The new, organizationally flexible center established by the Meiji oligarchs embodied no internal transformation of values.   The new national identity was couched mostly in terms of particularistic loyalty to the Emperor as Son of Heaven rather than in terms of his representation of any wider (transcendental) or universalistic values.   While this Imperial symbolism was flexible enough to absorb many new political orientations, the basic legitimation of the new political community and its activities did not transcend particularistic collective symbols.   Hence value orientations through which various new social forces could be legitimated and impinge on the center in autonomous terms, and through which support for various autonomous regulative mechanisms and frameworks could be provided, did not develop.[39]

Similarly, although the central groups possessed a relatively high degree of status flexibility at a relatively early stage of modernization, this flexibility was not bolstered by an autonomous basis for legitimation and self-perception.   The heavy neotraditionalism of the center did not foster the development of autonomous value orientations and hence limited the ability of various social groups to develop institutional frameworks for mediating among the interests of various groups and evolving a broad base of consensus.[40]

Only under the impact of external forces (i.e., military defeat) did Japanese modernization make a new start.   This new phase is also, as yet, overshadowed by problems from the past, especially the absence of an internal value transformation at the time of Japan's initial modernization.

INDIA

India is probably the only complex and highly differentiated historical civilization that has maintained its cultural integrity without being tied to any particular political framework.[41]   This is true not only of the last centuries under Muslim and later English rule but even before that.   In India there were small and large states and Imperial centers, but no single state with which the cultural tradition was identified.   Classical Indian religious thought did, of course, refer to political issues, and to the behavior of princes and the duties and rights of subjects.[42] But to a much higher degree than in many other historical Imperial civilizations, politics were conceived in secular terms.   The basic religious and cultural orientations, the specific cultural identity of Indian civilization, were not necessarily associated with any particular political or imperial framework; whatever partial identity of such kind might have existed during the period before Muslim domination has been greatly diminished since then.   The strength and survival of Indian civilization under alien rule is rooted in the very fact that it was not identified with any political framework.

This basic characteristic of Indian civilization had a very important influence on the initial modernization processes, which began under the aegis of the British and continued during the nationalist movement.   Because the cultural and political orders were more or less dissociated, modernization was relatively free of specific traditional-cultural orientations toward the political sphere.   The modern center was first established in terms of western symbols and was to some extent detached from the great Indian cultural tradition.[43]   In the Gandhian phase, the political aspirations of the Indian national movement were to some extent couched in traditional symbols or at least were legitimized by some interpretation of such symbols, but this did not create (as it did in Islam) too specific or intensive demands on the institutional structure.[44]

This dissociation was itself at least partially legitimized in terms of traditional ideological orientations.   Some of the symbols or values of the new center, expressed mostly in terms of such Western values as political and social justice, could be legitimized in older, classical Indian political terms.   This was reinforced by reformist tendencies among the upper strata of Hindu society after 1850, for, significantly enough, the new political-ideological center was to a large extent developed and borne by people coming from the strata—especially the Brahmanic groups—who were the bearers of the historical tradition in its non-political aspects and emphases.[45]

The second relevant aspect of Indian society has to do with the place of the political system in the system of stratification and the internal cohesion of broader social groups and strata.   In their identity and in their relation to the political order, these groups evinced a very high degree of autonomy.   Parallel to the relative independence of cultural traditions from the political center, castes, villages, and the various networks of communication were highly autonomous, self-regulating in terms of their own cultural and social identity, with but limited access to the political center or centers.[46]

For the process of modernization, this autonomy meant that the new political center could develop without intensive demands immediately impinging on it. The broader strata had their own mechanisms for coping with some of the problems of modernization, without becoming disorganized or making excessive demands on the political center.   By comparison, the situation in many new states is that broader groups depend on the center so heavily that it cannot crystallize. That this did not happen in India has greatly facilitated the development, first under British influence and then in the nationalist movement through the Congress, of a central, stable institutional structure which maintained order, established a modern framework, and is gradually expanding to incorporate broader groups.

Consequently, a concrete structural feature of modernization has been the continuous recrystallization of traditional frameworks, and especially of the various networks of caste relations. The configuration of castes has been transformed; caste groups have assumed new tasks and adapted readily to new economic and political frameworks.[47] Patterns of traditional caste-mobility persist: i.e., existing subcaste groups assume some new economic, political or ritual tasks more or less within the range set by traditional culture, or they attempt to obtain a better standing within the old, traditional ritual order. But side by side with this pattern a new one has developed, in which the older caste groups gave way to new broader, more differentiated and more flexible networks of caste associations, organized around modern economic, professional and political activities in a greaty variety of new organizational forms. Often though not always, these new associations crosscut the existing political, social and economic hierarchies of status.[48]

But in these developments there were points of weakness. Although the center was institutionally and organizationally strong and flexible, it did not develop common symbols in which elements of the new culture could be combined with the older traditions so as to create a relatively strong collective identity and commitments to it. This also reduced its ability to provide new symbols that would serve not only as foci of rebellion against the colonial rulers but also as flexible guidelines for institution building.[49] This weakness became especially critical when the center extended, through universal suffrage, the scope of its activities and consequently its dependence on broader groups. Then the lack of association between the cultural traditional and political framework, which was a point of strength in the beginning, became a point of weakness. The center must create new, binding symbols of collective identity to overcome the more "parochial"—mostly linguistic—symbols of the different regions and states and develop some feeling of political community. This is especially important because these parochial symbols tend to become more crystallized and better articulated as peripheral segments of the society are modernized. The explosive quality of the linguistic question in India today is a manifestation of this problem.[50]

A second problem has to do with the extent to which the permissiveness of the broad Indian cultural tradition and its reforming tendencies not only facilitates new institutional frameworks, under external influence, and the continuous adaptation of the traditional groups, but also develops innovative forces, and common integrative frameworks to support continuous institution building. Here the question is whether caste and other traditional groups will develop new, more flexible frameworks, cross-cutting different status hierarchies, and new values, orientations, and activities within them, or whether they will mainly reinforce the neo-traditional divisive symbols and groupings.[51]

The internal transformation of the great Asian societies, then, has been greatly facilitated by autonomy of social, cultural and political institutions. Cultural autonomy has made possible the development of new symbols supporting and legitimizing central institution building, while autonomy in the spheere of social organization has facilitated the crystallization of viable new organizational nuclei without disrupting the pre-existing order, thus enabling the new order to rely, at least to some extent, on the forces of the old one. The relatively strong internal cohesion of broader strata and of family groups, with some status autonomy and openness toward the center, has helped to develop positive orientations to the new centers and willingness to provide the necessary support and resources.

The precise institutional contours of emerging modern systems, as we have seen, depend on the concrete structural location of autonomous institutional spheres.

Conversely, so far as such autonomy is absent, and the social, cultural, and political orders are closely identified with one another, the development of viable modern structures has been greatly impeded. And where family and other groups are closed, they are likely to undermine the new institutional centers by making intensive and unregulated demands on them or by withholding resources. As the Chinese and Islamic examples show, the weak points in emerging new structures depend to some extent on the structural location of the mutually identified institutional spheres.

PROTESTANTISM AND MODERNIZATION IN THE WEST

I have confined the preceding analysis to great Asian civilizations that were drawn into modernization from the "base" of a relatively centralized and differentiated Imperial system. In this they differ greatly from African and Latin-American societies, which modernized either from relatively undifferentiated social structures without strong centers and a great cultural tradition or which, like most Latin American countries, were mainly peripheral to such centers. But it would be beyond the scope of this paper to examine the extent to which my analysis may be applied to these cases.

Even with regard to these more differentiated and centralized Asian societies, however, structural flexibility was not in itself—as the Indian and Japanese cases indicate—enough to assure the development and continuity of modern institutional frameworks. Flexibility, or the autonomy of different institutional orders, created the conditions under which more active groups and elites could attempt to institute new principles of cultural direction and social integration. But the mere existence of structural flexibility neither assured that such groups would appear nor indicated the type of integrative orientation they would develop.

Indeed, it is the extent to which such groups do develop that has been—especially in China, India, and some Islamic societies—perhaps the major problem facing these societies during their modernization. The root of the problem in these societies was that modernization was a matter of encounter with foreign forces, an encounter beset with the difficulties and ambivalences of colonial or semi-colonial relations. Modernization therefore required that the new elites create a national identity from the encounter with these foreign and often alien forces. The internal capacities of these societies for reformation or transformation may have been crucial to their adaptation to these external forces and to their success in building new institutional structures to cope with these problems. But the very nature of the modernization process in these societies was such that the sources and directions of the cultural transformation, and the potential creativity of different elite groups, were not necessarily given by the same factors that initiated their modern structural transformation.

The earliest modernization—that of Western Europe since the 18th century—permits a fuller analysis of the relative importance of structural flexibility and active cultural transformation in modernization, for here both processes were, from the very beginning, initiated mainly from within. In European—especially Western Christian European—culture the tradition of autonomous cultural, political, and social orders is strong, and here the first and most continuous impetus to modernization did indeed develop. But even in Western and Central European countries, the course of modernization was neither entirely continuous nor everywhere the same.

What requires explanation is the fact that background more or less common to all Western and Central European societies gave rise to different modern institutional frameworks, with greatly varying capacities to sustain change.

One approach to this question is to reexamine Weber's famous Protestant Ethic thesis and some recent criticisms of it. At first glance, it may seem that Weber was dealing not with the structural and cultural variables I have discussed, but mainly with the religious roots of orientations to new types of economic activity. But several recent discussions of Weber's thesis indicate that some of its broader implications may be relevant to the present discussion. Of special interest from this point of view are the comments of Luethy and Trevor-Roper.[52]

Luethy, and to some extent Trevor-Roper, deny Weber's thesis in the economic field proper, claiming that economic development in Europe was independent of the specific direct impact of Protestantism. They show, for instance, as others have before them, that the first impact of Protestantism on economic life was a restrictive one, as Calvin's Geneva demonstrates. For Luethy, however, the major impact of Protestantism on European history was in the political field. This impact was effected, according to him, through direct reference to the Bible in search of new bases to legitimate authority as well as through the new structural impetus to pluralistic politics which developed through the Counter-Reformation of the Wars of Religion.[53]

Both Luethy and Trevor-Roper admit—indeed, stress—that England and the Netherlands especially, and to some extent the Scandinavian countries, were more successful after the Counter-Reformation in developing viable modern institutions than were most of the Catholic countries. To this they attribute the ultimate, but not the initial success and continuity of modernization in Protestant countries.

Without going into the detailed merits of these criticisms of Weber's thesis,[54] it might be worthwhile to point out that in principle the criticism Luethy directs against Weber could easily be directed against his own thesis. For instance, one could show that the original political impulse of either Lutheranism or Calvinism was not in a "liberal" or democratic direction but rather in a more "totalistic" one.

But apart from such details, both Weber's and Luethy's analyses deal not with the direct economic or political "results" of certain religious beliefs or the activities of religious groups, but rather—as Troeltsch has already seen[55]—with their more indirect impact. Initially the Reformation was not a "modernizing" movement; it aimed to establish a purer "medieval" socio-political religious order. Protestantism produced an impetus toward modernity only after this initial socio-religious impulse failed. Hence theories that attempt to evaluate this influence or impact of Protestantism necessarily deal with the transformed social orientations of Protestant religious groups after they had failed to establish their initial militant, totalistic aims restricting autonomous activities in both the economic and the political field. From a comparative point of view, the special importance of Protestantism is that the basic Protestant value orientations and social organization contained within themselves the seeds of such transformation. The exact way in which this transformation worked out in the institutional framework of any given society, however, depended not only on the internal predispositions of the Protestant groups but also on some aspects of the preceding social structure and on the *initial* interaction between this structure and the original religious groups.

Here a question not considered by Luethy and Trevor-Roper is very pertinent: the extent to which the Protestant Reformation influenced the development of the social and political flexibility to which they attach so much importance. The Protestant Reformation did indeed have an enormous impact not only on the motivational orientations of its adherents but also, through the social and status orientations of various Protestant groups, on the central political sphere. This impact was not necessarily intended by the rulers who adopted Protestantism, yet it did facilitate the further development of a more flexible and dynamic social system. In the first Protestant societies—England, Scandinavia, the Netherlands, and later in the United States—perhaps even before the full development of a new motivational orientation, the central symbolic and political sphere, and the basic relations between the political and social spheres, were transformed through the incorporation of Protestant values and symbols. This not only reinforced the existing autonomy of these spheres but created new bases of political obligations and more flexible political institutions.[56]

Protestantism had a similar impact on the internal cohesion and autonomy of the more active social groups in these societies. Most of the Protestant groups developed a combination of two types of status orientation. First was their "openness" toward the wider social structure, rooted in the "this-worldly" orientations which were not limited to the economic sphere, but were gradually extended to demands for wider political participation and new, broader political frameworks and criteria. Second, their status orientations were characterized by a certain autonomy and self-sufficiency. Unlike countries or sectors with a more autocratic or aristocratic tradition, they were, from the point of view of the crystallization of their status symbols, virtually independent of the existing (i.e., monarchical or ecclesiastical) centers of political power.

But such orientations did not develop to the same extent among all Protestant groups in all countries. The full development and institutionalization of such orientations depended to no small degree on the flexibility or "openness" of the existing political and cultural centers, and that of broader groups and strata and their initial reaction to religious innovations. So far as this reaction was restrictive, the transformative potentialities of these orientations could not bear full fruit.

The various interactions between different transformative potentialities and existing structural flexibility could give rise to paradoxically similar—or divergent —results. The influence of the allegedly conservative Lutheranism, for example, took a variety of forms. In the German principalities Lutheranism was indeed very restrictive, because the existing political framework was not an appropriate setting for the development of a national identity and community or for the development of more autonomous and flexible status orientations in the broader strata.[57] Here, "traditional" or autocratic rulers of the small principalities adopted the new religious orientations, and in this context the more conservative among these orientations became predominant, often restricting further institutional development.

But in the Scandinavian countries these religious orientations were integrated into new, wider national communities and developed on the bases of the prior autonomy of the Estates. While they certainly did not impede the development of an absolutist state in Sweden they did help to make possible the subsequent development of these states in a more pluralistic direction.[58]

Similarly paradoxical results, also demonstrating the importance of restrictive prior situations, are evident in the institutionalization of Calvinism. Of special interest here is the Prussian case, where the institutionalization of these orientations by the absolutist, autocratic Hohenzollerns did not facilitate the development of a flexible and pluralistic political framework, though it did support development of more activist collective political goals.[59]

Thus, so far as the initial impact of the religious changes reinforced the seeds of autonomy, which were to a high degree present in all Western and Central European societies, it created the basis of a new political order, not only on the structural-institutional level, but also on the level of central values and symbols which both legitimized these institutions and prompted their further development. Under such conditions, potentially activist religious orientations could take various institutional directions—e.g., economic, or political as in Scotland, or scientific—and become institutionalized, thus reinforcing the continuous development of these societies. But so far as some of these conditions were lacking, these religious orientations were institutionalized in partial, relatively constrictive or discontinuous ways reducing their transformative potential.

The different Catholic countries, on the other hand, demonstrate the limitations of purely structural autonomy.   The first impetus of many modern developments —economic, scientific, cultural or politica—loccurred in Catholic countries too. But the continuity of these developments was greatly impeded by the initial response to many of their more far-reaching consequences and especially to their convergence with Protestantism, which minimized, at least initially, the possibility of continuous development of modern institutions.

The case of Spain[60]—in a way the first modern state—illustrates this pattern most clearly, but it is perhaps even more prominent in the case of France, where the potentially pluralistic impact of various modern trends, including Protestantism, was inhibited by the formation of the French state during the Counter-Reformation.   This provided the background for continuous rifts in the central political symbols—between traditional and modern (revolutionary), aristocratic and republican, religious and secular orientations—rifts that persisted till the end of the Third Republic.[61]

Only through the juxtaposition of the structural aspects with processes of elite formation and creativity can the transformative potential of any pre-modern society be fully evaluated.   The Asian societies with which this discussion began require still further analysis, for which this paper may, perhaps, serve as a starting point.

Notes

1. See Shmuel N. Eisenstadt, "Institutionalization and Change," *American Sociological Review*, 29 (1964), pp. 235–248.
2. On the concept of modernization see Shmuel N. Eisenstadt, *Modernization, Growth and Diversity*, Bloomington, Ind.: Indiana University Press, 1963, and Manfred Halpern, "Toward Further Modernization of the Study of New Nations," *World Politics*, 17 (1964), pp. 157–181.
3. The concept and conditions of such breakdowns are analyzed in Shmuel N. Eisenstadt, "Breakdowns of Modernization," *Economic Development and Cultural Change*, 12 (1964), pp. 345–367.
4. See Shmuel N. Eisenstadt, "Modernization and Conditions of Sustained Growth," *World Politics*, 16 (1964), pp. 576–594.
5. See Shmuel N. Eisenstadt, *The Political Systems of Empires*, New York: The Free Press of Glencoe, 1963, and "Religious Organizations and Political Process in Centralized Empires," *Journal of Asian Studies*, 21 (1962), pp. 271–294.   On the importance of the concept of center see Edward A. Shils, "Centre and Periphery in the Logic of Personal Knowledge," *Essays Presented to Michael Polani*, London: Routledge & Kegan Paul, pp. 117–131, and "Charisma, Order, and Status," *American Sociological Review*, 30 (1965), pp. 199–213.
6. See Etienne Balazs, *Chinese Civilization and Bureaucracy*, New Haven: Yale University Press, 1964, esp. Chs. 1 and 2, and Eisenstadt, *Political Systems of Empires, op. cit.*, which includes additional bibliography on all the societies analyzed here (except Japan).
7. Joseph Levenson, *Modern China and its Confucian Past*, New York: Doubleday Anchor Books, 1964, and the documents in Ssu-Yu Teng and John K. Fairbank, *China's Response to the West: A Documentary Survey 1839–1923*, New York: Atheneum, 1963.   See also Mary Wright, *The Last Stand of Chinese Conservatism: The T'ung-Chih Restoration, 1862–1874*, Stanford: Stanford University Press, 1957.
8. See Eisenstadt, "Religious Organizations and Political Process in Centralized Empires," *op. cit.*, and Balazs, *op. cit.*
9. Balazs, *op. cit.*

10. *Ibid.*

11. For the first analysis of Chinese familism from the point of view of modernization see Marion J. Levy Jr., *The Family Revolution in Modern China*, Cambridge: Harvard University Press, 1952. Levy has further elaborated and to some extent modified the point of view expressed there in his "Contrasting Factors in the Modernization of China and Japan," in Simon Kuznets, Wilbert E. Moore and Joseph J. Spengler (eds.), *Economic Growth: Brazil, India, Japan*, Durham, N.C.: Duke University Press, 1955, pp. 496–537.

12. Levenson, *op. cit.*, and Ssu-Yu Teng and Fairbank, *op. cit.*

13. For the institutional development of modern pre-Communist China see George M. Beckman, *The Modernization of China and Japan*, New York: Harper, 1962, especially Chs. 23 and 24, and William L. Tung, *The Political Institutions of Modern China*, The Hague: Martinus Nijhoff, 1964. For some of the problems of legal reform see Franz Michael, "The Role of Law in Traditional, Nationalist and Communist China," *The China Quarterly*, 9 (1962), pp. 124–148.

14. Claude Cahen, "The Body Politic," in E. von Grunebaum (ed.), *Unity and Variety in Muslim Civilization*, Chicago: University of Chicago Press, 1955, pp. 132–163.

15. Bernard Lewis, *The Arabs in History*, London: Hutchinson, 1960, and Hamilton A. R. Gibb, "The Evolution of Government in Early Islam," in *Studies on the Civilisation of Islam*, Boston: Beacon Press, 1962, pp. 34–47.

16. Erwin I. J. Rosenthal, *Political Thought in Mediaeval Islam*, Cambridge: Cambridge University Press, 1962.

17. The first overall exposition of modernization in Islam is probably Hamilton A. R. Gibb, *Modern Trends in Islam*, Chicago: University of Chicago Press, 1947. For further elaboration see Muhsin Mahdi, "Modernity and Islam," in Joseph M. Kitagawa (ed.), *Modern Trends in World Religions*, La Salle, Ill.: Open Court, 1959, and Marshall G. S. Hodgson, "Modernity and the Islamic Heritage," *Islamic Studies*, 1 (1962), Karachi.

18. Justus van der Kroef, "Recent Trends in Indonesian Islam," *The Muslim World*, 3 (1962), and "The Role of Islam in Indonesian Nationalism and Politics," *The Western Political Quarterly*, 11 (1958), pp. 33–54; Jan Prins, "Some Notes About Islam and Politics in Indonesia," *The World of Islam*, 6 (1959), pp. 124–126; Clifford Geertz, "Modernization in a Muslim Society: The Indonesian Case," in Robert N. Bellah (ed.), *Religion and Progress in Modern Asia*, New York: The Free Press, 1965; C. A. O. van Nieuwenhuize, *Aspects of Islam in Post Colonial Indonesia*, The Hague: W. van Hoeve, 1958, esp. Chs. 1, 2 and 5.

19. See F. Rahman, "Muslim Modernism in the Indo-Pakistan Subcontinent," in *Bulletin of the School of Oriental and African Studies*, 21 (1958), pp. 82–99; Louis Dumont, "Nationalism and Communism," *Contributions to Indian Sociology*, 7 (1964), pp. 30–70; Hafez Malik, *Moslem Nationalism in India and Pakistan*, Washington, D.C.: Public Affairs Press, 1963.

20. On problems of legal reform in modern Islam see James M. D. Anderson, *Islamic Law in the Modern World*, New York and London: Stevens, 1959; Joseph Schacht, "Problems of Modern Islamic Legislation," in Richard H. Nolte (ed.), *The Modern Middle East*, New York: Atherton Press, 1963, pp. 172–201; N. J. Coulson, *A History of Islamic Law*, Edinburgh: Edinburgh University Press, 1964.

21. See Leonard Binder, *The Ideological Revolution in the Middle East*, New York: John Wiley, 1964, and Nadav Safran, *Egypt in Search of Political Community*, Cambridge: Harvard University Press, 1961.

22. Leonard Binder, *Religion and Politics in Pakistan*, Los Angeles: University of California Press, 1961, and "Problems of Islamic Political Thought in the Light of Recent Development in Pakistan," *Journal of Politics*, 20 (1958), pp. 675–685.

23. See Clement H. Moore, "The Neo-Destour Party of Tunisia: A Structure for Democracy?" *World Politics*, 14 (1962), pp. 461–482; Charles A. Micaud, Leonard C. Brown and Clement H. Moore, *Tunisia: The Politics of Modernization*, New York: Praeger, 1964; Gabriel Ardant, *La Tunisie d'Aujourdhui et de Demain*, Paris: Calman-Levy, 1961.

24. Bernard Lewis, *The Emergence of Modern Turkey*, London: Oxford University Press, 1961.

25. Claude Cahen, "L'Histoire Economique et Sociale de l'Orient Musulman Médièval," *Studia Islamica*, 111 (1955), pp. 93–116, and "Les Facteurs Economiques et Socieaux dans l'Ankyklose Culturelle de l'Islam," in R. Brunschwig and G. E. von Grunebaum (ed.), *Actes du Symposium International d'Histoire de la Civilisation Musulmane*, Paris: Besson and Chautenerle, pp. 195–217.

26. Robert N. Bellah, *Tokugawa Religion*, Glencoe, Ill.: The Free Press, 1956, and "Values and Social Change in Modern Japan," *Asian Cultural Studies*, 3 (1962), pp. 13–56; David M. Earl, *Emperor and Nation in Japan—Political Themes of the Tokugawa Period*, Seattle: University of Washington Press, 1964.

27. See Marius B. Jansen, *Sakamoto Ryoma and the Meiji Restoration*, Princeton: Princeton University Press, 1961; Albert M. Craig, *Chossu in the Meiji Restoration*, Cambridge: Harvard University Press, 1961.

28. Ronald P. Dore, *Education in Tokugawa Japan*, Berkeley: University of California Press, 1964.

29. See on this, among others, Marius B. Jansen, "Changing Japanese Attitude Toward Modernization," in Marius B. Jansen (ed.), *Changing Japanese Attitudes Toward Modernization*, Princeton: Princeton University Press, 1965; Robert N. Bellah, "Values and Social Change in Modern Japan," *op. cit.*, and "Epilogue," in his *Religion and Progress in Modern Asia, op. cit.*; Herbert Passin, "Modernization and the Japanese Intellectual, Some Comparative Observations," in Jansen (ed.), *op. cit.*

30. Ronald P. Dore, "The Legacy of Tokugawa Education," in Jansen (ed.), *op. cit.*

31. Bellah, *Tokugawa Religion, op. cit.*, and Dore, *Education in Tokugawa Japan, op. cit.*

32. Herbert Norman, *Japan's Emergence as a Modern State*, New York: Institute of Pacific Relations, 1940; Levy, "Contrasting Factors in the Modernization of China and Japan," *op. cit.*; Craig, *Chossu in the Meiji Restoration, op. cit.*

33. Dore, "The Legacy of Tokugawa Education," *op. cit.*, and *Education in Tokugawa Japan, op. cit.*

34. Levy, "Contrasting Factors in the Modernization of China and Japan," *op. cit.*

35. *Ibid.*

36. Ezra Vogel, *Japan's New Middle Classes*, Berkeley: University of California Press, 1963.

37. *Ibid.*

38. Some of the basic data on this period in Japanese history are collected in Ivan Morris (ed.), *Problems in Asian Civilisations: Japan 1931–1945*, Boston: D. C. Heath, 1963. For analyses of the Japanese situation in that period see Talcott Parsons, "Population and the Social Structure of Japan," in his *Essays in Sociological Theory* (rev. ed.), Glencoe, Ill.: Free Press, 1959, pp. 275–298; Masao Maruyama, *Thought and Behaviour in Japanese Politics*, London: Oxford University Press, 1963; Dore, "The Legacy of Tokugawa Education," *op. cit.*; Passin, *op. cit.*

39. Masao Maruyama, "Patterns of Individuation and the Case of Japan: A Conceptual Scheme," in Jansen (ed.), *op. cit.*, pp. 489–533; Bellah, "Epilogue," *op. cit.*, and "Values and Social Change in Modern Japan," *op. cit.*; Herbert Passin, "Stratigraphy of Protest in Japan," in Morton Kaplan (ed.), *The Revolution in World Politics*, New York: John Wiley, 1963, pp. 12–113.

40. Dore, "Education in Tokugawa Japan," *op. cit.*, and "The Legacy of Tokugawa Education," *op. cit.*; Parsons, *op. cit.*

41. See Percival Spear, *India: A Modern History*, Ann Arbor: University of Michigan Press, 1961; Louis Renou, Jean Filliozet *et al.*, L'Inde Classique (2 vols.), Paris: Presses Universitaires, 1947, 1953; H. N. Sinha, *The Development of Indian Polity*, Bombay: India Publishing House, 1963.

42. This aspect of Indian political thought is elaborated from different points of view, in V. P. Varma, *Studies in Hindu Political Thought and its Metaphysical Background*, Benares: 1954; Louis Dumont, *La Civilisation Indienne et Nous*, Paris: Libraire Armand Colin, 1964, and "The Conception of Kingship in Ancient India," *Contributions to Indian Sociology*, 6 (1962), pp. 46–76; Charles Drekmeier, *Kingship and Community in Early India*, Stanford: Stanford

University Press, 1962. The best known classical text is the Arthashastra: see Rudrapatna Shammasastry (ed.), *Kautilya's Arthashastra* (5th ed.), Mysore Printing and Publishing House, 1960. Some additional texts can be found in William T. de Bary, Stephen N. Hay, Rayal Weiler and Andrew Yarrow, *Sources of Indian Tradition*, New York: Columbia University Press, 1958, pp. 236–258.

43. Spear, *op. cit.*

44. See, for instance, Lala Lajpat Rai, "The Remedy for Revolution," Jawahalal Nehru, "Satyagrapha," and Mohandras Karamchand Gandhi, "Face to Face with Ahimsa," all in D. M. Brown (ed.), *Indian Political Thought from Ranade to Bhave*, Berkeley: University of California Press, 1961; and Stanley A. Wolfert, *Tilak and Gohale in Revolution and Reform in the Making of Modern India*, Berkeley: University of California Press, 1962.

45. See the first chapter of the forthcoming work by Gopal Krishna, "The Development of the Organization of Indian National Congress, 1918–1932" (mimeo.). On the reforming potential of Hinduism see Joseph W. Elder, "Industrialism in Hindu Society: A Case Study in Social Change," unpublished Ph.D. thesis, Harvard University, 1959; and Milton Singer, *et al.*, "India's Cultural Values and Economic Development: A Discussion," *Economic Development and Cultural Change*, 7 (1958), pp. 1–12.

46. See Milton Singer (ed.), *Traditional India: Structure and Change*, Philadelphia: American Folklore Society, 1959, and Myron Weiner, "India's Two Political Cultures," in his *Political Change in South Asia*, Calcutta: Firma K. L. Mukhopadhyay, 1965, pp. 115–153. On the development of the "modern" center see Rajni Kothari, "The Congress System in India," *Asian Survey*, 4, (1964), pp. 1161–1174.

47. The best known analysis of these developments is M. N. Srinivas, *Caste in Modern India*, Bombay: Asia Publishing House, 1962, esp. Chs. 1, 2 and 4.

48. See André Beteille, *Closed and Open Social Stratification in India*, New Delhi (forthcoming), 1965; and Rajni Kothari and A. Maru, *Caste and Secularism in India—A Case Study of a Caste Federation*, New Delhi (forthcoming), 1965.

49. See Kothari, "The Congress System in India," *op. cit.*, and Weiner, *op. cit.*

50. See Selig S. Harrison, *India: The Most Dangerous Decades*, Princeton, N.J.: Princeton University Press, 1960; Paul Friedrich, "Language and Politics in India," *Daedalus*, 91 (1962), pp. 543–559.

51. On these different possibilities, see Lloyd I. Rudolph and Susanne Hoeber Rudolph, "The Political Role of India's Caste Associations," *Pacific Affairs*, 33 (1960), pp. 5–22; Beteille, *op. cit.*, and Srinivas, *Caste in Modern India, op. cit.*

52. Herbert Luethy, "Once Again—Calvinism and Capitalism," *Encounter*, January, 1964, pp. 26–39 and his earlier exposition in *La Banque Protestante en France de la Revocation de l'Edit de Nantes à la Revolution*, Paris: S.E.V.P.E.N., 1961, Vol. I, Ch. 1, and Vol. III, pp. 749–786; Hugh Trevor-Roper, "Religion: The Reformation and Social Change," *Historical Studies*, 4 (1965), pp. 18–45.

53. In this he is close to Michael Walzer, who stresses the Puritans' revolutionary ideology in "Puritanism as a Revolutionary Ideology," *History and Theory*, 4 (1963), pp. 59–90.

54. Cf. some of the older controversies around the Weber thesis in Robert W. Green, *Protestantism and Capitalism: The Weber Thesis and its Critics*, Boston: D. C. Heath, 1959, and Sidney A. Burrell (ed.), *The Role of Religion in Modern European History*, New York: Macmillan, 1964.

55. Ernest Troeltsch, *Protestantism and Progress*, Boston: Beacon Press, 1958; one of the most recent critical analyses of Weber which does not take this into account is Geoffrey R. Elton, *Reformation Europe*, London: Collins, 1963, pp. 312 ff.

56. For some of the very numerous analyses bearing on this see Enno van Gelder, *Revolutionaire Reformatie*, Amsterdam: Van Kayse, 1943; Charles H. George and Katherine George, *The Protestant Mind of the English Reformation*, Princeton: Princeton University Press, 1961; David Little, "The Logic of Order—an Examination of the Sources of Puritan-Anglican Controversy and of their Relation to Prevailing Legal Conceptions in the Sixteenth and Seventeenth Centuries," unpublished Doctor of Theology thesis, Harvard University, 1963.

57. See, for instance, Alfred L. Drummond, *German Protestantism Since Luther*, London: Epworth Press, 1951; John T. McNeill, *The History and Character of Calvinism*, New York: Oxford University Press, 1954; Gerhard Ritter, "Das 16. Jahrhundert als weltgeschichtliche Epoche," *Archiv für Geschichte der Reformation*, 35 (1938), and *Die Neugestaltung Europas im 16. Jahrhundert*, Berlin: Druckhaus Tempelhof, 1950, Ch. 3, esp. pp. 133–170; Alfred Adam, "Die nationale Kirche bei Luther," *Archiv für Geschichte der Reformation*, 35 (1938), pp. 30–62.

58. Hajalmar Holmquist, *Kirche und Staat im Evangelischen Schweden, Festgabe für Karl Müller*, Tübingen: J. C. B. Mohr, 1922, pp. 209–277; Heinz H. Schrey, "Geistliches und Weltliches Regiment in der Schwedischen Reformation," *Archiv für Gesschichte der Reformation*, 42 (1951) pp. 146–159; Georg Schweiger, *Die Reformation in den Nordischen Ländern*, München: Kozel Verlag, 1962; and Georg Ritter, *Die Neugestaltung, op. cit.*

59. Christine R. Kayser, "Calvinism and German Political Life," unpublished Ph.D. thesis, Radcliffe, 1961.

60. See Americo Castro, *The Structure of Spanish History*, Princeton: Princeton University Press, 1954.

61. See, for instance, Herbert Luethy, *France Against Herself*, New York: Frederick A. Praeger, 1955.

5 . Lévi-Strauss and the Primitive
Robert L. Zimmerman

Why are we so fascinated by the primitive? Why do we continue to investigate primitive man? Is it because we envy his simplicity and spontaneity? Does his animality excite and "eroticize" us? Or is it because our desire for self-knowledge—indeed, for more than that, for a self, an identity—drives us beyond our own beginning to the beginning of our race? Do we somehow know, as Hegel put it, that to become a person one must "ingest" the history of the race, become a We in order to become an I?

Although all of the above explanations no doubt have something to do with our continued investigation of the primitive, the last seems to me the most compelling. It is therefore somewhat paradoxical that one of the results of this investigation has been the fairly widespread acceptance of the view that, after all, the primitive is *not* like us; rather, he is a pre-man, a savage, a creature one cut above the beast. Most of us, in other words, have come to believe that the history of the race is analogous to the history of an individual, in that it has a beginning stage which is outgrown in time and which stands to what comes after it as the potential stands to the actual, the complete and the developed to the incomplete and undeveloped.

This view has had some formidable champions, among them Auguste Comte, Sir James George Frazer, Levy-Bruhl, Hegel, and others. In our time, it has had a formidable critic: Claude Lévi-Strauss, the distinguished French social anthropologist. In his many works, Lévi-Strauss has argued that this interpretation of the primitive is factually and theoretically indefensible. *The Savage Mind*,[1] the most recent of his books to be translated into English, contains perhaps the most thorough presentation of Lévi-Strauss's position, and is for this reason worth summarizing at some length, although it should be stated at the outset that no summary of the argument can do justice to its complexity or to the vast amount of evidence introduced to defend it.

In *The Savage Mind*, Lévi-Strauss undertakes an analysis of primitive thought in general—which, he argues, far from lacking a conceptual structure, rests upon a remarkably rich and complex one—and of primitive scientific thought in particular—which he argues is full-blown scientific thought and not, as we have been used to hearing, some pre-logical, non-rational counterfeit of it. Although primitive science is tied to the world of perception and imagination—the phenomenological world of the felt, immediate qualities of things—and organized in aesthetic and mythological terms, it does not follow, according to Lévi-Strauss, that it is therefore an inferior or theoretically defective science. It represents rather a method of approaching nature that is only *other than*, not less than, the one employed by modern science. As he puts it, there are

> . . . two distinct modes of scientific thought . . . two . . . levels at which nature is accessible to scientific enquiry: one . . . that of perception and imagination: the other at a remove from it. It is as if the objects of science . . . could be arrived at by two different routes, one very close to, and the other more remote from, sensible intuition.

The order of nature, that is to say, appears *on* its sensible surface as well as *beneath* it; the perceptible order of things reflects the imperceptible order of things, and is thus reachable by two routes: one which travels by way of the sensible features and felt qualities of things, the other which penetrates to what lies beneath and beyond them. Thus:

> Wild cherries, cinnamon, vanilla, and cherry are grouped together by the intellect as well as by the senses because they all contain aldehyde, while the closely related smells of wintergreen, lavender, and banana are to be explained by the presence of ester. On intuitive grounds alone we might group onions, garlic, cabbage, turnips, and mustard together even though botany separates liliaceae and crucifers. In confirmation of the evidence of the senses chemistry shows that these different families are united on another plane: they contain sulphur.

To be sure, not *every* link on the surface of nature signifies or reflects a link in its depths. But to say this is only to demonstrate the imperfect nature of a science based on the secondary properties of things, not to show that such a science is illegitimate.

The primitive, in other words, seeks the order of his world in sensible terms, and thus creates a science based on the sensible aspects of things. But this is not all. His search, according to Lévi-Strauss, is motivated not merely by a utilitarian, but also by a theoretical, interest. If it were otherwise, we could not explain, among other things, the existence in the primitive's language of terms which refer to objects or features of objects having little or no practical value. For example, although Indians of the Northeastern United States and Canada derive no economic benefit from reptiles, they nevertheless possess a herpetology with distinct terms for each genus of reptile, and other terms applying to particular species and varieties. And even when a known object *does* afford an economic benefit to the tribe, the process of "over-knowing" which takes place, and the elaborate terminology which is created to express it, suggest an interest or a drive which is more than practical. Thus, for instance, "The Hanunóo have more than a hundred and fifty terms for the parts and properties of plants. . . . Over six hundred named plants have been recorded among the Pinatubo . . . and one hundred terms [for] parts and characteristics of plants."

Furthermore, if the utility of an animal be taken as the reason for its being known, then the knowledge the primitive has of certain animals which, in his mind, have curative properties (like spiders for fertility, worms for rheumatism, or frozen bear excreta for constipation) must be said to be truly astounding. For surely it is absurd to claim that the primitive came to know about spiders, worms, and frozen bear excreta because they respectively cured sterility, rheumatism, and constipation. It seems more likely, as Lévi-Strauss observes, that ". . . animals are not known as a result of their usefulness; they are deemed useful . . . because they are first of all known."

Consider also the divination of omens. Among the Iban or Sea Dayaks of South Borneo, the songs and cries of certain birds are taken to be guides to the future:

> The rapid cry of the Crested Jay . . . is said to resemble the crackling of burning wood and so presages the successful firing of a family's swiddens. The alarm cry of the Trogon . . . is likened to the death rattle of an animal being slain and augurs good hunting.

Clearly the resemblances and associations between the cries and what they suggest are independent of any practical considerations. They are, rather, the spontaneous products of "free association": the apprehension of the phenomenological qualities of the cries. It is because this "logic" is at work that the cries become omens and take on signification. In other words, it is only *after* the cry has been associated with some event, and been given a "meaning," that it begins to function in a practical way, namely, as evidence of what is to occur.

In his science, then, the primitive exhibits a theoretical interest. He strives to detect the order and connections among the objects in his world to satisfy his "instinct" for order and connectedness. Contrary to the widely held belief, the primitive is not a "savage" who is governed only by his bodily impulses and who thinks, if at all, in merely utilitarian terms. His desires are not limited to those things which are "good to eat"; he is as much desirous of those things which are "good to think." Thus, if we accept the dual premise that disinterested inquiry and classification—*whatever* the principle of that classification might be—is the core of a genuine science, and that primitive science is an instance of such disinterested inquiry and classification, we come with Lévi-Strauss to the conclusion that primitive science is genuine science.

Lévi-Strauss continues his assault on the myth of the primitive as savage by turning to the phenomena of totemism and totemic classification. Through an analysis of these phenomena—first undertaken in *Totemism*[2] and present in its basic conclusions throughout the body of his writings—Lévi-Strauss tries to show, contrary to this myth, that primitive thought rests upon a rich and complex conceptual structure. More specifically, he argues, negatively, that totemism is an illusion and that the classic understanding of it is wrong (among other things, this understanding holds that members of a clan identify with the totemic object and literally believe it to be their ancestor); positively, he argues that totemism represents a highly sophisticated mechanism for ordering or classifying which has as its (unconscious) goal the differentiation and integration of units within society. Classification in terms of totemic objects stands in relation to *social* entities or phenomena as classification as such stands in relation to *natural* entities and phenomena: both, that is, signify and ratify the diversity-within-unity of what is. What this means can perhaps best be illustrated by some examples. In *Totemism*, Lévi-Strauss describes an Australian tribe ". . . which names its moieties after the parts of a tree. In the Ngeumba tribe Gwaidmudthen is divided into nhurai (butt) and wangue (middle) while Gwaigulir is equivalent to winngo (top). These names refer to the different portions of the shadow of a tree and refer to the positions taken up in camping." And in *The Savage Mind*, speaking about the class of the Chicksaw tribe, he observes:

> The Racoon people . . . live on fish and wild fruit, those of the Puma lived in the mountains . . . and lived principally on game. The Wild Cat clan slept in the daytime and hunted at night . . . Members of the Bird clan were up before daybreak. . . . The people of the Red Fox clan were professional thieves . . . the Redskunk lived in dugouts underground.

What these examples illustrate is the classificatory function of totemism. The totemic naming system is a device, a structure, a mechanism for distinguishing among *and* correlating the various groups within a tribe. As Rousseau observed (Lévi-Strauss is indebted to him in this), totemism, by superimposing a set of natural entities upon a set of social entities, translates the latter into the former. The facts of social life—such as the functions of different clans, their hunting duties and positions, spatial location within the village, position in the hierarchy, exogamous relations, etc.—are thus "coded" in terms of a symbolism or notation derived from the totemic objects themselves, i.e., from nature. The set of totemic objects, with its perceived internal distinctions and its overall organicity, stands in a symbolic or metaphorical relation to the set of units which comprise the social organism. Totemism is thus based upon symbolic or metaphoric reasoning. It can be thought of as a logic generated by a phenomenal awareness of an analogy between nature and society or among sets of things which contain similar differences. It provides a calculus for social ordering and makes the structure of society lucid and thinkable. Or—what comes to the same thing—it is a code which metaphorically represents the units within society, their various roles, and the relations they bear to one another.

There is much to say about this enormously fertile and provocative interpretation of totemism.   Not only does it salvage the phenomenon of totemism which, as classically conceived, had virtually become meaningless because of the wealth of counter-instances raised against it (e.g., the many clans which did not identify with the totemic object or in which totems were chosen willy-nilly with no pretense of literal ancestry); not only does it remove totemism from the narrow framework of magic or religion and place it within the broader framework of taxonomical activity as such; but, with one stroke, it re-establishes the continuity between primitive and modern man.   It accomplishes this because the function of totemism is now seen as a function which *any and every* society in search of cohesion and interplay must somehow symbolize and underwrite through some mechanism or other.   In other words, as Lévi-Strauss observes, when we deal with totemism:

> We are . . . dealing not with an autonomous institution which can be defined by its distinctive properties and is typical of certain regions of the world and certain forms of civilization, but with a *modus operandi* which can be discerned even behind social structures traditionally defined in a way diametrically opposed to totemism.

Deciphering the totemic code, the significations of the totemic objects both in themselves and as they relate to each other, is a complicated process.   The meaning of an object or an event is a function of that with which it is paired or associated, and since such pairing is rather variable (although not arbitrary), to re-establish the semantic value of a totemic name, or the relations among a group of totemic names, becomes a difficult task.   This, of course, is an instance of the larger difficulty of deciphering the meanings of objects and events as such.   For as we saw with respect to the meanings of bird cries, the linked entities (i.e., the cry and the event it brought to mind) are connected by an "informal" logic, a logic which utilizes the modalities and "feels" of things.   Such a logic, although not in itself irrational (we can understand the relations it fixes once we know what those relations are) is not based on reason and is thus difficult to reconstruct rationally.

Furthermore, primitive logic, the logic behind totemic and all primitive classification, utilizes many poles of reference in its ordering procedures.   Thus, according to Lévi-Strauss, although the basic structure or movement of primitive logic is the unification of opposites, the correlation of differences through pairing or binary thinking, this movement takes place in many ways and on many levels. In primitive logic objects can be paired in terms of contiguity and/or resemblance. These, in turn, are "many-valued" terms.   That is, resemblances can be based on considerations that are sensory (similar smells), metaphoric (bird cries), or almost anything else (among the Luapula of South India, the function of construction links bees and carpenters); contiguity, on the other hand, can be based on a juxtaposition which is diachronic or synchronic, static or dynamic. In addition, primitive logic will pair things which are compatible and things which are incompatible, objects whose presence excludes one another as well as objects whose activities include one another. And so on. Thus, although the "logic of the concrete," as Lévi-Strauss calls it, is a procedure of thought which orders and introduces system into what appears disordered and systemless, it does so in many different and subtle ways.

Nonetheless, once one grasps the way this logic "goes," all the classificatory schemas which operate within primitive societies become theoretically susceptible of analysis, since all of them make use of the same logical principles, or variants of these principles. Not only, for example, are colors, smells, foods, animals, plants and inanimate objects associated in terms of resemblance and contiguity but natural events (e.g., sunrise or sunset), a region of space (e.g., the sky), an animal activity (e.g., the cry of a bird), and human events (e.g., a man dies, a pregnant woman's body swells) are also given "meaning" in terms of the same principles in that they are associated with events which resemble or are contiguous with them (in any one of the number of ways two entities or events can be resembling or contiguous). These various classifications or quasi-classifications are thus *structurally* isomorphic, or at least are constructed in terms of the same set of logical principles.

Furthermore, just as the theoretical impulse behind these classifications is the unification of multiplicity, the establishment of connections among separate entities, so the impulse of society, so to speak (an unconscious impulse analogous to the "unconscious" grammar of a language) is the creation of liaison structures among its various component parts; thus, Lévi-Strauss argues, borrowing an insight from Marcel Mauss, relations among sub-groups within society, like exogamous ties or the ritualistic interchange of gifts, all serve the same end and are governed by the same logic. In each of these cases atomic units are taken up into a structure which makes them parts of an organic whole. As such they are homologous and intertranslatable.

Once social reality is conceived in this way as a logical system, any number of logical relations among social phenomena becomes apparent. Thus, a structure which has been used on one level with respect to a certain content can be transposed onto another level with respect to a different content. For example, food prohibitions—based upon a belief in the reincarnation of an ancestor in the form of a plant or an animal—reappear on the level of language as a prohibition against uttering any of the homophones of the name of the deceased. Or a structure which has appeared in one tribe can appear as an inverted or transformed structure in a different tribe. In certain tribes, before a man dies he sometimes indicates the animal in whose form he will be reincarnated; this becomes the animal which his descendants are henceforth forbidden to eat. In other tribes, a child will observe a food prohibition connected with an animal which the village "wise men" had associated with his mother's pregnancy. The content of these "systems"—food prohibitions, notions of reincarnation, etc.—can vary enormously, but the structures, the forms they assume, recur throughout, though sometimes in shapes which are transmuted versions of one another; and since these transmuted structures, according to Lévi-Strauss, are logically related, they admit, once we have learned the logical principles behind them, of structural interpretation. Hence, if we could gather all the data relating to a tribe's techno-economic, social, and religious structures, we could, with the help of a computer, determine all the logical principles at work in the ordering techniques of that tribe and show these structures and that society to be like a vast set of logically generated transformations. Using logic, cybernetics, game theory, and the like, the anthropologist can "unlock" the primitive society.

Primitive logic, then, however subtle, variable, and kaleidoscopically shifting it may be, *is certainly a logic*. Moreover, according to Lévi-Strauss, it is an ". . . elementary logic . . . the least common denominator of all thought . . . an original logic. . . ." As such, it is a logic which lies not only behind primitive thought (that is to say, all the ordering systems which primitive thought elaborates, as well as the structures of primitive life), but behind *all* thought and *all* life. And because it is omnipresent, it follows that there is really no such thing as "The Primitive Mind," or "The Modern Mind"; there is only "Mind-As-Such." To be sure, "Mind-As-Such" exhibits different contents at different times (primitive science, for instance, deals with the secondary properties of things while modern science deals with the primary properties of things), but its structures do not vary (in the cases of both primitive and modern science different contents are ordered and systematized in terms of opposition, contiguity, resemblance, etc.). We might add that it is the belief in such a Mind, or the efficacy of believing in such a Mind, with its invariant structures, that has convinced Lévi-Strauss that he can construct a model of Man and Society which will encompass all men and all societies. Indeed, it is just such a model which his work as a whole is an attempt to construct. By legitimizing the search for this model, or for closer and closer approximations to it (an activity which, although not antagonistic to empirical research, is *not* empirical research), Lévi-Strauss has significantly affected modern anthropological inquiry.

Lévi-Strauss's account of the savage mind is, of course, not immune from criticism; indeed, the very range and daring of his claims render debate probable. One can, for example, wonder whether he has not confused a phase of a developed science, that of classifying, with the essence of a developed science, that of constructing theoretical entities or models. Few would doubt—certainly in the light of the evidence Lévi-Strauss presents—that primitives classify or that primitives classify (at least some of the time) for the *sake* of classifying, i.e., that they are driven by a theoretical and not merely by a utilitarian interest. And, I suppose— although here there would be some controversy—many would at least be responsive to Lévi-Strauss's speculations, carefully hedged as they are, about the isomorphism which exists between the primary and secondary qualities of things, between what appears and what is inferred. In the area of epistemology, philosophers since Berkeley have been skeptical about the legitimacy of the distinction altogether; and psychologically, men have always balked somewhat at the notion that their perceptions and feelings yield up only a "subjective" reality, a realm of "phenomenal" events which exist only "in" and "for" their minds. The bias in favor of the given, of what is directly perceived and felt, is not something we have outgrown. Many of us still can't really believe that the colors and tastes and smells of things are not really real, or that what looks like human behavior in animals is really a mechanical response to a mechanical stimulus, or that what we introspect as our reasons for acting are not really the springs of our action. This, in the broadest sense of the word, "explains" why philosophers like Bergson, Whitehead, Dewey, Peirce, James, and Husserl have refused to succumb to the rationalized Parmenidean universe of science.

Yet even if we grant all this—that the primitive classifies, that the method he uses in classifying is formally congruent with the methods of modern science, and that he classifies for the sake of classifying—it does not necessarily follow that primitive science is full-blown science. One feels somewhat hesitant here since the meaning of science is not unequivocal and since the term is, to a degree, normative as well as descriptive. Nevertheless, it is commonly agreed that what is fundamental to developed, full-blown science—modern science—is not *classification* but *explanation*, and that the core of modern science is the construction of explanatory models and the testing of them through the verification of their implied, observable consequences. Notwithstanding the difficulties philosophers of science have run into in trying to pin down the concept of explanation, one thing is clear: *classification is not explanation*, and an inquiry into nature which merely classifies is not a scientific inquiry in the full sense of that term.

Thus, contrary to Lévi-Strauss, it is tempting to say that primitive science provided "Mind-As-Such" with a long period of time during which it looked at nature and, after a fashion, classified it. That this was a necessary precondition *for* science goes without saying; but *because it did only this* primitive science must be thought of as a precursor to a more profound inquiry into nature, i.e., as a precursor to, and not an equal of, modern science.

The issue is sharpened when we recognize that, in its most general sense, Lévi-Strauss's entire enterprise is at odds with his thoughts about primitive science. For if the essence of science is classification then the field that he himself engages in, anthropology, is something other than, or more than, science. For surely what Lévi-Strauss does is not classification; rather, in constructing models of "Mind-As-Such," he is seeking to delineate the set of invariant structures behind all human thought and life. This is an activity which transcends mere classification and reintroduces the very distinction he is seeking to eliminate. Conversely, if what Lévi-Strauss does is science, then what the primitive does is not science but rather a phase in the development of science. This is a crucial distinction.

In addition, we might also question the value of Lévi-Strauss's rationalism. As we saw, the forms of human thought and life are for him, in the end, determined by rational and logical principles. When primitive man thinks, his thought is logical. To be sure, the logic at work is not a conventional logic; it is a "concrete," "felt," "aesthetic" logic; it is "many-valued" and turns on many "axes." Nevertheless, it reveals itself to such conventional logical techniques as those of game theory, cybernetics, structural linguistics, and the logic of classes. It is thus systematic, it is not antagonistic to the laws of Aristotelian logic, and, more generally, it constitutes an ordering system which is both amenable to and reconstructable in terms of linear, sequential, "ordinary" thought. In addition, notwithstanding the complexities involved, it can be seen according to Lévi-Strauss that social phenomena like totemism, gift-giving, or the exogamous relations among clans, are determined by rational ends, i.e., the ends of societal order, stability, and coherence. Thus the image which emerges of man and society is of an organism which has set itself rational goals and has chosen rational, or what it takes to be rational, means to achieve these goals.

Before entering upon a criticism of Lévi-Strauss's rationalism, one must, first of all, bear in mind what he is *not* implying by this term. He does not, for instance, mean that men always reach conclusions which are rational or that social phenomena are always produced by means of careful rational deliberation. To interpret him in this fashion would be to misperceive the level of generality in his rationalism. Lévi-Strauss is not talking about the *content* of human thought and life but about its form: it is not the material, the "filling," but the structure of these phenomena that he would call rational and logical. Thus, from the point of view of their structures, as classificatory and ordering systems of nature, modern and primitive science are both logical and rational just as primitive and modern kinship systems, as classificatory and ordering systems within society, are both logical and rational. Once we recognize the nature of Lévi-Strauss's rationalism, its generality and formality, we should be less intuitively opposed to it; at the same time, however, we should also be less concerned or intellectually engaged with it. For given its generality and its abstractness, it seems to be a claim about man that at times borders on the trivial and insignificant and at times arbitrarily stretches and mishandles the meanings of terms. Is it not trivial to say that primitive and modern science are alike because they both are mechanisms which order nature? Considered as ordering mechanisms, *any* two human inquiries into nature are alike: men always order in some way or other when they inquire, even if they do so in a disorderly fashion. And do we not arbitrarily stretch and mishandle the meaning of the term "logic" if we apply it to both what Russell and Whitehead did in *Principia Mathematica* and to what the primitive does in divining bird cries or attributing medicinal value to spiders? Is it not trivial to say that primitive and modern kinship systems or marriage prescriptions are alike because they both are mechanisms which order relations among the elements within a society? What social institution *isn't* such a mechanism? Do we not, finally, arbitrarily stretch the meaning of the term "rational," if we use it to denote both a system which marks and codes distinctions and relations within a society metaphorically, and a system which marks and codes such distinctions and relations non-metaphorically? Surely the term "rational" denotes the latter and has as a boundary condition that it cannot be used of the former. To say that the former system is rational but relies on the imagination, while the latter system is rational but relies on the intellect is like saying that all humans are males but some are he-males and some are she-males.

One might set this latter point against a different background. Intuitively, we believe that man is both rational and irrational. Man is rational when he practices science and irrational when he relies on magic; man is rational when he uses his intelligence to decide the future course of events and irrational when he continues to rely on the mechanisms or institutions of magic. Now it is precisely this which Lévi-Strauss seems to deny. It would seem that these antitheses or oppositions have no place in his model. For according to that model man is rational both in practicing science *and* in relying on magic; man is rational both in using intelligence *and* in not using it; man is rational both in discarding ineffective mechanisms or institutions and in not discarding them. Surely the term "rational" is being misused when it is employed to identify such diverse, even contradictory human actions.

Finally, we might wonder at the discontinuity between nature and man which Lévi-Strauss's theories seem to imply. For in his rejection of the coming-into-being of man, in his insistence that man *qua* "Mind-As-Such" always was, he in effect is rejecting the existence of pre-humans who mediated the transition from nature to man. That is, in rejecting the notion that the primitive was a "Savage," a preman, he is also rejecting the notion that man as we know him evolved through a series of human-like forms.

Now, to be sure, the claim that there is discontinuity within nature is no longer objectionable (at an earlier time this would have been thought to be virtually a logical impossibility). Indeed in areas like sub-atomic physics and quantum mechanics discontinuity has virtually become a confirmed fact. There are, however, two considerations that must be dealt with. First, the discontinuity for which Lévi-Strauss argues allegedly occurred on the macroscopic level. Yet on this level all our experience points to the omnipresence of continuity, and in deference to this omnipresence, physicists have generally confined discontinuity to the microscopic sub-atomic level. The discontinuity which Lévi-Strauss alleges is thus exceedingly counter-intuitive. Second, Lévi-Strauss does not deal with the possibility that the discontinuity within nature which he proposes may not be a discontinuity at all, but rather a result of our inability to find those pre-human forms which would fill in the gap and eliminate the discontinuity, or even a result of our way of looking at and investigating primitives. That is, it may be that the alleged discontinuity is in fact a result of our inquiry's being incomplete or distorting, and not at all an objective fact about nature. (This was precisely the response of many to the finding of discontinuity in physics.) The importance of this possibility is obvious: one cannot ascribe to nature what is properly a consequence of one's method of inquiry. But Lévi-Strauss, even though he seems clearly aware of the issue—indeed he speaks of it often in *Tristes Tropiques*[3]— nonetheless seems essentially to disregard it. Moreover, his commitment to the construction of the model of "Mind-As-Such" seems not to *allow* him to consider it seriously, for the logic of models and of model-making tends to subvert the subjective-objective distinction. This is why all model-making—Lévi Strauss's, it seems to me, not excepted—runs the risk of becoming arbitrary and subjective, of becoming, in some cases, sheer speculation and indulgence in metaphysics.

Lévi-Strauss's belief in the existence of a Super-Mind, i.e., a quasi-Kantian set of invariant structures which all minds, and products of minds like societies, exhibit, leads him to some interesting reflections about human history. In a general sense his theory of history is anti-Marxian. This is all the more interesting since he often has suggested that his thought is greatly indebted to Marx. Thus, in *Tristes Tropiques*, he says:

> . . . rarely do I tackle a problem in sociology or ethnology without having first set my mind in motion by a re-perusal of a page or two from the *18 Brumaire of Louis Bonaparte* or the *Critique of Political Economy*.

And in *The Savage Mind*, speaking of Sartre, he says that ". . . in both our cases Marx is the point of departure of our thought." Nonetheless, at bottom, his thought moves in quite a different direction from that of Marx. What separates them is their respective attitudes toward historical change.

For Marx it seems clear that history is developmental. Man unfolds in history, and, like a seed, slowly comes to fruition. Moreover, the forms of life and of social organization at any given time are a function of the distance yet to be traveled and of the obstacles which impede, but paradoxically also further, the process; although dialectical, history for Marx is progressive. Time measures the progress of history; if it contains the seeds of contradiction, it also contains the seeds of consummation.

For Lévi-Strauss, on the other hand, it would seem that history and time are not developmental and progressive; they do not lead to successively better states of society and relations among men or even to a basic alteration of man's modes of consciousness and styles of living. (It is, by the way, on this point, although not solely on this point, that Lévi-Strauss criticizes Sartre in the last chapter of *The Savage Mind*. For Sartre, at bottom, retains a Marxian view of time and history. Thus, for example, Sartre distinguishes superior and inferior modes of consciousness in terms of historical position and context, and he is unwilling to grant that the primitive possesses "complex understanding" since such understanding could not have existed at that level of historical development.) For Lévi-Strauss, history is a series of combinations or clusters of modes of consciousness and life, individual and social, spread out in time. These different clusters represent the different contents or events which "fill in" the structures of "Mind-As-Such" in different historical epochs. Thus the existence of totemic clans, exogamy, gift-giving, etc. in the particular "piece" of history occupied by a primitive group represents the content or set of events in terms of which "Mind-As-Such" has "organicized" these particular group[s] of men living in that particular time. Those combinations which actually become manifest represent only some of the combinations which *could* have come about. The set of possible modes of consciousness and life is probably large but finite.* The diversity they exhibit, however, should not hide the fact that behind them, like Plato's Forms and Hegel's Categories, stand the invariant and recurring structures which they subserve and from which they derive their reality.

Lévi-Strauss rarely deals with the factors which lie beneath the structures of "Mind-As-Such." He does, however, speak of phenomena like demographic expansion, wars, drought, etc., as the generative factors underlying empirical change. Yet all these seem in the end reducible to the physical forces of nature. Thus, in speaking of the laws of primitive logic, the "original" and "elementary" logic which is the source of all thought, Lévi-Strauss remarks that these laws are ". . . a direct expression of the structure of the mind (and behind the mind, probably of the brain)." And lest the parenthetical "probably" be misconstrued, he goes on to say in *The Savage Mind:*

> . . . the ultimate goal of the human sciences (is) not to constitute, but to dissolve man. The preeminent nature of anthropology is that it represents the first step in a procedure which involves others. Ethnographic analysis tries to arrive at invariants beyond the empirical diversity of human societies. . . . However, it would not be enough to reabsorb particular humanities into a general one. This first enterprise opens the way for others . . . which are incumbent upon the exact natural sciences: the reintegration of culture in nature and finally of life within the whole of its physico-chemical conditions.

And, he adds, "the opposition between nature and culture . . . seems to be of primarily methodological importance."

The activities of the physical energies which govern all things have no point, no goal, no consummation; equally as surely one cannot speak of them as "progressing." And since these activities underlie the empirical and structural events which constitute human history, that history in turn cannot be said to progress. History and time are merely the space within which, on one level, the structures of Mind and the contents of those structures, exhibit their respective permutations and combinations. We have thus not progressed beyond the primitive; we have merely turned up on a different roll of the dice.

Now this vision of man and history, Lucretian in its broad outlines, can have a purgative and cathartic effect; it can loosen the grip of existence. Seen from the Olympian, timeless perspective of structuralism, our concrete concerns—our hopes, our struggles, our despairs—lose their flesh and blood, their urgency. The reality of our strivings and our failures, of our struggles with ourselves and others over principles and ideals, of our moral visions and political revolutions—

---

* Thus, speaking of customs in *Tristes Tropiques:* "The ensemble of a people's customs has always its particular style; they form into systems. I am convinced that the number of these systems is not unlimited, and that human societies, like individual human beings . . . never create *absolutely*; all they can do is to choose certain combinations from a repertory of ideas which it should be possible to reconstitute . . . one could eventually establish a periodic chart of . . . elements analogous to that devised by Mendeleyev. In this, all customs, whether real or possible, would be grouped by families, and all that would remain for us to do would be to recognize those which societies had . . . adopted.

in short, our humanity—fades, and like a God (or a crab) we are released from the demands and anxieties of being human.   Seeing it all from this remote, transcendent vantage-point produces a detachment, a disinterest, a purely theoretical frame of mind: our passions are subdued, calmed, muted.   It would be folly if, knowing this truth about things human, one remained within the frustrating, painful world of the passions.   In understanding and resigning before the reality of what is—the reality of human insignificance and cosmic indifference—man fulfills his destiny: self-realization lies in the adjustment of our humanity to our intellect.

Thus, if Lévi-Strauss's structuralism is Marxian, it is because it accepts Marx's demand that man be studied scientifically; its heresy, on the other hand, from a Marxian point of view, is its abstract, idealist conception of man as non-historical, non-social, non-existential Mind, and its undialectical mechanistic materialism which minimizes the reality of human purposes and principles, reads history as indifferent to such purposes and principles, and places no obligation upon us to work for them.   In these rejections lies the offensiveness of structuralism—its trivialization of our deepest instincts.

But to find structuralism offensive is neither to disprove it factually nor even to judge it wrong on the basis of some (necessarily relative) set of moral values.   For structuralism makes no factual claim but rather offers a way of interpreting facts; and any formative appraisal of it must of necessity be relative and arbitrary. Nevertheless, one cannot but be struck by its many internal irregularities and inconsistencies.   While rejecting the reality of the passions, structuralism passionately seeks release from them; while denying the reality of man's earthliness and finitude, it not only commits itself to a disciplined study of these phenomena but plays them off as a means of enlisting support for itself; while it implies an apolitical posture, it, in effect, pragmatically, seems to support the status quo and to express an ideology as conservative as historical Catholicism; while it implicitly prescribes that man seek fulfilment in intellect, it denounces prescription; while it concerns itself with the forms and structures of human thought and life and, indirectly, minimizes the reality of the content of human thought and life, it presents us nevertheless with its own clear message, namely, the dignity of the intellect and the folly of the passions; and while denying the existence of cross-cultural Truth, it solemnly, even scientifically, announces its existence.   All these inconsistencies within structuralism testify to the unavoidable reality of the very things which structuralism seeks to minimize and discredit.*

Is then, after all this, primitive man a savage different *in kind* from us, or is he essentially identical with us?   The work of Lévi-Strauss does not provide us with

* This conception of man and history seems to involve two apparently incompatible philosophical views.   On the one hand, in saying that man and human history are reducible to chemistry and physics, Lévi-Strauss is speaking like a materialist.   On the other hand, in maintaining that man and human history are governed by the forms and categories, the invariant and recurring structures of Mind-As-Such, he is speaking like an idealist.   And these two views, unless they are substantially qualified, contradict each other.

the answer—but then neither does the work of any anthropologist. This, however, should produce a cynicism about anthropology within us only if we misconceive the nature of the question, that is, if we believe it to be a rather straightforward empirical question amenable to the methods of scientific inquiry. It should be clear by now that the matter is not at all as simple as that. Rather, the nature of the question is perhaps best defined by its resemblance to such perennial philosophical questions as, "What is man?" "What is nature?" and "What is the relation between man and nature?" And with respect to these questions it is as important that we confront them and *attempt* to answer them as it is that we answer them conclusively. For only in that continuing confrontation do we define and redefine ourselves; and only by grappling with these questions of identity do we create an identity worth bothering about.

Notes

1. University of Chicago Press, 290 pp., $5.95.
2. Beacon Press, 116 pp., $3.95.
3. Atheneum, 404 pp., $2.85.

6 . Totem and Caste . Claude Lévi-Strauss

Both the exchange of women and the exchange of food are means of securing or of displaying the interlocking of social groups with one another. This being so, we can see why they may be found either together or separately. They are procedures of the same type and are indeed generally thought of as two aspects of the same procedure. They may reinforce each other, both performing the actual function, or one performing it and the other representing it symbolically. Or they may be alternatives, a single one fulfilling the whole function or if that is otherwise discharged, as it can be even in the absence of both procedures, then the symbolic representation of it:

> If . . . a people combines exogamy with totemism, this is because it has chosen to reinforce the social cohesion already established by totemism by superimposing on it yet another system which is connected with the first by its reference to physical and social kinship and is distinguished from, though not opposed to it, by its lack of reference to cosmic kinship. Exogamy can play this same part in types of society which are built on foundations other than totemism; and the geographical distribution of the two institutions coincides only at certain points in the world. (Van Gennep, p. 351).[1]

From Claude Lévi-Strauss, *The Savage Mind* (Chicago: 1966), pp. 109–117; 226–227, by permission of The University of Chicago Press. Reprinted also by permission of George Weidenfeld & Nicolson Ltd.

However exogamy, as we know, is never entirely absent. This is due to the fact that the perpetuation of the group can only be effected by means of women, and although varying degrees of symbolic content can be introduced by the particular way in which a society organizes them or thinks of their operation, marriage exchanges always have real substance, and they are alone in this. The exchange of food is a different matter. Aranda women really bear children. But Aranda men confine themselves to imagining that their rites result in the increase of totemic species. In the former, although it may be described in conventional terms which impose their own limits on it, what is in question is primarily a way of doing something. In the latter it is only a way of saying something.

Examples of "accumulation" of some kind have attracted particular attention, no doubt because the repetition of the same scheme on two different planes made them look simpler and more consistent. It is mainly this which has led to the definition of totemism by the parallelism between eating prohibitions and rules of exogamy and to making this supplementary set of customs a special object of study. There are, however, cases in which the relation between marriage and eating customs is one of complementarity and not supplementarity and where they are therefore dialectically related to each other. This form clearly also belongs to the same group. And it is groups in this sense, and not arbitrarily isolated transformations, which are the proper subject of the sciences of man.

In an earlier chapter [of *The Savage Mind*] I quoted a botanist's testimony with regard to the extreme purity of types of seed in the agriculture of so-called primitive peoples, in particular among the Indians of Guatemala. We also know that there is intense fear of agricultural exchanges in this area: a transplanted seedling may take the spirit of the plant with it, with the result that it disappears from its original locality. One may, then, exchange women but refuse to exchange seeds. This is common in Melanesia.

The inhabitants of Dobu, an island to the south-east of New Guinea, are divided into matrilineal lineages called *susu*. Husband and wife, who necessarily come from different *susu*, each bring their own seed yams and cultivate them in separate gardens without ever mixing them. No hope for a person who has not his own seed: a woman who has none will not succeed in marrying and will be reduced to the state of a fisherwoman, thief or beggar. Seed which does not come from the *susu* will not grow, for agriculture is possible only by the use of magic inherited from the maternal uncle: it is ritual which makes the yams swell.

These precautions and scruples rest on the belief that yams are persons: "Like women, they give birth to children ..." They go abroad at night and people wait for their return before harvesting. This is the source of the rule that yams may not be dug too early in the morning: they might not yet have returned. It is also the source of the conviction that the fortunate cultivator is a magician who has known how to persuade his neighbours' yams to move and establish themselves in his garden. A man who has a good harvest is reckoned a lucky thief (Fortune).

Beliefs of the same type were to be found even in France until recently. In the middle ages there was a penalty of death for "the sorceress who defiled and injured crops; who, by reciting the psalm *Super aspidem ambulabis*, emptied the fields of their corn to fill her own granary with this goodly produce." Not so long ago at Cubjac in the Perigord a magical invocation was supposed to assure the person using it of a good crop of turnips: "May our neighbours' be as big as millet seed, our relations' as big as grains of corn and our own as big as the head of Fauve the ox!" (Rocal, pp. 164–5).

Apart from the modicum of exogamy resulting from the prohibited degrees, European peasant societies practised strict local endogamy. And it is significant that at Dobu extreme endo-agriculture can act as the symbolic compensation for lineage and village exogamy which is practised with repugnance and even fear. In spite of the fact that endogamy within the locality—which consists of between four and twenty villages—is generally assured, marriage even into the next village is looked on as putting a man at the mercy of assassins and sorcerers and he him-self always regards his wife as a powerful magician, ready to deceive him with her childhood friends and to destroy him and his (Fortune). In a case like this, endo-agriculture reinforces a latent tendency towards endogamy, if indeed it does not express symbolically the hostility to the unwillingly practised rules of a pre-carious exogamy. The situation is symmetrically the reverse of that prevailing in Australia where food prohibitions and rules of exogamy reinforce one another, as we have seen in a more symbolic and clearly conceptual way in the patrilineal societies (where the food prohibitions are flexible and tend to be formulated in terms of moieties, that is, at a level which is already abstract and lends itself to a binary coding by pairs of oppositions) and in a more literal and concrete fashion in the matrilineal societies (where the prohibitions are rigid and stated in terms of clans which one might often be hesitant to regard as members of systematic sets, given the determining part of demographic and historic factors in their genesis).

Apart from these cases of positive or negative parallelism, there are others in which reciprocity between social groups is expressed only on one plane. Omaha rules of marriage are formulated very differently from those of the Aranda. Instead of the class of the spouse being precisely specified, as it is among the Aranda, any clan not expressly forbidden is permitted. On the plane of food, however, the Omaha have rites very similar to the intichiuma:[2] the sacred maize is entrusted to particular clans who annually distribute it to the others to vitalize their seeds (Fletcher and La Flesche). The totemic clans of the Nandi of Uganda are not exogamous; but a remarkable development of clan prohibitions, not only on the plane of food but also on those of technical and economic activities, dress and impediments to marriage based on some detail or other of the personal his-tory of the forbidden spouse, compensates for this "non-functionality" in the sphere of marriage exchanges (Hollis). No system can be constructed from these differences: the distinctions recognized between the groups seem rather to spring from a propensity to accept all statistical fluctuations. In a different form and on a different plane, this is also the method employed by the systems termed 'Crow-Omaha' and by contemporary Western societies to ensure the overall equilibrium of matrimonial exchanges.[3]

This emergence of methods of articulation more complex than those resulting just from rules of exogamy or food prohibitions, or even of both at once, is particularly striking in the case of the Baganda (who are near the Nandi) because they seem to have accumulated all the forms. The Baganda were divided into forty clans, *kika*, each of which had a common totem, *miziro*, the consumption of which was forbidden by virtue of a rule of food rationing: by depriving itself of the totemic food, each clan leaves more of it available to other clans. This is the modest counterpart of the Australian claim that by refraining from consuming its totem each clan retains the power to increase it.

As in Australia, each clan is characterized by its links with a territory, among the Baganda generally a hill. There is a secondary totem, *kabiro*, as well as the principal totem. Each Baganda clan is thus defined by two totems, food prohibitions and a territory. There are also prerogatives such as eligibility of its members for the kingship or other honours, the right to provide royal wives, making and caring for the royal emblems or utensils, ritual obligations to provide other clans with certain kinds of food, and technical specializations: the Mushroom clan, for instance, makes all the bark cloth, and all blacksmiths come from the clan of the Tail-less Cow, etc. Finally, we find some prohibitions, such as that the women of a particular clan cannot be the mothers of male children of the blood royal, and restrictions with regard to the bearing of proper names (Roscoe).

In cases like this it is no longer very clear what type of society is in question. There can, for instance, be no doubt that the totemic clans of the Baganda also function as castes. And yet at first sight it seems that nothing could be more different than these two forms of institution. We have become used to associating totemic groups with the most "primitive" civilizations and thinking of castes as a feature of highly developed, sometimes even literate, societies. Moreover, a strong tradition connects totemic institutions with the strictest exogamy while an anthropologist asked to define the concept of a caste would almost certainly begin by mentioning the rule of endogamy.

It may therefore seem surprising that between about 1830 and 1850, the first investigators of Australian societies often referred to their marriage classes as "castes" even though they had some idea of their function (Thomas, pp. 34–5). These intuitions which have the freshness and vivacity of a perception of societies which were still intact, and a vision undistorted by theoretical speculation, are not to be despised. Without going to the root of the problem now, it is clear that there are at least superficial analogies between Australian tribes and societies with castes. Each group has a specialized function indispensable to the collectivity as a whole and complementary to the functions assigned to other groups.

This is particularly clear in the case of tribes whose clans or moieties are bound together by a rule of reciprocity. Among the Kaitish and the Unmatjera, northern neighbours of the Aranda, anyone who gathers wild seeds in the territory of a totemic group named after these seeds must ask the headman's permission before eating them. It is the duty of each totemic group to provide the other groups with the plant or animal for whose "production" it is specially responsible. Thus a man of the Emu clan out hunting on his own may not touch an emu. But if, on the other hand, he is in company he is permitted and even supposed to kill it and offer it to hunters of other clans.   Conversely, when he is alone a man of the Water clan may drink if he is thirsty but when he is with others he must receive the water from a member of the other moiety, preferably from a brother-in-law (Spencer and Gillen, pp. 159–60).   Among the Warramunga each totemic group is responsible for the increase and availability to other groups of a particular plant or animal species: "The members of one moiety . . . take charge . . . of the ceremonies of the other moiety which are destined to secure the increase of their own food supply."   Among the Walpari as well as the Warramunga the secondary totemic prohibitions (applying to the maternal totem) are waived if the food in question is obtained through the agency of a man of the other moiety.   More generally and for any totem, there is a distinction between the groups which never eat it (because it is their own totem), those which eat it only if it is procured through the agency of another group (as in the case of the maternal totems), and those which eat it freely in any circumstances.   Similarly in the case of the sacred water-holes, women may never approach them, uninitiated men may approach but not drink from them, while some groups drink from them on the condition that the water is given to them by members of other groups who can themselves drink freely from them (Spencer and Gillen, pp. 164, 167).   This mutual interdependence is already to be seen in marriage which, as Radcliffe-Brown has shown in the case of Australia (but the same could equally well be said of other clan societies such as the Iroquois), was based on reciprocal gifts of vegetable food (feminine) and animal food (masculine): the conjugal family in these cases was like a miniature society with two castes.

There is thus less difference than would appear between societies which, like some Australian tribes, assign a distinctive magico-economic function to totemic groups and, for instance, the Bororo of Central Brazil, among whom specialists are in charge of the same function of "liberating" the food production—whether animal or vegetable—for the whole group (Colbacchini).   This leads one to doubt whether the opposition between endogamous castes and exogamous totemic groups is really radical.   There seem to be connections between these two extreme types, whose nature would appear more clearly if we could show that intermediate forms exist.

I have drawn attention elsewhere to a feature of so-called totemic institutions which in my own view is fundamental to them.   The homology they evoke is not between social groups and natural species but between the differences which manifest themselves on the level of groups on the one hand and on that of species on the other.   They are thus based on the postulate of a homology between *two systems of differences*, one of which occurs in nature and the other in culture. Indicating relations of homology by vertical lines, a "pure totemic structure" could thus be represented in the following way:

Nature: species 1 $\neq$ species 2 $\neq$ species 3 $\neq$ . . . . . species n
$\qquad\qquad\quad$ | $\qquad\qquad$ | $\qquad\qquad$ |
Culture: group   1 $\neq$ group   2 $\neq$ group   3 $\neq$ . . . . . group n

This structure would be fundamentally impaired if homologies between the terms themselves were added to those between their relations or if, going one step further, the entire system of homologies were transferred from relations to terms:

Nature: species 1 $\neq$ species 2 $\neq$ species 3 $\neq$ . . . . . species n

| | | |

Culture: group 1 $\neq$ group 2 $\neq$ group 3 $\neq$ . . . . . group n

In this case the implicit content of the structure would no longer be that clan 1 differs from clan 2 as for instance the eagle differs from the bear but rather that clan 1 is like the eagle and clan 2 like the bear.   In other words, the nature of clan 1 and the nature of clan 2 would each be involved separately instead of the formal relation between them.

Now, the transformation whose theoretical possibility has just been considered can sometimes be directly observed.   The islanders of the Torres Straits have totemic clans, numbering about thirty at Mabuiag.   These exogamous patrilineal clans were grouped into two moieties, one comprising terrestrial and the other marine animals.   At Tutu and Saibai this division seems to have corresponded to a territorial division within the village.   The structure was already in an advanced state of decay at the time of Haddon's expedition.   Nevertheless, the natives had a very strong sense of the physical and psychological affinity between men and their totems and of the corresponding obligation of each group to pursue the appropriate type of behaviour.   Thus the Cassowary, Crocodile, Snake, Shark and Hammer-headed Shark clans were said to love fighting and the Shovel-nosed Skate, Ray and Sucker-Fish clans to be peace loving.   The Dog clan was held to be unpredictable, dogs being of a changeable disposition.   The members of the Crocodile clan were thought to be strong and ruthless and those of the Cassowary clan to have long legs and to run fast (Frazer, vol. II, pp. 3–9, quoting Haddon and Rivers).   It would be interesting to know whether these beliefs are survivals from the old organization or whether they developed as the exogamous rules decayed.

The fact is that similar, though not equally developed, beliefs have been observed among the Menomini of the Great Lakes and among the Chippewa further north.   Among the latter, people of the Fish clan were reputed to be long-lived, frequently to go bald or to have thin hair, and all bald people were assumed to come from this clan.   Peoples of the Bear clan, on the other hand, had long, thick, coarse hair which never went white and they were said to be ill-tempered and fond of fighting.   People of the Crane clan had loud ringing voices and provided the tribe with its orators (Kinietz, pp. 76–7).

Let us pause for a moment to consider the theoretical implications of views like these.   When nature and culture are thought of as two systems of differences between which there is a formal analogy, it is the systematic character of each domain which is brought to the fore.   Social groups are distinguished from one another but they retain their solidarity as parts of the same whole, and the rule of exogamy furnishes the means of resolving this opposition balanced between diversity and unity.   But if social groups are considered not so much from the point of view of their reciprocal relations in social life as each on their own account in relation to something other than sociological reality, then the idea of diversity is likely to prevail over that of unity.   Each social group will tend to form a system no longer with other social groups but with particular differentiating properties regarded as hereditary, and these characteristics exclusive to each group will weaken the framework of their solidarity within the society.   The more each group tries to define itself by the image which it draws from a natural model, the more difficult will it become for it to maintain its links with other social groups and, in particular to exchange its sisters and daughters with them since it will tend to think of them as being of a particular "species."   Two images, one social and the other natural, and each articulated separately, will be replaced by a socionatural image, single but fragmented:[4]

| Nature: | species 1 | species 2 | species 3 | species n |
| Culture: | group   1 | group   2 | group 3 | group n |

It is of course only for purposes of exposition and because they form the subject of this book that I am apparently giving a sort of priority to ideology and superstructures.   I do not at all mean to suggest that ideological transformations give rise to social ones.   Only the reverse is in fact true.   Men's conception of the relations between nature and culture is a function of modifications of their own social relations.   But, since my aim here is to outline a theory of superstructures, reasons of method require that they should be singled out for attention and that major phenomena which have no place in this programme should seem to be left in brackets or given second place.   We are however merely studying the shadows on the wall of the Cave without forgetting that it is only the attention we give them which lends them a semblance of reality.

Notes

1. Van Gennep, A.: *L'Etat actuel du problème totémique*, Paris, 1920.
2. . . . the eating of totemic species, sometimes occurring in the Australian rites of increase known by the name of Intichiuma, cannot be treated as a primitive, or even an aberrant, form of sacrifice.   The resemblance is as superficial as that which would lead one to identify whales and fish.   Moreover, these rites of increase are not regularly connected with so-called totemic classifications; they do not always accompany them, even in Australia, and there are numerous and widespread examples of rites of increase without "totemism" and of "totemism" without rites of increase.

Above all, the structure of rites of the Intichiuma type and the implicit ideas on which they rest are very far removed from those we have discerned in sacrifice.   In such societies (magical) production and (real) consumption of natural species are normally separate as a result of an identity postulated between each group of men and a totemic species, and a proclaimed or ascertained distinction between different social groups on the one hand and different natural species on the other.   The role of the Intichiuma is therefore periodically and momentarily to re-establish the contiguity between production and consumption, as though human groups and natural species had from time to time to count themselves two by two and in pairs of allies, before each taking their own place in the game: species nourishing the men who do not "produce" them, and men "producing" the species which they are forbidden to eat.   In the Intichiuma, consequently, men momentarily confirm their substantial identity with their respective totemic species, by the two-fold rule that each group is to produce what it consumes and consume what it produces, and these things are the same for each and different for all. Thanks to this, there will no longer be a risk of the normal play of reciprocity creating confusions between fundamental definitions which must be repeated periodically. If the natural series is presented by capitals and the social series by small letters,

$$A \quad B \quad C \quad D \quad E \ldots\ldots\ldots N$$
$$a \quad b \quad c \quad d \quad e \ldots\ldots\ldots n$$

then the Intichiuma recalls the affinity between A and a, B and b, C and c, N and n, attesting that when, in the normal course of events, group b incorporates, by eating, species A, C, D, E . . . N, group a species B, C, D, E . . . N, and so on, what is in question is an exchange between social groups and an arbitrage between resemblance and contiguity, not the replacement of one resemblance by another resemblance nor one contiguity by another contiguity . . .

3. Rightly or wrongly, Radcliffe-Brown (in his "Introduction" in *African Systems of Kinship and Marriage*, A. R. Radcliffe-Brown and Daryll Forde, eds., Oxford, 1960, pp. 32–33), treats the Nandi kinship system as an Omaha system.

4. It will perhaps be objected that in the above mentioned work (*Totemism* [translated from the French by R. Needham], Boston, 1963), I denied that totemism can be interpreted on the basis of a direct analogy between human groups and natural species. But this criticism was directed against a theory put forward by ethnologists and what is in question here is an—implicit or explicit—native theory which indeed corresponds to institutions that ethnologists would refuse to class as totemic.

Bibliography

1. Colbacchini, P. A. et Albisetti, P. C. *Os Bororos Orientais*. São Paulo-Rio de Janeiro: 1942.
2. Fletcher, A. C. and La Flesche, F. "The Omaha Tribe," *27th Annual Report*, Bureau of American Ethnology (1905–1906). Washington, D.C.: 1911.
3. Fortune, R. F. *Sorcerers of Dobu*. New York: 1932.
4. Frazer, J. G. *Totemism and Exogamy*, Vol. 4. London: 1910.
5. Hollis, A. C. *The Nandi; their Language and Folklore*. Oxford: 1909.
6. Kinietz, W. V. "Chippewa Village. The Story of Katikitegon," *Bulletin No. 25*, Cranbrook Institute of Science. Detroit: 1947.
7. Rocal, G. *Vieux Perigord*, 3rd ed. Paris: 1928.
8. Roscoe, J. *The Boganda: An Account of their Native Customs and Beliefs*. London: 1911.
9. Spencer, B. and Gillen, F. J. *The Northern Tribes of Central Australia*. London: 1904.
10. Thomas, N. W. *Kinship Organization and Group Marriage in Australia*. 1906.

Microscale Frameworks

7 . Aspects of any Relationship
Marion J. Levy, Jr.

I. INTRODUCTION: DEFINITION AND EXPLANATION

This chapter gives explicit attention to a bit of analytic apparatus. I have developed it in greater detail elsewhere,[1] and I shall not try to reproduce it in full here. This will be the only chapter in this work [*Modernization and the Structure of Societies*] devoted primarily to an analytic tool.

I define a *relationship* as any set of social structures that define the action, ideally and/or actually in terms of which two or more individual actors interact. I define a *social structure* as any pattern (i.e., as any observable uniformity) in terms of which social action takes place. I define *social* as the adjective descriptive of any phenomenon that is not adequately explicable (for the purpose in hand) in terms of the heredity of the species of actors involved and the nonspecies' environment. Since we are only interested in human societies here, *social action* refers to any action of human beings that is not adequately explicable in terms of human heredity and the nonhuman environment. Thus any structures of behavior that adequately describe, for whatever purposes, the interaction between two or more human beings also describes their social relationship, provided of course the structures are not adequately explicable in terms of human heredity and the nonhuman environment. The structures of interaction of two friends

From "Aspects of any Relationship," pp. 133–174, in Marion J. Levy, Jr., *Modernization and the Structure of Societies: A Setting for International Affairs* (Princeton University Press, 1966); Princeton Paperback, 1969. Reprinted by permission of Princeton University Press.

constitute a relationship; the interaction of individual faculty members of a university is in terms of various relationship structures; the operations of the members *qua* members of any large-scale enterprise, be it a business or governmental enterprise or whatever, involve a complicated set of relationships; etc. All relationships are social systems or membership units or concrete structures or organizations. The number of members may be as small as two or indefinitely large. The most restricted possible relationship is the most restricted possible social system,[2] and all social systems consist of one or more relationships, involving two or more members.

Since all social systems can be conceived of as sets of relationship structures, the analysis of them may be used as a tool for the location of the more important social systems or organizations in terms of which social analysts must treat societies. The analysis of relationship structures is one of the tools with which we can combat the biases of ethnocentrism. There are certain social systems which we expect to find even if we study an unfamiliar society. We do not particularly expect to find these because there is anything "natural" about them, though this is frequently asserted. We expect to find them because we are familiar with them in our own experience and because most of the other societies with which we are familiar have also contained such organizations. Organizations such as families, governments, neighborhood units of various sorts, churches, business firms, friendship units, etc.—these are all organizations with which we are familiar. We are rather more surprised when we fail to find them elsewhere than when we do. Indeed, our initial approach to other societies is frequently to look for units of this sort. But there are also many types of units in many societies with which we are not at all familiar. It is quite impossible to approach any society without any conception of what you might find there. The idea that one deals with this sort of problem by approaching other peoples with a blank mind is a particularly virulent type of nonsense because it confuses inexplicitness with objectivity. To approach the analysis of any society (or of any other subject for that matter) with a completely blank mind would be like attempting to get to one's feet on a frictionless surface. In the latter case one would stay prone; in the former case one's mind would stay blank. Perhaps, if the members of that society were kindly, the person with a blank mind might be reared from scratch as though he were an infant and become thereby a member of their society but not an analyst of it.

In the absence of concepts of the specific types of units that are in fact present, one could always locate such units in a given society by observing the way in which individuals interrelate with one another and discovering which of these cluster in such fashion that one might refer to the people engaged as members of some common unit. This would be time consuming, but it would, in the long run, locate the organizations. Since we do not have blank minds and since there are some organizations common to all societies, we are never faced with the really costly problem of trying to locate all organizations by starting from scratch solely in terms of relationship structures. The analysis of any relationships is, however, useful as a tool when our preconceptions do not turn out to have a close fit with what we observe.

Another application of relationship structures is more important for present purposes. It leads to generalizations that cut across other distinctions and show common elements among them. For example, in the United States today, however different business firms and government may be, members of both organizations emphasize rationality, universalism, functional specificity, and avoidance. One can not only use these aspects of relationships to locate common features in different organizations of the sort just described; one can also use them to locate common features prominent in the conduct of different aspects of behavior. Again in the United States, outside of the family context the economic and political aspects of our behavior are, ideally speaking, carried out in terms of relationships which emphasize rationality, universalism, functional specificity, and avoidance. One may also use the same concepts to isolate variations across such lines. In the examples just given, although in business and governmental contexts we emphasize the same four aspects, and, I might add, relationships in both are hierarchically arranged, we usually expect business relationships to be predominantly individualistic whereas we expect government relationships to be predominantly responsible.[3] Thus in terms of all of the most general aspects of relationships developed here our business firms and government (and its subsystems) are identical, ideally speaking, except with regard to what will be called the "goal orientation" aspects (see below). By no means all of the distinctions between business firms and government are explicable in terms of this one difference, but many are, and other differences are understandable in terms of differences in more specific forms of the aspects in which they are identical on more general levels. Though rationality is stressed by both businessmen and members of the government, the rationality concerns quite different matters, and so forth.

II. ASPECTS OF ANY RELATIONSHIP

A. INTRODUCTION

The treatment here of aspects of any relationship is a development and adaptation of concepts that I have taken from the early work of Talcott Parsons. He, in turn, developed them partially on the basis of the work done by F. Töennies. The development here is not the form conceived by Töennies or favored by Parsons currently. Nevertheless, Töennies indirectly and Parsons directly are the sources from which these developments came.[4]

In selecting subcategories of relationship structures two considerations are paramount. First, the distinctions should be ones that are relevant for *any* relationship. Second, the subsidiary categories or aspects should be ones in terms of which some variability is possible. If a given subcategory has only a unique value, it is only useful as a constant in hypotheses about all relationships and can only be a variable in distinctions between relationship and nonrelationship structures.

For present purposes we need aspects of relationships with subcategories capable of binary distinctions at least. Rather than binary distinctions, I have chosen polar distinctions which permit considerable variation in degree of approximation to one extreme form or another of a given aspect. These distinctions could be converted into binary ones, but only at the expense of leaving out the vast majority of cases I wish to treat since they are not at one extreme or the other.

It is also essential that the distinctions are not such that virtually all of the cases fall in one subcategory as opposed to the other or close to one pole of the distinction as opposed to the other. For example, one of the aspects chosen here is the *cognitive aspect*. One could distinguish among cognitive aspects of different relationships on the basis of whether or not explicit biological knowledge were involved. If one did, only a small number of all the relationships one would wish to analyze would be ones involving such knowledge. To think of relationships as biologically cognitive or nonbiologically cognitive would be useful only for extremely limited questions. We need some set of distinctions of greater general utility if the tool is to be generally applicable for the comparative analysis of any set of relationship structures.

Six aspects of any relationship have been distinguished here. They are (1) the cognitive aspect, (2) the membership criteria aspect, (3) the substantive definition aspect, (4) the affective aspect, (5) the goal orientation aspect, and (6) the stratification aspect. For each of these aspects a polar distinction is offered. Those are respectively (1) rational-traditional, (2) universalistic-particularistic, (3) functionally specific-functionally diffuse, (4) avoidant-intimate, (5) individualistic-responsible, and (6) hierarchical-nonhierarchical. These categories are defined and discussed below.

B. PROBLEMS ABOUT THESE CONCEPTS

There are considerable theoretical shortcomings about these concepts. First, I have no satisfactory theoretical explanation of why six and only six aspects are distinguished. Second, I have no satisfactory explanation of why this set of six rather than another set of six is presented. The only answer I have to such questions is that it can be shown that these six and their subcategories are in fact useful in formulating hypotheses. One may use them and get at a great number of distinctions, and those distinctions turn out to be generally relevant for social analysis and particularly relevant for the analysis of the problems of relatively modernized and relatively nonmodernized societies which are of interest in this work.

Third, I have insisted that these distinctions not be used as binary distinctions. Technically, however, in all six of the cases about which I have been able to be fairly precise, I have defined one extreme of the scale residually relative to the other. Thus perfect rationality is different in kind from any element of traditionality; perfect universalism is different in kind from any particularism; etc. Perfect instances of these extremes may not exist at all, and most of the cases of interest to us are not pure cases of the extremes. Actual classification of relationships in terms of any of these aspects is always to some degree a function of the observer's judgment, and that, to some extent, is always arbitrary. Moreover, for theoretical reasons discussed shortly, no relationship can ever be completely and purely universalistic, and it is unlikely that any relationship be completely and perfectly rational. Therefore, the differences dealt with here are differences of degree. Moreover, it is quite useful in social analysis to distinguish whether ideal and/or actual emphases approach one extreme more closely than the other. Thus it is often useful to observe that employment structures characteristic of relatively modernized societies reflect overwhelming emphasis on universalism by contrast with those of other societies that reflect overwhelming emphasis on particularism. This is a relevant distinction despite the fact that there are *some* emphases on particularism, whether ideal or not, characteristic of even those relationships which reflect the most complete ideal structures of universalism in the most highly modernized society, and so forth. In general, to emphasize the nearly universal combinations of these elements a given relationship will be described as predominantly universalistic, rational, traditional, etc., if there is any possibility of confusion about whether the distinction intended is one of degree or kind.

C. USES OF THESE CONCEPTS

For the present two general uses of these concepts are asserted. First, as already mentioned, they can be used for the comparative analysis of any relationships. Implicit in this assertion, of course, is the assertion that they can be used to analyze any single relationship. Second, applications of the relationship aspects afford good reason to believe that different clusterings of certain of these relationship aspects are prominent features of societies, For example, if a relationship reflects heavy emphasis on rationality, it is likely also to be characterized by emphasis on universalism, functional specificity, and avoidance. This does not follow tautologically from the definition of the concepts involved. In the discussion of relatively modernized and relatively nonmodernized societies above, references have already been made to these relationship aspects. After detailed definition and illustration of these various aspects, their use for both comparative analysis and the formation of hypotheses about these clustering effects is discussed at some length.

D. RELATIONSHIP ASPECTS

1. COGNITIVE ASPECTS

Every relationship between two or more people involves some sort of knowledge, some sort of thinking, some sort of mental process, and that is defined here as its cognitive aspect. Subcategories of the cognitive aspects of any relationship are distinguished as follows: *rational* cognition is the kind of knowledge that, were it subjected to a theoretically omniscient scientific observer, would be found to violate none of the canons of science, that is to say, it would be in complete accord with the best scientific reasoning. Conclusions reached in terms of *traditional* cognition may coincide with conclusions reached on a purely rational basis. Even though this may often be the case, *traditional* cognition is defined as knowledge that is justified from the point of view of the individual who accepts it by argument to the effect that a given way of doing things is the prevailing and accepted way, and the way that should be continued because one's predecessors always did it that way. This is the essence of tradition in the social sense. Even when the conclusions of tradition coincide with those of rationality, the implications for action are importantly different. Having claimed this, let me go a bit behind this distinction and indicate some of the factors on which it rests.

This is one of those distinctions which, whatever its relevance to other species, is especially relevant to the human species. At the present stage of our development in the social sciences, it is fruitful to distinguish between the point of view of an observer and the point of view of an actor. The term *actor* is self-explanatory in this context. The term *observer* as used here is defined as a theoretically omniscient and objective scientific observer, literally a know-it-all. In considering any given act one may distinguish between the *end* of the act and the means (i.e., the methods, including use of materials) employed for that end. Either ends or means may be either empirical (i.e., can be analyzed in terms of sensory perception) or nonempirical. One may also distinguish as to whether from the point of view of the actor or the observer the ends and the means used are empirical or not. Thus if the action consists of going into a particular store to buy a pair of pliers, the end may be described as the purchase of a pair of pliers, and the means may be described as the selection of the particular store. Both ends and means are quite empirical. If the means selected by the actor are in fact adequate to the end he seeks, such action may be described as rational action. Even if he happens to have selected the wrong sort of store, such action is at least rationally oriented, although it is in fact *irrational*. On the other hand a given actor may simply pray that a pair of pliers be deposited on his desk. The end is still empirical, but the means contain an important nonempirical element. The physical act of prayer is quite empirical, but at least from the point of view of the actor the act of prayer is viewed as having some particular effect on some deity(ies) of some sort. This is quite nonempirical. The observer cannot tell one that he will not get a pair of pliers by use of such methods. The most that he can say is that many people who have behaved in that fashion have not ended up with pliers. There is no need here to elaborate on the various categories of nonrational and arational action which can be distinguished.[5] Value judgments such as the value of tradition itself in the last analysis always involve questions to which no observer can give a purely scientific answer.

In any social context the ultimate justifications of action from the point of view of the actors are standards of value to which no purely scientific solutions are possible. In this sense, if the range of action studied is enlarged, sooner or later one always encounters nonrational elements. Nevertheless, over a broad range of action, the selection of means may, ideally and/or actually, proceed much more importantly in purely scientific terms than not. When it does, I shall consider the emphasis, at least ideally speaking, to be on rational rather than on traditional action. The view that action should be as scientifically justifiable as possible is as much an evaluation as the view that action should be based on tradition as much as possible. Though both are evaluations which can be neither proved nor disproved by science, they are evaluations that have different implications for the actions of those who hold them. Those different implications can be studied scientifically and justify the distinction used here.

2. MEMBERSHIP CRITERIA ASPECTS

Every relationship is a system of action involving two or more actors who may be described as its membership. One may, therefore, always inquire why (or how) actors come to be members of such units. The reasons constitute the membership criteria. Following Parsons' early work, I have differentiated those into the two main categories of universalistic and particularistic. This distinction involves two lines of variation. The first has to do with the question of germaneness. Are the criteria concerned directly relevant to the purposes or main activities to be carried out in terms of the relationship? The second has to do with social barring. Is anyone prevented from participating in this particular relationship because of any social classifications which need not have anything to do with his abilities and/or accomplishments? The concept of social barring as used here is closely allied to the term *ascription* as it is ordinarily used by anthropologists and sociologists. Since to some extent one's life chances are always affected by one's kinship position, if one broadens the sphere of action enough, sooner or later, some criteria involving social barring come into play in every situation.

A relationship is defined as universalistic if the membership criteria contain no element of social barring and if they are germane. A relationship is defined as particularistic insofar as the membership criteria contain either nongermane elements, social barring, or some combination of the two. There are, therefore, three types of particularism: (1) *germane particularism*, i.e., involving social barring but germane criteria, (2) *capricious particularism*, i.e., involving no social barring but nongermane criteria, and (3) *ultimate particularism*, i.e., involving both social barring and nongermaneness.[6] I shall return to the three subcategories of particularism shortly. For the moment some more central considerations with regard to the basic distinction between universalism and particularism must be discussed, Membership criteria that tend to minimize but do not entirely eliminate particularistic elements will be called *predominantly universalistic*. Those that tend to minimize or eliminate universalistic elements will be called *predominantly particularistic*. Relationships may of course be ideally and/or actually *predominantly* universalistic or particularistic. The reason for insisting on these qualifications is simple. It is not difficult to find examples of relationships that are purely particularistic, ideally at least. The relationship between mother and son in many societies is such a relationship. Social barring is certainly involved. Unless a specifically different structure such as a structure of adoption is interposed, one and only one woman at any given point of time is eligible to stand in the relation of mother to a given son, if we define the term *mother* as it is defined in our own society. The criterion that only lords may join the hunt in a given forest is equally particularistic. A purely universalistic relationship is much more difficult to discover. As already mentioned, to some extent one's kinship position always affects one's life chances later on. Thus, if one considers the influences broadly enough, sooner or later one runs into some particularistic element since kinship considerations are inherently particularistic. On the other hand, *within a given setting*, the criteria concerned may be highly universalistic or even completely so, ideally speaking. For example, there are no doubt some particularistic elements in the determination of who is or is not admitted to Harvard College, but within the category of those admitted to Harvard College, admission to the Phi Beta Kappa honor society depends overwhelmingly, if not entirely, on qualifications that are germane to the selection for this relationship and that are criteria from which no Harvard undergraduate is socially barred.

In distinguishing between predominantly universalistic and particularistic classifications one must keep in mind the distinction between ideal and actual structures. In our own society, for example, relationships are frequently more nearly universalistic, ideally speaking, than they are in fact. Whenever one classifies a relationship as more or less particularistic or more or less nearly universalistic, he must be prepared to elaborate on the following questions if an explanation is called for: (1) From whose point of view is the relationship so classified? (2) Is the relationship so classified ideally and/or actually speaking, and again from whose point of view? (3) Within what setting is the relationship so classified?

Germane particularism may be defined as particularism in which social barring is present, but the social barring itself is highly relevant to the purposes of the relationship. Such a situation obtains in selection for succession to the throne of England. There the relationship may be considered one of sovereign to subject. At any given point in time, ideally and actually speaking, one and only one person is eligible to succeed. Eligibility for that succession is determined on the basis of kinship. The members of Parliament can, if they wish, set the whole structure aside, but if the system continues as at present, ideally speaking every individual save one at any given point in time is socially barred from succeeding to the throne. Since one of the main functions of that sovereign, however, is to symbolize a line of tradition and a family responsibility for the welfare of England, etc., the criteria involved are germane to the purpose of the selection. To the extent that such a situation obtains, a relationship will be considered more or less germanely particularistic. It is important to distinguish this kind of particularism because it combines more readily with a heavy emphasis on rationality than do the other types of particularism. Ordinarily, for example, there is an important element of kinship-oriented particularism in succession to positions of importance in a large number of family firms. The general emphasis on universalistic criteria may be great. Sons or sons-in-law of the directors of these enterprises may in fact be set aside if they do not have sufficient levels of ability, but there can be little doubt that in most cases the fact that they are sons or sons-in-law does give them a distinct differential advantage over other possible competitors. If the level of ability which they in fact achieve is sufficiently high and if to some extent the confidence of people who deal with them is importantly oriented to continuation of the family line, these predominantly particularistic criteria for succession may be easily combined with a heavy emphasis on rationality and on predominantly universalistic criteria elsewhere in the firm.

Capricious particularism is a quixotic possibility. Criteria that involve no social barring but that are irrelevant to the purpose for which selection is made may be insisted upon. In consideration of all these types one must pay close attention to the relationship involved since what would be nongermane criteria for one relationship might very well be germane ones for another. For example, the insistence that redheads and only redheads be hired to operate the pumps in a gasoline station would probably fall under the category of capricious particularism. No member of a society like our own is socially barred from being a redhead. There are no preferential mating structures that make redheadedness especially unlikely, there is no discrimination against redheaded infants at birth, etc. But redheadedness is not germane to one's ability to run a filling station. On the other hand for certain types of color film processes redheadedness might conceivably be highly germane. Thus, what would be an emphasis on capricious particularism in the one case might be a heavy emphasis on universalistic criteria in another.

If the criteria involve both social barring and nongermaneness, the relationship may be considered *ultimately particularistic*. Many forms of social discrimination fall into this category. Typical is the kind of discrimination based on so-called racial or religious distinctions. These certainly involve social barring, and in many settings they are not germane to the purposes of the relationship unless that relationship be extended to include the preservation of racial or religious distinctions as a basis of social barring. This sort of particularism, of course, raises the greatest difficulties when other emphases are on rationality, functional specificity, etc.

For most of the general purposes in this work the broad distinction between predominantly universalistic and purely or predominantly particularistic relationships will suffice, but for more detailed applications, the additional subcategories will prove useful.

3. SUBSTANTIVE DEFINITION ASPECTS

The substantive definition aspects of a relationship have to do with the precision or lack of precision of the definition and delimitation of the relationship. This is one way of describing what is involved in the relationship. The categories distinguished here are functionally specific and functionally diffuse. A *functionally specific* relationship is one in terms of which the activities, considerations, rights, obligations, or performances that are covered by the relationship are precisely defined and delimited. The modern business contract relationship is a typical example of a predominantly functionally specific relationship. In a modern contract relationship, ideally speaking, an attempt is made to state explicitly everything covered by the particular relationship. All questions among the members of such a relationship (*in verbis legitimis*: parties to the relationship) are supposed to be settled by specific reference to the contractual document itself. The burden of proof is on whoever wishes to claim some additional obligation under the contract. To show that the special request is not covered by the contract is sufficient defense. It is obvious, of course, that all contracts are not perfectly clear-cut documents, but ideally speaking at least that is one of the criteria of a good contract.

A *functionally diffuse* relationship is one that is more or less vaguely defined and delimited. The relationship between husband and wife is always predominantly functionally diffuse. Frequently many elements in a husband-wife relationship are carefully defined, but the relationship is always to some extent vaguely delimited. If a new situation raises a question of how husband and wife should behave toward one another, it is not customary to settle such matters by seeing whether or not the situation is covered in the fine print of the marriage contract, even if there is one. When the emphasis is on functional specificity, the burden of proof is on anyone who wishes to justify an additional obligation. When the emphasis is on functional diffuseness, the burden of proof is on anyone who wishes to evade an additional obligation under the relationship. Justification of such evasion is not ordinarily based on what was clearly understood at the outset of the relationship, but rather on citation of some more important obligation to which prior allegiance is recognized.[7]

It is important to distinguish degrees of functional specificity and of functional diffuseness. One can characterize relationships as placing greater or lesser emphasis on one or the other of the extremes. Detailed and precise measurement of variations along the scale may be exceedingly difficult, but for many rough purposes a common sense reference to differences in the degree of emphasis will serve well enough. In this distinction as the others, the distinction between ideal and actual structures is also of the greatest importance.

Some of the worst misunderstandings about relationships occur when a relationship is predominantly functionally specific from the point of view of one member and predominantly functionally diffuse from the point of view of another. Thus, again, one must be prepared to give some indication of the point of view from which he is describing a relationship.

Some of the implications involved in this distinction and the other two previously made should be fairly obvious by now. To the extent that a relationship is or becomes functionally diffuse, it is difficult to emphasize rationality and universalistic criteria. After all, if one does not know in advance what is likely to be involved in a relationship, how can one emphasize rationality in its conduct or make selections on a predominantly universalistic basis?

4. AFFECTIVE ASPECTS

I do not feel at home with the concept of affect.   The concept of affective aspects is an attempt to get at the kind of emotion, the degree of formality and informality, the feeling, etc., involved in a given relationship.   Relationships among the members of any given society or as among the members of different societies vary considerably in the kind of emotional or affective displays made, the intensity of such displays which is expected and permitted, etc.   There is no question but that the members of certain relationships are expected to emphasize elements easily recognizable as emotional displays and in considerable intensity.   For example, a mother and son of our society are expected to love each other and to show it. The ticklish question for present purposes is whether or not there are nonaffective relationships, that is to say, relationships in terms of which no affectivity of any significance whatsoever is involved.   This is a particularly important question if one wishes to handle relationships in a highly modernized society.   In such societies there are an enormous number of relationships that are of the most fleeting and casual sort.   To determine, either ideally or actually, whether precisely *no* emotional involvement is intended is even in principle a difficult proposition. Furthermore such a concept implies perfect indifference to a relationship of which one is at least in some sense aware.   Such indifference is almost certainly a feat of affective virtuosity, and rare.   For these reasons that concept is not used.   The distinction used here is that between *avoidance* and *intimacy*.   Here again the distinction is intended to be a polar distinction.   Perhaps no relationship is at either pole, but the gamut that can be run is wide.   It varies from relationships that are quite important for the parties concerned, but in terms of which the members must avoid any direct contact with one another, including seeing or being seen by one another, to relationships in terms of which direct, informal, almost constant contact with overt displays of emotion are both expected and demanded by the participants and/or by other members of the society.   The relationship between mother and infant in all societies is likely to be intimate in this latter sense.   Relations between ruler and subject or sacred figure and true believers often approximate the former.

The relationship between husband and wife is a predominantly intimate one in the modern United States.   It is also predominantly intimate in some contexts in traditional China, but in the latter case it is far less so than in the former.   There are also many social contexts in traditional China in which the relationship is not supposed to be an intimate one at all.   According to strict Confucian etiquette the husband and wife are expected to display genuine avoidance in many contexts. The term *avoidance* may be used to cover relationships that, ideally and/or actually, are supposed to be devoid of emotional involvement as well as those in terms of which the emotional involvement is supposed to be considerable though minimizing overt contacts, etc.   The most highly avoidant affect is probably that generally referred to as respect.   The opposite of respect is probably contempt, and it is not a matter of chance that there is a wise old saw in many languages which holds that "familiarity breeds contempt."   With regard to this aspect of relationships, as with the others, the prefix predominantly will be used. A relationship will be termed predominantly avoidant if it is one in terms of which the members or others emphasize restraint and/or formality in the overt display of affect and/or subordinate the overt display of affect to other aspects of the relationship. A relationship will be termed predominantly intimate if it is one in terms of which the members or others emphasize lack of restraint and informality in the overt display of affect and/or subordinate other aspects of the relationship to the overt display of affect. These affects may be of many different sorts. As indicated above, respect is one of the easiest affects to reconcile with avoidance; love, as that term is frequently understood, is one of the easiest to reconcile with intimacy.

For all the problems involved in their use, the concepts of avoidance and intimacy provide a highly generalized distinction among relationships in terms of their affective aspects. The distinction has been chosen because of its general relevance to the analysis of social structure. The line of theoretical speculation that justifies this particular choice may be briefly stated as follows. In all social contexts situations arise in which the unrestrained display of emotional responses would or could be highly disruptive. There are also situations in which overt emotional expression is to a high degree adaptive in its implications. Current work in the field of personality development would seem to indicate that rather lavish informal displays of affection for infants and children are critical for the development of stable adult personalities. The distinction used here is based largely on the distinction between types of regulation of affective expression and hence is germane to this sort of consideration. More specifically, in all societies the structures of allocation of power and responsibility are of central importance. Furthermore, there are always some situations in which a premium is placed upon the efficient and even rapid exercise of power. Even slightly uninhibited displays of emotion can be extremely disruptive in such situations. Hence it may be argued that in all such situations the institutionalization of predominantly avoidant rather than predominantly intimate relationships is of adaptive significance for the members of the organizations involved. One of the most obvious cases of such a relationship is that between superiors and subordinates in military organizations. That is by no means the only case. Similar factors are involved in the relationship between a traditional Chinese father and his son. Because of the manner in which the family structures of traditional China fits into the total social structure of Chinese society, the strength of the father-son relationship is far more important than in modern American society. In general, whenever the intimate type of affective expression is not a central element of the substantive definition of the relationship, or at least whenever it is subordinated to other aspects of such a definition of the relationship, a premium is placed upon avoidant affects. It is not enough to repress intimacy in such situations; formal modes of affective expression are also needed. Because of the ubiquitous relevance of such considerations as these, the particular polar dichotomy suggested here has been selected.

5. GOAL ORIENTATION ASPECTS

The goal orientation aspect of a relationship focuses attention on some of what might be called motivational aspects of the relationship. Insofar as the ends sought in terms of a relationship are manifest to one or all of the members of the relationship, what can be said about them which is generally useful in analysis? The concepts used here are *individualistic* and *responsible*. A given relationship is more or less *individualistic* to the degree that each of the members of the relationship may be expected to calculate how best to secure his own maximum advantage from action in terms of the relationship without regard to the goals sought by the other members of the relationship. A given relationship is more or less *responsible* to the degree that each of the members of the relationship is expected to safeguard, even at the expense of some of his own goals, the relevant goals of the other members of the relationship. Again these are polar terms. Pure cases of either extreme, if they exist, constitute only a small proportion of the relationships in any society. The use of the prefix predominantly is of service here as in the other categories. A relationship will be called *predominantly individualistic* if the emphasis is placed on each member of the relationship looking out for himself. A relationship will be called *predominantly responsible* if the emphasis is placed on one (or more) of the members of the relationship safeguarding the relevant goals of the others if he is (or they are) to achieve his (or their) own goals at all. This distinction has nothing whatsoever to do with egoism or altruism, nor with selfishness or the lack of it. A relationship may be so structured that even the most selfish person must make sure that the other members of the relationship realize their goals if he is to realize his. Correspondingly, one of the most altruistic of men in terms of another type of relationship may have to take the attitude that each other member must look out for himself. Ideally speaking, for example, the most selfish of doctors *has* to behave responsibly in this sense towards his patients. On the other hand, a businessman who intends to give all of his profits away to charity must nevertheless continue to be a driver of hard bargains if he is to compete successfully for profits.

Illustrations used here will be compared in greater detail below. A business relationship in the United States today is, ideally speaking, a predominantly individualistic one. Each member is expected to seek to maximize his own interests. The relationship is not devoid of responsible elements. Presumably negotiations are carried out in terms of a general framework of honesty. Straight misrepresentation is fraud, as is payment with a bad check. On the other hand, if the buyer is willing to pay twice as much as would be necessary if he knew the situation better, the seller is not necessarily expected to enlighten him or to price the property at the going-rate despite his customer's ignorance. Students of social change could no doubt trace an interesting development of the businessman-customer relationship in the United States. At no time was the maxim of *caveat emptor* completely without limit. Members of the judiciary stood ready to act on certain practices classified as illegitimate. Nevertheless, the change has certainly been marked, and deals that were commonplace in the heyday of "captains of industry" would be considered unethical today. Despite these changes, the good businessman is expected to be able to take care of himself and is not expected to look out for the interests of others. If his concern for the interest of others exceeds the expected levels of probity, and if that concern is to the detriment of his own interests, whatever may be the evaluation of him in other respects, he has shown himself to be a poor businessman, perhaps even something of a fool.

On the other hand, the doctor-patient relationship may be described as a predominantly responsible one. Ideally speaking, the doctor is expected to protect his patient's interests. The doctor is not only expected to avoid direct misrepresentation. The doctor is also expected to protect the patient from the patient's own ignorance. If the patient wishes an unnecessary operation, the doctor, whether to his own financial hurt or no, is expected to refuse to perform it. If the accepted scale of fees for patients of a given income group is five dollars a visit, it is not ethical for a doctor to charge such a patient ten dollars simply because the patient is ignorant of the situation. Again it must be insisted that this tells one nothing of the personal character of the doctor. A doctor who scrupulously observes such standards may be selfish in the extreme, and the businessman who follows the others may be the soul of generosity. The practice of medicine, is, however, differently structured than the conduct of business. The achievement of success in terms of the one is in part dependent upon the observance of this type of responsibility, and in terms of the other it is in part dependent upon the observance of this type of individualism. Two men almost identical in their personal ambitions for money, power, and prestige will behave quite differently in these respects if one is a doctor and the other a businessman. There is in all this every indication that socially acceptable behavior may be independent of individual personality factors to a high degree.

6. STRATIFICATION ASPECTS

This aspect is considerably simpler than those discussed above. *Stratification* may be defined as the particular type of role differentiation that distinguishes between higher and lower standing in terms of one or more criteria. In some relationships one member of the relationship is expected to have a higher ranking than another. The relationship between a traditional Chinese father and his son is of this type. There are also relationships such that, regardless of the rank of the members in their other roles, as members of this particular relationship their ranking is either considered equal or any question of differences in rank is considered irrelevant.

A relationship of the former type will be called a *hierarchical* one. A hierarchical relationship is defined as one for which the relative rankings of the members are different and in terms of which action is distinguished with regard to this ranking. The latter type of relationship mentioned above will be called a nonhierarchical one. A nonhierarchical relationship is one in terms of which no differential rankings of the members in any respect are considered relevant to the relationship.   When the relationship is one such that its members are specifically expected to treat one another without reference to differential rankings, it will be termed *egalitarian*.   The term egalitarian is used to distinguish this type of relationship from those in which differences in rank are irrelevant but are so simply by lack of definition of the relationship in this respect, e.g., in which the members are neither equals nor unequals ideally speaking.

Varying degrees of hierarchical relationships are familiar enough to require little or no comment.   The example of a traditional Chinese father and his son has been given, but other examples are even more obvious.   The relationship between officers and enlisted men, professors and associate-professors, employer and employee, union leader and union member, etc., are definitely of this sort. Nonhierarchical and egalitarian relationships are somewhat harder to find. Probably only relationships of short duration and ones such that any specific case of the relationship is socially defined as unimportant are non-hierarchical relationships of a nonegalitarian sort.   So pervasive are rank-order structures and so strategic, if not crucial, are they structurally speaking that strong, explicit structures are usually required to keep hierarchical considerations out of the picture.   Furthermore, only in rather fleeting relationships, specific cases of which matter little, would it be possible to have no definite structuring of hierarchical elements because of the great relevance of such elements to any action in terms of the relationship.   Relationships of the casual-meeting or crowd-contact sort would fall into this category.   This is not to argue that such relationships in the aggregate are unimportant for the society in which they occur. No relatively modernized society could exist unless a tremendous amount of action in terms of it could be carried out on the basis of the casual-meeting type of relationship.   On the other hand, in many relatively nonmodernized social contexts relationships of this sort are relatively infrequent, and any great expansion of such relationships would probably be a source of disorganization.

Egalitarian relationships, though considerably less frequent than the hierarchical ones, are quite familiar to most people.   Friendship is generally a relationship of this order in relatively modernized societies.   Friends are expected to treat one another as equals and to consider one another as such regardless of other factors.[8]   Strong egalitarian elements often enter relationships that are in other respects hierarchical.   In some respects the members of a university faculty are equals despite the fact that the hierarchy of professors, associate professors, assistant professors, and instructors is of great significance to us.   The faculty situation tenses instantly if we feel that the hierarchical aspects are being pushed beyond their proper sphere.   The emphasis on egalitarianism in the face of hierarchical distinctions is perhaps symbolized by the official university use of the term of address Professor for all three ranks of the professor category, and by the fact that faculty members among themselves frequently avoid such terms altogether and use the more neutral term Mister.

Particularly among those who believe or profess belief in democracy there are some misconceptions about hierarchical relationships.   The overwhelming proportion of all relationships in all societies contain hierarchical elements both ideally and actually.   In fact, it is difficult for most individuals to give examples, apart from friendship, of relationships that are ideally and/or actually egalitarian. Family relationships certainly aren't; bureaucratic relationships aren't; relationships within the government rarely are; universities aren't; business firms aren't, etc.   For men to be "equal before the law" does not imply a lack of hierarchy "before the law."   A judge may *order* the defendent or the plaintiff, etc.   It is common for those interested in either social analysis or social welfare to confuse predominantly universalistic criteria for treatment with egalitarian relationships. Societies could not persist on an egalitarian basis, nor could any other social system of any considerable membership or importance from the point of view of its members and other members in the society.   Relatively modernized societies could not exist at all if social structures combining predominantly universalistic emphases and hierarchical ones did not exist in great and varied panoply.[9]

For comparative purposes the distinctions concerned with the stratification aspects of relationships are often quite revealing.   Military systems seem on the whole to have been strictly hierarchical if their members were successful.   But other relationships show greater variations from one context to another.   Take, for example, the husband-wife relationship.   Although modern, urban, middle-class Americans do not regard the relationship, ideally speaking, as egalitarian, they at least favor as close an approach to egalitarianism in this relationship as men have ever achieved.   In traditional China it was definitely a hierarchical relationship with the husband much more highly ranked than the wife.   There are cases in which the relationship is hierarchical but with the wife ranked well above her husband in most respects.   With factual knowledge of only these three differences with regard to one aspect of one type of relationship, one can make a considerable number of predictions about other differences that must exist in these social contexts.[10]

E. APPLICATIONS

1. INTRODUCTION

First, the concepts discussed above are such that some statements can be made about any relationship, in any society, at any time in terms of them.   This means questions asked about these concepts are always capable of yielding some answers relevant for comparative purposes.   Second, they have been devised to illuminate the part played by specific relationships in more general social systems. Finally, like most sets of scientific concepts, these are designed to make possible the greatest accumulation of defensible knowledge about a given type of phenomena with the least amount of effort and to have that knowledge of maximum general relevance to the development of further generalized knowledge about the field concerned.   More specifically, however, this set of concepts is useful because it provides a framework in terms of which one may analyze and describe any single relationship and compare the following: (1) different types of relationships in a single society, (2) similar types of relationships in different societies, and

(3) different types of relationships in different societies. For the purposes of rapid sketching of examples the following table has been set up:

Table 1

	X	Y
1. Cognitive aspects	Rational	Traditional
2. Membership criteria aspects	Universalistic	Particularistic
3. Substantive definition aspects	Functionally specific	Functionally diffuse
4. Affective aspects	Avoidant	Intimate
5. Goal orientation aspects	Individualistic	Responsible
6. Stratification aspects	Hierarchical	Nonhierarchical

The symbol X_1 will be used for rational (i.e., predominantly rational), the symbol Y_1 for traditional (i.e., predominantly traditional), X_2 will be used for predominantly universalistic, etc. I devised the notation to make certain typical clustering effects which will be discussed below more readily obvious, but apart from this, it is arbitrary. One could mix the various polar types between the X and Y columns at random or change the order of the rows. To do so would make the discussion a bit more cumbersome, but it would not change the implications or the meaning of the discussion in any way. Using the notation as set up, a relationship that is described as X_1, X_2, X_3, X_4, X_5, X_6 is a relationship that is predominantly rational in its cognitive aspects, predominantly universalistic in its membership criteria aspects, predominantly functionally specific in its substantive definition aspects, predominantly avoidant in its affective aspects, predominantly individualistic in its goal orientation aspects, and predominantly hierarchical in its stratification aspects.

In order to illustrate the use of these concepts and this notation I shall compare: (1) the doctor-patient relationship and the businessman-customer relationship in modern United States society, (2) the businessman-customer relationship in modern United States society and in traditional China, and (3) the businessman-customer relationship in modern United States society and the gentry father-son relationship in traditional China.[11]

2. EXAMPLES

a. *The Doctor-Patient and the Businessman-Customer Relationships in Modern United States Society.* The doctor-patient relationship may be described in the terms used here as X_1, X_2, X_3, X_4, Y_5, Y_6. Ideally speaking, the doctor is expected to employ rational techniques in his treatment of the patient. It is well understood that, given the limitations of knowledge and the fallibility of man, the doctor sometimes acts irrationally, but the range of irrational actions is limited, and attempts are made to limit them further. Many medical errors are considered inescapable and nonculpable, but others, for example, repeated failures to diagnose correctly common ailments appearing in common uncomplicated forms, are likely to result in pressures of some sort being brought to bear on the doctor. Some irrational actions are considered sufficiently egregious to be grounds for civil suits against the doctor, and some are even grounds for his loss of license to practice. The latter form of discipline is relatively rare, probably because of the reluctance of qualified personnel to testify. This reluctance is by no means wholly understandable in terms of a "guild" or "There but for the grace of God go I" feeling. It is, at least in part, understandable in terms of the reluctance to shake by such exposure the element of public confidence in medical men. This element of confidence is certainly vital to the current forms of medical practice. Whether it would be broken down or bolstered by more frequent exposures of this sort is as yet an undetermined point. The fact that overt sanctions are not so evident as might seem justified on the basis of expressed licensing standards, medical society membership criteria, etc., does not mean that sanctions of this sort are totally lacking.

Doctors may in fact act nonrationally, or traditionally as the term is used here, in their treatment of patients. The use of traditional techniques which are not necessarily rationally justified is either definitely condemned or is not considered proper to the relationship. The complete substitution by a doctor of nonempirical means for empirical ones in the treatment of a patient is never sanctioned. Nonempirical means of some sort, for example prayers in terms of one of the established religious systems of society, are acceptable as a means supplementary to the application of scientific knowledge, but such activities are definitely not a central part of the relationship. They may be tolerated, sometimes even approved, but they are not required. Nonempirical means of other sorts are strongly condemned and are considered applications of superstitions or magic, both of which are felt to have no place in this field and to be bad. Doctors frequently carry out practices because that is the way they have been done in the past, but the usual traditional arguments are not considered justifications in this field. The argument, "We have always done it that way, and it's a good way to do it because we've always done it that way," is not in general acceptable. The argument, "We have not yet got a better scientific way of doing this than the one we have been using for quite some time," is as far as medical ethics permit the doctor to go.[12]

The patient on his side is also expected to act rationally in the following respects. He is expected to choose his physician on the basis of predominantly universalistic criteria. This involves an element of rationality since there is rationality involved in the process of understanding what criteria are germane to the end sought and in the process of judgment as to whether the doctor chosen in fact measures up to such criteria. Another rational element enters from the patient's point of view in that he is expected to know within limits when it is and is not necessary to consult his doctor (i.e., initiate the relationship), and he is expected to follow his doctor's orders rationally. The emphasis on his rationality, however, is much less well institutionalized[13] than for the doctor.

The doctor-patient relationship is, ideally speaking, a predominantly universalistic one.   The patient is expected to choose his doctor on grounds of competence and availability.   The doctor is expected, within quite broad limits, to accept patients on the basis of need for treatment.   These ideal structures often fail to coincide with actual ones.   Patients often choose or reject doctors on bases that are medically irrelevant.   Such considerations may range from liking a doctor's looks to not liking his political or religious affiliations.   Doctors, on the other hand, sometimes choose or reject their patients on the basis of the patient's ability to pay, social position, etc.   Again, the structure seems to be better institutionalized for the doctors than for the patient in both conformity and sanction aspects.   Although the ideal structures are often violated from both points of view, the remarkable feature of the situation is that they are not violated more often, given, among other relevant factors, on the one hand the medical ignorance of the patient and on the other hand the tremendous relevance of monetary income as a symbol of success in such societies.

Ideally speaking, the relationship is functionally specific.   It is the doctor's obligation to do what he can medically for the patient, and all of his orders and access to the patient must be justifiable on the grounds of their relevance to the patient's health.   The patient on his part is expected to follow the doctor's orders (and to pay his fees unless he is being treated on a charity basis).   The doctor with respect to fixing fees is expected to take into consideration the patient's ability to pay.   Often functionally diffuse elements creep into the relationship, particularly in the case of the general practitioner or family doctor, who may be a close friend and advisor of the patient in matters otherwise as well as medical.   The appearance of functionally diffuse elements in the relationship almost inevitably go hand in hand with predominantly intimate rather than predominantly avoidant structures.   Again, the lead in breakdowns in these respects is more likely to be taken by the patient than by the doctor.

The relationship is ideally a predominantly avoidant one; the more so the more it is strictly confined to medical matters.   Departures on the doctor's part are only in theory justified if they contribute to the patient's health.   Departures on the patient's part may range from the often unobjectionable combining of a friendship relationship with that of doctor and patient, to excursions into intimacy of a sort most strongly condemned.   Both doctor and patient may be strongly condemned for some of these departures in the direction of intimacy, and the profession as a whole, as well as the public, is well aware of this.   Doctors are so thoroughly aware of it that elaborate precautions and procedures have been set up to eliminate such breakdowns.

The relationship is ideally predominantly responsible rather than individualistic.   The doctor rather than the patient is primarily concerned here since he has the more active role in the relationship.   The whole structure of prestige in the medical profession is so set up as to require even the most selfish of doctors to place the interests of his patients, both actual and potential, before any goals of his own that do not involve their medical welfare.   The selfish doctor dares not acquire a widespread reputation for demanding assurance of payment before treating an emergency case or for ordering profitable but medically unnecessary operations and the like.   Again, the experts in the field are reluctant to testify openly in such cases, but the sanctions brought to bear are none the less strong. The patient on his part is expected to heed the doctor's advice and pay his fees, but the question of individualism or responsibility is not quite so relevant from the patient's point of view, since he has little possibility of sacrificing the doctor's interest for his own.   Both he and the doctor in theory share the end of restoring the patient's health.   Other goals such as minimizing the doctor's fee, etc., are not supposed to enter since the doctor's responsibility covers making such fees reasonable.

Finally, the relationship is of a relatively nonhierarchical sort.   Of course, the roles are sharply differentiated, but as far as general social standing the doctor may be of either higher or lower rank than the patient.   In theory at least, none of the action takes place because one member of the relationship is a superior of the other in any power sense.   A doctor's orders are not orders in the ordinary sense that implies an enforcement agency outside the person ordered and the possibility of orders not to the subordinate's best interest.   Ideally, the doctor's orders are given the patient only so that the patient may achieve his own goal, i.e., restoration or maintenance of health.   The only hierarchical aspect involved, ideally speaking, is that of medical knowledge, but even this is by no means a hard and fast requirement since doctors are usually patients of doctors other than themselves, sometimes of less able ones.   However the members of the society as a whole may rank doctors relative to patients, and in this there is certainly a hierarchical element, the treatment by the doctor of the patient, ideally speaking, is determined by medical criteria and not by criteria of any other relative social standing.[14]

The relationship between a businessman and his customer in the modern United States may be described as an X_1, X_2, X_3, X_4, X_5, and Y_6.   Both the businessman and his customer are expected to deal rationally with one another.   Not to do so is bad business, and in terms of this relationship both parties are expected to behave in a businesslike fashion.   Irrational action on the part of either member is the mark of a fool.   Traditional action or other departures from rationality in general, simply are not considered good business, and in some cases come in for harsh criticism.   The emphasis on rationality in the businessman-customer relationship is by no means complete.   Some important traditional elements are still maintained, but the trend is overwhelmingly in the opposite direction.   The mark par excellence of maintenance of traditional emphases is likely to be the presence of a family firm, but these in the old fashioned sense are becoming increasingly rare in all highly modernized societies.

The criteria for membership in the relation are predominantly universalistic. Both parties are expected to pick fellow members on the basis best calculated to serve the empirical ends sought.   The businessman seeks to make a profit; the customer seeks to get the best possible value for his money.   To refuse to sell at a profit to second generation Scandinavian citizens because one does not like them is bad business, as is refusal to buy from them on this ground.   There are many departures from these standards by both types of members, but such departures become increasingly less common as business becomes large scale. Representatives of large-scale firms such as some of the automobile manufacturers would find insuperable obstacles in trying to enforce such predominantly particularistic criteria. Individual customers find their effect in such matters negligible and such activities likely to fall into the category of "cutting off your nose to spite your face." The accepted criteria for businessmen in selecting customers is their ability to pay, and that of customers in selecting businessmen is the ability to deliver the best goods at the lowest price.

The relationship is generally kept as functionally specific as possible. Ideally speaking, it is perfectly so from both points of view. The contract relationship is the archetype of this quality. If a contract is vague, it is a bad contract, at least from the point of view of the person who may find added unanticipated obligations as a result of such vagueness. In only a fraction of such relationships are actual contracts drawn, but the usual structures of a one-price market makes such things quite clear. A customer buys a soft drink. His obligation is confined to the payment of the price; the dealer's obligation is to deliver the product as defined by quite specific standards. If there is an insect in the drink, the dealer is liable; if the payment is less than the stated price, the customer is liable. To leave the obligations of such a relationship vague is always potentially bad business from someone's point of view.

Ideally speaking, the relationship is a predominantly avoidant one. Often there are departures in the direction of intimacy, but these departures are more likely to characterize small firms with a restricted, relatively unchanging set of customers. On the whole, the attitude in this respect is that business is business and that emotional involvement with one's customers, insofar as it is permissible, becomes inadmissible if it interferes with the profit goals of enterprise. Roughly the same situation exists from the customer's point of view.

The relationship is a predominantly individualistic one. It is not, however, completely individualistic with a completely unhindered *caveat emptor* outlook. There are restrictions on both parties. Certain standards of honesty, for example, are not only expected but are enforceable at law. Yet, neither member is held responsible for protecting the other against his own ignorance as is the case with the doctor-patient relationship. Within a certain framework of mutual regard for each other's interests, the businessman and his customer operate on an "every man for himself" basis. Ideally, this is never true of the doctor's relation with his patient.

Finally, this relationship is, ideally, nonhierarchical and in some respects even egalitarian. The customer has neither higher nor lower rank than the businessman in general, and of course, one individual may at any time be playing both roles in different operations. Ideally the members of such relationships deal with one another as equals. Proof of deliberate tinkering with this equality may be the basis for setting aside such transactions legally. Much of the antimonopoly legislation rests on the legal philosophy that the parties to a valid contract should be equals from many points of view for the purposes of that transaction. Of course there are many departures from the ideal structures in this respect.

I shall now compare these two relationships briefly on three levels. First, I shall compare them on the most general level discussed here. In that comparison the basic difference between the doctor-patient and the businessman-customer relationship lies in the fact that the former is predominantly responsible and the latter is predominantly individualistic. On this level the two relationships are identical in all other five aspects. Now, there is considerable feeling that the doctor-patient relationship, ideally as well as actually, is different from that of the businessman and his customer. For purposes of comparative analysis of the two, it is best first to see how much of the differences between the two can be explained in terms of the difference between X_5 and Y_5. Some of the differences, which we feel so strongly should and do exist, hinge on this difference at this level.

If differences on the most general level are not sufficient to explain the differences we wish to understand, we must proceed to the second level of analysis. Both relationships institutionalize structures of predominantly rational action and predominantly universalistic criteria. The specific contents of the rationality and of the universalistic criteria are, however, quite different. In the one case rational action is oriented to the restoration and maintenance of health, and in the other it is oriented to the allocation of goods and/or services. In other words, both are predominantly rational but their members are interested in rationality about different matters. In theory at least, those differences between the two relationships which are not explicable in terms of differences between X's and Y's (i.e., differences on the most general level) may be explicable in terms of the differing contents of the similar X's or Y's (e.g., both of the relationships described here are predominantly rational, but about quite different matters). If the second level differences are insufficient to explain the differences noted between two relationships being compared, then one of four possibilities remains: (1) differences on the first level of generalization have been overlooked, (2) differences on the second level of generalization have been overlooked, (3) the list of aspects of relationships needs reformulation and/or additions at least on lower levels of generalization, or (4) some combination of the three foregoing difficulties is present.

In the third of the foregoing possibilities lies the third level of comparison mentioned above. If two relationships are in fact different in their structures but also in fact identical on the two levels of procedure cited above, the difference must be in aspects of one of the other or both of the relationships not given in the original list of six aspects. Even if the relationships are not identical on the two levels previously cited, additional differences on this third level may still be present. Any failure to explain differences between relationships on the previous two levels should lead to exploration of this third level. Its exploration may also lead to further development by discovering an aspect(s) which is (are) empirically observable in *any* relationship and hence should be added to the original list of six aspects.[15]

It is possible to discuss the doctor-patient relationship at great length, and its contrast with that of the businessman-customer in modern United States society is revealing about both spheres and about the society in general, but most of the relevant differences between these two relationships are, in fact, to be subsumed under either the most general differences in the goal orientations aspects and lower level differences in the other aspects.

b. *The Businessman-Customer Relationship in Modern United States Society and in Traditional China.* The material on the businessman-customer relationship in modern United States society need not be repeated. In traditional China the relationship took one of two forms. If the relationship was the expected predominantly particularistic one, it took the form Y_1, Y_2, Y_3, X_4, Y_5, X_6. Ideally speaking, it was expected to be based on particularistic criteria such as friendship, family connections, and neighborhood considerations which were already present or established by a go-between. If predominantly particularistic connections of this sort did not exist the relationship was likely to take the form X_1, X_2, X_3, X_4, X_5, X_6.

This difference between the businessman-customer relationship in China when based on predominantly particularistic rather than on predominantly universalistic criteria of choice, explains many differences in accounts as to the reliability or honesty of the Chinese businessman. If he were dealing with a friend or relative or family members who had dealt with his family members for years, or a person from his own village or a person introduced by a go-between who possessed one or some combination of these connections with both businessman and customer, the businessman emphasized the preservation of the relationship. He operated in a predominantly traditional fashion. The relationship was by definition highly particularistic, but it was also predominantly functionally diffuse. Extra requests by the customer might well be granted. Although something like friendship might dominate the relationship and displays of affect in terms of it were by no means out of the question, it must be borne in mind that the members of that society generally placed a heavy emphasis on highly formalized predominantly avoidant relationships. Given the fact that, ideally speaking, the position of merchant was frequently a lowly one, the relationship might be prominently avoidant. Most importantly, it was a highly responsible relationship. The merchant was expected to protect his customer at all costs even to the extent of his own financial ruin in some extreme cases. The relationship might be hierarchical in different ways. If the merchant were dealing with a gentry customer, the relationship was certainly hierarchical with the customer of higher rank than the merchant, of course. In other cases it might be hierarchical in the opposite direction. The differences between ideal and actual structures were especially important. In the strictest ideal sense the merchants ranked below gentry, peasants, and artisans. Actually, of course, if they were at all well off, they certainly outranked the latter two as well as many of the gentry.

On the other hand, if the expected predominantly particularistic connections did not exist, the picture was almost exactly opposite.   A ruthlessly *caveat emptor* situation existed and was carried as an ordinary matter to an extreme that United States businessmen have not tolerated for some decades.   Indeed, if the business-man could get by with it, his attitude was not simply "every man for himself," but rather "'It's every man for himself and God for us all,' said the elephant as he danced among the chickens."   Under these circumstances both businessman and customer acted as rationally as possible in an attempt to maximize their material gains from the relationship.   The relationship was as functionally specific as either party could make it to his own advantage, and it was an avoidant one.   It was ruthlessly individualistic, and that within a framework in which force and fraud were only limited by what the parties concerned thought they could get by with.   It would be hierarchical with each party attempting to utilize hierarchical factors to secure an advantage.   Thus, insofar as possible, it becomes a relation-ship of the X_1, X_2, X_3, X_4, X_5, and X_6 type.   It must be emphasized that it was not institutionally expected that the businessman-customer relationship would be of this second type, and the Chinese tried to avoid this type of relationship if they could possible do so.   Cases of it, however, were frequently observable.   If one entered such a relationship without establishing proper predominantly particu-laristic grounds either directly or via a go-between and was badly treated in terms of it, one was considered a fool for having gotten oneself involved in such a situa-tion in the first place.

In comparing the businessman-customer relationship in modern United States society and in traditional China, one should first consider the differences in the relationship in China.   Here the distinctions are almost, if not com-pletely, understandable in terms of differences on the most general level of relationship aspects.   In comparing either of the Chinese structures with those of the United States, differences on both the most general level and the second level of generalization mentioned above are significant.   These relationships have been set up in Table 2, below, along with several others for ease of comparison.

In this tabular form, it is immediately obvious that the differences between Type A and Type B in traditional China apparently lie on the most general level since the structures tend to opposite poles except with regard to the possibilities of variation in the affective and the stratification aspects.   The differences between Type A and the United States type again lie apparently almost wholly on the first level of procedure, but the differences between Type B and the United States type obviously must be sought in considerable part on the second level of generaliza-tion or on the third (i.e., in some additions to the list of relevant aspects).   Actu-ally, in comparison of the United States type and Type B the differences lie largely in differences in the cognitive aspects and the goal orientation aspects, both of which on the first level emphasize rationality and individualism.   Most of the differences may be subsumed under the goal orientation aspects.   The much greater individualism possible in Type B behavior in China makes it possible for the cognitive aspects to be far more ruthlessly rational than would be counte-nanced in the modern United States case.   Approved rationality in the latter case does not permit taking into consideration the possible rational implications of applications of force and fraud as in the Chinese Type B. The differences between Type A Chinese relationships and the United States type are the ones conventionally associated with discussions of the contrast between traditional

Table 2

RELATIONSHIP	RELATIONSHIP ASPECTS					
	1	2	3	4	5	6
1. Doctor-patient	X	X	X	X	Y	Y(?)
2. U.S. businessman-customer	X	X	X	X	X	Y
3. Traditional Chinese businessman-customer						
Type A	Y	Y	Y	X	Y	X
4. Type B	X	X	X	X	X	X
5. U.S. husband-wife	Y	Y	Y	Y	Y	X
6. Traditional Chinese husband-wife	Y	Y	Y	X(Y)	Y	X
7. U.S. employer-employee	X	X	X	X	X	X
8. Traditional Chinese employer-employee	Y	Y	Y	X	Y	X
9. U.S. lawyer-client	X	X	X	X	Y	Y(?)
10. U.S. architect-client	X	X	X	X	Y	Y(?)
11. U.S. father-son	Y	Y	Y	Y	Y	X
12. Traditional Chinese father-son	Y	Y	Y	X	Y	X
13. Japanese Emperor-Crown Prince						
Old	Y	Y	Y	X	Y	X
14. New	Y	Y	Y	Y	Y	X
15. Engineer-client	X	X	X	X	Y	Y(?)
16. Certified public accountant-client	X	X	X	X,	Y	Y(?)

Chinese ways of doing business and modern, "objective," etc., forms of business-man-customer relationships.

c. *The Businessman-Customer Relationship in Modern United States Society and the Father-Son Relationship in Traditional China.* The United States business-man-customer relationship has already been described above. It takes the form X_1, X_2, X_3, X_4, X_5, and Y_6. The father-son relationship in traditional

China takes the form Y_1, Y_2, Y_3, X_4, Y_5, and X_6. On the most general level these different types of relationships in different societies have only one element, predominantly avoidant affective aspects (X_4), in common. On the most general level the relationships are almost wholly different from one another, but there are critical differences on lower levels as well. For example, the matters about which the members of the one emphasize rationality and those of the other emphasize tradition are quite different. Even in the one similarity on the most general level, there are differences on lower levels, since the types and degrees of avoidance are quite different. Whether this particular comparison is interesting may be doubtful. Some comparisons of radically different types of relationships in different types of societies are, however, of considerable importance.

d. *Other Examples.* In Table 2 additional examples have been given. For example, the employer-employee relationship in the United States is ideally expected to take the form X_1, X_2, X_3, X_4, X_5, and X_6. Insofar as one can speak about the employer-employee relationship in most of the relatively nonmodernized areas, those relationships, ideally speaking, take the form Y_1, Y_2, Y_3, X_4, Y_5, and X_6 as illustrated by the employer-employee relationship in traditional China. The husband-wife relationship in the United States ideally takes the form Y_1, Y_2, Y_3, Y_4, Y_5, and X_6.[16]

Since this set of concepts can be used to analyze *any* two or more different relationships, it follows that it can also be used to analyze the same type of relationship at different points in time. Thus it can be used to analyze questions of changes in a given relationship over any given span of time. For example, a dramatic change has recently been reported in the structures of the Royal Family in Japan. This appears in Table 2 as the example of the relationship between the Japanese Emperor (or the Crown Prince) and the Emperor's (or Crown Prince's) son, i.e., the present or future Crown Prince) according to previous custom and present practice. In the old days that relationship took the form Y_1, Y_2, Y_3, X_4, Y_5, and X_6. According to the present reported decision of the Crown Prince to rear his own son within a more ordinary modern family setting in Japan, the relationship would now take the form Y_1, Y_2, Y_3, Y_4, Y_5, and X_6. There is every reason to believe that the relationship between the present Crown Prince and his son will be a predominantly intimate one at least by contrast with the overwhelmingly avoidant one previously characteristic of this relationship.[17]

For purposes of comparison, Table 2 also includes the husband-wife relationship in the United States and in traditional China, the lawyer-client relationship in the United States, the architect-client relationship in the United States, the engineer-client relationship in the United States, the certified public accountant-client relationship in the United States, the father-son relationship in the United States, and the father-son relationship in traditional China. Given the detailed illustrations above, these should be sufficiently clear to support subsequent allusions to them.

III. USE OF THE RELATIONSHIP ASPECTS FOR THEORY FORMATION

A. GENERAL EXAMPLES

The examples given above illustrate comparative analysis of different types of relationships in terms of the concepts suggested here. Four sources of differences have been suggested. Differences arise from: (1) differences on the most general level (i.e., differences in X or Y classification), (2) differences on lower levels of generalization (i.e., the relationships whether similar or different on the most general level may be different in the kind and/or degree of "X-ness" or "Y-ness"), (3) differences in aspects on the most general level of relationships or on lower levels for which no concepts have been provided (i.e., aspects of any relationship or of specific ones not included in the present list of six general aspects), or (4) some combination of the three foregoing differences. The diverse choice of relationships used for illustrations constitutes an attempt to indicate that *any* relationships, however different or similar, in the same or different societies can be compared usefully in these terms. Insofar as analysis of this sort is successful, one in effect forms theories (or gets useful insights, if one prefers), by locating differences in relationships that are relevant to the analysis, whatever the purpose of the analysis may be.

Inferences drawn from the comparison of the doctor-patient and businessman-customer relationships illustrate this. As modernization increases, if a considerable amount of decision about the allocation of goods and services is left in the hands of members of private enterprises, there is nevertheless observable a continual increase in the level of bureaucratization of those private enterprises. This increase has caused growing talk about the professionalization of the business role. The patterns of X's and Y's characteristic of the doctor-patient relationship are also characteristic of a substantial number of so-called professional man-client relationships. For example, the lawyer-client relationship is, ideally speaking of the same form, and so are those of architect and client, certified public accountant and client, and engineer and client. There are important differences among all of them on the second level of generalization, e.g., they are not expected to be rational about the same matters, but the one difference between all of them and the ordinary businessman-customer (including other businessmen) relationship is that they are predominantly responsible. Given the line of analysis suggested here and the history of the well-established professions, the inference is that, as the professionalization of the business role increases, the most general alteration in the relationship of businessmen with their customers (including other businessmen) will be an increase in emphasis on the responsibility of the more expert members of those relationships for the interest of all others involved in them.[18] Modern business history shows an increase in emphasis on responsibility by contrast with individualism. Probably nothing else is more characteristic of the discipline of the modern business school, and few themes appear more frequently in the pronouncements of leading business figures. Even so marked lapses such as those implicit in recent alleged violations of standard and generally accepted antimonopoly rules continue to crop up,[19] the ticklish question in modern business development is not *whether* such increases in emphasis on responsibility will take place, but only *how* they will take place.

In many spheres this development has gone quite far. Veblen made much of the concept of sabotage as deliberate interference with efficiency for the sake of profit. It was Veblen's irony that a word developed from a desperate labor practice of throwing a wooden shoe into machinery to confound businessmen should be applied to business practices. Today some of Veblen's irony has come full circle. For many business leaders, particularly those associated with communications, the use of "strategic withdrawals of efficiency" to gain profit are virtually out of the question. The range of choice open to labor leaders is often larger than the range of choice open to business leaders. Certainly there are emphases on individualism in the relationships between union leaders and their "customers," whether those customers be representatives of their own government or of private business firms which are at least the equal of any emphasis on individualism characteristic of other businesslike leaders in our society.

The prediction of increased emphasis on predominantly responsible goal orientations can be broadened. Not only will there be an increase in emphasis on responsibility in businessman-customer (including other businessmen) relationships, but the same will also be increasingly true of relationships involving any leaders strategically placed in terms of bureaucratic organizations of considerable relevance to the allocation of goods and/or services. Thus there will be an increasing emphasis on responsibility in the relationships between union leaders and the customers of labor and between governmental leaders whose policy decisions can seriously affect economic allocations and members of all other organizations whether those be local, state, or federal agencies on the one hand, or private enterprises or labor unions on the other. At present, the major differences of these relationships from professionalized relationships in the ordinary sense inhere overwhelmingly in the emphasis on individualism as opposed to responsibility. In every bureaucratic sphere of any importance in which the emphasis, either ideally or actually, on individualism continues at a high level that emphasis is shifting in the direction of an emphasis on responsibility. With all increases in modernization it will continue to do so, if the systems concerned are to be stable and probably even if they are not. From this one may draw a still further inference, a riskier one: With the increase of modernization and the attendant increase of bureaucratization, all roles in bureaucracies tend to become increasingly professionalized.

I shall give one further example of such theorizing. The major difference between the traditional Chinese father-son relationship and the United States father-son relationship, is that the latter is predominantly intimate and the former is predominantly avoidant. There has already been considerable discussion of family developments in relatively modernized societies as opposed to relatively nonmodernized ones above, and there will be more below (pp. 377–435 [of *Modernization and the Structure of Societies*]). Suffice it to say here that in all increasingly modernized social contexts there will be an increasing emphasis on intimacy in the father-son relationship, if that emphasis did not exist before. The attempt of the Chinese Communists to carry out their commune policies in greatest detail does not alter the tenability of this proposition. It is characteristic of all other societies as they change in the direction of modernization.

B. THE CLUSTERING EFFECT

Inspection of Table 2 discloses clusters of relationship aspects. If a relationship is predominantly X in any of the first three aspects it is predominantly X in the other two and correspondingly with the Y aspects. Furthermore, if there is any X in any one of the first three aspects there is an X in the fourth aspect as well.[20] What does such clustering mean? If an emphasis on rationality, universalism, functional specificity, and avoidance must go together *by definition*, and if an emphasis on tradition, particularism, and functional diffuseness must go together *by definition*, such clustering effects would add nothing to what we already know. But, they do not cluster by definition. Emphases on rationality, functional specificity, universalism, and avoidance are likely to cluster, and if they fail to, one can make further predictions from that variation. When rationality is involved, both ends and means must be empirical and to a high degree explicit. Functionally diffuse elements are likely to interfere with rational emphases and force inclusion of traditional or nonrational elements if only by adding vagueness to an otherwise explicit situation. Again rational factors are likely to be interfered with by particularistic selections, especially if the particularism is not germane particularism, since such selection will not maximize or safeguard the ability of the members of the relationship to carry out rational action in terms of the relationship. Intimacy, as opposed to avoidance, is more likely to involve departures in the direction of traditionality (or nonrationality), functional diffuseness, and particularism. It is difficult to confine activity to rational considerations or to specifically defined and delimited factors or to objective selections when a person is intimately involved with others. These four elements by no means always go together. For example, rather close approaches to universalism are sometimes maintained by picking wives for one's sons, whereas this relationship may be and commonly is, predominantly traditional, functionally diffuse, and intimate. Also there may be radical differences between the ideal structures and the actual structures of the relationships. The ideal structures of relationships that are predominantly X in the first four categories are extremely difficult to live up to. One of the major developments in social science in the twentieth century came from the developments of the Harvard Business School studies of just such questions. The famous studies by Roethlisberger and Dickson[21] stressed the importance of the entry of particularistic considerations even into settings that were ideally speaking predominantly universalistic.

In Part I, above [of *Modernization and the Structure of Societies*], one of the major distinctions between relatively modernized and relatively nonmodernized societies was the different emphases in different spheres that the members of those societies placed on the X and Y forms of the relationship aspects. Throughout this work, there is a great deal of hypothesizing that the role of changing emphases on different clusters of the relationship aspects is of the first importance in the transition from relatively nonmodernized to relatively modernized societies. Many problems of the transitions can be understood in these terms. The exploration of just how these relationship aspects tend to cluster and under what conditions these and other clusterings take place, has only recently begun in social science. The two major clustering effects illustrated in Table 2 may be rather confidently relied upon. For any relationship in which there is a switch in emphasis from a Y to an X category in any of the first three aspects, one should expect a shift from an emphasis on a Y category to an X category in the other two as well. There would also be a switch toward X_4 if the emphasis was previously on Y_4. If such a switch does not take place, or if one finds an emphasis on an X in any one of the first three aspects and not in the other of the first four, he can draw one of two possible inferences: (1) the relationship concerned will prove to be highly unstable, or (2) it will be fitted into and buttressed by other relationships in a peculiar fashion.[22]*

There is another general avenue for theory formation in these terms. Certain emphases on relationship aspects are characteristic not only of different societies but more importantly of their various subsystems. This has many implications for general theories of social change. One of the major reasons that the structures of relatively modernized societies are in fact a sort of universal social solvent of the social structures of other societies is that for certain structures likely to be imitated intentionally or unintentionally, the members of relatively modernized societies emphasize X qualities in the first four aspects whereas members of most of the relatively nonmodernized societies emphasize Y qualities in at least the first three aspects. Moreover, the disintegrative impact of the importation of such structures is never confined to the minimal departures from emphasis on the Y categories necessary to establish firmly an emphasis on the X categories for altogether new relationships. The disintegration may go quite far even though the emphases on the X category are not at all firmly established. For example, contrary to many sentimental views, the stability of the traditional Chinese family did not inhere in the fact that it was a type of family devoid of stressful implications for its members. The stresses and strains on family members were of considerable intensity at different periods of their lives, but there were many reasons why relatively few people attempted to run away. One of those reasons certainly had to do with the fact that they had little or no place to go. Ordinary employment was in a family context on, of course, predominantly particularistic grounds. If one sought employment elsewhere, there was also a heavy emphasis on particularistic criteria. One of the main criteria was a person's filial character. A runaway defied family structures and was for that reason alone not to be trusted. The possibility of viable alternative employment on relatively objective grounds, if one defied one's family head and fled, hardly existed. Family rebels were likely to be forced into the byways of the society in terms of which life, though rarely

[* See Supplement, p. 124.]

solitary, was likely to be nasty, brutish, and short.   With the coming of the structures of relatively modernized societies, for the first time in two thousand years, the possibility of viable alternative employment on relatively objective grounds began to crop up.   The threat of the disaffected to run away unless treated better became an effective possibility.[23]   The modification of the authority of the family head was far-reaching.   This was one of the reasons why family structures, relatively stable for two thousand years, had already begun to change radically long before the Communist regime, despite the fact that the actual development of modernization in terms of large numbers of modern factories and the like was modest.

IV. FINAL CAUTION

Let me recapitulate and warn about the use of this tool.   First, it is a set of categories in terms of which any relationship in any society can be analyzed.   Second, it is a tool in terms of which any two or more relationships or any particular relationship at different points in time can be compared with one another.   Third, it is a tool that provides a systematic procedure for seeking out some of the major differences and similarities relevant to any particular problem.   Fourth, even elementary applications of the tool for purposes of illustration reveal that certain of these relationship aspects tend to cluster with one another.   Fifth, certain types of clusters are characteristic of some social systems and not of others. Sixth, the fact that certain of these clusters are characteristic of some subsystems and not of others has considerable relevance for theories of social change in general and for those of change from relatively nonmodernized societies to relatively modernized societies in particular.   Given the state of the social sciences, none of these claims is modest, but I would claim more and maintain that it is quite unlikely that either the problems of modernization of relatively nonmodernized peoples or the problems of stability of highly modernized peoples can be studied at all without some form of these concepts being explicit or implicit in the analysis.

There are, however, two major cautions which anyone should observe in using this tool of analysis.   First, as I have tried to indicate nontechnically, it is by no means a perfectly developed tool of analysis.   There are serious problems of a theoretical nature in its present state of development—let alone its further refinement and development.   As a set of scientific concepts, it leaves a great deal to be desired.   Second, insofar as it is at all well developed, critical acumen is still necessary.   In the treatment above I have stressed again and again that combinations of say universalistic and particularistic elements are more likely than pure cases of either, even if pure cases are possible.   It is, therefore, always legitimate for anyone to inquire "Why has this particular relationship been classified as 'predominantly,' or even 'more,' X_1 than Y_1?"   In answering such a question one must specify not only what the criteria for such judgments are but also the set of actors alleged to make these emphases.   For example, if I claim that the relationships between employer and employee in the United States today are predominantly universalistic, I may justify it by saying that, ideally speaking, from the point of view of virtually everyone in the society, the feeling is that no one should be barred from employment on the basis of race, creed, or color and that the only legitimate criteria are the possession of skills relevant to the job for which selection is being made.   Any of those empirical allegations is subject to either confirmation or disproof.

In addition to the justification of the classification of a structure as predominantly X rather than predominantly Y there is also another kind of comparison. One may wish to maintain that the emphasis in the United States doctor-patient relationship is predominantly X_1, whereas that in the traditional Chinese doctor-patient relationship is predominantly Y_1.   If challenged, one must be prepared not only to substantiate the classifications in the sense discussed immediately above, but also to say in what respect, if any, one justifies differences in the comparison as between the American and the Chinese case.   If the emphasis is predominantly X_1 in one case and a predominantly Y_1 in the other, such justifications are relatively simple.   If both are predominantly X_1 relationships, the statement that one of them is more predominantly X_1 than the other may be difficult to demonstrate.   Nevertheless, it is at least in principle possible to make such statements.   For example, with regard to the employer-employee relationship in ordinary manufacturing concerns in the United States by contrast with those in Japan there are far more elements of functional diffuseness in the Japanese than in the American case.   In many areas of Japanese production the acceptance of a job and the acceptance for a job imply a lasting obligation of employee to employer and vice versa.   This is a less prominent feature of the Japanese labor market than once was the case, but it is often still the case.   In this sense the relationship between employer and employee is less precisely delimited in the Japanese than in the United States case.[24]

This tool of analysis shares a common tragic defect with all tools of analysis. No matter how infatuated one may become with it, it is never a substitute for either hard work or good ideas.   Within any given frame of creativity and hard work, however, its use does at least facilitate the development of implications.

Notes

1. *The Structure of Society*, Princeton University Press, 1952, Chap. 6.
2. The most restricted possible social system would consist of structures interrelating only two members for a single act.
3. The terms *individualistic* and *responsible* as used in this connection will be explained below.
4. In my book cited above I have discussed the distinctions between the scheme as presented there and that of Parsons.   The differences are considerably greater today than they were then.   In Parsons' work these aspects of relationships have developed into the famous "patterned variables."   I have continued to use a form based on his earlier versions.   The earlier versions

(e.g., T. Parsons, "The Professions and Social Structure," *Social Forces*, vol. XVII, no. 4, May, 1939, reprinted, pp. 185–199, in T. Parsons: *Essays in Sociological Theory: Pure and Applied*, The Free Press, Glencoe, 1949), as qualified and amplified here are considerably less subject to confusion than the "patterned variables." There is another more technical reason for not using the present Parsonian version. Parsons insists that the distinctions drawn are binary distinctions. Thus a relationship is either *particularistic* or *universalistic*. Empirically this is simply not the case. The concepts so defined must always be used in a manner other than their definitions would lead one to expect. In fact the uses of the distinctions by Parsons in his own works and in that of his followers are almost always differences of degree rather than of kind. To insist that differences of degree are in fact differences of kind and to try to handle consequent overstatements by *ad hoc* qualifications to the effect that of course other elements are involved to some degree is to beg the very question one intends to answer.

5. For further elaboration see, *The Structure of Society*, pp. 240–248.

6. The treatment of the cognitive aspects of relationships is an abridgement of the treatment presented in *The Structure of Society*. The treatment of the membership criteria aspects is an enlargement on the treatment there.

7. In this connection, one must be careful about the use of the term *contract*. The modern business contract used as the example par excellence of a predominantly functionally specific relationship is quite a different matter from a marriage contract or a feudal contract. These contracts contain many elements of precise definition, but characteristically the extent of the relationships is vaguely delimited, even deliberately so.

8. During World War II the egalitarian character of friendship as opposed to the hierarchical character of the officer–enlisted-man relationship was a frequent theme of conflict in comic strips, in the movies, on the radio, etc. Bosom friends who met but could not eat together because of the military distinction appeared in all sorts of stories. Whether or not old friends in uniform, meeting in a nonmilitary context, could treat one another as equals became, as it were, a test of the strength of the friendship, etc.

9. See below, pp. 296–300 and 670–671 [of *Modernization and the Structure of Societies*].

10. Predictions based on these three facts taken alone might be extremely risky, but they would tell something, and the more such facts one has, the less risky prediction becomes.

11. These relationships have been chosen to illustrate the three major comparative applications of this scheme of analysis. I do not wish at this point to get sidetracked into any discussion of the validity of the assertions made about any of the relationships. I have not knowingly misrepresented any of the structures, but my hypotheses about the facts may be false.

The material used on the doctor-patient relationship was first brought to my attention in lectures delivered at Harvard by Professor Talcott Parsons more years ago than either of us cares to remember. Much of the material also appears in his article already cited above (p. 136) [of *Modernization and the Structure of Societies*] as one of the original sources for the development of this particular taxonomy of relationship structures. Professor Parsons is, of course, not to be held responsible for the present form of this material or any of the uses made of it despite the indebtedness of this treatment to his work.

I have not bothered to illustrate the analysis of a single relationship separately because that analysis can be illustrated by the description of the first two relationships discussed below.

12. As is well known, this is an area in which there is great pressure on the professional man to act. In similar circumstances in many societies, magical practices are frequent. They are specifically denigrated in the medical sphere. It is not a matter of accident'that medical faddism is so prominent a phenomenon. Many wise doctors have pointed out that the most difficult thing for a doctor to do when his knowledge is inadequate is literally to do nothing. Fortunately, perhaps, the constantly changing nature of medical faddism—in this respect it is almost exactly the opposite of magical practices—probably minimizes any harm done by uncritical pursuit of any particular medical fad.

13. The term *institution* is defined as a normative pattern, conformity with which is generally to be expected, and failure to conform with which is generally met with the moral indignation of those individuals who belong to the same general social system and are aware of the failure—or

by some other sanctions from that source. The term normative pattern refers simply to any pattern involving a standard of conduct. Thus, "men should have only one wife at a given point in time," "no one should bully anyone else," "patients should select their doctors on the basis of their medical qualifications," etc., are normative patterns. A normative pattern may be more or less well institutionalized with regard to the level of conformity expected in terms of it or the degree and kind of moral indignation and sanctions which greet a failure to live up to this ideal structure. There is an extended discussion of this concept in the *Structure of Society*, pp. 101–109. The details of that discussion need not detain us here. All institutions in this sense are social structures.

14. There is not space here to go into the question of how these peculiar structures developed or what their implications may be. It is important, however, to keep in mind the fact that the doctor-patient relationship, as we take it for granted, is a peculiar and unusual relationship in world history. To an unusual degree one member has a great deal of knowledge relative to the other member's concern, and the other member usually has little knowledge. In that sense the doctor could potentially do the patient great harm, if he took advantage of his knowledge. It is also interesting to keep in mind that we permit the doctor a kind of access to our bodies that is literally permitted to no one else in the society. Such access is deemed vital to modern medical treatment, but such access made available to any one on a nonmedical basis would immediately raise questions of proper conduct in general and of proper sexual behavior in particular. It is not a matter of chance that members of modern societies feel so strongly about doctors or that so much attention is given to the way in which the doctor-patient relationship is exemplified.

15. Two colleagues, Miss Kazuko Tsurumi and Mr. Andrew Effrat, have suggested further developments of this scheme. Miss Tsurumi has suggested a *communications aspect* with a polar distinction between *secret* and *open* relationships. Mr. Effrat in an unpublished paper has suggested a *volitional aspect* with a distinction between voluntaristic and nonvoluntaristic relationships plus some six mixed forms. Both suggestions are promising, but I have not explored them enough to use them here. One of the rough rules of thumb of theory, however, is that once one exceeds six or seven distinctions on any one level (and these two aspects would give us eight) some more general less complicated level should be sought.

16. That is to say, even in the United States there is still a vestigial expectation that the relationship be a hierarchical one with some male precedence. Some might argue that Y_6 should be substituted here, taking the position that this relationship should be an egalitarian one. Whatever *should be* the case, even in America, the relationship retains hierarchical elements (with male precedence) even ideally speaking. It may also be argued that the pressure is not toward egalitarianism but toward female precedence.

17. Under previous custom the Imperial children were literally reared almost entirely by persons who were not their parents.

18. One can generalize as follows: All relationships characterized by high emphases on rationality will involve members who have a high probability of being cognitive equals or will be characterized by high emphases on responsibility or will be instable.

19. Even in these instances, however, the reaction of the accused parties, much of the general reaction of other businessmen, and certainly that of the general public is censorious of such behavior to a degree hard to imagine some decades ago. Sworn testimony in court established clearly that many, if not all, of those convicted of these lapses were violating explicitly professed standards of their organizations.

20. It does not follow that if there is an X in the fourth aspect that there are X's in the first three. Although one can generalize to the effect that if there is X_1 or X_2 or X_3, there is also X_4, one can not generalize to the effect that if there is Y_1 or Y_2 or Y_3, there is usually Y_4.

21. F. J. Roethlisberger and William J. Dickson, *Management and the Worker*, Harvard University Press, Cambridge, 1941.

22. In changes in relationship aspects generally it makes a great deal of difference not only whether there is a switch from an X emphasis to a Y emphasis (or vice versa) or from one type of X emphasis to another (e.g. from an emphasis on rationality about health to one about

wealth), but also the sequence of changes is important especially when clustering effects are relevant.

23. In addition, the Chinese family was the only general structure of social insurance for the aged. If the son ran away and was able to establish himself elsewhere, he not only won his own freedom, he also left his father and mother, if they survived into old age, without anyone to take care of them.

24. Once again I must emphasize that the statements of fact in this illustration may not be tenable, but at least in theory they are susceptible of confirmation or disproof.

Supplement

Whenever an emphasis is placed on predominantly rational, predominantly universalistic, predominantly functionally specific, and predominantly avoidant relationships, the following hypotheses can be maintained:

1. The longer such a relationship is maintained, the greater is the probability that there will be a breakdown ideally and/or actually in the direction of predominantly traditional, predominantly particularistic, predominantly functionally diffuse, and predominantly intimate relationships. Some such breakdown will always take place with regard to the actual structures even if it does not take place with regard to the ideal ones. In other words, the longer X_1, X_2, X_3, and X_4 emphases are maintained, the greater is the probability that they will break down in the direction of predominantly Y_1, Y_2, Y_3, and Y_4 emphases.

2. It is exceedingly improbable that any breakdowns in predominantly X_1, X_2, X_3, and X_4 relationships will be in the direction of other predominantly X_1, X_2, X_3, and X_4 relationships.

3. It is extremely improbable that breakdowns in predominantly Y_1, Y_2, Y_3, and Y_4 relationships will be in the direction of predominantly X_1, X_2, X_3, and X_4 relationships.

4. Whenever predominantly Y_1, Y_2, Y_3, and Y_4 relationships break down, they break down in the direction of other predominantly Y_1, Y_2, Y_3, and Y_4 relationships.

5. Only under conditions of rapidly increasing modernization are there continuous increases in emphases on predominantly X_1, X_2, X_3, and X_4 relationships, and most of these will take the form of new types of relationships rather than alterations or subversions of the old, though the latter are by no means out of the question, especially in the sphere of governance.

6. The above hypotheses pose very special problems with regard to the stability of highly modernized society. Not only are these instable in respects already discussed in *Modernization and the Structure of Societies* with regard to relationship aspects, but the predominantly X_1, X_2, X_3, and X_4 emphases are vulnerable in respects not characteristic of the predominantly Y_1, Y_2, and Y_3 emphases characteristic of relatively nonmodernized societies in corresponding relationships.

If the above propositions are true, it would seem that not only is mankind much less habituated to the X_1, X_2, and X_3 type of emphases, but that there is also built into them a kind of instability which is not built into Y_1, Y_2, Y_3, or Y_4 emphases. It is important to note that the X_4 emphasis (predominantly avoidant) is not necessarily less frequent in relatively nonmodernized societies than in highly modernized ones and that it is more likely to be met with inside kinship contexts in relatively nonmodernized societies than in relatively modernized ones. The instability of high emphases on avoidance is built into any society. Human beings are rarely virtuosi of avoidance. I do not emphasize the difference in breakdown with regard to this because it is constant to all societies, although there may be important differences of incidences of this breakdown. (Personal communication from Marion J. Levy, Jr.)

8 . On Role Systems . Siegfried F. Nadel

The definition of social structure which we made our starting point stipulated the ordered arrangement, system or network of the social relationships obtaining between individuals 'in their capacity of playing roles relative to one another'. We therefore regarded the role system of any society, with its given coherence, as the matrix of the social structure. But we found this matrix broken up by logical cleavages and by the factual dissociation of roles. More simply stated, a great many actors never can 'play their roles relative to one another', simply because the roles have no common locus, logically or empirically. The absence of a common logical locus precludes the assumption of a unitary, coherent system; indeed, there seem to be as many separate systems as there are logical role frames. Between them, there is only the linkage provided by recruitment rules, defining the flow or 'circulation' of persons between disparate sets of roles and the chances of their belonging to several at once. Where the logical cleavages are absent, the factual dissociation of roles still makes it impossible to relate certain roles with one another since the actors in these roles never meet in that capacity in social intercourse. Rather, one of the actors in his role would face a more or less

Reprinted with permission of The Macmillan Company and Routledge & Kegan Paul Ltd. from *The Theory of Social Structure* by Siegfried F. Nadel. First published in the United States of America by The Free Press, a Corporation, 1957. Nadel used the title "Degrees of Abstraction."

broad public, of indeterminate role composition, so that the 'ordered arrangement' of relationships contains so-to-speak zones of indeterminacy. Finally,
the relational or correlative character of roles will tend to isolate the respective
relationships from one another, in the manner of enclaves. The result, then, is
that our 'ordered arrangement', far from being a total one, must remain fragmentary. In a word, it seems impossible to speak of a social structure in the
singular.

Figure 1

	a	b	c	d	α	β	γ	δ
a		+	+	+	+	+	+	+
b	+		+	+	+	+	+	+
c	+	+		+	+	+	+	+
d	+	+	+		+	+	+	+
α	+	+	+	+		+	+	+
β	+	+	+	+	+		+	+
γ	+	+	+	+	+	+		+
δ	+	+	+	+	+	+	+	

Let me show this graphically. If there were such a thing as a fully coherent
role system and a unitary social structure, a role system containing roles belong-
ing to two different logical frames (a, b, c, d and α, β, γ, δ) could be represented
in a matrix every cell of which would be filled [as shown in Figure 1].

Figure 2

	a	b	c	d	α	β	γ	δ
a		+	+	+				
b	+		+	+				
c	+	+		+				
d	+	+	+					
α						+	+	+
β					+		+	+
γ					+	+		+
δ					+	+	+	

The logical cleavages on the other hand, since they preclude relationships between
logically disparate roles, would introduce blank spaces [as shown in Figure 2].
   The reduction of role-to-role relationships to relationships of the actor-public
kind, though it would fill the matrix, would fill it in an indeterminate fashion, the

former links being submerged in the collective orientations upon 'customers', 'audience', 'congregation', or simply 'the rest of society'. This may be indicated in the following fashion [see Figure 3]. And the enclaves produced by correlative roles would give this picture (a-a, b-c, d-d being three such pairs of roles, like and unlike, e.g. friend-friend, host-guest, freemason-freemason) [see Figure 4].

Figure 3

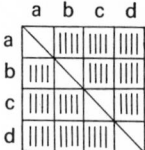

This lack of coherence and unity in any presumed social structure might not apply to the same degree if we changed our whole approach and considered the attachment of relationships to concrete persons, to the Toms, Dicks and Harrys of any society, rather than to the roles they choose or are made to play. For in view of the possible summation of roles, concrete individuals, unrelated to one another in the sense of certain of their roles, might yet be related in the sense of

Figure 4

	a	b	c	d
a	+			
b				
c		+		
d				+

others. We could in fact think of situations where a whole set of people, considered as total persons, exhibits a fully coherent, single network of relationships while the analysis of their roles would yield only one that is discontinuous or fragmentary. The model below illustrates such a situation for four persons, A, B, C and D [see Figure 5].

But this cannot mean that we should give up talking about roles and actor relationships and refer instead to concrete people and the ties between them, because by this method we shall find it easier to construct a coherent 'structure'. Nor am I exaggerating the difficulties of this task—difficulties readily overcome if we are prepared to change our methods. For the approach through person-to-person relationships can only imply one of two things. Either it leads to provisional findings, leaving it unexplained on what principle (by what 'brief') the individuals in question actually assume their various relationships: which means that the enquiry into the role-to-role connections is only postponed. Or the approach means, if we also disregard the principles or 'brief' underlying the relationship, that we are treating them as purely 'personal' and accidental occurrences, concerning particular people in particular circumstances: which is not what we have agreed to understand by 'social structure'.

In a sense, however, I have been exaggerating the lack of coherence in any given social structure; for to some extent it will be corrected or rendered less relevant by a number of factors. Thus in simple, homogeneous societies certain of the 'blanks' in the structure will not matter; since, in such societies, numerous roles,

Figure 5

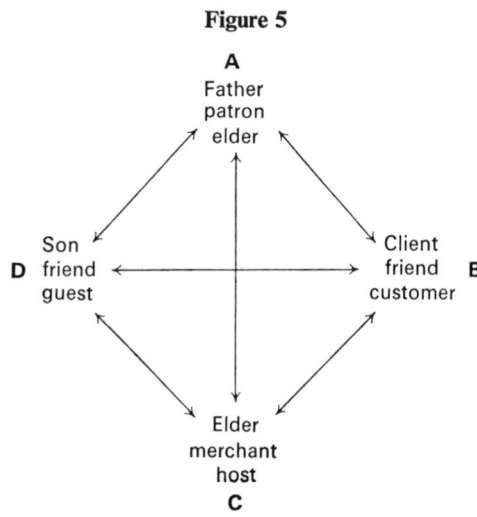

including disparate ones, invariably coincide (we remember our paradigm, the family head-cum-manager-cum-priest), the need to trace relationships between the persons playing these roles simply does not arise. Again, a high degree of 'personalization' will partly eliminate or reduce some of the 'zones of indeterminacy.' And dichotomization will bridge the mutually isolated enclaves. But for the society as a whole, for the total collection of existing roles and relationships, these gaps and breaks cannot be entirely spirited away. More important, even where they do not apply, perhaps in selected, restricted sectors of social life, other difficulties will arise. We may indeed know that all the roles we are concerned with (for example, in such a selected sector) are linked in relationships and that all the relationships combine to form a single network. If so, it would seem that all we have to do is to describe or somehow indicate the character—the *orderly* character—of the combination. But to be able to do this we must deal with data which are in fact comparable and 'combinable'. And it is here that we meet with new obstacles.

Let us consider a small area of roles and relationships (another 'miniature system') represented by the nuclear family, that is, by the set of roles exemplified by a man ('father' and 'husband'), his wife ('wife' and 'mother'), and say two sons ('sons' and 'brothers'). There are, of course, no cleavages or lacunae in this situation; all roles are interrelated, both logically and through actual behaviour. We have in fact that most coherent network, corresponding to a full matrix [as shown in Figure 6]. Here if anywhere our data should prove entirely comparable and combinable. Yet while we continue to think of roles and relationships in the way we have done so far, this is simply not the case.

Roles, we remember, were for us series of behavioural attributes, each with its peculiar content of aims, tasks, expectations, entitlements, obligations; relationships in turn referred to the constancies of behaviour, still conceived with this kind of content, between people described in role terms. In other words, all our formulae had to contain the letters, a, b, c . . . n, indicative of the particular contents and qualities. Now from this point of view the relationship between a

Figure 6

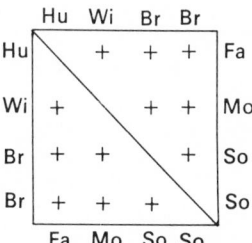

father and a son implies 'paternal' care and authority and 'filial' respect and love, and would lose its very identity without this implication; the relationship between husband and wife implies, among other things, sexual intimacy; the relationship between brothers, sibling rivalry or solidarity. Obviously, this list can be extended further, to include many other qualities. The point is that it always does include qualities, and hence *differentiae* of an irreducible nature. How then can we combine them in some overall design? Or how can we extract, even from this miniature system, any embracing order while still paying attention to these qualitative characteristics? As it stands, each relationship contains unique features which render it incomparable with the others, offering nothing in the way of a common criterion or dimension. All we can do, apparently, is to enumerate and describe the diverse relationships and place them side by side, as so many disparate entities.

We can in fact do a little more; for we can indicate also the interlocking of relationships and thus the extension of the dyadic to triadic and perhaps higher-order relationships, ultimately to the whole network. Thus we should note the 'concern' of each parent in the proper execution of the sibling relationship, as seen by them. We should note the concern of the mother in the relationship between her husband and the sons, which might be such as to express an authoritarian and disciplinarian attitude, as against her own attitude of love and care. The father would similarly pay attention to what he considers the appropriate relationship between a mother and sons. In either case the husband-wife relationship would be adjusted to and affected by the relationship of each towards the children. The sibling relationship in turn would be determined by the particular attitude of the parents towards each sibling, say, partiality towards a younger son; and each son-parent relationship would be determined by the enactment of the relationship between the parents, for example, by any disturbance of the latter by quarrels, jealousy, infidelity, etc.

But this picture is still too heavily invested with qualitative features to yield any clear order or overall design. Though the picture does indicate a complete and coherent network, with all its strands interlocking, the very ways and points of interlocking retain a great deal that is pure 'quality'. The mother's concern over her husband's harshness or mildness towards the sons; the parents' concern over the brotherly feelings of the sons; and the sons' concern over the marital relations of their parents—all these are still incomparable and, from the point of view of any overall order, intractable. Again, all that we seem able to do is to enumerate and describe separately each triadic or higher-order relationship.

If we were to extend the system of kinship roles, this would not necessarily mean a proportionate increase in the incomparability of the relationships involved, simply because some of the added relationships would prove to be identical or similar to those contained in the miniature system. For example, the father's brother's relationships with his brother's sons might merely duplicate (or approximately duplicate) the father-son relationship. Yet where this extension beyond the miniature system implies the inclusion of differentiated roles and relationships, the "intractability" we discussed a moment ago will in fact be increased. And much the same intractability would characterize any other coherent role system. Think of the diversified relationships and their ways of interlocking involved in any productive enterprise of some complexity (which would include managers, foremen, consultants, and workers in different or like tasks), or in any political-administrative set-up, with its diverse offices, responsibilities and channels of communication. Even in a relatively simple organization like a school there will be the diverse and incomparable relationships between teachers, between teachers and pupils, between the pupils, and between the parents and the teachers. . . .

I now want to suggest my own criteria for . . . [a] level abstraction that defines the positional picture of societies. The conditions which such criteria must satisfy . . . must enable us to synthesize the efficacy of roles and relationships in numerous situations, and must do so on the grounds of some acceptable principle of relevance. I can think of two criteria of this kind: (i) The first applies to roles between which there is no 'dissociation,' that is, to roles which we know to involve specific relationships with actors in other roles, and which are rendered incomparable only by the qualitative diversity of the relationships. The criterion here is the differential *command over one another's actions*.   (ii) The second criterion, though it applies to the first case also, is meant to overcome the 'zones of indeterminacy' in actor-public relationships.   In order to do this we reinterpret the 'roles played relative to one another' of individuals so that they have an extraneous reference point; this can be found in the differential *command over existing benefits or resources*.

Employing the first criterion, we have no difficulty in comparing such relationships as father-child, husband-wife, and brother-brother: schematically expressed (using *ca* to indicate 'command over actions')—

$$\text{Fa } (ca) \text{ Ch} > \text{Hu } (ca) \text{ Wi} > \text{Br } (ca) \text{ Br} \tag{18}$$

the latter relationship being, for example, such that

$$\text{Br}_1 \ (ca) \ \text{Br}_2 = \text{Br}_2 \ (ca) \ \text{Br}_1$$

Identifying 'father' with 'husband' and 'wife' with 'mother', considering brothers on different generation levels, and including various other kinship degrees, we can express the total 'order' of relationships in a chain formula, thus—

$$\text{Fa } (ca) \text{ So} > \text{Mo } (ca) \text{ So} > \text{Fa } (ca) \text{ Mo} \tag{19}$$

$$< \text{FaBr } (ca) \text{ FaBrSo} > \text{MoBr } (ca) \text{ WiSo}$$

$$> \text{FaFa } (ca) \text{ SoSo} = \text{MoFa } (ca) \text{ FaSo etc.}$$

This is, of course, a fictitious example, though a realistic one.   There is nothing very new in the attempt as such to represent systematically a whole order of command relationships; the familiar charts illustrating the 'chain of command' in administrative organizations are based on much the same principle, though they deal with infinitely simpler data.   Nor do I claim that one such set of formulae will summarize all the relevant relationships.   Equivalent command as, for example, in sibling relationships might have to be expressed separately.   We may also need additional symbols, e.g. for zero command, for the peculiar 'negative command' implied in avoidance relationships, and perhaps for command exercised illegitimately.   Equally, we must be able to indicate the fluctuating, tug-of-war situation between competitors and rivals, e.g.

$$\text{E } (ca) \text{ A} \gtrless \text{A } (ca) \text{ E,} \tag{20}$$

as well as true conflict relationships, where the actors have incompatible expectations as to their command over one another.   Let me leave this last point for the moment and only suggest that, with relatively few additions or changes, sets of formulae of the kind here outlined can give a complete and accurate positional picture.   There is only this proviso, which merely repeats a point made already: the picture can be complete or accurate only for a given sector of the society—any sector for which comprehensive role-to-role relationships can at all be constructed.

The positional character of the picture is evidenced by the strictly relational, mathematical symbols ($<$, $>$, $=$) which now replace the qualitative signs (a, b, c . . . n) of our previous formulae.   Let us note also that the new formulae allow for the interlocking of relationships, i.e. for their transitiveness.   For if a person E in his particular role stands in relationship to A such that

$$E \, (ca) \, A, \qquad (21a)$$

it means that E can also influence and will normally be concerned in any relationships with 'third parties' in which A might be engaged.   Thus the formula above can be expanded to

$$E:(A:T) \qquad (21b)$$
$$\therefore ErA \rightleftarrows Tr \, (A, E),$$

which is, in transposed form, our crucial formula (17b).[1]

The second criterion permits the direct comparison and interrelation of roles which would otherwise yield only the broad opposition of an actor with his more or less anonymous 'public'.   We remember the situation indicated by the diagram below:

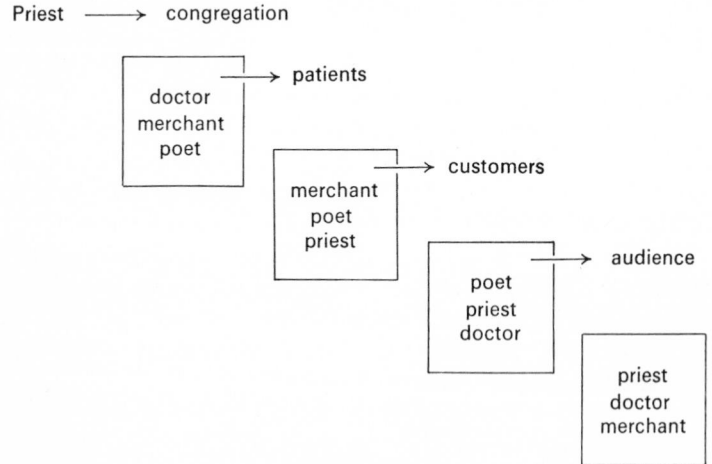

With the aid of the second criterion each role can be singled out and compared with any other as to their relative 'command over services and benefits' (*crb*); the blanketing collectivities then drop out, being replaced by a series of role-to-role relations for example—

$$\text{doctor} \, (crb) > \text{merchant} \, (crb) > \text{priest} \, (crb) = \text{poet} \, (crb)$$

If, in this criterion, I am combining existing benefits *and* resources I do so in order to indicate in a single phrase both the gratifications current and favoured in a society and the instrumentalities for their attainment. Differently expressed, the phrase is meant to indicate the possessions and conditions access to which is valued in the society, in a given degree. The employment of the criterion therefore presupposes our ability to construct the appropriate scale of valuation, whether it approximates to the precise 'preference scale' of economists or corresponds to a more abstract and broadly conceived 'scale of worthwhileness', as I have phrased it elsewhere. Yet there is the diversity of the things valued by human beings: which means, in many though not perhaps in all societies, a mingling of scales of valuation similarly diverse and not entirely reducible to one another. Thus we may have to reckon with several discrete value areas or dimensions, or with some combination of them: (i) material resources and benefits; (ii) social dignity (prestige, esteem, status in a hierarchical sense); (iii) cognitive values (learning, knowledge); (iv) emotional, sensual, and aesthetic gratifications; (v) moral values (the fulfilment of duties and 'missions'); and (vi) transcendental values (the 'spiritual' benefits of religion).

This splitting up of *crb* does not however weaken the efficiency of the criterion; in a sense it enhances it since it permits us to demonstrate significant interrelations between the different types of this command. Let $>$ and $<$ now stand for greater and lesser command; then societies may be characterized by the fact that, for example,

$$crb \text{ (i)} > \rightleftarrows crb \text{ (vi)} <, \quad \text{or} \tag{22}$$
$$crb \text{ (i)} > \rightleftarrows crb \text{ (ii)} >.$$

The first formula would apply to societies which believe in the spiritual value of poverty; the second, to the many societies where wealth means prominence.

Obviously, like the command over the actions of others, the command over resources and benefits implies the possibility of conflict, when people, in virtue of their roles, have incompatible expectations or make incompatible claims concerning their access to the existing desiderata. But the two criteria are altogether closely related and even overlap. Command over resources will clearly often lead to command over the actions of others. The latter, in turn, is one of the instrumentalities for the attainment of material benefits, the benefits of 'social dignity', and perhaps others as well. Also, command over other people's actions may itself be considered a 'benefit' (as when 'power' is considered desirable for its own sake), additional to if not coinciding with the other instances of 'social dignity'.

The link between this value area and the command over the actions of others is even closer. For the benefits exemplified by prestige or esteem, as they are attainable through command over the actions of others, also imply a measure of this command by definition. As suggested before, having prestige, gaining the esteem or enjoying the deference of others, already means being able to command their actions in some respect. Symbolically expressed—

$$ca \rightarrow crb \text{ (ii)} \supset ca \tag{23}$$

This formula, incidentally, represents a true sociological 'law'; for the circularity expressed in it is a fundamental aspect of prestige and similar states of social dignity, which may always be both sources of command and consequences of it (as when a man with a large following gains prestige for this reason, and can then count on further people offering their deference). In this sense the command over the actions of others is cumulative, through leading to some form of social dignity and expanding in virtue of it.

The interrelation between the two command criteria has a further significance, more germane to the issue under discussion. The second criterion might seem to belong to the purely distributive level of structure, merely demonstrating the way in which benefits or access to them are allocated to the various classes of people making up the society. But this is not so. Since such access always has something to do with the command people exercise over one another, it is also to that extent evidence of interactive alignments. Let me put it this way: it is because other people facilitate or hinder my attainment of certain commonly valued benefits that I in fact attain them in such-and-such measure. More generally speaking, it is in consequence of all the possible relationships between actors that each actor also receives his allocation of benefits: so that the measure of this allocation also synthesizes numerous, perhaps all, interactive relationships and demonstrates their interlocking. Somewhat modified, our formula (17b) once more lends itself to defining the situation; replacing the symbol for the 'third' actor (T) by the sign indicating command over resources and benefits, great or less great, we can write:

$$\text{if } E:A \; [\gtrless (crb)] \text{ is such that} \tag{24}$$

$$ErA \supset E \, (ca) \, A$$

$$\therefore ErA \; \rightarrow \; A \; [\gtrless (crb)].$$

It is important to stress that this dependence of crb upon all the ca relationships in which a person is involved is not reversible. Although one's command over resources and benefits is likely to lead to some command over the actions of others, it need not do so with regard to all the persons with whom one comes in contact. A high degree of crb (i), especially, may well go together with low or zero ca towards certain people, that is, with unassuming, familiar, or 'democratic' behaviour. This means that certain relationships can properly be described only by combining the two criteria. And this, in turn, has far-reaching consequences. For if we use both criteria together we can let one (crb) represent the role typified by it and employ the other to indicate the relationships in which the actors so described are involved. The actors then become simply anonymous persons— any person in any role characterized by the given degree of crb: while the ca relationship will characterize their command over other persons similarly anonymous. It will be seen that by this method we can carry abstraction to a point where even the last element of 'quality' disappears—roles described as such. In other words, we are finally able to deal purely with 'positions', and we are able to do so without being trapped by tautologies.

As for the practical advantage of this method of exposition, it renders structural descriptions infinitely transposable. Let me illustrate this with the help of our earlier paradigm, the juxtaposition, in many kinship systems, of two complementary relationships, one disciplinarian, the other friendly; as we suggested at the time, the same principle may well apply also to widely different situations, e.g. in politics or business (see pp. 105f. [of *The Theory of Social Structure*]). To demonstrate this wider validity means, in concrete terms, to find a general proposition covering all the following cases: a father who is a 'friend' while the mother's brother is the 'disciplinarian'; a father who is a disciplinarian while the grandfather is the friend; a political leader whose authoritarian position is balanced by that of a 'people's tribune'—a man still of leadership status but on familiar and equal terms with the subjects; and a strict 'boss', assisted by a more approachable deputy or 'public relations man'. Let me restate the positional picture common to all these situations: it lies in the fact that a superiority rigidly exercised goes together with a superiority softened and minimized. Put in yet another way, we have a triad involving two persons in 'superior' roles, one of whom acts authoritatively towards the subordinates, the other, in a friendly and more egalitarian fashion.

The superiority in question, whether it derives from kinship position, leadership status, or rank in the business organization, inevitably implies a relatively great *crb* (i or ii). Let *crb* therefore stand for all the roles so characterized; and let *ca* stand for the behaviour evinced by the actors, authoritarian or friendly. The common positional picture is then characterized by this proposition: if two persons (in whatever roles) are so related that

$$A\ (crb) \geqslant E\ (crb), \text{ and} \tag{25a}$$
$$A\ (ca)\ E \geqslant E\ (ca)\ A,$$

there is a third person T such that

$$T\ (crb) > A\ (crb), \text{ yet (approximately)} \tag{25b}$$
$$T\ (ca)\ A = A\ (ca)\ T.$$

If the proposition as here stated really holds, it amounts to a general social regularity or 'law'. Whether or not it does hold, is an empirical question, and beyond this context. What is important in the present context is that the very expression of the law would depend on the employment of the two criteria of command.

These, however, could be criticised on other grounds. It might, for example, be objected that I have taken it for granted too readily that we can in fact accurately locate, identify and measure the two kinds of command. But if I have taken it for granted, I have done no more than affirm a familiar competence of social enquiry. Though it may still be in need of considerable refinement, we constantly exercise it; that is, we freely rank values and notions of 'worthwhileness' and operate with such concepts as power, authority, or hierarchical status, assessing their magnitudes; which is precisely what we are doing when applying the criteria of command. And if, in view of this, it is argued that the 'social structure' I am envisaging is little more than a power, authority or status structure, I would reply that this seems to me the only "dimension" both sufficiently abstract for our purpose and still sufficiently relevant, in the sense of being important in human and social existence. Let me make it clear that in saying this I do not wish to suggest anything in the way of universal human motivations or desires inherent in 'human nature'. I am making no assumptions whatever about people's love of command or thirst for power, and I have not argued in the way I did because I believe that it is 'necessary and justifiable to assume that a conscious or unconscious wish to gain power is a very general motive in human affairs.'[2] All that it is 'necessary and justifiable' for us to accept is a certain degree of abstraction, and the fact that command relationships exemplify it most satisfactorily.

The two criteria yield these or similar descriptive categories: The first—dominance, submission, equality; superordination, subordination, co-ordination; symmetry and asymmetry in relations; and onesided or reciprocal dependence. The second—superiority, inferiority, equality; and degrees of access and entitlement, with the limiting values of complete inclusion or exclusion. Each set of categories could be translated into the appropriate formulae, though this is too obvious to need illustration. Nor are the categories themselves in any way new or unfamiliar. Significantly, they are used in much the same sense as names for relationships seen structurally, in the 'pure' or 'formal' sociology of Simmel and von Wiese.[3] Are they too 'pure' and 'formal', too empty of context and hence uninformative? The answer is that this rigorous formalism, and the consequent 'emptiness' of the description, are the price we must pay for the extraction of an embracing and strictly positional picture of societies. Whether or not this is too great a price we may for the moment leave undecided.

This is not denying that, in practice, it is rarely feasible to exclude descriptions in qualitative terms altogether, even from the most consistent structural analysis. How far this intrusion or concession should go is a question of usefulness and convenience, on which there are no firm rules. There are, however, two elements or aspects of human relationships the omission of which would seriously impair any social analysis. The first is their emotionally *loaded* or *neutral* character; the second, the actors' expectations as to the *retention* or *relinquishment* of the relationships.[4] The two aspects clearly hang together; we know enough about human relationships to predict that their expected retention will tend to involve some emotional bond (or 'sentiment'), and the anticipation of their change, some strain or perhaps hostility. The two aspects are, however, of a logically different order. For the emotional loading of relationships is merely one of the qualitative features which a rigorous abstraction might ignore or 'bracket away', and which we now suggest should be 'put back'; while the retention or relinquishment of relationships bears on an element in the structure itself, namely, its dynamic properties. This is a new problem, not so far considered, to which we shall return in a different context.

It is hardly necessary to stress, in conclusion, that the positional criteria here developed apply to the 'external' order of groups no less than to their 'internal' order, that is, to the relationships between sub-groups of the society no less than to the relationships between actors or persons. The former exhibits the same positional possibilities—superordination, subordination, coordination, domi-nance and equality, inclusion in and exclusion from benefits and resources, etc. We need only remember that, here as elsewhere, the interrelation of sub-groups basically rests on the actions of individuals—now individuals exercising the given command or access in a representative capacity, in virtue of corporate entitle-ments vested in their groups.

It follows that there need be no congruence between the position of actors when enacting their roles within their groups and their position when acting in their corporate capacity *vis-à-vis* or relative to other groups. Sub-groups which have a hierarchical internal structure may be equivalent within the society at large (e.g. parallel descent groups or segments, each with its different command position derived from descent-cum-age); or the internal hierarchical structure may be cancelled by the external one (e.g. when leadership or seniority in a low caste group is compared with inferior position in a high caste group); or finally, the equivalence of roles in a sub-group may go together with a hierarchical ordering of that sub-group in the wider society (as when an egalitarian association or religious sect is placed high or low among other associations or sects).

These are all straightforward issues, which involve no new problems. It is, in fact, easy to see that our three instances of incongruence between the internal and external order of sub-groups are the only possible ones, and that they can be directly deduced from the conjunction of the two principles, the dichotomization of roles, and the progressive abstraction of relationships to mere command differentials.

Notes

1. Nadel wrote, on page 87 of *The Theory of Social Structure:* 'Writing. . . E (ego) and A (alter) for . . . relational roles, and T for any actor or actors completing (the) 'triad', we can apply this brief calculus—

$$\text{if } E \supset A \text{ (and } vice\ versa\text{), so that} \tag{17a}$$

$$E\,(a \ldots n)\!:\!A, \text{ and}$$

$$\therefore \text{ ErA,}$$

then, in virtue of the dichotomization of roles, there is a role T so that

$$[E(a \ldots n)]\!:\!T \tag{17b}$$

$$\therefore \text{ ErA } \rightleftarrows \text{ Tr(E,A).}$$

Formula (17b), then, symbolizes that crucial juncture in the coherence and orderliness of social structures, the interlocking of relationships. Differently expressed, it symbolizes the *transitiveness* of relationships. And I would argue, more generally, that when we try to trace the orderly interconnectedness of any plurality of relationships, such as might fill and 'hold together' a group or society, we shall find that it corresponds to the situation described by this set of formulae.'

2. E. R. Leach, *Political Systems in Highland Burma*, p. 10.

3. *The Sociology of Georg Simmel*, ed. K. H. Wolff, part III; L. von Wiese, *System der Allgemeinen Soziologie*, 1933, vol. I, pp. 205, 216–217.

4. The emotionally loaded or neutral character of relationships corresponds to the first of the five 'basic pattern variables' determining the character of social actions in Parsons's theoretical system (there called 'affectivity—affective neutrality'). The categories 'retention' and 'relinquishment' appear as the two basic possibilities in the 'primary mechanisms of adjustment'. (See Talcott Parsons and Edward Shils, *Toward a General Theory of Action*, 1951, pp. 77, 256.) The analogy, however, does not go beyond this very general correspondence.

9 . Regulation of Want Conversion: Structural Mechanisms . David Easton

Wants do not appear on the political scene as demands in some mysterious or inexplicable way. Members of the system must do the converting. They must give voice to a want in such a way as to indicate that they feel it ought to be handled through the formulation of binding decisions. Every demand will, therefore, have a concrete and in principle, determinable point of entry into a system through some member or group. This is our anchor point and although it may appear to be emphasizing the obvious, we can easily lose sight of the fact that the input of demands is the product of identifiable, observable behavior on the part of a person or a group.

But if this is so, who can be expected to voice wants as demands, introducing them into the system for the first time? In principle there is no reason why the selection of such members could not be a totally random process. In practice, we find that there are stable points of entry for demands. We shall be able to identify loci in the political structure where it is more rather than less likely that conversion of wants will take place.

From David Easton, *A Systems Analysis of Political Life* (New York, 1967), pp. 74–75, 85–99, by permission of John Wiley & Sons, Inc., Publishers.

If it is true that wants do gain entry to systems through determinable and stable points in the political structure, clearly we have here a specific class of means for regulating the inflow of demands. In thus turning to the structural means whereby conversion takes place, we shall acquire the added dividend of putting ourselves in a position to sharpen our conceptualization of the demand input process, the first stage in the whole chain of events whereby demands may be shunted aside or become transformed into outputs.[1]

TYPES OF STRUCTURAL REGULATORS

I shall define structure in the broadest sense to include, on the one hand, the interrelationships among all political roles, individually considered, and on the other, such goal-oriented collections and combinations of roles as are embodied in groups and organizations. All members of a political system occupy some political role if only that of "general member of the system" who may be called a citizen, subject or in primitive systems, a kinsman or tribesman. Insofar as a member of a system has any regularized voice in the conversion of wants to demands, the role in which he is acting will have some significance for the input of demands. We may not be able to identify a role that is exclusively or even largely devoted to the tasks of want conversion. It will be enough to establish that, in some roles, an appreciable part of the activities are devoted to voicing wants as demands. If this turns out to be the case, the occupants of these roles in the political structure will have some say over the kinds of demands that become part of political life. They will thereby help to regulate the inflow of demands.

In most political systems that have any degree of structural differentiation, regulators fall into two types. First, in all but the simplest political systems, intrasystem structural differentiation is such that there are a number of kinds of roles functionally distinct from that of general member of the system. In this event, it will be worth considering the part that such internally differentiated political roles play in the initial stages of processing demands. As we shall see, such components of a political structure as parties, interest groups, legislators, opinion leaders, administrators, executives, or tribal chiefs represent elements of political structures that have many and varied consequences for the operation of a system. Among them, however, the expression of wants as political demands plays an unmistakable part.

But there is a second type of structural regulation in which the points of entry of demands are far more diffusely spread throughout a system. This occurs particularly in those systems in which the cultural norms permit or conduce to popular involvement. However, few systems can avoid it to some limited extent. To the degree that relatively large numbers in a system are able to convert their wants to demands directly, conversion is the result of a more widely spread and less easily located set of processes. In principle, every occupant of the role "general member of the political system" is a potential converter. To establish the point of entry of any want empirically is more difficult than in the case where demands enter through specific and numerically more limited political roles such as those of leaders, parties and the like.

But if it is not practical to specify the precise point of entry of a demand in cases where the conversion takes place in relatively undifferentiated sectors of the political system, at least we should be able to identify the type of structural component that is activated. Specifically, for this second type of structural regulation, even though we cannot locate the exact member who first politicizes a want, under certain circumstances we should be able to identify the type of source. We will be able to say that it is the membership of the system at large that does the converting or some isolable segment of it. For the first class of structural regulator, however, we can always pinpoint some special roles or role combinations such as legislator, political activist, party, interest group, or mass medium.

What this discussion brings out is that persons who engage in converting wants to demands, those who put demands into the system by being the first to give expression to them, may be located in different parts of the political structure, depending upon the rules of the regime. At the extremes, conversion may be permitted to all or it may be restricted to a few leaders or even one chief extraordinary. In reality, any system will fall somewhere between these two poles.

GATEKEEPING

If we now [consult] Diagram 1 we can fit the preceding discussion more systematically into our general scheme of analysis. To anticipate briefly what will later be dealt with more fully, as wants are transformed into demands, some of them may have an extremely abbreviated life. They may move no further in the system than their point of entry. Having been asserted, they expire. Typically, however, at least some demands must flow right through the system to points of decision and implementation, otherwise the system could get no political work done. If this is so, the point of entry into a system may be viewed analytically as the beginning of a pathway, network or what I shall usually call a channel, along which demands may move.

We may now re-interpret what each position marked with a D, R or I stands for in the diagram. Structurally, it represents a check point on the channel where, through the role activities of specific or general members of the system, a demand may find itself stopped completely from continuing on to other points and where it may be modified in some way as to content. Perhaps the most appropriate way to characterize these structural points in the system is to designate them as gateways regulating the flow along the demand channels. The occupants of the roles, whether they are individuals or groups, are the gatekeepers. They form the key structural elements in determining what the raw materials of the political process will be. As we shall see, gatekeepers are not only those who initiate a demand by first voicing it; the term also designates those whose actions, once a demand is moving through the channels of the system, at some point have the opportunity to determine its destiny.

BYPASSING THE GATEKEEPERS

Later chapters [of *A Systems Analysis of Political Life*] will analyze the functions of those gatekeepers who are located well along the communication channels in a system. Here I shall restrict my remarks to those at the boundary.

Before anything can be said about them, it is important to recognize that there are rare moments in the history of political systems when it is possible to bypass them entirely. Wants may then be converted to demands without falling into the hands of these gatekeepers. Conversion of wants may occur spontaneously, entirely without benefit of gatekeepers, unless we attenuate the meaning of the word so thinly that it loses its specific content.

For example, in the case of popular upheavals, gatekeepers may find themselves unceremoniously swept aside or their regulative powers seriously impaired. Since the conversion of wants occurring in this way would be direct, we might describe the demands they spawn as *unmediated inputs*. Unmediated demands will normally reflect popular responses to special situations of distress, emergency or catastrophe, a common reaction to similar conditions that leads to the contagious and widespread popular conversion of wants almost instantaneously. The want is transmitted as a demand directly from its holders to the authorities without formal or informal intermediaries.

In the Unites States such a conversion took place at the end of World War II when a spontaneous grassroots movement arose around the feeling that the government ought to "bring the boys back home." Swift decisions were taken in the wake of this popular outcry; the want was almost instantaneously transformed into a demand and soon thereafter into an output.[2]

The decision need not be favorable, however. Historically, spontaneous demands may pour forth in the form of uprisings, jacqueries or other manifestations of discontent that are genuinely unorganized and unpremeditated—rare occurrences in politics. In such cases the outputs may be of a negative character, rejecting or suppressing the demands entirely.[3]

Genuinely spontaneous grassroots movements are quite extraordinary but they do represent one kind of conversion of wants in which, at the very least, the gatekeeping kind of regulation is minimal. There are other cases of popular political expression of wants that appear to be equally spontaneous and unmediated but which, upon close scrutiny, turn out to be spurious.

At one time or another every system has witnessed the apparent direct expression of wants through the medium of violent outbursts, street demonstrations, assassinations, or other types of militant and direct action. In many transitional systems today, this has come to be the expected mode of behavior and in some, where the regular and free expression of demands may be difficult, it may be the only kind available.

But appearances are frequently misleading. Popular outbreaks such as these seldom partake of the character of a groundswell of sentiment, uninspired and essentially undirected. Inquiry into the origins and patterns of diffusion of these mass demonstrations frequently reveals a concealed, underlying leadership that

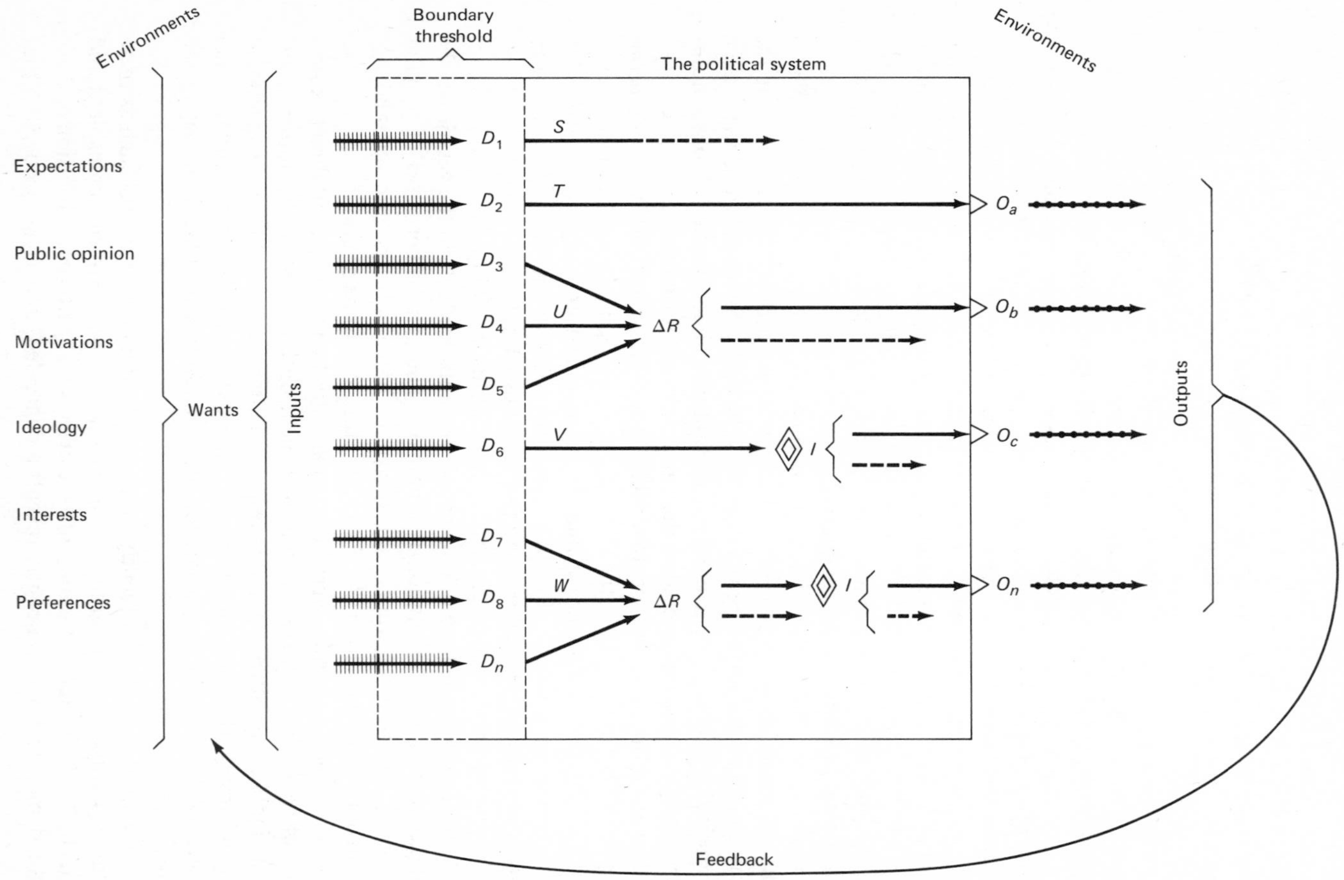

Diagram 1. Types of Demand Flow Patterns

Environments

Outputs

Environments

The political system

Feedback

O_a

O_b

O_c

O_n

Boundary
threshold

Inputs

Wants

S

T

U

V

W

ΔR

ΔR

I

I

D_1 D_2 D_3 D_4 D_5 D_6 D_7 D_8 D_n

Expectations

Public opinion

Motivations

Ideology

Interests

Preferences

142

Legend and Explanations

Environments: These include the intra- and extra-societal environments indicated on Table 1, in Chapter 2 [of *A Systems Analysis of Political Life*].

Boundary threshold: This is shown as a broad band, indefinite as to limits, in order to indicate that it matters little whether we interpret the conversion of wants as taking place in the environments or in the system.

Wants: By definition this term refers to expectations, opinions, motivations, ideology, interests and preferences, out of which demands arise or by which demands are shaped.

Conversion points:

SYMBOL	REFERENCE	INTERPRETATION
⊞⊞⊞⊞⊞↑	D_{1-n}	*Voicing of demands*: The shaded arrows represent the points of entry and inflow of demands. They indicate that varying wants have been voiced as demands. The letters D and their subscripts identify different demands.
↑↑↑	S to W	*Flow channels and patterns*: The solid arrows represent the channels along which demands flow, and the broken arrows suggest the disappearance of the demands. The letters identify the five basic types of flow patterns that demands may take.
△	R	*Reduction and combining points*: Once a demand is part of the political processes, it may be modified or combined with others, thereby reducing the total number of demands in the system.
		Reducing units: These are not shown but may consist of any individuals or groups in the system. Typically, in modern systems they take the form of parties, opinion leaders, elites, interest groups, legislators, administrators, and the like.
◈	I	*Conversion to issues*: At some stage demands are transformed into issues; from these a selection is ultimately made for conversion to outputs.
△	O_{a-n}	*Conversion to outputs*: Demands in their original or processed form are turned into decisions and associated actions. The subscripts identify different outputs. The circled arrows represent the flow of the outputs into the environments. Output units: Outputs are produced and implemented by the authorities.

FEEDBACK: Although this is shown as a single line, in fact it represents extremely numerous feedback channels. They represent the paths taken through the environment by outputs as they influence prior wants and demands.

guides and manipulates larger aggregates, giving point and content to the outpouring of sentiments. In such cases, we may designate these unobtrusive persons as the real gatekeepers.

THE POWER OF THE GATEKEEPERS

Without a closer examination of the role of those gatekeepers who stand at the boundary of a political system, it would be difficult to understand one essential source of control and power over the numbers and kinds of demands entering a system and, thereby, over the agenda for discussion in the system. Even if many and varied wants are created in the environment of the system and even if the political culture, to be examined next, permits their conversion to demands, whether or not they do gain admission will hinge on the characteristics and behavior of these gatekeepers who straddle the channels of admission to the system.

From a structural point of view, the probability that a want will be converted to a demand will be closely tied to the number of alternative gatekeepers who regulate the admission process and the rules under which they operate. Where the gatekeepers are widely distributed throughout a membership, less control over conversion will exist and there will be greater danger of input overload, discounting entirely, for the moment, restraints imposed by the political culture. At the same time, if the conversion of wants falls into relatively few and specialized hands, the opportunities for keeping the input of demands within critical limits increases enormously.

Here our analysis leads us to consider the consequences of different structural arrangements only from the perspective of the persistence of some kind of system, regardless of its type or ethical merit. But it is clear from what I have just said that the control over inputs has major consequences for the achievement of the ideals of democratic systems. With respect to them, we find that effects move in conflicting directions. From the point of view of the persistence of the system, some means must be found to keep the input of demands below a critical level. But in the light of the objectives of democratic systems, the intent is to maximize the expression of every point of view on Colonel Rainboro's maxim in the Putney Debates during the Puritan Revolution that "the poorest he that is in England hath a life to live as the richest he."[4] We shall discover in the following chapter [of *A Systems Analysis of Political Life*] that the tension between these two requirements is eased by the emergence in democratic systems of cultural means to inhibit the flow of demands into the system.

THE DISTRIBUTION OF GATEKEEPERS

Each type of system—democratic, non-literate, and dictatorial—has different sets of rules applying to the input of demands. But if we hold these constant for the moment, fundamentally the overall distribution and numbers of gatekeepers will be a function of the degree of specialization as between the political system and the rest of society as well as within the political system itself. Where the degree of structural differentiation between a political system and the rest of society is low, the capacity to convert wants to demands will be widely distributed throughout the system. Typically this is the case in those traditional systems in which there is even very little structure in the way of a well-defined set of authorities. In small, non-literate systems composed of lineages, clans, and tribes, the communication and formulation of demands is no more distinctively associated with a given role than is the case of most other activities. Elders, councils, lineages, clans, age-sets, occupational and craft organizations, villages, and similar groups perform many different kinds of social activities, religious, economic, and ritualistic, as well as political. Among these will be included want-conversion.

Where political roles are thus imbedded in other social roles and scarcely distinguishable from them, there is likely to be maximal diffusion of the capacity to convert wants to demands. There are few structural check-points for limiting the input of demands. Cultural restraints, to which we shall come, must bear the whole burden, at least at this point in the network of demand channels. There are no structural barriers to anyone voicing a demand and, in fact, in these societies each adult member tends to his own gate. This is what gives all life in small non-literate societies an intense and overriding political character seldom if ever achieved in structurally more differentiated societies.

Keesing has put this well when he comments that "a distinction may be noted between a traditionally habituated society such as Samoa and the modern Western setting in the degree to which specific issues are institutionally assigned or delegated. This is not just a function of size or massiveness of organization, though this factor undoubtedly is influential. In Samoa problems are easily referable to the responsible decision-makers."[5] The fact that members of traditional systems of this sort are able to turn naturally and constantly to the authorities in the society for the resolution of differences has meant that in the dislocations occasioned by contact with Western civilization, the tendency has been great to politicize problems rather than to seek extra-political solutions. This customary ease of converting new wants into political demands has made an important contribution to the enormous increase in the volume of demands already noted with regard to transitional societies today.

THE EFFECTS OF STRUCTURAL DIFFERENTIATION

Where, however, structural differentiation prevails, whatever other source there may be for an increase of the inflow of demands, the fact that conversion may fall into specialized hands provides an important means for regulating volume and content. Among the varied roles arising in those systems that are structurally well-differentiated from the rest of society and that manifest considerable internal role specialization as well, we shall be able to identify roles with respect to which want conversion is particularly closely associated.   By thus narrowing the points of entry into the system, the regulation of conversion is more readily facilitated.

THE IMPACT OF RULES GOVERNING THE FREEDOM TO CONVERT WANTS

Although reduction of the number of converters automatically reduces the input load that gatekeepers as a class can transmit to the system, nevertheless the volume they do let through will be inextricably bound up with the rules under which they operate.   Strictly speaking, we should put off discussion of these rules until the next chapter [of *A Systems Analysis of Political Life*].   They consist of part of the response mechanism that I shall call cultural regulation.   But it would be artificial to postpone consideration of this element of political culture since it fits logically at this point.   It would be awkward to attempt to analyze the effects flowing from structural differentiation in and of itself.   We need to discuss it with respect to two kinds of cultural rules: the regime rules that forbid conversion to all but a few members in the system and those rules that throw conversion open to any and all members of the system.   Although we cannot examine all structural types of systems that conform to these criteria, I shall be able to illustrate the consequences for the conversion process by citing two cases, dictatorial and democratic systems under conditions of modern industrialism.

GATEKEEPERS IN DICTATORIAL SYSTEMS

Modern totalitarian or dictatorial systems present an instance of structural differentiation as related to want conversion that is about as divergent from the small traditional systems we have been looking at, as we can expect to find empirically. In such dictatorial systems the capacity to set the agenda for political discussion is a crucial instrument of control.   If the regime is to endure, its rules must carefully and drastically restrict the number and variety of gatekeepers.

The operating rules of regimes such as these require that any want seeking political expression must secure validation through the approval of the leadership or of cadre groups in an approved political party which is close enough to the leadership to be able to interpret its desires and intentions.   By thus imposing limits on those who may act as gatekeepers in the conversion of wants to demands, access to the political process is limited and the leadership is able effectively to help regulate the entry of demands.   In systems such as these, based as they are on the limitation of want conversion, input overload would scarcely be likely to occur or even threaten.

DIFFUSE GATEKEEPERS IN DEMOCRATIC SYSTEMS

Democracies, under conditions of structural differentiation such as we find in industrialized societies, present us with a type of system that falls somewhere between the least inhibited expression of demands typical of small non-literate systems and the severely restricted range in dictatorial systems. In democracies as we know them today, the formal capacity to convert wants to demands is broadly diffused throughout the system. Each person may tend to his own gate, is even encouraged to do so by injunctions to participate actively in politics, always of course within the permissible limits of the other aspects of the political culture.

Although nominally each person may be able to cry out politically when the shoe pinches, in fact only certain kinds of persons or groups are likely to do so. Even where the rules impose few formal restrictions upon conversion, whether it be a small intimate system or a mass democracy, the political structure is likely to create differential opportunities. Some roles will provide greater power over the conversion process than others. Furthermore, it is utopian to believe that each member in a democracy is interested enough in politics, sufficiently well-informed and aware of what is possible, or endowed with a sufficiently vibrant sense of efficacy to desire to express his wants as political demands or to feel able to do so. The number of persons able and willing to voice demands is undoubtedly drastically lower than those formally entitled to do so.

If not every man becomes his own converter, even in a democracy, those who in fact do engage in this activity will help to set the content and level of input of demands. To be sure, as long as we continue to consider the popular gatekeepers, we shall be looking at members who are diffuse, ill-defined and low in visibility, dispersed as they are through the system. But in spite of this, they cannot be ignored if we are not to neglect one of the important points of regulation over the input of demands.

In the following chapter [of *A Systems Analysis of Political Life*] I shall discuss the cultural rules in conformity with which such popular gatekeepers will operate. These will serve to limit the range and number of demands that they are likely to convert. But here we must recognize that in spite of limits imposed by realistic considerations, popular gatekeepers do constitute numerous, widespread structural points through which demands may enter a system. Because of the potentially large number of gatekeepers that they represent, they are a possible source of stress for democratic systems.[6] Implicit here is the suggestion that, other things being equal, the greater the number of gatekeepers or points of entry for demands, the greater are the number of demands that can gain entry into a system. Accordingly, the greater is the importance that must attach to non-structural regulatory means in a democratic system, the special significance of which I shall consider in the next chapter.

WELL-DEFINED GATEKEEPERS IN DEMOCRATIC SYSTEMS

To some minimal extent then, especially in a democracy in which conditions encourage popular interest rather than apathy, each person is his own converter. But there are no data as yet that would permit us to hazard a guess as to the proportion of wants that are converted at the hands of the general members, natural spokesmen of this sort, who occupy no special or clearly differentiated role as converters of wants. However little data we may have of the extent to which they contribute toward the conversion of wants, there can at least be much less doubt that a very considerable amount of this activity is performed by others, namely by those who do hold well-defined political roles such as that of opinion leader, politician, legislator, or administrator, or by organizations such as an interest group, legislature, political party, or newspaper.

Stable roles and organized centers of political discussion and action of which these are representative, perform many kinds of tasks in a political system. The conversion of wants need not even reflect the major contribution of any one of the roles or groups just mentioned. Yet even the low salience of a function in the total behavior does not necessarily reduce the significance of this part of the political structure for the operation of the system as a whole. Regardless of whether or not want conversion is dominant, one of the characteristic activities of the occupants of these roles and members of these organizations is that they reflect the wants of others as well as their own, by voicing them as demands.

Thus, a labor organization not only sums up the demands of its membership in the area of politics; it may also sort out, summarize and evaluate their wants, anticipate their needs, and decide what political demands can be formulated around them. Indeed, interest groups, and in some systems, although not usually the American, political parties, may conceive it as part of their task to sense in advance what the wants of their followers and sympathizers may be and to formulate these as a program for political discussion and action.

Certainly such highly differentiated structures as interest groups are constantly searching for expressed or latent wants that, within the framework of their beliefs, they can appropriately adopt and around which they may formulate political policy alternatives. In modern industrialized systems, interest groups are specific structures for the conversion of wants. In fact, it is well known that the bureaucracies of such groups require a constant flow of dissatisfactions and complaints to justify the organization's continued existence. An alert leadership of an interest group will anticipate wants, at times even attempt to create them when they do not exist, if it seems necessary to assure the active survival of the group as a political instrument.

Within the limits of their positions and roles, parties, opinion leaders, the intelligentsia—where they are a political force—and the mass media similarly may search out the wants of what may in this context appropriately be called the silent ones in the system, the less articulate. And as in the case of interest groups, each of these units may also initiate demands as a reflection of their own, independently felt wants.

Hence, these members or organizations are critical gatekeepers standing at the boundary of the system, at the point marked D in Diagram 1, and controlling the initiation of demands. As we shall see, it is possible for the same unit to play a significant part at quite different points along the flow channels of demands. The fact that I locate them at the boundary for purposes of conversion will not prevent us from recognizing that they may also appear at other loci well within the system.

How much more they do with regard to the passage of demands through the system—and it is considerable—and at what other points in the system, will appear in later chapters.

THE AUTHORITIES AS SPECIFIC CONVERTERS

In modern systems to a considerable extent and in transitional types to an even greater extent, demands may be initiated by government bureaucracies such as the administrative services, the military establishment, political leaders in the role of the executive, and by the legislative representatives.[7] These are differentiated structural elements that, collectively, make up the authorities. Indeed, we can generalize this proposition by stating that wherever the authorities constitute a distinguishable set of roles, part of their activities is inevitably devoted to want conversion.

A variety of reasons may motivate them to put in demands. It may be that they are responding to direct pressure from citizens or subjects. They may undertake to convert what they view as the wants of members in the system in the anticipation that if they did not, they would be subject to considerable pressure to do so in any event. Thereby they anticipate and abort the input of demands on the part of others.

But aside from inspiration under the threat of sanctions of others, the authorities may convert wants quite independently, in response to internal moral norms that inspire them to live up to the ideal expectations of the culture with regard to what is expected of the authorities in the system. For example, the absolute monarchs of seventeenth century Europe were not entirely capricious or arbitrary in the selection of demands that they sought to fulfill. They were limited to some extent by compelling expectations of others with respect to how the authorities ought to behave. And what is true of such systems as these is equally the case, in some degree, of all political systems. In primitive systems, the paramount chief may by convention be expected to take the initiative to propose moving out of the hills down into the river valleys in simple anticipation of the dry season.

Numerous other reasons may induce the authorities to generate demands themselves and introduce them into the system for consideration according to the normal rules of the regime. The government leaders may be responding to their own image, not of what is expected of them, but of what they view in any event to be necessary. They may state demands as formal proposals for legislation if prior economic projections or developmental studies show such policies to be a necessary step in the achievement of agreed-upon ends.

At times, the authorities may simply be adjusting to the logic of previous actions which imposes upon them the need to voice certain demands. For example, a developing nation that commits itself to a large military establishment thereby sets in motion a whole chain of inescapable demands. To consummate such a policy, one or another segment of the authorities must be prepared to raise the request for a program and funds for training technological experts, for the purchase of modern equipment, for the education of medical personnel to maintain the health of the armed forces, and for equipment to make possible the use of advanced methods of communication and transportation.[8] Like so many other types of demands, the demand for a capable military force proves to be a breeder demand under modern conditions of military competition. Once it has been introduced, it gives birth to vast second and third generation sets of wants.

But whatever the source of inspiration for authorities to convert wants to demands, it is a task that is always closely associated with their roles in any system. It is easy to neglect the fact that the authorities, no less than any general or specific member of the system, are to be found among the structural regulators of the input of demands. We tend to think of them only as producers of binding decisions; but as an intrinsic part of this task, authorities at all times and places have themselves taken the initiative in proposing action.

The authorities must, therefore, be viewed as spanning the boundary between a system and its environment, on the input side. Later we shall see that they perform the same function on the output side. What this demonstrates once again is that it will not be inconsistent with our analysis to locate a structure at more than one point along the flow channels. This is just another, but theoretically more precise way, of observing that a given structure may perform many functions in a system.

In this chapter I have been identifying the gatekeepers who stand athwart the demand channels at the very beginning. Theoretically, there are many other matters regarding the gatekeepers that have to be answered before we can understand the regulative power and control of variable types of structures over the volume and content of demands.

In the first place, the number and content of wants themselves, as validated by the general culture and influenced by historical events, would determine the reservoir from which a selection could be drawn. But since we consider that wants are formed in the environment, we may take them as givens, even if these givens themselves are subject to considerable change over time.

In the second place, which of whose wants are likely to be converted, what the gatekeepers read into the situation and interpret as a want, which of these are selected for conversion, and how many they are ready to act upon and convey to the political system will depend upon more than the general structure of gatekeeping as already described.

In the third place, a number of other factors need to be taken into consideration. Among these it would be important to look at the characteristics of the gatekeepers as related to their socio-economic origins, the processes through which they arrive as gatekeepers, the ideological perspectives within which they operate, the motivations underlying their actions, the communication processes through which the wants of others may be impressed upon them, the resources for conversion at their disposal, and their differential responsiveness to the wants of others as compared to their own goals.

But among all of these factors operating on the gatekeepers, one type looms large as a major category of regulative means relevant to input overload. This is what we may call the cultural norms that inhibit or promote conversion. Without minimizing the importance of those that have just been mentioned, nevertheless many of them are themselves derivative of the kind of culture of which the gatekeepers are part. The norms act as the operating rules according to which behavior in the system is expected to take place. Which wants get through as demands and which never assume this form will therefore be decisively influenced by the kind of cultural rules prevalent in the political system. We shall concern ourselves with this in the following chapter [of *A Systems Analysis of Political Life*].

Notes

1. For a suggestive statement of the conditions under which wants are likely to be converted to demands, see W. C. Mitchell, *The American Polity* (New York: Free Press, 1962) p. 280 ff. There is an interesting and relevant discussion of the conversion process in R. E. Lane, *Political Life: Why People Get Involved in Politics* (Glencoe, Illinois: Free Press, 1959), chapters 5 and 6.
2. "In 1945 the very memory of this war was sickening, and in America there began a dash to dismantle the greatest military force the world had known. Angry mothers marched on Washington demanding that their sons be returned home ... Everywhere Americans were clamoring for an end to the austerity of war and the high cost of maintaining a large military establishment to oversee the peace. In 1946, a Congressional year, few men ran for office on platforms of continued wartime controls. By the end of that year the U.S. Army had been effectively emasculated ..." R. Leckie, *Conflict: The History of the Korean War, 1950–1953* (New York: Putnam, 1962), p. 28.
3. If we inflexibly insisted upon theoretical rigor, however artificial its outcome, we could interpret unmediated inputs as instances in which the tenders of the gates in the communication channels are maximally diffused through the system. In that event we could describe the situation as one in which virtually each person was his own gatekeeper. His actions would represent a common response to similar circumstances. Each gatekeeper could be seen as opening the gate to a similar want and converting it to an identical political slogan. But an intellectually more relaxed construction might be put upon the matter. Where popular sentiments swell to overwhelming strength in a short span of time, the gatekeepers are simply swamped in the flood of demands and find themselves helpless to stem it even if they so desired. Each person genuinely raises his voice in unison with others; the conversion of demands is direct and unmediated.
4. Cited by A. D. Lindsay, *The Modern Democratic State* (New York: Oxford University Press, 1943), vol. 1, p. 118.
5. F. M. and M. M. Keesing, *Elite Communication in Samoa* (Stanford: Stanford University Press, 1956), p. 97.
6. If we move from the theoretical to the empirical level, we have some clues as to who the converters are likely to be. Coleman refers to the fact that there is a direct relationship between the degree of involvement of members in a community and the frequency with which they raise issues. J. S. Coleman, *Community Conflict* (Glencoe, Illinois: Free Press, 1957), p. 3.

In an unpublished Master's dissertation, *The Conversion of Wants into Demands: A Theoretical Statement and An Exploratory Case Study* (University of Chicago, 1959), Elliott White reports on a study specifically directed to the problems of conversion of the kind raised in this chapter. In this study, a survey was conducted in Marshfield, a pseudonym for a small neighborhood housing development in the city of Chicago. Using this as a democratic political subsystem, White sought to discover the characteristics of those who are most likely to voice the grievances, wants and discontents of the persons of Marshfield. The developer of the community had provided for a Council, resembling a ratepayers association, with some legal powers, and it is here that grievances were typically raised and negotiated.

White found that those persons who became converters of wants held by themselves and others usually had the following characteristics. (1) The person must himself adhere to the want with a minimal intensity of conviction. Since he is not usually a professional politician he has little to gain aside from status and satisfaction of achieving his own purposes. (2) He must be able to recognize similar wants on the part of others and if he is to express their wants, he must feel that he speaks for them as well as for himself. (3) He must be able to generalize on the basis of this awareness so that the want can be validated by reference to others favoring the same one. (4) He must have such minimal knowledge of political life that he is at least aware of the fact that there are political units to which he can direct his wants. (5) He must feel efficacious, that his voice can be made to count in some way.

This study suggests that the members of the small political system under consideration who were more likely to possess these characteristics, were those who had a greater number and variety of interpersonal and organizational contacts, especially with regard to the area of life in which the wants being traced lay, that is, in the broader community adjacent to the neighborhood itself. The interpretation is that the broader the range of relevant contacts, the more likely is a person to be aware of the means available for meeting a want, to assess its possibilities realistically, and to feel able to do something about them, given the total cultural and political context. It may also enable him to anticipate wants sensitively even before those who have the needs become aware of them.

Finally, it is suggested that the skills and responses so developed by want converters tend to reinforce themselves. Habit, success and self-confidence will encourage increased reliance on such persons as gatekeepers of wants. In this way some stability for the occupant of the role of want converter ensues.

7. Cf. L. W. Pye, *Politics, Personality and Nation Building* (New Haven: Yale University Press, 1962), p. 43: "Indeed, the initiative for change [in transitional societies] more often than not comes from those in command of the arbitrarily introduced structures [of government], and instead of the government responding to pressures from the society, the process is in many respects essentially reversed."

8. F. W. Riggs, "Prismatic Society and Financial Administration," 5 *Administrative Science Quarterly* (1960) 1–46, especially on pp. 15–6.

Part Two | Concerning Models

Models are probably the central ingredients of scientific theories. Ideally, they are precise yet generalized statements about relationships among things that one can know. They are deliberately abstract, since they are statements about *aspects* of things that exist in the concrete world by lifting them out of their full embedment in a concrete setting. Models combine simplicity and a degree of completeness. They unite appreciation of the aesthetically pleasing with tough-minded search for orderliness. Finally, they are gambles: some variables are included and taken very seriously, whereas other variables are deliberately excluded, and predictions are made and checked in such a way that the inadequate model can be shown to be wrong.[1] In short, they substitute precise thinking for fuzzy thinking.

The importance of models is sometimes ignored by scientists as they become immersed in the gathering, sorting, and evaluation of data. This preoccupation can detract attention from deliberate production and utilization of theory. Twentieth-century American sociology has been timid in generating and using models. Within the social sciences, sociology lags behind economics in the production of useful models. Economic models have been quite effective in predicting trends and in helping to control large portions of economic activity in industrialized societies.

It is understandable that work with models is not the first preference of all scientists—social scientists in particular. The arbitrariness of deliberately dealing with *aspects* of reality can seem to do violence to its complexity. After all, "real life" involves exceedingly diverse, interwoven, and frequently untractable forces. Models invariably and inevitably fail to catch many of these complexities. The search for generalizations, the rigorous quest for *some* truths, may seem alien to anyone who has a sense of involvement and participation in the world. From another viewpoint, it may seem that the criteria of elegance and beauty in models belong to an unwarrantedly artistic view of science. Finally persons believe that the uncovering of truth requires not only sterilized laboratory equipment, but sterilized thinking. For these persons, models hold no charm, and most of science is cold, calculated business.

The distinction between frameworks and models is arbitrary. Both incorporate abstract categories for the purpose of demonstrating that some order exists in the real world. The distinction is useful, however, if one thinks of models as dealing with a more limited sector of reality than frameworks. This does not mean that models cannot focus on large empirical realities, such as whole societies. They are limited *conceptually*. The use of models requires a willingness to view a few interrelated assumptions very seriously, taking them as far as they will go, and at the same time holding other, possibly competing, assumptions in abeyance. An example of the distinction can be found in the field of chemistry. The periodic table is a framework; chemical formulas and equations are models. Another example, a mathematical proof, is a model of the process of getting from one level of understanding to another. Its power comes from its stark exclusion of elements not essential to arrival at a particular conclusion. By the same token, it might not be well suited to arrival at a fundamentally different conclusion.

Models need not only represent static conditions.   There are models of change involved in theories of modernization, evolution, revolution, riots, social movements, assimilation, and many other social processes.   An example of the structural character of change is clearly shown in Magoroh Maruyama's model "The Second Cybernetics," which is included in this book.[2]

MACROSCALE MODELS

Amitai Etzioni's paper, "Toward a Macrosociology," advocates the development of what might be called macro-models.   He presents a model that integrates pairs of approaches that were traditionally thought to be opposed to one another. These "opposing" approaches include (1) the view of social units as cohesive organic entities, as opposed to potentially divided social units comprised of reluctantly amalgamated individual decision-makers; and (2) the view that ascribes much social activity to inertia and uncontrollable factors as opposed to a view based on a notion of the possibility of deliberate "guidance" of social processes. Etzioni recommends that attention be given to the controlling forces that exercise power.   He also recommends analysis of participation by the people in some form of consensus (or alienation).   The cybernetic emphasis on the acquisition and utilization of information is fundamental to this approach.   Etzioni believes that his model can be used to assess objectively the effectiveness of a society's command over its own destiny.   Presumably, this development would open the way for social engineering to improve a society's potential for determining its own objectives and achieving them.

The selection by Percy Cohen, "The Two Models of Society: A Critique," presents a review of the "consensus" and "conflict" models of society.   Among sociologists, adherence to one or the other of these two models is often marked by a zealousness that leaves little room for charity toward nonbelievers.   Cohen injects a measure of balance into the picture: "to say that a room is half-full is not to deny that it is half-empty."   He finds that each model contains some discrepancies and shows that neither model totally excludes the other.   Cohen's essay reinforces the idea that models are man-made constructs that require periodic reevaluation to see whether all their components are really firmly welded together.   A scholarly dissective analysis such as Cohen's serves a useful purpose. But so does a firm embrace of a particular model.   This enables one to discover how well it will serve as a tool for generating theory.

The selections by David Easton and Anatol Rapoport are discussions about models rather than being specific substantive models themselves.   Both men discuss models in terms of general systems theory, a type of approach that is becoming increasingly popular in many sciences.   The selection by Easton, "The Environment of a Political System," deals with the specific problems of defining the boundaries and describing the environments of such systems.   This discussion highlights two very general problems in developing models: (1) The apparent boundaries may not be the real boundaries.   To decide what belongs in a system, one must deal with analytic criteria, and this focus may do violence to common-sense notions. (2) In addition, the separateness of different systems and the manner of interaction between systems depends very much on the kind of theoretical model one uses. The process of developing models is highly arbitrary.

The selection by Anatol Rapoport, "Mathematical Aspects of General Systems Analysis," emphasizes that general systems models attempt to combine two traditional points of view. One of these is the mechanistic view, which has been the source of much of the success of classical physics, largely because it lent itself to the development of a certain type of mathematics that "to this day remains *the* model of completely rigorous science." The other is the organismic view which, along with several other approaches, includes the idea that the whole is greater than the sum of its parts. Mechanism tends to be blind to "organized complexity," and to reduce complex systems to the characteristics of their component parts. Organicism, according to Rapoport, has never been able to shake off the ghost of teleology; parts are seen in terms of their contribution to a larger whole, and this contribution becomes a causal factor in the explanation of the parts themselves. Rapoport suggests that organized complexity can often be formulated in lean, precise mathematical models and that mathematics can, in turn, help to clarify analyses. In sociology, the use of mathematical models is still in its infancy. Rapoport's paper suggests that not only can mathematics be tailored to general systems theory, but that general systems theory can be tailored to sociology.

The two selections by Gerhard Lenski, "Conservatives and Radicals" and "Inequality in Industrial and Agrarian Societies," are taken from his larger study which attempts to develop a model for explaining the distributive system— "who gets what and why?"—in different societies. The main independent variable for comparing societies is the level of technological development. A variety of other social and personal features are included among the other independent variables. These include ideologies, types of political organization, demographic conditions, and others. Lenski hopes to create a bridge between the conservative and radical ideological commitments that have permeated sociological studies.

The chief reason for including these selections is that they illustrate Lenski's idea that sociological theorizing should continually alternate between deductive and inductive reasoning—between fairly audacious generalized reasoning and continuous consultation of data that may force reformulation of the theoretical scheme. In "Inequality in Industrial and Agrarian Societies" the particular formulation that is being reformulated is his own prediction that as one moves toward more technologically advanced societies one finds that social inequality decreases.

Shirley Terreberry's selection, "The Evolution of Organizational Environments," presents a model of the relationship between organizations and their environments. The emphasis is on "turbulent" environments to which organizations must, somehow, adapt. Organizational studies have traditionally focused on the dynamics within organizations. In contrast, Miss Terreberry suggests that environments of organizations can and should be analyzed. Underlying this conception is the realization that organizations can be regarded as basic component units of modern societies and, for this reason, organizations are increasingly becoming part of the environment for other organizations.

In "The Second Cybernetics" Magoroh Maruyama proposes a new cybernetic model. The earlier concept emphasized deviation-counteracting processes. That is, some sort of equilibrium tends to be maintained when, following a deviation from an existing pattern of activity, processes are set in motion to return the system to its previous state. Maruyama proposes a "second cybernetics" characterized by the process of deviation-amplification in which deviations become cumulative as sequential development takes place. Both of these, the "morphostatic" and the "morphogenetic" processes, involve a mutual causation among the component units of a system; thus no outside force need be included within the model.

Maruyama's essay is a very clear example of work with a conceptual model. He illustrates the model with drastically diverse empirical subject matter. Indeed, traditional disciplines are largely irrelevant as conceptual boundaries. All that matters is that the model and the theory be effectively illuminated. The implication is that amid the profusion of new knowledge and multiplication of disciplines, unifying theoretical approaches are possible. The essay is also a clear example of the fact that one can devise structural models that clarify many aspects of social change.

The first cybernetics, then, describes systems where deviations occur but the system counteracts them. The "second cybernetics" describes systems in which deviations find a more hospitable situation. In the latter, the deviations and other system components reinforce each other to amplify a process of development.

One can conceive of two additional types of cybernetics. In one type, deviations are not merely counteracted; they are prevented from occurring. In the second type, deviations occur and influence the system with uncontrolled abandon. When deviation is prevented it is likely that there is "dead" rigidity. One might call these systems "morphorigoric"; they are frozen to the extent that no flexibility remains. Such systems cannot take advantage of any existing deviations and they do not permit new deviations to occur. In the pattern in which deviations prevail freely, the situation is characterized by the second law of thermodynamics. This law states that in an isolated system, entropy, that is, unstructuredness or unavailable energy, tends to increase. In cybernetic terms, there are systems that appear unable to cope with deviations—they can neither prevent them, nor control them so that their impact on the system is minimized, nor harness them in a growth or other adaptive process. Instead, the deviations become dominant and create amorphousness and entropy. One might call these systems "morphentropic"; they are moving toward a state of dissolution.

Economists have been far more successful than sociologists in developing and using models on a macroscopic, that is, societal, scale. This is the reason for including the selection by Alvin H. Hansen, "The Keynesian Model." The components of this model—particularly, the proposition that massive government spending and deficits can lead to full employment—are not crucial to sociologists, although unemployment levels are socially important. The willingness and ability to isolate a few significant, interrelated, quantifiable variables are important. The manipulation of these variables can have a rational, calculable impact on major social processes. Such ideas as morphogenesis and equifinality are implicit in the Keynesian models. Some of Keynes' proposals for economic intervention amount to coaxing the society into the initial kick of morphogenetic processes.

The selection by Martin Shubik, "Simulation of Socio-Economic Systems," presents ways of simulating economic development in several Latin American countries. Unlike most purely economic models, Shubik's model includes a variety of behavioral and social policy factors. In his own words, his approach is "casual empiricism." To the sociologist it also exhibits some of the attractiveness—the potential for rigor, especially—of quantified macroscopic models.[3]

MICROSCALE MODELS

"Management Conflict and Sociometric Structure," by Harrison White, deals with conflict within one organization: a manufacturing firm that is also heavily involved in research to create new products. It offers a description of interdepartmental conflict that stems from a tug of war over competing and overlapping spheres of activity. It also provides sociometric information about contacts among persons and about the affective states that characterize these contacts. The model blends psychological features (likes, dislikes, avoidance, attraction) with social-organizational ones. It also blends "soft and hard" techniques of sensitizing interviews and relatively precise formulations of social relationships.

James Geschwender's "Continuities in Theories of Status Consistency and Cognitive Dissonance" concerns the conflicting pressures that may impinge on individuals, and their patterns of response to such pressures. Geschwender summarizes and synthesizes a body of literature that touches on this subject—literature including theories of status inconsistency, dissonance, social certitude, and expectancy congruence. For example, he considers the questions of what is likely to happen to individuals who have low ethnic status and high educational attainment or who have low educational attainment and high occupational attainment. The assumption is that "dissonance is an upsetting state and will produce tension for the individual." The resolution, in turn, is apt to follow some sort of pattern and may, therefore, take a predictable direction. This type of sociology makes the individual the focus of analysis.[4] The individual is regarded as a system that strives for some sort of equilibrium.

Theorists of this persuasion make social predictions, especially in predicting about social aggregates. But the aggregates are not fused into social systems that have emergent properties of their own.   Instead, the focus is on types of individual coping behavior, based on forms of status conflict.   Some scholars claim that this approach is essentially psychological reductionism.[5]   Yet the possibility of making predictions about social aggregates suggests that the approach has sociological relevance.

The selection by Peter Blau, "Social Exchange," is taken from his larger study, which focuses on exchange processes in social interaction.   The present selection formulates some of the major premises for the claim that many interactions among individuals can be looked upon as exchange processes.   The scheme includes a recognition of the distinction between intrinsic and extrinsic components in interactions, and a judgment of the precision with which goods are calculated. For instance, social exchanges, in contrast with economic exchanges, typically do not specify the price of the goods to be received in return for something given. Despite this difference, Blau's scheme does seem to imply an "economy" in his model of the life of the individual—there is calculation in one's interactions and there is scarcity of social resources.   Although the present selection is concerned with the individual, it must be noted that in the latter part of his study, Blau attempts to join the person-to-person model of exchange process with more macroscopic features of social organization.

Notes

1. See John R. Platt, "Strong Inference," *Science*, Vol. 146, October 16, 1964.
2. E. R. Leach is one of many scholars who have criticized structure-functionalists for their emphasis on stable equilibrium.   See E. R. Leach, *Political Systems of Highland Burma*, Cambridge, Mass.: Harvard University Press, 1954, pp. 7 ff.
3. For additional models of economic development that appear to have potential for sociologists, see Irma Adelman and Erik Thorbecke, eds., *The Theory and Design of Economic Development*, Baltimore: Johns Hopkins Press, 1966.
4. Phenomenological sociology places an even greater emphasis on models that focus on the individual and his way of seeing the world around him.   See, for example, Aaron V. Cicourel, *Methods and Measurement in Sociology*, New York: Free Press, 1964.
5. For an eloquent attack on psychological reductionism, see Rodney Needham, *Structure and Sentiment: A Test Case in Social Anthropology*, Chicago: University of Chicago Press, 1960. This book is a critique of George C. Homans and David M. Schneider, *Marriage, Authority, and Final Causes: A Study of Unilateral Cross-Cousin Marriage*, Glencoe, Ill.: Free Press, 1955.   Psychological reductionism is the subject of considerable debate among sociologists and anthropologists.

Macroscale Models

10 . Toward a Macrosociology[1]
Amitai Etzioni

INTRODUCTION

A macrosociology is needed both on theoretical and on pragmatic grounds. Theoretically I suggest societies and polities have *emergent* properties, which it is fruitful to treat as the subject of a distinct subtheory, macrosociology. Such a theory is not to replace general theory, which deals with the *universal* properties of all social units, from the dyad to the world community (e.g., level of integration). But both macro- and micro-sociology are additional tiers on the top of this shared base, one dealing with the particular properties of macro-units (e.g., nations, classes), the other with properties of micro-units, such as family, work teams, and friendship groups. While sociological theory holds for general, micro- and macro-sub-theories, history is a macroscopic process. It is on this level that sociological and historical perspectives can be authentically and systematically joined.

From a pragmatic viewpoint, a disciplined study of the substantive problems of society—such as modernization, democratization, change of status relations among major collectivities, societal reallocation of wealth, and political integration of previous autonomous units—cannot be much advanced without a systematic analysis of macroscopic factors.

From R. William Millman and Michael P. Hottenstein (eds.), *Promising Research Directions: Papers and Proceedings of the 27th Annual Meeting of the Academy of Management* (Washington, D.C., December 1967), pp. 12–33, by permission of the Academy of Management.

The most basic distinction here, for reasons that will become evident below, is between guided and ongoing change. The higher the ratio of guided change over ongoing change, the greater the danger of rebellion of instrumentality against the primacy of societal goals, and that collectivities whose vested interests rest in the realm of instruments might divert societal guidance to serve their goals. Hence, as has often been pointed out but never made the cornerstone of a sociological theory, the key problem of guided change is the development of more effective methods of societal guidance that will ensure the primacy of societal goals.

I. A MACROSOCIOLOGICAL PERSPECTIVE

1. MACROSOCIOLOGY DEFINED

We suggest that macroscopic (social) units have emergent properties, above and beyond those of microscopic (social) units and beyond universal social properties. One can support this suggestion on tentative pragmatic grounds: let us try it out and see if it will enable us to gain some insight into substantive societal problems. One can further support the suggestion on empirical logical grounds: that macroscopic emergent properties account for a significant part of the variance of sociological data; i.e., explanation of those data cannot be reduced, without a significant residue or unaccounted variance, to propositions drawing only on microscopic or universal properties. Finally, it can be supported on mere logical grounds: a three-level referent structure—of units, sub-units, and supra-units—can be applied at any level of analysis, e.g., roles, families, and neighborhoods. There is in principle no reason why one cannot apply the same structure to societies, sub-societies, and supra-societies. Thus, this differentiation is a private case of a universe of formal, hierarchical relations.

Whatever track one follows, the units of analysis need to be substantively designated. In doing so we adhere to a functional approach in that acts are defined as macroscopic if their consequences are macroscopic, i.e., affect the properties of macroscopic units. An act, let us say a peasant uprising, is in itself neither micro- nor macroscopic; its consequences might be both microscopic (a few families were destroyed) and macroscopic (a change of political institutions and stratification was forced). The same act might thus be studied from both viewpoints. However, because of the hierarchical nature of the concepts, while acts that have macroscopic consequences always also have microscopic ones, those with microscope consequences may or may not have macroscopic ones. (Some cutoff point in time is always to be specified because in the long run there might be consequences to consequences that would move from the microscopic to the macroscopic level.) Macroscopic theory deals with the acts that have macroscopic consequences and with the relations of these consequences to each other, not exploiting their microscopic effects as long as they, in turn, do not have macroscopic consequences within the period specified.

We characterize social units according to where the majority of their consequences lie. Macroscopic units are those whose primary acts effect changes in properties of societies, sub-societies, or supra-societies. General Motors is macroscopic for American society; the Chinese restaurant next door probably is not. Families are usually not macroscopic, but that of an absolute ruler is. Units that are part of the referent framework—societies, sub-societies, and supra-societal units—are macroscopic by definition. Small groups—such as families, teams, friendship groups—are the units of microsociology.

2. TWO KINDS OF REDUCTIONISM

Two kinds of reductionism are prevalent in the social sciences. One reduces social or political analysis to the level of a universal theory of action or to psychology. This reductionism in effect denies both sociology and political science as distinct theoretical disciplines. It is widely embraced by philosophers, anthropologists, and psychologists. Sociologists and political scientists tend naturally to profess to realize that their disciplines require a distinct theory, but their actual analyses are often—and, it seems, increasingly—psychological or draw entirely on universal variables. This is particularly common in studies that use survey data about attitudes of individuals, e.g., studies of political sociology that deal only with aggregate data about various categories of voters, explaining their voting by attitudes they hold (e.g., on a conservatism-liberalism scale) or personality variables (e.g., degree of authoritarianism). The explanatory processes are clearly intra-personal. For instance, an individual who holds one attitude will tend to hold others that are consonant because dissonant attitudes cause a psychic cost or pain; or, aggressive attitudes toward foreigners fulfill a superego need. While various procedures for transition from such data to social analysis and suggestions for combination of such data with "global" data about the social units themselves have been advanced,[2] most studies do not carry out such analysis.

The second kind of reductionism is to microsociology, on the ground that micro- and macro-sociological theories are isometric and hence studying small groups will provide all the theoretical statements needed to understand relations among macroscopic variables (e.g., studies of cohesion of small groups are used to explain class solidarity), or else the existence of macroscopic emergent properties is *a priori* denied. The reductionism from macrosociology to microsociology, which has already been forcefully called to our attention,[3] is much less widely acknowledged by the majority of sociologists and political scientists who work with empirical data than is psychological reductionism. Here, it is not just a matter of a threshold that is disregarded in actual research, but one whose very claim is questioned.[4]

3. SUBSTANTIVE ASSUMPTIONS

Those engaged in macro-theory tend to follow one or two major approaches to what substantive assumptions are to be made about the nature of the macroscopic units, their properties, and their dynamics. We suggest a combination of the two approaches and add a third ingredient. Before we turn to explore these approaches, the criteria used for differentiation among them are briefly noted.

We are interested in developing a general theory for macroscopic (social) change, which is a formal concept for socio-political (or societal) history. Societal change, obviously, is affected both by factors which the participants control and by those beyond their control, a mix of guided and ongoing change. *The approaches under discussion differ in the assumptions they make about the ratio of one kind of change as against the other.* The collectivistic theories see chiefly ongoing changes; voluntaristic ones focus on guided change. The collectivistic view of society—as an actor oriented toward itself—is rather passive; the voluntaristic is hyper-active. A third approach, which we favor, balances these two approaches.

We are dealing here with analytic languages (or meta-theories), each one of which is used to formulate several theories. As we are concerned only with laying bare their most basic assumptions, no attempt is made to do justice to any specific theory or to assumptions concerning other dimensions than the one explored: their position toward societal change.

Sociologists are most familiar with collectivistic theories. Social system theories, functionalist models, anthropological-cultural theories of configuration as well as phenomenological ones are collectivistic and basically passive. They do not recognize systematically a seat of action on the macroscopic, societal level. Scanning major theoretical writings of these traditions shows that concepts such as goals, knowledge, decision-making, and strategies—all typical concepts needed to characterize an actor who guides a change process—are absent or appear only infrequently and mainly in relation to micro-units and not macroscopic ones. The typical society under study is treated as if it had no government, and political processes are described only as ongoing.

Differentiation is representative of many other theories that could be utilized as an example. The concept is increasingly used over recent years by Parsons, Smelser, Eisenstadt, and others,[5] to relate societal change to functional-structural analysis. The core-image which is typical of the collectivistic approach, is taken from biology, where we find "simple" units that split into two or more, each one more "specialized" than the previous. All the functions carried out by the simple unit are also carried out by the differentiated ones, except that now each of the functions has a substructure of its own, a "differentiated" unit. Most biological studies do not ask what propels the transition, or to what degree the transition may be guided by a unit other than units which are being differentiated. Those who did raise those questions in biology dealt with the function of codes in guiding the transition from a simple to a differentiated unit. The code, which is found in the undifferentiated unit, holds in an "abstracted" form (as information pattern or model) a full differentiated design of the future unit toward which the simple unit is to evolve. Research focuses on what the code specifically contains and how its "messages" are transmitted to the evolving unit.[6] In sociology so far, by and large the question which the conception of a code answers for biology, i.e., what guides differentiation, has not been raised. The patterns of societal differentiation and its *consequences* are studied, but [not] its guidance mechanism.[7] In other words, the process is viewed as ongoing and the unit merely subject to it, i.e., as passive.

The voluntaristic approach is almost unknown in contemporary sociology. Voluntarism was quite influential in political science until recently, especially in the study of international relations between the two world wars and in studies of administration or formal organizations.[8] It is at the heart of "general system" theories, cybernetics, and communication theories. The central assumption of this approach, often implicit, is that there is a central unit that is able to guide the other member units of the particular system and more or less control them in accordance with its will. The voluntaristic theories divide sharply according to their assumptions about the nature of this will (and central unit) and its "ties" to the other units. Some assume a rationalistic model, others an irrational one, but all share a view of a highly active guiding mechanism.

One of the best known voluntaristic-rationalistic models is the legal-constitutional approach to societal change. Its adherents hold that new societal systems, e.g., unions of states, can be generated by forming a constitution or revising it, and that societal structure, e.g., the steepness of the stratification, can be drastically altered by legislation. The 1789 meeting in Independence Hall in Philadelphia is viewed as having created an American polity out of a confederation, and enactment of inheritance and progressive tax laws is expected to level economic differences, just as Civil Rights Acts are believed to be a major instrument for desegregation. Without asking here if and under what conditions these assumptions are valid, the model of societal change used should be noted. It is that of a group of sensible leaders—Founding Fathers, Congress—who, having examined a problem and found a solution, bring it into being by their action. A limited degree of "unanticipated consequences" is anticipated, but distortion of processes due to latent dysfunctions, replacement of goals, and above all, failure to proceed significantly due to resistance of the body of society, are not part of this view. It had direct parallels in the scientific management school and "formal organizational" theory, where managements draw up blueprints and charts and implement them.[9]

For our purposes, one rationalistic-voluntaristic model is of particular interest for reasons that will become evident below, namely the cybernetic model. The source of the model, it is important to realize, is the mechanical guidance of machines, that is, the development of machines that take over control functions the way "lower order" machines, the supervised ones, took over earlier performance ("work") functions. The cybernetics model most frequently applied entails a decision-making center, and a communication network that carries the messages from the center to the units under supervision and feedback messages from the units to the center. The underlying assumption of the model, is that in principle the center can guide the system. "Disturbances" are recognized, e.g., over-loading of the decision-making center; various solutions are worked out assessing priorities to messages. Similarly, gaps in the communication networks might appear, let us say, due to poor relay, and correction is provided (e.g., by including redundant lines).

When this model is applied to societal analysis, the government is viewed as the cybernatorial overlayer of society which provides it with a decision-making center, a communication network to member units, and feedback mechanisms. One of the most distinguished and influential political scientists of this generation, Karl W. Deutsch, has developed this application of the cybernatorial model.[10]

The irrational-voluntaristic model is held mainly by psycho-analysts who write about societies, some psychologists, and a few anthropologists.[11] The tendency is to view society as man writ large, each society interacting with other societies basically the way one individual interacts with others. For instance, the United States and the Soviet Union misunderstand each other, which leads to frustration, which generates aggression, etc. Improved communication between the sides is expected to increase their reality-testing and cooperation. Charles E. Osgood, a former President of the American Psychological Association, is one of the best known representatives of this approach.[12] While it is diametrically opposed to the rationalistic approach in terms of the substantive assumptions about the mechanisms at work, which here are subconscious and emotional, the parallelism is complete as this voluntarism too views society as basically acting as a mono-lithic unit, being able to change, for instance, from a hostile to a cooperative mood as if it had one will.[13]

All the voluntaristic approaches see one main seat of action, and in principle recognize no limitations to "Man's," i.e., society's, capacity to change. In that sense they are all hyperactive, because these theories do not include as an integral part variables that can account for the forces that resist change, that block or distort implementation of the will.

4. TOWARD A SYNTHETIC APPROACH

We suggest that a synthesis of the collectivistic approach, which in effect focuses upon *ongoing* processes and change, and a voluntaristic-cybernatorial approach, largely concerned with *guided* processes and change, would provide for a more balanced theory of societal change, especially of modern societies in which both kinds of changes are prevalent. It also balances the non-rational focus of the collectivistic approach, which tends to stress the study of societal ties of senti-ments and values, with the rationalistic perspective cybernetics often exhibits. A third major element that both approaches tend to neglect is added, that of a conception and theory of power.[14] By power we mean a relational attribute which indicates the capacity of one unit to overcome the resistance of the other(s).[15]

The central position of power for our theory is manifest in our seeing in each society (and in each societal unit) an internal struggle between the guidance mechanisms and the passive elements, and not just an external, interunit struggle. The outcome of this struggle significantly determines the capacity of a societal unit to act upon itself (to effect its own change) as well as to act externally and hence also to influence the patterns of the supra-unit of which it is a unit. Supra-units are composed of units that have at least some cybernatorial capacities and power, as well as having, in principle, some such capacities and power of their own, on the supra-unit level.

The collectivistic approach sees the members of the collectivity, configuration, or system as closely tied to each other. While some leeway or "play" is recognized, basically units cannot be moved around or changed unless other units change more or less simultaneously. If they do not, various pathologies are expected, described in such concepts as social lag and imbalance.[16] And, as no guidance center is assumed—a center whose assumption would entail also assuming moveable and changeable, less "tied" units—the question of the source of the capacity to transform the units or the ties does not arise. Power has at best a marginal, external role and a theoretical status. As a matter of fact, most collectivistic theories do not include the concept of power at all, while in others it is tacked on, *post hoc*.

The voluntaristic cybernatorial model stresses the importance of communication and information, the manipulation of symbols, and largely excludes power other than that involved in manipulation of symbols. No resistance of the units is in principle expected. It focuses on the problems of generating well-calculated messages, of relaying the messages from the center of the units, and of providing reliable feedbacks, but once the messages reach the performing units, no power is assumed necessary to overcome their resistance to the message. If the feedback indicates that the message did not trigger the expected action, the assumption is that the message was inappropriate (and the effective center is expected to revise it) or was distorted on its way because of communication difficulties, not that the message was appropriate and was "read" loudly and clearly, but was not backed up by enough power. Symbols, changes in patterns of information or meaning are transmitted, not power;[17] it is a matter of the nerves, not the muscles of government.[18]

Rather than characterizing our approach as one of collectivistic-voluntaristic power analysis, we shall refer to it as cybernatorial sociology or *sociobernetics*. (Cybernetics is the one voluntaristic tradition we attempt to synthesize with a social-collectivistic perspective.) While the term violates one rule of linguistics, it meets another well; although we drop one syllable of a root word, the resulting term is more euphonious than sociocybernetics. We shall attempt here and in future work to lay out the main elements of such a theory.[19]

While sociobernetics thus draws on both the collectivistic and the voluntaristic approaches, it differs significantly on one major dimension from both—it does *not* assume that the societal unit it deals with is a monolithic or highly integrated unit. Authors of both traditions have argued that this assumption is just a heuristic device, a standard against which reality can be measured, and not an assumption about the nature of reality itself.[20] However, even for those who remember that they are dealing only with a heuristic device, these models introduce the mistaken perspective that deviations from the standard are pathological, limited, and correctable; and they provide no model for the study of low integration or low compliance situations, which are abundant.   We assume no particular relationship between the societal actors under study.   The actors might relate to each other completely externally without any shared bonds, a situation approximated by nations in a state of all-out war.   Or, the actors might be related by complementary or shared interests, which bind them with ties that are limited to the transactions themselves and which are inherently unstable, because changes in the environment or in the actors that will change the interests concerned will lead to an abandonment of the relationship.   Further the actors might be bound by shared values and institutionalized norms, which bind in a more "generalized" and stable way because commitments are non-rational and may have a moral force.

Relations might be classified accordingly as coercive, utilitarian, or normative. It should be stressed that while there are symbolic elements in all three kinds of relationships (e.g., threats to use force play an important role in coercion), and one—normative—is a relationship where the primary link is symbolic, the core of the other two relationships is non-symbolic.   Utilitarian relationships draw heavily on interests and material objects, and besides the symbolic relation to the object (as has been stressed in the institutions of property), the nature and the distribution of the objects themselves are of much importance.   The same holds for means of violence as the basis of coercive relations; too much has been made by contemporary sociologists of the symbolic elements of legitimation in the concept of authority and too little of the other component, the actual capacity to use force.

We have argued elsewhere that these three kinds of relationships are analytically exhaustive, i.e., that every concrete relationship can be analytically classified in terms of various combinations of these three basic ones.   The threefold conception of bases of societal order seems to answer the criticism raised by Dahrendorf and others on the symbolistic and non-conflict nature of prevailing sociological theory.[21]   It should be noted that each of these relationships can be either horizontal or hierarchical, i.e., a relationship either of actors having similar values, interests, or force, or of actors that are subject to an actor who has power of one kind or another over them.   All the members of a cohesive group are committed to each other, but the commitments of leaders and followers are asymmetric. Exchange between roughly equal units, and between those which are not, is basically different.   This difference between hierarchical and horizontal interactions, neglected in many traditional as well as more recent writings, is central to the present approach.

5. SYSTEM, STRUCTURE, AND TRANSFORMABILITY

Over the last decades the term system has been applied increasingly loosely, to a degree that it has lost an essential quality of a concept, the ability to differentiate one referent from another. There is no relationship which has not been at one point or another directly or by implication characterized as a social system, including the relationships between the drivers of cars on the freeway. The essence of the concept as used in sociology, it seems, is collectivistic; no relationship makes a system unless there are non-trivial feedback effects among the members. If half of the American housewives were to have a cup of change-of-pace tea instead of another cup of coffee, the Brazilian economy would be damaged. This does not make the distinguished ladies and the Brazilian coffee plantations one system, however, because what happens to the Brazilian economy will not have significant feedback effects on the American housewives.

We see three kinds of relations: *situations* in which there are inter-unit relations but no feedback loops; *systems* which assume non-trivial interdependence among the member units; and *communities* which assume an integrative supra-unit capacity. Each of these three concepts covers a sector of a "closeness"-of-interaction continuum, and hence within each sector one might refer to more or less "tight" relationships (e.g., more vs. less integrated units).

A system might be a relatively concrete concept referring to relations among units of action—tribes, nations, organized classes—or a relatively abstract one, referring to relations among variables. Systems of either kind have boundaries which should not be confused with their structures. Boundaries determine which unit or variable is a member and which is not; structures characterize the specific pattern of relationship among the members. Boundaries change much less frequently than structures; the same system may have, over time, many structures.

Societal units whose structure includes an overlayer can partially guide the change of their *non-societal* situation, their relations to other actors, and their own internal structure. Relatively passive actors are those who react to environmental changes more than they introduce changes in their environment. They adapt by changing their internal makeup, but the nature of their adaptation is itself often affected by external factors, including more active societal units. More active units are more able to initiate change both in themselves and in their environments, in accordance with their preferences.

Second, relatively passive units tend to be *ultra-stable*, in the sense that when challenged they tend to introduce variants of the existing structure, attempting to maintain the same basic institutional solutions. More active units have a *self-transforming capacity*, i.e., they can create on the cybernatorial level a map of a not-yet existing future-system, and guide their self-change toward the realization of a new structure, which is not a variation of the existing one but a basically new pattern. This capacity allows them to (a) adapt successfully to a much larger variety of environmental changes, (b) participate much more actively in changing the environment, and (c) actualize more of their own values. The study of the conditions under which the capacity for self-transformation increases and of the elements involved is an integral part of sociobernetics; it ties systematically the study of encompassing societal changes, planned and unplanned, to structural-functional analysis.

The tension between ongoing processes and guided ones is central to the study of sociobernetics.   To realize his values, an actor seeks to guide processes; but in doing so he faces the constraining effects of other actors in the situation, his system- or community-ties to others, and the institutionalized consequences of both his and their earlier actions.[22]

The degree to which an actor is active depends on his cybernatorial capacities, his power, and his consensus-formation capacity.   Each one of these factors has both an internal and an external dimension; how much he knows about himself and about others, how much he can mobilize power over members *and* over non-members, to what degree he can gain the support of sub-units and of external units.   As for many purposes it is useful to refer to both cybernatorial and power capacities together, we shall refer to them jointly as his ability to *control*.   When his skill in mobilizing consensus is also taken into account, we refer to his ability to guide.   As we grant to the sub-units and other units in principle the same capacities as to the actor under study, his capacity to be active is obviously not optimized by maximizing his control capacities but by optimizing the combination of control and consensus formation—that is, by maximizing the capacity of his guidance mechanisms.

We turn now to explore these factors in some detail.   Our approach is at first analytic, in that each factor is explored as if all the others were held constant; in the following section we shall take a more synthesizing and historical view of actors that are becoming more active generally, on all major dimensions.   In the analytic section we compare briefly both societies and sub-societies.   (Supra-societies are not discussed here.)   The societies we focus on are political—that is, encapsulated in a state which serves as their organizational tool for both control and consensus formation.   Similarly, the sub-societal actors are collectivities that have organizational "arms," such as working classes which have labor parties and unions.   Collectivities which have not been organized are treated mainly for comparative purposes.

The purpose of the following discussion is strictly to illustrate the kind of factors our theory focuses on and not to provide here a set of propositions (not to mention data) in support of the theory.   The statements, however, have the basic structure of propositions; each proposes that if all other conditions were equal, a change of the specific variable discussed would correlate in the way specified with the active capacity of the unit under study.

II. CONTROL FACTORS

1. CYBERNATORIAL CAPACITIES

Knowledge input.   Societal units differ in their capacity to collect, process, and use information.   This holds not only for corporations that compete over a market, but also for political parties (Kennedy is believed to have used social sciences more effectively than Nixon in the 1960 campaign), federal agencies (the Air Force is thought to be superior in this respect to the Navy and the Army), and civic organizations (the NAACP's capacity to use information has increased between 1955 and 1965).

The input of knowledge into a societal unit follows, we suggest, the same basic patterns other inputs do; that is, it might be blocked (and hence partially or completely lost for action purposes) at each stage of the process. Societal units have varying facilities for collecting information ("raw material" input). This capacity seems to be associated with economic affluence but not in a one-to-one relationship. If we were to order countries (or other societal units) by their income per capita and then score their information collection capacity, e.g., in terms of expenditure on research, we expect the most affluent units would have much higher capacity than the next affluent ones, and all the other units would have few such capacities at all. Three powerful federal agencies in the U.S. spent more of the federal research-and-development (R. & D.) funds than the other 34 agencies together. Three affluent states out of 50 gain more than 50% of these R. & D. funds.[23] Societal units that spend highly on information spent more in the last generation than in all previous generations combined. In short, patterns of inter-unit distribution of information seem significantly more inegalitarian than are those of distribution of economic assets.

The ratio of investment in *collecting* over *processing* information is an indicator of the sophistication of the cybernatorial overlayer and the knowledge-strategy to which the particular unit subscribes. The U.S. and Great Britain, it seems, tend to invest relatively highly in collection; France, at least until recently, has stressed relatively more processing.[24] A societal unit that emphasizes disproportionally the collection of information will, we expect, have a fragmented view of itself and its environment; it will have many bits but no picture, like a survey study before tabulation. Such processing, we suggest, will tend to be associated with drifting (or passivity) as information that is not sufficiently processed is in effect not available for active societal guidance.

On the other hand, a unit that overemphasizes *processing* is expected to have an "unempirical" view of itself and its environment, because it will tend to draw more conclusions from the available information than are warranted; it is similar to acting on the basis of a poorly validated theory. Thus, overprocessing is expected to be associated with hyperactivity, as the actor assumes he knows more than he does. Master plans used to guide economic development are typically hyperactive in their assumptions. Finally, societal units whose collection and processing are relatively balanced (not in absolute amounts but in terms of intrinsic needs of the guidance mechanisms) are expected to have comparatively more effective controlling overlayers, all other things being equal, and to be active without being hyperactive.

Information that has been processed might still be wasted as far as the societal unit is concerned if it is not *systematically introduced into the unit's decision-making and implementation overlayer*,[25] where the main societal "consumption" of information takes place. Two major variables seem useful for characterizing the different arrangements societal units have for interaction between the knowledge-producing and the decision-making units; one concerns the relative degree of autonomy of production, the other, the effectiveness of communications of the "product." It is widely believed that structural differentiation between the producers and consumers of information is necessary; fusion of the two kinds of units—for instance, in the management of a corporation—is viewed as dysfunctional both for production of knowledge and for decision-making. For societal units whose knowledge and decision-making units are differentiated, various modes and forms of articulation and communication exist whose relative effectiveness remains to be explored. Here we can touch on only one aspect of this intricate subject.

The controlling overlayer itself has layers upon layers; processing is superimposed on the collecting of information, both in the logical sense that the one presupposes the other, and in the structural sense that those engaged in processing have higher ranks and more power to mold the societal input of knowledge than those who collect information.[26] Differences in the internal *structure* of the control overlayer affect the total action capacity of societal units. The division between those who work within a given knowledge framework and those who seek to transform it, and the structural relations between them, seem to be of much cybernatorial importance. Consumption and, to a degree, processing of knowledge are inevitably in part political processes. That is, which part of the available knowledge is used and what conclusions are reached on the basis of the knowledge is in part determined by political factors. These include considerations of the knowledge-producers in terms of the internal politics of the organizations in which knowledge is processed, their affiliations with political groupings in the society at large; and the differential absorption by various political actors of the knowledge produced, according to its political rather than intrinsic value. The core of the politicization of knowledge lies not in deliberate or subconscious slanting of facts but in the interpretive and judgmental elements most items of knowledge include. It is not, as some students of administration would have it, that knowledge-units simply produce information and the political decision-making elites add the judgment. The producers of knowledge play an active role in formulating the judgments.

Within this context, one issue is of special significance for the study of sociobernetics: the effect of the relative investments in two sections of the cybernatorial overlayer—viz., transforming versus "stable" knowledge production. Transforming knowledge re-checks and potentially challenges the basic assumptions of a system. "Stable" knowledge elaborates and re-specifies, even revises, secondary assumptions within the framework of a basic set which is taken for granted. Most decision-making elites most of the time seem to prefer "stable" over transforming knowledge production, to seek closure on basic knowledge assumptions precisely because they cannot be selected and reviewed on wholly empirical grounds. Hence, once consensus has been reached on the basic assumptions of a world view, a self-view, a view of others, strategic doctrine, etc., it is expensive politically, economically, and psychologically for the elites to transform these assumptions. They hence tend to become *tabooed* assumptions, and knowledge production to become limited to specifics within the limits of the assumptions.   At the same time, the ability to transform basic perspectives is sharply reduced and with it the capacity for *societal* self-transformation.   The societal units survive as long as the range of tolerance of their knowledge and societal pattern allows for sufficient adaption to environmental changes, but such adaptation tends to become increasingly costly.

More active units have supra-layers that can be activated to review and transform tabooed assumptions.   A comparison of corporations that have shifted to a new line of products, re-structured their internal organization, and found new markets when their old markets were gradually lost, with those whose sales and profits declined or "died" because of lack of innovations, suggests that transforming corporations maintained R. & D. units which were not only exempt from the tabooed assumptions but were also, among other things, expected sporadically to review these assumptions.   That is, part of their institutionalized role was to engage in "search" behavior precisely where the decision-making elites would otherwise settle for "satisfying" solutions.[27]

The societal parallel of this cybernatorial arrangement is not difficult to see. The intellectual community acts as one major societal R. & D. unit, as a critical examiner of tabooed assumptions.   Under what economic, political, and sociological conditions it can fulfill this function and what, if any, functional alternatives exist are questions social scientists have much feeling about—but there is surprisingly little systematic research.[28]

These questions can be studied for any society and any societal unit.   As the input of knowledge becomes a major *guided* societal activity (more than 75 per cent of expenditure of the R. & D. funds is federal), as the ratio of this input as compared to other societal inputs is increasing, both in relative expenditure and in socio-political importance, the macrosociology of knowledge becomes an unavoidable part of studies of societal change.   Typically, earlier studies of a society stressed the size of its population, territory, and GNP; the present approach adds the number of Ph.D.'s a society "turns out," the size of its professional manpower, and its investment in research and development as indicators of a major societal variable.   Sociology of knowledge traditionally focused on the social conditions under which true statements are made;[29] macrosociology of knowledge focuses on the societal conditions under which knowledge for societal purposes is produced and consumed, opening a whole new field of inquiry for study of societies.[30]

2. SOCIETAL DECISION-MAKING

The head of the societal control overlayer is a decision-making elite—the socio-political equivalent of the electronic center.   The elites choose between alternative policies, issue signals to the performing units (guide the underlayer), and respond to feedback information.   (The body of the overlayer is made up of communication networks which tie elites to other member units and a power hierarchy.)   Sociologists have studied elites by asking how "closed" versus "open" they are to members of various societal units, how dispersed control is among them, and how they relate to each other.   But these are not cybernatorial considerations.   They belong under the heading of consensus-formation (e.g., closed and completely open elites are believed less effective for consensus formation than relatively open ones) and the study of power relations (e.g., hierarchy plus decentralization is believed more effective than monopolization of control by one elite or its fragmentation among several).   Cybernatorial aspects of elites have been studied largely by non-sociologists and have not been systematically related to analysis.[31]   The cybernatorial study of elites concerns the procedures used by the decision-making elites, the strategies employed, and the communication networks that lead from the elites to the performing units and back.

When elites engage in decision-making they draw on an implicit or explicit societal theory as to what the relations among the units under control are like, and as to how much and by what means these can be guided by the elites.[32]   The validity of these theories varies from elite to elite; the greater the validity, the more effective one would expect the decision-making to be, which in turn is positively associated with the degree to which a social unit is active.   This proposition is not earthshaking, nor are many other ones concerning the conditions under which decision-making is effective.   However, the inclusion or omission from a societal theory of a set of propositions about effective decision-making is of much importance.   It is indicative of a central position regarding the nature of society and of societal change.

In seeking to explain the action or change of a societal unit, most sociologists are more inclined to explore "background" conditions, from the level of economic resources the unit commands to the educational opportunities of elite members, than to study the decision-making procedures the elites follow.   There is a widely held assumption that such "background" factors constitute the basic substructure which both sets the main limits of variability of societal action and change (e.g., poor countries lack the capital needed to develop) and specifies the main factors which determine what divisions will be made among whatever options are left open (e.g., because of the revolution of rising expectations democratic elites cannot defer an increase in consumption).   Differences in decision-making procedures are considered either "dependent" variables or trivial.   In comparison, sociobernetics views the societal actors as having more autonomy.   "Background" factors are viewed as setting a broad frame; which course is followed within its limits is affected by cybernatorial factors, among which decision-making procedures are significant elements.   An effective elite might defer consumption increase in a poor country, and thereby lead toward a stable development.

Actually many of the undeveloped nations are not poor in resources or overpopulated, but poor in cybernatorial capacities, among which the quality of their elites ranks high in importance.   For instance, in 1930 the economic indicators of Canada and Argentina were similar.[33]   Canada since then has continued to develop, while Argentina remains underdeveloped.   A typical "background" conditions approach would stress the presence of the Protestant element in the one country and its absence in the other, as well as the differences in the Catholic stock in the two countries (in Argentina it is more that of Southern Spain and

Italy, in Canada that of the French). These differences are expected, a la Weber, to correlate with attitudes favorable to capitalism.

An elite study would add the difference between the responsive-democratic government of Canada and the authoritarian leadership of Argentina. True, this difference in leadership is in part due to differences in societal structure; e.g., Canada would not "tolerate" a Peron. But unless one assumes a one-to-one relationship between background factors and elite conduct and assumes that elite conduct has no significant independent effect on background factors, the analysis of the nature of the elites has to be included as an integral part of a theory of societal processes. It suffices to contrast the development of each country under different governments following different decision-making procedures, e.g., Peron and Illia in Argentina, to highlight the importance of systematically including the study of elites.

One typical decision societal elites in charge of guided change often have to make, at what are relatively critical turning points, is between acceleration and deceleration of the processes of change they guide. When a societal change is initiated—whether it be collectivization of farms, federation, or desegregation—resistance tends to accumulate because existing patterns are backed up by vested interests which are often threatened by the changes. As a change advances there is often at least one critical turning point at which resistance rises to a point where it endangers the control of the elites. The President thinks he might not be re-elected, the government believes it might be overthrown, or a part of the country might secede. The decision the elites then face is between acceleration, in hope of "overpowering" the opposition and reaching a stage at which the support of those that will benefit from the new pattern will rise, or slowing down to give more time for the opposition to be worked out, circumvented, educated, or otherwise dealt with.

Obviously the question is not which one procedure or strategy is in the abstract the more effective; the question is under what societal conditions one is more effective than the other *and* under what conditions an elite chooses the suitable, as against the unsuitable, strategy. In a comparative study of four cases we found two elites that accelerated and two that decelerated in face of a "premature" situation, i.e., a situation where opposition was high and forces in support of the change weak. The accelerating elites lost control (in the UAR Syria rebelled and seceded; the West Indian Federation was disbanded). The decelerating elites are still in control, though in one of the two cases (the Scandinavian system) the elite had to decelerate so much that the process of change (unification) came to a standstill, while only in the fourth case (the European Economic Community) was continuation of the process assured by deceleration.[34]

Other societal decisions, often debated ideologically but rarely studied analytically and systematically, concern the conditions of militancy versus moderation, or confrontation versus coalition politics, and the wholistic versus the gradualist approach. These and similar strategic decisions draw on explicit or implicit theories about the nature of societal linkages and control factors, such as how far a government can be relied upon as an agent of transformation, what will be the result of mass activation of apathetic publics, or how much will "spillover" in one societal sector generate change in others. Here lies the main link between the study of societal decision-making and of societal input of knowledge.

The quality of decision-making gains in importance the more active a societal unit is by other criteria. Obviously the more activated a unit is and the more assets it has, the more advantages it can gain by effective use of them, and the more it can waste them if it uses them ineffectively. For passive units, which barely guide their own processes, "background" factors are of much importance; for units that react more creatively to their environmental as well as to internal challenges, it is the quality of decision-making that is of much importance. Under what structural conditions elites make more effective decisions, all other conditions being equal, is a question that has been barely explored sociologically.

Cybernatorial factors other than processing of information and decision-making include various attributes of societal goals, such as the clarity of their formulation, and the degree of compatability of the various goals a unit pursues. Also important is the quality of the communication networks that lead from the decision-making elites to the performance units and back, including number and intensity of gaps, "noise" on the line, etc. As our purpose here is not to list all these factors, but to illustrate the main categories, we turn now from cybernatorial factors to the second element of control, power.

3. CONTROL: POWER, ITS SOURCES AND ITS MOBILIZATION

Societal Assets and Power. Societal structures are not just patterns of interaction of actors, patterns of expectations and symbols, but also patterns of allocation of societal assets, the possessions of a societal unit. These can be classified analytically as coercive, utilitarian, and normative, concerning respectively the distribution of means of violence, material objects and services, and symbols. A measure of the assets a societal unit or sub-unit possesses is *not* in itself an indication of its actual power, but only of its *potential.* Assets might be used to generate more assets, be consumed or stored, *or* used to overcome the resistance of other actors, which is what by definition societal power means. (This does not mean necessarily to force other actors; their resistance might be overcome, for instance, by offering a pay-off.) In exploring the relations between assets and power, it is essential not to shift the frame of reference in mid-analysis. Conversion of assets into power in time one might lead to more assets in time two; in time one, however, the generation of power entails a "loss" of assets.

A central predisposition of sociobernetics is that the relationship between assets and power is a "loose" one—that is, the amount of assets allocated to a societal unit in a given structure is a poor predicator of how much societal power the unit will have. The amount of power generated depends significantly on the intra-unit allocation of the assets among alternative usages. A unit poor in assets can in principle command more power than a much more affluent one, if the poor unit assigns more of its assets to power "production." (With half the GNP, the U.S.S.R. maintains a defense budget similar to that of the U.S.)

What fraction of the assets a unit possesses is converted into power is itself influenced by the societal context and not freely set by the societal actor (e.g., that Negro-Americans are less politically active than Jewish-Americans is in part due to differences in educational opportunities). However, we suggest, the degree of intra-unit assignment of assets to power is a relatively more malleable attribute than the amount of assets the unit possesses (at any given point in time). It is here that an important element of voluntarism enters the societal structure. A comparison of colonial societies in the years immediately preceding the "take-off" of national independence movements with those immediately after they won their independence seems to show that the "take-off" involved more change in the relative *use* of assets for power than in the assets base. Similarly, the American civil rights movement, which between 1953 and 1965 transformed important segments of the American Negro from a passive to an active grouping, entailed much more of a change in mobilization of power than in amount of assets.[35]

Mobilization.   Each societal unit has at any given point in time a *level of activation* which we define as the ratio of its assets that are available for collective action over its total assets.   The percent of the GNP spent by the government, the percent of the labor force employed by it, and the percent of knowledge producers that work for it are crude indicators of national activation level.   *Mobilization* refers to an upward change in the level of activation, to an increase in the fraction of the total assets possessed by a unit that are made available for collective action by that unit.   (De-mobilization refers to a reduction in that level.)

The level of activation of most societal units most of the time is very low; if all their assets are taken into account, usually less than ten percent are available for unit action.   Hence relatively small percentage changes in the level of mobilization may largely increase the action capacity of a unit.   E.g., an increase of ten percent in the assets of a unit that are mobilized might more than double its action capacity.   Major societal transformations, such as revolutions and the gaining of national independence, usually involve relatively high mobilization.   The secret of the power of social movements lies in part in the relatively high mobilization which their asceticism and the intense commitment of their members allows for.

Aside from the asset-base a collectivity possesses and the amount of power it is mobilizing, the *kind* of power mobilized also affects the action capacity of the unit.   To employ power is, by definition, to overcome resistance, but in society as in nature each application of power generates a counter-power, a resistance of its own (the result of the alienation of those who were made to suspend their preferences in favor of those of the power wielders).   While all power applications have this effect, some generate more alienation than others.

In estimating the effect of the use of a particular kind of power on the relationships between the power wielder and the subjects, it is essential to take into account that this is as a rule a "generalized" relationship.   That is, while a particular instance of exercise of power may generate little alienation, repeated use may generate much.   Even when no alienation is manifest, it might accumulate covertly and express itself indirectly.

We suggest that when the power relationship is explored (and not just described), if the power used is coercive, all other things being equal, resistance will tend to be high; if utilitarian, lower; and if normative, even smaller. (Actually even some net gains in future capacity to act may be achieved when normative power is applied, as it may reduce resistance to future acts.)   Most power wielders may prefer to use the less alienating kinds, but there are limitations on their capacity to mobilize these kinds as well as on their understanding of the dynamics involved, with the consequence that they may opt to use the more alienating kinds of power,[36] even where this is not otherwise necessary.

A study of control thus adds to the exploration of the asset base of a unit, the degree to which it is mobilized for collective action and which kinds of power are mobilized.   These added factors in turn determine to a considerable degree how alienating control will be, and whether relations between the elites and the other units will be those of open conflict, encapsulated conflict, or cooperation.

III. CONSENSUS FORMATION

1.   CONSENSUS DEFINED

So far guidance of change has been explored from a "downward" view, from the controlling overlayer to the controlled underlayer; even the discussion of communication feedback and subject resistance has been from the viewpoint of a controlling center.   The main difference, though, between societal and electronic cybernetics is that in the societal we take into account systematically that the controlled units have some of the controlling capacities themselves: they input knowledge, make decisions, pursue goals, and exercise power.   Hence the capacity of any one unit to act is determined only in part by its ability to control the others; it is similarly affected by the degree to which the goals it has chosen to pursue and the means it employs are compatible or in conflict with those preferred by other units, i.e., degree of consensus.

Consensus, the congruence of preferences of the units concerned, is viewed by typical collectivistic theories as largely given (or changing under the impact of ongoing processes); voluntaristic theories tend to view it as open to manipulation by charismatic leadership and/or mass media.   From a sociobernetic viewpoint consensus is the result of a process in which given preferences *and* guided efforts affect the outcome, which is a changing consensus.   Many studies have applied such a perspective; in sociobernetics it finds a theoretical home.   How much consensus is actually achieved changes with a variety of socio-political factors and can not be explored here.

2.   CONTROL AND CONSENSUS

There is a trade-off curve between control and consensus; that is, for any given level of activation, the more consensus, the less need for control, and the less consensus gained the more need for control. Which "mix" is used is of course not without consequences; it affects the level of alienation and of resistance, and hence the future capacity to act. It is important to realize that when both consensus *and* control are higher, more change can be guided than when both are lower, without an increase in alienation. (The additional consensus absorbs the additional alienation which the additional control would generate.)

3. CONSENSUS FORMATION STRUCTURES

To illustrate a sociobernetical study of consensus formation, we briefly compute "built-in" to "segregated" consensus formation structures. In a built-in structure, consensus formation is by and large the output of ongoing interactions among the societal units. Consensus formation in smaller and less complex preliterate tribes seems to rely largely on ongoing interaction between the member families. Consensus is to a degree produced in the Soviet society in the process of interaction between factory managements, union leaders, and party officials, though the prime function of these interactions is not consensus formation but is economic and administrative in nature (in the downward guidance sense of the term).[37] In a segregated structure, political units (such as parties and legislatures) exist as distinct from societal ones, and societal differences are translated into political ones before consensus concerning collectivization is worked out. Segregated structures seem more effective for consensus formation than built-in ones, though they can produce only enough to back up comparatively low levels of activation. They are like a sophisticated machine that cannot be used for heavy duty.

In the search for a structure that would allow for more guided change and higher consensus, a search that is far from completed, "voluntary planning" as developed in France in the post-war years and by the European Economic Community has gained much attention. There is less segregation of political and societal units than in the segregated structure (typical of traditional democracies) but more than in built-in structures (typical of totalitarian regimes). Above all, the knowledge input units are not related only to the decision-making units but are also tied into the consensus forming process, thus informing the controlled and not just the controlling units, and remodeling the judgments that information units produce— on the basis of interaction with *both* groupings.

Comparative studies of consensus formation ought to supplement and in part to replace the comparative study of constitutions and formal studies of governments. To supplement, because we need studies of both the political institutions and consensus formation which will relate these institutions to societal groups and relations among them. To replace in part, because the studies of political shells have proved too rigid and simplistic for many purposes. The study of democracy might illustrate this point.

As democracy was traditionally defined—the rule of the majority—the concept was unable even to distinguish between totalitarian and democratic regimes.

The more subtle definition, provision for the institutionalized change of the party in office, still disregarded less formal democratic mechanisms, such as changes in the coalition partners and the factions represented inside the ruling party in response to changes in societal power, and defines countries such as West Germany and Israel as non-democratic. Neither the Christian Democratic Union nor Mapai has been voted out of office since the establishment of the two states, and whether or not these parties can be voted out is an open question. Also, the formal study focuses on parliaments and parties as the consensus formation agents, but these are rapidly losing their effectiveness as the power of the executive rises. Thus, a polity that meets all the criteria of a formal democracy might still not generate enough consensus for the prevailing level of activation, not to mention increased levels which are both needed and occurring, thus leaving the society with substandard consensus leading either to accumulative alienation or curtailment of activity.

Similarly, important differences among the consensus formation of various totalitarian societies and of authoritarian ones, a mode of government which prevails among the new nations and in Latin America, as well as their changes over time, can scarcely be studied in formal terms (which characterization of regimes as totalitarian or authoritarian are) or by the classification of regimes as one-, two-, or multi-party states. In comparison, a sociobernetic study of consensus formation provides a less institutional and more "societal" approach.

IV. A SYNTHESIZING VIEW: THE ACTIVE SOCIETY

We turn now to illustrate the synthesizing perspective on societal change that can be attained once our understanding of the various components of sociobernetics is more advanced, since at the present stage little more than a brief illustration can be provided. Using control (cybernatorial capacities and power) and consensus formation as two dimensions of a property space, we characterize, in an ideal-typical manner, a society which is high on both as comparatively active; low on both as passive; high on control but low on consensus as over-managed; and low on control but high on consensus as drifting.

The *passive society* is approximated by highly primitive societies. Their low level of societal self-control is obvious. Their consensus is collectivistic and static, but it is largely not mobilized around societal goals and there is little machinery to *form* consensus when additional consensus is needed. Hence while "background" consensus might be high, the consensus *formation* capacity is low. One indicator of this low capacity is that when primitive societies do act, coercion often plays a rather central role in overcoming resistance.[38]

The *active society* maintains a level of activation that is not lower and is possibly even higher than that of over-managed societies and it forms at least as much consensus as drifting societies. This is possible because the active society commands more effective control and consensus formation mechanisms; it can rely more on the less alienating kinds of power, especially on the normative. Also, high consensus requires a high level of activation and realization of some of the variety of goals the various sub-societies and the society as a unit are committed to. Effective control, in turn, requires support of those subject to the control; hence raising the level of control without at the same time raising alienation requires a high capacity to form consensus. Thus, high control and high consensus, high activation and low alienation are mutually reinforcing. Finally, the active society has the highest capacity of the four ideal-types for self-transformation, which is the ultimate safeguard against widespread alienation as it makes possible that the rise of radically different goals and sub-societies may still be accommodated within the same system.

The active society is largely a utopia which does not exist, though it is not a utopia in the sense that no society might become one, for its functional requirements do not appear to violate any sociological law. Social-movement societies, such as Israel in 1948, approximate such an active society. A main difference between a social-movement society and the active one is that the latter stabilizes some social-movement features such as high consensus formation and intense commitment, rather than merely passing through such a phase. The mechanisms for stabilization can not be discussed in the present limits of space.

The *over-managed*, high control, low consensus type is approximated by the totalitarian societies. Typically they have inadequate consensus formation structures, and those they [have] are mainly of the built-in type. Societal action is oriented to hyper-active goals, which later are scaled down, as consensus mechanisms here do not allow discovery beforehand of where and how much resistance will be encountered in the various sub-societies as various societal changes are introduced. Typically, too, use of alienating kinds of power is high.

Whether over-managed societies are transformable and what kind of societies they will become if they are, are two widely debated questions. The argument is between those who see democratization as taking place and those who argue that the totalitarian societies are ultra-stable.[39] This dichotomy seems not to exhaust the possibilities. Democratization seems unlikely because democracies are themselves no longer well adapted, as their present control and consensus mechanisms are insufficient for the higher level of activation needed, and because there is no legitimation of democracy or democratic experience in the history of most contemporary totalitarian societies. On the other hand, it seems hard to maintain that totalitarian societies are not transformable in view of the far-reaching changes of the U.S.S.R. since 1917.

The direction of any such change might be toward an active society whose level of control is relatively closer to that of totalitarian societies than of the democratic ones, whose less-segregated consensus-formation structure is closer to the totalitarian built-in one than the democratic segregated one, and whose social-movement character can draw on legitimation of the most charismatic period of totalitarian societies. The sharpest transition needed would be from reliance on force and propaganda as central means of compliance to a focus on education and normative power; such a transformation, as drastic as it is, may be easier than a shift to a utilitarian focus characteristic of capitalistic democracies. In fact, this is the direction of change already evidenced by the U.S.S.R.

Drifting societies are approximated by capitalist democracies. Their most important relevant feature is that they act as societies to introduce significant structural change only when the need to act is "overdue,"[40] is a "crisis," when broad consensus can be mobilized before action is taken. Second, the action taken often does not remove the lag as the changes introduced are the fruit of compromise between the the more conservative and the more change-oriented sub-societies. The second major reason why capitalist democracies are drifting societies is that the more powerful sub-societies draw societal assets for their own consumptions and power, either by neutralizing the societal controls or by slanting them to serve their sub-societal interests. In either case, as far as the society at large is concerned, it is not guiding its processes and change.

CONSENSUS, EQUALITY, AND ACTIVATION

Here a conceptual addition must be introduced to tie the concept of consensus formation to those of asset analysis and alienation, an addition found in the concept of equality. Equality is higher the closer the distribution curve of assets approximates a straight line, i.e., groupings of the population that are equal in size possess equal amounts of assets. No society is completely egalitarian, but there are obviously significant differences in the degree of inequality. These in turn are associated, though of course not on a one-to-one basis, with differences in power. Now when consensus is formed it reflects the power relations among the members; the policy agreed upon tends to be closer to that preferred by the more powerful sub-societies. It is as if the weaker members say to themselves that they had better go along with a suggested policy, in which their concurrence is traded for some concessions—for fear that otherwise the powerful would impose a policy even more removed from their preferences. The amount of alienation that remains in the weaker units, however, is clearly related to the measure of inequality. Consensus which leaves little or no alienation can be formed only under conditions of comparatively high equality.

While this cannot be demonstrated here, we suggest that there is a secular historical trend toward a reduction in inequality among the sub-societies making up the capitalistic democracies although so far this reduction has been limited. (The trend is fairly obvious as far as political rights and status symbols are concerned; it is less clear with regard to economic well being.) Continuation and acceleration of such a trend, if it were to take place, would move democratic societies in an active direction by allowing the formation of more consensus with less alienating undertones, and more facing of societal problems before they are overdue, i.e., toward a high level of activation. A major force which propels the transition from a drifting to an active society is the mobilization of the weaker collectivities; this is triggered by the spread of education, by changes in employment opportunities, and other factors that generate imbalanced status sets, as well as by the priming effect of elites, especially intellectual ones. As this statement is rather central to our conception of societal change as far as the transition of Western societies into the post-modern (see below for definition) period is concerned, the assumptions implied should be briefly outlined.

As we see it, transformation of capitalist democracies is not propelled by *conflict* among *classes*, but by *interaction* among *organized collectivities*. Thus, the societal units may be an ethnic group, a race, a national community, and not just a class; the relationship might be of coalition, limited adversary, etc., rather than all-out conflict; and, above all, the unit of action is not the collectivity *per se*, but that part of it which has been mobilized into organizational structures. Thus, history is not affected by the working class as such, which is a passive unit, but by labor unions, labor parties, social protest movements that mobilize a segment of the working class. (The same could be said about the civil rights movement and the Negro-Americans, national independence movements and colonial people, etc.)

Collectivities are bases of *potential* power, but generally only a small fraction of these potentialities are actualized for purposes of societal action and change. The capacity of any societal actor to influence the pattern of societal change, i.e., his actual societal power, depends as much on his capacity to mobilize—i.e., *on the outcome of the internal struggle between mobilizers and the apathetics*—as on the actor's potential power base.

It might be said that the capacity to mobilize is itself determined by the distribution of assets *among* the collectivities; that the more powerful units hold down the capacity to mobilize of the weaker societal units. While this is a valid observation, it is also true that the mobilization of any collectivity reduces the capacity of other collectivities to hold it down. For each point in time, hence, it is necessary to study not only the power potential of a societal actor but also his mobilization capacity, which affects his actual power at this point in time. The dynamic analysis then proceeds by comparing changes in potential and actual power over time and the effects of changes in the power of some actors over that of the others. A study of societal change which focuses largely on the stratificational relations among collectivities (as Marx did and in which he was corrected to a degree by Lenin),[41] not to mention one which excludes power analysis altogether, provides at best a fragmental theory of societal change.

What does all this imply for the change of capitalistic democracies? In these societies, too, most members of most collectivities have a formal right to participate in the political process, i.e., an egalitarian political institutional status unmatched in their societal positions. An increasing number are also gaining an education, which has a mobilizing effect.[42] For historical reasons which need not be explored here, campus groups, professionals, clergy, middle-class members of ethnic minorities, all of which command political skills, are allowed to act as mobilizers, though under various constraints. And, we suggest, with weaker collectivities becoming increasingly mobilizable, and with an increase in the number of mobilizers, the total effect is increased societal power of the heretofore weaker and underprivileged collectivities. The effect of the mobilization of weaker collectivities, which is only in part neutralized by counter-mobilization of more powerful collectivities, is to transform the society in the direction of a relatively more egalitarian and active one. Whether such transformation will sooner or later lead to a showdown between the powerful and the mobilizing collectivities, or the mobilization will run out of steam on its own, or the scales will be tipped for an active society—that is, whether a structural transformation will take place—are questions our study of sociobernetics points to but cannot at present answer.

Both over-managed and drifting societies seem tending in the direction of an active society (rather than either of the less active types becoming the prevalent type). The new means of communications and of knowledge-technology may be working in this direction in both kinds of societies; continued mobilization of the weaker collectivities in capitalist societies and increased pluralism in totalitarian societies may also be supportive of such a transformation. Under what conditions an active society will be advanced is a major subject of macrosociology. The new cybernatorial capacities that are increasingly available since 1945 offer a new range of societal options and hence mark a period that might be referred to as the post-modern one. 1945 marks also the opening of the atomic age and hence suggests that a major issue for macrosociology, not touched upon here, is that of changing not the systems' structures but their boundaries. The question of which conditions favor and which block the rise of active societies and the transformation of an anarchic world into a communal one, we suggest, is regained for systematic sociological study by such approaches as that of sociobernetics.

Notes

1. This is an extensively revised version of my paper presented to the 1967 annual meeting of the Academy of Management. A much more detailed treatment of the subject will be found in my *The Active Society: A Theory of Societal and Political Processes* (New York: The Free Press, 1968). The study benefited from a grant from the National Science Foundation, No. GS-1475. Segments of the second part of this article were previously published in a different version.

2. Paul F. Lazarsfeld and Herbert Menzel, "On the Relation Between Individual and Collective Properties," in Amitai Etzioni (ed.) *Complex Organizations: A Sociological Reader* (New York: Holt, Rinehart, and Winston, 1961), pp. 214–247.

3. C. Wright Mills *The Sociological Imagination* (New York: Grove Press, 1959); Barrington Moore, Jr., *Political Power and Social Theory* (Cambridge: Harvard University Press, 1958), pp. 111–159; Sheldon Wolin, *Politics and Vision* (Boston: Little, Brown & Co., 1960), pp. 429–434.

4. Raymond W. Mack and Richard C. Snyder, "Approaches to the Study of Conflict: Introduction by the Editors," *Journal of Conflict Resolution*, 1 (1957), pp. 107–108. Morton Deutsch, "The Social Psychology of Interpersonal Bargaining," paper delivered at the 1965 meetings of the American Psychological Association, New York.

5. Talcott Parsons, "Some Consideration on the Theory of Social Change," *Rural Sociology*, Vol. 26 (1961), pp. 219–34. Talcott Parsons and Robert Bales, *Family, Socialization and Interaction Process* (New York: Free Press, 1953), 134 ff.; Neil Smelser, *Social Change in the Industrial Revolution* (Chicago: University of Chicago Press, 1959), CH VIII–X; Morris Zelditch, Jr., "Role Differentiation in the Nuclear Family: A Comparative Study," in Parsons and Bales, *op. cit.*, pp. 307–51. Studies of favorable environmental conditions are not to be confused with those of guidance mechanisms. There are inputs and not system qualities by which the reaction of the system is to be explained and which cannot be assumed. Most of these are *ad hoc* anyhow—dealing with the contact of non-whites with the white civilization.

6. F. S. Grodius, *Control, Theory and Biological Mysteries* (New York: Columbia University Press, 1963). For results of experiments with animals in which the brain was disassociated from the embryo and the effects of such disassociation on the embryo's development, see: Heinz-Joachim Pohley, *Roux' Archiv für Entwicklungsmechanik*, Vol. 1953 (1961), pp. 443–58.

7. For an attempt to analyze differentiation from this viewpoint, see: Amitai Etzioni, "The Function Differentiations of Elites in the Kibbutz," *American Journal of Sociology*, 64 (1959), pp. 476–87; "The Epigenesis of Political Communities at the International Level," *American Journal of Sociology*, 68 (1963), pp. 407–21.

8. Among the contemporary writers along this line, see those who believe that changes in the United Nations charter, especially weighted voting, would significantly enhance world government, and that direct election to a European Parliament would lead to the United States of Europe. See: L. Goodrich, *United Nations* (New York: Crowell, 1959); Eric Stein, "The European Parliamentary Assembly," *International Organization*, Vol. 13 (1959), 233–54, J. B. Scott, *Law, the State, and the International Community* (New York: Columbia University Press, 1939). For a more sophisticated approach, see: E. Jackson, *Meeting of Minds* (New York: McGraw-Hill, 1952). Most writings in the "conflict resolution" and "problem solving" traditions are voluntaristic, often to a high degree.

9. An important segment of decision-making studies view the actors as being able to make rational decisions, while lack of complete information and computation capacities limit his capacity to guide the unit for which he decides. These are viewed as *ad hoc* limitations. In principle, the more information he collects and the better his computers, the more effective decisions he is expected to make. For a recent collection of presentations most of which are in line with this position, see: William J. Gore and James Dyson (eds.), *Making of Decisions* (New York: Free Press, 1964); L. Gulick and L. Urwick (eds.), *Papers on the Science of Administration* (New York: Institute of Public Administration, Columbia University, 1937). See, also: J. W. Buchanan and G. Tulloch, *The Calculus of Consent: Logical Foundations of Constitutional Democracy* (Ann Arbor: University of Michigan Press, 1962). For a study of "group" behavior explained in terms of individualistic goals, see: Mancur Olson, Jr., *The Logic of Collective Action* (Cambridge: Harvard University Press, 1965).

10. Karl W. Deutsch, *The Nerves of Government* (New York: Free Press, 1963).

11. Nathan Leites, "Psycho-Cultural Hypotheses about Political Acts," *World Politics*, Vol. 10 (1958), pp. 102–119. K. N. Waltz, *Man, The State, and War* (New York: Columbia University Press, 1959). For a discussion of a suggestion to consider the state as a person, see J. Buchanan, "The Pure Theory of Government Finance," *Journal of Political Economy* LVII (1949), pp. 496–505.

12. Charles E. Osgood, *An Alternative to War or Surrender* (Urbana: University of Illinois Press, 1962).

13. Voluntarists, who face the question of the nature of the actor of the differing units of analysis, maintain their monolithic assumption by assuming a close relationship among the units, for instance, between the President (or power elite) and public opinion. See, for instance, Osgood, *op. cit.*

14. Voluntarism neglects mainly the relationship between the guiding mechanism and the "body" of the actor, and less so in the relationship among actors.

15. Much has been written about the difficulties of defining power. To go into all the objections here would require more space than this entire article. We shall present our reasons for holding that the above definition is operational in ... *The Active Society, op. cit.*

16. Ragnar Nurkse, *Problems of Capital Formation in Underdeveloped Countries* (New York: Oxford University Press, 1963), Ch. 1.

17. Symbols are cognitive, not expressive, and hence have no motivational power.

18. Deutsch, *op. cit.*, p. ix.

19. For the main presentation, see *The Active Society, op. cit.*

20. See, for instance, Thomas C. Schelling, "Nuclear Strategy in Europe," *World Politics*, Vol. 14 (1962), pp. 421–432. See also Thomas C. Schelling, *The Strategy of Conflict* (Cambridge: Harvard University Press, 1960).

21. Ralf Dahrendorf, "Out of Utopia," *American Journal of Sociology*, 64 (1958), pp. 115–127; Lewis Coser, *The Functions of Social Conflict* (New York: Free Press, 1964), pp. 20–26.

22. He faces other factors, too, such as conditions of the non-social environment, but those are not the focus of the present study.

23. Based on preliminary figure for 1962–63. U.S. Bureau of the Census, *Statistical Abstract of the U.S.*, 1964, *New York Times*, October 25, 1964, p. 49 and *Christian Science Monitor* (Boston), December 12, 1964.

24. This is one meaning that is implied when the Anglo-Saxon tradition is characterized as "pragmatic" and the French as rationalistic. For some evidence, related to differences in economic planning, see Andrew Shonfield, *Modern Capitalism: The Changing Balance of Public and Private Power* (New York: Oxford University Press, 1965), pp. 151–175.

25. George E. Homans, *The Human Group* (New York: Harcourt, Brace & World, 1950), pp. 369–414. On the societal level, see Don K. Price, *The Scientific Estate* (Cambridge, Mass.: Belknap Press of Harvard University Press, 1965), pp. 120–62.

26. Roger Hilsman, *Strategic Intelligence and National Decisions* (New York: Free Press, 1956), pp. 141–161.

27. Herbert A. Simon, "A Behavioral Model of Rational Choice," *Quarterly Journal of Economics*, Vol. 69 (1955), pp. 99–118.

28. For one of the few sociological studies, see Lewis Coser, *Men of Ideas* (New York: Free Press, 1965).

29. For an overview of this sociology of knowledge, see Robert K. Merton, *Social Theory and Social Structure* (rev. ed., New York: Free Press, 1957), pp. 456–488.

30. For studies of this field so far conducted almost exclusively by non-sociologists, see Viscount Hailsham, Q.C., *Science and Politics* (London: Faber and Faber, 1963), Don K. Price, *The Scientific Estate* (Cambridge, Mass.: Belknap Press of Harvard University Press, 1965), pp. 120–162; Jerome A. Wiesner, *Where Government and Science Meet* (New York: McGraw-Hill, 1965).

31. Deutsch, *op. cit.*; Alfred Kuhn, *The Study of Sociology: A Unified Approach* (Homewood, Ill.: Richard D. Irwin, 1963).

32. David A. Zinnes, "A Comparison of Hostile Behavior of Decision-Makers in Similar and Historical Data," *World Politics*, Vol. 18 (1966), pp. 474–502. See also seven essays in part one of Herbert C. Kelman, *International Behavior: A Social-Psychological Analysis* (New York: Holt, Rinehart & Winston, 1965), pp. 43–334.

33. See *El Desarrollo Economico de la Argentina*, E-CN. 12-429-Add. 4 (1958), pp. 3–5.

34. Amitai Etzioni, *Political Unification: A Comparative Study of Leaders and Forces* (New York: Holt, Rinehart & Winston, 1965), *passim.*

35. For this pre-mobilization state, see James Q. Wilson, *Negro Politics* (New York: Free Press, 1965), esp. pp. 3–7.

36. Amitai Etzioni, *A Comparative Analysis of Complex Organization* (New York: Free Press, 1961), pp. 3–22.

37. Joseph Berliner, *Factory and Manager in the U.S.S.R.* (Cambridge, Mass.: Harvard University Press, 1957), pp. 231–78. Samuel P. Huntington, *Political Power: U.S.A.-U.S.S.R.* (New York: Viking Press, 1965), pp. 129–190.

38. Max Gluckman, *Order and Rebellion in Tribal Africa* (New York: Free Press, 1963), pp. 39–40.

39. The transformation view is presented by Gabriel Almond, *The American People and Foreign Policy* (New York: Frederick A. Praeger, 1960), p. xvi, the opposite one by Philip E. Mosely, "Soviet Foreign Policy since the 22nd Party Congress," *Modern Age*, VI (Fall 1962), 343–52.

40. Etzioni, *Political Unification, op. cit.*, pp. 81–82, 95.

41. Sheldon Wolin, *Politics and Vision, op. cit.*, pp. 421–424.

42. For a review of several studies which show correlations between education and political activation, see Lester W. Milbrath, *Political Participation* (Chicago: Rand McNally, 1965), pp. 42–54.

11 . The Two Models of Society: A Critique .
Percy S. Cohen

One of the principal substantive issues in the recent literature of social theory has been the debate concerning the compatibility of two models of society: the first is called the 'consensus' or 'integration' model, while the second is called the 'coercion' or 'conflict' model. It is clear from the two alternative sets of names that the proponents of the first model are alleged to emphasize the importance of both consensus and integration in society, while the proponents of the second claim to emphasize the significance of both coercion and conflict; the assumption is that consensus and integration are either the same thing or that they are empirically correlated, and that coercion and conflict are similarly connected.

One might characterize the controversy, such as it is alleged to be, by saying that one model attributes to social systems the characteristics of commitment, cohesion, solidarity, consensus, reciprocity, cooperation, integration, stability and persistence, while the other attributes to it the characteristics of coercion, division, hostility, dissensus, conflict, malintegration and change. One could also say that the first model emphasizes the significance of norms and legitimacy, while the second emphasises those of interests and power. These two opposed models can now be set out as below (Cf. the models proposed by Dahrendorf).[1]

Model 'A'

i. Norms and values are the basic elements of social life.
ii. Social life involves commitments.

iii. Societies are necessarily cohesive.
iv. Social life depends on solidarity.

v. Social life is based on reciprocity and cooperation.
vi. Social systems rest on consensus.

vii. Society recognizes legitimate authority.
viii. Social systems are integrated.

ix. Social systems tend to persist.

Model 'B'

i. Interests are the basic elements of social life.
ii. Social life involves inducement and coercion.

iii. Social life is necessarily divisive.
iv. Social life generates opposition, exclusion and hostility.

v. Social life generates structured conflict.
vi. Social life generates sectional interests.

vii. Social differentiation involves power.
viii. Social systems are malintegrated and beset by 'contradictions'.

ix. Social systems tend to change.

Excerpted from *Modern Social Theory* by Percy S. Cohen, © 1968 by Percy S. Cohen, Basic Books, Inc., Publishers, New York. Reprinted also by permission of Heinemann Educational Books Ltd.

Reasoned arguments underlie the defence of either or both of these two models. The theoretical defence of Model A is as follows. If social life is not possible without the existence of norms, then there must be commitment to these norms and, therefore, consensus on the values which underpin them. All divisions are countered by a fundamental unity, cohesion and solidarity. All social roles, including those which involve the exercise of power must, in the long run, be governed by norms mutually acceptable to all parties; thus all power ultimately becomes legitimate authority, and it is exercised in the pursuit of those goals which are defined in terms of the fundamental values of society. The exercise of power within a legitimate system is both a reward for special qualities as well as a facility for the achievement of social goals. The underlying system of values influences the particular sets of norms which operate in any institutional sphere; therefore, all institutions tend to be integrated through their conformity to basic value orientations.

Given all these conditions, it follows that there is a widespread interest in the status quo and a relative harmony between the different parts of the social system. The social system tends, therefore, to be in a state of equilibrium: any tendencies to deviant conduct are controlled within certain limits or call forth responses which restore support for the institutional structure: the social system tends to persist. Insofar as social change occurs it is largely an adaptive process, though some forms of change can occur largely as a result of the failures of socialization to ensure adequate commitment to values.

The argument underlying Model B is very different, but succeeds equally in linking the various assumptions. Society exists because it serves men's interests. Interests are never identical for all individuals and groups and the division of society into different statuses and classes with differential access to a variety of privileges, itself generates conflicts of interest. Insofar as there is consensus, it is the gradually formed consensus of those who share certain life-chances and whose interests are structured by these. Insofar as there are believed to be common values in society this belief is part of the ideology of the powerful; the so-called basic values of society are only the values of the ruling class. Privilege in one sphere creates favourable conditions for the acquisition of privilege in other spheres; power tends to become generalized. The maintenance of power and privilege requires inducement and coercion; coercion breeds conflict, which in turn leads to further coercion. The stability of society is constantly threatened by the fundamental conflicts of interest and by opposition to coercive power. Thus the social mechanisms which are employed to inhibit change must always provoke pressure for change. There may be some degree of institutional integration which results from the pressures of the ruling class—for example, the various forms of power are brought into close relation with one another—but this can not endure; the various conflicting interests ensure that different institutional sectors will strive for autonomy and this, ultimately produces 'contradictions' between them. Societies, except, perhaps for the most primitive, are unstable systems; normally they tend to change.

Some commentators on this matter would agree that the theory behind each model is, more or less, acceptable, even if one model is preferable to the other. Dahrendorf, who has himself constructed models similar to this, recognizes that an 'integration' or 'consensus' model, is applicable to some cases, but not, on the whole to those in which he is interested.[2]   Rex gives little support to model A, except to acknowledge that consensus and solidarity may be characteristic of relationships within conflicting groups or parties.[3]   But neither Dahrendorf nor Rex seems to question the theory underlying each model: *in short they assume that, on the whole, if one item in a model is accepted then acceptance of all other items follows.*   This view is not quite accepted by Parsons who argues that conflict, tension and normative strain are inherent in all systems, but that they must be kept within certain limits if the system is to operate as a 'going concern'.[4] Coser[5] and Gluckman,[6] following Simmel, have shown that they do not accept the theories underlying the two models: they both agree that conflict, for example, does not necessarily lead to change, and they even go so far as to recognize that it may even strengthen a system; and Gluckman argues that even conflicts of principle—normative or value inconsistency—may be contained within a system.[7]

Gouldner has also questioned the theories behind these two models.   In discussing the preoccupation of Comte, Marx and Durkheim with the problems of consensus and conflict, he recognizes that these characteristics are not mutually exclusive, but may coexist, possibly in tension, within the same system.[8]

Lockwood distinguishes two separate aspects of social systems: 'social integration' and 'system integration'.[9]   The first term refers either to consensus, solidarity or cohesion; Lockwood is not quite clear on this.   The second term refers to functional interdependence.   Lockwood's argument is both important and correct: the existence of integration in one sense does not imply its existence in another.   He argues that the 'integration model' may well be applicable to societies with structured conflict insofar as it emphasizes the functional interrelation between the material base and the different parts of the institutional structure; a system may be integrated in this sense without displaying social solidarity, consensus, etc.   This view is in line with Lockwood's neo-Marxism; for Marx strongly emphasized the close connection between the infra-structure and the various levels and parts of the superstructure of the social system.   Lockwood applies these ideas to the analysis of several cases of social change, showing how they result as much from the interaction between incompatible system parts as they do from social conflict.   But even Lockwood seems to despair of ridding social theory of the two opposed models.   He finds it comforting, but not convincing to be told that some reconciliation is possible.[10]

On all this, two points need to be made.   The first is that the two models do not really need to be reconciled, for the propositions of A and B are not mutually exclusive.   The two models are not genuine alternatives: to say that a room is half-full is not to deny that it is half-empty.   The second point is more complicated.   Assume that it is recognized that the two sets of propositions are not mutually exclusive.   It may still be claimed that they argue for a difference of *emphasis,* and that it is possible to establish two models of society in which two lists of interrelated predominant characteristics are opposed to one another. The gist of the second point is that this is to assume that the existence of one *predominant* characteristic implies the existence of another. The argument against this is that it is perfectly possible to conceive of models which would contain some of the predominant characteristics of model A and some of those of model B. In short, it may be possible, and desirable, to construct several models of social systems, rather than only two; this is certainly discomforting to those who think in binary terms.

The first point—that the two sets of statements are not mutually exclusive—has really been made earlier in this chapter. But it is worth repeating for emphasis. It may be that the possession of a particular characteristic in the most extreme form would exclude the possession of its opposite. But no one could surely suggest that societies usually have only the characteristics listed under A or those listed under B. They usually possess each characteristic and its opposite in tension with one another. The difference, of course, is in the degree to which they are characterized by the emphases listed under A or those listed under B. But some of the opposed items are not even mutually exclusive when both assume an extreme form. For example, the use of coercive power may co-exist with legitimate authority; though clearly the more coercive the power becomes the less it rests on legitimacy.

The second point is not difficult to establish. Consensus does not necessarily mean persistence as opposed to change: there may be consensus on the direction and forms of change; while a lack of consensus, or a marked expression of sectional interests may produce an impasse which inhibits planned change. Similarly, a recognition of legitimate authority does not necessarily suggest a lack of change; while the use of coercive power may inhibit or slow down the process of change. Conflict may be compatible with functional integration; and solidarity may be compatible with malintegration, which may cause role conflict for the individual.

In some cases several of the predominant characteristics of model A are found together. In some simple societies there is a close connection between the high degree of integration, cohesion and solidarity and the tendency of the social system to persist. But it is doubtful whether this simple, binary conception of system models is applicable to all types of society.

The assumption that an emphasis on change is necessarily linked with the other characteristics of model B, while an emphasis on stability is necessarily linked with the other characteristics of model A, probably owes much to ideology, whether conservative or radical. This is not, in itself, a bad thing; unless wishful thinking displaces evidence. It is, of course, true that much nineteenth century sociology did emphasize the role of conflict in explaining social change and that much recent sociology has neglected both conflict and change. But while this may signify the influence of values, it does not establish a necessary logical or empirical connection between these two things.

Notes

1. R. Dahrendorf, *Class and Class Conflict in Industrial Society* [Stanford, 1959], pp. 160–5.
2. R. Dahrendorf, *loc. cit.*
3. J. Rex, *Key Problems of Sociological Theory* [Routledge, 1951], esp. pp. 110–14.
4. Talcott Parsons, *The Social System* [Free Press, 1951], esp. pp. 490–6.
5. Lewis A. Coser, *The Functions of Social Conflict*, Routledge, 1958.
6. Max Gluckman, *Custom and Conflict in Africa*, Oxford, 1959.
7. Max Gluckman, *ibid.*
8. Alvin W. Gouldner, 'Introduction' to Emile Durkheim, *Socialism*, Collier, New York, 1962, pp. 7–31.
9. David Lockwood, 'Social Integration and System Integration' in George K. Zollschan and Walter Hirsh (eds.), *Explorations in Social Change*, Routledge, 1964, pp. 244–56.
10. *Ibid.*

12 . The Environment of a Political System
David Easton

If a political system is to be identified in the way we have done it in the previous chapter [of *A Framework for Political Analysis*], the other side of the coin could be expected to reveal those things that are not included within the system. But if we are to entertain the notion that there are things outside of a system, latent in our minds must be the complementary idea that there are boundaries of some kind that demarcate a political system from whatever is not included within it. If that is so, in one way or another we must be able to indicate the nature of the boundary that tells us when something is happening in the environment or non-political sphere. At the very least, such a boundary should not be conceptually ambiguous. It should have sufficient empirical referents so that positive clues are available to tell us when a person is acting as a member of a political system and when his interactions occur outside this area.

Furthermore, once the idea of a boundary between systems is introduced, it should make sense to say that if something happens in the nonpolitical arena, it may influence the political system. An exchange will have taken place across the boundaries of the two systems. Except for this possibility, there would be little point in seeking conceptual clarity with respect to the environment of a political system.

David Easton, *A Framework for Political Analysis*, © 1965. Reprinted by permission of Prentice-Hall, Inc., Englewood Cliffs, New Jersey.

AMBIGUITIES IN THE CONCEPT "SYSTEM BOUNDARIES"

It seems reasonable to impose conceptual requirements such as these in connection with systems terminology. Yet when we look at the phenomenal systems, we encounter certain apparent difficulties and ambiguities. To consider a relatively simple obstacle, by way of illustration, are families, as structural units, to be excluded from political systems? If we were considering solely primitive, nonliterate societies, we might not be predisposed to do so too hastily. There, interactions within and between both nuclear families and extended kinship groups are highly charged with political content; this was equally true in earlier days among the aristocratic classes of many European societies. In at least two ways most families in modern societies continue to play a part in politics: through the contribution they make to the socialization of their own maturing members with respect to political attitudes, knowledge, and values; and in a diffuse way through the continued molding of the political attitudes and opinions of adult members. But the bulk of a family's activities relates to matters that cannot be labeled political. Yet because of its transparent participation in the vital area of political socialization and attitude formation, does this suggest that the family as a structure should normally be placed within the boundaries of the political system? To do so would be counter to common sense.

In a like vein, we might point to the investment policies and other activities of powerful financial houses in an industrialized society. These have at times been critical for the political destinies of a political party and government, as in the case of the influence presumably exercised by the Bank of England during the financial crisis of the Ramsay MacDonald Government in the thirties.[1] For that time are we to consider that the Bank of England and its specific actions lay inside the boundaries of the English political system? We would probably decide against inclusion of this structure on the grounds that the Bank was primarily an economic institution and therefore fundamentally part of the economy, especially since at the time it was privately dominated. Does this signify that if we are to be consistent, we must view a structure like this as part of two systems or that we at least ought to see it as oscillating between the political and economic systems?

At worst, this imagery seems to invite excessive reification or unpalatable analogizing; at best it confronts us with the real difficulty of deciding how we are to describe the boundaries of a political system so that we know what we can usefully include and exclude. For that matter, it raises the even more serious question as to whether we can intelligibly continue to speak of the boundaries of a system of interactions and of movement or exchanges across such boundaries.

THE SIGNIFICANCE OF SYSTEM BOUNDARIES

If the questions as to whether boundaries were real or mythical, simplifying or complicating, had little consequence or relevance for our subsequent analysis, there would be little point in pursuing the discussion any further. We shall find, however, that the idea of exchanges between a political system and its environment plays a critical role in the theoretical approach being developed. The concept "boundaries" will represent an essential analytic tool, and this for two reasons.

CLOSED AND OPEN SYSTEMS

In the first place, an explicit conception of boundaries will aid us immeasurably in simplifying, interpreting, and understanding the way in which changes in the environment are communicated to a political system and the way in which a system seeks to cope with these influences. It is obvious that many changes in a political system may be owing to factors internal to it. Its own form of organization may be the source of major difficulties, such as those attributed to the separation of powers in the American political system.

Other significant kinds of stress may derive from the fact that a system is open to influences from its environment. Although this is an inescapable observation, an empirical truism need not always provide the groundwork for a theoretical analysis. For some purposes it is often necessary and useful to violate what is known, temporarily at least, in order to build a simplified model even if it bears only a remote resemblance to reality. It is entirely possible to conceive of a mode of analysis that would follow some models of physical systems and interpret political life as a closed system, one that conceived it to be isolated from the influences of its environment. Such an interpretation would require us to account for what happens in a political system solely in terms of its internal activities.

This is not quite so farfetched as it may seem. In the past considerable research with respect to political life did leave the impression that insufficient account was being taken of the parameters of political behavior. Personality, culture, and social structure, three of the major parametric systems, have only episodically been used as central explanatory variables until recent years. But no political scientist could neglect the obvious effects of at least some of the nonpolitical aspects of social life.

Nevertheless, if for initial analytic purposes we were to adopt the assumption that a political system is entirely closed, we would be forced to conclude that the system would have to move toward what could be called maximal social entropy. We would be rather hard put, however, to describe just what is implied in the notion of a political system "running down" in any sense comparable to its use in the physical sciences from which the ideas of closed system and entropy are borrowed.

As meaningless as the term might be for a political system, it does serve the vital purpose of forcing us to conceptualize the nature of the relationship between a system and its environment. That is, it raises what has been a latent assumption to a conscious level so that we recognize that we have indeed been conceiving of political life as an open system. Because this notion has been latent, its implications have not been fully understood nor has its theoretical significance been clear or fully exploited.

Once we raise the notion of an open system to the level of theoretical conscious-ness, it impels us to clarify the meaning conveyed by the idea of a system as distinct from its environment.   To say that a system is open to outside influences makes sense only if we can distinguish inside from outside.   But we cannot do this satisfactorily except by examining the properties of a presumed boundary that separates the two.   At a later point the logic behind the idea of an open system will also make it necessary to seek to develop concepts that will enable us to handle an analysis of the exchanges between a system and its environment.   At that time we shall find the ideas of inputs and outputs invaluable for this purpose. Here again the idea of exchanges or flows of effects would make little sense unless we were able to think of boundaries across which such transactions took place.

IDENTIFICATION OF DEPENDENT VARIABLES

In the second place, the adoption of boundaries as a concept will also represent a strategic step toward the simplification of reality, an essential condition for any scientific research.   It will provide us with a criterion for determining which politically important elements need to be explored in depth as our major depen-dent variables and which may be accepted as given in the form of external vari-ables.   Each of these types of elements, the internal and the external, will be crucial for an understanding of our problems concerning political systems, but each will have a different theoretical status in the conceptual model that we are in the process of constructing.

THE GENERAL PROPERTIES OF SYSTEM BOUNDARIES

How are we to distinguish between a political system and its setting?   Does it make empirical as well as theoretic sense to say that a political system has a boundary dividing it from its environment?   If so, how are we to define the line of demarcation?

The difficulties that beset us in seeking to answer these questions can be ex-posed, if not fully clarified, if we briefly consider other types of behaving or em-pirical systems with respect to which the existence of system boundaries is in much less doubt.   By examining these systems and discovering the true signifi-cance of boundaries as a concept, we shall be in a better position to appreciate the utility and reality of attributing apparently similar boundaries to systems of social interaction, such as political systems.

THE BOUNDARIES OF PHYSICAL AND BIOLOGICAL SYSTEMS

All types of systems that have been found useful for research in the natural sciences are alike at least in that none of them functions in a vacuum in the phenomenal world.   They are all imbedded in some kind of environment in fact, even though for heuristic purposes it may be necessary to exclude the influence of the setting temporarily, as in the case of the study of gravity under conditions of a frictionless world. Yet even though all systems are to be found in some kind of setting, they are able to maintain their identity with sufficient distinctiveness so that it is relatively easy for us to distinguish them from their environment.

From this perspective a boulder is one of the simplest of physical systems. Its density separates it from the surrounding air, and its parts share a common destiny as long as it retains its character as a boulder. Thereby we are able to distinguish it from adjacent boulders and the ground upon which it rests. The boundary between the boulder and other things is clear and unmistakable

Our solar system, consisting of the sun and its satellites, similarly represents by its very designation a physical system of interest. Imaginatively and literally, given the technology, we could draw a line around it to designate its physical boundary. We can even consider the interaction of its parts as though, for the moment, it were not affected by the gravitational field of its own galaxy or even larger segments of the universe. Yet we know that the destiny of the solar system is irrevocably linked to the broader environment outside its spatial boundaries.

A waterfall as well may be considered a system of behavior, even though in this instance there is the complication that after a brief stay each drop of water constantly leaves the system never to appear again. This rapid flow of the water through the system does not lead us to confuse the waterfall with the precipice over which it cascades, the river feeding the water and drawing it away, or the winds contributing to its turbulence. Indeed, even though disturbances to the system may change the rate of flow of the water, the boundaries will usually change only marginally. They tend to be quite stable during short intervals of time.

An apple is an organic system isolated from its environment by a skin. We take it for granted that if our task is to understand the processes occurring within the apple itself as it matures and decays, we need to take into consideration factors outside of the skin itself. The soil in which the apple tree grows, the nature of the tree itself, and when parted from this, the humidity, temperature, and circulation of the atmosphere in which the apple is stored are all of decisive importance for the life of the apple as a system. Yet, from the point of view of the horticulturalist, these elements are variables external to the apple as an organic system. The boundary is well defined by the skin.

The human body is another biological system whose boundaries consist not of an imaginary line but of an epidermis that seems to mark it off unambiguously from its environment. In the maturation process we quickly learn not to confuse things bounded by our skin and those outside.

In each of these examples of physical or biological systems the boundaries seem simple enough to perceive. They form the spatial or material limits to the collection of variables in which we are interested. Either they in fact contain these variables, like an envelope, as the skin of an apple or of the human body, or it requires very little stretching of the imagination to conceive of some kind of shell surrounding them, as for the boulder, waterfall, or solar system. Such a container would decisively mark off the relevant variables from their surroundings.

But a system of social interactions, such as a political system, is normally so diffused throughout a society that we have considerable difficulty in accommodating the same imagery to these actions, taken collectively, that we apply so easily to physical and biological systems. A system of social interaction need not and usually does not include all of the actions of the person or group. Of course, if we were thinking of a specific political organization, such as a legislature, political party, interest group, or court, it is not beyond the bounds of our imagination to think of each of these organizations as possessing a physical boundary. At least we could think of scooping up all the members identified with these organizations and containing them within the walls of one building, if it could be built large enough.

We know that political interactions do not occur only within such well-defined goal-oriented structures. Much behavior occurs in other contexts, entirely outside a political organization, as in the illustrations mentioned earlier with regard to the family or an economic organization such as a bank. Furthermore, persons may act in political roles only intermittently, in the course of behaving economically or religiously, so that they may well seem to be popping in and out of a political system, as it were. We often talk politics at work, at social gatherings, and the like. When we take into account all kinds of political behavior, suffused as they are throughout society, it certainly seems to put a considerable strain on language as well as imagery to think of containing political interactions in some sort of envelope or within spatial boundary lines.

THE GENERAL CHARACTER OF ALL BOUNDARIES

The circumscribing of boundaries for physical and biological systems seems to be simple enough. They do not seem to depend upon a decision on the part of the investigator but appear to be given in nature as though the systems were indeed purely natural in kind. But the simplicity in conceptualization of the boundaries is quite deceptive. These boundaries are, in fact, not phenomenally out there waiting to be identified. They conform to our general conclusion about the character of systems, that they are products of analytic selection; this is also true with regard to the boundaries of political systems.

We select the density of a boulder, the imaginary celestial line around our solar system, the form of the waterfall, and the skin of the apple and of the human being because we are particularly interested in understanding what happens to a set of variables defined by these limits. Although these are boundaries that we have become habituated to accepting, they stem from decisions that indicate the nature and limits of the theoretical or, for the layman, the practical interests on the part of the observer. If we had so wished, we could have ignored these boundaries and drawn entirely different ones. We could have considered each of these systems to be subsystems of a broader suprasystem consisting respectively of all rock formations constituting, say, the Pre-Cambrian shield, the Milky Way

Galaxy, a river system, an orchard, and (with Patrick Geddes) the human biological organism as part of the ecological system. In fact, with regard to the human skin, as cytologists move in the opposite direction and reduce it to its component cells, at a given point of refinement in analysis they have difficulty in differentiating the epidermal cells from the surrounding air. The skin as an apparently natural boundary disappears.

In many cases, therefore, we may be able to draw a physical line to represent a boundary for a system, but this is an accidental although useful empirical property of some systems only. Conceptually a boundary is something quite different from its possible physical representation. A boundary line stands rather as a symbol or spatial embodiment of the criteria of inclusion–exclusion with respect to a system. It is a summary way of referring phenomenally to what we have included in or left out of a system. If, for systems in which space is a significant dimension, we can point to a line or a container, we know immediately that what is inside is part of the system and what is outside may belong to other systems.

For systems in which spatial location is not well defined or highly differentiated with regard to other systems and in which there may be considerable interlacing of behavior from different systems, we need other ways of describing or identifying the boundaries. Since the systems cannot be spatially and wholly separated from each other, the boundaries can be identified by the criteria in terms of which we can for each interaction determine whether it falls inside or outside the system. For the political system, as I have indicated, the test is whether the interactions are more or less directly related to the authoritative allocations of values for a society.

Accordingly, what we choose to put inside our system, to consider within its boundaries, will depend upon what we wish to examine in detail; for scientific purposes we also expect that these variables will show considerable inter- relationship and coherence. What we leave outside, as part of its environment, will be those factors that we can accept as givens. They represent the independent variables or parameters of the system. In identifying them we thereby relieve ourselves of the need to go into detail about how they arise and what induces them to take the values that they do.

The external as compared to the internal or dependent variables may well have major consequences for the operation of the system. The fact that we consider them to be parameters of the system is not to be interpreted as indicating their irrelevance or lesser significance for understanding the functioning of the system. Their exclusion from the system for purposes of analysis says nothing at all about their contribution to the persistence or transformation of the system. All that it indicates is that the interrelationship of those elements or variables included in the system is what we wish to understand. They are the strictly political variables. We leave the explanation of variations in the parameters to others who are specialists in those areas. We need to know how the parameters vary, but we usually accept these variations as "givens" and seek to trace out their impact on the dependent internal or political variables.

Here we are fundamentally in no different a methodological position than those who study the physical or biological systems already mentioned. The gravitational forces of the universe compose part of the relevant environment of the solar system; large changes in these forces may destroy this system. In the analysis of the functioning of the solar system, however, it is quite satisfactory to assume these changes, to ignore their causes, and to confine our interest exclusively to the behavior of our solar system.

Similarly with regard to the human organism as a biological system, inadequate provision of nourishment can lead to its destruction. Yet in order to be able to cope with the unique range of problems that confront them as specialists, biologists are not called upon to become professional students of agriculture or of the system of distribution and exchange within a society.

We do not need to conclude from this generalized description of what is involved in the delineation of boundaries that, once established, they are eternally fixed. If it should turn out that owing to some mistaken interpretation or lack of insight, in order to improve our understanding of the political system we must include within it some element previously assigned to the environment, we are faced with no crisis. We simply redefine the system to meet our analytic needs. Each time that we enlarge our system we simultaneously shrink the environment. If this seems to introduce an element of indeterminacy into our conceptualization, I can only refer to our discussion of what we mean by a system. It is a device to help us to understand a defined and redefinable area of human behavior, not a strait jacket to imprison analysis permanently within a preconceived mold or model.

THE DECEPTIVE CHARACTER OF GEOGRAPHIC BOUNDARIES

It might appear that I am overstating the case against the spatial delineation of a political system. After all, we do have maps of societies and the boundaries on these maps represent positive constraints on the behavior of persons in the society. Are these not the physical boundaries of a political system? They are often referred to as geopolitical boundaries.

On the surface it may seem plausible to utilize geographic boundaries as coincident with our analytic ones. In fact, these are not the kind of limits which I am speaking of here. Geopolitical boundaries have important and obvious consequences for a political system and to that extent form an important variable. They do help to define the claims to and acceptance of the jurisdiction of a particular set of authorities, but they stand as the politically defined boundaries for the whole society, not solely of the political system in that society. Geopolitical boundaries do not help us to differentiate those interactions *within* the society that are political from those that are economic, religious, educational, or the like. They tell us when a person moves from the jurisdictional claims of one set of authorities into those of another; they do not help us to understand when this person moves from an economic setting to a political one. The geopolitical boundaries circumscribe all interlaced social systems of the society, not any specific social system.

From this discussion we must conclude that, in their theoretical status, boundaries of systems need not always be spatial in nature. Analytically, the boundaries of all systems may be interpreted as the criteria of inclusion in or exclusion from the systems forming the focus of interest. The fact that empirically a system of political interaction cannot be contained, unmixed with other social systems, by a line drawn on a map or cannot symbolically be put within an envelope of some sort that separates it unmistakably from other systems of social interaction does not weaken the utility of the concept "boundaries" as an analytic tool. It just compels us to recognize that physical boundaries are only one way of empirically separating systems.

EMPIRICAL INDICATORS OF BOUNDARIES OF POLITICAL SYSTEMS

Although empirically there is no physical line across which we might step as we move from one system to another, experience, nevertheless, lends reality to the existence of a boundary between political and other systems in a society. Most societies provide some clues as to when we move from one system of behavior to another, although the absence of manifest telltales need not be conclusive proof that an exchange between systems has not taken place.

The most distinctive indications of such exchanges occur in societies with a high degree of structural differentiation, as in modernized social systems. In such societies there is usually a sharp demarcation of many political roles from other kinds of roles. Members of a society will have different expectations with regard to the way persons will behave in political as compared with religious or familial roles, for example. As we move from a strictly religious or family setting to a political one, we are expected to change our rules of behavior in some known degree. If we did not, we would be looked upon as odd or ignorant. In other words, in a structurally highly differentiated society regularized patterns of expectations with regard to how we act in different situations provides one empirical test of the existence of boundaries between systems. This is so clearly the case that in ordinary conversation we often speak of a person "stepping out" of his role, say, as a religious leader or scientist and undertaking to act as a political prophet or politician.

In many societies, though, the analytically distinguishable kinds of behavior may be empirically fused. In various traditional, nonliterate societies, for example, a few structures may perform all the major tasks. Through the kinship structure alone all of the activities necessary for the persistence of the society may be carried out, such as the production of goods and services, transmission of cultural norms, inculcation of motivations, and the making of binding allocations. Under these conditions the political system would be completely embedded in this major structure and its components. A chief might act not only as the political chief, but as the ceremonial leader, the main economic decision maker, and the ultimate head of the kinship unit in its familial aspects. And in practice he might perform these varied kinds of actions virtually simultane-ously. That is to say, a person might act in any analytically differentiated role without changing his setting or empirical role.

Under conditions such as these, empirical indicators of the boundary between the political and other social systems would be considerably more obscure than in modern societies. Even here, the society is not entirely devoid of empirical clues corresponding to the analytically distinguished kinds of behavior. A meeting of the elders of the clan, a council of war, or the introduction of a wand of authority in a ritual, cue the participants to the change of setting or of activity. In that sense, these cues provide evidence that the boundary into the political system of the society has beeen crossed.

It has been suggested that the degree of differentiation of political systems from other social systems and therefore, we may add, the clarity of the boundary be-tween them is signalized by the following properties: (1) the extent of distinction of political roles and activities from other roles and activities, or conversely the extent to which they are all imbedded in limited structures such as the family or kinship groups; (2) the extent to which occupants of political roles form a sepa-rate group in the society and possess a sense of internal solidarity and cohesion; (3) the extent to which political roles take the shape of a hierarchy which is distin-guishable from other hierarchies based upon wealth, prestige, or other non-political criteria; and (4) the extent to which the recruitment processes and criteria of selection differ for the occupants of political as contrasted with other roles.[2] If we used indicators such as these, it would be possible to rank societies on a con-tinuum with regard to the sharpness of definition and empirical delineation of intersystem boundaries.

THE ENVIRONMENT OF POLITICAL SYSTEMS

THE INTRASOCIETAL SYSTEMS

Those aspects of a society that fall outside the boundaries of a political system can be generalized by stating that they consist of all the other subsystems of the society. They constitute the environment of the political system. Environment embraces the social as well as the physical environment. Unless the context indicates otherwise, the concept will be used, henceforth, in both senses. But this uni-versal environment, with its variety of differentiable systems, has two major aspects: that is, the numerous systems external to a political system are composed of two basically different types, intrasocietal and extrasocietal. Table 1 depicts this dichotomy and indicates the various kinds of systems that are included within each of these two major types.

Let us consider the classification scheme. By the environment we may be referring to that part of the social and physical environment that lies *outside* the boundaries of a political system and yet *within* the same society. This is the

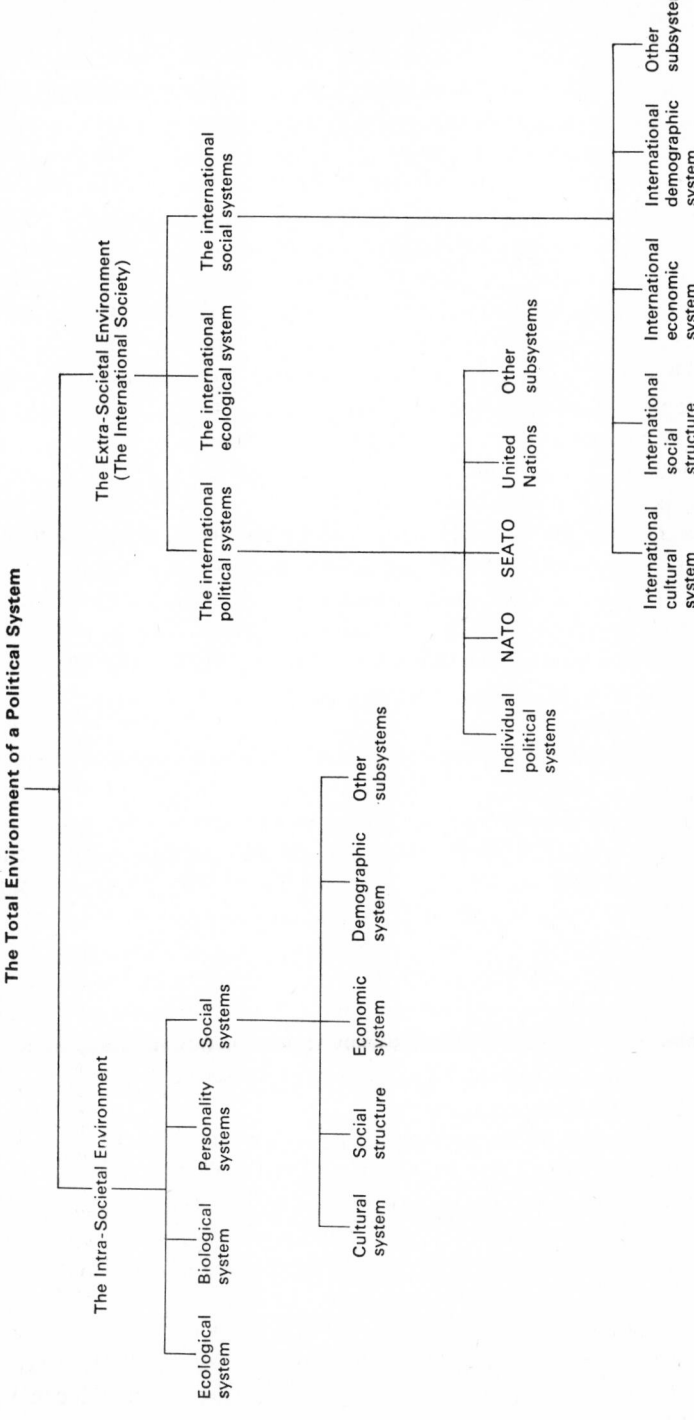

The Total Environment of a Political System

Table 1. Components of the Total Environment of a Political System

intrasocietal part of the environment. In examining the impact of the environmental changes on a political system, we would be referring to changes that occur in these other social systems. A depression in the economy, a change of values and aspirations in the culture, or a shift in the class structure may each have consequences for a political system. These changes occur in areas outside of what is normally conceived to be the political system; yet they take place within the same society as the one that contains the political system. This part of the total environment will engage a considerable share of our attention. When we move beyond it into the extrasocietal systems, we are in effect dealing with what we normally call the international political system.

This intrasocietal part of the environment of a political system may be classified in many ways, but it will be helpful to simplify and order it by dividing it into several systems. The following may be identified as some of the major external intrasocietal systems of importance to the persistence and change of political systems: the ecological, biological, personality, and social systems.

There is nothing predetermined or sacrosanct about this classification scheme. Alternative formulations could be easily visualized. Since the mode of analysis to be explored does not rest definitively on the specific categorization of the environment of the political system, we do not need to pause very long over it. The important point, rather, requires that we recognize the fact of the environment and the theoretical problems it occasions. Without this, we could not proceed to suggest a kind of analysis designed to shed light on the way in which political systems are able to persist and change or cope with the stresses to which they are constantly exposed.

To indicate what is involved in the major intrasocietal environmental systems, we shall examine each in turn, but only very briefly. The ecological system encompasses the physical environment and the nonhuman organic conditions of human existence. In the physical part of the ecological system may be included geographical or spatial characteristics such as the nature of the physical resources, topography, size of territory, climate, and similar properties that influence the conditions of all existence including the political. The nonhuman organic aspects of the environmental systems refer to the nature, location, and accessibility of food supply and other flora and fauna that can be utilized by members of a political system. Variations in food supply, both for nomadic and sedentary societies, are known to affect the structure and processes of political systems, if technology is accepted as a constant.[3]

The biological system in the environment draws attention to the fact that in seeking to understand political processes, it is easy to neglect the hereditary properties that may help to determine human motivation in political as well as other social contexts. It refers to that aspect of political interactions that is determined or influenced by the biological make-up of human beings. To the extent that genetic characteristics impose limits upon the behavior of individuals, this may have implications for political life. Capacities for pacific or rational behavior, for cooperation as compared to conflict, are said to be related to the genetic inheritance of human beings. Orthodox Freudians have insisted on the inherent aggressive drives which all social arrangements, including the political, can ignore only at their peril.[4] The validity of this proposition is not at stake here; rather the only point that is politically relevant biological traits cannot be neglected as part of the total environment in which a political system operates. The fact that political science tends to do so, does not, of course, reduce either their theoretical or empirical importance.

Personality and social systems have received the widest and most detailed attention in the traditional literature. Social systems may be classified into several types: cultural, social structural, economic, and demographic. Here again the precise subdivision is not crucial.

Variations in the nature of the personalities and acquired motivations of members of a political system have long drawn the attention of students of politics. The science of ethology toward which John Stuart Mill was reaching and recent efforts around the theme of national character and variable kinds of political behavior presumed to be associated with different types of personalities reflect a firm recognition of the role of this major parameter.[5]

Fluctuations in the social culture by which personalities are shaped and in the economy, shifts in the general structure of society or in specific aspects of it (as in the number and size of group formations or of social classes) and changes in the size, rate of growth, composition, and distribution of populations are known to have high significance for what happens in the relevant political system. A great deal of the effort of political research has gone into seeking to trace out, informally at least, the relationships between the political system and these environmental or parametric systems. Although I shall not interpret it as the task of an introduction to systems analysis to seek to extract systematically the actual relationships that exist between any of these parametric systems and the political system, nevertheless, a major effort will be directed toward devising a satisfactory set of categories for doing so.

EXTRASOCIETAL SYSTEMS

The systems just identified are part of the same society of which the political system itself is a social subsystem. In this sense, these systems are external to the political system. Any influence they exert on the political system must derive from the fact that actions bridge the boundary between one or another of them and of the political system. This is the first sense in which a system may be said to be external to or in the environment of a political system.

But a system is external to a political system in a second and different sense. It may lie outside the society of which the political system itself is a social subsystem; yet it may have important consequences for the persistence or change of a political system. Instances of this are societies and political systems that are different from the society and political system under consideration. From the point of view of the United States, France is a society and contains a political system the consequences of the actions of which may cross the boundary of the American political system and help to shape its destinies.

We can broaden considerably this image of the external environment if we also view the whole international society as a unit external to any given political system. We may consider it a vital part of the extrasocietal environment. In fact, it is a summary way of referring to the whole of this environment, including the individual societies as subsystems of the international society. From this point of view, as components of the international society, we would find an international ecological system, an international political system, and such international social systems as an international culture, an international economy, an international demographic system, and so forth, just as in the case of the domestic societies. The international society as a whole or any of its subsystems would constitute parameters in the extrasocietal environment of a given political system and would have to be taken into account as possible sources of influence upon what happens within the given system. Among the international subsystems would also be found various collections of political subsystems such as NATO, SEATO, the United Nations, or the Soviet bloc, and each of these might have separate effects on a given political system.

The task will be to devise a conceptual structure for systematically and economically tracing out the exchanges of the extra- and intrasocietal parameters with a given political system. Diagram 1 provides a highly and inexpressibly oversimplified version of the relationships just discussed. It is presented here as another way of interpreting the classification shown in Table 1 and offers a simple spatial representation of the exchanges between a system and the various components of its environment. At a later point I shall be able to modify this diagram so as to show, first, the dynamic relationship of a political system to its environment and, second, the flow of the influences of the environment through the system.

In reply to the questions with which we began this discussion, we have seen that political life may be described as a set or system of interactions defined by the fact that they are more or less directly related to the authoritative allocation of values for a society. Although similar allocations occur within other organizations, I shall find it useful to include within our range of theoretical concern only societal political systems rather than parapolitical systems. However, much of our conceptual structure might apply equally well, with the necessary modifications, to the parapolitical systems of organizations.

What happens to a political system, its stability or change, will in part be a function of the operations of internal variables, the elements we are primarily concerned with understanding and explaining. The way in which they function, the stresses imposed upon them, and the behavior that occurs as a response to such stress will also be a product of what takes place in the total environment of the political system. A political system is an open one in the sense that it is exposed, in varying degrees, to the events that occur in its environment. The concepts "boundary" and "environment" help to order our analysis with these desiderata in mind. A major effort with which we shall shortly be confronted will be to devise a further set of concepts adequate for simplifying and systematizing the study of the *relationships* between a system and its total environment.

Before proceeding to this task, we require additional preparation. I have specified the nature of a system as such, identified the characteristics of the system I shall be calling political, and called attention to the easily neglected setting in

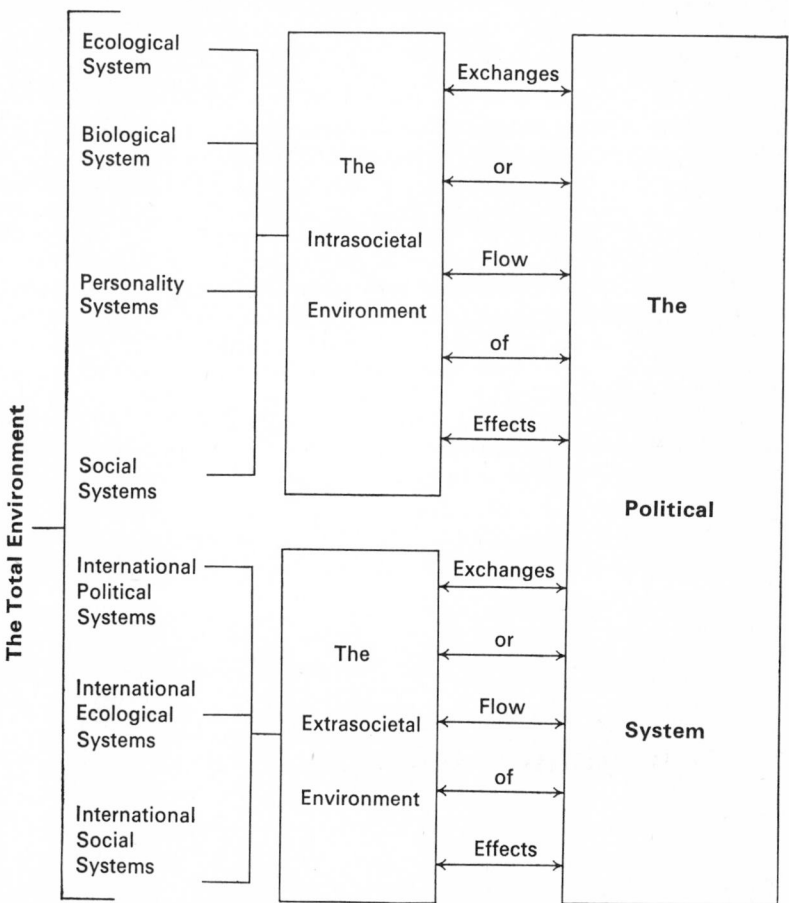

Diagram 1. Exchanges Between the Political System and the Total Environment

which this system must exist. This puts us in a position to open the door fully to the kind of theoretical analysis that becomes possible now that we have taken these first small steps. In the process of doing so we shall be able to explore additional significant properties of the political system as a system of behavior.

Notes

1. R. Basset, *Nineteen Thirty-One: Political Crisis* (London: Macmillan & Co., Ltd., 1958), Chap. 4, especially p. 62.
2. See Eisenstadt, *The Political Systems of Empires* [New York: Free Press, 1963].

3. E. R. Leach, *Political Systems of Highland Burma* (Cambridge: Harvard University Press, 1954), in which political structure seems to shift with movement from plains to hill agriculture; Schapera, *Government and Politics in Tribal Societies*, especially Chaps. I and VI and p. 219.
4. See S. Freud, *Group Psychology and the Analysis of the Ego* (New York: Liveright Publishing Corp., 1951) and *Civilization and Its Discontents* (New York: Doubleday & Company, Inc., 1958); E. F. M. Durbin and J. Bowlby, *Personal Aggressiveness and War* (New York: Columbia University Press, 1938), and the same authors with others, *War and Democracy* (London: Routledge & Kegan Paul, Ltd., 1938).
5. See N. J. Smelser and W. T. Smelser, eds., *Personality and Social Systems* (New York: John Wiley & Sons, Inc., 1963); J. S. Mill, *A System of Logic*, Book VI, especially Chap. V which is significantly entitled "Of Ethology, of the Science of the Formation of Character"; L. W. Pye, *Politics, Personality and Nation Building* (New Haven: Yale University Press, 1962); Lipset and Lowenthal, *Culture and Social Character*; R. E. Lane, *Political Life* (New York: Free Press of Glencoe, Inc., 1959), especially Part III and the many references found there, and *Political Ideology* (New York: Free Press of Glencoe, Inc., 1962), especially p. 400 ff.; A. Inkeles and D. J. Levinson, "National Character: The Study of Modal Personality and Sociocultural Systems," in *Handbook of Social Psychology*, G. Lindzey, ed. (Cambridge, Mass.: Addison-Wesley, 1954), II, 977–1020, and an extensive bibliography therein; D. Tomašić, *Personality and Culture in Eastern European Politics* (New York: George W. Stewart, Publisher, Inc., 1948); F. L. K. Hsu, ed., *Psychological Anthropology: Approaches to Culture and Personality* (Homewood, Ill.: The Dorsey Press, Inc., 1961), especially the essay by A. Inkeles, "National Character and Modern Political Systems," pp. 172–207.

13 . Mathematical Aspects of General Systems Analysis . **Anatol Rapoport**

"General system theory" subsumes an outlook or a methodology rather than a theory in the sense ascribed to this term in science. The salient feature of this outlook is, as its name implies, an emphasis on those aspects of objects or events which derive from general properties of systems rather than from the specific content. Clearly, then, the power and the scientific fruitfulness of general system theory depends on whether in fact there exist properties common to all systems, and if so whether important consequences can be derived from these properties. This, in turn, depends on the way "system" is defined or, in a pragmatic sense, on what portions of the world one chooses to regard as systems.

The system-theoretic point of view received its impetus from two sources: first,

From "The Social Sciences: Problems and Orientations," The Hague/Paris, 1968, Mouton/ Unesco, pp. 320–334. Reprinted by permission of The Society for General Systems Research, UNESCO, and the author.

a realization of the inadequacy of "mechanism" as a universal model; second, a tendency to counteract the fractionation of science into mutually isolated specialties. A radical critique of the mechanistic outlook was voiced already in the 1920's by Alfred North Whitehead (in *Science and the Modern World*). A principal thesis in that book was a warning that the store of fundamental ideas on which the then contemporary science was based (the "intellectual capital," as Whitehead called it) was becoming depleted. The implication was that unless a new source of ideas were tapped, science would face a dead end. Whitehead suggested that the concept of "organism," hitherto neglected in physical science, might be a source of new ideas.

Actually the concept of organism has always been fundamental in biology. Its exclusion from physics marked the beginning of modern physical science. This exclusion was necessary in order to free physics from the dead hand of Aristotelian philosophy with its emphasis on teleological goal-seeking determinants of motion. In this framework of thought, philosophers sought to explain the falling of stones by the "nature" of stones and the rising of smoke by the "nature" of smoke. The "nature" of an object or a substance was supposed to prescribe for it its proper or natural position, and so motion was explained by the supposed striving of each object or substance to attain its natural position.

This teleological conception of motion proved to be sterile and was rejected by Galileo and his successors in favor of the mechanistic conception. In this conception, it was not some final sought-after state of affairs, but the combination of forces acting on a body at a given moment, that determined its motion, namely via instantaneous changes of velocity. The observed motion was a sequence of these instantaneous changes. In this scheme, the "nature" of the moving body and of its "proper position" has no place.

The phenomenal success of classical physics (which was nurtured entirely on the mechanistic view) attests to the fruitfulness of this view. The difficulty of incorporating in it the behavior of living systems attests to its limitations. Both the strength and the limitations of the mechanistic outlook reside in the mathematical methods used in the construction of mechanistic theories. The fundamental tool of this method is the differential equation which is essentially a precise statement about how certain quantities and their rates of change are related. For example, the law of motion of a particle in a gravitational field is expressed by a relationship involving the acceleration suffered by the particle and the strength and direction of the field at a particular time in a particular place. But the strength and direction of the field depend on the position of the particle, and its acceleration involves the second derivatives (the rates of change of the rates of change) of the position coordinates. In other words, a law of motion is expressed by a differential equation. The solution of such a differential equation gives the position of the particle for all time to come, once the initial position and velocity and the nature of the gravitational field are known. The immense predictive power of celestial mechanics derives from this deterministic character of the differential equation.

If several bodies are involved, the gravitational field associated with each of them affects the accelerations of all of them.   Their motions would then be described by a *system* of differential equations in which the relations between the positions and the accelerations are all interwoven by a network of interdependencies.   Now if the differential equations comprising a system are linear, i.e., if the variables and their rates of change appear at most in the first degree, the same general methods of solution apply regardless of how many equations are involved.   However, the differential equations describing motions of bodies in the gravitational field associated with them are not linear (since the gravitational forces are inversely proportional to the squares of distance, between the bodies).   Consequently the equations are not solvable by the known general methods.

Fortunately for the success of the mechanistic method, the solar system, with which classical celestial mechanics was concerned, constituted a special, tractable case of several bodies in motion.   The sun is so huge compared even to the largest of the planets that the mutual gravitational forces among the planets can be neglected in the first approximation.   That is to say, the motion of each planet can be calculated with good approximation as if it and the sun were the only two bodies in the universe.   This is the so-called two-body problem, which can be solved by classical methods.   To obtain better approximations, the mathematicians of the eighteenth and nineteenth centuries made use of the so-called perturbation method, in which the influences of the other planets were superimposed on the solutions of the separate two-body problems.   The success of these methods was assured by the weakness of interdependence among these separate two-body problems.   Had these interdependencies been strong (if, for example, the masses of the planets were comparable to that of the sun), the mathematicians would have been faced with an N-body problem, which has not been solved in the general form to our day.

Thus the specific nature of the solar system had both a stimulating and an inhibiting effect on the development of applied mathematics.   On the one hand, the success of mathematical methods made the physicists supremely confident in the power of these methods and led to the creation of mathematical physics, which to this day remains *the* model of completely rigorous science.   On the other hand, the successful methods became "fixated" in the minds of workers in applied mathematics, who sought to formulate problems in ways which made them tractable by those methods.   Consequently, many phenomena remained outside the scope of mathematized (i.e., completely rigorous) science.

The most important of these phenomena are those involving instances of "organized complexity."   Mathematically an "organized complexity" can be viewed as a set of objects or events whose description involves many variables, among which there are strong mutual interdependencies, so that the resulting system of equations cannot be solved "piece-meal," as in the case of classical celestial mechanics, where perturbations can be imposed on two-body problems.

In our experience, the living organism is the most obvious example of "organized complexity."   Attempts to represent the living organism as a mechanism have been unsuccessful except in extremely limited contexts, usually quite tangential to the central problem, that of describing the living process (including behavior) in mechanistic terms. Awareness of this limitation propelled some philosophers (for example, Bergson) and some biologists (for example, H. Driesch) toward vitalism, which excludes the prospect of eventually explaining living processes in terms of known physical and chemical processes. The vitalists postulated special "vital forces" to account for phenomena associated with life. Other philosophers, while avoiding the refuge of ad hoc concepts like "vital force," emphasized the necessity of re-organizing or extending the conceptual repertoire of science in order to bring "organized complexity" within its scope. This was the meaning of A. N. Whitehead's warning that the intellectual capital accumulated in the seventeenth century (i.e., the mechanistic method of analysis) was becoming depleted.

The mechanistic method of analysis can be understood in a sense broader than that of classical mechanics. It includes all forms of analysis which seek to explain the working of a whole in terms of the working of its parts. Such an approach characterizes not only classical celestial mechanics (in which the behavior of the solar system emerges from the behavior of individual "point masses" which comprise it) but also the methods of physiology in which the life process is viewed in terms of sequences of chemical reactions; the method of behavioristic psychology which conceives of behavior as a totality of "responses to stimuli"; classical market economics, which pictures the economic process as a totality of actions of individuals motivated to buy or to sell by the fluctuations of supply and demand, etc. In short, in a broader sense the mechanistic outlook is an extension of the Laplacian idea that the universe (or any portion of the universe singled out by our attention) can be explained if the laws governing its constituent atomic units are known. Roughly speaking, it is a view which holds the whole to be the sum of its parts. The often cited negation of this view, "The whole is greater than the sum of its parts," should be regarded not as a denial of a well known tautology but rather as an expression of the inadequacy of the mechanistic view.

An antithesis to the mechanistic outlook is a view which makes some "whole" the starting point of investigation. According to this view, the laws governing the behavior of the whole are taken as primary. To the extent that one is interested in the behavior of the parts, one seeks to deduce them from the laws governing the behavior of the whole. Thus one would seek to deduce the behavior of individuals from the roles they play in an institution or a society, which is supposedly governed by laws relevant to *that* level of organization. In this approach, the problem of synthesizing the behavior of the whole from that of the parts is by-passed. This view, which can be called the organismic, still prevails in certain areas of biological and social science. For example, when a physiologist explains the action of an organ in terms of its contribution to the survival of the organism, or when a cultural anthropologist of the "functionalist" school explains a practice or belief in terms of how it fits into a "culture pattern," each is using the organismic approach.

The organismic approach brings into focus the "whole," which often eludes the methods of the mechanistic approach. The weakness of the organismic approach stems from its tendency toward teleological explanation, which, as we have already seen, had led pre-Galilean physical science into an impasse.

General system theory, or at least its mathematical aspect, can be viewed as an effort to fuse the mechanistic and the organismic approaches so as to utilize the advantages of each. A system is not merely a totality of units (particles, individuals), each governed by laws of causality operating upon it, but rather a totality of *relations* among such of these units. The emphasis is on organized complexity, i.e., on the circumstance that the addition of a new entity introduces not only the relation of this entity to all others but also modifies the relations among all the other entities. The more tightly interwoven is the network of relations, the more organized is the *system* comprised by the relations. *Degree of organization*, then, becomes the central concept of the system-theoretic view. Theories engendered by this view have been called (among other things) contributions to general system theory.

A second impetus to general systems theory came, as we have said, from a perceived need to counteract the excessive specialization in science which had been threatening to sever all communication among scientists in different fields, or even different subfields of the same field, for want of a common technical language. This view was forcefully voiced by Norbert Wiener in his book, *Cybernetics*.[1] Cybernetics is an example of a discipline which cuts across the established disciplines of science and by doing so provides opportunities for communication among scientists from different disciplines.

While the organismic view, proposed by Whitehead and other philosophers of similar persuasion, was hardly more than an expression of awareness of the problem posed by the inadequacy of the mechanistic view, cybernetics became a concrete example of how the system concepts could be developed without departing from the standards of rigor demanded in physical science. For cybernetics is a mathematical method specifically developed to describe "organized complexity."

Cybernetics has been defined as the science of communication and control. It first developed in the context of problems associated with the development of complex weapons systems equipped with automatic guidance and control devices. Similar problems arose also in the design of communication systems and of high speed computers. Almost simultaneously, Wiener, a pioneer in cybernetics, and Claude E. Shannon, who first formulated rigorously the foundations underlying the mathematical theory of communication, recognized the cardinal principle involved in all of these problems, namely that of "amount of information." The concept of information is as central in cybernetics and communication engineering as the concept of energy is in classical physics.

Energy had been the unifying concept underlying all physical phenomena involving work and heat. Information became the unifying concept underlying the working of organized systems, i.e., systems whose behavior was under control so as to achieve some pre-set goals. This control is accomplished by processes involving the coding, the storage, and the transmission of information. In this way the organismic, "teleological" notions of goal-seeking behavior were reintroduced into the theory of physical processes. In this modern version, however, these notions are derived not from metaphysical speculations on the "nature" of the behaving entities but from the mathematical structure of systems characterized by organized complexity.

Since "amount of information" is defined in purely mathematical terms, this concept is applicable to the analysis of all phenomena in which organized, specifically goal-seeking behavior is involved. Thus the ideas of cybernetics have served not only in extending rigorous mathematical methods to the study of organized complexity but also as a source of concepts cutting across the disciplines. In this way the ideas of cybernetics have been instrumental in counteracting the alienation between scientists who had become isolated from each other by virtue of the barriers set up by specialized technical language.

An example of this integrating function of cybernetics is seen in the fusion of biological and physical concepts which cybernetics has stimulated. The concept of "the amount of information" has played an important part in this fusion. "The amount of information" required to describe some state of affairs is roughly related to the average (expected) amount of guessing required to guess the actual state of affairs among all the possible ones. Thus, if I ask you to guess the number which I have arbitrarily selected from the numbers between one and one million, it will take you (on the average) more guesses to determine this number than if I had selected it from one to one hundred. (A "guess" is understood as a question which can be answered by "yes" or "no.")

It can be easily seen that a number from one to one hundred can always be guessed in seven guesses, while a number from one to a million can always be guessed in twenty guesses. To do this one needs to make guesses in such a way as to eliminate one half of the remaining range. In the case of a million one starts with "Is it less than 500,000?" If yes, "Is it less than 250,000?" If no, then "Is it less than 375,000?" etc. Since one million is less than 2^{20}, it will take at most 20 such dichotomies to determine the number.

So far we have assumed that the selection of each number in the range is equally probable. If this is not the case, the "amount of information" is reduced. Specifically, let p_n be the probability that the number n has been selected from the range $1 \leqslant n \leqslant N$. Then it can be shown that $H(n) = -\sum_{n=1}^{N} p_n \log_2 p_n$ is the average number of guesses required to guess the number. Accordingly, $H(n)$ is defined as the amount of information associated with the situation.

Now Wiener has noted that this expression of "the amount of information" was formally identical (as a mathematical expression) with the formula which designates the *entropy* of a physical system. In this interpretation, p stands for the probability that the system is in a particular "molecular state," as defined by the configuration of its molecules and of their velocities. This formula was derived in statistical mechanics and provided a link between the kinetic theory of gases and classical thermodynamics. The concept of entropy had been developed in the latter discipline in connection with the formulation of its so-called Second Law. The Second Law of Thermodynamics states that if a physical system (in this context, simply a portion of the physical universe) is isolated from its environment, then the amount of entropy in the system can only increase toward a maximum (never decrease). *Physically,* this means that although the total amount of energy in the system will remain constant (a consequence of the First Law of Thermodynamics), the amount of so-called "free energy" (i.e., energy which can do work on the environment) can only decrease. To put it in another way, the tendency in an isolated system is for its energy to be "degraded," i.e., to become heat energy, which becomes unavailable for "useful work" (i.e., work upon the environment). *Statistically* this means that isolated systems tend to drift from less probable configurations to more probable ones, or, which is the same thing, from more "organized" states to more "chaotic" ones.

For a while the vitalists cited the Second Law in support of their contentions. It appeared to them that living organisms violated the Second Law; for, at least in the process of embryonic development, an organism becomes *more* organized, not less. Only after death does the process of disorganization set in, until the organism disintegrates and gradually becomes undifferentiated from the environment. The vitalists sought, therefore, to explain the entropy-reducing capacity of living organisms by a vital principle outside the scope of physical law.

It did not take long to point out the basic error in the vitalists' conclusion. The Second Law of Thermodynamics applies only to *isolated* systems. An isolated system cannot be a living system (at least not for long). Therefore an argument based on the supposed circumvention of the Second Law by living systems collapses. However, the vitalists' argument, although it was in itself unsound, served a constructive purpose in calling attention to a fundamental aspect of the living process previously unnoticed, namely that the food ingested by living organisms serves not only as a source of energy but also as a source of *free* energy, which compensates for the increase of entropy associated with physical and chemical processes in accordance with the Second Law. As E. Schroedinger put it picturesquely, "life feeds on negative entropy." Food ingested by animals and sunlight absorbed by plants are rich in "negative entropy" (free energy), and this supplies the living organisms not only with energy used in maintaining the living process, but also with means to maintain and even to increase the "organized complexity" which characterizes them as living systems and so to resist the trend toward disorganization inherent in the operation of the Second Law.

Wiener's insight into the meaning of the mathematical connection between entropy and information provides further clarification of the fundamental principle of the living process. Increase of entropy can be viewed as "destruction of information." Conversely, information can be used to reduce entropy. A simple analogy will serve to illustrate this principle. Consider a deck of playing cards as it comes from the factory, i.e., arranged in perfect order. If we know the order, we can name with certainty the card which follows any given card. Putting it in another way, knowledge of what card has been picked gives us much information about what card follows. Let now the deck be shuffled by repeated cuttings of the deck. After only a few cuttings we can still frequently guess what card follows a given card (if the two happened not to have been separated by a cutting). However, as the number of cuttings increases, we shall make more and more errors in our guesses. Eventually the cuttings will completely "randomize" the deck and so we shall guess the card following a given card with no more than chance frequency (once in fifty-one times). That is, all the information provided by a given card about the next card has been destroyed by the shuffling. This process is analogous to the operation of the Second Law of Thermodynamics. The deck goes from an ordered (improbable) state to a chaotic (probable) state. We cannot reverse this process by continued shuffling: the original order will almost certainly not be restored.

We can, however, restore the original order by "feeding information" into the deck. This can be done in the following manner. Imagine a position assigned to each card according to the original order, i.e., 1–52. Look at each successive card of the shuffled deck; and if it has moved forward from its original position, move it one position backward, and vice versa. In doing so we are "injecting" information (in the form of either-or decisions) into the deck. Eventually the original order of the cards will be restored. In other words, a process analogous to a reversal of the Second Law may well occur if interventions in the form of decisions are allowed.

This way of looking at the Second Law of Thermodynamics led Clerk Maxwell to formulate an interesting idea, namely that a being with perceptions sufficiently keen to observe and control the positions and velocities of single molecules (Maxwell's Demon), could reverse the process of increasing entropy (disorder) even in an isolated system. To an outside observer, such a system would appear to be violating the Second Law of Thermodynamics.

Maxwell's argument, however, contains a basic fallacy. If the demon is placed inside the system, the processes going on within *him* must also be taken into account in computing the total change in entropy. It was subsequently shown by L. Szilard and later by L. Brillouin that the processes within the demon (whether he is a mechanism or an organism) must be such that the decrease in entropy effected by his intervention is at least compensated (in general, over-compensated) by an increase of entropy in the demon. If, on the other hand, the demon intervenes from outside the system, then the system can no longer be considered to be isolated, and the Second Law does not apply.

It was this fundamental distinction between isolated and non-isolated systems that led L. Bertalanffy to formulate his approach to general system theory. The distinction, argued Bertalanffy, leads to a crucially important insight into the nature of life.

The most fundamental property of a living organism is its ability to maintain its "organized" state against the constant tendency toward disorganization implied by the operations of the Second Law of Thermodynamics. We have seen that this ability is inherent in the fact that a living organism is an open (non-isolated) system. Therefore, biology must be rooted in the theory of such systems. In particular, the characteristic properties of living organisms—for example, the maintenance of steady states (homeostasis), the principle of equifinality (the attainment of final states, irrespective of initial conditions), the apparently purposeful behavior of organisms, etc.—ought to be derivable from general properties of open systems.

To the extent that such general properties of systems are describable in a language independent of the specific nature of the systems, general system theory can provide the framework for integrating the specialized disciplines and in this way alleviate the estrangement between workers in fields separated by over-specialized language.

The language of mathematics is eminently qualified to serve as the language of general systems theory, precisely because this language is devoid of content and expresses only the structural (relational) features of a situation.

As an example, consider a system of chemical reactions in which the rate of change of concentration of each of the substances involved is a linear function of the concentrations of all of the substances. The behavior of such a system is described by a system of first order linear differential equations of the following form:

$$\frac{dx_i}{dt} = \sum_{j=1}^{n} a_{ij}x_j + b_i \quad (i = 1, 2 \ldots n), \tag{1}$$

where x_i is the concentration of the i-th substance, and a_{ij} represents the effect of substance j upon the rate of change of substance i. This effect is facilitating if a_{ij} is positive, and inhibitory if negative. The constant b_i represents an outside source of the i-th substance (if positive) or a sink (if negative).

Suppose now we are interested in a steady state of the system, i.e., a state of affairs in which all of the rates of change are zero. We can obtain such a steady state if we set the left-hand side of every equation equal to zero and solve for the x_i, thus obtaining the concentrations which guarantee a steady state. Suppose first, that the system is isolated, i.e., has neither sources nor sinks. Mathematically this means that all the b_i are zero. The resulting system of equations is then a *homogeneous* system of n linear equations in n unknowns. It is known that the only unique solution of such a system is $x_i = 0$. In other words, the only steady state which is uniquely determined by our conditions would be the trivial one, where all the concentrations are zero. However, we have omitted an important condition if we are speaking of a real physical system, namely the fact that the total mass of all the substances must remain the same (the law of conservation of mass). Mathematically this law is expressed by the condition:

$$\sum_{i=1}^{n} \frac{dx_i}{dt} = 0. \tag{2}$$

But if the condition holds, we get only $n - 1$ independent equations when we set $dx_i/dt = 0$. Such a system has an infinity of solutions. A *unique* solution can be obtained only if an additional condition is imposed. If the system is isolated, this additional condition must be a statement concerning the total mass (or the sum of the concentration) of the substances, e.g.,

$$\sum_{i=1}^{n} x_i = C \quad \text{(a constant).} \tag{3}$$

Now the system has a unique steady state; but what this steady state is depends on C, i.e., on the sum of the initial concentrations.

Suppose now, on the contrary, that the system is open, i.e., contains sources and sinks. Now the b_i are not all zero; the system of equations is non-homogeneous and (except in some very special cases) has a unique steady state solution. This steady state does *not* depend on the initial concentrations. Consequently, if we tamper with the system, i.e., increase or decrease various concentrations, it will nevertheless tend to the *same* steady state as soon as we leave it alone. This steady state will depend only on the a_{ij} and on the b_i, that is, on the *relations* within the system and between the system and the outside world. Such a system will exhibit "equifinality," i.e., will seem to an observer to "seek" a final state "appropriate" to it. A naive observer may be induced to invoke teleological notions or to attribute purposeful behavior to a system of this sort, whereas mathematical analysis shows that the apparently purposeful behavior of the system is a consequence strictly deduced from the fact that it is open, not closed.

The question of the existence of a steady state independent of initial conditions is only one of many questions one can ask with reference to the behavior of a system. Other important questions relate to the stability of steady states, if they exist. A steady state is stable if small departures from it result in an ultimate return of the system to the same steady state. If, however, small departures tend to be "magnified" so that the system moves even further away, the steady state is unstable. Next, there may be several steady states if the differential equations describing the system are not linear. The number and stability of the steady states, as well as the behavior of the system in moving over intermediate states toward or away from the steady states, are thus completely determined by the structure of the *mathematical model* which describes the system.

Mathematical aspects of general system theory are those that concern the structure of mathematical models which describe the systems. The shift of attention from the specific nature of systems (physical, biological, social) to their mathematical structure makes possible a rigorous definition of "system," suggests ways of linking the organismic view with the mechanistic, and opens excellent opportunities for bridging the gap between specialized disciplines.

A system from a mathematical point of view is any portion of the world which at any given time can be described by ascribing specific values to a number of variables. The totality of these values constitutes a *state* of the system. A static or structural theory of a system is the totality of assertions which relate the values of these variables to each other, when the system is in some state singled out for attention (for example, an equilibrium or steady state). A dynamic theory of a system is one which indicates how changes in the values of some of the variables depend on the values or on the changes in the values of other variables. Thus a dynamic theory is the totality of assertions from which the behavior of the system, as it goes from state to state, can be mathematically deduced.

The system is the more complex, the more variables are required to describe a state of the system. The system is the more organized, the more it is equipped to resist disturbances in "pursuing a chosen goal." The phrase in quotation marks is to be understood metaphorically. No conscious striving for goals needs to be ascribed to a system. A "goal" in its general sense is simply some end state to which a system tends by virtue of its structural organization (as was made clear in the chemical reaction example above).

Organization and complexity are correlated. For example, the essence of automation is the capacity of machines to adjust to changing conditions (as in an automated oil refinery). The adjustments require "sense receptors" (which take readings from the environment), communication networks, correction devices, etc. All of these make for greater complexity, since the state of each device is an additional variable in the state of the system.

As has been pointed out, the system-theoretic view provides a link between the mechanistic view, which does not encompass the workings of a complex system as a whole, and the organismic view, which relies on ad hoc teleological notions and often sacrifices rigor in the interest of suggestive descriptions of system behavior. The most important advantage of the mathematical system-theoretic view, however, is in the natural integrative function of mathematical theory.

From the standpoint of a mathematical theory, two systems are the more closely related the more structural similarity there is between the mathematical models that describe them. As an example, consider the following system of differential equations,

$$\frac{dx_i}{dt} = \sum_{j=1}^{n} \sum_{k=1}^{n} a_{jk}^{(i)} x_j x_k + \sum_{j=1}^{n} b_{ij} x_j + C_i \quad (i = 1, 2 \ldots n). \tag{4}$$

This system is of the second degree, since products of pairs of variables appear on the right, in addition to the variables themselves and the constant terms. This system of equations is a reasonable description of a system of chemical reactions in which reactions occur as a consequence of collisions between molecules of the different substances involved. The frequencies of such collisions are roughly proportional to the products of the corresponding concentrations, as reflected in the quadratic terms. The linear terms represent the monomolecular reactions, while the constant terms represent, as in the previous example, sources and sinks. However, there is nothing about these indications that suggests an interpretation in terms of chemical reactions. The variables might well represent populations of several species of organisms in an ecological system. If the members of such populations prey on each other, then the rates of population increase or decrease may well depend on the frequencies with which individuals "collide," since a collision between a predator and its prey may result in the demise of the prey and in an increase in the mass of the predator. Similarly, reproduction depends upon meetings of members of the same species of opposite sex. Therefore equations (4) may represent a rough model of an ecological system as well as of a chemical one.

Finally, consider a population of human beings divided into groups, each characterized by a certain behavior pattern or a complex of opinions or beliefs (i.e., members of sub-cultures, religions, political parties, and the like). Contacts between members may result in shifts or modifications of behavior patterns, beliefs, or the like, consequently in increases or decreases of the sub-populations. Thus equations (4) may be imagined to be also a model of some social process.

How accurately a mathematical model can describe a real system is an important question but is not central to a general system theory. In order to answer this question, an intensive empirical study is required of the system in question. Such a study is centered on the *content* of the events examined. General system theory, however, is primarily concerned with the *structures* of systems as defined by the relations which the parts of a system have to each other, in the way these relations determine the dynamic behavior of the system (its passage from state to state), and with the history of the system, i.e., its own development as a result of the interactions between it and its environment.

A mathematical general system theory provides descriptions of these three aspects of systems, namely structure, behavior, and evolution, in abstract mathematical language. A typology of systems, accordingly, becomes a mathematical typology. Two systems are identical if the mathematical structures of their respective models are identical (or *isomorphic*, to use the mathematical expression). The degree of similarity between the systems is estimated by the degree in which their mathematical models are related.

The shift of emphasis from the content to the structure of events helps in the resolution of many controversies of questionable fruitfulness. For example, in the light of the organismic approach to a theory of social systems, many analogies suggest themselves. An institution can be easily imagined to be an organism. Its organizational structure can be thought to correspond to "anatomy," its modus operandi to "physiology" or "psychology," its history to the development of the organism; while the history of the *type* of institution can be compared to the evolution of the organism. The analogy may be extremely suggestive, but suggestiveness is not an index of reliability. One does not know the limits to which the analogy can be pushed; nor how to answer those who decry any theory inspired by "mere analogy." After all, an institution is *not* a biological organism, and the resemblance brought out by the analogy may be as spurious as the resemblance of some cloud formations to animals, or of thunder to an angry outburst.

Another familiar example of a heated controversy concerning the validity of analogy is that raging around the question of whether "the brain is a computer." This controversy is obscured by clashing philosophical convictions. There are people who relish the idea of reducing all phenomena, including mental operations and emotions, to physical events; and there are others who are repelled by this idea. The general system theorist by-passes this issue. He is interested in the *extent* to which the operation of a brain can be likened to that of a computer. The answer to this question is not to be found in what a brain and a computer "are" (such questions are vestiges of prescientific metaphysics), but rather in what brains and computers *do*. *To the extent* that certain operations of the brain can be represented as the behavior of a system having some hypothesized structure and dynamic properties, and *to the extent* that such a system can be simulated by a computer, both the brain and the computer appear to be realizations of a certain general system type. [Note that this is not the same as saying that the brain "is" a computer.] The actual extent to which this analogy can be carried out becomes an empirical question rather than a metaphysical one. Clearly, any such re-statement of a problem facilitates a meaningful search for new knowledge both in the realm of automated information processing (computer technology) and in the realm of brain physiology. In this context, the concept of "amount of infor-mation," discussed above, serves the function of binding together theoretical frameworks of widely different content but of similar structure.

Still another example of how putting system-theoretic ideas into a mathe-matical framework clarifies certain issues of long standing is seen in the recent mathematical approaches to certain aspects of international relations. The idea of balance of power has been for a long time important in the conceptualization of international relations. The idea clearly derives from an analogy with phys-ical equilibria. As such it is open to all the objections raised against analogical thinking. It is, however, possible to construct various mathematical models of power relations among states. The aim is to see what theoretical consequences can be rigorously (e.g., mathematically) drawn from the various models. We have already seen how mathematical analysis brings out crucial distinctions between stable and unstable equilibria (steady states). The property of stability is a general system property. If the totality of relations among states vying with each other for power constitutes a system, then this system too has certain prop-erties of stability or instability, depending on the parameters of its dynamics.

Economic systems are also characterized by degrees of stability or instability in certain phases of their existence. To the extent that certain aspects of an econom-ic system (fluctuation of production levels, prices, or investment capital) can be cast into a mathematical model, questions about equilibria and their stability can be answered by rigorous mathematical deduction rather than by intuitive guesses.

It would be rash to draw definitive conclusions about the stability of the eco-nomic or international system from the properties of various hypothetical sys-tems offered as models. However, an examination of these purely theoretical consequences cannot fail to be instructive in the sense of enlarging the conceptual repertoire of the theoreticians. Mathematical models bring to our attention aspects of phenomena which might not otherwise have occurred to us.

In recent years increasing emphasis has been put upon probabilistic or stochas-tic aspects of processes. The corresponding models are based on the assumption that the transitions of a system from state to state are governed by probabilities. The question arises whether a system so defined is still an instance of "organized complexity," since one ordinarily thinks of organization in terms of well-defined contingencies of events rather than in terms of events determined by chance. To this one can reply along two lines. First, the distinction between deterministic and probabilistic contingencies is not sharp. Probabilities tend toward certainty as the probability of one of the possible events approaches one. Therefore a probabilistic system theory provides a useful intermediate theoretical framework between chaos and organization.   Indeed, the degree of organization of a system can be conveniently defined in terms of the departure of the observed behavior from a base line, determined by purely chance events.   Second, in a large population of systems, probabilities become frequencies, and so determinism is in a sense re-established in the observed distributions of system characteristics.

The introduction of probabilistic and stochastic models to describe systems puts the entire conceptual apparatus of the theory of stochastic processes at the disposal of general system theory.   Like all other mathematical concepts, those derived from the theory of stochastic processes are content-free and therefore provide additional opportunities for integrating theories of widely different content.   The statistics of accidents, of divorces, of strikes, of elections, etc., are all derivable from appropriate stochastic models.   The parameters of these models constitute the corresponding system characteristics.   These parameters are structural parameters independent of content, and therefore are suitable building blocks of corresponding unified theories cutting across the special concepts derived from special contents.

In calling attention to the methodological advantages of general system theory, particularly of its mathematical formulations, one should not, of course, forget the limitations of this approach.   Conclusions about structural similarities between two or more systems are valid only if the corresponding mathematical models are sufficiently faithful representations of the systems.   As a matter of fact, however, the formulation of a mathematical model is often an extremely difficult task.   Some systems defy all attempts at mathematical descriptions. So far, all the suggestions for constructing mathematical models of a brain have remained merely suggestions.   No such model exists; nor does one seem feasible, if by a model one means more than a description in mathematical terms of some very special features of neural functioning.

Too strong confidence in mathematical general system theory, therefore, may have one of two unfortunate consequences.   First, far from adequate models may be taken too seriously, for want of better models which remain tractable. Second, effort may be wasted in trying to subject to mathematical analysis systems so complex that they cannot possibly yield to such analysis, with the consequent neglect of other approaches, for example, the purely organismic approach which, after all, has been considerably successful in classical biology.   It would be wise, therefore, to consider mathematical general system theory as an important addition to the conceptual repertoire of the scientist rather than a method destined to drive all the older methods into obscurity.

Notes

1. The singling out of authors as proponents of views does not imply priority.   Thus L. Bertalanffy, to whom, incidentally the term "general system theory" is credited, anticipated Wiener
in pointing out the necessity of counteracting the fractionation of science.   We mention Wiener

in order to emphasize the importance of cybernetics in providing a framework of concrete ideas which have stimulated recent developments in general system theory.

References

Bertalanffy, L. Von. "General System Theory, a Criticial Review." *General Systems*, Vol. 7, pp. 1–22 (1962).

Brillouin, L. "Life, Thermodynamics, and Cybernetics." *American Scientist*, Vol. 36, pp. 554–568 (1949).

Schroedinger, E. *What Is Life?* New York: The Macmillan Co., 1945.

Shannon, C. E. and Weaver, W. *The Mathematical Theory of Communication.* Urbana, Ill.: University of Illinois Press, 1949.

Szilard, L. "Über die Entropieverminderung in einen thermodynamischen System bei Eingriffen intelligenter Wesen." *Zeitschrift für Physik*, Vol. 1, 53, pp. 840–856 (1924).

Whitehead, A. N. *Science and the Modern World.* New York: Pelican Mentor Books, 1948.

Wiener, N. *Cybernetics.* New York: John Wiley & Sons, 1948.

14 . Conservatives and Radicals
Gerhard Lenski

Before concluding this chapter [of *Power and Privilege: A Theory of Social Stratification*], it is important to review and summarize the basic issues which have emerged out of the historic controversy between conservatives and radicals. Any truly synthetic theory must address itself to these issues.   Hence, this summary will serve not only as the conclusion to this historical review but also as the point of departure and foundation for all that follows.

In summarizing a controversy as extensive and protracted as this one has been, some degree of oversimplification is inevitable.   Conservatives have not always agreed among themselves, nor have radicals.   The only belief common to all conservatives has been their belief that the existing system of distribution was basically just; the only belief common to all radicals has been their belief that it was basically unjust.   On other matters there has been no single conservative or radical position to which each and every adherent subscribed.   Nevertheless, given the basic assumption about the justice or injustice of the system, other views tend to follow, with the result that most conservatives have lined up on one side of the key issues and most radicals on the other.   It is these dominant tendencies with which we are concerned here.

One of the most basic issues dividing radicals and conservatives over the centuries has been that concerning the nature of man himself.   Historically, conservatives have been distrustful of man's basic nature and have emphasized the need for restraining social institutions.   By contrast, radicals have been distrustful of these restraining institutions and have taken an optimistic view of man's nature.   This difference can be seen quite clearly in the French Revolution, where the conservatives put their trust in the monarchy and the Church and the radicals in man himself, emancipated from the restraints of these "corrupting" institutions.

A second basic issue has been that concerning the nature of society.   As noted before, conservatives have traditionally viewed society as a social system with various needs of its own which must be met if the needs and desires of its constituent members are to be met.   Radicals, by contrast, have tended to view society more as the setting within which various struggles take place; it is significant chiefly because its peculiar properties affect the outcome of the struggles.

Third, radicals and conservatives have also differed on the question of the degree to which systems of inequality are maintained by coercion.   Radicals have generally emphasized coercion as the chief factor undergirding and maintaining private property, slavery, and other institutions which give rise to unequal rights and privileges.   Conservatives, on the other hand, have argued that coercion plays only a minor role and inequality arises as a necessary consequence of consensus (i.e., because of values which are shared widely throughout society, even by the less privileged elements) and/or innate differences among men.

Fourth, proponents of the two traditions have differed concerning the degree to which inequality in society generates conflict.   Radicals have seen this as one of the chief consequences of inequality; conservatives have generally minimized it.

Fifth, a genuine disagreement exists concerning the means by which rights and privileges are acquired.   Radicals have laid great emphasis on force, fraud, and inheritance as the chief avenues.   Conservatives, by contrast, have stressed more justifiable methods such as hard work, delegation by others, and so forth.

Sixth, conservatives have always regarded inequality as inevitable.   Radicals, or at least those in the egalitarian tradition, have taken the opposite view, though in the case of Marxian theory they concede its inevitability at certain stages of societal development.

Seventh, a major disagreement has always existed with respect to the nature of the state and of law.   Radicals have commonly regarded both as instruments of oppression employed by the ruling classes for their own benefit.   Conservatives have seen them as organs of the total society, acting basically to promote the common good.

Eighth, and finally, conservatives have tended to regard the concept of class as essentially a heuristic device calling attention to aggregations of people with certain common characteristics. Radicals, however, have been much more inclined to view classes as social groups with distinctive interests which inevitably bring them into conflict with other groups with opposed interests. Perhaps we might summarize much of the foregoing by saying that conservatives have tended to be realists with respect to the concept "society" and nominalists with respect to the concept "class," while radicals have generally taken the opposite position.

These, then, are the basic issues. In the chapters [of *Power and Privilege: A Theory of Social Stratification*] which follow we shall return to them repeatedly since the synthesis must either take a position with respect to each of them or reformulate them. It may not be inappropriate to say at this point that we shall adopt the latter course as often as the former.

15 . Inequality in Industrial and Agrarian Societies . **Gerhard Lenski**

Of all the types of societies we have examined, none illustrates better than the industrial, the difficulties and limitations of a *purely* deductive and highly general approach to stratification theory. Given the vastly increased productivity of this type of society and the greatly enlarged powers of industrial states, nothing would be more logical than to predict inequalities in power and privilege even greater than those found in agrarian societies. However, even a limited survey of the contemporary scene suggests that this is not the case, and a more intensive examination confirms this impression. If anything, inequalities in power and privilege seem usually somewhat *less* pronounced in mature industrial societies than in agrarian. In short, *the appearance of mature industrial societies marks the first significant reversal in the age-old evolutionary trend toward ever increasing inequality.*

The evidence supporting these assertions takes several basic forms. To begin with, a comparison of the political systems of agrarian and industrial societies makes it clear that political power is much more concentrated in the former. In agrarian societies, the powers of government were nearly always vested in the hands of the few; the great majority were *wholly excluded* from the political process. In industrial societies this is a minority pattern, limited only to those societies in the earlier stages of industrialization and to those ruled by totalitarian parties. In the majority of industrial societies, all adult citizens not only enjoy voting privileges but, far more important, the right to organize politically to promote their own special interests or beliefs, even when these are in opposition to the interests or beliefs of those in power.[1]   While this does not mean that all inequalities in political power are eliminated or the democratic millennium ushered in, it does mean a significant reduction in political inequality and a substantial diffusion of political power, both of which are readily evident when these societies are compared with agrarian.   This can be seen most clearly in the case of the Scandinavian democracies, where Socialist Parties have been the dominant political force in recent decades, but the pattern is also evident in countries such as the United States and France, where the political influence of the lower classes has not been nearly so great.   It should also be noted that even in some of those industrial societies where democracy was not permitted, as in post-Stalinist Russia or Peron's Argentina, the political elite used much of its power to promote programs designed to benefit the lower classes, a practice virtually unknown in agrarian societies.

A second indication of declining inequalities can be found in data on the distribution of income.   Earlier we saw evidence which indicated that in agrarian societies the top 1 or 2 per cent of the population, usually received *not less than half* of the total income of the nation.[2]   In the case of industrial societies the comparable figure is substantially less.   According to official governmental reports, the top 2 per cent of the population of democratic nations receives about 10 per cent of the total personal cash income after taxes.   For example, British figures for 1954 indicate that the top 2 per cent received 8.5 per cent of the total income after taxes; Swedish figures for 1950 show the top 1.8 per cent received 9.9 per cent before taxes; Danish figures for 1949 show the top 1.1 per cent received 10.3 per cent *before taxes*; United States figures for 1958 show the top 1.3 per cent received 8.1 per cent, and the top 2.3 per cent received 11.6 per cent, *before taxes*.[3]

These figures cannot, of course, be taken at face value.   As a number of recent writers have pointed out, they do not include many billions of dollars of income, sometimes because of fraud and evasion by taxpayers, but more often because the tax statutes do not define certain forms of income as income.[4]   For example, as Gabriel Kolko has shown, in the United States such factors have led to underreporting of cash income to the extent of more than $30 billion each year; in addition, corporate expense account outlays are estimated to have been between $5 and $10 billion.[5]   Kolko suggests that, conservatively, a third of the corporate expense account outlay represented income-in-kind for the top 10 per cent of the population, and that from a third to a half of the errors and evasions should be assigned to the same group.   If one accepts these estimates (and they are not likely to be low, given Kolko's evident political sympathies), this means that the upper-income tenth received from $12 to $18 billion more in annual income than was reported in their tax returns.   If, to avoid *any* danger of conservative bias, we assume that almost all of this went to the upper 2 per cent of the population, we arrive at an error estimate of $10 to $15 billion for this group.   Offsetting this in part, however, is the balance of the evasions and errors estimate, totaling roughly $20 billion, which must be assigned to the remaining 98 per cent of the population. Taking the higher estimate for underreporting by the upper-income group, i.e., $15 billion, we arrive at the conclusion that, before taxes, 15.5 per cent of the personal income of the American people went to the top 2.3 per cent.

Even this figure, however, is far short of the 50 per cent estimated to be the elite's share of the gross national product in agrarian societies. This difference arises, in part, because the revenues of government are included in agrarian societies but not in industrial. On first inspection this may seem both arbitrary and unjust. Actually it is neither. In agrarian societies government functions almost entirely, as we have seen, as an instrument of, by, and for the few. In modern industrial societies, this is no longer the case. While it is true that the upper classes still benefit disproportionately from the actions of government in every industrial society, it is also true that the masses of ordinary citizens benefit to an extent undreamed of in the agrarian societies of the past, or even in those which still survive.

It is impossible to determine with any precision what percentage of the benefits of government go to the top 2 per cent of the population and what percentage to the remainder in industrial societies. However, even if one were to assume that they went *entirely* to the elite, the total would still fall short of the agrarian figure of 50 per cent. In most industrialized societies, the costs of government at all levels, from local to national, constitute only 20 to 30 per cent of the gross national product, with an average of about 25 per cent.[6] If this average figure were added to our earlier estimate that up to 15 per cent of *personal income* (which means about 12 per cent of the gross national product), goes to the upper 2 per cent, then less than 40 per cent of the gross national product would go to the equivalent of the agrarian elite, i.e., the top 2 per cent. If we were to assume, more realistically, that only as much as half of the benefits of government went to the favored 2 per cent, the elite's share of the gross national product would drop to only 25 per cent.[7] Thus, while it may not be possible to determine precisely what percentage of the gross national product is enjoyed by the top 2 per cent in mature industrial societies, it is safe to conclude that the percentage is considerably less than in agrarian. In fact, it is probably no more than half so large, and quite possibly less than that.[8]

Since the foregoing estimates are all based on data from democratic nations, one may properly ask whether the situation in totalitarian states is not different. This question is not easily answered owing to the paucity of trustworthy quantitative data. However, such as we have indicates that in the Soviet Union, at least, income inequality is substantially less than in the United States. According to one recent study, the minimum Soviet wage is 300 rubles monthly, and the average from 800 to 900. By comparison, highly placed executives in Soviet industry received from 4,500 to 7,500 rubles per month, fifteen to twenty-five times the minimum and five to ten times the average.[9] These figures are very similar to those reported by others who have studied the subject.[10] However, one other recent report adds that top incomes in the Soviet Union "reach a million rubles a year," or about 80,000 rubles per month.[11] This is nearly three hundred times the minimum and about a hundred times the average. As in the case of non-Communist nations, these figures omit many very tangible benefits for the rich as well as the poor. It appears, however, that these are roughly proportional to cash incomes and thus have no great effect on the ratios.

Turning to the United States, we find that one who currently earns the minimum wage for businesses engaged in interstate commerce would, if fully employed, receive about $2,500 per year. The median income reported in 1958 tax returns was about $4,000 per year.[12] The earned incomes of important executives in major industries in recent years have ranged from $50,000 to over $500,000 a year and have almost always been supplemented appreciably by unearned income from stock and bond holdings.[13] At the upper end of the income ladder, we have definite knowledge of one officially reported income of over $28 million in 1960, and if it is true, as reported, that J. Paul Getty owns assets valued at $2 billion, and if he obtains no more than a modest 4 per cent return on his investments, he should have an income of about $80 million per year (though obviously most of this would not be classified as "income" by the government).[14] Putting all these figures together, we find that American industrial executives receive from twenty to two hundred times the income indicated by the minimum wage law, and from 12 to 125 times the median income. Ignoring estimates of Getty's income, and taking as the maximum the more modest figure of $28 million, we find that this is eleven thousand times the minimum and seven thousand times the average. All these ratios are substantially larger than the corresponding Soviet ratios, which suggests that income inequality is much less pronounced in the Soviet Union than in the United States, a conclusion in keeping with the unsystematic and impressionistic observations of most trained visitors to Russia. Thus, it appears that the Soviet Union provides no exception to the conclusion about the historic decline in income inequality formulated on the basis of data from democratic nations.

CAUSES OF THE REVERSAL

From the theoretical standpoint, the decline in political and economic inequality associated with the emergence of industrial societies is extremely important. This constitutes a reversal in a major historical trend, and the reasons for this reversal are by no means obvious. On the contrary, given the increased productivity of industrial societies and the growth in the powers of the state, one would normally predict even greater inequality than in agrarian societies. The fact that the opposite occurred indicates either that one or more of the basic postulates with which we began is in error, or that other factors are at work which were not taken into account (or, at least, not sufficiently) in our original, highly general formulation. The evidence, as I shall show, favors the latter interpretation, indicating again the serious difficulties which attend any effort to develop a general theory by purely deductive means.

Among the factors not considered in our earlier assumptions about the nature of man and society, was the relationship between technological and cultural complexity on the one hand, and administrative efficiency on the other. In modern industrial societies, technology in particular, and culture in general, are far more complex than in even the most advanced agrarian societies.[15] In fact, they are so complex that it is no longer possible for those in positions of high command to begin to understand the work of all those beneath them. In effect, there is a growing "ignorance" on the part of those in positions of command. This is not to say that those in authority in industrial societies are less intelligent or knowledgeable than their counterparts in agrarian societies, but rather that they are masters of *a smaller proportion* of what they need to know to maintain effective control over those beneath them. Thus, because of the many gaps in their knowledge, they are often compelled either to issue commands based on insufficient information, or to leave matters to the discretion of their subordinates, thus opening the door to encroachments on their prerogatives. In the former case, authority is preserved, but at the expense of efficiency and productivity, while in the latter case a measure of authority is sacrificed to increase efficiency and productivity. In short, *the relationship between productivity and authority appears to be curvilinear in industrial societies, at least up to the present time.*[16] Thus, unless political authorities are willing and able to sacrifice productivity, it is unlikely that they will be able to rely on the technique of command to the extent their agrarian counterparts did. However, to the degree that they delegate authority or rely on market mechanisms, they facilitate the diffusion of power and privilege.

A second factor which seems to have contributed to the reversal in the historic trend toward greater inequality is *the rapidity and magnitude of the increases in productivity.* In societies in which the gross national product and per capita income are rapidly rising, and promise to continue rising, elites find themselves in the paradoxical situation in which they can maximize their *net* input of rewards by responding to pressures from below and making certain concessions. By granting the lower classes some share in the economic surplus, they can reduce worker hostility and the accompanying losses from strikes, slowdowns, and industrial sabotage. In an expanding economy, an elite can make economic concessions in *relative* terms without necessarily suffering any loss in *absolute* terms. In fact, if the concessions are not too large, and the rate of the economy's growth is great enough, relative losses can even be accompanied by *substantial* absolute gains. For example, an elite would enjoy a substantially greater income if it took 40 per cent of the gross national product in a \$100 billion economy, than if it stubbornly fought to maintain a 50 per cent share and thereby held the economy at the \$50 billion level. *If we assume that the majority of men would willingly make modest relative concessions for the sake of substantial absolute gains, and if we also assume that leading members of the elites in industrial societies have an awareness of the benefits they can obtain from concessions, then we can only predict they will make them.*

A willingness to make concessions may also be encouraged by the principle of marginal utility. This principle serves as a reminder that the first million dollars normally has greater value to a man than any subsequent million he may acquire.

In societies with very productive economies, many members of the elite may be prepared to make some *economic* concessions in order to maximize other kinds of rewards, such as safety, respect, and leisure.   In other words, after a certain level of wealth has been attained, elites may prefer to sacrifice a portion of the economic surplus in order to reduce hostility and the dangers of revolution, and to win for themselves a greater measure of respect and affection.   Or, they may find it impossible to maintain tight control over political and economic organizations and at the same time enjoy the benefits of leisure, and so permit a portion of the economic surplus to pass into other hands.   In short, *because elites have multiple goals, and are not concerned with maximizing material rewards alone, they may be willing to make certain economic concessions in a highly productive and expanding economy.*

Yet another factor which has played a role in reducing inequality is the development of new and highly effective methods of birth control.   In the past, the natural tendency of the human race to multiply usually had the effect of offsetting whatever economic gains might otherwise have resulted from technological advance.   Numbers tended to increase up to the carrying power of the economy *except as limited by the development of tyrannical political systems which diverted the "economic surplus" to the elite at the expense of further population increase.* One consequence, of course, was the large and wretched class of expendables, whose very presence served to prevent any substantial long-run improvement in the lot of the peasants and artisans with whom they constantly competed for employment.

Today the situation is rapidly changing, and promises to change even more in the future.   For the first time in history, mankind has found safe, simple, and effective means of controlling population growth.   In societies where these have been most widely used, the rate of population growth has been slowed to the point where real and substantial gains in per capita income have been achieved in a fairly short time, thus reducing the intensity of the competitive pressures.   Now, for almost the first time in centuries, the lower classes are able to bargain for wages in markets no longer perennially glutted with labor.   This development has almost certainly contributed to the decline in inequality.

Another factor that has probably contributed to the decline in inequality is the great expansion in human knowledge.   In the past, the dominant class chiefly needed unskilled labor, and thanks to human fecundity, this was always plentiful. This put the vast majority of men in a poor bargaining position, and hence the price of labor was minimal.   Today, in the more advanced industrial societies, the situation is radically changed.   Because of the great functional utility of so much of the new knowledge, a host of occupational specialists have appeared who are not interchangeable to any great degree.   This introduces into the labor market certain rigidities which favor the sellers of labor, especially in an era in which the demand for technical skills is rapidly rising.   Furthermore, even if the dominant classes could obtain the necessary labor for a subsistence wage, it is doubtful that this would prove expedient.   The efficiency of work requiring mental effort or alertness can be seriously reduced when those performing it are not physically fit.   Two men working at 50 per cent efficiency in this situation are not the equal of one man working at top efficiency, as in work requiring brute strength alone.   Moreover expensive machines and tight production schedules are vulnerable to the mistakes of inattentive workers to a degree that is not characteristic of agrarian societies.   These factors all prevent the dominant classes from driving the wages of this increasingly numerous segment of the population down to the subsistence level, and prevent the system from reaching the level of economic inequality that is found in agrarian societies, both past and present.

The egalitarian trend in modern industrial societies is evident in the *political* area no less than in the economic.   In many respects the trend toward greater political equality is more surprising than the corresponding economic trend, because the struggle for political power is essentially a zero-sum "game," i.e., gains by one party necessarily entail corresponding losses by opponents.   The struggle for privilege, on the other hand, is a positive-sum "game," thanks to the constantly rising level of productivity.   Thus in the political realm the privileged classes cannot accept losses in relative terms and still realize absolute gains.

All the reasons for the spread of democratic government are still not completely understood.   Obviously, it has not been dictated by economic necessity, as shown by the vigor of a number of nondemocratic, totalitarian nations.   On the other hand, the relative frequency of democratic government in industrial states and its virtual absence in agrarian, strongly indicate some connection.   Specifically, this suggests that industrialization creates conditions favorable to the growth of democracy, but does not make it inevitable.

One favorable condition is the spread of literacy and the extension of education.   An illiterate peasantry lacking access to mass media of information is in a poor position to participate in the political process; a literate middle and working class with many media of information available is much more favorably situated.   Advances in the level of living have a similar effect.   Peasants and artisans living at, or near, the subsistence level cannot afford the luxury of sustained political activity; workers in an industrial society have more leisure, energy, and money to devote to this.   Still another factor favoring the growth of democracy is the modern pattern of warfare which involves the entire population to an extent unknown in agrarian societies.[17]   As many observers have noted, the traditional distinction between the military and civilian segments of the population has been almost obliterated, and military men have come to regard urban centers of production as prime military targets.   If Andrzejewski and other writers are correct, this trend should have an egalitarian influence, since inequality tends to be most pronounced where military activities are limited to the few.

More important than any of these, however, has been the rise and spread of *the new democratic ideology* which asserts that the state belongs to the people.[18]   This ideology is not simply a reflection of changing economic conditions, though, as we have seen, it has been affected by them.   Rather, the historical record indicates it had its origin in religious and philosophical developments of the seventeenth century and spread rather widely in the eighteenth century in countries which were still thorougly agrarian in character, e.g., the United States and France.   In fact, there appears to be as much justification for the thesis that this new ideology contributed to the emergence of industrial societies as for the converse.

In any case, this new ideology became an important force in the political life of industrial societies.   It captured the imagination of all kinds of men, even some of the political elite, thus making the traditional monopoly of political power increasingly untenable.   As the democratic ideology spread, those who governed had to make substantial concessions in order to avoid massive challenges to their power—challenges which would have been costly to resist, and might even have led to their overthrow.   The idea that the state should be the servant of all the people continues to be a major force in the modern era, mobilizing the egoistic impulses of the disadvantaged classes in an idealistic cause, thereby uniting morality and egoism in a manner reminiscent of their union under the banner of "the divine right of kings," but with the opposite effect.

Wherever democratic theory has become institutionalized, a dramatic new possibility has arisen: *now the many can combine against the few, and even though individually the many are weaker, in combination they may be as strong or stronger.* With this development, the door is opened to a host of revolutionary developments in the distributive realm.

Notes

1. In some countries the right of opposition is limited to those who are willing to support democratic procedures, with the result that Communist and Fascist parties are excluded by law, but even this limitation is absent in the majority of democratic nations.
2. [*Power and Privilege: A Theory of Social Stratification*], p. 228.   This figure includes the income of the ruler as well as that of the governing class.
3. British figures are calculated from G. D. H. Cole, *The Post-War Condition of Britain* (London: Routledge, 1956), p. 223; Swedish figures are from George R. Nelson (ed.), *Freedom and Welfare: Social Patterns in the Northern Countries of Europe* (sponsored by the Ministries of Social Affairs of Denmark, Finland, Iceland, Norway, and Sweden, 1953), p. 54; Danish figures are from K. Lemberg and N. Ussig, "Redistribution of Income in Denmark," in Alan Peacock (ed.), *Income Redistribution and Social Policy* (London: Cape, 1954), p. 72; United States figures are calculated from *The World Almanac, 1961*, p. 744.   All figures are from official governmental sources.
4. See, for example, Gabriel Kolko, *Wealth and Power in America: An Analysis of Social Class and Income Distribution* (New York: Frederick A. Praeger, 1962), especially chap. 1 or Philip Stern, *The Great Treasury Raid* (New York: Random House, 1964), on the United States.   See Richard M. Titmuss, *Income Distribution and Social Change* (Toronto, Canada: University of Toronto Press, 1962) on Britain.
5. Kolko, pp. 16–23.
6. See Dewhurst, *Europe's Needs*, p. 407.   See also Dewhurst, *America's Needs*, p. 579.
7. Critically minded readers may wonder why lower estimates of the elite's share of governmental benefits have not been used.   In part this is because it is not necessary to prove the basic point.

In part, however, it is because it appears that the privileged classes benefit from the actions of government to a far greater degree than we ordinarily suppose. For example, it is the wealthy owners of private property who are the chief beneficiaries of the expenditures for defense and police services. It is they, not the poor, who would be the chief losers if their country were conquered, or could not protect its interests abroad, or if internal anarchy developed. They also benefit disproportionately by highways and other governmental services which facilitate trade and commerce. They even benefit to a considerable degree from the technical education their nation provides, since this insures their industries a ready supply of skilled technicians, engineers, and scientists. By contrast, welfare expenditures, which go chiefly to the lower classes, are only a minor cost of government in comparison–despite the heated controversies they create. Thus, all things considered, it is probably not unrealistic to estimate that one-third to two-thirds of the value of all governmental services redound to the benefit of the most privileged 2 per cent.

8. For evidence on declining inequality in France in recent centuries, see Jean Fourastié, *The Causes of Wealth*, translated by Theodore Caplow (New York: Free Press, 1960, first published 1951), chap. 1.

9. David Granick, *The Red Executive* (Garden City, N.Y.: Doubleday Anchor, 1961), p. 92.

10. See, for example, Nicholas DeWitt, *Education and Professional Employment in the USSR* (Washington, D.C.: National Science Foundation, 1961), especially pp. 537–545 and appendix table 6-W. DeWitt states that the Russian government reported that the average wage was 710 rubles in 1955, and estimated that this had risen to 800 rubles by 1960. He also shows that wages reported in official Soviet publications sometimes ranged up to thirteen times the average without bonuses, and that with bonuses, which were largely limited to upper income groups, wage differentials would be increased 20 to 50 per cent. See also Emily Clark Brown, "The Soviet Labor Market," in Morris Bornstein and Daniel Fusfeld (eds.), *The Soviet Economy* (Homewood, Ill.: Irwin, 1962), fn. 19, pp. 201–202, who reports a range for manual workers from 450 to 2,500 rubles per month, with the latter apparently very exceptional. She reports average earnings for production workers in five large plants as ranging from 750 to 1,000 rubles per month. Margaret Dewar reports that after the reforms scheduled for 1962, there would probably be a 15 to 1 differential in income between the extremes in Soviet industry, i.e., between top managers and workers at the minimum wage. See "Labour and Wage Reforms in the USSR," in Harry G. Shaffer (ed.), *The Soviet Economy: A Collection of Western and Soviet Views* (New York: Appleton-Century-Crofts, 1963), p. 222.

11. Klaus Mehnert, *Soviet Man and His World*, translated by Maurice Rosenbaum (New York: Frederick A. Praeger, 1961), p. 24.

12. See *The World Almanac, 1961*, p. 744.

13. See, for example, Mabel Newcomer, *The Big Business Executive* (New York: Columbia University Press, 1955), p. 124, or the annual reports in *United States News and World Report*.

14. For the reported income of $28 million in 1960, see the speech of Sen. Paul Douglas, reported in *The Washington Post*, Dec. 14, 1963, p. A-4. On Getty's wealth, see Philip Stern, p. 21, or *Newsweek*, July 15, 1963, p. 48. As Stern makes clear, only half of capital gains are classified as "income" if taken during one's lifetime and none are so classified if the assets are kept until death (pp. 91–92).

15. One of the best evidences of this is the rapid growth of vocabulary in the language of every industrial society.

16. Recent events in the Soviet Union provide a good illustration of this. The increasing reliance on market mechanisms in economic decision making represents a deliberate effort to increase efficiency and productivity while sacrificing centralized authority. This development was forced on Soviet authorities by the physical impossibility of developing an adequate, workable, and comprehensive plan for the whole Soviet economy. According to reports, one Soviet economist predicted that unless there were drastic reforms, planning work would increase thirty-six-fold by 1980, and would require the services of the entire adult population, and this presumably would not raise the level of efficiency of the planning procedures. Another Soviet economist is reported to have argued that a sound plan must take acount of all the possible

interrelationships between products in the plan and the number of these interrelations is the square of the number of products.   Since the Soviet machine industry alone now turns out 125,000 different products, a comprehensive plan for this one industry would require provision for more than 15 billion interrelations.   See Joseph Alsop, "Matter of Fact," *The Washington Post*, Jan. 13, 1964.   While the use of modern high-speed computers will undoubtedly alleviate the problems of planners to a considerable degree, it is not likely that in the foreseeable future the curvilinearity in the relationship between productivity and authority can be eliminated, especially in societies in which the diversity of goods and services produced is constantly increasing.

17. See, for example, Walter Millis, *Arms and Men: A Study of American Military History* (New York: Putnam, 1956).

18. In one sense this ideology is not at all new, as shown in Chap. 1 [of *Power and Privilege: A Theory of Social Stratification*] and also in the practices of hunting and gathering and simple horticultural peoples.   In another sense, however, modern democratic beliefs can be said to derive from the work of seventeenth-century political theorists such as John Locke, who put this ancient idea in a modern form which made it a significant force first in the intellectual world and then in the political.

16 . The Evolution of Organizational Environments . Shirley Terreberry

Darwin published *The Origin of Species by Means of Natural Selection* in 1859. Modern genetics has vastly altered our understanding of the variance upon which natural selection operates.   But there has been no conceptual breakthrough in understanding *environmental* evolution which, alone, shapes the direction of change.   Even today most theorists of change still focus on *internal* interdependencies of systems—biological, psychological, or social—although the external environments of these systems are changing more rapidly than ever before.

INTRODUCTION

Von Bertalanffy was the first to reveal fully the importance of a system being open or closed to the environment in distinguishing living from inanimate systems.[1] Although von Bertalanffy's formulation makes it possible to deal with a system's exchange processes in a new perspective, it does not deal at all with those processes in the environment *itself* that are among the determining conditions of exchange.

From *Administrative Science Quarterly*, March 1968, pp. 590–613, by permission of *Administrative Science Quarterly*.

Emery and Trist have argued the need for one additional concept, "the causal texture of the environment."[2]   Writing in the context of formal organizations, they offer the following general proposition:

> That a comprehensive understanding of organizational behaviour requires some knowledge of each member of the following set, where L indicates some potentially lawful connection, and the suffix 1 refers to the organization and the suffix 2 to the environment:

$$L_{11}\, L_{12}$$
$$L_{21}\, L_{22}$$

L_{11} here refers to processes within the organization—the area of internal inter-dependencies; L_{12} and L_{21} to exchanges between the organization and its environment —the area of transactional interdependencies, from either direction; and L_{22} to proc-esses through which parts of the environment become related to each other—i.e., its causal texture—the area of interdependencies that belong within the environment itself.[3]

We have reproduced the above paragraph in its entirety because, in the balance of this paper, we will use Emery and Trist's symbols (i.e., L_{11}, L_{21}, L_{12}, *and* L_{22}) to denote intra-, input, output, and extra-system interdependencies, respectively. Our purpose in doing so is to avoid the misleading connotations of conventional terminology.

PURPOSE

The theses here are: (*1*) that contemporary changes in organizational environ-ments are such as to increase the ratio of externally induced change to internally induced change; and (2) that *other* formal organizations are, increasingly, the important components in the environment of any focal organization.   Further-more, the evolution of environments is accompanied—among viable systems—by an increase in the system's ability to learn and to perform according to changing contingencies in its environment.   An integrative framework is outlined for the concurrent analysis of an organization, its transactions with environmental units, and interdependencies among those units.   Lastly, two hypotheses are presented, one about organizational *change* and the other about organizational *adaptability*; and some problems in any empirical test of these hypotheses are discussed.[4]

CONCEPTS OF ORGANIZATIONAL ENVIRONMENTS

In Emery and Trist's terms, L_{22} relations (i.e., interdependencies within the en-vironment itself) comprise the "causal texture" of the field.   This causal texture of the environment is treated as a quasi-independent domain, since the environ-ment cannot be conceptualized except with respect to some focal organization.

The components of the environment are identified in terms of that system's actual and *potential* transactional interdependencies, both input (L_{21}) and output (L_{12}).

Emery and Trist postulate four "ideal types" of environment, which can be ordered according to the degree of *system connectedness* that exists among the components of the environment (L_{22}). The first of these is a "placid, random-ized" environment: goods and bads are relatively unchanging in themselves and are randomly distributed (e.g., the environments of an amoeba, a human foetus, a nomadic tribe). The second is a "placid, clustered" environment: goods and bads are relatively unchanging in themselves but clustered (e.g., the environments of plants that are subjected to the cycle of seasons, of human infants, of extractive industries). The third ideal type is "disturbed-reactive" environment and con-stitutes a significant qualitative change over simpler types of environments: an environment characterized by similar systems in the field. The extinction of dinosaurs can be traced to the emergence of more complex environments on the biological level. Human beings, beyond infancy, live in disturbed-reactive en-vironments in relation to one another. The theory of oligopoly in economics is a theory of this type of environment.[5]

These three types of environment have been identified and described in the literature of biology, economics, and mathematics.[6] "The fourth type, however, is new, at least to us, and is the one that for some time we have been endeavouring to identify."[7] This fourth ideal type of environment is called a "turbulent field." Dynamic processes "arise from the *field itself*" and not merely from the inter-actions of components; the actions of component organizations and linked sets of them "are both persistent and strong enough to induce autochthonous processes in the environments."[8]

An alternate description of a turbulent field is that the accelerating rate and complexity of interactive effects exceeds the component systems' capacities for prediction and, hence, control of the compounding consequences of their actions.

Turbulence is characterized by complexity as well as rapidity of change in causal interconnections in the environment. Emery and Trist illustrate the tran-sition from a disturbed-reactive to a turbulent-field environment for a company that had maintained a steady 65 percent of the market for its main product—a canned vegetable—over many years. At the end of World War II, the firm made an enormous investment in a new automated factory that was set up exclusively for the traditional product and technology. At the same time postwar controls on steel strip and tin were removed, so that cheaper cans were available; surplus crops were more cheaply obtained by importers; diversity increased in available products, including substitutes for the staple; the quick-freeze technology was developed; home buyers became more affluent; supermarkets emerged and placed bulk orders with small firms for retail under supermarket names. These changes in technology, international trade, and affluence of buyers gradually interacted (L_{22}) and ultimately had a pronounced effect on the company: its market dwindled rapidly. "The changed texture of the environment was not recognized by an able but traditional management until it was too late."[9]

Sociological, social psychological, and business management theorists often still treat formal organizations as closed systems.   In recent years, however, this perspective seems to be changing.   Etzioni asserts that interorganizational relations need intensive empirical study.[10]   Blau and Scott present a rich but unconceptualized discussion of the "social context of organizational life."[11]   Parsons distinguishes three distinct levels of organizational responsibility and control: technical, managerial, and institutional.[12]   His categories can be construed to parallel the intraorganizational (i.e., technical or L_{11}), the interorganizational (i.e., managerial or L_{21} and L_{12}), and the extra-organizational levels of analysis (i.e., the institutional or L_{22} areas).   Perhaps in the normal developmental course of a science, intrasystem analysis necessarily precedes the intersystem focus.   On the other hand, increasing attention to interorganizational relations may reflect a real change in the phenomenon being studied.   The first question to consider is whether there is evidence that the environments of formal organizations are evolving toward turbulent-field conditions.

EVIDENCE FOR TURBULENCE

Ohlin argues that the sheer rapidity of social change today requires greater organizational adaptability.[13]   Hood points to the increasing complexity, as well as the accelerating rate of change, in organizational environments.[14]   In business circles there is growing conviction that the future is unpredictable.   Drucker[15] and Gardner[16] both assert that the kind and extent of present-day change precludes prediction of the future.   Increasingly, the rational strategies of planned-innovation and long-range planning are being undermined by unpredictable changes.   McNulty found no association between organization adaptation and the introduction of purposeful change in a study of 30 companies in fast-growing markets.[17]   He suggests that built-in flexibility may be more efficient than the explicit reorganization implicit in the quasi-rational model.   *Dun's Review* questions the effectiveness of long-range planning in the light of frequent failures, and suggests that error may be attributable to forecasting the future by extrapolation of a noncomparable past.   The conclusion is that the rapidity and complexity of change may increasingly preclude effective long-rang planning.[18]   These examples clearly suggest the emergence of a change in the environment that is suggestive of turbulence.

Some writers with this open-system perspective derive implications for interorganizational relations from this changing environment.   Blau and Scott argue that the success of a firm increasingly depends upon its ability to establish symbiotic relations with other organizations, in which extensive advantageous exchange takes place.[19]   Lee Adler proposes "symbiotic marketing."[20]   Dill found that the task environments of two Norwegian firms comprised four major sectors: *customers*, including both distributors and users; *suppliers* of materials, labor, capital, equipment, and work space; *competitors* for both markets and resources; and *regulatory groups*, including governmental agencies, unions, and interfirm associations.[21]   Not only does Dill's list include many more components than are accommodated by present theories, but all components are themselves evolving into formal organizations. In his recent book, Thompson discusses "task environments," which comprise the units with which an organization has input and output transactions (L_{21} and L_{12}), and postulates two dimensions of such environments: homogeneous-heterogeneous, and stable-dynamic. When the task environment is *both* heterogeneous and dynamic (i.e. probably turbulent), he expects an organization's boundary-spanning units to be functionally differentiated to correspond to segments of the task environment and each to operate on a decentralized basis to monitor and plan responses to fluctuations in its sector of the task environment.[22] He does not focus on other organizations as components of the environment, but he provides a novel perspective on structural implications (L_{11}) for organizations in turbulent fields.

Selznick's work on TVA appears to be the first organizational case study to emphasize transactional interdependencies.[23] The next study was Ridgway's 1957 study of manufacturer-dealer relationships.[24] Within the following few years the study by Dill[25] and others by Levine and White,[26] Litwak and Hylton,[27] and Elling and Halebsky[28] appeared, and in recent years, the publication of such studies has accelerated.

The following are examples from two volumes of the *Administrative Science Quarterly* alone. Rubington argues that structural changes in organizations that seek to change the behavior of "prisoners, drug addicts, juvenile delinquents, parolees, alcoholics [are] . . . the result of a social movement whose own organizational history has yet to be written."[29] Rosengren reports a similar phenomenon in the mental health field whose origin he finds hard to explain: "In any event, a more symbiotic relationship has come to characterize the relations between the [mental] hospitals and other agencies, professions, and establishments in the community."[30] He ascribes changes in organizational goals and technology to this interorganizational evolution. In the field of education, Clark outlines the increasing influence of private foundations, national associations, and divisions of the federal government. He, too, is not clear as to how these changes have come about, but he traces numerous changes in the behavior of educational organizations to interorganizational influences.[31] Maniha and Perrow analyze the origins and development of a city youth commission. The agency had little reason to be formed, no goals to guide it, and was staffed by people who sought a minimal, no-action role in the community. By virtue of its existence and broad province, however, it was seized upon as a valuable weapon by other organizations for the pursuit of their own goals. "But in this very process it became an organization with a mission of its own, in spite of itself."[32]

Since uncertainty is the dominant characteristic of turbulent fields, it is not surprising that emphasis in recent literature is away from algorithmic and toward heuristic problem-solving models;[33] that optimizing models are giving way to satisficing models;[34] and that rational decision making is replaced by "disjointed incrementalism."[35] These trends reflect *not* the ignorance of the authors of earlier models, but a change in the causal texture of organizational environments and, therefore, of appropriate strategies for coping with the environment. Cyert and March state that "so long as the environment of the firm is unstable—and predictably unstable—the heart of the theory [of the firm] must be the process of short-run adaptive reactions."[36]

In summary, both the theoretical and case study literature on organizations suggests that these systems are increasingly finding themselves in environments where the complexity and rapidity of change in external interconnectedness (L_{22}) gives rise to increasingly unpredictable change in their transactional interdependencies (L_{21} and L_{12}). This seems to be good evidence for the emergence of turbulence in the environments of many formal organizations.

INTERORGANIZATIONAL ENVIRONMENT

EVIDENCE FOR INCREASING DEPENDENCE ON ENVIRONMENT

Elsewhere the author has argued that Emery and Trist's concepts can be extended to *all* living systems; furthermore, that this evolutionary process gives rise to conditions—biological, psychological, and social—in which the rate of evolution of environments exceeds the rate of evolution of component systems.[37]

In the short run, the openness of a living system to its environment enables it to take in ingredients from the environment for conversion into energy or information that allows it to maintain a steady state and, hence, to violate the dismal second law of thermodynamics (i.e., of entropy). In the long run, "the characteristic of living systems which most clearly distinguishes them from the nonliving is their property of progressing by the process which is called evolution from less to more complex states of organization."[38] It then follows that to the extent that the environment of some living system X is comprised *of other living systems*, the environment of X is *itself* evolving from less to more complex states of organization. A major corollary is that the evolution of environments is characterized by an increase in the ratio of externally induced change over internally induced change in a system's transactional interdependencies (L_{21} and L_{12}).

For illustration, let us assume that at some given time, each system in some set of interdependent systems is equally likely to experience an internal (L_{11}) change that is functional for survival (i.e., improves its L_{21} or L_{12} transactions). The greater the number of other systems in that set, the greater the probability that some system other than X will experience that change. Since we posit interdependence among members of the set, X's viability over time depends upon X's capacity (L_{11}) for adaptation to environmentally induced (L_{22}) changes in its transactive position, or else upon control over these external relations.

In the case of formal organizations, disturbed-reactive or oligopolistic environments require some form of accommodation between like but competitive organizations whose fates are negatively correlated to some degree. A change in the transactional position of one system in an oligopolistic set, whether for better or worse, automatically affects the transactional position of all other members of the set, and in the opposite direction (i.e., for worse or better, as the case may be).[39] On the other hand, turbulent environments require relationships between dissimilar organizations whose fates are independent or, perhaps, positively correlated.[40] A testable hypothesis that derives from the formal argument is that the evolution of environments is accompanied, in viable systems, by an increase in ability to learn and to perform according to changing contingencies in the environment.

The evolution of organizational environments is characterized by a change in the important constituents of the environment. The earliest formal organizations to appear in the United States (e.g., in agriculture, retail trade, construction, mining)[41] operated largely under placid-clustered conditions. Important inputs, such as natural resources and labor, as well as consumers, comprised an environment in which strategies of optimal location and distinctive competence were critical organizational responses.[42] Two important attributes of placid-clustered environments are: (1) the environment is itself *not* formally organized; and (2) transactions are largely initiated and controlled by the organization (i.e., L_{12}).

Later developments, such as transport technology and derivative overlap in loss of strength gradients, and communication and automation technologies that increased economies of scale, gave rise to disturbed reactive (oligopolisitc) conditions in which similar formal organizations become the important actors in an organization's field. They are responsive to its acts (L_{12}) *and* it must be responsive to theirs (L_{21}). The critical organizational response now involves complex operations, requiring sequential choices based on the calculated actions of others, and counteractions.[43]

When the environment becomes turbulent, however, its constituents are a multitude of other formal organizations. Increasingly, an organization's markets consist of other organizations; suppliers of material, labor, and capital are increasingly organized, and regulatory groups are more numerous and powerful. The critical response of organizations under these conditions will be discussed later. It should be noted that *real* environments are often mixtures of these ideal types.

The evolution from placid-clustered environments to turbulent environments[44] can be summarized as a process in which formal organizations evolve: (*1*) *from* the status of systems within environments not formally organized; (*2*) *through* intermediate phases (e.g., Weberian bureaucracy); and (*3*) *to* the status of subsystems of a larger social system.

Clark Kerr traces this evolution for the university in the United States.[45] In modern industrial societies, this evolutionary process has resulted in the replacement of individuals and informal groups by organizations as *actors* in the social system. Functions that were once the sole responsibility of families and communities are increasingly allocated to formal organizations; child-rearing, work, recreation, education, health, and so on. Events which were long a matter of chance are increasingly subject to organizational control, such as population growth, business cycles, and even the weather. One wonders whether Durkheim, if he could observe the current scene, might speculate that the evolution from "mechanical solidarity" to "organic solidarity" is now occurring on the *organizational level*, where the common values of organizations in oligopolies are replaced by functional interdependencies among specialized organizations.[46]

INTERORGANIZATIONAL ANALYSIS

It was noted that survival in disturbed-reactive environments depends upon the ability of the organization to anticipate and counteract the behavior of similar systems. The analysis of interorganizational behavior, therefore, becomes meaningful only in these and more complex environments. The interdependence of organizations, or any kind of living systems, at less complex environmental levels is more appropriately studied by means of ecological, competitive market, or other similar models.

The only systematic conceptual approach to interorganizational analysis has been the theory of oligopoly in economics. This theory clearly addresses only disturbed-reactive environments. Many economists admit that the theory, which assumes maximization of profit and perfect knowledge, is increasingly at odds with empirical evidence that organizational behavior is characterized by satisficing and bounded rationality. Boulding comments that "it is surprisingly hard to make a really intelligent conflict move in the economic area simply because of the complexity of the system and the enormous importance of side effects and dynamic effects."[47] A fairly comprehensive search of the literature has revealed only four conceptual frameworks for the analysis of interorganizational relations outside the field of economics. These are briefly reviewed, particular attention being given to assumptions about organization environments, and to the utility of these assumptions in the analysis of interorganizational relations in turbulent fields.

William Evan has introduced the concept of "organization-set," after Merton's "role-set."[48] Relations between a focal organization and members of its organization-set are mediated by the role-sets of boundary personnel. "Relations" are conceived as the flow of information, products or services, and personnel.[49] Presumably, monetary, and legal, and other transactions can be accommodated in the conceptual system. In general, Evan offers a conceptual tool for identifying transactions at a given time. He makes no explicit assumptions about the nature of environmental dynamics, nor does he imply that they are changing. The relative neglect of interorganizational relations, which he finds surprising, is ascribed instead to the traditional intraorganizational focus, which derives from Weber, Taylor, and Barnard.[50] His concepts, however, go considerably beyond those of conventional organization and economic theory (e.g., comparative versus reference organizations and overlap in goals and values). If a temporal dimension were added to Evan's conceptual scheme, then, it would be a very useful tool for describing the "structural" aspects of transactional interdependencies (L_{21} and L_{12} relations) in turbulent fields.

Another approach is taken by Levine and White who focus specifically on relations among community health and welfare agencies. This local set of organizations "may be seen as a system with individual organizations or system parts varying in the kinds and frequencies of their relationships with one another."[51] The authors admit that interdependence exists among these local parts only to the extent that relevant resources are not available from *outside* the local region, which lies beyond their conceptual domain. Nor do we find here any suggestion of turbulence in these local environments. If such local sets of agencies are increasingly interdependent with other components of the local community and with organizations outside the locality, as the evidence suggests, then the utility of Levine and White's approach is both limited and shrinking.

Litwak and Hylton provide a third perspective. They too are concerned with health and welfare organizations, but their major emphasis is on coordination.[52] The degree of interdependence among organizations is a major variable; low interdependence leads to *no* coordination and high interdependence leads to merger, therefore they deal only with conditions of moderate interdependence. The type of coordinating mechanism that emerges under conditions of moderate interdependence is hypothesized to result from the interaction of three trichotomized variables: *the number* of interdependent organizations; the degree of their *awareness* of their interdependence; and the extent of *standardization* in their transactions. The attractive feature of the Litwak and Hylton scheme is the possibility it offers of making different predictions for a great variety of environments. Their model also seems to have predictive power beyond the class of organizations to which they specifically address themselves. If environments are becoming turbulent, however, then increasingly fewer of the model's cells (a $3 \times 3 \times 3$ space) are relevant. In the one-cell turbulent corner of their model, where a large number of organizations have low awareness of their complex and unstandardized interdependence, "there is little chance of coordination,"[53] according to Litwak and Hylton. If the level of awareness of interdependence increases, the model predicts that some process of arbitration will emerge. Thus the model anticipates the interorganizational implications of turbulent fields, but tells us little about the emerging processes that will enable organizations to adapt to turbulence.

The fourth conceptual framework available in the literature is by Thompson and McEwen.[54] They emphasize the interdependence of organizations with the larger society and discuss the consequences that this has for goal setting. "Because the setting of goals is essentially a problem of defining desired relationships between an organization and its environment, change in either requires review and perhaps alteration of goals."[55] They do not argue that such changes are more frequent today, but they do assert that reappraisal of goals is "a more constant problem in an unstable environment than in a stable one," and also "more difficult as the 'product' of the enterprise becomes less tangible."[56]

Thompson and McEwen outline four organizational strategies for dealing with the environment. One is competition; the other three are subtypes of a cooperative strategy: bargaining, co-optation, and coalition. These cooperative strategies all require direct interaction among organizations and this, they argue, increases the environment's potential control over the focal organization.[57] In bargaining, to the extent that the second party's support is necessary, that party is in a position to exercise a veto over the final choice of alternative goals, and thus takes part in the decision. The co-optation strategy makes still further inroads into the goal-setting process. From the standpoint of society, however, co-optation, by providing overlapping memberships, is an important social device for increasing the likelihood that organizations related to each other in complicated ways will in fact find compatible goals. Co-optation thus aids in the integration of heterogeneous parts of a complex social system. Coalition refers to a combination of two or more organizations for a common purpose and is viewed by these authors as the ultimate form of environmental conditioning of organization goals.[58]

The conceptual approaches of Levine and White and of Litwak and Hylton therefore appear to be designed for nonturbulent conditions. Indeed, it may well be that coordination *per se*, in the static sense usually implied by that term is dysfunctional for adaptation to turbulent fields. (This criticism has often been leveled at local "councils of social agencies."[59]) On the other hand, Evan's concept of organization-set seems useful for describing static aspects of interorganizational relations in either disturbed-reactive *or* turbulent-field environments. Its application in longitudinal rather than static studies might yield data on the relationship between structural aspects of transactional relations and organizational adaptability. Lastly, Thompson and McEwen make a unique contribution by distinguishing different *kinds* of interorganizational relations.

As an aside, note that Evan's extension of the role-set concept to organizations suggests still further analogies, which may be heuristically useful. A role is a set of acts prescribed for the occupant of some position. The role accrues to the position; its occupants are interchangeable. If formal organizations are treated as social actors, then one can conceive of organizations as occupants of positions in the larger social system. Each organization has one or more roles in its behavioral repertoire (these are more commonly called functions or goals). The organization occupants of these social positions, however, are also interchangeable.

INTEGRATIVE FRAMEWORK

MODEL

It is assumed that the foregoing arguments are valid: (*1*) that organizational environments are increasingly turbulent; (*2*) that organizations are increasingly less autonomous; and (*3*) that other formal organizations are increasingly important components of organizational environments. Some conceptual perspective is now needed, which will make it possible to view any formal organization, its transactional interdependencies, and the environment itself within a common conceptual framework. The intent of this section is to outline the beginnings of such a framework.

A formal organization is a system primarily oriented to the attainment of a specific goal, which constitutes an output of the system and which is an input for some other system.[60] Needless to say, the output of any living system is dependent upon input into it. Figure 1 schematically illustrates the skeletal structure of a living system. The input and output regions are partially permeable with respect to the environment, which is the region outside the system boundary. Arrows coming into a system represent input and arrows going out of a system represent output. In Figure 2, rectangles represent formal organizations and circles represent individuals and *non*formal social organizations. Figure 2 represents the *statics* of a system X and its turbulent environment. Three-dimensional illustration would be necessary to show the *dynamics* of a turbulent

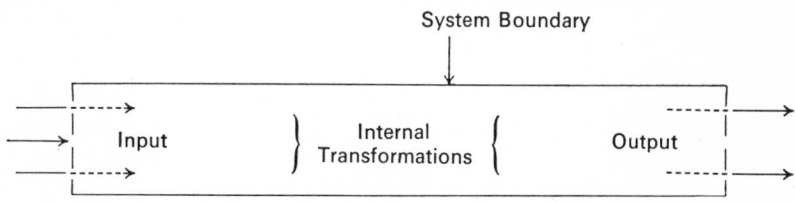

Figure 1. Structure of living systems such as a formal organization

environment schematically. Assume that a third, temporal dimension is imposed on Figure 2 and that this reveals an increasing number of elements and an increasing rate and complexity of change in their interdependencies over time. To do full justice to the concept of turbulence we should add other sets of elements even in Figure 2, although these are not yet linked to X's set. A notion that is integral to Emery and Trist's conception of turbulence is that changes outside of X's set, and hence difficult for X to predict and impossible for X to control, will have impact on X's transactional interdependencies in the future. The addition of just one link at some future time may not affect the supersystem but may constitute a system break for X.

This schematization shows only one-way directionality and is meant to depict energic inputs (e.g., personnel and material) and output (e.g., product). The organization provides something in exchange for the inputs it receives, of course, and this is usually informational in nature—money, most commonly. Similarly the organization receives money for its product from those systems for whom its product is an input. Nor does our framework distinguish different kinds of inputs, although the analysis of interorganizational exchange requires this kind of taxonomic device. It seems important to distinguish energic inputs and outputs from informational ones. Energic inputs include machinery, personnel, clientele in the case of service organizations, electric power, and so on. Informational inputs are not well conceptualized although there is no doubt of their increasing importance in environments which are more complex and changeable. Special divisions of organizations and whole firms devoted to information collecting, processing, and distributing are also rapidly proliferating (e.g., research organizations, accounting firms, the Central Intelligence Agency).

An input called "legitimacy" is popular in sociological circles but highly resistant to empirical specification. The view taken here is that legitimacy is mediated by the exchange of other resources. Thus the willingness of firm A to contribute capital to X, and of agency B to refer personnel to X and firm C to buy X's product

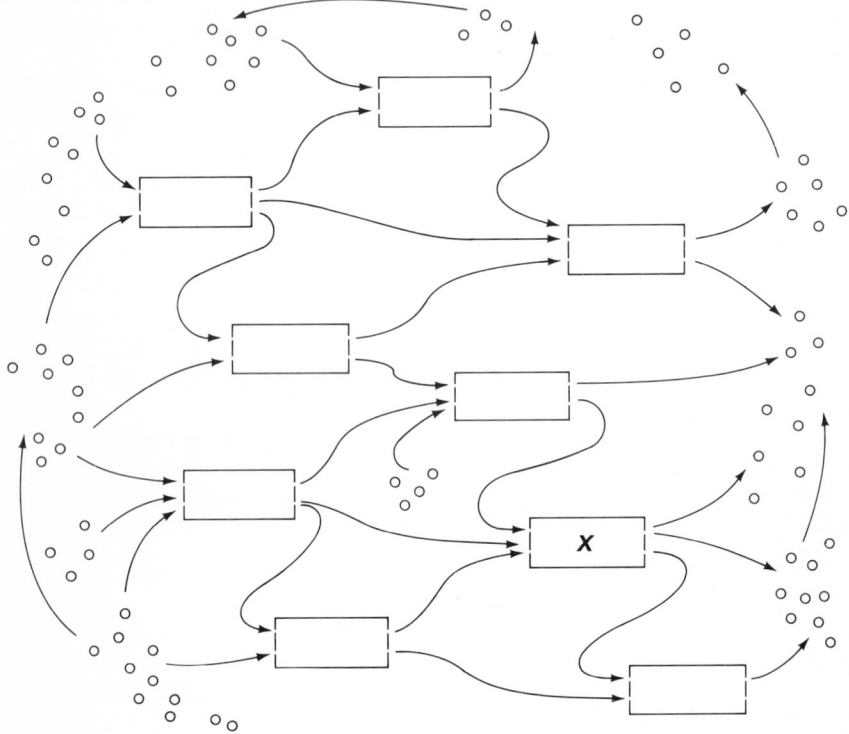

Figure 2.   Illustration of system X in turbulent environment

testifies to the legitimacy of X. This "willingness" on the part of organizations A, B, and C, however, can best be understood in terms of informational exchange. For example, A provides X with capital on the basis of A's information about the market for X's product. Or B refuses to refer skilled workmen to X since B has information on X's discriminatory employment practices and also knows of consequences to itself from elsewhere if it is party to X's practice. Technology is also sometimes treated as an input to organizations. We use the term, however, to refer to the complex set of interactions among inputs which takes place in the internal region shown in Figure 1. It is technology which transforms the inputs of the system into the output of the system. Transportation and communication technologies, however, are of a uniquely different order; the former constitutes an energic and the latter an informational transcendence of space-time that enabled the evolution of the more complex environments (L_{22}) which concern us here. Automation and computer technologies are roughly equivalent (i.e., energic and informational, respectively) but on an intraorganizational (L_{11}) level.

Our attention to "legitimacy" and "technology" was tangential to our main theme, to which we now return. Our simplistic approach to an integrative framework for the study of organizations (L_{11}), their transactional interdependencies (L_{21} and L_{12}), and the connectedness within their environments (L_{22}), gives the following conceptual ingredients: (1) units that are mainly formal organizations, and (2) relationships between them that are the directed flow[61] of (3) energy and information. The enormous and increasing importance of informational transaction has not been matched by conceptual developments in organization theory. The importance of information is frequently cited in a general way, however, especially in the context of organizational change or innovation. Dill has made a cogent argument on the need for more attention to this dimension.[62]

The importance of communication for organizational change has been stressed by Ohlin, March and Simon, Benne, Lippitt, and others.[63] Diversity of informational input has been used to explain the creativity of individuals as well as of social systems.[64] The importance of boundary positions as primary sources of innovative inputs from the environment has been stressed by March and Simon[65] and by Kahn et al.[66] James Miller hypothesizes that up to a maximum, which no living system has yet reached, the more energy a system devotes to information processing (as opposed to productive and maintenance activity), the more likely the system is to survive.[67]

Evolution on the biological level is accompanied by improvement in the ability of systems to discover and perform according to contingencies in their environments. The random walk which suffices in a placid-randomized environment must be replaced by stochastic processes under placid-clustered conditions, and by cybernetic processes in disturbed-reactive fields. Among biological/psychological systems, only man appears to have the capacity for the purposeful behavior that may permit adaptation to or control of turbulent environments. There is some question, of course, as to whether man actually *has* the capacity to cope with the turbulence that he has introduced into the environment.

Analogous concepts are equally applicable to the evolution of social systems in general and to formal organizations in particular. The capacity of *any* system for adapting to changing contingencies in its environment is inversely related to its dependence upon instinct, habit, or tradition. Adaptability exists, by definition, to the extent that a system (L_{11}) can survive externally induced (L_{22}) change in its transactional interdependencies (L_{21} and L_{12}); therefore viability equals adaptability.

HYPOTHESES

Hypothesis 1. Organizational change is largely externally induced.
Any particular change may be adaptive or maladaptive, and it may be one of these in the short run and the other in the long run. There is *no* systematic empirical

evidence on the relative influence of internal versus environmental antecedents to organizational change. The empirical task here is to identify organizational changes, and the internal or external origins of each change.

It is crucial to distinguish change on the organizational level from the multitude of changes that may occur in or among subsystems, only some of which give rise to change on the system level. Many social psychologists, for example, study change in individuals and groups *within* organizations, but with no reference to variables of organizational level. Likert's book is one noteworthy exception.[68] The important point is that change on the organizational level is analytically distinct from change on other levels.

Organizational change means any change in the kind or quantity of output. Ideally, output is treated as a function of inputs and of transfer functions (i.e., intraorganizational change is inferred from change in input-output relations). Haberstroh illustrates the use of these general system concepts in the organization context.[69] An excellent discussion of the efficiency and effectiveness of organizations, in an open-systems framework, is given in Katz and Kahn.[70]

However, the input-output functions in diversified industries and the outputs of many service organizations are resistant to objective specification and measurement. An empirical test of this hypothesis, with presently available tools, may have to settle for some set of input and internal change that seems to be reasonably antecedent to output change.

The identification of the origin of change is also beset by difficulties. An input change may indeed have external antecedents, but external events may also be responses to some prior internal change in the focal organization. And internal change may be internally generated, but it may also be the result of an informational input from external sources. Novel informational inputs, as well as novel communication channels, often derive from change in personnel inputs. Increasingly, organizations seek personnel who bring specialized information rather than "manpower" to the organization. The presence of first, second, and higher order causation poses a problem for any empirical test of this hypothesis.

Hypothesis 2. System adaptability (e.g., organizational) is a function of ability to learn and to perform according to changing environmental contingencies.

Adaptability exists, by definition, to the extent that a system can survive externally induced change in its transactional interdependencies in the long run. Diversity in a system's input (L_{21}) and output (L_{12}) interdependencies will increase adaptability. The recent and rapid diversification in major industries illustrates this strategy. Flexible stucture (L_{11}, e.g., decentralized decision making) will facilitate adaptation. Beyond this, however, adaptability would seem to be largely a function of a system's perceptual and information-processing capacities.[71] The following variables appear crucial: (*1*) *advance information* of impending externally induced (L_{22}) change in L_{21} or L_{12} transactions; (*2*) *active search* for, and activation of, more advantageous input and output transactions; and (*3*) *available memory store* (L_{11}) of interchangeable input and output components in the environment.

Advance information and active search might be empirically handled with Evan's concept of the role-sets of boundary personnel, along with notions of channel efficiency. For example, overlapping memberships (e.g., on boards) would constitute a particularly efficient channel. Likewise, direct communication between members of separate organizations, while less effective than overlapping memberships, would be a more efficient channel between agencies A and B than instances where their messages must be mediated by a third agency, C. Efficiency of interorganizational communication channels should be positively associated with access to advance information, and be facilitative of search, for example. The members of an organization's informational set may become increasingly differentiated from its energic set. Communication channels to research and marketing firms, universities, governmental agencies and other important information producing and distributing agencies would be expected to increase long-run viability. The third variable, memory store, is probably a function of the efficiency of past and present informational channels, but it involves internal (L_{11}) information processing as well.

Lastly, *any* internal change that improves an organization's transactional advantage (e.g., improved technology) will also be conducive to adaptability. Since organizational innovation is more often imitation than invention,[72] these changes are usually also the product of informational input and can be handled within the same integrative framework.

SUMMARY

The lag between evolution in the real world and evolution in theorists' ability to comprehend it is vast, but hopefully shrinking. It was only a little over one hundred years ago that Darwin identified natural selection as the mechanism of evolutionary process. Despite Darwin's enduring insight, theorists of change, including biologists, have continued to focus largely on internal aspects of systems.

It is our thesis that the selective advantage of one intra- or inter-organizational configuration over another cannot be assessed apart from an understanding of the dynamics of the environment itself. It is the environment which exerts selective pressure. "Survival of the fittest" is a function of the fitness of the environment. The dinosaurs *were* impressive creatures, in their day.

Notes

1. Ludwig von Bertalanffy, General System Theory, *General Systems*, 1 (1956), 1–10.
2. F. E. Emery and E. L. Trist, The Causal Texture of Organizational Environments, *Human Relations*, 18 (1965), 21–31.
3. *Ibid.*, 22.
4. I am particularly grateful to Kenneth Boulding for inspiration and to Eugene Litwak, Rosemary Sarri, and Robert Vinter for helpful criticisms. A Special Research Fellowship from

the National Institutes of Health has supported my doctoral studies and, therefore, has made possible the development of this paper.

5. The concepts of ideal types of environment, and one of the examples in this paragraph, are from Emery and Trist, *op. cit.*, 24–26.

6. The following illustrations are taken from Emery and Trist, *ibid.*: For random-placid environment see Herbert A. Simon, *Models of Man* (New York: John Wiley, 1957), p. 137; W. Ross Ashby, *Design for a Brain* (2nd ed.; London: Chapman and Hall, 1960), Sec. 15/4; the mathematical concept of random field; and the economic concept of classical market.

For random-clustered environment see Edward C. Tolman and Egon Brunswick, The Organism and the Causal Texture of the Environment, *Psychological Review*, 42 (1935), 43–72; Ashby, *op. cit.*, sec. 15/8; and the economic concept of imperfect competition.

For disturbed-reactive environment see Ashby, *op. cit.*, sec. 7; the concept of "imbrication" from I. Chein, Personality and Typology, *Journal of Social Psychology*, 18 (1943), 89–101; and the concept of oligopoly.

7. Emery and Trist, *op. cit.*, 24.

8. *Ibid.*, 26.

9. *Ibid.*, 24.

10. Amitai Etzioni, New Directions in the Study of Organizations and Society, *Social Research*, 27 (1960), 223–228.

11. Peter M. Blau and Richard Scott, *Formal Organizations* (San Francisco: Chandler, 1962), pp. 194–221.

12. Talcott Parsons, *Structure and Process in Modern Societies* (New York: Free Press, 1960), pp. 63–64.

13. Lloyd E. Ohlin, Conformity in American Society Today, *Social Work*, 3 (1958), 63.

14. Robert C. Hood, "Business Organization as a Cross Product of Its Purposes and of Its Environment," in Mason Haire (ed.), *Organizational Theory in Industrial Practice* (New York: John Wiley, 1962), p. 73.

15. Peter F. Drucker, The Big Power of Little Ideas, *Harvard Business Review*, 42 (May 1964), 6–8.

16. John W. Gardner, *Self-Renewal* (New York: Harper & Row, 1963), p. 107.

17. James E. McNulty, Organizational Change in Growing Enterprises, *Administrative Science Quarterly*, 7 (1962), 1–21.

18. Long Range Planning and Cloudy Horizons, *Dun's Review*, 81 (Jan. 1963), 42.

19. Blau and Scott, *op. cit.*, p. 217.

20. Lee Adler, Symbiotic Marketing, *Harvard Business Review*, 44 (November 1966), 59–71.

21. W. R. Dill, Environment as an Influence on Managerial Autonomy, *Administrative Science Quarterly*, 2 (1958), 409–443.

22. James D. Thompson, *Organizations in Action* (New York: McGraw-Hill, 1967), pp. 27–28.

23. Philip Selznick, *TVA and the Grass Roots* (Berkeley: University of California, 1949).

24. V. F. Ridgway, Administration of Manufacturer-Dealer Systems, *Administrative Science Quarterly*, 2 (1957), 464–483.

25. Dill, *op. cit.*

26. Sol Levine and Paul E. White, Exchange as a Conceptual Framework for the Study of Interorganizational Relationships, *Administrative Science Quarterly*, 5 (1961), 583–601.

27. Eugene Litwak and Lydia Hylton, Interorganizational Analysis: A Hypothesis on Coordinating Agencies, *Administrative Science Quarterly*, 6 (1962), 395–420.

28. R. H. Elling and S. Halebsky, Organizational Differentiation and Support: A Conceptual Framework, *Administrative Science Quarterly*, 6 (1961), 185–209.

29. Earl Rubington, Organizational Strain and Key Roles, *Administrative Science Quarterly* 9 (1965), 350–369.

30. William R. Rosengren, Communication, Organization, and Conduct in the "Therapeutic Milieu," *Administrative Science Quarterly*, 9 (1964), 70–90.

31. Burton R. Clark, Interorganizational Patterns in Education, *Administrative Science Quarterly*, 10 (1965), 224–237.

32. John Maniha and Charles Perrow, The Reluctant Organization and the Aggressive Environment, *Administrative Science Quarterly*, 10 (1965), 238–257.

33. Donald W. Taylor, "Decision Making and Problem Solving," in James G. March (ed.), *Handbook of Organizations* (Chicago: Rand McNally, 1965), pp. 48–82.

34. James G. March and Herbert A. Simon, *Organizations* (New York: John Wiley, 1958), pp. 140–141.

35. David Braybrooke and C. E. Lindblom, *A Strategy of Decision* (Glencoe: The Free Press, 1963), especially ch. 3, 5.

36. Richard M. Cyert and James G. March, *A Behavioral Theory of the Firm* (Englewood Cliffs, N.J.: Prentice-Hall, 1963), p. 100.

37. Shirley Terreberry, "The Evolution of Environments" (mimeographed course paper, 1967), pp. 1–37.

38. J. W. S. Pringle, On the Parallel Between Learning and Evolution, *General Systems*, 1 (1956), 90.

39. Assuming a nonexpanding economy, in the ideal instance.

40. Emery and Trist argue that fates, here, are positively correlated. This writer agrees if an expanding economy is assumed.

41. Arthur L. Stinchcombe, "Social Structure and Organizations," in March (ed.), *op. cit.*, p. 156.

42. Emery and Trist, *op. cit.*, 29.

43. *Ibid.*, 25–26.

44. The author does not agree with Emery and Trist, that *formal* (as distinct from social) organization will emerge in placid-random environments.

45. Clark Kerr, *The Uses of the University* (New York: Harper Torchbooks, 1963).

46. Emile Durkheim, *The Division of Labor in Society*, trans. George Simpson (Glencoe: The Free Press, 1947).

47. Kenneth E. Boulding, "The Economies of Human Conflict," in Elton B. McNeil (ed.), *The Nature of Human Conflict* (Englewood Cliffs, N.J.: Prentice-Hall, 1965), p. 189.

48. William M. Evan, "The Organization-Set: Toward a Theory of Interorganizational Relations," in James D. Thompson (ed,), *Approaches to Organizational Design* (Pittsburgh, Pa.: University of Pittsburgh Press, 1966), pp. 177–180.

49. *Ibid.*, pp. 175–176.

50. *Ibid.*

51. Levine and White, *op. cit.*, 586.

52. Litwak and Hylton, *op. cit.*

53. *Ibid.*, 417.

54. James D. Thompson and William J. McEwen, Organizational Goals and Environment, *American Sociological Review*, 23 (1958), 23–31.

55. *Ibid.*, 23.

56. *Ibid.*, 24.

57. *Ibid.*, 27.

58. *Ibid.*, 25–28.

59. Examples include: Robert Morris and Ollie A. Randall, Planning and Organization of Community Services for the Elderly, *Social Work*, 10 (1965), 96–103, Frank W. Harris, A Modern Council Point of View, *Social Work*, 9 (1964), 34–41; Harold L. Wilensky and Charles N. Lebeaux, *Industrial Society and Social Welfare* (New York: Russell Sage Foundation, 1958), especially pp. 263–265.

60. Talcott Parsons, "Suggestions for a Sociological Approach to the Theory of Organizations," in Amitai Etzioni (ed.), *Complex Organizations* (New York: Holt, Rinehart, and Winston, 1962), p. 33.

61. Dorwin Cartwright, "The Potential Contribution of Graph Theory to Organization Theory," in Mason Haire (ed.), *Modern Organization Theory* (New York: John Wiley, 1959), pp. 254–271.

62. William R. Dill, "The Impact of Environment in Organizational Development," in Sidney

Mailick and Edward H. Van Ness (eds.), *Concepts and Issues in Administrative Behavior* (Englewood Cliffs, N.J.: Prentice-Hall, 1962), pp. 94–109.

63. Ohlin, *op. cit.*, 63; March and Simon, *op. cit.*, pp. 173–183; Kenneth D. Benne, "Deliberate Changing as the Facilitation of Growth," in Warren G. Bennis *et al.* (eds.), *The Planning of Change* (New York: Holt, Rinehart, and Winston, 1962), p. 232; Ronald Lippitt, *The Dynamics of Planned Change* (New York: Harcourt, Brace, and World, 1958), p. 52.

64. For example: Floyd H. Allport, *Theories of Perception and the Concept of Structure* (New York: John Wiley, 1955), p. 76; William F. Ogburn and Meyer F. Nimkoff, *Sociology* (4th ed.; Boston: Houghton Mifflin, 1964), pp. 662–670.

65. March and Simon, *op. cit.*, pp. 165–166, 189.

66. Robert L. Kahn *et al.*, *Organizational Stress* (New York: John Wiley, 1964), pp. 101–126.

67. James G. Miller, Toward a General Theory for the Behavioral Sciences, *The American Psychologist*, 10 (1955), 530.

68. Rensis Likert, *New Patterns of Management* (New York: McGraw-Hill, 1961).

69. Chadwick J. Haberstroh, "Organization Design and Systems Analysis," in March (ed.), *op. cit.*, pp. 1171–1211.

70. Daniel Katz and Robert L. Kahn, *The Social Psychology of Organizations* (New York: John Wiley, 1966), especially pp. 149–170.

71. Igor Ansoff speaks of the "wide-open windows of perception" required of tomorrow's firms, and offers a perspective on the future that is fully compatible with that presented here; see The Firm of the Future, *Harvard Business Review*, 43 (September 1965), 162.

72. Theodore Levitt, Innovative Imitation, *Harvard Business Review*, 44 (September 1966), 63–70.

17 . The Second Cybernetics: Deviation-Amplifying Mutual Causal Processes
Magoroh Maruyama

Since its inception, cybernetics was more or less identified as a science of self-regulating and equilibrating systems. Thermostats, physiological regulation of body temperature, automatic steering devices, economic and political processes were studied under a general mathematical model of deviation-counteracting feedback networks.

By focusing on the deviation-counteracting aspect of the mutual causal relationships however, the cyberneticians paid less attention to the systems in which

From *American Scientist*, June 1963, pp. 164–179, by permission of *American Scientist*. For a technical treatment of the subject, see my article "Morphogenesis and Morphostasis," *Methodos*, 12, no. 48, 1960.

the mutual causal effects are deviation-amplifying. Such systems are ubiquitous: accumulation of capital in industry, evolution of living organisms, the rise of cultures of various types, interpersonal processes which produce mental illness, international conflicts, and the processes that are loosely termed as "vicious circles" and "compound interests"; in short, all processes of mutual causal relationships that amplify an insignificant or accidental initial kick, build up deviation and diverge from the initial condition.

In contrast to the progress in the study of equilibrating systems, the deviation-amplifying systems have not been given as much investment of time and energy by the mathematical scientists on the one hand, and understanding and practical application on the part of geneticists, ecologists, politicians and psychotherapists on the other hand.

The deviation-counteracting mutual causal systems and the deviation-amplifying mutual causal systems may appear to be opposite types of systems. But they have one essential feature in common: they are both mutual causal systems, i.e., the elements within a system influence each other either simultaneously or alternatingly. The difference between the two types of systems is that the deviation-counteracting system has mutual negative feedbacks between the elements in it while the deviation-amplifying system has mutual positive feedbacks between the elements in it.

Since both types are systems of mutual causal relationships, or in other words systems of mutual feedbacks, they both fall under the subject matter of cybernetics. But since the deviation-counteracting type has predominantly been studied up till now under the title of cybernetics, let us consider its studies *the first cybernetics*, and call the studies of the deviation-amplifying mutual causal relationships "*the second cybernetics*." The deviation-counteracting mutual causal process is also called "morphostasis," while the deviation-amplifying mutual causal process is called "morphogenesis."

Though the second cybernetics as defined here is lagging behind the development of the first cybernetics at the present moment, the germination of the concept of deviation-amplifying mutual causal process is not entirely new. The concept was formulated in some fields even before the advent of cybernetics and was applied fruitfully. The field of economics is a good example.

For many years the economists had claimed that it was useless to try to raise the standard of living of the lower class, because, they argued, if the income of the population in the lower class should increase, they would produce more children and thus reduce their standard of living to the original level; the poor stay poor and the rich stay rich. This was a morphostatic model of mutual deviation-counteracting between the income level and the number of children. This theoretical model led the policy makers to the action of laisser-faire policy. On the other hand, it was also known that "the more capital, the more rapid the [rate] of its increase"; in other words, the poor become poorer and the rich become richer. This was a morphogenetic model of deviation-amplifying process.

Subsequently J. Tinbergen and H. Wold have given more elaboration and mathematical sophistication to the theory of mutual causal process in the theory of economics.[1]   More recently G. Myrdal has pointed out that, while in the economically well-developed countries the regional, social, and hierarchical differences in economical level tend to decrease, in the economically underdeveloped regions the difference between the poor and the rich increases.   In an economically well-developed society, transportation, communication, education, insurance systems, and welfare programs equalize the economical level throughout the society.   In an economically underdeveloped society, on the other hand, under the laisser-faire policy and free play of market forces, the few privileged people accumulate more wealth and power while the living standard of the poor tends to fall.   Low standard of living, poor health, and low efficiency in work aggravate one another.   Racial or social discrimination, and other social, psychological and cultural factors may be added in the "vicious circle."   Likewise, between nations, world free trade is profitable for rich countries and detrimental for poor countries.   This morphogenetic reformulation of the economic theory affects the public policy toward the direction of planned economy within economically underdeveloped countries and controlled international trade.

Myrdal[2] further points out the importance of the direction of the initial kick, which determines the direction of the subsequent deviation amplification in the planned economy.   Furthermore, the resulting development will be far greater than the investment in the initial kick.   Thus, in the economically underdeveloped countries it is necessary not only to plan the economy, but also to give the initial kick and reinforce it for a while in such a direction and with such an intensity as to maximize the efficiency of development per initial investment. Once the economy is kicked in a right direction and with a sufficient initial push, the deviation-amplifying mutual positive feedbacks take over the process, and the resulting development will be disproportionally large as compared with the initial kick.

We find the same principle of deviation-amplifying mutual causal relationships operating in many other happenings in the universe.   Take, for example, weathering of rock.   A small crack in a rock collects some water.   The water freezes and makes the crack larger.   A larger crack collects more water, which makes the crack still larger.   A sufficient amount of water then makes it possible for some small organisms to live in it.   Accumulation of organic matter then makes it possible for a tree to start growing in the crack.   The roots of the tree will then make the crack still larger.

Development of a city in an agricultural plain may be understood with the same principle.   At the beginning, a large plain is entirely homogeneous as to its potentiality for agriculture.   By some chance an ambitious farmer opens a farm at a spot on it.   This is the initial kick.   Several farmers follow the example and several farms are established.   One of the farmers opens a tool shop.   Then this tool shop becomes a meeting place of farmers.   A food stand is established next to the tool shop.   Gradually a village grows.   The village facilitates the marketing of the agricultural products, and more farms flourish around the village.   Increased agricultural activity necessitates development of industry in the village, and the village grows into a city.

This is a very familiar process.   But there are a few important theoretical implications in such a process.

On what part of the entire plain the city starts growing depends on where accidentally the initial kick occurred.   The first farmer could have chosen any spot on the plain, since the plain was homogeneous.   But once he has chosen a spot, a city grows from that spot, and the plain becomes inhomogeneous.   If a historian should try to find a geographical "cause" which made this spot a city rather than some other spots, he will fail to find it in the initial homogeneity of the plain.   Nor can the first farmer be credited with the establishment of the city.   The secret of the growth of the city is in the process of deviation-amplifying mutual positive feedback networks rather than in the initial condition or in the initial kick.   This process, rather than the initial condition, has generated the complexly structured city.   It is in this sense that the deviation-amplifying mutual causal process is called "morphogenesis."

A sacred law of causality in the classical philosophy stated that similar conditions produce similar effects.   Consequently, dissimilar results were attributed to dissimilar conditions.   Many scientific researches were dictated by this philosophy.   For example, when a scientist tried to find out why two persons under study were different, he looked for a difference in their environment or in their heredity.   It did not occur to him that neither environment nor heredity may be responsible for the difference.   He overlooked the possibility that some deviation-amplifying interactional process in their personality and in their environment may have produced the difference.

In the light of the deviation-amplifying mutual causal process, the law of causality is now revised to state that similar conditions may result in dissimilar products.   It is important to note that this revision is made without the introduction of indeterminism and probabilism.   Deviation-amplifying mutual causal processes are possible even within the deterministic universe, and make the revision of the law of causality even within the determinism.   Furthermore, when the deviation-amplifying mutual causal process is combined with indeterminism, here again a revision of a basic law becomes necessary.   The revision states: A small initial deviation, which is within the range of high probability, may develop into a deviation of very low probability (or more precisely, into a deviation which is very improbable within the framework of probabilistic unidirectional causality).

Not only the law of causality, but also the second law of thermodynamics is affected by the deviation-amplifying mutual causal process.   [See the Appendix immediately following this selection.]   Let us return to the example of the growth of a city in an agricultural plain.   The growth of the city first increases the internal structuredness of the city itself.   Secondly, it increases the inhomogeneity of the plain by its deviating from the original prevailing condition.   Thirdly, the growth of a city at a spot may have an inhibiting effect upon the growth of another city in the vicinity, just as the presence of one swimming pool may discourage an enterpriser from opening another pool right next to it, and just as the presence of large trees inhibits with their shades the growth of some species of small trees around them.   A city needs a *hintergrund* to support it, and, therefore, cities have to be spaced at some intervals. This inhibiting effect further increases inhomogeneity of the plain.

This gradual increase of inhomogeneity is a process against the second law of thermodynamics. In a few words, the second law of thermodynamics states that an isolated system spends with a great probability most of its time in high-probability states. Hence, if an isolated system is in an improbable state, it will most probably be found in the future in a more probable state. Under the assumption of randomness of events, homogeneous states are more probable than inhomogeneous states. For example, uneven distribution of temperature is less probable than even distribution of temperature. Under the assumption of the second law of thermodynamics, an isolated system in an inhomogeneous state will most probably be found in a future in a more homogeneous state. The second law of thermodynamics is in this sense a law of decay of structure and of decay of inhomogeneity.

Any process such as biological growth which increases structuredness and inhomogeneity was against the second law of thermodynamics and was an embarrassing problem for scientists. This embarrassing question was temporarily ignored by the argument that an organism is not an isolated system. But what process and principle make it possible for an organism to increase its structure and to accumulate heat was never squarely answered. Now, under the light of deviation-amplifying mutual causal process this mystery is solved.

The process of evolution, or in other words phylogenetic morphogenesis including the pattern of behavior, is deviation-amplifying in several ways.

First, there is deviation-amplifying mutual process between the mutations and the environment. For example, suppose that some mutants of a species can live at a lower temperature than the "normal" individuals. Then the mutants may move to an environment which is colder. Further mutations occur. Some of the mutants are unfit for the low-temperature environment and die off. But some other mutants are able to live in a much colder climate than their parents. They move to a still colder environment. The cold climate eliminates any new mutants that are unfit for cold climate. The "average" individuals of the survivors are then fit for cold climate. The chances of the species, or at least some members of the species, to move to a still colder environment are now greater than before. Thus the selection of, or accidental wandering into, a certain type of environment and the direction of survivable mutations amplify each other.

Not only the organism may move into a new environment, but it may also create its own environment. *Homo sapiens* is a typical example. A "civilized" man lives in an environment which he created, and which is relatively free from the bacteria of certain diseases such as typhoid. His resistance against typhoid decreases as a result of living in such an environment. The decreased resistance necessitates him to make his environment more germ-free. This decreases his resistance further.

Secondly, there is interspecific deviation-amplification. For example, a species of moth has predators. Because of the predators, the mutants of the moth species which have a more suitable cryptic coloration (camouflage) and cryptic behavior than the average survive better. On the other hand, those mutants of the predators which have a greater ability than the average in discovering the moth will survive better. Hence, the cryptic coloration and the cryptic behavior of the moth species improve generation after generation, and the ability of the predators to discover the moth also increases generation after generation.

Thirdly, the intraspecific selection has a deviation-amplifying effect. For example, many animals prefer supernormal (above-average) members of [their] species to normal members for mating and for carrying on other cooperative activities. By giving more responses to supernormal stimuli than to normal stimuli, the members of the species amplify, by favoring supernormal mutants, the deviation in the direction of supernormality. The deviation in turn may increase either the number and the intensity of the members' responses to the supernormal stimuli, or the level of the supernormality of the members' characteristics.

The response to supernormal stimuli may be inborn or culturally conditioned. For example, an oystercatcher (*Haematopus ostralegus*) prefers a large artificial egg given by an experimenter to its own egg, and tries to sit on the large egg even though the egg may be as large as the bird's body.[3] This response is inborn. On the other hand in *homo sapiens*, what is considered "supernormal" often depends on the culture. In the contemporary American culture, female legs which are more slender and longer than normal are supernormal stimuli, while in Polynesia obese young girls used to be supernormal stimuli. In this way, culture may influence the direction of the evolution of the human species while, at the same time, the evolution influences the culture. We may say that "cultural selection" rather than natural selection is the mechanism of human evolution since much of man's environment is man-made. But the matter is not very simple because certain cultures like ours, with medical science and technology, make it possible for constitutionally "unfit" individuals to "survive." Perhaps fitness should be defined not in terms of the capacity of the individual without tools, but in terms of the tools which he can mobilize.

In any case, man is responsible for his own evolution because of his capacity to create his own culture which is his environment and to choose his criterion of supernormality. Incidentally, to "create" is no longer a concept which violates the law of physics. As we have seen, creation *ex nihilo* [of structure, though not of material], or rather almost *ex nihilo*, is scientifically possible because the secret is no longer in the Prime Mover or in the Creator, but in the process of deviation-amplifying mutual positive feedback network.

Fourthly, the effect of inbreeding is deviation-amplifying for purely statistical reasons. Marriages between close relatives produce individuals in whom certain characteristics are extremely amplified. In fact, if people were to practice intra-family marriages only, each family would develop into a separate species because there is no interbreeding between families. In a more extreme case, if the reproduction were always sexless, i.e., if an individual produced its offspring without any help from another individual, then each individual's descendants would develop into a separate species. In fact, "species" would be non-existent [unless the intraspecific ecology weeds out the "deviants"].

Many times cooperation between individuals facilitates life,[4] and therefore the existence of species facilitates the life of the individual. The sexual reproduction, as compared with asexual reproduction, acts as a stabilizer of the species.

Here we have seen that mating may amplify the deviations or stabilize the species. This is not a contradiction. Whether mating is deviation-amplifying or deviation-counteracting depends on whether the inbreeding component or the interbreeding component is predominant. S. Wright[5] has made this relationship clear. When the mutation rate is high as compared with the population size, random matings will produce more inbreeding than interbreeding, and the deviation-amplifying effect is predominant. On the other hand, when the population size is large as compared with the mutation rate, random matings will produce more interbreeding than inbreeding, and the deviation-counteracting effect is predominant. The direction of deviation in a small population with a high mutation rate is unpredictable since it depends on the initial kick which is random. But once the deviation started, it is systematically amplified in the same direction.

When the mutation rate is neither too high nor too low as compared with the population size, neither inbreeding nor interbreeding predominates. The result is neither deviation-amplifying nor deviation-counteracting, but a combination of both which results in random drift. At one time, a random initial kick produces a deviation in a certain direction. Deviation-amplification takes over and this deviation is amplified consistently in the same direction. But this does not last very long. Soon, deviation-counteracting takes over, and the population becomes fixed at a certain point of deviation. After a while, another random initial kick produces a deviation in a new direction. Deviation-amplification takes over again and the population drifts consistently in this direction for a while. But soon, deviation-counteracting takes over and the population becomes fixed at a new point in the new direction of deviation. Then another initial kick starts a deviation in a new direction. The process repeats itself with unpredictable drifts.

The maximum speed of evolution is found, not in one colony with a high rate of mutation and a small size of population, but in the interaction between colonies which have a moderate mutation rate. When the mutation rate is too high as compared with the population size, the mutant characteristics may amplify themselves at a speed beyond the possibility of finding a new environment and new intraspecific and interspecific ecological conditions which are suitable for the mutant characteristics, and beyond the possibility of allowing other variations of mutants, which have characteristics greater in survival value, to develop. The species may become extinct, or it may reach the limit of mutability and become fixed there, or the mutant characteristics may become so dominant and homogeneous as to become deviation-counteracting.

A moderate mutation rate produces a more viable and changeable evolution. Moreover, when there are occasional exchanges of immigrants between colonies, the introduction of a new strain, which has proved to be viable in one colony, into another colony has the same effect as producing viable mutants, and tends to favor evolution.

This seems to be true of human cultures also. When there is enough separation, not necessarily geographical, between cultures to allow them differentiation and variety, with enough exchange between them to allow mutual enrichment and new combinations, the human civilization seems to progress most efficiently.

As we have seen, evolution is deviation-amplifying in several ways. For this reason we called evolution "phylogenetic morphogenesis." But more traditionally, "morphogenesis" is used for ontogenesis, i.e., for the development of the embryo into an adult individual. Is the new usage of the word "morphogenesis," meaning deviation-amplifying mutual causal process, in any way contradictory to the traditional usage? By no means so. As we see in the following, the development of the embryo also involves deviation-amplifying mutual causal process.

There is one basic difference between ontogenesis and phylogenesis. Mutation and natural selection, which are the basis of phylogenesis, are absent in ontogenesis. In fact, while phylogenesis has the randomness of mutation, ontogenesis lacks this randomness and seems to be based on a strictly detailed, deterministic planning. But this detailed planning is *generated* within the embryo by a deviation-amplifying mutual causal process in a deterministic scheme.

Biologists have been puzzled by the fact that the amount of information stored in the genes is much smaller than the amount of information needed to describe the structure of the adult individual. The puzzle is now solved by noticing that it is not necessary for the genes to carry all the information regarding the adult structure, but it suffices for the genes to carry a set of rules to generate the information. This can be illustrated by a model.

Let us imagine, for the sake of simplicity, a two-dimensional organism. Let us further imagine that its cells are squares of an equal size. Let us say that the organism consists of four types of cells: green, red, yellow, and blue. Each type of cell reproduces cells of the same type to build a tissue. A tissue has at least two cells. The tissues grow in a two-dimensional array of squares. Let us give a set of rules for the growth of tissues:

1. No cells die. Once reproduced, a cell is always there.
2. Both ends of a tissue grow whenever possible, by reproducing one cell per unit time in a vacant contiguous square. If there is no vacant contiguous square at either end, that end stops growing. If there are more than one vacant contiguous squares at either end, the direction of the growth is governed by the preferential order given by Rules 3, 4, and 5.
3. If, along the straight line defined by the end cell and the penultimate cell (next to the end cell) there are less than or equal to three cells of the same type (but may be of different tissues) consecutively, the preferred direction is along the same straight line. If that direction is blocked, follow Rule 5.
4. If, along the straight line defined by the end cell and the penultimate cell, there are more than or equal to four cells of the same type (but may be of different

tissues) consecutively, the preferred direction of the growth is a left turn. If a left turn is impossible, make a right turn.

5. If, when a straight growth is preferred, the straight growth is impossible because the square ahead is already occupied, do the following: If the square to which the straight growth would take place is filled with a cell of the same type as the growing tissue, make a left turn. If the square ahead is filled with a cell whose type is different from that of the growing tissue, make a right turn.

6. The growth of the four types of tissues is timewise out of phase with each

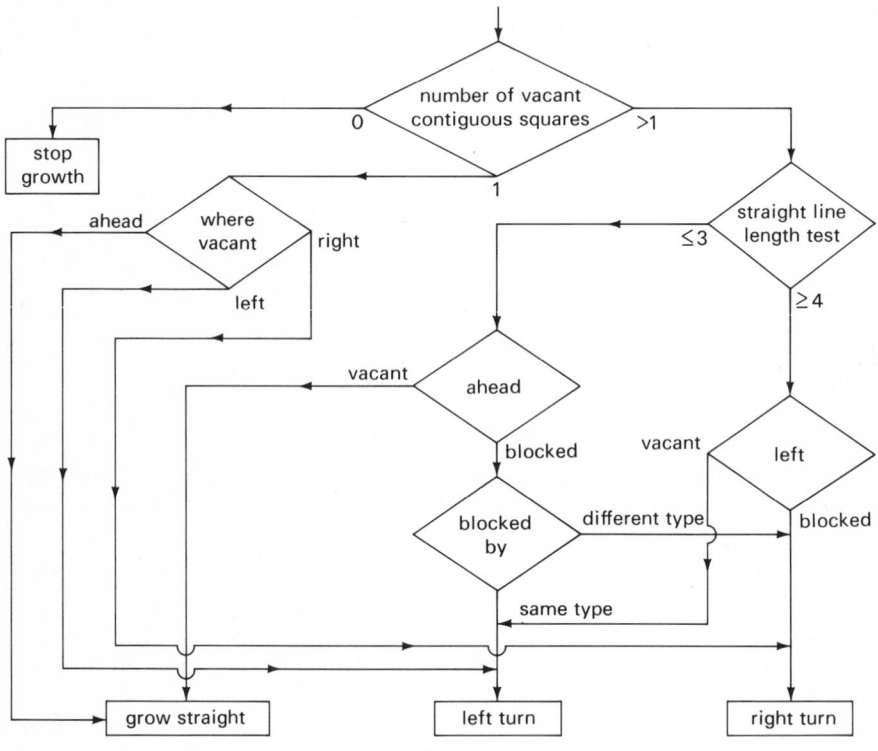

Figure 1

other: green first, red second, yellow third, and blue last within a cycle of one unit time.

Rules 2, 3, 4, and 5 can be diagrammed together as in Figure 1.

Using these rules, we can compute the growth of the tissues when the locations of the initial tissues are specified. For example, let us say that, in Figure 2, only the squares marked by 1's are filled with cells of the types indicated by the colors. At the end of the second unit time, the squares marked by 2's are filled. And at the end of the nth unit time, all squares marked by numbers less than [or equal to] n are filled. At the end of the 44th unit time all tissues have completed the growth, and the organism has attained its full differentiation.

In this example we started with four tissues of the minimum length, one tissue of each of the four types.   But already the result is a fairly complex structure. If we start with a slightly larger number of tissues at the beginning, the resulting pattern becomes disproportionately more complex.   The amount of information to describe the resulting pattern is much more than the amount of information to describe the generating rules and the positions of the initial tissues.   The pattern

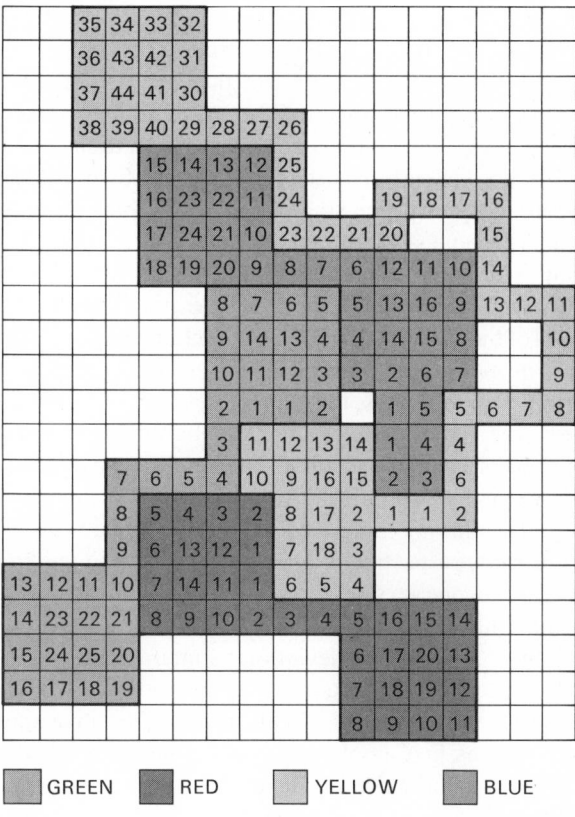

Figure 2

is generated by the rules and by the *interaction* between the tissues.   In this sense, the information to describe the adult individual was not contained in the initial tissues at the beginning but was generated by their interactions.

Besides generating information, this type of process has two additional features. First, it is strictly deterministic.   When the locations of the initial tissues are identical in two embryos, the resulting adults, no matter how complex, will be exactly identical.

Secondly, it is in most cases impossible to discover the simple generating rules after the pattern has been completed, except by trying all possible sets of rules. When the rules are unknown, the amount of information needed to discover the rules is much greater than the amount of information needed to describe the rules. This means that there is much more waste, in terms of the amount of information, in tracing the process backwards than in tracing it forward.   A geneticist would waste much time and energy by trying to infer the characteristics of the embryo from the characteristics of the adult organism.   It would be more profitable to perform experiments in embryonic interference and embryonic grafting.   The same is true also for the study of other deviation-amplifying mutual causal processes such as history or mental illness.

Since information is generated by the interaction between various parts of the embryo, it is not necessary for each part of the embryo to contain information regarding the body part it is destined to become.   It partly receives the information from other parts of the embryo and from its relationships to them.   For example, in the embryo of certain species, if the part which would become an eye is transplanted at an appropriate stage of the embryonic development into the part which would become skin, the eye-tissue becomes skin.   It receives information for its growth from its surroundings.

We have discussed mainly the structure-generating aspect of the interaction between the parts of the embryo.   But the interaction has also a structure-stabiliz-ing aspect.   Let us look at the example of the grafted eye tissues again.   When they were grafted on skin tissues, the skin tissues made the would-be-eye tissues into skin tissues, against the possibility that the would-be-eye tissues might become an eye.   This process is "morphostasis" in the traditional terminology.

Thus, the usage of the words "morphogenesis" and "morphostasis" in the sense of deviation-amplifying mutual causal process and deviation-counteracting mutual causal process, respectively, does not contradict their traditional usage in the sense of ontogenetic structure-generation and structure-stabilization. The new usage not only extends the old usage, but gives a functional definition in terms of deviation-generating and deviation-counteracting, and in terms of posi-tive and negative feedback networks.

Let us now examine more closely what is meant by positive and negative feed-back networks.   Let us first emphasize that the presence of influences in both directions between two or more elements does not necessarily imply mutual causation.   If the size of influence in one direction is independent of the size of influence in the other direction, or if their apparent correlation is caused by a third element, there is no mutual causation.   Only when the size of influence in one direction has an effect upon the size of the influence in the other direction and is in turn affected by it, is there a mutual causation.

For example, Eisen Iron Co. makes iron from iron ore.   Dexter Tool Co. manufactures tools made of iron.   Dexter buys iron from Eisen, and Eisen buys tools from Dexter.   There is some mutual relationship between the two com-panies.   But suppose Dexter buys iron from several companies.   When Eisen's output drops, Dexter's purchase of iron from other companies increases.   When Eisen's output goes up, Dexter's purchase of iron from other iron companies decreases.   The amount of tools Dexter can suplpy to Eisen does not depend on the amount of iron Dexter buys from Eisen.   Furthermore, Dexter has other customers besides Eisen. Whether Eisen buys no tools or 10,000 tools from Dexter does not matter much to the operation of Dexter. In this case, though there is traffic of merchandise in both directions between Eisen and Dexter, the amounts of traffic in two directions have no mutual causal relationship.

Suppose that, suddenly, some ship industry develops in the vicinity, and both iron and tools are in great demand. Consequently, both Eisen's output and Dexter's output increase simultaneously. But this simultaneous increase was not caused by a mutual causal relationship between Eisen and Dexter, but by a third element which is the ship industry.

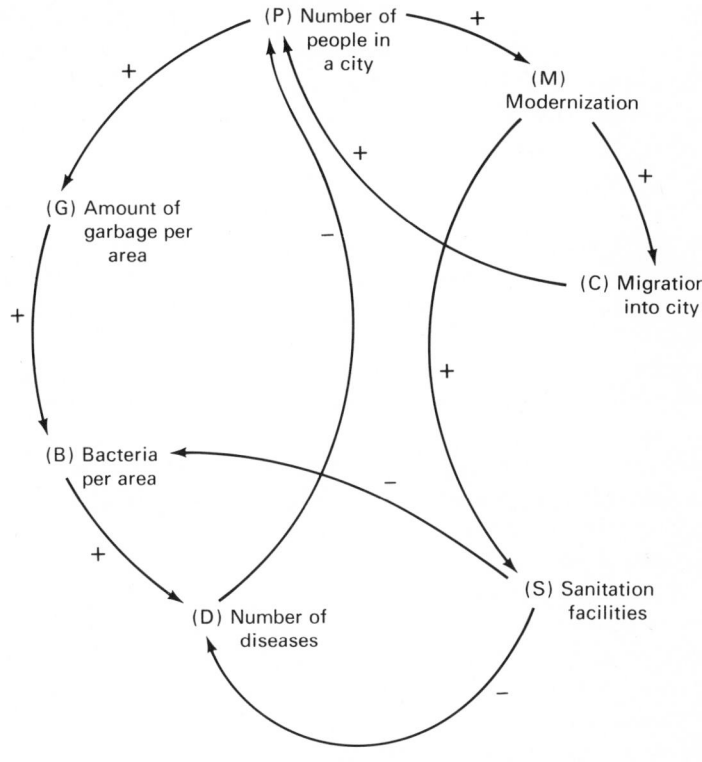

Figure 3

On the other hand, if the amount of Dexter's output depends on the amount of Eisen's output and varies with it either in the same or opposite direction, and the amount of Eisen's output depends on the amount of Dexter's output and varies with it either in the same or opposite direction, then there is a mutual causal relationship between Eisen's output and Dexter's output.

Mutual causal relationships may be defined between more than two elements. Let us look at Figure 3. The arrows indicate the direction of influences. + indicates that the changes occur in the same direction, but not necessarily positively. For example, the + between G and B indicates that an increase in the amount of garbage per area causes an increase in the number of bacteria per area.

But, at the same time, it indicates that a decrease in the amount of garbage per area causes a decrease in the number of bacteria per area. The − between S and B indicates that an increase in sanitation facilities causes a decrease in the number of bacteria per area. But, at the same time, it indicates that a decrease in sanitation facilities causes an increase in the number of bacteria per area.

As may be noticed, some of the arrows form loops. For example, there is a loop of arrows from P to M, M to C, and C back to M. A loop indicates mutual causal relationships. In a loop, the influence of an element comes back to itself through other elements. For example, in the loop of P-M-C-P, an increase in the number of people causes an increase in modernization, which in turn increases migration to the city, which in turn increases the number of people in the city. In short, an increase in population causes a further increase in population through modernization and migration. On the other hand, a decrease in population causes a decrease in modernization, which in turn causes a decrease in migration, which in turn decreases population. In short, a decrease in population causes a further decrease in population through decreased modernization and decreased migration. Whatever the change, either an increase or a decrease, amplifies itself. This is so when we take population as our criterion. But the same is true if we take modernization as a criterion: an increase in modernization causes a further increase in modernization through migration and population increase; and a decrease in modernization causes a further decrease in modernization through decreased migration and decreased population. The same holds true if we take the migration as the criterion.

In a loop, therefore, each element has an influence on all other elements either directly or indirectly, and each element influences itself through other elements. There is no hierarchical causal priority in any of the elements. It is in this sense that we understand the mutual causal relationships.

Let us take next the loop P-G-B-D-P. This loop contains a negative influence from D to P. In this loop, an increase in population causes an increase in the amount of garbage per area, which in turn causes an increase in the number of bacteria per area, which in turn causes an increase in the number of diseases, which in turn causes a decrease in population. In short, an increase in population causes a decrease in population through garbage, bacteria and diseases. On the other hand, a decrease in population causes a decrease in garbage, bacteria and diseases, and thus causes an increase in population. In this loop, therefore, any change in population is counteracted by itself. Likewise, any change in the amount of garbage per area is counteracted by itself. The mutual causal relationship in this loop is a deviation-counteracting mutual causal relationship. Such a deviation-counteracting process may result in *stabilization* or *oscillation*, depending on the time lag involved in the counteraction and the size of counteraction.

Let us further consider the loop P-M-S-D-P. This loop has *two* negative influences. An increase in population causes an increase in modernization, which in turn causes an increase in sanitation facilities, which in turn causes a decrease ... in the number of diseases, which in turn causes an increase in population. This is therefore a deviation-amplifying loop. Two negative influences cancel each other and become positive in the total effect.

In general, *a loop with an even number of negative influences is deviation-amplifying, and a loop with an odd number of negative influences is deviation-counteracting.* Besides the three loops mentioned above, there is another loop P-M-S-B-D-P, which is deviation-amplifying because of the two negative influences contained in it. The system shown in [Figure 3] contains several loops, some of which are deviation-amplifying and some of which are deviation-counteracting. Whether the system as a whole is deviation-amplifying or deviation-counteracting depends on the strength of each loop. A society or an organism contains many deviation-amplifying loops as well as deviation-counteracting loops, and an understanding of a society or an organism cannot be attained without studying both types of loops and the relationships between them. It is in this sense that our *second cybernetics* is essential to our further study of societies and organisms.

Not only are there deviation-amplifying loops and deviation-counteracting loops in the society and in the organism, but also under certain conditions a deviation-amplifying loop may become deviation-counteracting, and a deviation-counteracting loop may become deviation-amplifying. An example is the principle of diminished return. An increase in investment causes an increase in capital, and an increase in capital makes more investments possible. Before the profit reaches a certain level the effect of income tax is negligible. But, as the profit becomes greater, the influence of income tax becomes greater and eventually stabilizes the size of the capital.

A culture may follow a similar process. Sometimes one may wonder how a culture, which is quite different from its neighbouring cultures, has ever developed on a geographical background which does not seem to be in any degree different from the geographical conditions of its neighbours. Most likely such a culture had developed first by a deviation-amplifying mutual causal process, and has later attained its own equilibrium when the deviation-counteracting components have become predominant, and is currently maintaining its uniqueness in spite of the similarity of its geographical conditions to those of its neighbours.[6]

The second cybernetics is useful also in such fields as psychiatry. In many cases, interpersonal conflicts are generated by mutual deviation-amplification between persons and are later maintained at the deviated (but not necessarily deviant) pattern. Mutual amplification may occur within a person, for example, between loss of self-confidence and poor performance in a neurotic person. The established pattern, no matter how deviated, is not necessarily "pathological" if it enables a constructive life. But, if the pattern results in a reduction of conflict-free, constructive energy, then a therapy becomes necessary. The therapy aims at breaking the stabilized unsatisfactory pattern and at initiating a new deviation-amplification in the direction of developing a satisfactory pattern.

The second cybernetics will be useful also in the technological fields such as in the design of a machine which invents. A trial-and-error machine is inefficient because it has no directivity. But it has a great flexibility. A deviation-amplifying inventing machine, on the other hand, works in the direction specified by the initial kick, and, for this reason, is efficient. It is not built for any specific direction, because the direction is a variable which is specified by the initial kick. In this sense it is flexible. But in another sense it is not flexible because once the direction is set, it will persist in that direction. A machine that incorporates randomness, deviation-amplification and deviation-counteracting may be both efficient and flexible. It can search for all possibilities. It can try to amplify certain ideas in various directions. It can stay at a relevant idea (which may change from time to time during the invention) and bring back to it other ideas for synthesis. In fact, openness to strange hunches, ability to elaborate on them and to bring them back to a synthesis are what is found in the process of human creative minds.[7]

The elaboration and refinement of the second cybernetics belong to the future, and we may expect many fruitful results from them.

Notes

1. Tinbergen, J. (1937). An Econometric Approach to Business Cycle Problems. Paris.
———(1939). Statistical Testing of Business Cycle Theories. Geneva.
———(1951). Business Cycles in the United Kingdom 1870–1914. Amsterdam.
Wold, H. (1956). *J. Royal Stat. Soc. ser. A, 119*, pp. 28–61.
———(1958). *Rev. Inst. Internat. Stat., 26*, pp. 5–25.
———(1960). *Econometrica., 28*, no. 2, pp. 417–463.
2. Myrdal, G. (1957). Economic Theory and Underdeveloped Regions. London.
3. Tinbergen, N. (1951). The Study of Instinct. Oxford. p. 45.
4. Allee, W. C. (1951). Cooperation Among Animals.
5. Wright, S. (1931). Evolution in Mendelian Population. *Genetics, 16*, pp. 97–159.
———(1932). Roles of Mutation. *Proc. 6th Internat. Congr. Gen., 1*, pp. 356–366. Also see Ref. 4, pp. 85, 86, 88, 91, 92.
6. Maruyama, M. (1961). The Multilateral Mutual Causal Relationships among the Modes of Communication, Sociometric Pattern and the Intellectual Orientation in the Danish Culture. *Phylon, 22*, no. 1, pp. 41–58.
7. Barron, F. (1953). Some Personality Correlates of Independence of Judgment. *J. Personality, 21*, no. 3, pp. 287–297.
———(1957). Originality in Relation to Personality and Intellect. *J. Personality, 25*, no. 6, pp. 730–742.
Rokeach, M. (1960). The Open and Closed Mind. New York.

18 . Appendix to "The Second Cybernetics"
Magoroh Maruyama

We have to distinguish several *logical levels* of the second law of thermodynamics.

The first logical level has two logically equivalent forms which are linked together by the following definition of entropy: An infinitesimal increase of the entropy of a system is defined as an infinitesimal quantity of heat received by the system divided by the absolute temperature of the system.

The two forms are: "The entropy of the system of two bodies A and B, having different temperatures, in contact increases"; and "Heat flows from a warmer body A to a cooler body B when they are in contact."

Let:

T_1: temperature of A.
T_2: temperature of B.
   $T_1 > T_2$.
q_1: quantity of heat input of A.
q_2: quantity of heat input of B.
S_1: entropy of A.
S_2: entropy of B.

then $q_1 = -q_2$ (by virtue of the first law of thermodynamics regarding the conservation of energy)

$$dS_1 = q_1/T_1$$
$$dS_2 = q_2/T_2 \quad \text{(by the definition of entropy)}$$
$$dS_1 + dS_2 = q_1/T_1 + q_2/T_2 = (1/T_2 - 1/T_1)q_2$$

Since $T_1 > T_2$, we have

$$1/T_2 - 1/T_1 > 0$$

By assuming that heat flows from A to B, we obtain $q_2 > 0$, and hence

$$dS_1 + dS_2 > 0 \qquad \text{entropy increases}$$

On the other hand, by assuming that the entropy increases, we obtain $dS_1 + dS_2 > 0$, and therefore $q_2 > 0$. Heat flows from A to B.

The second logical level is given by the Boltzmann-Planck formula:

$$S = k \ln P$$

where S is the entropy of the system under consideration, k is Boltzmann's constant and P is the number of "elementary complexions." An elementary

From *American Scientist*, Vol. 51, No. 3, September 1963, pp. 250A, 252A, 254A, 256A, by permission of *American Scientist*.

complexion is a configuration of quantized discrete finite structures of atoms and molecules in the system. A number of different elementary complexions may have a same level of entropy, and thus each entropy level is associated with the number of the elementary complexions having the same level of entropy. It thus turns out that S is large when P is large. A state, which can be produced by a great number of elementary complexions, in other words, which has a choice of alternatives from among a great number of elementary complexions, is a highly probable state. Hence the higher the entropy of the state, the more probable the state. Thus a high entropy state is a high probability state. The Boltzmann-Planck formula by itself does not indicate the direction of the change of entropy. But, as will be seen later, when combined with other assumptions, it serves as a basis for deriving the direction of the change of entropy.

The third logical level is defined by Brillouin's formula:

$$-S = I = r \log (P/P_c)$$

where I is the amount of information, which is the negative of entropy, r is a positive constant, P is the number of apriori equally probable alternatives and P_c is the number of alternatives falling under the specification given by the message. This formula is not directly a formula for thermodynamics, but is a formula for the entropy of information.

The higher the specificity related to the state, the lower the entropy. This formula is important because it not only shows the distinction between the apriori probability and the aposteriori structuredness, but also defines the entropy as a function of the ratio between them.

The fourth logical level is given by Shannon's formula:

$$I/G = -r \sum_i p_i \log p_i$$

where G is the length of the message, and p_i is the probability of the ith symbol appearing at each position within the message.

This formula can be derived from Brillouin's formula when the following assumptions are made: the message is sufficiently long to permit the approximation of the logarithm of a factorial by Stirling's formula; and for each symbol its occurrence has an equal probability at all positions along the length of the message.

The fifth logical level is the consideration that an isolated system spends with great probability most of its time in most probable states.

The sixth logical level is that an isolated system, if it is found in an improbable state, is likely to be found in a more probable state at a later time. This may be looked at as derived from the consideration on the fifth logical level. Assuming that the state at time $T_0 + t$ is independent of the state at time T_0, the system at time $T_0 + t$, in view of the consideration on the fifth level and regardless of the state at T_0, will most likely be in a probable state. Likewise, the system was, with a great probability, in a probable state at a past time $T_0 - t$. Hence this consideration is time-symmetrical with respect to the future and to the past.

The seventh logical level is that it is highly unlikely that random changes accumulate systematically and monotonically into one direction. A corollary of this consideration is that independent random changes tend to destroy structure rather than to build a structure: if a structure is built at all, it has to be built by a sudden change rather than by a gradual and monotonical increase of structuredness. This was the basis of Reichenbach's argument that, given a motion picture of an event in which the structuredness gradually changes, there is only one direction the film can be run to make sense.

Deviation-amplifying mutual causal processes and the second law of thermodynamics: Now the question is at what logical level the deviation-amplifying mutual causal processes contradict the second law of thermodynamics. Or, more precisely, at what logical level the assumptions made are violated by deviation-amplifying mutual causal processes.

There is no contradiction at the first level. At the second level, however, a reorganization of thinking is necessary. High level of entropy was associated with a large number of elementary complexions corresponding to the level of entropy, and the probability of an entropy level was associated with the number of elementary complexions. The rationale behind this reasoning was an assumption of spatial independence of the probability of the states of the atoms and the molecules. This assumption permitted each configuration to be weighted equally in the probability calculation.

Deviation-amplifying mutual causal processes violate the assumption of the spatial independence of probability. On the contrary, deviation-amplifying mutual causal processes assume the spatial interdependence resulting from the interactions between the spatial parts. Deviation-amplifying mutual causal processes assume not only space-wise interactions, but also time-wise dependence of the present upon the past as stochastic processes.

The Boltzmann-Planck formula still holds, provided we keep in our minds that any inference based on the assumption of direct relationship between the entropy level and its probability is no longer valid.

At the third level behind Brillouin's formula, there is an assumption of apriori equally probable alternatives. This assumption is again violated by deviation-amplifying mutual causal processes.

It is worth while underlining that while the assumption behind Brillouin's formula is not satisfied by deviation-amplifying mutual causal processes, Shannon's formula is capable of handling deviation-amplifying mutual causal processes. This is so in spite of the fact that Shannon's formula can be derived from Brillouin's formula. This is because Shannon has made, in his conceptualization, provisions for conditional probabilities as well as for independent probabilities.

However, in the conditional probability the direction of condition is one-way. If conditional probability is to be used in mutual causal spatial relationship rather than in temporal relationship, it has to be mutual-conditional probability rather than unidirectional-conditional probability. The study of mutual-conditional probability belongs to the future.

Meanwhile, there is a way to analyze deviation-amplifying mutual causal processes as temporal relationship and consequently as stochastic processes. In this case we use multivariable time-wise-unidirectional conditional probabilities, and Shannon's formula is useful.

The reasoning at the fifth logical level is not contradicted by deviation-amplifying mutual causal processes provided we do not equate probable states with random states. We note, however, that, frequently, probable states are equated with random states, and in such a case deviation-amplifying mutual causal processes contradict the reasoning. The same comments apply at the sixth logical level.

At the seventh level, the reasoning was correct as long as it dealt with random processes. The error was in the overlooking of the possibility of deviation-amplifying mutual causal processes which are systematic rather than purely random. This oversight caused Reichenbach to impute finality or teleology to events involving gradual and monotonical increase of structuredness.

The above discussions answer our question as to the logical level at which the underlying assumptions are violated by deviation-amplifying mutual causal processes. When an assumption is violated, the version of the second law of thermodynamics combined with that assumption becomes invalid.

What we learn from the foregoing discussions is that the seven logical levels (no hierarchical order between the levels is necessarily implied) should be distinguished; that we should be aware of the assumptions made at each logical level; and that if we assume spatial interdependence the statements at various logical levels have to be considerably modified.

There are two more questions to be examined. The first is: How great is the probability of a deviation-amplifying mutual causal process getting started? The answer is that the probability, per unit time, of a deviation-amplifying mutual causal process *getting started* may be very low, but the probability of it maintaining itself is rather high. Given a long period of time and a large space, the probability of some kind of deviation-amplifying mutual causal process getting started somewhere sometime is large, even if the probability per unit time in a unit space is small. And, once started, such a process may maintain and multiply with a great probability.

The second question is: Can an *isolated system* decrease its entropy within itself? . . . Consider the following example. Let the entire universe be our closed system. Suppose all particles are evenly and thinly distributed in it with low even temperature and with random distribution of motion. Suppose further that by some chance two particles come a little closer to each other than other particles. The decreased distance increases the gravitational force, and this will decrease the distance still more. Eventually the two particles join together. This union produces a large particle with a larger gravitational field. This will attract additional particles to it, and the mass grows. Increased bombardments and collisions produce a high temperature. Thus the distribution of the particles as well as the distribution of the temperature become uneven, and the closed system decreases entropy within itself.

19 . The Keynesian Model . **Alvin H. Hansen**

J. R. Hicks, in his first review article on the *General Theory* (*Economic Journal*, June, 1936), singles out this feature for special mention. The "use of the method of expectations," said Hicks, "is perhaps the most revolutionary thing about this book."[1] Keynes believed that the current economic theory was frequently unrealistic because it assumed too often a "static state where there is no changing future to influence the present."[2]

The *General Theory* is, however, cast mainly in terms of equilibrium analysis. Keynes's method, in much of the book, can indeed be described as comparative statics. But in his hands comparative statics becomes a useful device for thinking about practical problems in a manner which is essentially dynamic. Hicks was the first to see this quite clearly. "It is a theory of shifting equilibrium *vis-à-vis* the static or stationary theories of general equilibrium such as those of Ricardo, Böhm-Bawerk, or Pareto."[3]

In static analysis, certain parameters such as tastes, income, etc., being assumed as given, a functional relation is posited between two variables, say price and quantity demanded. At a higher price less will be demanded. But this is purely static analysis. If a change in anticipations is introduced so that prices are expected to rise further, Demand will probably increase—*more* will be purchased in anticipation of further price increases. This represents a dynamic situation. If a given *higher* price is regarded as permanent, the static Demand schedule will again control the quantity taken. But if it is expected that prices will continue to rise, a higher price will call forth an increase in Demand; *i.e.*, under the impact of the element of anticipations the static Demand schedules will shift up or to the right. The *change* from one equilibrium position to another is the subject matter of comparative statics. Comparative statics is a study of "the way in which our equilibrium quantities will change as a result of changes in the parameters taken as independent data."[4]

Comparative statics should assist us to discern the direction and magnitude of changes in the variables when certain data change so as to cause a movement to a new equilibrium condition. Pareto, says Samuelson, "laid the basis for a theory of *comparative statics* by showing how a change in a datum would displace the position of equilibrium."[5]

In comparative-statics analysis, we investigate "the response of a system to changes in given parameters."[6] In *period analysis* and in *rates-of-change analysis* we investigate the behavior of the system which results from the passage of time. Comparative statics leaps over the time involved in the transition to the successive positions of equilibrium. But in period analysis we have an economy *in motion*, an economy *undergoing change*. Comparative statics "involves the special case where a 'permanent' change is made, and only the effects upon final levels of stationary equilibrium are in question."[7] Dynamic analysis proper gives us a "description of the actual path followed by a system in going from one 'comparative static level' to another."[8]

Hicks pointed out that the subject matter for Keynes's study and analysis was not the "norm of the static state," but rather the "changing, progressing, fluctuating economy." This has "to be studied on its own, and cannot usefully be referred to the norm of the static state." Accordingly, while static theory has ordinarily assumed that tastes and resources are given, Keynes introduced into his comparative statics a new and vitally significant element, namely, "people's anticipations of the future."[9] "Once the missing element—anticipations—is added, equilibrium analysis can be used, not only in the remote stationary conditions to which many economists have found themselves driven back, but even in the real world, even in the real world in 'disequilibrium.'"[10]

Thus while Keynes's method is formally that of comparative statics, it is nonetheless a highly useful method of studying an economy undergoing change. "The equations of comparative statics are then a special case of the general dynamic analysis."[11]

In Keynes's method the lagging adjustment that the economic system makes in response to the introduction of a disturbance is indeed often skipped over, and attention is directed to the equilibrium (or normal) magnitudes and relationships of the relevant variables. Now it is the system's power of adjustment or adaptation (not indeed the lagged response, but the *normal* or *equilibrium* response) that primarily interests Keynes. "The point of the method," said Hicks, "is that it reintroduces determinateness into a process of change."[12] The method is, he concludes, "an admirable one for analysing the impact effect of disturbing causes."[13]

* * *

The *General Theory* is something more than just static theory. Over and over again Keynes is thinking in highly dynamic terms. Sometimes this involves brief excursions into period analysis (taking account of lags), and sometimes the analysis proceeds in terms of a moving equilibrium (continuous rates of change). And for the rest, his comparative statics is concerned not with the problems of equilibrium at one point alone but rather with the factors that cause a shift from one equilibrium position to the next. Comparative statics is in short *a* method of studying *change*.

All this is well-illustrated in Chap. 5, where he discusses Expectation as Determining Output and Employment. He begins by introducing *time:* "Time usually elapses, however—and sometimes much time—between the incurring of costs by the producer (with the consumer in view) and the purchase of the output by the ultimate consumer." The entrepreneur has to form the "best expectations he can as to what the consumers will be prepared to pay when he is ready to supply them." The modern entrepreneur, since he must produce by "processes which occupy time," has no choice but to be "guided by these expectations."[14]

These expectations fall into two groups. One class relates to the *producer*, and these may be called "short-term expectations." The second relates to the prospective returns which can be anticipated from a long-term, durable asset. These may be called "long-term expectations." Short-term expectations have to do with the outlook for *sales*; long-term expectations have to do with *investment in fixed capital*.

Keynes is here thinking in terms of period analysis. A "*change* in expectations (whether short-term or long-term) will only produce its full effect on employment over a considerable period." A lagged adjustment is here envisaged. "The change in employment due to a change in expectations will not be the same on the second day after the change as on the first, or the same on the third day as on the second, and so on, even though there be no further change in expectations." Thus "some time for preparation must needs elapse before employment can reach the level at which it would have stood if the state of expectation had been revised sooner." And in the case of changed long-term expectations leading to investment outlays, "employment may be at a higher level at first, than it will be after there has been time to adjust the equipment to the new situation" (pp. 47–48).

"If we suppose a state of expectation to continue for a sufficient length of time for the effect on employment to have worked itself out" completely, then the "steady level of employment thus attained may be called the long-period employment corresponding to that state of expectation" (p. 48). This is certainly a statement of interest from the standpoint of dynamics. Moreover, Keynes is careful to point out that this long-period employment once reached is not necessarily a *constant* amount. "For example, a steady increase in wealth or population may constitute a part of the unchanging expectation" (footnote, p. 48). Thus there may be a continuous rate of change.

Keynes has a good deal to say (in Chap. 5 and elsewhere) about the lags involved in the process of transition. Read in this connection what he says on pages 48 to 50. Here we have a good example of period analysis involving lagged adjustments. Changes in long-term expectations will first cause increases in the investment industries (the "earlier stages") and only later in the consumption industries (the "later stages"). "Thus the change in expectation may lead to a gradual crescendo in the level of employment, rising to a peak and then declining to the new long-period level. . . . Or again, if the new long-period employment is less than the old, the level of employment during the transition may fall for a time *below* what the new long-period level is going to be. Thus a mere change in expectation is capable of producing an oscillation of the same kind of shape as a cyclical movement, in the course of working itself out" (p. 49).

The discussion of involved lagged adjustments continues. "An uninterrupted process of transition, such as the above, to a new long-period position can be complicated in detail. But the actual course of events is more complicated still.

For the state of expectation is liable to constant change, a new expectation being superimposed long before the previous change has fully worked itself out; so that the economic machine is occupied at any given time with a number of overlapping activities, the existence of which is due to various past states of expectation." Thus "the level of employment at any time depends, in a sense, not merely on the existing state of expectation but on the states of expectation which have existed over a certain past period" (p. 50).

These quotations describe precisely the kind of dynamic model that econometricians are fond of elaborating. During this complicated process of adjustment, "past expectations," he says, "have not yet worked themselves out" (p. 50).

With respect to short-term expectations there is a "large overlap between the effects on employment of the realised sale-proceeds of the recent output and those of the sale-proceeds expected from current input." But "in the case of durable goods, the producer's short-term expectations are based on the current long-term expectations of the investor" (p. 51).

Expectations play a role in all Keynes's basic functional relations. Expectations underlie the investment-demand schedule, the liquidity preference schedule, and the instantaneous multiplier. All this will be explained in later chapters [of *A Guide to Keynes*], where we consider these functions in more detail. Here it is sufficient to note that Keynes's emphasis on expectations introduces a dynamic element—the difference between expected and actual rates of flow, and the difference between expected and actual stocks.

Nonetheless it is quite true that he was primarily interested in an analysis of the factors tending toward *equilibrium*, and especially in an explanation of the condition of underemployment equilibrium. This was the question that J. M. Clark had raised, namely, the "chronic limitation of production owing to limitation of effective demand."[15] Clark rightly saw, as did Keynes, that this question could not be answered by cycle theories of the type which merely stress oscillation, i.e., dynamic theories of disequilibrium, which merely show how the economy sways up and down. Thus it is quite true that Keynes's primary interest was in *equilibrium* analysis. But about this, together with the related problems of statics and dynamics, we shall have much more to say in the chapters which follow [in *A Guide to Keynes*].

* * *

The Consumption Function [in the Keynesian model]

FUNCTIONAL RELATIONS AND ECONOMIC ANALYSIS

If the Keynesian system of economics consisted simply of definitional equations such as $I = S$ and $I + C = Y$, we could safely dismiss the *General Theory* from serious consideration. Economic analysis cannot make progress with such truisms as "*actual purchases* (demand) always equal *actual* sales (supply)"; nor is our understanding of the functioning of the economy deepened significantly by the proposition that "*actual* investment equals *actual* saving."

But when a demand schedule is set over against a supply schedule, we can then begin to learn something about the determination of price. Similarly with the Keynesian theory of income determination.

The student who reads widely in the critical literature on Keynes will not infrequently get the impression that the Keynesian analysis runs in terms of *ex post* or *realized* magnitudes. This is not correct. In the first place the Keynesian analysis takes account of expectations, as we have already pointed out[16] and shall have occasion to point out again and again. In the second place it is based on *functional relationships*. The moment *functions* (as distinct from *realized* or *observed* points in the schedules) are introduced, we are dealing with a hypothesis which can be verified or disproved as a pattern of economic behavior.

That Keynes's analysis does not run in terms of sterile ex post equations is evident at once in the opening paragraph of Chap. 8, where he resumes the argument broken off at the end of Book I. Ex post equations explain nothing; instead, Keynes begins his argument with the proposition that "the volume of employment is determined by the intersection of the aggregate supply function with the aggregate demand function" (p. 89).

The Aggregate Supply function involves few, if any, considerations not already well-known. But it is the Aggregate Demand function which has been neglected. To explain it requires an analysis of (1) the consumption function and (2) the investment-demand function. This is something very different from simply presenting the ex post equation $Y = I + C$, namely, that Aggregate Demand equals investment plus consumption.

The Aggregate Demand *function*, Keynes explains, relates any given level of employment to the expected proceeds from that volume of employment (p. 89). What the expected proceeds will be depends upon the expected outlays on consumption and the expected outlays on investment (p. 98). Accordingly it becomes necessary to analyse (1) the factors underlying consumption outlays and (2) the factors underlying investment outlays. The former involves a study of the consumption function; the latter a study of the investment-demand function.

With respect to consumption, we may consider either the function relating consumption to employment or, alternatively, the function relating consumption

to real income.   In the short run, employment and real income will usually increase or decrease together more or less proportionally.   But over the long run,
real income tends to rise *in relation to* employment, owing to technological improvements which raise the per capita output.   In the short run, however, output
(real income) cannot be increased readily without an increase in employment.

Accordingly, it is a permissible and useful approach to translate the functional
relation of consumer demand to employment into a functional relation of consumption expenditures (in real terms) to real income (p. 90).   We may therefore
translate the function $D_1 = {}_x(N)$ into $C = C(Y)$, where C is consumption in real
terms and Y is real income.   Keynes, as we have seen, deflated the nominal
monetary values into real terms by means of an index of wage rates (wage units).
Accordingly he writes the consumption function as $C_w = X(Y_w)$, in which the
subscript w indicates that C and Y are stated in terms of wage units (p. 90).

In setting up this function, Keynes advanced the hypothesis that consumption
depends primarily upon real income.[17]   Income is singled out as the main determinant of consumption just as in the case of the familiar demand curve, price is
singled out as the primary determinant of the quantity taken.   With respect to
any such functional relation, however, it is always assumed that all other determining factors are *given and remain uncharged.*   Other things remaining equal, the
consumption function shows what changes can be expected in consumption from
given changes in income.

The functional relation between consumption and income may be stated in the
form of a schedule or table showing the aggregate amount consumed at each
assumed income level; or again the relation may be presented as a curve in a
diagram.

Now the curve will *shift* up (or down) if any significant change occurs in the
"other factors."   If any of the "other factors" change, we can say that the *parameters* of the function have changed.   Thus an important parameter of the familiar demand curve is "consumer taste."   If tastes change substantially, the
demand curve for pork, for example, may rise sharply.   At the same price more
will be demanded than before.   When any parameter of the function changes,
the curve will *shift* (p. 96).

The greater part of Chaps. 8 and 9 are devoted to a consideration of the factors
which underlie the consumption function and determine its *form* (i.e., the *slope*
and *position* of the curve).   One section (pp. 91–95), however, is devoted to
factors which cause *shifts* in the function.

The factors in question are classified under two broad heads, (1) the objective
factors (exogenous, or external to the economic system itself) and (2) the subjective
(endogenous) factors.   These latter include (a) psychological characteristics of
human nature and (b) social practices and institutions (especially the behavior
patterns of business concerns with respect to wage and dividend payments and
retained earnings) and social arrangements (such as those affecting the distribution of income).

The subjective factors "though not unalterable, are unlikely to undergo a
material change over a short period of time except in abnormal or revolutionary

circumstances" (p. 91).   Being deeply rooted in established behavior patterns, they are likely to be fairly stable.   These slowly changing factors fundamentally determine the *slope* and *position* of the consumption function and serve to give it a fairly high degree of stability.   But the external factors may at times undergo rapid change and in these circumstances may cause marked *shifts* in the consumption function.   We are thus concerned with two highly important matters, (1) the *form* (slope and position) of the function, and (2) *shifts* in the function.

These matters are treated by Keynes with great acumen and rich insight.   But the argument is not well-arranged, and having in mind the literature which has appeared since the *General Theory*, one could easily think of many ways in which these two chapters could be improved.   One must never forget, however, that, writing in 1936, Keynes was breaking quite new ground.

* * *

The essentials of Keynes's discussion of the trade cycle can be summed up as follows:

1. The cycle consists primarily of fluctuations in the rate of investment.

2. Fluctuations in the rate of investment are caused mainly by fluctuations in the marginal efficiency of capital.

3. Fluctuations in the rate of interest have indeed at times played a significant role, but, more typically, changes in the liquidity preference schedule, induced by fluctuations in the marginal efficiency of capital, reinforce and supplement the primary factor (*i.e.*, changes in r).

4. Fluctuations in the marginal efficiency of capital, r, are due to (a) changes in the prospective yields (the R series) of capital goods and (b) changes in the replacement cost of capital goods C_R.   Fluctuations in the cost of capital goods are due to changes in the rate at which investment is produced in a given period, in other words, to the extreme pressure placed upon the capital-goods industries during the boom.   Fluctuations in costs are secondary and supplementary to the primary initiating factor, which is the fluctuation in the prospective yields of new capital goods.

5. Toward the end of a boom the decline in prospective yields on capital is due in the first instance to the growing abundance (and therefore lower marginal productivity) of capital goods.   This is an *objective* fact, which in turn may induce a wave of pessimistic expectations (a psychological factor) so that the anticipated yield, once the turning point is past, is usually lower than the facts, coolly considered, justify.

6. In the absence of more thoroughgoing measures (e.g., fiscal policy) a variable rate of interest may be useful as a means to stabilize the cycle.   Keynes, however, prefers a maintained low rate of interest in conjunction with other more radical measures designed to regularize the cycle.

7. Even boom-time levels of investment have typically failed to produce full employment.   Thus in order to achieve sustained full employment it is not even enough to keep the boom going.   Accordingly, Keynes did not believe it to be sound policy to choke off the boom.   He was not impressed with the analysis

which alleged that the depression is the inevitable consequence of the distortions of the boom. Any distortions that might exist could progressively be overcome by a program of sustained full employment. Merely to choke off the boom by an increase in the rate of interest "belongs to the species of remedy which cures the disease by killing the patient" (p. 323).

Keynes did not come to grips with the possible inflationary implications of a deliberate program of sustained full employment. Still more difficult are the maladjustments and distortions caused by wars and postwar restocking booms. Keynes, to be sure, was thinking, in this chapter, about normal peacetime conditions and not about the overfull employment of war and postwar booms.

* * *

NOTES ON EARLY ECONOMIC THINKING

... Keynes attacked dominant orthodox theories; he attacked conventional dogmas with respect to practical policy;[18] and he attacked the doctrine that reliance can be placed on automatic adjustment processes. He labeled as outstanding faults of the modern economy, failure to provide full employment and an inequitable distribution of wealth and income.

He contended that his analysis leads to directly opposite conclusions from those reached by orthodox economics with respect to the effect of measures (e.g., taxation) designed to lessen the existing inequality of income. Greater equality will raise the consumption function; and an increase in the propensity to consume will serve to increase the inducement to invest[19] (p. 373). Yet he states, as part of his faith, a belief in the "social and psychological justification for significant inequalities of incomes and wealth," though not as large as those which existed in 1936 (p. 374).

Similarly his analysis leads, he thought, to diametrically opposite conclusions from those reached by classical theory with respect to capital formation. According to the classicals, a high propensity to save is the source of high capital formation; and a high volume of saving was thought to be promoted by (1) a low propensity to consume and (2) a high rate of interest. As Keynes saw it, the opposite is true: a high level of investment is promoted by a low rate of interest and by a high propensity to consume. Basically, of course, the explanation for these different conclusions must be sought in the fact that the classicals were thinking of full-employment conditions, while Keynes had in mind the condition of under-employment.[20]

Keynes explicitly pointed out that a system of highly progressive taxes might reduce the net rate of return, after taxes, sufficiently to cause a low level of investment even though the rate of interest were low. "I must not be supposed to deny the possibility, or even the probability, of this outcome" (p. 377). Thus steeply progressive taxes might have the effect of preventing the optimum volume of capital formation. Here as so often in economics one encounters a dilemma:

highly progressive taxes are favorable to a high level of consumption since such taxes promote greater equality of income, but they tend to have a deterrent effect on investment.

Keynes expressed forcibly the view that a program of continuous full employment would provide so high a rate of capital formation, assuming no radical change in the consumption function, that, within a generation or so, the marginal efficiency of capital would be driven down to zero (i.e., the capital stock would increase until the condition of *full investment* is reached). Necessary conditions for this eventuality to occur would be (1) a fairly inelastic marginal efficiency schedule and (2) relatively small upward shifts in the schedule (i.e., inadequate investment outlets due to a sluggish technology and a slow rate of population growth).

In line with his faith, often expressed, in the virtues of active enterprise (in contrast with the passive virtues of thrift) he unfurled the banner for the intelligence, determination, and executive skill of the entrepreneur (p. 376) while complacently foreseeing the gradual euthanasia of the *rentier* class.

He affirmed his faith in individual initiative and private enterprise. He was opposed to a system of state socialism. Nevertheless, the role of the State must, he thought, be greatly increased. "The State will have to exercise a guiding influence on the propensity to consume partly through its scheme of taxation, partly by fixing the rate of interest, and partly, perhaps, in other ways" (p. 378). Banking policy alone, via a low rate of interest, will not provide sufficient investment, he thought, for full employment. Public investment (but Keynes did not go into details) will be needed. Mixed companies—public authority combined with private initiative—have already played an important role in many countries, and such ventures may be expanded.[21] State control of investment in housing— low-cost public housing, lending, insurance, and guaranteeing operations—have become standard policies in all advanced countries. State action to ensure adequate investment, public and private, together with a tax policy designed to raise the consumption function—these are the types of measures which seemed promising. "It is not the ownership of the instruments of production which it is important for the State to assume" (p. 378). What is needed is "an adjustment between the propensity to consume and the inducement to invest" (p. 379). It is no more necessary, he thought, to socialize economic life now than formerly.

Once sustained full employment is achieved, classical theory comes into its own. At full employment, the price system can be expected to direct productive resources, economically and wisely, into the right channels. What we suffer from is not misdirected employment but underemployment. The "free play of economic forces" can be trusted to give us efficient use of the factors of production (p. 379). In support of Keynes's position, one may cite the miraculous productivity and efficiency which the American economy has displayed ever since 1941 under the stimulus of a high level of Aggregate Demand.

Keynes was keenly aware of the advantages of individualism and free enterprise —the play of self-interest, the safeguard of personal liberty, the exercise of personal choice, and the variety of life which these institutions encourage. Indeed

Keynes averred that he defended the enlargement of the functions of government (designed "to adjust the propensity to consume to the inducement to invest") as the "only practicable means of avoiding the destruction of existing economic forms" and promoting the "successful functioning of individual initiative" (p. 380). The world will not continue to tolerate unemployment. What is needed is a "right analysis . . . to cure the disease whilst preserving efficiency and freedom" (p. 381).

Notes

1. J. R. Hicks, "Mr. Keynes' Theory of Employment," *Economic Journal*, June, 1936, p. 240.
2. Keynes, *General Theory*, p. 145.
3. Hicks, *op. cit.*, p. 238.
4. Samuelson, *Foundations of Economic Analysis*, Harvard University Press, 1947, p. 257.
5. *Ibid.*, p. 351.
6. *Ibid.*
7. *Ibid.*, p. 352.
8. *Ibid.*
9. Hicks, *op. cit.*, p. 240.
10. *Ibid.*
11. Samuelson, *op. cit.*, p. 262.
12. Hicks, *op. cit.*, p. 241.
13. *Ibid.*
14. All quotations in this paragraph are from the *General Theory*, p. 46.
15. J. M. Clark, *Economic Reconstruction*, Columbia University Press, 1934, p. 105.
16. See Chap. 2 [in *A Guide to Keynes*].
17. The demand for one category of consumer expenditures (namely, consumers' durables) depends very much upon the stock already acquired. Thus when the public generally is well-stocked with new automobiles and other consumers' durables, demand will fall off even though real incomes and employment continue to remain high, owing, for example, to continued high military expenditures.
18. With respect to the two leading policy dogmas—the gold standard and the balanced budget—Keynes attacked the first directly but the second rather vaguely, though he stanchly supported loan expenditures as a means of raising Aggregate Demand. His earlier substitute for the gold standard was flexible exchanges, but later (Bretton Woods) his substitute was international machinery to permit exchange-rate adjustments and cooperation with respect to international investment and also with respect to domestic full-employment policies. With respect to a balanced budget, he did not hesitate to advocate loan expenditures, but he never faced up to the debt problem. After the First World War he advocated a capital levy, and in his pamphlet, *How to Pay for the War*, he still showed leanings toward this proposal. He never explored the implications of a growing public debt, the problems of debt management, or the important role of public debt as a means of providing adequate liquid assets in a growing economy.
19. Without expressly saying so, this is one of the few instances in which Keynes in fact invokes the acceleration principle.
20. The optimism of the classicals rested on the assumption of unlimited investment opportunities. On this basis, the higher the propensity to save, the greater the *amount* of capital formation.
21. The illustrations given in this and the sentence following are not drawn from Keynes.

20 . Simulation of Socio-Economic Systems Part II An Aggregative Socio-Economic Simulation of a Latin American Country
Martin Shubik

1. INTRODUCTION

The simple model constructed here is built to serve as an illustration of the uses of simulation and as a first approximation for a socio-economic model to be used in connection with the investigation of development problems in parts of Latin America.

The technique of simulation serves as an excellent data organizing device and framework for the conceptual scheme behind a national economic accounts system and aggregate financial reporting system. This simulation utilizes in part the national economic accounts format developed in the Country Study Program of the Yale Economic Growth Center[1] and the financial statistical reporting of the International Monetary Fund and World Bank.[2]

Although this first model is based primarily upon an aggregated national income system of a variety that is well known to economic studies, it contains several parameters and relations of a socio-economic variety, which are not commonly found in national income models.

The simulation described below has been constructed in a manner that employs what can at best be called "casual empiricism." It has been used to provide a structure for joint discussion and as a possible basis for research between anthropologists, economists, political scientists, sociologists, and others. The eventual goal, however, is to demonstrate that this type of simulation is a natural integrating device to provide a basis for discourse among operating planners, those concerned with the gathering of information or the administration of data-gathering and information systems, as well as behavioral scientists.

From Ludwig von Bertalanffy and Anotal Rapoport (eds.), *General Systems*, Vol. XII, 1967, pp. 159–175, by permission of the Society for General Systems Research. Research undertaken by the Cowles Commission for Research in Economics, Yale University, under Contract Nonr-3055(01) with the Office of Naval Research. The author is indebted to Marshall Pomer and Joel Rubinstein who participated considerably in the work involved in revising this model. I wish also to thank J. Friedman who worked together with me on an earlier version of this paper, as well as R. and N. Ruggles for their comments, cooperation, and assistance. Furthermore, I am indebted to G. Blanksten, R. Holt, S. Mintz, W. Robichek, and many others whose ideas and conversations on the possibility of interdisciplinary work led me to construct this model.

Part of the motivation behind this work is to show that relatively interesting and thought-provoking models can be constructed and examined quickly and relatively cheaply by means of computer simulation. Before validation problems must be faced, pre-validation problems must be overcome. These involve the sorting out of variables, the organization of common sense, uncommon sense, insights and "guesses," and the "playing" with models as a preliminary to well-defining structural relationships and devising methods for empirical verification of the chosen relationships.

Accuracy and validity should depend upon the question to be answered; models and questions which appear to be vague to the econometrician may thus have a place and use to the policy maker, political scientist, administrators, and others. These comments should *not* be interpreted as a defense of sloppy thinking. The gaps separating policy oriented studies, economic theory and econometrics as well as highly relevant sociological and political studies are large. The work here is addressed to providing an interlinkage for the different approaches.

1.1. SOCIOLOGICAL AND POLITICAL FACTORS

This simulation is directed towards portraying some of the basic features of a Latin American country with a large Indian population. Peru, Ecuador, Bolivia, Honduras, Guatemala, and Nicaragua fall into this category.

Models of different countries undoubtedly have much in common; however, it is our belief that we are a long way from the "all-purpose" general simulator. A common methodology, data-gathering procedures, and common output formats with which to carry out comparative studies can be achieved. However, in detail models will differ from country to country.

Eventually it will be highly desirable to deal directly with such factors as degree and speed of urbanization, the effects of religious beliefs, and political structure.[3] At this point neither time nor resources permit including these in the rudimentary model constructed here. Nevertheless the point that is fundamental to the approach adopted here is that in the study of socio-economic and political systems the best disaggregation may be a mixed disaggregation. For many purposes the choice between a disaggregation into, say, 40 economic sectors or 10 economic sectors and 4 social sectors should be made in favor of the mixed economic and social disaggregation.

Formal data often follow theories and purpose. Thus, the argument that the data do not exist or are hard to quantify is not a sufficient reason to abandon factors which may serve to provide much more explanation of processes of growth or change than do available, easily quantifiable variables. A poor guess as to the effect of an important but hard to quantify variable may easily be of more use than an elegant time series of a tangentially relevant variable.

In keeping with the above remarks, in this simulation the population of the country is broken down into four sociological groups which are broadly described as "commercial white" (which will be assumed to include resident foreigners), "agricultural white," mestizo, and Indian. It should be emphasized that these are sociological and not racial categories. A full-blooded Indian could easily have the social status of a "commercial white."

Another way of looking at this breakdown sociologically would be:

	Low Status	High Status
modern	mestizo	"commercial white"
traditional	Indian	"agricultural white"

2. GROSS NATIONAL PRODUCT OR EXPENDITURE

In the following sections we return to the more or less traditional path of listing the various identities and relations of a national accounting scheme. These are integrated with the breakdown into social classes and a scheme for social mobility. The economic system may be regarded as providing a framework upon which social and political factors that are the more difficult to identify and quantify can be added.

We begin by presenting the major expenditure components of gross national product. These show the basic components of GNP (consumption, investment, government, etc.), and the relationship of GNP to other important concepts such as personal income and disposable income. Functional relationships relating the major expenditure components to relevant variables are also set up. These may be interpreted as behavior and policy relations.

Gross national product is computed separately, both from the expenditure and income sides of the balance sheet. In general these calculations do not match and the discrepancy is explained in terms of changes in the price level. Details of this are discussed in Section 4.3.

Let Y_t = gross national product in period t in current currency

I_t = gross private and public capital formation in current currency

C_t = total consumption in current currency

$G_{2,t}$ = government expenditures on health, education, and welfare in current currency (see 2.2.1 for further discussion and breakdown)

$G_{3,t}$ = other government current expenditures

X_t^1 = exports of goods and services in current currency (f.o.b.)

M_t^1 = imports of goods and services in current currency (c.i.f.)

$M_t^{2,1}$ = factor income received

$X_t^{2,1}$ = factor income paid. (From here on all references are to current domestic currency, unless stated otherwise.)

We have the accounting identity defining GNP from the viewpoint of expenditures:

$$Y_t = I_t + C_t + G_{2,t} + G_{3,t} + (X_t^1 - M_t^1) + (M_t^{2,1} - X_t^{2,1}) \tag{1}$$

Eq. (2) specifies that total personal income equals Gross National Product minus depreciation, retained earnings, and indirect business taxes and plus transfer payments. (We assume that international transfers to individuals are negligible for these countries.) This may also be regarded as the sum of factor payments augmented by transfers. $\pi_{6,t}$ is profits of government-owned enterprise.

Y_t^1 = total personal income

D_t = depreciation (Capital Consumption Allowances) in constant currency

T_t = total taxes

T_t^1 = indirect taxes

Y_t^0 = gross domestic product in constant currency

P_t = domestic price level

T_t^2 = direct taxes on business

R_t = net transfer payments to individuals

CS_t = retained earnings

π_t = total profit

$\pi_{i,t}$ = profit of the ith group ($i = 1, \ldots, 6$)

$$Y_t^1 = (Y_t^0 - D_t)P_t + (M_t^{2,1} - X_t^{2,1}) - T_t^1 + R_t - T_t^2 - CS_t - \pi_{6,t} \tag{2}$$

where the first two terms express gross national product calculated from the production side of the accounts.

We consider the population to be broken down into four socio-economic categories in the countries of our interest (for example: Peru, Bolivia, Ecuador, Mexico, and Guatemala). They are: "Commercial" Whites ($i = 1$), "Agricultural" Whites ($i = 2$), Mestizos ($i = 3$), and Indians ($i = 4$). The color divisions are not actually racial in South and Central America. An approximate criterion is that a detribalized Indian becomes a mestizo. A mestizo who attains an appropriate degree of wealth and education may become a white. These divisions will be discussed in further detail in subsequent sections. The subscript 5 is used to denote foreign enterprise in the country (the income of foreign residents is assumed to be included in the first class), while 6 refers to government.

$Y^1_{i,t}$ = personal income of the ith socio-economic category.

We have the identity:

$$Y^1_t = Y^1_{1,t} + Y^1_{2,t} + Y^1_{3,t} + Y^1_{4,t}. \tag{3}$$

In Eq. (4) disposable personal income (Y^2_t) is defined as personal income minus taxes levied on personal income.

Y^2_t = disposable income

T^3_t = direct taxes on households

$Y^2_{i,t}$ = disposable income of ith socoi-economic category

$$Y^2_t = Y^1_t - T^3_t = Y^2_{1,t} + Y^2_{2,t} + Y^2_{3,t} + Y^2_{4,t}. \tag{4}$$

2.1. CONSUMPTION

All of the above equations have been accounting identities. At this point we must specify the first behavioral relationships.

C_t = total consumption

$C_{i,t}$ = consumption of the ith group

N_t = total population

$N_{i,t}$ = population of the ith socio-economic group

η_j = random variables.

Eq. (5) is a mere accounting identity summing up consumption in the different classes.

$$C_t = \sum_{i=1}^{4} C_{i,t}. \tag{5}$$

$$C_{i,t} = \alpha_{i,1} N_{i,t} + \alpha_{i,2} Y^2_{i,t} + \eta_j \tag{6}$$

In Eq. (6) we have assumed as a first approximation that per capita consumption can be described as a linear function of per capita disposable income. If we believed that (6) held for all incomes and over considerable lengths of time, we would run into difficulties with assigning values of $\alpha_{i,1} > 0$, as this would leave open the possibility that individuals with no income could continue to consume indefinitely.

The $\alpha_{i,1}$ are not dimension free parameters but must be measured in terms of (money/people). As an economy develops one might wish to introduce credit effects on consumption.

$$S_{i,t} = Y^2_{i,t} - C_{i,t}; \tag{6a}$$

where

$$S_{i,t} = \text{savings of the } i^{th} \text{ group.}$$

2.2. GOVERNMENT

Government activities may be grouped, for national accounts purposes, into two broad categories: expenditures, which represent an allocation of part of gross national product; and taxes and transfers, which are, of course, means of redistributing income. The next section takes up government expenditures, and although taxes and transfers do not necessarily belong here, they are taken up in Section 2.2.2.

2.2.1. GOVERNMENT EXPENDITURES

Government expenditures in our model are divided into four categories, which we believe are particularly relevant for a development study: gross investment; health, education, and welfare; transfers; other expenditures. These are denoted:

$G_{1,t}$ = gross investment by government

$G_{2,t}$ = government expenditures on health, education, and welfare

$G_{3,t}$ = other government current expenditures

R_t = transfers and subsidies

The breakdown of government expenditures will be determined by the group in power and represents one of the politico-economic aspects of this model which needs to be investigated in detail. For example, it appears to be worthwhile to distinguish between two types of "revolutionary" change in a Latin American state: the first, a change in the "palace guard" which might result in a shift in the biases between landed and commercial or industrial interests; the second, a deep social revolution such as that of Mexico in 1911 or the recent Cuban revolution.

In the content of this model we eventually will wish to introduce political control alternatives explicitly. The method for doing this is indicated in the flow diagram below. However, we limit ourselves by the assumption that the governmental group in power will remain fixed over the period under consideration.

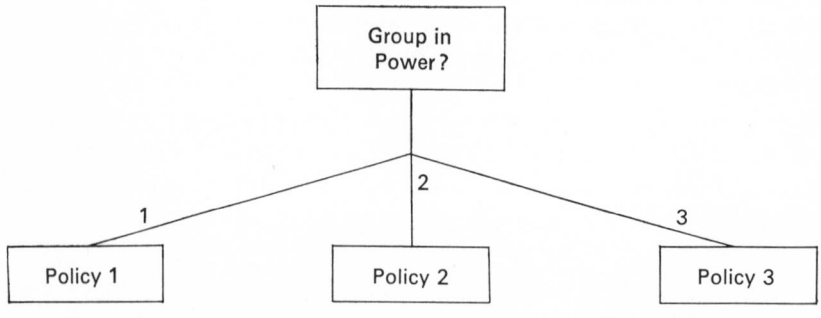

Until a satisfactory first approximation for adding political features has been made, two approaches are adopted for the next three behavioral equations.

The first is to leave them open for exogenous inputs. This procedure can be defended in several ways.

In many countries government policy may be a critical item in the determination of growth and welfare. Given the current state of social, political, and economic information, and the difficulties in constructing models of politico-economic process, in checking previous histories, and in testing the effects of policies, the use of historical data or of plans both simplifies problems of validation and permits experimentation with planning procedures.

Once more it must be stressed that such an approach is not offered as an alternative to econometric methods. In the construction of models for developing, planning, and the control of economies, it appears to be desirable to distinguish between behavioral relations which are or are not amenable to economic analysis and those which depend upon large numbers of independent actions and/or exhibit some special features leading to stability in structure over a reasonable period of time. Those which exhibit these properties are amenable to an econometric approach. Those which do not, yet may be important in describing growth processes, must be approached differently.

Reasons for opposing this approach are that it introduces too many additional degrees of freedom into the model and increases the complexity and unwieldiness of the input.

The second approach is to ignore all the above caveats and to try to specify behavioral equations.

As a simple first approximation, we assume that government gross domestic capital formation is given by

$$G_{1,t} = \beta_1 + \beta_2 Y_{t-1} + \beta_{34}[M^{2;2}_{t;6} + M^{2;3}_{t;6}] \tag{7}$$

Here government investment is a simple linear function of lagged gross national product and transfers and long term capital flows from abroad.

$M^{2;2}_{t;6}$ = net capital inflows to government

$M^{2;3}_{t;6}$ = net transfer payments from abroad to government

Government expenditures on health, education, and welfare are assumed to depend on gross national product and total population during the previous period. This allows for an increase in health, education, and welfare expenditures as either population or GNP rises. This is shown below in Eq. (8).

$$G_{2,t} = \beta_3 + \beta_4 Y_{t-1} + \beta_5 N_{t-1} \tag{8}$$

Other government expenditures are assumed to grow with population. (It is of interest to note that the Ecuador Central Bank bulletin recommends that the government adjust its expenditures to accord with revenue.[4])

$$G_{3,t} = \beta_6 N_t P_{t-1} \qquad (9)$$

In Ecuador there is considerable earmarking of taxes, with the result that automatic transfer of revenues to various of the 18 provinces, 97 municipalities, and around 700 other autonomous entities dilutes the Central Government's abilities to use the national public resources.

2.2.2. GOVERNMENT REVENUE AND TRANSFERS

Revenues can be considered in three broad headings:

Direct taxes.

Indirect taxes, and

Non-tax revenue.

Under the first there are income tax, inheritance and gift taxes, and export taxes. Indirect taxes include excise taxes, consumption and sales taxes, and import taxes. The non-tax revenues include income from property and charges for services.

In this relatively simplified model only four taxes, two direct and two indirect, are considered. They are personal income tax, profits, indirect business taxes other than tariffs, and tariffs.

The basic tax identities are given below.

$$T_t = T_t^1 + T_t^2 + T_t^3 \qquad (10)$$

$$T_t^1 = T_t^{1,1} + T_t^{1,2} \qquad (11)$$

T_t = total tax revenue

T_t^1 = indirect business taxes

T_t^2 = taxes on profits

T_t^3 = personal income taxes

$T_t^{1,1}$ = indirect business taxes, except tariffs

$T_t^{1,2}$ = tariffs

Eq. (10) gives total tax revenue as the sum of indirect business taxes ($T_t^1 = T_t^{1,1} + T_t^{1,2}$) and income taxes ($T_t^2 + T_t^3$). In Eqs. (12) and (13) $T_t^{1,1}$ is assumed proportional to gross national product, and $T_t^{1,2}$ to imports of goods and services.

$$T_t^{1,1} = \beta_7 Y_t \qquad (12)$$

$$T_t^{1,2} = \beta_8 M_t^1 \qquad (13)$$

The tax on profits is assumed proportional to profits earned in the private sector, except that it does not become negative.

$$T_{i,t}^2 = \max[\beta_9,\ \pi_{i,t},\ 0] \qquad i = 1, 2, 3, 5. \tag{14}$$

$\pi_{6,t}$ are profits of government owned enterprise and hence are not taxed.

Personal income taxes are assumed proportional to personal income; however, the constant of proportionality will not be the same for all four socio-economic groups; there are progressive tax rates, not fully reflected in this approximation.

$$T_{i,t}^3 = \alpha_{i,3} Y_{i,t}^1 \tag{15}$$

$$T_t^3 = \sum_{i=1}^{4} T_{i,t} \tag{16}$$

It is clear from Eq. (2) that personal income includes the after tax profits of the four socio-economic groups. Thus profits are double-taxed in this model. Tax laws vary considerably from country to country on this point.

Transfers to the government from abroad are assumed exogenous to the model, being determined by the foreign policies of the country and of other nations. Net transfers scheduled by the government to the four socio-economic groups are given below. (Subsidies should be accounted for by a separate equation if they are large.)

$$R_t = \sum R_{i,t} \tag{17}$$

$$R_{i,t} = \alpha_{i,4}Y_{t-1} - \alpha_{i,t} - [(Y_{t-1} - Y_{t-2}), 0] \tag{18}$$

Eq. (18) by definition cannot have a negative value. This equation should be considered as a key policy control and should either be exogenous or merits careful empirical investigation. Here a crude approximation has been used linking transfers to GNP with a simple countercyclical term. For most countries this fits the facts poorly as both specific changes in policy and reporting methods can be observed in the series.

Total government expenditure is

$$E_t = G_{1,t} + G_{2,t} + G_{3,t} + R_t + J_t; \tag{19}$$

where

$J_t = $ interest on public debt,

and total revenues are

$$REV_t = T_t + M_{t;6}^{2;3} + \pi_{6,t}; \tag{20}$$

where

$E_t = $ government total expenditures

$REV_t = $ government total revenues

$M_{t,6}^{2;3}$ = net transfers and payments to the government from abroad

$R_{i,t}$ = transfers by the government to the ith socio-economic group

and

$$J_t = \beta_{10} \, DET_t; \tag{21}$$

where

DET_t = government debt

$$SC_t = REV_t - E_t + G_{1,t}; \tag{21a}$$

where

SC_t = surplus on current account

$$DEF_t = SC_t - G_{1,t}; \tag{21b}$$

where

DEF_t = government surplus

$$BOR_t = BOR_{1,t} + BOR_{2,t} + M_{t,6}^{22}; \tag{21c}$$

where

BOR_t = total borrowing

$M_{t,6}^{22}$ = foreign borrowing

$BOR_{1,t}$ = borrowing from banking system (net increase in the claims of the banking system)

$BOR_{2,t}$ = borrowing from out of the banking system

Without detailed information it is easiest to treat foreign borrowing as exogenous. Furthermore in many planning uses, foreign borrowing is a critical decision variable.

$$DET_t^1 + DET_{t-1}^1 \left(\frac{FEXCH_t}{FEXCH_{t-1}}\right) + M_{t,6}^{22}(FEXCH_t); \tag{21d}$$

where

DET_t^1 = foreign debt (in dollars, U.S.)

$FEXCH_t$ = foreign exchange rate

$$DET_t^{21} = DET_{t-1}^{21} + BOR_{1,t}; \tag{21e}$$

where

DET_t^{21} = bank held domestic debt (net outstanding claims; liabilities of the government to the banking system net of its deposits)

$$DET_t^{22} = DET_{t-1}^{22} + BOR_{2,t}; \tag{21f}$$

where

DET_t^{22} = non-bank held domestic debt.

$$DET_t^2 = DET_t^{21} + DET_t^{22} ; \qquad (21g)$$

where

DET_t^2 = total domestic debt.

A behavior or policy equation is needed to explain the relative sizes of bank and non-bank government borrowing.

2.3. INVESTMENT IN PHYSICAL CAPITAL

Eight special symbols which are used below are now noted:

$$\hat{G}_{1,t}, \ \hat{G}_{2,t}, \ \hat{G}_{3,t}, \ \hat{R}_t, \ \hat{I}_{1,t}, \ \hat{I}_{2,t}, \ \hat{I}_{3,t} \ \text{and} \ \hat{I}_{5,t}.$$

Their detailed definitions are given in 4.2.3; briefly they account for possible leakages of funds: $\hat{G}_{1,t}$ stands for "effective" government investment as contrasted with $G_{1,t}$ which stands for government investment; and similarly for the others.

$$\hat{G}_{1,t} = (1 - \alpha_{1,22} - \alpha_{2,22})G_{1,t}. \qquad (22)$$

There are similar equations for all of the others.

In this section we consider gross investment by the four socio-economic groups and by foreign enterprises. Government investment was discussed above in Section 2.2.1. One feature related to government investment needs to be specified. That is capital stock.

$$K_{6,t} = (1 - \alpha_{6,8})K_{6,t-1} + \hat{G}_{1,t}/P_t . \qquad (23)$$

$K_{i,t}$ = the capital stock owned by members of the ith socio-economic group.

The poorness of capital stock estimates is well known even in highly developed countries. Nevertheless, even a crude approximation is of value.

2.3.1. GROSS INVESTMENT BY COMMERCIAL WHITES

Without specifying the country and combining some casual empiricism with sociological and economic considerations, one form of an investment function for the commercial group which might be worth investigation is given in (24a):

$$I_{1,t} = \max \left[0, \left\{ \alpha_{1,6} \left(\frac{Y_{t-1} - Y_{3,t-1}^2}{P_{t-1}} \right) - \left(\frac{Y_{t-2} + Y_{3,t-2}^2}{P_{t-2}} \right) \right. \right.$$
$$\left. \left. + \alpha_{1,7} \left(\frac{Y_{3,t-1}^2}{P_{t-1}} - \frac{Y_{3,t-2}^2}{P_{t-2}} \right) + \alpha_{1,8}(K_{1,t-1})(P_{t-1}) \right\} \right] \qquad (24a)$$

It is the sum of two accelerator terms and a depreciation term. The first accelerator term involves changes in GNP, leaving out changes in mestizo disposable income; the second accelerator term involves changes in mestizo disposable income. It is assumed that change in mestizo income is of particular import to investment in an economy, as its growth represents the possible expansion of a lower middle class market. A serious drop in this income may also be an important factor in the growth of political instability.

The determination of reasonable investment functions is obviously one of the most critical empirical problems in the construction of this type of model. In the case of Ecuador, bank policy, the availability of foreign long term finance, and the size of the export market appear to have been dominant factors. "Betting on bananas" appears to have been a policy followed recently.

In view of the considerations noted above, an alternative gross investment function which we use is suggested in (24b):

$$I_{1,t}^1 = \max[(\{\alpha_{1,6} X_{t-1}^1 + \alpha_{1,8} K_{1,t-1}\}P_{t-1} - \alpha_{1,32}\beta_8), GC_t^1, BC_t] \qquad (24b)$$

where

GC_t^1 = government direct control limit on private capital imports

BC_t = credit limit

$I_{1,t}^1$ = private sector imported capital goods.

This states that investment is primarily dependent upon previous exports modified to some extent by import tariffs and constrained by credit limitations and direct governmental controls. In some countries with imperfectly developed capital markets, limits may play a more important role than the rate of interest.

Eq. (24b) suggests a priority in investment considerations; the amounts to be imported are considered first here with a fixed proportion assumed between local and foreign procurement. If substitutability is low this is a reasonable assumption. Furthermore an investor will try not to be stuck with an almost completed project, to find that he cannot obtain some vital overseas parts due to restrictions.

$$I_{1,t}^2 = \alpha_{1,33} I_{1,t}^1; \qquad (24c)$$

where

$I_{1,t}^2$ = capital goods of domestic origin purchased by local enterprise.

$$I_{1,t} = I_{1,t}^1 + I_{1,t}^2. \qquad (24d)$$

Depreciation in fixed currency is given by:

$$D_{i,t} = \alpha_{i,8} K_{i,t-1} \qquad (25)$$

Capital stock for the commercial class is given by:

$$K_{1,t} = (1 - \alpha_{i,8})K_{1,t-1} + \hat{I}_{1,t}/P_{1,t}. \qquad (26)$$

The description of investment leaves out terms of trade, import and export elasticities, all of which are obviously important in a reasonably competitive market, but are far less so in international oligopolistic or oligopsonistic markets. The implications of the model here are that for at least some commodities one sells what one can at whatever prices one can obtain above variable costs. This description could be little more than part of a mythology concerning trade in underdeveloped countries; at least we may explore its implications in a formal model here with relative ease.

2.3.2. GROSS INVESTMENT BY AGRICULTURAL WHITES

Investment in this group is taken to depend on disposable income within the group. For these people investment may be more a matter of status than of rational calculation. It has been suggested, for instance, that the social role of "patron" is in some areas still of importance. Thus, the additions to the hacienda, finca, or estancia may be a manifestation of the role rather than a pure economic act. Investment would be predominantly internal.

Once more it is stressed that even though the following equation might be regarded as a caricature of the "patron," a valuable role of a simulation is to serve as a method for formalizing, categorizing, and testing the folklore.

$$I_{2,t} = \alpha_{2,6} + \alpha_{2,7} Y^2_{2,t-1} + \alpha_{2,8}(K_{2,t-1})(P_{t-1}) \tag{27}$$

if
$$\frac{Y^2_{2t,-1}}{N_{2,t-1}} \geqslant \beta_{31} P_{t-1} ,$$

$$= \alpha_{2,8}(K_{2,t-1})(P_{t-1})$$

if
$$\frac{Y^2_{2,t-1}}{N_{2,t-1}} < \beta_{31} P_{t-1} .$$

Capital stock for the second socio-economic group is given by

$$K_{2,t} = (1 - \alpha_{2,8})K_{2,t-1} + \hat{I}_{2,t}/P_t \tag{28}$$

2.3.3. GROSS INVESTMENT BY MESTIZOS AND INDIANS

In general, mestizos have little surplus for investment; nevertheless we assume that

$$I_{3,t} = Y^2_{3,t-1} - C_{3,t-1} . \tag{29}$$

This indicates that they invest their savings, but with a time lag. At first glance and historically, this factor may be small; yet as far as policy, social mobility, and political stability are concerned, it may be of considerable importance.

There is the standard accounting equation for capital stock, as follows:

$$K_{3,t} = (1 - \alpha_{3,8})K_{3,t-1} + \hat{I}_{3,t}/P_t . \tag{30}$$

Our initial assumption is that investment by the Indian sector is negligible. In this model we omit further consideration of it.

2.3.4. GROSS INVESTMENT BY FOREIGN FIRMS

The final category of investment is investment by foreign enterprises. Foreign investors are probably more ready, willing, and able to pull out of a country when the country appears to be heading toward social or political instability than are the local citizens. One simple way to represent this is with a "domestic stability index." The index could be a function of the length of time the present government has been in power, the recent growth rate of gross national product, and the growth rates of real wages for the various socio-economic groups. Usually the index will be the higher, and the country the more stable, the higher are these variables. If the index is below a crucial value, the foreign investors seek to pull out at the fastest possible rate, which is the maximum depreciation rate. (It is possible that some assets can be transported out of the country, but in general this is unlikely.) The diagram below represents the investment decision for foreign investors.

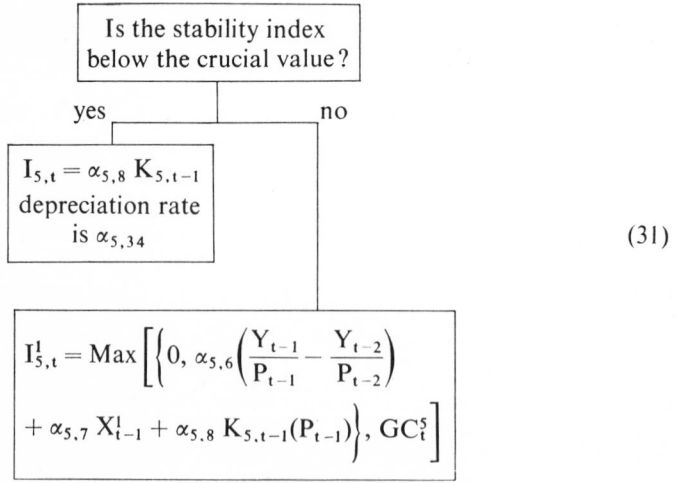

$$(31)$$

$I_{5,t}$ = the rate of gross investment of foreign nationals

GC_t^5 = government limit on import of capital goods

Investment is broken into imports and local procurement:

$$I_{5,t}^2 = \alpha_{5,33} I_{1,t}^1 \tag{31a}$$

$$I_{5,t} = I_{5,t}^1 + I_{5,t}^2 . \tag{31b}$$

$$K_{5,t} = (1 - \alpha_{5,7})K_{5,t-1} + \hat{I}_{5,t}/P_t \tag{32}$$

Thus, if the index is below the crucial value, gross investment may equal net investment and is $-\alpha_{5,34}K_{5,t-1}$ in constant currency. On the other hand, if the index is sufficiently high, investment is determined by depreciation and the change in gross national product between the previous period and two periods prior; it is the greater of zero or the amount calculated from these considerations. We note that there are two depreciation rates above, $\alpha_{5,8}$ and $\alpha_{5,34}$. Through hard driving and poor maintenance, capital can be made to depreciate faster than it would with careful use and maintenance. The actual rate of depreciation for a capital good will depend on the cost of replacement, expected returns on it, and the cost of various levels of maintenance. A foreign investor wishing to pull out of a country due to the instability of the political situation may expect expropriation or wholesale destruction of his investment. If so, he may want to work his capital as hard as possible without spending anything on it until it has no value left. Thus $\alpha_{5,34}$ is the maximal rate of depreciation relevant to when the capital is used up as quickly as possible; $\alpha_{5,8}$ is the "normal rate," applicable when the investor expects to stay in the country indefinitely. It will be seen later that the stability index has a bearing on international capital movements.

In many debates on policy the role of foreign investment is usually discussed. The actual nature of the foreign investment function may depend heavily upon explicit laws, special economic opportunities and the faith placed in the political and economic ambiente.

An interesting use of a model of this type is to carry out gaming exercises for the exploration of policy. A way in which the simulation can be used for gaming is to have a set of players select foreign private investment and other capital flows exogenously, while the other team controls tariffs and other aspects of government policy.

2.4. EXPORTS AND IMPORTS OF GOODS AND SERVICES

The demand for exports is assumed to be autonomous, being determined by conditions abroad which are essentially unaffected by developments in the country. In some countries such as Ecuador or Guatemala, four or five items account for 75–90% of exports. (In Ecuador, for example, bananas, coffee, cacao, and rice form more than 90% of exports.) A reasonably satisfactory model for exports could be constructed by including some features of prices and demands for these specific commodities [see note 3]. Even this disaggregation is not completely satisfactory, as it is in general the case that the commodities traded are highly subjected to oligopolistic influence. Hence a good model of foreign trade needs to take this into account.

We treat the demand for exports as exogenous. Exports could, of course, be considerably less than the demand for exports; however, for crops such as bananas or rice, it is possible to increase production in a year.

From the viewpoints of operational gaming, planning, and growth studies, it is desirable to experiment with alternative conditions on exports and to carry out separate studies to locate the factors to which exports are sensitive.

Imports depend upon consumption, investment, foreign transfers, and credit conditions, as well as export and import price levels, tariffs, and direct controls and bank policy. These are reflected in Eq. (34). The term $G_{I,t}^1$ may be very small unless the government has important nationalized sectors of the economy.

$$X_t^1 = \text{an exogenous series for exports} \tag{33}$$

$$M_t^1 = I_{I,t}^1 + I_{5,t}^1 + C_t^1 + G_{I,t}^1; \tag{34}$$

where

$C_t^1 = $ imports generated by consumption

$G_{I,t}^1 = $ government investment imports.

As with investment, we assume that part of consumption calls for imports. This is often directly controlled and results in large contraband operations which are not fully reflected here.

$$C_t^1 = \beta_{11} C_t \tag{34a}$$

$$C_t = C_t^1 + C_t^2 . \tag{34b}$$

3. HUMAN CAPITAL

A very important ingredient in successful growth for an underdeveloped country, indeed for any country, is investment in a healthy, educated population. The importance of attempting to measure the effect of health, education, and welfare (HEW) expenditures on productivity is obvious, as are the difficulties in doing so.

Below we sketch two models for the measurement of human capital. The first is an input-output model which we do not utilize at present. It is included because it is our hope that this basic approach may eventually prove feasible and fruitful. The second approach, which is utilized for the first approximation, includes a method (primarily suggested and devised by James Friedman) for converting the labor force of each socio-economic group into standard labor units which are comparable between classes. The number of standard labor units into which a member of the labor force converts depends on the HEW expenditures made on members of his group. While this method leaves something to be desired, it does represent a beginning at the difficult task of measuring labor productivity as a function of HEW.

3.1. INPUT-OUTPUT MODEL

In Table 1 following appears a simple input-output scheme. Each column is an activity. The negative coefficients are outputs and the positive, inputs. Thus, looking at the first activity, it shows that if we put in one infant $\gamma_{6,1}$ of social and medical resources and $\gamma_{7,1}$ of education resources, we will get as outputs one child and $\gamma_{8,1}$ of labor.

Table 1

Infants:	+1				
Children:	−1	+1			
Young adults:		−1	+1		
Middle aged:			−1	+1	
Old:				−1	+1
Costs: social, medical:	$\gamma_{6,1}$	$\gamma_{6,2}$	$\gamma_{6,3}$	$\gamma_{6,4}$	$\gamma_{6,5}$
Costs: education:	$\gamma_{7,1}$	$\gamma_{7,2}$	$\gamma_{7,3}$	$\gamma_{7,4}$	$\gamma_{7,5}$
Labor output:	$\gamma_{8,1}$	$\gamma_{8,2}$	$\gamma_{8,3}$	$\gamma_{8,4}$	$\gamma_{8,5}$

We have divided the life span into five stages here and have implicitly assumed that at each stage there will be a linear relationship linking the labor output (measured in some standard unit) with the HEW inputs.

In order to study the effectiveness of the HEW programs, we might wish to expand the number of activities shown in Table 4 to account for different inputs in education, for example. As a good second approximation, four social groups, each portrayed by five activities, should provide sufficient information for the estimation of human capital.

If we are able to measure labor output in terms of a standardized dollar, and if we are willing to specify a discount factor in the economy, we can calculate a value for an individual in the t-th age group.

$$V_t = \sum_{i=t}^{5} \rho^{i-t+1}(\gamma_{8,i} - \gamma_{6,i} - \gamma_{7,i})$$

where

V_t = the human capital value of an individual in age group t

ρ = discount rate

$\gamma_{k,i}$ = input-output coefficient

3.2. THE CURRENT MODEL

The model which we look at in this section averages over all members of a socio-economic group identically, regardless of age and sex. It would not be difficult to expand it to keep track of the population within each socio-economic group

by age groups.   The steps in the model are two: (1) the size of the population is computed, taking into account births, deaths, and transfers from one class to another.   (2) The labor force is converted into standard labor units, taking into account the per capita HEW expenditures made in recent years.
Let

N_t = total population in time t

$N_{i,t}$ = population of i-th group in time t

A_t = deaths in total population during period t

$A_{i,t}$ = deaths in i-th group

B_t = births in total population

$B_{i,t}$ = births in i-th group

$F_{1,t}$ = number of people who transfer from 3rd (mestizo) group to group 1 (Commercial White)

$F_{3,t}$ = number who transfer from 4th (Indian) group to 3rd.

Some basic bookkeeping relationships which involve the variables defined above are

$$N_t = N_{t-1} + B_{t-1} - A_{t-1} \tag{35}$$

$$N_{1,t} = N_{1,t-1} + B_{1,t-1} - A_{1,t-1} + F_{1,t-1} \tag{36}$$

$$N_{2,t} = N_{2,t-1} + B_{2,t-1} - A_{2,t-1} \tag{37}$$

$$N_{3,t} = N_{3,t-1} + B_{3,t-1} - A_{3,t-1} - F_{1,t-1} + F_{3,t-1} \tag{38}$$

$$N_{4,t} = N_{4,t-1} + B_{4,t-1} - A_{4,t-1} - F_{3,t-1} \tag{39}$$

Eq. (35) gives total population in period t as population in period $t-1$ plus births and minus deaths during period $t-1$; (36) through (39) are the analogous equations for each group.   Two values of inter-group transfer are allowed for in (42) and (43).   The relationships governing births and deaths are given below.

$$A_{i,t-1} = \alpha_{i,30} N_{i,t-1} \tag{40}$$

$$B_{i,t-1} = \alpha_{i,31} N_{i,t-1} . \tag{41}$$

Transfers from one class to another are considered to occur when a mestizo acquires sufficient wealth and position to be, in fact, a member of the commercial white community; or when an Indian turns outward from his tradition-bound environment and tries to get along in the more market-oriented part of society. The two transfer equations are

$$F_{1,t-1} = \alpha_{1,9} N_{3,t-1} \left(\frac{N_{1,t-1} \cdot N_{3,t-1}}{(N_{1,t-1} + N_{3,t-1})^2} \right)$$

$$\left(\alpha_{1,10} \frac{Y_{3,t-1}^2}{N_{3,t-1}} + \alpha_{1,11} \frac{H_{3,t-1}}{N_{3,t-1}} \right) \cdot \frac{1}{P_{t-1}} \quad (42)$$

$$F_{3,t-1} = \alpha_{3,9} N_{4,t-1} \left(\frac{N_{3,t-1} \cdot N_{4,t-1}}{(N_{3,t-1} + N_{4,t-1})^2} \right)$$

$$\left(\alpha_{3,10} \frac{Y_{4,t-1}^2}{N_{4,t-1}} + \alpha_{3,11} \frac{H_{4,t-1}}{N_{4,t-1}} \right) \cdot \frac{1}{P_{t-1}} \quad (43)*$$

In both these equations, the first expression in brackets is the proportion of the combined population of the two groups which is in one of the classes multiplied by the proportion in the other. This proportion is modified by a parameter, $\alpha_{i,9}$, and by an expression involving per capita disposable income for the group and HEW expenditures. The result is modified by the size of the group from which people will transfer. The equations are modified for the effect of price level. It is assumed that as HEW and per capita income rise, the numbers which will transfer rise.

The next step is to determine the labor force for each group and then convert into standard labor units.

$$N_{i,t}^1 = \alpha_{i,12} N_{i,t} \quad (44)$$

$$N_{i,t}^2 = e^{\left(\alpha_{1,13} - \frac{\alpha_{i,14}}{RH_{i,t}^1 + \alpha_{1,15}} \right)} N_{i,t}^1 \quad (45)$$

where

$H_{i,t}$ = total effective HEW spent on group i

$N_{i,t}^1$ = labor force of group i

$N_{i,t}^2$ = number of standard labor units represented by the labor force of group i

$RH_{i,t}^1$ = real per capita HEW on group i, summed for $\beta_{16} + 1$ years.

$\alpha_{i,12}$ is the proportion of the i-th group which is in the labor force. (Further study is needed to consider the meaning of implicit unemployment in an under-developed economy.) The general shape and characteristics of Eq. (45) are

* A consistency check requires that $\alpha_{3,9}[1/2][...] \leqslant 1$. Otherwise the size of population transfer would be greater than the population.

illustrated in Figure 1. The minimum value of $N_{i,t}^2$, when $RH_{i,t}^1$ is zero, is $N_{i,t}^1 e^{\alpha_{1,13} - \alpha_{1,14}/\alpha_{1,15}}$. This is constrained to be non-negative.

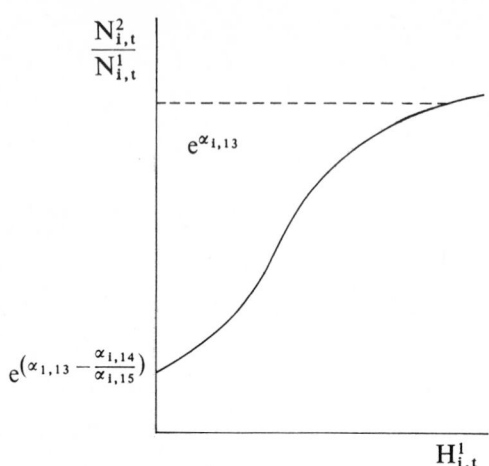

Figure 1

HEW shows increasing, then decreasing returns. The marginal product of HEW in terms of labor units is almost positive, although it is asymptotic to zero and total labor units are asymptotic to $N_{i,t}^1 e^{\alpha_{1,13}}$.

The derivation of $RH_{i,t}^1$ remains

$$H_{i,t} = \alpha_{i,16} + \alpha_{i,17} C_{i,t} + \alpha_{i,19} \hat{G}_t^2 \tag{46}$$

$$\sum_{i=1}^{4} \alpha_{i,19} = 1 \tag{47}$$

$$RH_{i,t} = H_{i,t}/P_{t-1} \tag{48}$$

$$RH_{i,t}^1 = \sum_{\theta=t-\beta_{16}}^{t} \frac{RH_{i,\theta}}{N_{i,\theta}} = RH_{i,t-1}^1 - \frac{RH_{i,t-\beta_{16}-1}}{N_{i,t-\beta_{16}-1}} + \frac{RH_{i,t}}{N_{i,t}} \tag{49}$$

According to Eq. (46), the HEW expenditures on the ith group are a linear function of the consumption expenditures of the group and of government HEW expenditures. This implies in particular that we should count private expenditures on education and health as affecting productivity of the group spending. Eq. (47) is merely a constraint to assure that the whole of $\hat{G}_t^2$ is parceled out among the four groups. Eq. (48) changes the current HEW expenditure into fixed currency terms. Eq. (49) is the sum of per capita HEW in group i for the current year and the β_{16} preceding years.

It must be noted that the definition of HEW expenditures presents several diffi-cult problems both in theory and in national accounts classification.

4. PRODUCTION AND DISTRIBUTION

In this section the treatment of production and distribution is outlined. The product side of the model utilizes an aggregate Cobb-Douglas production function. The assumptions about distribution are a variant of traditional marginal productivity theory.

The program includes the more general C.E.S. production function for purposes of experimentation; however, the worth of this extension is doubtful and discussion here is limited to the Cobb-Douglas.[4] In any expansion of a model of this type a natural step would be to replace this total aggregate by a small input-output table.

4.1. PRODUCTION

We assume the existence of three factors: capital, labor, and the "institutional" factor. The third of these is not represented directly in the production function, and is discussed below.

Let

Y_t^0 = gross domestic product in constant currency

$$P_t Y_t^0 = Y_t - M^{2,1} + X^{2,1} . \tag{50}$$

Eq. (50) contains an accounting identity which defines gross domestic product as the sum of all goods and services produced within the country. Eq. (51) expresses gross domestic product, as an output, related to the labor force and capital stock as inputs. This "aggregate production function" we have assumed to be a Cobb-Douglas function, modified by the term $e^{\beta_{32}t}$ to account for technological progress.

$$Y_t^0 = \beta_{17} \ K_{t-1}^{\beta_{18}}(N_t^2)^{1-\beta_{18}} \ e^{\beta_{32}t} \qquad (0 < \beta_{18} < 1) \tag{51}$$

$$K_t = \sum_{i=1}^{6} K_{i,t} . \tag{52}$$

Eq. (52) is an accounting equation for the total worth of capital stock. It is evident that for many policy purposes it would be desirable to disaggregate the production function and consider at least an agricultural and other sector separately.

4.2. DISTRIBUTION OF PRODUCT

We assume that, generally, labor and capital are paid in proportion to their marginal productivity, with the exception of the Indian sector of the population where institutional rigidities have an influence. In many Latin American countries there are extreme rigidities in payments to government employees, and in places such as Chile, Argentina, and Uruguay, union and government negotiations play an important role.

An allocation of income is also made to an "Institutional Administrative" factor. The appropriate licenses, administrative blessings, cooperation of local authorities, adequate protection against institutional delays, etc., all are part of a production process and may be regarded as very valuable factors. They are, in general, resources with increasing returns to scale. Essentially it costs the mayor little extra to sign additional permissions to build, but each permission is nevertheless needed as a factor. There is possibly an upper bound or a capacity beyond which an individual cannot go without dipping too heavily into his "political capital" (a quantity we do not attempt to measure at this point); hence, a given administrative system may be regarded as having a capacity in the way as does a bridge or railway system. (Up to a point the administrator may actually be increasing his "political capital" when he grants permissions.)

4.2.1. WAGES

The returns to labor in the several groups are given by

$$W_{i,t} = \alpha_{i,20} \frac{\partial Y_t^0}{\partial N_t^2} (N_{i,t}^2)(P_{t-1}) \qquad i = 1, 2, 3 \tag{53}$$

and

$$W_{4,t} = \left\{ \alpha_{4,20} \frac{\partial Y_t^0}{\partial N_t^2} (P_{t-1}) + \beta_{19} + \eta_j \right\} N_{4,t}^2 \tag{54}$$

where the $\alpha_{i,20}$ for $i = 1, \ldots, 4$ are proportionality factors, which will be discussed further below.

$W_{i,t}$ = labor income of ith social group in constant currency

β_{19} = a traditional constant component of income to Indians

η_j = a random variable.

In Eqs. (53) and (54) P_{t-1} is used to show the effect of price level indicating a "price-stickiness" in the adjustment of wages.

Eq. (53) is merely the standard returns to labor in a competitive economy modified by the $\alpha_{i,20}$; (54) is a modified version of (53) where we assume that the income to the Indians has three components: the first is in proportion to marginal productivity, the second is a constant in money terms determined from socioeconomic considerations, and the third is a random variable determined by such things as weather and crop conditions. (There is the difficult problem of imputing national income monetary returns to groups only partially in the money economy.)

4.2.2. GROSS PROFITS

Given the way we have written the production function for gross domestic product, the profit equations must include depreciation coverage as part of the returns to capital. In a competitive market we would have

$$\pi_{i,5} + D_{i,t} P_t = \alpha_{i,21} \frac{\partial Y_t^0}{\partial K_{t-1}} K_{i,t-1} P_t \quad i, \ldots, 6 \tag{55}$$

where $\alpha_{i,21} =$ factors of proportionality in return to capital.

4.2.3. INCOME TO THE INSTITUTIONAL FACTOR

The third set of equations (56) to be given represents the sources of payments to the institutional administrative factors. We assume that there are primarily seven sources, being respectively government investment and transfers, and private investment. $\pi_{5,t}$ includes all factor costs paid abroad including royalties and commissions.

$Z_{i,t} =$ income to the institutional factor supplied by the ith social group.

$$Z_{i,t} = \alpha_{i,22} G_{1,t} + \alpha_{i,23}(G_{2,t} + G_{3,t}) + \alpha_{i,24} R_t + \alpha_{i,26} I_{1,t}$$
$$+ \alpha_{i,27} I_{2,t} + \alpha_{i,28} I_{3,t} + \alpha_{i,29} I_{5,t} \quad i = 1, 2 \tag{56}$$

We assume that income from this source accrues only to the commercial and agricultural whites. It indicates that they obtain a part of the funds spent by government, in transfers and in investment, in their role as controllers of the bureaucratic structure of the country. A more socio-politically oriented model would have these shares depend upon the party in power and its major backing.

There remains the problem of consistency checking that the identity

$$P_t Y_t^0 = \sum_{i=1}^{4} W_{i,t} + \sum_{i=1}^{6} \pi_{i,t} + P_t D_t + \sum Z_{i,t} + T_t^1 - \alpha_{i,24} R_t \tag{57}$$

must hold. This can be ensured in the manner shown in the flow diagram below.

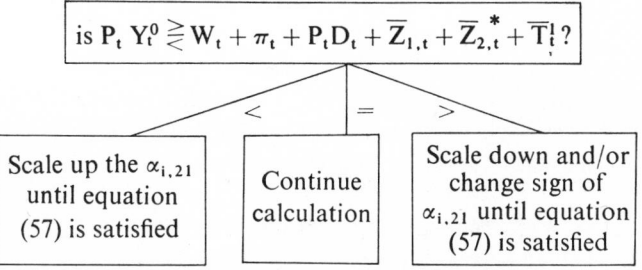

* For ease of solution, as we wish to exclude transfers we may define $\bar{Z}_{i,t} = Z_{i,t} - \alpha_{i,24} R_t$.

In order to guarantee that (57) holds, we adjust the scale factors to the returns to capital. This implies that administrative costs and indirect business taxes, then labor, have the priority in being satisfied. After they have been met, then the residual is paid to the other factor. A full explanation of the adjustment is given below.

4.3. THE CONSISTENCY OF INCOME AND EXPENDITURE

A mixture of behavior and accounting equations has been written to describe the income and expenditures of all sectors and the interaction of foreign trade and financial flows. In order to bring consistency to the income and expenditure sides, we introduce a gross correction in terms of a price level which is assumed to be endogenous to the system. The model given here for the whole economy is treated as open in the sense that foreign exchange levels are treated as exogenous.

Eqs. (50)

$$P_t Y_t^0 = Y_t - M^{2,1} + X^{2,1}$$

and (1)

$$Y_t = I_t + C_t + G_{2,t} + G_{3,t} + (X_t^1 - M_t^1) + (M_t^{2,1} - X_t^{2,1})$$

are sufficient to fix a price level when combined with (57).

Y_t^0 is determined directly from the Cobb-Douglas equation (51). $M_t^{2,1}$ [see (64) and below] does not involve P_t or the necessity to determine any set of variables simultaneously. This is not the case with the identity (57). If we require this to hold, we can do so by violating (55) and defining profits to be a residual. We make a further simplification that all profit sectors are hit equally by changes in economic conditions and the value of money. (This should be modified, as it appears that governmental revenues are derived from a monopolistic sector and are more institutionally inflexible than the others.) This is equivalent to assuming that there exists a variable x modifying the parameters $\alpha_{i,21}$. We may rewrite (57) as

$$\left[Y_t^0 - x \sum_{i=1}^{6} \alpha_{i,21} \frac{\partial Y_t^0}{\partial K_{t-1}} K_{i,t-1} \right] P_t = \sum_{i=1}^{4} W_{i,t} + \sum_{i=1}^{2} \overline{Z}_{i,t} + T_t^1 \tag{I}$$

Substituting (50) into (1) we obtain:

$$P_t Y_t^0 = I_t + C_t + G_t^2 + G_t^3 + (X_t^1 - M_t^1). \tag{II}$$

We may solve (I) and (II) simultaneously in order to obtain the x and the P_t.

In (II) the C_t are dependent on current profits; hence involve both the x and the P_t, as is seen below:

$$C_{i,t} = \alpha_{i,1} N_{i,t} + \alpha_{i,2} Y_{i,t}^2 \quad \text{from (6)} \qquad i = 1, \ldots, 4$$

$$Y_{i,t}^2 = (1 - \alpha_{i,3}) Y_{i,t}^1 \quad \text{from (3 and 15)} \qquad i = 1, \ldots, 4$$

and

$$Y_{i,t}^1 = x(1 - \beta_9)(\alpha_{i,25})\alpha_{i,21} \frac{\partial Y_t^0}{\partial K_{t-1}} K_{i,t-1} P_t + w_{i,t}$$

$$+ \bar{Z}_{i,t} + R_{i,t} + \alpha_{i,35} J_t \qquad i = 1, \ldots, 4 \quad (III)$$

Eq. III, and the relation based on (3) and (15) to link personal income with disposable income, imply that transfers and payments to the administrative factor are also subject to income tax. Where the poor pay no income tax and the rich obtain little welfare payments, the approximation is reasonable. The term $(1 - \beta_9)$ represents profits tax paid before entrepreneurial income is obtained.

Summing over $i = 1, \ldots, 4$ to obtain C_t using (III), (6), and (3) and (15), we may write (II) as

$$P_t Y_t^0 = I_t + G_t^2 + G_t^3 + (X_t^1 - M_t^1)^* + \sum_{i=1}^{4} \alpha_{i,1} N_{i,t}$$

$$+ \sum_{i=1}^{4} \alpha_{i,2}(1 - \alpha_{i,3})[W_{i,t} + \bar{Z}_{i,t} + R_{i,t}]$$

$$+ x(1 - \beta_9) \sum_{i=1}^{4} \alpha_{i,2}(1 - \alpha_{i,3})\alpha_{i,21} \frac{\partial Y_t^0}{\partial K_{t-1}} K_{i,t-1} P_t \quad (IV)$$

which is of the form

$$P_t Y_t^0 = A_1 + A_2 x P_t . \qquad (V)$$

In (I) we know that $T_t^1 = \beta_7 Y_t^0 P_t + T_t^{1,2}$. Hence we may rewrite it as

$$P_t[1 - \beta_7)Y_t^0 - A_3 x] = A_4 . \qquad (VI)$$

Solving (V) and (VI) we obtain

$$x = \frac{[A_4 - A_1(1 - \beta_7)]Y_t^0}{[A_2 A_4 - A_1 A_3]}$$

$$P_t = \frac{[A_1 A_3 - A_2 A_4]}{Y_t^0[A_3 - (1 - \beta_7)A_2]} ;$$

where

$$A_1 = I_t + G_{2,t} + G_{3,t} + (X_t^1 - M_t^1) + \sum_{i=1}^{4} \alpha_{i,1} N_{i,t}$$

$$+ \sum_{i=1}^{4} \alpha_{i,2}(1 - \alpha_{i,3})[W_{i,t} + \bar{Z}_{i,t} + R_{i,t}].$$

* In different versions equations may be considered which imply more or less simultaneity. This must be checked in the following calculations.

$$A_2 = \sum_{i=1}^{4} \alpha_{i,2}(1 - \beta_9)(1 - \alpha_{i,3})\alpha_{i,21} \frac{\partial Y_t^0}{\partial K_{t-1}} K_{i,t-1}$$

$$A_3 = \sum_{i=1}^{6} \alpha_{i,21} \frac{\partial Y_t^0}{\partial K_{t-1}} K_{i,t-1}$$

$$A_4 = \sum_{i=1}^{4} W_{i,t} + \sum_{i=1}^{2} \overline{Z}_{i,t} + T_t^{1,2} .$$

The mechanisms of monetary flows, banking regulations, and price adjustment are probably among the more important features needing explicit description in an adequate developmental model. At this level of model construction only the barest formal consideration has been given to a rudimentary price adjustment mechanism.

4.4. RETAINED EARNINGS

We assume that corporate enterprise is owned primarily by the commercial class and by foreign firms. In order to determine the income of the commercial class, it is necessary to distinguish those parts of profits which are paid out and those which are retained earnings.

$$RET_{i,t} = (1 - \beta_9)\pi_{i,t} - DIV_{i,t} \qquad i = 1, 5; \tag{58}$$

where

$$DIV_{i,t} = \alpha_{i,25}(1 - \beta_9)\pi_{i,t} . \tag{59}$$

Eq. (59) states that paid out profits are a percentage of earnings.

5. INTERNATIONAL CAPITAL FLOWS AND TRANSFERS

Economic relations between a country and the rest of the world may be viewed in the context of imports and exports of goods and services, and imports and exports of capital. Imports and exports of goods and services have been discussed above; however, international capital movements have received little attention. These flows are a barometer reflecting basic conditions and problems within the country. Thus an adverse trade balance will show up here and perhaps give an indication of whether devaluation, stricter exchange control, or other such measures are needed. A developing social condition inimical to the wealthier segment of the population may cause substantial short term capital movements out of the country which aggravate any balance of payments problems which might previously have existed.

The country's central bank, development banks, the World Bank, I.M.F., and other international monetary agencies, together with the ministerio de hacienda form the dominant complex of institutions influencing capital flows. In any direct application of simulation for planning purposes, along with the internal price adjustment mechanism, they merit a more explicit treatment than is given here.

Capital inflows may be under any of three categories: transfers, long term flows, and short term flows. The distinction between a transfer and another long term inflow is that no indebtedness or servicing is incurred on the former; they are essentially international gifts or accounting settlements and appear on current account.

A policy such as that of AID contains an intermix of transfer and other long term capital inflow where loans (even though they may be on very favorable terms) are dominant.

5.1. GOVERNMENT CAPITAL FLOWS AND TRANSFERS

$M_{t,6}^{2,2}$ = net government borrowing from abroad

$M_{t,6}^{2,3}$ = net transfer payments to government from abroad.

We treat both of these phenomena as exogenous, as they are primarily determined by policy and specific bargaining and do not lend themselves to easy behavioral equation modeling. [Eqs. (60) and (61) are omitted for the two exogenous series.]

5.2. LONG TERM PRIVATE CAPITAL FLOW, EXPATRIATED EARNINGS, AND TRANSFERS

PM_t^{22} = long term net private capital inflow

$PM_{1,t}^{22}$ = direct investment (investment of foreign owned firms)

$PM_{2,t}^{22}$ = other long term capital (loans).

$$PM_t^{22} = PM_{1,t}^{22} + PM_{2,t}^{22} \tag{62}$$

This is merely an accounting equation to denote that long term private investment consists of the sum of the two components noted above. (In the program this disaggregation is not made, owing to lack of information.)

$$PM_t^{22} = (1 + \beta_{12})I_{5,t} \tag{63}$$

Eq. (63) states that long term private capital inflow will be somewhat greater than private foreign investment by working capital requirements.

PM_t^{23} = net private international transfers.

This item is sufficiently small that it is assumed to be approximately zero.

$$X_t^{2,1} = \pi_{5,t} - T_{5,t}^2 + \beta_{13}DET1_tFEXCH_t \tag{64}$$

Factor income paid abroad includes expatriated earnings, interest, and commissions. M_t^{21} is approximately zero.

5.3. SHORT TERM PRIVATE CAPITAL FLOWS

$BK_{1,t}$ = net foreign assets of banking system

$DBK_{1,t}$ = change in net foreign assets of banking system

$$DBK_{1,t} = BK_{1,t} - BK_{1,t-1} . \tag{65}$$

$M_t^{2,4}$ = short term private capital inflow.

BOP_t = balance of payments surplus.

$$BOP_t = M_t^{2,4} + DBK_{1,t} . \tag{66}$$

The balance of payments surplus equals short term private capital inflow plus the change in foreign assets of the banking system. We may define this as a residual as is shown in (66).

$$BOP_t = (X_t^1 - M_t^1) + (M_t^{2,1} - X_t^{2,1}) - \beta_{10} DET_t^1$$
$$+ (M_{t,6}^{22} + PM_t^{22}) + (M_{t,6}^{23} + PM_{t,6}^{23}) \quad (67)$$

where the first term is trade balance; the second is net factor payments from abroad; the third is public debt interest payment to abroad; the fourth is foreign borrowing; and the fifth is foreign transfers.

$$M_t^{2,4} = \text{exogenous series.} \tag{68}$$

Short term private capital inflow may be regarded as exogenous.

6. BANKING SYSTEM

The banking system of an underdeveloped country can usually be divided into (1) the central bank, (2) private banks, (3) development banks. For the purposes of this model, the assets and liabilities of these three institutions are aggregated. This eliminates interbank credit and liability accounts.

The international assets and liabilities of the banking system are treated net under the concept, Net Foreign Assets. Similarly, the Net Claims on Government represent the credit of the banking system to government less the deposits of the government in the banking system. Bank credit to the private sector is denoted by the concept, Claims on Private Sector. The liabilities of the banking system to the private sector are divided into two categories: (1) Money supply (currency and demand deposits), and (2) Non-Monetary Liabilities (time and savings deposits, bonds, and capital accounts).

The categories used to divide up the assets and liabilities of the banking system are derived from those used in the monthly IMF publication, *International Financial Statistics*.[5] Under the heading, "Monetary Survey," the IFS data gives the total liabilities of the banking system, including the development banks. In our application of the simulation to Ecuador we have included the development banks because the Central Bank of Ecuador in its own policy discussions defines Money Supply to include demand deposits at development banks. Another departure from the IFS system of accounts is that we have collapsed the government assets and liabilities of the banking system into one account, and the foreign assets and liabilities of the banking system into one account.

Banking System Assets:

$BK_{1,t}$ = net foreign assets

$BK_{2,t}$ = net claims on government

$BK_{3,t}$ = claims on private sector.

Banking System Liabilities:

$BK_{4,t}$ = non-monetary liabilities to private sector

$BK_{5,t}$ = money supply

$BK_{1,t} = BK_{1,t-1} + DBK_{1,t}$ where

$DBK_{1,t}$ = change in net foreign assets of banking system.

$$BK_{3,t} = BK_{3,t-1} + DBK_{3,t} \tag{69}$$

where

$DBK_{3,t}$ = change in credit to private sector during time t.

$$DBK_{3,t} = \beta_{20} + \beta_{21} I_{1,t} \tag{70}$$

As a first approximation, this states that the change in credit outstanding is a linear function of private investment. This is interdependent with the level of fixed investment not financed from abroad.

$$BK_{4,t} = BK_{4,t-1} + DBK_{4,t} \tag{71}$$

where

$DBK_{4,t}$ = change in non-monetary deposits of the private sector during time t.

$$DBK_{4,t} = \beta_{22} + \beta_{23}(S_{1,t} + S_{2,t} + S_{3,t}) \tag{72}$$

where

$S_{i,t}$ = personal saving of group i.

Eq. (71) represents change in non-monetary deposits of the private sector, and is determined by the level of personal saving.

$$BK_{5,t} = BK_{1,t} + BK_{2,t} + BK_{3,t} - BK_{4,t} \tag{73}$$

Eq. (73) is the accounting relation for the money supply.

7. CONCLUDING COMMENTS

The previous sections have outlined a general aggregate model in which several features not usually common to macroeconomic models have been included. A later paper, Part III [of "Simulation of Socio-Economic Systems" in *General Systems*], is devoted to specializing the model to reflect the basic features of Ecuador, and then experimenting with simulations based on the specialized model.

There remain several further general comments before we turn to the operation of the model. They concern the relationship between this model, economic, political, and social theory, and simulation as a form of economic history.[6] Two other topics noted are the technical details of this model as a simulation, and the relationship between data processing and the input-output scheme adopted.

7.1. DESCRIPTION OF THE SIMULATION

The model constructed above is primarily macroeconomic with a four social sector disaggregation. Except for several logical switches, which enable the program to execute policy or other decision changes, the system is composed of a series of interlinked difference equations.

In general, difference equation models of economic processes are purely sequential; however, in this instance some of the relationships are simultaneous. This has made it necessary to solve a small simultaneous linear equation system in order to determine the price level.

Random variables do not play an important explicit conceptual role in the model, although they can be directly introduced in the input so that parameters, instead of being regarded as fixed, may be given variable values and outputs can be obtained in the form of average values together with standard deviations. This use of randomness aids in the exploration of the sensitivity of the system and plays a role when econometric measurement is attempted. Error terms may be added with ease to any equation. As is the case with all simulation, optimization is implicit rather than explicit.

The simulation here is a "representative unit," "fixed clock" model. This means it is so highly aggregated that any sector such as "the mestizos" is represented by a solitary behavior equation rather than a sample of behavioral units (as in the simulation of Orcutt).[7] The fixed clock feature of the model implies that all activities are updated at regular time intervals. There are no distributed lags to smooth the behavior of the behavioral units.

Among the natural extensions of this model would be to disaggregate production into at least agricultural and some industrial sectors. In some cases input-output matrices exist for the economy, thereby offering an available basis for disaggregation.

The current model contains approximately 135 equations, of which 65 are accounting; 60 are behavioral; and 10 are planning or policy relations which are for the most part treated as exogenous. Further interdisciplinary work might result in the specification of explicit relationships for variables currently left to be exogenous.

7.2. SIMULATION, THEORY, AND ECONOMIC HISTORY

What is different in this approach from an input-output model? Is it not more confusing, arbitrary and ad hoc than a simple mathematically expressed and analyzed model? Does it not confuse economic, social, and other variables? What does it prove? How can one validate this type of model? Is it not of less value than a good verbal description?

The above questions are all relevant to work of this type and must be considered seriously.

The prime thesis behind this application of simulation is that it is a natural complementary approach to the currently more accepted methods in economic theory, econometrics, institutional studies, national income accounting, data processing, and planning. It has considerable potential as an integrative device. Its role in a data system is discussed in 7.3 below. Here the other aspects of the use of this approach are considered.

No technique or methodology can be of use itself when applied by those without a substantive knowledge and an understanding of basic theory. Hence "simulation" is no more an answer to the problems of the behavioral sciences than is "calculus." However, given a sufficient background, simulation offers a cheap and flexible method to augment the exploration of mathematical models of production growth and income. Sociological, political, and other hypotheses are often suggested. Before a heavy investment is made in research, theory, development, and empirical work, it appears to be desirable to be able to obtain insights and estimations of the possible effects of various "guesstimates" on the structure of the environment.

A preliminary sensitivity analysis may be of considerable use in guiding the direction of deeper research. The model described here is offered in this spirit. It would be foolish to accept it, as it stands, as sufficiently detailed and trustworthy for detailed planning purposes.

By the judicious selection of parameter values at 0 or 1, many standard economic models can be obtained. If we believe in the Cobb-Douglas production function and competitive markets, limiting the allocation of product only to labor and capital according to marginal productivity, this can be conformed with in this model by cutting out the leakages to the institutional factor. If, however, we wish to check the effects of the conjecture that there are drains in administration, we are in a position to do so.

Difference equation and other time dependent economic models are conjectural economic histories which up to some degree (not easy to define) may have some econometric validation. In general it appears that, were it not for human inability to analyze the system, many socio-economic phenomena call for mathematical models in the form of non-linear simultaneous stochastic systems with distributed time lags and with logical switches and discontinuous functional forms.

We do not often construct models of the complexity noted above, because they appear to be so intractable both from the viewpoint of analysis and statistical validation. This leaves us, for the most part, with a theory for and statistical approach to simple mathematical models on the one hand, and verbal description on the other. The type of model suggested here offers a third alternative. We are able to generate time series from structures of considerable complexity but may not have at this time adequate procedures for statistical validation; nevertheless, they provide a means for experimentation and "sweetening the intuition." Having experimented with alternative models and parameter values, the simulation may serve to aid in the selection of simpler models of greater realism and relevance than might otherwise have been constructed.

7.3. OUTPUT DISPLAY, INPUT FORMAT, AND DATA BANKS

Data processing and data gathering are expensive occupations; but both are subject to vast external economies. It is my contention that more often than not the availability of data follows either theory or recognized need or both. The more a model constructed for the purposes of theory or planning is compatible with an ongoing data-gathering system, the greater are the economies in the obtaining of information, in influencing data-gathering procedures, and in communicating with others working on allied problems.

In the forthcoming Part III [of "Simulation of Socio-Economic Systems" in *General Systems*], both the input format and output display associated with this model are discussed in detail. It must be restressed at this point that the output display is directly related to and cross-referenced with the economic data-reporting system for AID devised at the Economic Growth Center at Yale. The selection of this output format was so that the simulation would be intimately related to a data processing system and a data bank and would have an output in a format that makes it easily available to and understandable by many.

The construction and use of large scale socio-economic models call for coordinated work by individuals with considerably varied training and skills. The costs of communication and coordination of effort are high. This approach is directed at least partially towards lessening them.

Notes

1. Country Analysis Program of the Yale Economic Growth Center, Yale University.
2. Memoria del Gerente General del Banco Central de Ecuador, 1965, p. 148.

International Monetary Fund, *International Financial Statistics*, XVI, 1, Washington, D.C., January 1963.
3. See for example Cornblit, O., T. S. DiTella, and E. Gallo, "Politics in New Nations," *Instituto Torcuato Di Tella*, August 1966.

Rosen, G., "Political and Economic Interrelationships in the Economic Development Process," RAND Corporation, Santa Monica, P-3266, December 1965.

Gillespie, R. W., in E. P. Holland and with R. W. Gillespie, *Experiments on a Simulated Underdeveloped Economy: Development Plans and Balance-of-Payments Policies*, Part II, M.I.T. Press, 1963.
4. Nelson, R. R., "The CES Production Function and Economic Growth Projections," *Rev. of Economics and Statistics*, XLVII, 3, August 1965, pp. 326–328.
5. International Monetary Fund, *op. cit.*
6. Nerlove, Marc, "Two Models of the British Economy: A Fragment of a Critical Survey," *Intnl. Econ. Rev.*, 6, 2, 1965, pp. 127–128.
7. Orcutt, G. H., M. Greenberger, J. Korbel, and A. H. Rivlin, *Microanalysis of Socioeconomic Systems—A Simulation Study*, New York: Harper, 1961.

Microscale Models

21 . Management Conflict and Sociometric Structure . **Harrison White**

This paper has two objectives.   One is substantive: to analyze the organizational significance of the chronic conflicts among departments of a manufacturing corporation regarding research and development.   The other is the development of a model for inferring the structure of personal relations within a permanent organization subject to conflict, a model which integrates the affective qualities and the contact frequencies revealed by choices on sociometric questions.   The opposing cliques of managers derived from the model are consistent with the conflict analysis; each approach can enrich and validate the other.

The problems of incorporating scientists into creative research programs within existing organizations of government and business bring into sharp relief issues of importance to social psychologists and to students of organization. The growth in number of studies of research and development activities (hereinafter abbreviated "R & D") has paralleled the enormous expansion of R & D

From *American Journal of Sociology*, Vol. LXVII, No. 2, September 1961, pp. 185–199, by permission of *American Journal of Sociology*.   This paper is based in part on a Ph.D. dissertation submitted in May, 1960, to the Department of Economics and Sociology of Princeton University. Helpful suggestions were given by Professors F. F. Stephan and W. E. Moore.   The financial support of the Office of Special Studies of the National Science Foundation, which is gratefully acknowledged, was granted under a contract with the Graduate School of Industrial Administration at the Carnegie Institute of Technology, where the author was a member of the Innovation Project.   The name and other characteristics of the company studied are disguised.

the United States.[1]   Unlike most of the social science studies of R & D, this paper deals with external rather than internal relations of the R & D department.[2]

In analyzing conflict and consensus on the program in research and development among departmental groups in upper management, a heuristic theory of the behavior of subunits in organization proposed by Selznick is used as the framework.[3]   By Selznick's model the complexity of company goals leads to delegation of authority, from which develops specialization in personnel and ideology between different departments and a parallel growth in interdepartmental conflict.   Uncertainty will be a prominent concept in the study: the manipulation of and the views on uncertainty by departments were constrained by the influence of outside opinion, and both uncertainty and outside opinion entered differently into the types of conflict.

The key assertion is that conflict regarding R & D shows every sign of having been continuous, there being several types of it, no one of which was ever resolved more than temporarily and for specific topics.   The issues were categorized by whether the primary goal of one side is invasion, expansion, or insulation. Chronic conflict, fueled by continuous departmental drives for more secure autonomy, implies reliance on bargaining and politics rather than on persuasion or rational problem-solving, and the price the organization paid was recurrent reorganizations of program and structure.[4]

The Forthright Corporation produces for other manufacturing companies a variety of specialty products which can be grouped into alloys and abrasives. Forthright is highly exposed to the business cycle's fluctuations, but normal sales are about $20 million a year and total employment about 2,500.   As demand grows for a specialty product, the giant steel companies commonly enter and capture the market with their large-scale facilities for production and distribution. Therefore, Forthright, like its immediate competitors, has had to shift to new specialty products repeatedly over the years.   In the late 1940's ownership of Forthright passed from a family to a large investment trust.   The new president brought with him from a giant metallurgical firm several men as replacements and additions to top management and he attached great importance to the newly established R & D department.   Several reorganizations took place under the new president among all departments, but top management remained the same except for the addition of an executive vice-president.

Within either the production or the sales department, alloys and abrasives were handled by separate groups of managers, between whom little co-ordination was needed.   R & D was concentrated in the area of abrasives, although 75 per cent of the sales of Forthright were in the relatively few and well-established alloy products.   The chief metallurgist, who supervised the development work in alloys, was responsible to the production vice-president for control of quality and trouble-shooting in alloys production, which took up most of his time.   For simplicity the treasurer, the comptroller, the personnel chief, and the president's trouble-shooter will be considered as one department, "staff."

The titular head of R & D, the co-ordinator, had little direct authority over other R & D managers, but he handled routine administrative matters and coordinated all R & D proposals in both alloys and abrasives for submission to a technical management committee and thence to a general management committee on R & D. These committees, which approved of more projects than could be carried out, were more effective as channels of information than as control groups. Several promising new products in abrasives were the personal work of the innovator, a man of great energy who had involved himself in many aspects of R & D since his transfer a few years before from a prominent government laboratory to Forthright. He and the co-ordinator together directed specialized programs of research in abrasives. The R & D machine manager directed development of a novel abrasives machine, the only entry by Forthright in the field of production equipment. The glamor-products manager, the only old-timer at Forthright among the R & D managers, worked alone in co-ordinating R & D, sales, and production for recondite new materials related to abrasives and of interest primarily to the United States Department of Defense. Of the twenty-odd professional R & D personnel, only the latter manager and the innovator had Master's degrees.

Interviews lasting from a half-hour to three hours took place, by appointment in the offices of the managers during normal business hours. Extensive notes were taken, and immediately afterward an approximately verbatim account was dictated for transcription. On the basis of this information a questionnaire of 110 elementary items was developed. Each item was posed orally to each manager, and the answers recorded verbatim, a process which took up to one and one-half hours. A variety of company reports and records was used.

The sociometric analysis and, to a large extent, the analysis of conflicts are based on responses to the questionnaire and interviews of the sixteen managers involved in decisions on R & D.

INFLUENCE OF OUTSIDE OPINION

In response to a questionnaire item, managers from all departments except production stated that the results of abolishing the R & D program would be disastrous in the long run. The production managers said that the results would be "somewhat unfavorable" over a short period but ventured no estimate as to the long run. Yet there was almost no agreement among the managers in any department as to what were the most important benefits to be expected from R & D; the new products developed by the R & D department during the eight years of its effective existence had not sold in large quantities and showed no clear promise of doing so.

Forthright's budget for R & D had remained relatively constant, once the initial build-up was completed, yet net sales had declined sharply several times in this period, and average net income had been low—about the same size as R & D expenses. After the postwar change in ownership, forthright stock was listed on a major stock exchange, and the quotations on its stock had tended to decline. Forthright bonds were classified by a leading investment guide as "*Ba*-speculative elements; their future cannot be considered as well assured. . . . Uncertainty of position characterizes bonds of this class."

There was consensus among the managers on the desirability of a sizable R & D program at Forthright, carried on as a full-time activity by permanent personnel financed only by the company. This unanimity should be attributed neither to favorable experience with R & D at Forthright nor to ease in financing it. The inference is that the climate of opinion favorable to R & D in the segments of United States industry with which Forthright managers had close connections was the dominant influence, directly or indirectly.

Even if management had not come to agree with opinions favorable to R & D, there were many reasons for their acting as if they did. Forthright had had to obtain renewals of several very large loans from banks during this decade, primarily to finance its modernization program, and in the prevailing climate of opinion a company like Forthright without an R & D program would seem to lack prospects for the future to justify loans. The Board of Directors of Forthright would probably not have remained as quiescent as it had been if the top management they installed slighted R & D. Forthright's product line was changing rapidly; the average of estimates by sixteen managers was that 35 per cent of then current production was in products not made three years before. The most important new products had been obtained by some kind of license arrangement, and both R & D managers and executives agreed that other firms are much more willing to grant licenses if there is the possibility of eventual reciprocation with results from one's own R & D program in that area.

There were differences in orientation to outside opinion which influenced the internal conflicts over R & D among Forthright departments as described below. The executive, R & D, and sales departments were more directly responsive to and exposed to outside opinion than were the production and staff departments.[5] Throughout the interviews it struck the observer that production and staff managers' skepticism about particular R & D projects derived in large part from their absorption in the internal operations of the firm, with the inevitable series of crises in accomplishing even technically simple tasks. The other managers discounted the concrete difficulties with an R & D project relative to both its potential technical importance and its importance in improving the company image.

Sales managers asserted that the R & D laboratory should be a facility for impressing visiting firemen as much as a producer of important innovations. Even the most professionally oriented R & D managers appeared more interested in the general trade's opinion of the results of Forthright R & D than in the opinions of colleagues in other firms. The president, sensitive to the views of top executives in other firms, was convinced of the necessity and feasibility of major innovations through R & D, more so than any other manager.

CHRONIC CONFLICTS

One can distinguish five issues on which the R & D department had been and was likely to continue to be in opposition to some other departments. As noted earlier, Selznick's view of the development of conflict among organizational subunits as an unanticipated consequence of the delegation of authority aptly describes the general nature of these specific conflicts. The task of managing a sizable company is so complex that there must be considerable delegation of authority to a set of top managers, and this leads in a familiar way to specialization in training, experience, and promotion. There ensues a development of the loyalty of each manager to the autonomy and the specialized goals or ideology of his department. Conflicts among departments develop, and decisions become oriented more and more to the strategy of internal disagreement over autonomy and goals.

The president of Forthright followed a conscious policy of delegating authority as much as possible. Ambiguity of responsibilities and of formal relations among departments had developed from frequent reorganizations. The latter were in large part the result of this policy of maximum delegation and hence minimum imposed co-ordination, which led to crises resolved by reorganization. Wide scope was offered internal conflicts.

The R & D managers did not constitute a well-knit unit with a common view of the goals of R & D. In several conflicts the chief metallurgist and the glamor-products manager were in opposition to the other R & D managers, but this is consistent with their acting to maximize their own autonomy to pursue the goals of their work as they saw them. In each instance the effect of their opposition to the other R & D managers was the evasion of more centralized co-ordination with R & D activities in abrasives, at the relatively low cost of some "control" by managers not expert in technological matters. Hereafter the designation "R & D department" refers only to the trio of the co-ordinator, the machine-developer, and the innovator, unless otherwise indicated.

The conflict issues are of three types, distinguished by whether a drive for autonomy is aimed at accepted functions of another department, at claims to functions necessarily involving more than one department, or at assertions of independence of the company as a whole.

COUNTERPART UNITS I

In the literature on administrative behavior the tendency of a line department to develop a "counterpart unit" of experts to match a centralized staff department has often been noted.[6] The explanation, in essentials, is as follows: A staff department, while nominally in an advisory capacity to the line department, in fact tends to develop effective control over the relevant aspects of the line department's work, perhaps through the authority to insist on standard procedures of its own choosing. To be able to negotiate with the staff department on even terms, the line department needs a group of men themselves expert and experienced in the given specialty. Chronic conflict can develop between the staff department and the counterpart unit, since their interpretations of the general principles of their speciality are biased by the interests and goals of their respective units.

The production department had operating control over the chief metallurgist, who directed the group of engineers working on R & D for alloys. This group functioned as a counterpart unit to the R & D department, and the standard explanation seems to fit. Historically, the production department had simply retained effective control of this group through the successive reorganizations of the formal R & D department set up after World War II.

The R & D co-ordinator had "administrative control" over this counterpart group in R & D in alloys, and in a number of ways he tried to develop fuller control. Meanwhile, the R & D budget for alloys, partly as a result of pressure from the R & D co-ordinator, was less than a fifth that for abrasives, when each is measured as a fraction of the respective sales.

The production managers on several occasions resisted introducing newly, and often only partly, developed abrasives products into production and used the expert knowledge of the alloy R & D group in the resulting negotiations. Moreover, production managers had stated that the abrasives R & D managers did not give enough help to the production men with their regular bread-and-butter problems. The alloy R & D group was used mainly for such routine, predictable development work, and production managers pointed to the benefits of this work in arguing for modification of the general R & D policy.

COUNTERPART UNITS II

A converse type of counterpart unit was also found at Forthright. The R & D managers made a determined and successful effort to be allowed to do job-shop production of moderate quantities of several novel abrasives products. The standard explanation of counterpart units can be turned around: The R & D department needs experience in production to deal effectively with the "it can't be done" arguments production managers advance in opposing new products. This need is particularly crucial in the metallurgical industry, where the great difference in size between R & D laboratory runs and production lots of a new product can lead to wholly unanticipated performance of the R & D laboratory process in production.

There were other advantages to R & D in job-shop production, not least the very high profit rate obtainable on novel products, which helped to reduce the uncertainty felt by R & D managers as to the value of the R & D program as a whole. Executives and sales managers were pleased with the advertisement and good-will value of providing even small quantities of novel products to regular customers who needed them. The accounting and personnel managers, on the other hand, tended to oppose job-shop production by R & D on the grounds that it complicated their duties unnecessarily. According to the R & D managers concerned with abrasives, the intermittent opposition by production to their job-shop operations was vitiated by the fact that production had often rejected or terminated the same novel products as too much trouble for too little volume.

MARGINAL FUNCTIONS I

Quality control is a function marginal between the R & D and production departments. R & D has to set the formula for a new product, but practical production problems and schedules require some flexibility in adherence to it. The R & D department, when founded, carried out quality control on abrasives products. Argument over the acceptability of production batches was chronic. The production managers took back control of abrasives' quality in 1952. One of their chief arguments was the anomaly of having to deal with different personnel in control of quality and standards for the abrasives products and the alloys products; this argument was an additional dividend from having kept control of R & D for alloys.

Conflict continued over the adequacy of control of quality of abrasives. Just at the end of the field work for this study one of the R & D managers, the innovator, was transferred to control of a new "abrasives technical activities" division in the production department, which was to have considerable autonomy to effect improvement in the quality of abrasives products. It is unlikely that this is the final resolution.

This conflict can be viewed as a struggle over the bargaining power inherent in the authority to reject production lots on grounds of quality. It can also be seen as the result of incompatibility between the R & D department's goals of maximizing and standardizing quality and the production department's goals of minimizing costs as well as uncertainty in delivery time and cost.

MARGINAL FUNCTIONS II

Until fairly recently, most products at Forthright had been new products. The power inherent in the choice of potential products to develop affected all departments. Unitary control by R & D managers of this choice would perhaps most directly challenge the autonomy of the executives, in their role of formulating company goals and co-ordinating company activities.

A complex set of activities and a high level of uncertainty are associated with developing and introducing a new product. Two negative generalizations can be made about development of new products at Forthright: the set of development activities had never been the same for any two distinct new products, and the administrative responsibility had never been held by the same sequence of managers. The most common procedure had been the creation of a semiautonomous new unit to co-ordinate the development of a group of new products. The R & D machine manager, the R & D glamor-products manager, and the president's trouble-shooter each headed such a unit. Typically, the effective control of such a unit shifted from one department to another over a period of time. In several instances impatience on the part of the executives with a new unit led to the assignment of an additional manager to that group of products as an independent "trouble-shooter."

Several R & D managers tried at different times to stake claims to the over-all control of various types of new products until they reached routine status. At least one R & D manager, the co-ordinator, was explicitly willing to sacrifice the mission of carrying out the technical research work in Forthright laboratories to the mission of co-ordinating the successful establishment at Forthright of new products, from whatever source. However, the two autonomous new-product units directed by R & D managers were partly under the control of other departments, and the other two new-product units were currently managed by others than R & D managers.

Although the new-product situations have been complex and varied, the actions of the production and staff managers appeared to be consistent with an attempt to bar R & D managers from control over ramifications beyond the more technical aspects of R & D. The rapid introduction of new products favored by the R & D department would most directly create problems and uncertainty for the production and staff departments. The sales managers were inclined to support the R & D managers in favoring the introduction of numerous new products, which enhanced the sales appeal of Forthright product lines, but they favored only those types of products salable through existing connections.

The executives made the decisive moves regarding the various groups of new products. Ambiguity in the administration of the over-all process of new-product development, in large part due to the executives' actions, had the effect of reducing the influence of other managers, particularly the R & D managers, relative to the executives' influence. Like the R & D managers and, to some extent, the sales managers, but, unlike the production and staff managers, the executives were inclined to favor attempts at dramatic innovations. Often the ideas for these innovations came to them from executives in other companies. However, the executives were as concerned with writing off as with introducing dramatic new projects. In this they were rather successfully opposed by the R & D managers, who pushed the elaboration of new variants of initial dramatic ideas. In his interviews the president suggested (at one point in the presence of the R & D machine manager) that the R & D managers resorted to obscurantism in conveying technical information.[7] By increasing uncertainty in evaluation, an R & D manager may secure the continued development of a problematic product in new variants.

BUDGETARY INDEPENDENCE

The fifth conflict was over redistributed costs and, more generally, the budgetary independence of the R & D department. The desire of R & D managers in abrasives to earn their own way through job-shop production has already been noted. A standard accounting practice at Forthright, as in other companies, was the "redistribution" of costs from one department to another.[8] The costs redistributed to R & D from production remained fairly constant and represented largely "housekeeping" charges. Initially, R & D, like other staff units, redistributed no costs to production. Later, during a business recession in which the R & D managers felt their budget was being cut drastically, the R & D department began the practice of charging for trouble-shooting and other services to production, and later to sales. This move provoked controversy, and sales and production cut down on their requests for help from R & D.

The R & D managers covered as much as half their budget by these specific financial credits for contributions to company welfare in providing advice and service to other departments. Production, staff, and sales managers fought it: they felt that R & D services could not be realistically assessed by cost tags but should be included in general company overhead as part of the total R & D budget. (However, in the case of products under development which were not related to current production items, production and staff managers sought strict accounting of expenses while R & D managers favored flexibility.) The more general motivation of the conflict was the desire of the R & D managers, opposed by production and staff, to secure a constant R & D expenditure independent of immediate R & D performance and of the company's fluctuating sales.

SUMMARY

A summary of the positions inferred for the sixteen managers in the five conflicts is appropriate, since in the next section an independent sociometric analysis of the structure of conflict will be developed for comparison. In the simplified description which follows, for each conflict area two opposed groups of managers are listed, the omitted managers being considered neutral. The "A" label is reserved for the side of a conflict taken by R & D managers in abrasives.[9]

Counterpart units, I, Group A: Co-or., Mach.; *Group B:* Met.; VP-P; E-VP.
Counterpart units II, Group A: Co-or., Mach., Inno., Glam.; VP-S, Ab-S, AVP-S; Pres., E-VP; *Group B:* VP-P,Ab-P; T.S., Pers.
Marginal functions I, Group A: Co-or., Mach., Inno.; Ab-S; *Group B:* Met., Glam.; VP-P, Ab-P; Pers.
Marginal functions II, Group A: Co-or., Mach., Inno.; *Group B:* Met., Glam.; VP-P, Ab-P; Pres.; Acc., Treas., T.S., Pers.
Budgetary independence, Group A: Co-or., Mach.; VP-S; Pres.; *Group B:* Ab-P; Acc.

This bare listing of opposed groups conceals one especially important aspect of the conflicts. In each conflict area, members of Group A disagreed among themselves considerably more than did members of Group B. There was less competition both over personal advancement and over the reasons for their stand in each of the five areas among the members of Group B.[10]

STRUCTURE OF PERSONAL RELATIONS

During the period of the field work, the summer and fall of 1958, since the sixteen managers were more often in conflict on R & D issues than on any other, it is natural to seek in the pattern of their personal relations a reflection of their participation in conflicts over R & D.

SOCIOMETRIC CHOICES

A series of questions on their personal relations was put to each manager:

1. Could you list the two or three managers with whom you have the most dealings in the course of your work?
2. Do any of your personal friends work at [Forthright]? Who? How regularly do you see them away from work?
3. Would you single out the one or two people in [Forthright] whose ideas about business policy and procedure are most similar and congenial to yours?
4. Who do you guess might single you out as one of those with similar ideas about business policy and procedure?
5. Who is the individual in [Forthright] whom you most respect for great knowledge? For ability to deal effectively with people?
6. With what persons in [Forthright] do you find it most uncomfortable to associate?—not that you dislike them, just that you find it awkward to deal with them.
7. Who might think you were one of the people it was most uncomfortable to associate with?

Of the two hundred choices made, thirty-three choices of managers not in the group of sixteen respondents were excluded.

Direct inspection of the tables of choices reveals that less than half the guesses on questions 4 and 7 were confirmed by the actual choices.[11] With one exception, one-quarter or less of the choices on a given question are reciprocated; the exception is question 2, where sixteen out of twenty-six choices of friends are in reciprocal pairs.   Of the eight friendship pairs, five were between sales managers and the three abrasives R & D managers, one between R & D managers in abrasives, and one between sales managers.   On the other hand, on questions 6 and 7, the one pair of mutual choices, the one pair of mutual guesses, and the two confirmed guesses are each between some R & D manager in abrasives and some production manager.   The observer's first-hand impression was that the abrasives R & D managers were anxious to be personal friends with other Forthright managers. Not only the number (nine) of friendship choices they made, but also the fact that in each of the five sales—R & D friendship pairs the abrasives R & D manager reported about twice as many visits per month (average of 5.4) as did the sales manager (average of 2.5), tended to confirm the impression.

To obtain a more general picture of the structure of interpersonal relations, it is desirable to classify these choices by the affective quality and by the familiarity implied.   The naming of a manager in question 2, 3, 4, or 5 implies a positive feeling of the respondent for him.   A negative feeling is implied by the naming in questions 6 and 7.   An idea of the structure of the feelings of managers about each other is given in Table 1.   Here an entry "p" means that the manager in whose row the entry lies has named the manager in whose column the entry lies on one *or more* of the four "positive" questions, and similarly for the "n" entries. Where there is no entry in a cell of Table 1, no choices in questions 2 through 7

Table 1. Affective Quality of the Feeling of Each Manager for Each Other Manager*

CHOSEN

CHOOSER		R & D managers					Sales managers			Production managers		Executives		Staff managers			
		Co-or.	Mach.	Met.	Inno.	Glam.	VP-S	Ab-S	AVP-S	VP-P	Ab-P	Pres.	E-VP	Acc.	Treas.	T.S.	Pers.
R & D managers	Co-or.	p	p				p			n		p	n	p			
	Mach.	p					p	p		n		p					
	Met.						p	p		p		p					
	Inno.				p	p		p	p	n	n	p	n		p		
	Glam.			p		p			p			p	p		p		
Sales managers	VP-S.	p		p				p	p	n		p		p			
	Ab-S.	p		p		n			p	n	n	p	n	p	p		
	AVP-S.	p								n		p			p	p	
Production managers	VP-P.	n			p	p	p				p	p				p	
	Ab-P.				p	p				p							
Executives	Pres.	n					a			p		p	n	p		p	
	E-VP.			n						p		p		p			
Staff managers	Acc.	n					p			p		p		p		p	
	Treas.									p		p		p			
	T.S.									p		p	p	p			
	Pers.									p		p					

* Here p = positive, n = negative, a blank = neutral, and a = ambivalent quality; e.g., the vice president-sales (VP-S) has a negative feeling for the vice president-production (VP-P), whereas the latter has a neutral feeling for the former. See text for relation of entries to sociometric choices made and n. 9 for abbreviations of managers' titles.

Table 2. Perceived Frequency of Contact*

		R & D managers					Sales managers			Production managers		Executives		Staff managers			
CHOOSER		Co-or.	Mach.	Met.	Inno.	Glam.	VP-S	Ab-S	AVP-S	VP-P	Ab-P	Pres.	E-VP	Acc.	Treas.	T.S.	Pers.
R & D managers	Co-or.		1				1		1	1		1	1	1			
	Mach.	1					1	1	1	1		1	1				
	Met.	1					1	1		1							
	Inno.	1				1	1		1	1					1		
	Glam.	1			1		1		1			1	1	1	1		
Sales managers	VP-S.	1					1		1	1		1	1	1			
	Ab-S.	1			1		1		1	1	1		1	1	1		
	AVP-S.	1			1												
Production managers	VP-P.						1			1							
	Ab-P.									1	1	1					
Executives	Pres.						1			1				1			
	E-VP.						1			1		1		1			
Staff managers	Acc.	1					1			1		1	1				
	Treas.											1	1				
	T.S.									1		1	1	1			
	Pers.												1				

CHOSEN

* The manager named in the stub of a row indicated he had most contact with the managers named in the column headings of those cells in the row which contain the entry "1." See text for relation of entries to sociometric choices and n. 9 for abbreviations of managers' titles.

321

were made by the manager named in the stub of the row of that cell, of the manager named at the head of the column in which the cell lies. The president named the vice-president for sales on both types of questions; so the feeling of the president for the VP-S is called "*a*" for ambivalent.

The feeling of one manager for another is often not reciprocated at all or not in kind; for example the R & D co-ordinator indicated a positive feeling for the president, but the president indicated a negative feeling for the R & D co-ordinator. Since the same entry, *p*, is used whether there were one or several choices in questions 2–5, only quality, not strength of feeling, is indicated, and similarly for negative and ambivalent entries. When there is no entry in a cell, the affective quality of the corresponding feeling is considered neutral.

A choice in questions 1 or 2 implies that the chooser knows the chosen manager fairly well through frequent contact, whatever the affective quality of the relation. In Table 2 an entry "1" means the manager in that row chooses the manager in that column in question 1 and/or in question 2. One manager's perception of frequent contact with another often is not reciprocated, since the levels of activity and the frames of reference of the two managers may be different.

Responses to questions touching several aspects of positive feeling—similarity in ideas, personal attraction, respect—are combined in deriving the *p* entries in Table 1. Managers in Forthright were loath explicitly to indicate various kinds of clearly negative feelings for a colleague. They were even loath to respond to the discreetly worded questions on discomfort, but it seemed that all the more obvious cases of antipathy were indicated by the *n* entries in Table 1. The manager's guesses as to the positive and negative feelings of others toward him (questions 4, 7) were included as equivalent to choices because the more senior managers seemed to feel it beneath their dignity to indicate positive and negative feelings for their juniors and subordinates on the direct-choice questions. The rareness of confirmed guesses noted earlier to some extent justifies this treatment of guesses as surrogate choices. Table 2 was based on question 2 as well as question 1 in order to tap social as well as on-the-job occasions of interaction among the managers.

INFERRED QUALITIES OF FEELING

Any picture of the structure of conflict in interpersonal relations should refer to the frequencies of contact as well as the affective quality in the relations between pairs of managers. Furthermore, to speak of the structure of relations is to speak of the interrelations of the various choices. Modifications of the affective quality of the relations shown in Table 3 between pairs of managers will be inferred following a set of plausible rules which combine the information in Table 2 with that in Table 1.

It will be assumed that, if manager A likes manager B who likes manager C, and if manager A sees enough of manager B to know his preferences, then manager A will tend to like manager C. Here "likes" is taken to mean the "*p*" quality of feeling, "dislikes" means the "*n*" relations, and "sees enough of" means the "1" relation.   The assumption can be abbreviated as: if ApB and if BpC, and if A1B, then ApC.   Note that ApB does not imply BpA, and so on, as noted earlier.

A second and complementary assumption should also be made: One manager who sees a lot of another will tend to like him if they have a mutual friend.   In symbolic terms, if ApB and if CpB and if A1C, then ApC.   Several additional equally plausible assumptions will be made;[12] in the symbolic notation they are:

> If ApB and if BnC and if A1B, then AnC
> If ApB and if CnB and if A1C, then AnC
> If AnB and if CpB and if A1C, then AnC
> If AnB and if BnC and if A1B, then ApC
> If AnB and if CnB and if A1C, then ApC

Given this set of assumptions, a large number of inferences can be drawn from our data as to the affective qualities of the relations between pairs of managers. The rules by which different inferences as to the feeling of manager A for manager B should be combined to reach a net inference are almost self-evident.   Any number of inferences of p quality, when combined, simply yield the net inferences of a p quality, since no attempt is made to measure strength of feeling; and similarly for the combination of different inferences of n.   Combination of one or more p inferences with one or more n inferences naturally yields a net inference of an ambivalent quality (a).   Finally, combination of an inference of an ambivalent quality with any other inference will still yield the net inference of an a quality.   The use of these rules can aptly be termed "qualitative addition."

OPPOSING CLIQUES

A manifest quality of feeling given in Table 1 is to be combined with the net inferred quality by exactly the same rules of qualitative addition.   It is assumed that an inferred quality of feeling will tend to be realized under the stimulus which conflict situations exert on interpersonal relations.   Since no attempt was made to measure the strength either of the original or of the net inferred feeling, it is natural to combine them on an equal footing by qualitative addition.   The resultant affective quality of the feeling by each manager for each other manager is shown in Table 3,[13] in which the rows and columns have been rearranged to indicate more clearly the grouping of managers found.   As before, a blank cell indicates that the affective quality is neutral and feelings are not necessarily reciprocated.

Clique membership is to be determined by a search procedure using as criterion that a member has some positive but no negative feelings toward other members of the clique.[14]   A brief rationale for this is that purely negative feeling, but not simply ambivalence, will imply conflict and that in conflict a coalition will tend to be formed by a group of men among whom there are positive, and possibly ambivalent, feelings but no negative feelings.   Nothing in the

Table 3. Net Emotional Quality of the Feeling of Each Manager for Each Other Manager*

CHOSEN

CHOOSER	"White" clique							"Black" clique								
	Co-or.	Mach.	Inno.	VP-S	Ab-S	AVP-S	Pres.	Met.	Glam.	VP-P	Ab-P	E-VP	Acc.	Treas.	T.S.	Pers.
"White" clique:																
Co-or.		*p*	*a*	*a*	*p*	*p*	*a*	*n*	*a*	*a*		*a*	*a*	*p*	*a*	
Mach.	*a*		*p*	*a*	*p*	*p*	*a*	*n*	*a*	*a*	*n*	*n*	*p*	*p*	*p*	
Inno.	*p*	*p*		*p*	*a*	*p*	*a*	*a*	*a*	*a*	*n*	*a*	*p*	*p*	*a*	
VP-S	*a*	*p*	*p*		*p*	*p*	*a*	*n*	*a*	*a*			*a*	*p*	*a*	
Ab-S.	*p*	*p*	*a*	*a*		*p*	*p*	*a*	*a*	*n*	*a*	*a*	*p*		*p*	
AVP-S.	*a*	*p*	*a*	*p*	*p*		*p*	*p*	*p*	*n*	*n*	*n*	*a*	*p*	*p*	
Pres.	*a*	*a*	*n*	*a*	*a*	*a*		*p*	*p*	*a*			*a*		*p*	
"Black" clique:																
Met.	*n*		*n*	*n*			*p*		*p*	*p*					*p*	
Glam.	*a*		*a*	*a*	*p*		*a*	*p*		*a*	*n*	*a*	*p*	*p*	*p*	
VP-P.	*n*		*n*				*p*	*p*			*p*				*p*	
Ab-P.	*a*	*p*	*n*	*a*	*p*		*p*	*p*	*p*	*p*					*p*	
E-VP.	*n*		*n*	*a*			*p*	*p*	*p*	*a*			*p*		*p*	
Acc.	*a*	*a*	*n*	*a*	*p*		*a*		*p*	*a*		*p*				
Treas.							*p*									
T.S.	*n*		*n*	*a*			*a*	*p*	*p*	*p*		*a*	*p*			
Pers.								*p*	*p*	*p*		*p*	*p*			

* Inferred from Tables 1 and 2. See text for clique criterion and n. 9 for abbreviations of managers' titles.

procedure requires that all managers will fall into two opposing cliques, and the "Black" and "White" cliques defined in Table 3 do not, in fact, fully meet the criterion. The president really is a "swing" man, belonging to neither clique, which makes sense considering the president's role as chief co-ordinator and final arbiter. The feeling of the glamor-products R & D manager for the abrasives production manager is negative, although both are assigned to the "Black" clique.

The sociometric finding that, using a reasonable definition of clique, one discovers two opposing cliques with the memberships indicated in Table 3 tends to confirm the previous analysis of the five specific conflicts. To a good approximation the seven members of the White clique include those and only those managers listed in Group A, at the end of the previous section, for one or more of the five conflicts, and similarly for the relation of Group B to the nine members of the Black clique.

To summarize the results in Table 3: Between cliques there is not only a far higher percentage of negative feeling than within cliques but also a much lower percentage of positive feelings. The feelings of the White clique toward the Black clique are given by the percentage of the appropriate set of entries which are positive (22 per cent), negative (17 per cent), ambivalent (29 per cent), and neutral (32 per cent). The appropriate set of entries is the upper right bloc in Table 3, that is, all sixty-three entries which are in one of the first seven rows and in one of the last nine columns. The corresponding percentages for the feelings of Black toward White are 17, 22, and 43 per cent.

Relations within the Black clique taken as a whole are bland; 58 per cent of the seventy-two entries are neutral, and almost all the remaining entries are positive— 33 per cent p, 1 per cent n, and 7 per cent a. In the five specific conflicts these managers are found only in Group B; their departmental interests tend to be parallel. Moreover, they tend to have the same departmental ideologies, particularly in regard to outside opinion and to uncertainty.

Within the White clique, relations taken as a whole are intense and ambivalent; there are no neutral feelings, and nearly as many of the feelings are ambivalent (45 per cent) as are positive (52 per cent), only 2 per cent of the forty-two entries being negative. Here, too, there is agreement with the results of the earlier analysis of conflicts. Managers in the White clique are generally in Group A in the five conflict areas but are also found in Group B. They tend to be more partisan in more of the areas of conflict than do members of the Black clique, and they differ more in their attitudes toward uncertainty and outside opinion.

The two opposing cliques found by applying the clique criterion to the direct sociometric choices as classified in Table 1 would be the same as those found from Table 3. However, the texture of clique relations would be markedly different, and the texture in Table 3 represents better the actual situation found earlier from analysis of the conflicts on five R & D issues.

The sociometric results are a partial confirmation of the R & D conflicts derived earlier from interviews. It is desirable to recast and integrate the analysis to bring out ideas which might be fruitful beyond this case study.

Uncertainty is the key variable, as one might expect in a study of R & D conflicts. A major technique of negotiation was the manipulation of the opposition's uncertainty on specific issues. A major aspect of ideological conflicts was divergent evaluations of uncertainty in the different criterion variables dear to one department or another.[15]

The ideology which the R & D department wished to further by increasing its autonomy, and which it used as a weapon for doing so, is most clearly evident in the second conflict over marginal functions. Not only the three R & D managers, treated here as the heads of an R & D department, but also the glamor-products R & D manager were more concerned with developing radically new products than with gradually improving existing standard products. All sixteen managers treated here were aware of this bias and tended to see the production and staff managers as taking the opposite view.[16] When their preference for novel R & D projects was effective, the R & D managers were in a stronger position for controlling general decisions on the development of new products, since they had a greater relative advantage in technical knowledge and a lesser relative disadvantage in knowledge of production and sales.

All managers agreed that many years must be allowed before major R & D projects can be properly evaluated. However, the above four R & D managers took an extreme position in explicitly claiming that a good R & D program, on the one hand, was necessarily uncertain because it was concerned with the frontier of knowledge but, on the other hand, needed a constant high level of support to have a good chance of success. The R & D managers tried, as in "Counterpart Unit II," to reduce the uncertainty of their contribution to Forthright, but on occasion they increased uncertainty by initiating new variants of development projects that appeared to be failures. Executives and sales managers also believed creative experimentation with new products was essential for growth and survival and required tolerance of the associated uncertainty.

Each department tolerated least well a particular aspect of uncertainty, being willing to trade less uncertainty in that aspect for more uncertainty in other aspects. R & D managers favored trading uncertainty in investment and time for certainty in quality and variety of new products, whereas executives and sales managers seemed to give priority to certainty of the company's growth. A desire by production and staff managers for certainty in the variables important to them, cost and accountability, led them to oppose uncertain experimentation, stringent standards of quality, and novelty in products.

The influence of outside opinion dominated objective uncertainty as to the general worth of the R & D program. In spite of a ten-year record of costly but minor successes and incompleted projects, there was consensus among the managers as to the necessity of a sizable R & D program. Thus conflicts on specific issues could not be resolved by eliminating R & D. The variation between departments on orientation to uncertainty in part reflected differential sensitivity to outside opinion and in part followed from differences in their tactical positions in conflicts.

Conflicts about R & D could be chronic because of the departmental autonomy practically required of the company by the rapid change in its environment and the complexity of its operations. In Forthright the drive for autonomy was greatest in those areas where hostility among departments was greatest and the interrelation of tasks was highest, a finding contrary to the propositions advanced by Dill after a comparison of two Norwegian firms.[17]

When the delegation of authority is extensive, it is unnecessary to distinguish horizontal from vertical autonomy.[18] The president is the most influential figure at Forthright, however: close inspection of Tables 1–3 reveals that relations with the president are the single most important set of choices in determining the texture of social relations, given the postulates of the sociometric model.

Recurrent minor reassignments of responsibility among departments and reorganization of departments were the distinctive concomitants of chronic conflict in Forthright. There is considerable similarity between the study of chronic interdepartmental conflict and of research in the Sherif tradition on intergroup conflict outside formal organizations.[19] The departments share common goals for the company and basically accept each other's distinctive roles. For this reason the distinctions drawn among counterpart, marginal, and independent types of conflicts are meaningful.

Notes

1. For examples of documentation of these two trends see the bibliography in R. Anthony, *Management Controls in Industrial Research Organizations* (Cambridge, Mass.: Harvard University Press, 1952); and *Science and Engineering in American Industry: Final Report on a 1953–54 Survey* (Washington, D.C.: National Science Foundation, 1956).
2. The role conflicts among the group of men who co-ordinate R & D with the other activities of the company at the same time as they motivate the activities of the R & D scientists are the subject of another paper (H. C. White, "Role Conflict and Information Structure: A Case Study of Industrial R & D Managers" [unpublished]).
3. A clear and concise description of Selznick's model is given by James G. March and Herbert A. Simon in *Organizations* (New York: John Wiley & Sons, 1958), pp. 40–44. The basic reference is Philip A. Selznick, *TVA: The Grass Roots* (Berkeley: University of California Press, 1949).
4. See March and Simon, *op. cit.*, p. 129, for the definition of these four types of reaction to conflict. Their assumption that internal conflict is not a stable condition for an organization seems naïve and certainly does not fit this case.
5. No consistent differences among departments in the numbers and lengths of visits at Forthright in a nine-month period were found from receptionists' entries in appointment books. However, R & D managers and executives named many more outsiders with whom long discussions were regularly held than did the other managers. Furthermore, R & D managers, sales managers, and executives spent far more days on out-of-town visits, as recorded in expense-account statements, than did production and staff managers. In view of the difficulties of measurement it seemed artificial to conceptualize the material in this section either in terms of reference-group theory or in terms of "the pattern of inputs from the environment to the

organization," the approach favored by W. R. Dill in "Environment as an Influence on Managerial Autonomy," *Administrative Science Quarterly*, II (March, 1958), 409–43.

6. See, e.g., H. Simon, D. Smithburg, and N. Thompson, *Public Administration* (New York: Alfred A. Knopf, Inc., 1950), pp. 291 ff.

7. Research-and-development managers were not influential sources of information, however, and there was great inconsistency in their attitudes (see n. 2).

8. J. Neuner, *Cost Accounting* (Homewood, Ill.: Richard D. Irwin, Inc., 1957), pp. 291 ff.

9. Abbreviations of managers' titles used here and in tables are as follows:

R & D department: "Co-or." = Co-ordinator; "Mach." = R & D machine manager; "Met." = chief metallurgist; "Inno." = innovator; "Glam." = glamor-products manager.

Sales department: "VP-S" = vice-president–sales; "Ab-S" = manager of abrasive sales; "AVP-S" = assistant to the VP-S.

Production department: "VP-P" = vice-president–production; "Ab-P" = manager of abrasives production.

Executives: "Pres." = president; "E-VP" = executive vice-president.

Staff department: "Acc." = comptroller; "Treas." = treasurer; "T.S." = president's troubleshooter (who works both on special production and special R & D missions); "Pers." = personnel manager.

10. A number of questions were asked of each manager regarding potential promotions he anticipated. All conflicts among the anticipations of different managers revolved around the ambitions of R & D managers.

11. The full data for this and other topics discussed are contained in the thesis, which is available on microfilm through University Microfilms, Inc., Ann Arbor, Michigan.

12. Many aspects of the sociometric model are adapted from a paper dealing with the formally similar topic of the analysis of attitude structures (R. Abelson and M. J. Rosenburg, "Symbolic Psychologic: A Model of Attitudinal Cognition," *Behavioral Science*, III [January, 1958], 1–15). The primary difference between the set of assumptions they discuss at length and the ones here lies in the necessity to modify inferences according to the presence or absence of the "1" relation. It may be that many puzzling aspects of results of prior sociometric case studies would be clarified if "affect" and "contact" choices were integrated in some such fashion as that proposed here. For an excellent review of the literature on measures of sociometric structure see M. Glanzer and R. Glaser, "Techniques for the Study of Group Structure and Behavior, I: Analysis of Structure," *Psychological Bulletin*, LVI (1959), 317–31. Representation of choices by directed graphs, discussed in this review (on pp. 329–30), is an alternative to the representation by relational algebra used in the present paper, and the reader may find it helpful to rewrite the postulates for inferring relations in terms of patterns of directed lines of three kinds among three points representing managers A, B, and C.

13. Matrix algebra was used to develop and combine inferences systematically and efficiently. Tables 1, 2, and 3 can be treated as 16×16 square matrices; denote them by R, M, and T respectively. Number the rows and columns from 1 to 16 in each matrix; the entry in the ith row and the jth column of R, for example, can then be compactly denoted by r_{ij}. The possible values of r_{ij} are p, n, a, and o, for neutral quality. The possible values of m_{ij} are 1 and 0. For ordinary matrix multiplication use the symbol "$\cdot$"; then $Q = R \cdot M$ means that

$$q_{ij} = \sum_{k=1}^{16} r_{ih} m_{ki}.$$

A different type of matrix multiplication, "application," denoted by α, is defined as the formation of a product matrix by multiplication of corresponding elements in the two initial matrices; i.e., if $Q = R\alpha M$, then

$$q_{ij} = r_{ij} m_{ij}.$$

The rules for adding and multiplying the individual entries r_{ij} are given in verbal form above; e.g., $p + p = p, p + n = a, p + o = p, pp = p, pn = a$, and $po = o$. Only multiplication is possible between entries in M and entries in R; the rules are obvious—$p1 = p$, $p0 = o$, etc. Finally, define $\bar{R}$ as the transpose of the matrix R; i.e., $\bar{r}_{ij} = r_{ji}$. In terms of this notation Table 3, the matrix T, can be expressed as

$$T = R + (RaM) \cdot R + (R \cdot \bar{R})aM,$$

using the standard rule of matrix addition.   Parentheses indicate the order in which successive multiplications are to be performed.   Calculated in this way, T contains entries in the diagonal cells, but they are meaningless in this context and are to be ignored.

14. This criterion bears some resemblance to the n-clique definition introduced by Luce, but the membership of a clique is determined primarily by the absence of one- and two-step negative relations among members rather than by each pair of members being connected by a positive chain of at most n lines (see R. D. Luce, "Connectivity and Generalized Cliques in Sociometric Group Structure," *Psychometrika*, XV [June, 1950], 169–90).

15. Much of the literature on formal organization overlooks the role of uncertainty in ideology and tactics although it treats the impact made by unplanned uncertainty in internal functions and environmental inputs (but see A. W. Gouldner, *Patterns of Industrial Bureaucracy* [London: Routledge & Kegan Paul Ltd., 1955], p. 27 and chap. vii).

16. Each manager was asked in the questionnaire to identify the colleagues who habitually used seven phrases which had been culled from the transcripts of interviews.   "Romancing about it," "blue-sky research," and "they may be wooden nickels," all phrases indicating skepticism of radical R & D programs, were attributed to production and staff managers.   Apparently, these managers did not use the phrases, and statistical analysis indicated that attribution to them, in general, had no correlation with actuality.

17. See "tentative inferences" 1 and 2 in Dill, *op. cit.*, pp. 438–39.   Note however that Dill's propositions refer to managers as individuals.

18. *Ibid.*, p. 412.

19. M. Sherif and C. W. Sherif, *Groups in Harmony and Tension* (New York: Harper & Bros., 1953), pp. 191, 210, 211.

22 . Continuities in Theories of Status Consistency and Cognitive Dissonance
James A. Geschwender

The concept of status consistency (status crystallization or status congruence) is gradually assuming greater prominence in the literature of social stratification. Its major weakness lies in its use as a structural characteristic predicting behavioral consequences without an explicitly stated social-psychological theory of motivation to account for these predictions.   Three such theories have been proposed. They are Homans' Theory of Distributive Justice,[1] Zaleznik's Theory of Social Certitude,[2] and Sampson's Principle of Expectancy Congruence.[3]

James A. Gechwender, "Continuities in Theories of Status Consistency and Cognitive Dissonance," *Social Forces*, Vol. 46, December 1967, pp. 160–171, by permission of the University of North Carolina Press.

The last-named is an attempt to explain the findings of status consistency research within the framework of Festinger's Theory of Cognitive Dissonance.[4] Sampson's approach is similar to that of Zaleznik but has the advantage of being more general. However, it is still incomplete as it does not adequately explain all consequences of status inconsistency. It is suggested herein that the Theory of Distributive Justice can bridge this gap if it can be integrated into a dissonance framework. Two attempts to do this have been made.[5] However, they represent mere beginnings as they are limited as to degree of specification and detailed analysis. The present paper hopes to complete the task and to spell out in some detail further implications of the combined theory.

The strategy of attack will be to briefly describe the Theory of Social Certitude and the Principle of Expectancy Congruence, to relate them to each other, and to evaluate this combination. The Theory of Distributive Justice will then be described and integrated into dissonance theory. This combination will subsequently be evaluated as to its ability to explain the empirical findings of status consistency and further theoretical implications will be derived.

SOCIAL CERTITUDE AND EXPECTANCY CONGRUENCE

The essence of the Theory of Social Certitude is the assumption that each status position carries with it a set of behavioral expectations regarding both the behavior of the occupant of said position and the behavior of all persons with whom he interacts. Each individual occupies several positions and possesses several sets of behavioral expectations which may either reinforce or contradict one another.

The status consistent possesses sets of behavioral expectations which either reinforce or are consistent with one another. A condition of social certitude exists and social relations are fluid and satisfying. The status inconsistent possesses sets of expectations which conflict with one another. A condition of social certitude does not exist. Anxiety is produced for all concerned and social relations are hampered and unsatisfying. This sets in motion forces tending toward the creation of status consistency.

The Principle of Expectancy Congruence and the Theory of Social Certitude have much in common. The major difference between them is that the former is stated within the framework of the more general dissonance theory while the latter stands alone. Sampson bases his analysis upon the following assumption:

> Let us make the assumption that one aspect of each position—or set of positions along a given status dimension consists of certain expectations for the behavior of the occupant of that position. Thus, for example, a person ranking high in education may meaningfully be said to have certain expectations held by others and by himself for his behavior. A similar parallel between rank position and expectation can be drawn for other dimensions along which persons can be ranked.[6]

From this point, the analysis is identical to that proposed by Zaleznik. Incongruent expectations are a problem for everyone and interfere with interaction.

Congruent expectations simplify interaction. Thus, there is a pressure on all participants to create and maintain a congruence of expectations. This is why status inconsistency is an undesirable state which produces pressure toward changing the situation.

EVALUATION OF SOCIAL CERTITUDE AND EXPECTANCY CONGRUENCE

The Principle of Expectancy Congruence has the advantage of being derivable from a more general theory of motivation. This makes it more attractive than the Theory of Social Certitude as it may be more easily related to findings in other areas. However, the ultimate test of any theory is how well it explains empirical findings. It is at this point that the principle breaks down.

Research has demonstrated a relationship between status inconsistency and tendencies toward social isolation, mobility striving, political liberalism, psychosomatic symptoms of stress, and preference for changes in the social order or actual attempts to bring about these changes. This research will be discussed below. Some of these findings are explainable within an expectancy congruence approach and some are not.

The frustrations and anxieties produced by a lack of expectancy congruence might easily produce psychological symptoms of stress. They might interfere with social interaction and produce a tendency for inconsistents to withdraw into social isolation. They might also produce mobility strivings to achieve a state of expectancy congruence. However, this approach does not do a very good job of explaining the status inconsistent's preference for a change in the social order and predisposition for participation in social movements. Actually, mobility strivings are only partially explained. This approach does not supply us with any means of predicting which response to inconsistency a status inconsistent will be likely to select. An expanded theory which integrates the Theory of Distributive Justice into dissonance theory might perform this function.

THE THEORY OF DISTRIBUTIVE JUSTICE

An author can usually state his own ideas better than someone else can summarize or paraphrase them. Thus, it is best to quote Homans' description of his theory:

> A man in an exchange relation with another will expect that the rewards of each man will be proportional to his costs—the greater the investments, the greater the profits. ... Finally, when each man is being rewarded by some third party, he will expect the third party, in the distribution of rewards, to maintain the relation between the two of them. ... The more to a man's disadvantage the rule of distributive justice fails of realization, the more likely he is to display the emotional behavior we call anger. ... men are rewarded by the attainment of justice, especially when just conditions are

rewarding in other ways. For instance, I am more likely to demand justice when justice would bring me more money than when it would bring me less. . . . Not only do men display anger, or less predominantly, guilt when distributive justice fails in one way or the other, but they also learn to do something about it. They learn to avoid activities that get them into unjust exchanges; they learn to emit activities that are rewarded by the attainment of justice. . . .[7]

Homans suggested that certain status dimensions could be viewed as investments into a social situation while others could be viewed as rewards received from that situation. The four dimensions that Lenski utilized in his analysis of status consistency may be classified according to this framework. Education and ethnicity may be seen as investment dimensions. There are universalistic norms in American society which lead one to expect that he will be rewarded in terms of his level of education. There are also particularistic norms which lead one to expect that he will be rewarded in terms of his ethnic status. Thus, education may be classified as an achieved investment and ethnicity as an ascribed investment.

Occupation and income may be viewed as reward dimensions. Income is clearly a reward as it determines one's standard of living. Occupation may also be seen as a type of reward. Some occupations are preferable to others in terms of the amount of physical labor demanded by them, the cleanliness of the work, and the amount of individual autonomy allowed. Thus, occupation may be classified as a social reward and income as a material reward.

Using these definitions, it could be concluded that a state of distributive justice exists when individuals who possess greater investments (higher education and/or ethnicity) also possess greater rewards (higher occupation and/or income). Those persons whose investments are higher than rewards (level of occupation and/or income below level of education and/or ethnicity) will experience a felt injustice and feel anger. It is reasonable to assume that this anger may be directed against the society which fails to maintain distributive justice and may lead to behavior designed to change society in order to eliminate this inequity.

Those persons whose investments are lower than their rewards (education and/or ethnicity below level of occupation and/or income) would experience a felt injustice and feel guilt. It may be assumed that individuals who are over-rewarded will not attempt to reduce guilt feelings by lowering their reward level. It is more likely that they will develop a political philosophy which, if implemented, would ameliorate the consequences of being short-changed for those who are under-rewarded. They might also develop a philosophy which defines ascribed investments as irrelevant to rewards. In short, they may become political liberals. If educational investment is the low dimension, they may either attempt to raise their level of education to one consistent with rewards received or else develop a definition of education as being "ivory tower" and impractical, which would lead to anti-intellectualism. It is to be noted that the Theory of Distributive Justice is not equipped to handle an explanation of the consequences of either investment (education–ethnicity) or reward (occupation–income) inconsistencies.

RELATION OF DISTRIBUTIVE JUSTICE TO DISSONANCE THEORY

It is possible to incorporate the Theory of Distributive Justice into dissonance theory with the addition of a few assumptions.   We may assume that every individual includes within his cognitive set cognitions concerning his status level in the educational, occupational, ethnic, and income hierarchies.   We may assume that he possesses cognitions defining education as an achieved investment, ethnicity as an ascribed investment, occupation as a social reward, and income as a material reward.   We may also assume that he possesses cognitions which define the proper relation that should hold between investment and reward dimensions.   This definition of the proper relation between investments and rewards would be based upon the individual's perception of that relation which normally exists in society.

Thus, experiencing a state of felt injustice is reduced to experiencing cognitive dissonance resulting from inconsistency among simultaneously held cognitions.   The empirical consequences of felt injustice may be seen as behavioral attempts to reduce dissonance.

This may be combined with Sampson's assumption that each status position carries with it expectations regarding behavior that should be forthcoming from, or directed toward, the occupant of that position.   Congruent sets of expectations facilitate the development of satisfying patterns of social interaction and incongruent sets of expectations impede this development.   Thus, status inconsistency leads to the development of cognitive dissonance, and attempts to cope with this inconsistency represent behavioral attempts to reduce dissonance.   Other behavioral responses may be non-coping responses indicating an inability to reduce dissonance.   Dissonance theory, thus expanded, may enable us to explain the empirical consequences of status inconsistency which have been observed and to predict others not yet observed.

EVALUATION IN RELATION TO FINDINGS

The research literature has demonstrated six different types of responses to status inconsistency.   These are enhanced mobility striving, withdrawal into social isolation, psychosomatic symptoms of stress, political liberalism, preference for and attempts to change the social order, and prejudice.   The findings in each of these areas of research will be considered separately and in relation to the foregoing theoretical approach.

MOBILITY STRIVING

Benoit-Smullyan proposed the existence of a status equilibration process.[8]   He stated that individuals are ranked or have status on three major dimensions: the economic, political, and prestige hierarchies. These types of status are analytically distinguishable and often empirically independent, but there is a tendency for one to be transformed into the others through a status equilibration process.

Implicit in Benoit-Smullyan's analysis is the assumption that possession of discrepant statuses in different hierarchies creates strain for individuals and causes them to follow a course of action designed to bring their statuses into line with one another. This assumption was not tested. Fenchel et al. did attempt to test this hypothesis with an undergraduate population at CCNY.[9] They had the students rate themselves as to their general standing in five potential reference groups and as to where they would like to stand. The difference between the two ratings was taken as an index of status striving. The hypothesis was supported as the students did tend to strive for a common ranking in all reference groups.

Homans reinterpreted one of his earlier studies into a framework which lends support to the equilibration hyopthesis.[10] This was a study of female clerical workers and involved two categories of jobs—cash posters and ledger clerks. The line of promotion was from cash poster to ledger clerk. The general evaluation was that the position of ledger clerk was a better job, carried more responsibility, and conveyed more status. However, the same salary was paid to both positions. Ledger clerks protested demanding that they be paid more than the cash posters as would befit their more important jobs. They were status inconsistent because their material rewards were not comparable to their occupational status. They were attempting to reduce dissonance by raising their lower-ranking status to a level consistent with their higher-ranking one.

The literature does not deal with variations in response by pattern of status inconsistency. However, it does yield implications for it. It suggests that persons experiencing dissonance resulting from status inconsistency may attempt to reduce this dissonance by altering their ranking on one or more of the dimensions of status. This would not be equally possible for all types of inconsistents. Persons who are low ethnically but high on the other dimensions could not normally be expected to alter their ethnic status through individual mobility. But a person who is high in education and low in occupation and/or income might hope to reduce dissonance through hard work, individual effort, and mobility on the occupational and/or income dimensions. More will be said about this below.

POLITICAL LIBERALISM

Lenski studied the relationship between status inconsistency and political liberalism.[11] A sample of persons were asked their views toward a government-sponsored health insurance program, price controls, and a general extension of governmental powers. Their responses were classified along a continuum of liberalism. The more liberal responses were found to be associated with low status consistency. Democratic voting was taken to be an indication of relative liberalism and was found to be associated with low status consistency.[12]

Both of these associations held when general status levels were controlled.

Certain patterns of inconsistency were more closely associated with liberalism than others. A person of low ethnic status and high income, occupational, or educational status tended to be more liberal than the reverse combinations. Individuals with low educational and high occupational statuses tended to be more politically liberal than did those with the opposite combination. An inconsistent with high occupational and low income status was more likely to be liberal than was the reverse combination. In fact, the high income–low occupation inconsistent was less likely to be liberal than were consistents.

Lenski's findings have been interpreted as indicating that status inconsistents may be prone to engage in social movements designed to bring about major changes in society. This may be erroneous. The particular items that Lenski used to measure political liberalism appear to be more closely related to a mild reformist perspective as might be incorporated into a welfare state or great society philosophy rather than the type of outlook that would motivate a person to join a social movement with more sweeping aims.

These findings suggest that a person who experiences dissonance resulting from status inconsistency may try to reduce his dissonance through the development of a liberal political outlook. The relationship of particular types of inconsistents to political liberalism is suggestive. Inconsistents with low educational and high occupational statuses and inconsistents with low ethnic and high occupational or income statuses are types of inconsistents categorized above as over-rewarded. Their investment dimensions are lower than their reward dimensions. They would be expected to feel guilt. Their attempts to reduce dissonance might be expected to take the form of attempting to ameliorate the consequences for others of their getting more than their share, and to develop a belief that ethnicity should not be related to rewards. Both of these are indications of political liberalism.

The inconsistent with low ethnicity but a high educational status represents a different type. He has brought his achieved investment to a level higher than his ascribed investment. In this sense, he is a success. One might expect that, in this sample, this type of inconsistent is also high on reward dimensions. This is based on the fact that inconsistents with high education and low occupation are lower on the liberalism scale. Thus, they may also be over-rewarded and react as the others described above. However, I would suggest that we reserve judgment of this type of inconsistent. It might be necessary to know his position on reward dimensions before making any predictions about him. Similarly, we should reserve decision on the two types of reward inconsistents (high income–low occupation and high occupation–low income). It is difficult to draw any conclusions regarding the relative importance of income and occupation as types of rewards.

SOCIAL ISOLATION

Lenski also studied the relationship between status inconsistency and tendencies toward social isolation.[13] He found that status inconsistents were less likely than status consistents to interact with neighbors and fellow workers outside of business hours, to be members of voluntary associations, to be regular participants in those voluntary associations in which they were members, and less likely to report sociable motives (noneconomic reasons) for those voluntary ties that they had. No attempt was made to analyze the relation between types of inconsistency and tendency toward social isolation.

Homans provided data which suggest that this tendency toward social isolation may not always be voluntary.[14] He found that the status inconsistent members of a work group were high on initiating interaction for others but were low on the receipt of interaction from others. Generally the interaction that they initiated took the form of horseplay or joking. Homans suggested that joking may be the reaction of the inconsistent to the insecurities in the situation, while the reaction of others is a tendency to avoid the inconsistent.

These results are explainable with the assumptions that Sampson makes in his Principle of Expectancy Congruence. Status inconsistency creates a situation in which there exist conflicting sets of behavioral expectations. This interferes with the development of fluid tension-free interaction. Thus, interaction becomes unpleasant and tends to be broken off. It may be possible that the earliest stage of this process is found in other persons avoiding the inconsistent and in the inconsistent resorting to joking. Withdrawal on the part of the inconsistent may represent the final acceptance on his part of the impossibility of creating satisfying patterns of interaction. Suicide is the most extreme form of withdrawal, and Gibbs and Martin found a relationship between status inconsistency and propensity toward suicide.[15]

PREFERENCE FOR SOCIAL CHANGE

Lenski postulated that status inconsistents might be prone to react against society by participating as leaders in social movements and that a society with widespread status inconsistencies was unstable and generated pressures toward change.[16] However, he never empirically tested this proposition. Benoit-Smullyan made a similar suggestion when he stated, "There are historical grounds for supposing that when legal, customary, or other barriers seriously hamper the equilibrating tendency, social tensions of revolutionary magnitude may be generated."[17] He cited as evidence the fact that support for the Nazi Party came from large classes of persons who became impoverished but retained their former prestige statuses.

There are other historical examples of status inconsistents who have supported social movements. Frazier noted that Negro support for organizations like the Urban League and the NAACP tends to come from middle-class Negroes.[18] Lipset pointed out that urban middle-class leaders in the C.C.F. tended to come from minority groups, while the urban middle-class leaders in the Liberal and Conservative Parties tended to come from the Anglo-Saxon majority group.[19] Michaels noted that middle-class Jews were quite prominent in European Socialist parties.[20] These last three examples are all of status inconsistents whose ethnic status was lower than their occupational status. It is worth noting at this point that the examples show low ethnicity–high occupation inconsistents supporting leftist movements and high occupation–low income inconsistents supporting rightist movements.

Ringer and Sills found a high proportion of status inconsistents among political extremists in Iran. They were overrepresented among the extremists on the revolutionary left and the nationalistic right.[21] The inconsistents were of a high educational level and only a moderate economic status. The degree of inconsistency was sharpest for the revolutionary left. Both types of extremists were anti-colonialist and this common antagonism to vestiges of colonialism may have been more important in attracting adherents than their left–right differences. These data show a tendency for under-rewarded inconsistents with a high level of education to take an extremist position in reacting against the social order. The data regarding the NAACP, C.C.F., and Jewish socialists show over-rewarded inconsistents with a low ethnic status taking a more moderate reformist position when reacting against the social order.

Goffman related status inconsistency to preferences for change in power distributions within society.[22] Status inconsistency was measured using the educational, occupational, and income hierarchies. Preference for change was measured by asking respondents to check their perceptions of the amount of influence in the conduct of national affairs presently held by, and the amount of influence that they prefer be held by, state governments, big business, labor unions, businesses that were not big, and the national government. Status inconsistents exhibited a greater preference for change than did status consistents. This relation held with general status levels controlled. No attempt was made to analyze differences between status types. It is not possible to discuss the left–right direction of these preferences for change without knowing more detail about the responses than Goffman provided.

These findings suggest that there is reason to believe that status inconsistents may attempt to reduce dissonance by reacting against the social order, or at least by expressing a preference for a change in the present distribution of power within society. They further suggest that under-rewarded inconsistents are more likely than over-rewarded inconsistents to take an extreme reaction against the social order. This is predictable from the assumptions incorporated into dissonance theory from the Theory of Distributive Justice. Homans states that anger is a stronger emotion than guilt. The angry (under-rewarded) inconsistent would be expected to experience a sharper form of dissonance and a more extreme reaction than would guilty (over-rewarded) inconsistents.

PSYCHOSOMATIC SYMPTOMS

Elton Jackson studied the relationship between status inconsistency and the exhibition of psychosomatic symptoms.[23] Consistency was measured in terms of the ethnic, educational, and occupational status dimensions. He found a significant relationship between status inconsistency and the exhibition of psychosomatic symptoms.   He also found a significant difference between types of inconsistents.

Jackson noted that two types of inconsistents (high ethnicity combined with either low occupation or low education) had high rates of psychosomatic symptoms, while the opposite types (low ethnicity combined with high education or high occupation) did not have symptom rates which differed from that of status consistents.   He noted that Lenski had found the two types of status inconsistents with high symptom rates to exhibit only a slight tendency toward political liberalism and the two types with low symptom rates to exhibit strong tendencies toward political liberalism.   He suggested that the important determinant is the relationship between achieved and ascribed ranks.   Those with high ascribed and low achieved ranks are likely to see themselves as failures and to develop high psychosomatic symptom rates.   Persons with low ascribed and high achieved ranks are likely to see themselves as successes—they have made it despite their ethnic handicap.   Thus, they will direct their response to stress outward.   This will take a political form for many.

The major difficulty with this interpretation of political and psychosomatic responses as alternative ways of reacting to inconsistency is that it does not seem to apply equally well to all types of inconsistents.   Jackson included in his table, but did not discuss, psychosomatic symptom rates and tendencies toward political liberalism for high occupation–low education and high education–low occupation inconsistents.   Both types of inconsistents have symptom rates higher than consistents and also exhibit a stronger tendency toward political liberalism. The one possible support for viewing political and physical reactions as alternative responses comes from the fact the symptom rates for these two types of inconsistents are lower than those with high physical, low political responses and their tendency toward political liberalism is less than those with high political, low physical responses.   Possibly these results show a tendency for some persons experiencing this type of inconsistency to react physically and others to react politically.

Jackson advanced one other tentative proposition that bears examination. He found male inconsistents with high occupation and low educational statuses to have a symptom rate much higher than did status consistents.   Those males who had high educational and low occupational statuses exhibited a symptom rate lower than that of status consistents.   He suggests that mobility opportunities might explain this.   The latter type of inconsistent is likely to see the possibility of future mobility bringing about consistency, while the former type cannot look forward to this possibility.   More mobility would simply cause greater inconsistency.   Jackson indicated elsewhere the existence of the relation of mobility possibilities and age.[24]   Younger inconsistents, who had status profiles which could become consistent through mobility, had lower levels of psychosomatic symptoms than older inconsistents with similar profiles.   This could indicate that with advanced age mobility would be defined as less likely and persons would give up striving and develop physical responses.

Jackson's major contribution came in demonstrating that failure to reduce dissonance through either mobility or political reactions might force one to attempt to live with dissonance. Dissonance is tension-producing and, in the absence of dissonance-reducing behavioral attempts, might easily produce a physical response leading to psychosomatic symptoms.

PREJUDICE

There is currently very little research relating status inconsistency to prejudice.[25] However, we can draw indirect inferences regarding this relationship if we accept membership in the Ku Klux Klan as an indication of racial prejudice. Vander Zanden has pulled together the names and occupations of 153 members of the Klan.[26] Ninety-eight of these were found in occupations (skilled labor, marginal businessmen, and marginal white-collar occupations) which are the occupations in which Negroes are making the greatest inroads.[27] The rest are transportation workers, semiskilled or unskilled laborers. These are occupations in which whites have been receiving competition from Negroes for many years. It is reasonable to assume that in the South, the status attributed to an occupation declines with increases in the proportion of Negroes. Thus, KKK members are status inconsistent because their occupational status fails to come up to their high ethnic status.

If membership in the KKK is not accepted as a valid indication of racial prejudice, it certainly is an indication of willingness to express and/or act out hostility toward members of a racial minority. Thus, we can see that under-rewarded status inconsistents may attempt to reduce dissonance by directing hostility against members of a minority group.

DISCUSSION

It would appear that all research findings to date dealing with consequences of status inconsistency can be explained within the framework of an expanded version of dissonance theory. This would require combining the initial premises of the theory with Sampson's assumptions and a series of assumptions derived from the Theory of Distributive Justice. A brief statement of the assumptions would go as follows:

1. All persons hold sets of cognitions which include some that are reality-based, some which are definitional, and some that are normative. Reality-based cognitions describe the existing state of affairs while normative cognitions describe the state of affairs which should exist.

2. Any set of cognitions may stand in a relation of dissonance, consonance, or irrelevance depending upon the internal relations which hold among reality-based and normative cognitions. If the conjunction of a reality-based and a normative cognition implies another reality-based cognition in the set then a state of consonance exists. If this conjunction implies the negation of another reality-based cognition in the set then a state of dissonance exists. If this conjunction

implies neither another reality-based cognition nor the negation of one in the set then a state of irrelevance exists.

3. Reality-based cognitions will include perceptions of one's status in the educational, occupational, income, and ethnic hierarchies. They will also include perceptions of behavior expected from, and expected to be directed toward, the occupants of positions in each of these hierarchies. Definitional cognitions will include the definition of ethnicity as an ascribed investment, education as an achieved investment, occupation as a social reward, and income as a material reward. Normative cognitions will include beliefs regarding the proper relation that should exist among the various status positions. Particularly, they will include the belief that rewards received should be proportional to investments. Possession of a higher level of ascribed investments than achieved investments will be defined as failure. The reverse combination will be defined as success.

4. Dissonance is an upsetting state and will produce tension for the individual. This tension will lead to an attempt to reduce dissonance by altering cognitions, adding new cognitions, or deleting old ones. Attempts to alter reality-based cognitions will involve attempting to change the real world. Attempts to alter normative cognitions will involve attempts to change evaluations of the real world and will take place within the cognitive system.

5. Status inconsistents whose rewards received are less than believed to be proper for their investments will feel anger and inconsistents whose rewards exceed investments will feel guilt. Anger is a sharper form of dissonance than guilt. The perception of failure produces a sharper form of dissonance than the perception of success. The intensity of dissonance-reducing behavior will be directly proportional to the sharpness of dissonance.

6. Dissonance-reducing attempts will take the form of coping responses, attempts to change the real world, when possible. When coping responses are not possible, dissonance-reducing attempts will take the form of attempting to withdraw from interaction. When neither changing the real world nor withdrawal from it is possible, dissonance will remain and the tension will be manifested in psychosomatic symptoms.

7. Dissonance-reducing attempts will move from the simple to the complex. That is, the simplest types of alterations in reality that would reduce dissonance will be attempted first. If these attempts are unsuccessful, a shift will be made to increasingly complex attempts. The simplest form of altering reality is to attempt to change one's own status through individual mobility. Downward mobility would create sharper dissonance by causing a comparison with rewards received in the past, and therefore believed possible, and rewards currently received. Thus, only upward mobility would be a dissonance-reducing move. The next most simple form of altering reality is to strike out against individuals and categories of individuals (e.g., prejudice and discrimination). The most complex form of attempting to change reality is attempting to alter society. The simplest form of withdrawal is social isolation, and the most complex form of withdrawal is suicide.

These assumptions enable us to make deductions for each of the patterns of inconsistency which would explain the empirical findings to date. These patterns are presented in Table 1.

Under-rewarded status inconsistents whose high investment dimension is ethnicity would feel sharp dissonance (anger). Mobility might possibly be a way of reducing dissonance depending on their level of education. If it is possible, it will be attempted first. If it is not possible, or if it is unsuccessful, attempts to reduce dissonance will shift to attacking categories of persons. It would be expected that this type of inconsistent would be highly prejudiced and would engage in discrimination. Any attempt to change the society would likely take the form of trying to create a state of affairs in which ethnicity has increased importance—a racist social movement. If none of these attempts are successful, then one would expect a tendency toward social isolation and a high level of psychosomatic symptoms.

Under-rewarded inconsistents whose high investment dimension is education would experience sharp dissonance (anger). Mobility for them is possible and will be attempted as a means of reducing dissonance. If mobility attempts are unsuccessful or blocked (e.g., if they are minority group members) then the individual will shift to more complex forms of dissonance reduction. Prejudice and discrimination may develop but could hardly result in changing reality if they were directed against members of the majority group. Thus one would be prone to attempt to change society and this attempt would take a more extreme form (social movements or revolution). A requirement for participating in social movements and revolutions is the belief that one has the power to be successful. If this is lacking, or the change attempt fails, then the inconsistent would be forced into social isolation and/or exhibition of psychosomatic symptoms.

Over-rewarded status inconsistents whose low investment dimension is ethnicity will not be able to reduce dissonance through mobility. They may develop anti-majority group prejudices but this will do them little good. Thus, they will be forced to attempt to reduce dissonance by changing society. Their mild state of dissonance (guilt) will produce a moderate change response such as political liberalism or participation in a moderate reform social movement. It is doubtful if they will be forced into social isolation or exhibition of psychosomatic symptoms, as they will be able to define themselves as successes for overcoming their ethnic handicap.

Over-rewarded inconsistents whose low investment dimension is education will probably not be able to reduce dissonance through individual mobility, nor would they benefit by attacking other categories of people through prejudice. Thus, it is likely that they would start their dissonance-reducing attempts at the level of societal alteration. Their mild state of dissonance (guilt) would lead to a moderate response such as political liberalism. It is possible that this would fail and force them into social isolation, but the mild degree of dissonance might make it unlikely that they would develop psychosomatic symptoms to any great extent.

Investment inconsistents could not be considered as either over- or under-

Table 1. Status Consistency Pattern and Reactions to Dissonance

Responses	UNDER-REWARDED INCONSISTENTS		OVER-REWARDED INCONSISTENTS		INVESTMENT INCONSISTENTS		REWARD INCONSISTENTS	
	High ethnicity (Low occupation income)	High education (Low occupation income)	Low ethnicity (High occupation income)	Low education (High occupation income)	High ethnicity (Low education)	High education (Low ethnicity)	High occupation (Low income)	High income (Low occupation)
Emotional reaction	Anger	Anger	Guilt	Guilt	Definition as failure	Definition as success	Ambiguity	Ambiguity
Mobility possibility	Possible, depends upon level of education	Possible, depends upon age	Not possible	Unlikely	Unlikely	Not possible	Unlikely, but depends upon age	Not possible
Prejudice	If no mobility, then high prejudice and discrimination likely	If no mobility, then possible prejudice against majority or minority groups (unlikely to aid in coping)	May develop antimajority prejudice (unlikely to help cope) or prejudice against other minorities	May develop prejudice, but this is unlikely to aid in coping	Prejudice and discrimination highly probable	May develop antimajority prejudice (unlikely to help cope) or prejudice against other minorities	Possible, but probably not aid in coping	Possible, but probably not aid in coping
Social change attempt	If neither mobility nor prejudice proves adequate, then possibly joins a racist social movement	If other coping responses fail (as is likely), then prone to join extremist social movements—providing perception of adequate power	If prejudice fails to reduce dissonance, then moderate change response such as liberalism or moderate reform social movement	Moderate change response such as political liberalism or participation in moderate reform social movement possible	Prone to join racist social movements	Moderate change response such as political liberalism or participation in reform social movement likely	No prediction. Data show tendency toward *both* political liberalism and extremist movements	No prediction. Data show no tendency toward liberalism
Social isolation	If coping responses fail, then tendency to withdraw into social isolation	If coping responses fail, then tendency to withdraw into social isolation	Doubtful, even if coping responses fail	Doubtful, even if coping responses fail	If coping responses fail, tendency toward social isolation	Doubtful, even if coping responses fail	Tendency toward social isolation quite probable	Tendency toward social isolation quite probable
Symptoms of stress	If coping responses fail and withdrawal impossible, then symptoms likely	If coping responses fail and withdrawal impossible, then symptoms likely	Doubtful, even if coping responses fail	Doubtful, even if coping responses fail	If coping responses fail, and isolation impossible, symptoms likely	Doubtful, even if coping responses fail	If social isolation not possible, symptoms quite probable	If social isolation not possible, symptoms quite probable

Coping Responses (Emotional reaction, Mobility possibility, Prejudice, Social change attempt)

Non-coping (Social isolation, Symptoms of stress)

rewarded.   Those with ethnicity as the higher dimension are failures and those with ethnicity as the lower dimensions are successes.   Failures would not be able to expect mobility.   They would probably develop hostility toward minority groups, and might be prone to join racist social movements.   If these dissonance-reducing attempts fail, they would be forced into social isolation and be prone to display psychosomatic symptoms.   The successes could not expect social mobility and would not gain from attacking categories of persons.   Their mild dissonance might lead them into attempts to reduce dissonance by moderate attempts at social change such as developing a liberal political philosophy or supporting moderate reform movements.   If these attempts are unsuccessful, it is unlikely that they would exhibit strong psychosomatic symptoms though they may be forced into social isolation.

Reward inconsistents could not be defined as over- or under-rewarded, successes or failures, without knowledge of their investment dimensions.   The only prediction one could make about them is that they would exhibit a tendency toward social isolation and possibly the exhibition of psychosomatic symptoms. However, one might expect that high occupation–low income inconsistents would also have a high level of education and be prone to act like other under-rewarded–high education inconsistents.

CONCLUSIONS

Sampson made a major contribution to the development of a motivational theory which would explain the behavioral consequences resulting from status inconsistency.   He did this by placing reactions to status inconsistency within a cognitive dissonance framework through the addition of an expectancy congruence assumption.   The present paper attempts to develop this further by adding a set of assumptions derived from the Theory of Distributive Justice.   The task is hardly finished.   Considerable refinement of these assumptions and empirical testing of derived propositions is required.   Nevertheless, it is hoped that the present paper is a step in the right direction.

Notes

1. George C. Homans, *Social Behavior: Its Elementary Forms* (New York: Harcourt, Brace & Co., 1961).
2. A. Zaleznik, C. R. Christenson, and F. J. Roethlisberger, in collaboration with George C. Homans, *The Motivation, Productivity, and Satisfaction of Workers* (Cambridge: Harvard University Press, 1958), pp. 56–66.
3. Edward E. Sampson, "Status Congruence and Cognitive Consistency," *Sociometry*, 26 (June 1963), pp. 146–162.
4. Leon Festinger, *A Theory of Cognitive Dissonance* (Evanston, Illinois: Row, Peterson & Co., 1957).
5. James A. Geschwender, "Explorations in the Theory of Social Movements and Revolutions,"

unpublished manuscript; and C. Norman Alexander, Jr. and Richard L. Simpson, "Balance Theory and Distributive Justice," *Sociological Inquiry*, 34 (Spring 1964), pp. 182–192.

6. Sampson, *op. cit.*, p. 153.

7. Homans, *op. cit.*, pp. 332–333.

8. Emile Benoit-Smullyan, "Status, Status Types, and Status Interrelations," *American Sociological Review*, 9 (April 1944), pp. 151–161.

9. Gerd H. Fenchel, Jack H. Monderer, and Eugene H. Hartley, "Subjective Status and the Equilibration Hypothesis," *Journal of Abnormal and Social Psychology*, 46 (October 1951), pp. 476–479.

10. Homans, *op. cit.*, pp. 237–242.

11. Gerhard E. Lenski, "Status Crystallization: A Non-Vertical Dimension of Social Status," *American Sociological Review*, 19 (August 1954), pp. 405–413.

12. Kenkel's retest of this hypothesis produced results which did not support it. See William F. Kenkel, "The Relationship Between Status Consistency and Politico-Economic Attitudes," *American Sociological Review*, 26 (June 1961), pp. 365–368. However, this retest was severely criticized. See Gerhard E. Lenski, "Comments on Kenkel's Communication," *American Sociological Review*, 26 (June 1961), pp. 368–369. Lenski maintained that Kenkel erred in using different indices of status. His lack of results may have resulted from not using those that Lenski believed had a central place in American society. For the purposes of the present analysis, it will be useful to assume that Lenski's criticisms are correct.

13. Gerhard E. Lenski, "Social Participation and Status Crystallization," *American Sociological Review*, 21 (August 1956), pp. 458–464.

14. George G. Homans, *Sentiments and Activities* (Glencoe, Illinois: The Free Press, 1962), p. 100.

15. Jack P. Gibbs and Walter T. Martin, "Status Integration and Suicide," *American Sociological Review*, 23 (April 1958), pp. 140–147. For other research documenting the fact that status inconsistency interferes with the development of free communications and satisfying interaction see Stuart Adams, "Status Congruency as a Variable in Small Group Performance," *Social Forces*, 32 (October 1953), pp. 16–22; Ralph V. Exline and Robert C. Ziller, "Status Congruence and Interpersonal Conflict in Decision-Making Groups," *Human Relations*, 12 (April 1959), pp. 147–162; and Arlene C. Brandon, "Status Congruence and Expectations," *Sociometry*, 28 (September 1965), pp. 272–288.

16. Lenski, "Status Crystallization . . ." p. 412.

17. Benoit-Smullyan, *op. cit.*, p. 160. For supporting documentation see also William Kornhauser, *The Politics of Mass Society* (Glencoe, Illinois: The Free Press, 1959), p. 181. Lipset cites unpublished research by Robert Sokol which found a relationship between perceived status discrepancy and support of McCarthy, but patterns of discrepancy were not discussed. See Seymour M. Lipset, "Three Decades of the Radical Right," in Daniel Bell, *The Radical Right* (New York: Anchor Books, 1955), p. 403.

18. E. Franklin Frazier, *Black Bourgeoisie* (Glencoe, Illinois: The Free Press, 1959), pp. 98–104.

19. Seymour M. Lipset, *Agrarian Socialism* (Berkeley: University of California Press, 1950), p. 191.

20. Robert Michels, *Political Parties*, (trans.) Eden and Cedar Paul (New York: Dover Publications, 1959), pp. 260–261.

21. Benjamin B. Ringer and David L. Sills, "Political Extremists in Iran," *Public Opinion Quarterly*, 16 (Winter 1953), pp. 689–701.

22. Irwin W. Goffman, "Status Consistency and Preference for Change in Power Distribution," *American Sociological Review*, 22 (June 1957), pp. 275–288.

23. Elton F. Jackson, "Status Consistency and Symptoms of Stress," *American Sociological Review*, 27 (August 1962), pp. 469–480. Dunham has also found that persons with high education and low occupation exhibit a tendency toward both schizophrenia and psychopathies, though he raises questions regarding the causal direction. See H. Warren Dunham, Patricia Phillips, and Barbara Srinivasan, "A Research Note on Diagnosed Mental Illness and Social Class," *American Sociological Review*, 31 (April 1966), pp. 223–227.

24. Elton F. Jackson, "Status Consistency, Vertical Mobility, and Symptoms of Stress," unpub lished Ph.D. dissertation, University of Michigan, 1960, p. 95.

25. See Donald J. Treiman, "Status Discrepancy and Prejudice," *American Journal of Sociology*, 71 (May 1966), pp. 651–664. Treiman attempted to evaluate the relative utility of a status consistency and an additive hypothesis for the explanation of prejudice. He concluded that the additive hypothesis was adequate for the explanation of prejudice without making the complex assumptions involved in a status consistency hypothesis. His treatment is unsatisfactory for three reasons. First, he limited himself to a consideration of education–income inconsistents. Second, he used family income rather than individual income. This does not give an individual status profile as one does not know how many people contribute to total family income. Third, and most important, he used a system of classification which produced some "inconsistents" which could be more accurately classified as consistents. This does not mean that his findings are necessarily wrong—merely that they are questionable.

26. James W. Vander Zanden, *Race Relations in Transition* (New York: Random House, 1965), pp. 42–43.

27. For a description of these inroads see James A. Geschwender, "Social Structure and the Negro Revolt: An Examination of Some Hypotheses," *Social Forces*, 43 (December 1964), pp. 248–256; James A. Geschwender, "Desegregation, the Educated Negro, and the Future of Social Protest in the South," *Sociological Inquiry*, 35 (Winter 1965), pp. 58–68.

23 . Social Exchange ... Unspecified Obligations and Trust . **Peter M. Blau**

The concept of exchange can be circumscribed by indicating two limiting cases. An individual may give another money because the other stands in front of him with a gun in a holdup. While this could be conceptualized as an exchange of his money for his life, it seems preferable to exclude the result of physical coercion from the range of social conduct encompassed by the term "exchange." An individual may also give away money because his conscience demands that he help support the underprivileged and without expecting any form of gratitude from them. While this could be conceptualized as an exchange of his money for the internal approval of his superego, here again it seems preferable to exclude conformity with internalized norms from the purview of the concept of social exchange.[1] A social exchange is involved if an individual gives money to a poor man because he wants to receive the man's expressions of gratitude and deference and if he ceases to give alms to beggars who withhold such expressions.

From Peter M. Blau, *Exchange and Power in Social Life* (New York, 1964), pp. 91–106, by permission of John Wiley & Sons, Inc.

"Social exchange," as the term is used here, refers to voluntary actions of individuals that are motivated by the returns they are expected to bring and typically do in fact bring from others. Action compelled by physical coercion is not voluntary, although compliance with other forms of power can be considered a voluntary service rendered in exchange for the benefits such compliance produces, as already indicated. Whereas conformity with internalized standards does not fall under the definition of exchange presented, conformity to social pressures tends to entail indirect exchanges. Men make charitable donations, not to earn the gratitude of the recipients, whom they never see, but to earn the approval of their peers who participate in the philanthropic campaign. Donations are exchanged for social approval, though the recipients of the donations and the suppliers of the approval are not identical, and the clarification of the connection between the two requires an analysis of the complex structures of indirect exchange, which is reserved for chapters eight and ten [of *Exchange and Power in Social Life*]. Our concern now is with the simpler direct exchanges.

The need to reciprocate for benefits received in order to continue receiving them serves as a "starting mechanism" of social interaction and group structure, as Gouldner has pointed out.[2] When people are thrown together, and before common norms or goals or role expectations have crystallized among them, the advantages to be gained from entering into exchange relations furnish incentives for social interaction, and the exchange processes serve as mechanisms for regulating social interaction, thus fostering the development of a network of social relations and a rudimentary group structure. Eventually, group norms to regulate and limit the exchange transactions emerge, including the fundamental and ubiquitous norm of reciprocity, which makes failure to discharge obligations subject to group sanctions. In contrast to Gouldner, however, it is held here that the norm of reciprocity merely reinforces and stabilizes tendencies inherent in the character of social exchange itself and that the fundamental starting mechanism of patterned social intercourse is found in the existential conditions of exchange, not in the norm of reciprocity. It is a necessary condition of exchange that individuals, in the interest of continuing to receive needed services, discharge their obligations for having received them in the past. Exchange processes utilize, as it were, the self-interests of individuals to produce a differentiated social structure within which norms tend to develop that require individuals to set aside some of their personal interests for the sake of those of the collectivity. Not all social constraints are normative constraints, and those imposed by the nature of social exchange are not, at least, not originally.

Social exchange differs in important ways from strictly economic exchange. The basic and most crucial distinction is that social exchange entails *unspecified* obligations. The prototype of an economic transaction rests on a formal contract that stipulates the exact quantities to be exchanged.[3] The buyer pays $30,000 for a specific house, or he signs a contract to pay that sum plus interest over a period of years. Whether the entire transaction is consummated at a given time, in which case the contract may never be written, or not, all the transfers to be made now or in the future are agreed upon at the time of sale.

Social exchange, in contrast, involves the principle that one person does another a favor, and while there is a general expectation of some future return, its exact nature is definitely *not* stipulated in advance. The distinctive implications of such unspecified obligations are brought into high relief by the institutionalized form they assume in the Kula discussed by Malinowksi:

> The main principle underlying the regulations of actual exchange is that the Kula consists in the bestowing of a ceremonial gift, which has to be repaid by an equivalent counter-gift after a lapse of time. . . . But it can never be exchanged from hand to hand, with the equivalence between the two objects being discussed, bargained about and computed. . . . The second very important principle is that the equivalence of the counter-gift is left to the giver, and it cannot be enforced by any kind of coercion. . . . If the article given as a counter-gift is not equivalent, the recipient will be disappointed and angry, but he has no direct means of redress, no means of coercing his partner. . . .[4]

Social exchange, whether it is in this ceremonial form or not, involves favors that create diffuse future obligations, not precisely specified ones, and the nature of the return cannot be bargained about but must be left to the discretion of the one who makes it. Thus, if a person gives a dinner party, he expects his guests to reciprocate at some future date. But he can hardly bargain with them about the kind of party to which they should invite him, although he expects them not simply to ask him for a quick lunch if he had invited them to a formal dinner. Similarly, if a person goes to some trouble on behalf of an acquaintance, he expects *some* expression of gratitude, but he can neither bargain with the other over how to reciprocate nor force him to reciprocate at all.

Since there is no way to assure an appropriate return for a favor, social exchange requires trusting others to discharge their obligations. While the banker who makes a loan to a man who buys a house does not have to trust him, although he hopes he will not have to foreclose the mortgage, the individual who gives another an expensive gift must trust him to reciprocate in proper fashion. Typically, however, exchange relations evolve in a slow process, starting with minor transactions in which little trust is required because little risk is involved. A worker may help a colleague a few times. If the colleague fails to reciprocate, the worker has lost little and can easily protect himself against further loss by ceasing to furnish assistance. If the colleague does reciprocate, perhaps excessively so out of gratitude for the volunteered help and in the hope of receiving more, he proves himself trustworthy of continued and extended favors. (Excessive reciprocation may be embarrassing, because it is a bid for a more extensive exchange relation than one may be willing to enter.) By discharging their obligations for services rendered, if only to provide inducements for the supply of more assistance, individuals demonstrate their trustworthiness, and the gradual expansion of mutual service is accompanied by a parallel growth of mutual trust. Hence, processes of social exchange, which may originate in pure self-interest, generate trust in social relations through their recurrent and gradually expanding character.

Only social exchange tends to engender feelings of personal obligation, gratitude, and trust; purely economic exchange as such does not. An individual is obligated to the banker who gives him a mortgage on his house merely in the technical sense of owing him money, but he does not feel personally obligated in the sense of experiencing a debt of gratitude to the banker, because all the banker's services, all costs and risks, are duly taken into account in and fully repaid by the interest on the loan he receives. A banker who grants a loan without adequate collateral, however, does make the recipient personally obligated for this favorable treatment, precisely because this act of trust entails a social exchange that is superimposed upon the strictly economic transaction.

In contrast to economic commodities, the benefits involved in social exchange do not have an exact price in terms of a single quantitative medium of exchange, which is another reason why social obligations are unspecific. It is essential to realize that this is a substantive fact, not simply a methodological problem. It is not just the social scientist who cannot exactly measure how much approval a given helpful action is worth; the actors themselves cannot precisely specify the worth of approval or of help in the absence of a money price. The obligations individuals incur in social exchange, therefore, are defined only in general, somewhat diffuse terms. Furthermore, the specific benefits exchanged are sometimes primarily valued as symbols of the supportiveness and friendliness they express, and it is the exchange of the underlying mutual support that is the main concern of the participants. Occasionally, a time-consuming service of great material benefit to the recipient might be properly repaid by mere verbal expressions of deep appreciation, since these are taken to signify as much supportiveness as the material benefits.[5] In the long run, however, the explicit efforts the associates in a peer relation make in one another's behalf tend to be in balance, if only because a persistent imbalance in these manifestations of good will raise questions about the reciprocity in the underlying orientations of support and congeniality.

Extrinsic benefits are, in principle, detachable from the source that supplies them, but their detachability is a matter of degree. At one extreme are economic commodities, the significance of which is quite independent of the firm that supplies them. The value of a share in a corporation is not affected by the broker from whom we buy it. At the other extreme is the diffuse social support we derive in a love relationship, the significance of which depends entirely on the individual who supplies it. The typical extrinsic benefits socially exchanged, such as advice, invitations, assistance, or compliance, have a distinctive significance of their own that is independent of their supplier, yet an individual's preferences for them are also affected by his interpersonal relations with the supplier. Although the quality of advice determines its basic value for an individual, regardless of who furnishes it, he tends to prefer to consult a colleague whose friendly relations with him make it easy for him to do so rather than a more expert consultant whom he hardly knows.[6] The ease with which he can approach a colleague, the jokes and conviviality that surround the consultation, and other rewards he obtains from the association combine with the quality of the advice itself to determine the value of the total transaction for him. Indeed, the exchange of instrumental assistance may sometimes largely serve the function for participants of providing opportunities for exchanging these other more salient rewards. Going over and helping a fellow worker with his task might simply be an excuse for chatting with him and exchanging social support.

Since social benefits have no exact price, and since the utility of a given benefit cannot be clearly separated from that of other rewards derived from a social association, it seems difficult to apply the economic principles of maximizing utilities to social exchange.[7] The impersonal economic market is designed to strip specific commodities of these entangling alliances with other benefits, so to speak, and thus to make possible rational choices between distinct alternatives with a fixed price. Even in economic exchange, however, the significance of each alternative is rarely confined to a single factor, which confounds rational decision-making; people's job choices are affected by working conditions as well as salaries, and their choices of merchants, by the atmosphere in a store as well as the quality of the merchandise. Although the systematic study of social exchange poses distinctive problems, the assumptions it makes about the maximization of utilities implicit in choice behavior are little different from those made by the economist in the study of consumption.

In production and in marketing, profit is at a maximum "when the marginal cost and the marginal revenue are equal,"[8] and since both these quantities are defined in dollars, an unequivocal criterion for maximizing exists. But in consumption maximizing involves equating the marginal utilities obtained from expending an extra dollar in alternative ways, and this comparison of utilities poses, in principle, the same problem the study of social exchange does. Indeed, economists typically do not attempt to measure utilities directly to ascertain whether they are equated but simply infer that they are from the distribution of consumer expenditures or from other economic decisions. Thus, if a scientist accepts an academic job at a lower salary than he could command in industry, the so-called psychic income he obtains from his university position is assumed to equal or exceed in utilities the difference in salary. Similar inferences can be made from the observable conduct in social exchange. Moreover, these inferences about the value the social rewards exchanged have for individuals can be used to derive testable hypotheses concerning the group structures that will emerge among them and the structural changes that will occur under various conditions, as will be exemplified in chapter seven [of Exchange and Power in Social Life].

Impressionistic observation suggests that people usually discharge their social obligations, even though there is no binding contract that can be enforced, in contrast to the contractual obligations in economic exchange, which can be enforced through legal sanctions. The reason is that failure to discharge obligations has a number of disadvantageous consequences, several of which do not depend on the existence of a norm of reciprocity. Suppose an individual to whom a neighbor has repeatedly lent some tools fails to reciprocate by doing his neighbor a favor when an opportunity arises. He can hardly borrow the tools again next time he needs them, and should he be brash enough to ask for them the neighbor may be reluctant to lend them to him. The neighbor is also likely to become less friendly toward an individual who refuses to do favors after he accepts some.   Besides, the neighbor will probably distrust him in the future and, for example, be disinclined to trust him to repay for having their common fence painted but ask him for payment in advance.   Chances are, moreover, that the neighbor will tell other neighbors about the ingratitude of this individual, with the result that this person's general reputation in the community suffers.   Specifically, the neighbor's complaints will prompt numerous others to think less well of him, to hesitate to do him favors, and generally to distrust him.   The first neighbor and the others have reason to act in this manner even if they were only concerned with protecting their own self-interest.   The existence of a norm of reciprocity among them further reinforces their disapproval of him and their disinclination to do favors for him, now as a punitive reaction against a violator of a moral standard as well as to protect their own interest.   Finally, an internalized norm of reciprocity would make him feel guilty if he fails to discharge his obligations, subjecting him to sanctions that are independent of any actions of others.   The multiple penalties that failure to discharge social obligations evokes constitute pressures to discharge them.

CONDITIONS OF EXCHANGE

A variety of conditions affect processes of social exchange: the stage in the development and the character of the relationship between exchange partners, the nature of the benefits that enter into the transactions and the costs incurred in providing them, and the social context in which the exchanges take place.

The initial offer of a favor to a stranger or an acquaintance is of special significance, whether it takes the form of a few friendly words, a cigar, the first invitation to one's home, or some helpful suggestions.   It entails the risk of rejection of the offer itself and the risk of rejection of the overture implied by it through failure to reciprocate and enter into a friendly relationship.   By taking these risks, an individual brings to an end the complete indifference between himself and another and forces on the other a choice of two alternatives, as Lévi-Strauss has noted: "From now on it must become a relationship either of cordiality or hostility."[9]   The offer cannot be refused without being insulting, and acceptance of it invites some friendly exchange, if only of greetings and a few cordial words.   Simmel took the extreme view that the first kindness of a person can never be fully repaid, because it alone is a spontaneous gesture of good will for another, whereas any future favor is prompted by the obligation to reciprocate.[10]

The establishment of exchange relations involves making investments that constitute commitments to the other party.   Since social exchange requires trusting others to reciprocate, the initial problem is to prove oneself trustworthy.   We have already seen how the gradual expansion of exchange transactions promotes the trust necessary for them.   As individuals regularly discharge their obligations, they prove themselves trustworthy of further credit.   Moreover, the investments an individual has made by fostering a friendly relation with another, in which it is easy to exchange services of various sorts, and by neglecting to cultivate other associates, who might constitute alternative sources of such services, commit him to the relationship. His commitment, which would make it disadvantageous for him to abandon the partnership in favor of another, gives the other additional reasons to trust him not to evade his obligations in their relationship.[11] Both partners gain advantages from a stable exchange partnership, but the greater commitment of one constitutes a particular advantage for the other. Here again we find, as we did in the discussion of social integration and in that of love, a situation that resembles a mixed game with some common and some conflicting interests—the common ones in the partnership and the conflicting ones concerning who makes the greater commitment. The partner with fewer alternative opportunities tends to be more dependent on and committed to the exchange relation than the other.

Since trust is essential for stable social relations, and since exchange obligations promote trust, special mechanisms exist to perpetuate obligations and thus strengthen bonds of indebtedness and trust. In the Kula expeditions of the Trobriand islanders, for example, the ceremonial gifts received cannot be returned until the next expedition many months later,[12] and while exchanges between partners who live in proximity to one another are more frequent, hasty reciprocation here too is condemned as improper.[13] In our society, similarly, the custom of giving Christmas gifts prevents us from reciprocating for an unexpected Christmas present until a year later or, at least, until another suitable occasion arises. Although an invitation to a party can be repaid any time, it is not proper to do so too promptly. Generally, posthaste reciprocation of favors, which implies a refusal to stay indebted for a while and hence an insistence on a more businesslike relationship, is condemned as improper. "Excessive eagerness to discharge an obligation is a form of ingratitude."[14] Social bonds are fortified by remaining obligated to others as well as by trusting them to discharge their obligations for considerable periods.

The nature of social rewards can be distinguished along several lines. First, some social rewards cannot be bartered in exchange, notably intrinsic attraction to a person, approval of his opinions and judgments, and respect for his abilities, because their significance rests on their being spontaneous reactions rather than calculated means of pleasing him. These evaluations of a person or his attributes reward him only if he has reason to assume that they are *not* primarily motivated by the explicit intention to reward him. Rewarding actions, in contrast to evaluations, can be bartered in social exchange since the fact that they are intended as inducements does not infringe on their inherent value as rewards. Social acceptance in a group to which a person is attracted, instrumental services of various kinds, and compliance with his wishes constitute rewards for him even if he knows that they are furnished in exchange for benefits expected of him. Second, within each of these two categories, rewards that are intrinsic to the association between individuals, such as personal attraction and social acceptance, can be distinguished from extrinsic ones, such as approval of decisions or opinions and instrumental services. Third, rewards that individuals may mutually supply for each other, as the four types just mentioned, can be distinguished from those that are necessarily unilateral, which are manifest in the general respect for a person that bestows superior prestige on him and in the prevailing compliance with his requests that bestows superior power on him. The six types of rewards delineated can be presented in this schema:

	Intrinsic	*Extrinsic*	*Unilateral*
Spontaneous Evaluations	Personal attraction	Social approval*	Respect-prestige†
Calculated Actions	Social acceptance*	Instrumental services*	Compliance-power†

* Entails investment costs for suppliers in addition to those needed to establish the social association.
† Entails the direct cost of subordination for suppliers.

The person who receives rewards from associating with another has an incentive to furnish inducements to the other to continue the association, and this is also the case if the rewards are spontaneous reactions that must not be bartered in exchange. Since it is rewarding for an individual to associate with others who accord him high respect, he is likely to provide sufficient inducements for them to continue the association unless he suspects them of simulating respect in order to obtain benefits from him. Positive evaluations of a person must not be bartered lest they cease to be accepted as genuine and thus lose their significance, but they do make social associations rewarding and worth some cost to the recipient and consequently enable the evaluator to reap some benefits from associating with him. Men sometimes take advantage of this fact and express approval of another in a calculating manner to obtain benefits from him in exchange, but this strategy of the sycophant can succeed only as long as its calculating intent remains hidden.

The cost incurred in providing social rewards in exchange for others may be thought of as "investment cost," "direct cost," and "opportunity cost." Investments in time and effort are necessary to acquire the skills required for furnishing many instrumental services, and such investments are also necessary to command respect for one's approval and thereby make it valuable for others. A group's investments that benefit its membership determine the value of social acceptance in the group and the contributions it can demand in exchange for acceptance. The supply of other social rewards usually entails no investments beyond those needed to establish the exchange relations. The most distinctive direct cost in social transactions is the subordination involved in expressing respect or manifesting compliance, that is, in rewarding another with prestige or with power. The most general cost incurred in supplying any social reward is the time required to do so in social associations. Since the significance of this time depends on the alternatives foregone by devoting it to a given exchange relation, it may be considered an opportunity cost. Time is not the only limited resource that may have to be withdrawn from alternative uses, thereby engendering opportunity costs, although it is probably the most widely significant one in social life.

The rewards an individual obtains from a social association cost him the opportunity to devote the time (and other limited resources) spent to another association where he could have obtained rewards. The mutual support in a love relationship and the social acceptance in an artistic circle, the endeavors made to court the approval of others or to command their respect, the efforts devoted to providing benefits to others in exchange for needed services or for compliance with one's wishes—all entail the cost of alternatives foregone as the result of the decision to expend time and energy in these associations rather than elsewhere. This time and effort could have been spent to obtain the same kinds of rewards from another source, possibly at less cost or of a better quality, and it could have been spent to obtain different rewards. As long as these alternatives appear tempting, individuals are inclined to explore them, but once they decide on what they consider the best alternative, they are likely to become committed to an exchange partnership and stop further exploration, with the result that they may not be able to take advantage of better opportunities that do become available.

If an individual obtains gratification from doing something in social interaction that is also gratifying for his associate, he provides the associate with a social reward without any cost to himself. Although there is a cost in time for him, this cost should be allocated to the reward he himself experiences rather than to the one he simultaneously furnishes the other. Such costless rewards are typical of mutual love, where each individual derives gratification in the very process of furnishing it to the other, but they also can be observed in instrumental associations. Giving advice to a colleague costs time and effort, and the colleague is expected to recompense the consultant for this cost, at least by expressing appreciation and respect for his expert counsel. Instead of asking for advice, however, a competent individual who encounters complex problems may tell his colleagues about his interesting case, as was actually often observed in a study of government officials.[15]

Such discussions of intricate problems in the presence of fellow experts can be considered consultations in disguise. The attentive listening and appreciative comments of his colleagues provide the speaker, in effect, with needed advice and confirmation by indicating to him whether he is on the right track while "thinking out loud," thus helping him to arrive at decisions that he might not have been able to make when alone. Since listening to and commenting on an interesting presentation of a complex case is instructive and enjoyable, the implicit advice of the listeners does not entail any cost to them for which the speaker would be obligated to recompense them. He obtains advice free, except for the indirect cost of his investment in his competence, without which he could not present complex discussions others find stimulating enough to want to hear.[16]

What exactly is it that enables a person to obtain social rewards from associates without incurring obligations to reciprocate? It is basically the fact that their actions that reward him are experienced by them not as a net cost but as a net gain, that is, as sufficiently rewarding to themselves to motivate them to engage in these actions.[17] The perception of relative advantage of the exchange partners, however, may complicate the situation. For example, if one neighbor enjoys chopping wood and another wants to have his wood chopped, the first can provide the other with a service by an action from which he directly profits himself (chopping wood), and vice versa (letting wood be chopped), so that initially neither is indebted to the other.   But if either or both should come to think that the advantages one gains from the transaction are greater than those of the other, one will feel obligated to supply additional favors to the other, who will feel justified in accepting or even requesting favors.   The *comparative* net advantage one person gains from an action that also rewards another is what frees the other from the obligation to reciprocate for the rewards he receives.

In the analysis of the cost in an exchange transaction, it is important to differentiate between the cost to A of obtaining a given reward and the cost to B of supplying it.   If B's cost in alternatives foregone are amply repaid by the gratification he receives in the very process of rewarding A, he can supply these rewards at no net cost to himself.   Nevertheless, obtaining these rewards may be costly for A, because the disproportionate benefits he derives obligate him to make a return to B at some expense to himself.   An individual can cut his costs by obtaining rewards from actions of others that are profitable rather than costly to them, if this is possible.[18]   Thus, consulting others indirectly by telling them about difficult problems is a more economical method of receiving help with decision-making than directly asking for advice, but only experts whose discussions of problems others find stimulating can avail themselves of this method of obtaining help without becoming obligated to reciprocate for it.   Social exchange can also be made less costly and more profitable by supplying social rewards that simultaneously benefit and obligate several others.   The person who makes important contributions to an entire group illustrates this way of multiplying the benefits produced by one's actions and so does, to a lesser extent, the individual who mediates disagreements between friends.   A manipulative case of this type is illustrated by Proust:

> He would now and then agree to act as an intermediary between two of his friends who had quarrelled, which led to his being called the most obliging of men.   But it was not sufficient for him to appear to be doing a service to the friend who had come to him to demand it; he would represent to the other the steps which he was taking to effect a reconciliation as undertaken not at the request of the first friend but in the interest of the second, an attitude of the sincerity of which he had never any difficulty in convincing a listener already influenced by the idea that he saw before him the "most serviceable of men."   In this fashion, playing in two scenes turn about, what in stage parlance is called "doubling" two parts, he never allowed his influence to be in the slightest degree imperilled, and the services which he rendered constituted not an expenditure of capital but a dividend upon some part of his credit.[19]

The social context in which exchange transactions take place affects them profoundly in several respects, which must be briefly adumbrated in this discussion of the conditions of exchange, although a more complete analysis of the interrelations between exchange processes and social structure is reserved for later chapters.   First, even if we abstract the exchange transactions in a single pair, they are influenced by the "role-set" of each partner,[20] that is, by the role relations either has by virtue of occupying the social status relevant to the exchange, since these role relations govern the alternative opportunities of the two. The larger circle of acquaintances of the members of a clique who exchange invitations, for example, or the dating opportunities of two lovers, define the alternatives foregone by each and hence affect the cost each incurs in order to obtain rewards from his present association.

Second, the entire exchange transactions in a group determine a prevailing rate of exchange, and this group standard puts pressure on any partnership whose transactions deviate from it to come into line. These are not normative pressures in the sense of moral standards supported by group sanctions that enforce conformity but pressures resulting from existing opportunities. The demand for and supply of certain mechanical skills in a group of factory workers, for instance, influence how much respect and other benefits a highly skilled worker can command on the average for helping others with their tasks. Considerable departures from this average in a given exchange partnership create strong inducements for one of the partners to abandon it, inasmuch as more profitable opportunities for social interaction are elsewhere available to him. Third, potential coalitions among the weaker members of a collectivity tend to restrain its stronger members from fully exploiting their advantageous position in exchange transactions. Fourth, the differences in power to which exchange processes typically give rise in a group subsequently modify these processes, since established power enables an individual to compel others to provide services without offering a fair return, although the danger of the formation of coalitions to destroy his power may discourage its exploitative use.

Finally, the social situation exerts a subtle but important influence by making the transactions in a given exchange relation part of other exchanges that occur in the background and that may, nevertheless, be the more salient ones. A person may give a waiter a large tip to elicit the approval of his companions at the table for his generosity, not primarily to earn the waiter's gratitude. A worker may kindly help a newcomer and refuse any return offered because he wants to impress his supervisor or senior colleagues. If we look only at the apparent exchange in these cases, the individual appears to be uninterested in profiting from it, but the reason is that he is oriented toward a different exchange, and his unselfish behavior in one exchange is designed to profit him in another by winning him the approval of significant others. The opposite type of case is that of the individual who fully exploits every advantage to extract maximum instrumental benefits from some exchange relations in disregard of the disapproval he thereby incurs, because he needs these benefits to court the approval of other parties who are more significant for him. In either case, the immediate exchange processes cannot be understood without taking into account other exchange transactions that impinge on them.

People want to gain approval and they want to gain advantage in their social associations, and the two desires often come into conflict, since heedless pursuit of advantage tends to elicit disapproval. The multigroup affiliations of individuals in modern societies help to resolve this conflict. The resources needed to win social approval in some groups are typically acquired in other groups whose approval is less significant and can be dispensed with, as mentioned earlier.   The money the businessman earns driving hard bargains that make him more feared than liked among his business associates enables him to earn the approval of his friends with his generosity.   The politician humbly ingratiates himself with voters in order to achieve a position where he can wield power.   The miserly secretary saves all year despite the ridicule of her companions in the hope of impressing another social circle with her affluence during her vacations.   The juvenile delinquent willingly draws upon himself the condemnation of the larger community for acts that command respect in his gang.   Multigroup affiliation entails social costs, as shown by the last illustration, particularly.   It enables individuals in modern society to make the informal, and partly even the formal, sanctions of the community at large ineffective by organizing themselves into subcollectivities whose social approval alone is considered important.

Notes

1. Ludwig von Mises refers to this type as autistic exchange.   "Making one-sided presents without the aim of being rewarded by any conduct on the part of the receiver or of a third person is autistic exchange.   The donor acquires the satisfaction which the better condition of the receiver gives to him.   The receiver gets the present as a God-sent gift.   But if presents are given in order to influence some people's conduct, they are no longer one-sided, but a variety of interpersonal exchange between the donor and the man whose conduct they are designed to influence." *Human Action*, New Haven: Yale University Press, 1949, p. 196.
2. Alvin W. Gouldner, "The Norm of Reciprocity," *American Sociological Review*, 25 (1960), 161–178, esp. p. 176.
3. This is not completely correct for an employment contract or for the purchase of professional services, since the precise services the employee or professional will be obligated to perform are not specified in detail in advance.   Economic transactions that involve services generally are somewhat closer to social exchange than the pure type of economic exchange of commodities or *products* of services.
4. B. Malinowski [*Argonauts of the Western Pacific*, New York: Dutton, 1961], pp. 95–96.
5. See Erving Goffman, *Asylums*, Chicago: Aldine, 1962, pp. 274–286.
6. See Blau, *The Dynamics of Bureaucracy* (2d ed.), University of Chicago Press, 1963, pp. 129–131.
7. George C. Homans [*Social Behavior*, New York: Harcourt, 1961], p. 72.
8. Kenneth E. Boulding, *Economic Analysis* (3d ed.), New York: Harper, 1955, p. 552.
9. Claude Lévi-Strauss, "The Principle of Reciprocity," in Lewis A. Coser and Bernard Rosenberg, *Sociological Theory*, New York, Macmillan, 1957, p. 90.
10. Georg Simmel, *Soziologie*, Leipzig: Duncker und Humblot, 1908, pp. 595–596.
11. Commitment has been conceptualized as a side bet that promotes trust by making it disproportionately disadvantageous for a person to violate an agreement; see Thomas C. Schelling, *The Strategy of Conflict*, Cambridge: Harvard University Press, 1960, Chapter ii; and Howard S. Becker, "Notes on the Concept of Commitment," *American Journal of Sociology*, 66 (1960), 32–40.
12. Malinowski, *op. cit.*, pp. 210–211.
13. *Ibid.*, p. 96.

14. François La Rochefoucauld, *The Maxims*, London: Oxford University Press, 1940, p. 73 (No. 226).

15. Blau, *op. cit.*, pp. 132–135.

16. He also incurs a cost in time but not an obligation to reciprocate. Individuals who ask advice pay, at least, respect to the superior ability of others implicitly by requesting their advice. In contrast, individuals who present discussions on the complex problems in their cases *earn* respect by doing so successfully, although they do incur the risk of losing respect should their analysis prove incorrect, and this discourages the less competent individuals from resorting to this practice.

17. Although I emphasized in my study the significance of a person's *intention* of rewarding another in this connection (*ibid.*, p. 134), I now think that the crucial factor is not his intent but whether he himself profits in the very process of rendering a service to the other.

18. He will cut his cost, although not to nothing, even if they profit less than he does from these actions.

19. Marcel Proust, *Remembrance of Things Past*, New York: Random House, 1934, Vol. I, 703.

20. For the concept of role-set, see Robert K. Merton, *Social Theory and Social Structure* (2d ed.), Glencoe: Free Press, 1957, pp. 369–370.

Part Three | Concerning Concreteness

If in a short time we cannot reach the same stage of reason and morality in the control of society and of our own natures that we have reached in technology, the social order will collapse. We should be neither sociologists nor even scientists if we were willing to let the matter rest with such a general diagnosis and vague prophecy.[1]

KARL MANNHEIM

. . . we seem to have lost our taste, our nerve, and our imagination for conceiving new forms of social relationships, new structures of social organization and community . . .[2]

ALVIN GOULDNER

Karl Mannheim says that potent sociological knowledge is urgently needed and that this knowledge must be applied. Alvin Gouldner calls for imaginative consideration of alternatives to existing social structures. We live in an age when knowledge in the physical and biological sciences is almost mass-produced. This knowledge, furthermore, is quickly utilized.[3] But the social sciences— sociology in particular—have not fared well. To be sure, in recent years there has been great expansion of sociological research that relates to the concrete world in which we live.[4] In recent years, also, sociologists have increasingly been asked to give advice on policy matters. But the results have been mixed. Sociologists have not made major contributions toward solving the crucial problems of our time. A popular view of this situation is expressed by Martin Mayer: "Action sociology . . . has a relatively short and almost entirely unhappy history."

There are many complexities involved, not only in the mechanics of developing theory about concrete reality, but in the determination of the place of sociological theory in relation to the concrete world. There is the problem of determining the best *type* of theory for immediate relevance to concrete reality, and the problem of actually applying theory to concrete reality. The development of theory ties in with the hoary sociology-of-knowledge question: What are the social conditions under which valid sociological knowledge emerges? This question is too broad for our purposes. Karl Deutsch and Richard Meier suggest in the following pages that one can gather a large amount of data in a relatively orderly and sophisticated manner and thereby achieve significant practical explanatory power. The assumption is that practical, useful generalizations are bound to emerge. Similarly, James Ridgeway suggests that game theory and computer simulation provide a good deal of bread-and-butter theory for the practitioner who is expected to solve tangible problems. This touches on the second issue: which type of theory is best suited for dealing with concrete reality? This sort of theory need not have the analytic purity of a framework; different orientations can be combined. In fact, concretists may operate without any clear framework. The models may be composites of variables that happen to work when explored through a computer-simulation process. The following selections exhibit eclectic use of existing frameworks, as well as the courage to organize data even when no clear framework or model is available.

A discussion of concretely usable theory should consider the history and fate of concretist theorizing in sociology. There have been many attempts to build sociological theory around publicly recognized problems. There have been, and still are, flourishing sociological efforts at developing theory applicable to such problems as facilitating the adjustment of immigrants to America, increasing marital happiness, and producing penal reforms. The most pressing problems of the present era are poverty and racial exploitation. If the past is any guide, current problems will continue to receive the enthusiastic attention of researchers until new problems become popular. But the payoff in new theories will be meager. The reason for this theoretical paucity surely includes the fact that a pressing practical problem must be drastically refocused if it is to serve as an important conceptual problem. All too frequently the sociologist is expected to accept the layman's version of the problem; often he merely dresses it up in technical language. There is something strongly seductive in crushingly real problems. The problems speak so loudly that it is often difficult to hear the conceptual confusion. The present inability of sociologists to devise viable concrete services to society may be due chiefly to inadequate analytic theories—theories that have validity in abstractly conceived systems, but are then available for adaptation to the concrete world by the applied sociologist. Stated differently, the professional theorist's posture toward knowledge is fundamentally different from that of the applied scientist. This distinction needs some further exploration, because it is a central aspect of the process of applying theory to concrete reality.

Much valid scientific knowledge has been acquired through rigorous work with abstractions. This involves both focus on aspects of reality rather than full reality and a distinctively detached posture toward the world of daily living. Knowledge of the concrete world involves a very different challenge. It includes translating abstract knowledge into concretely usable knowledge, tackling problems for which completely adequate knowledge seldom exists, constantly accepting feedback for the purpose of reformulating theory and practical strategies, and developing a posture toward social participation that combines rights and duties of the citizen with the expertise of the scientist.

The translation process involves the amalgamation of very different sorts of knowledge as one concentrates on a particular concrete problem; this requires definite skills. The physician who makes decisions about a patient must frequently utilize knowledge of anatomy, physiology, and biochemistry, while also considering the immediately available medical facilities, the patient's economic resources, customs and habits, social and cultural status, and emotional state. The doctor often takes all of these considerations into account quite routinely. His training has made him a specialist in the art of amalgamating different sorts of knowledge. In contrast, the "pure" scientist feels uncomfortable when different sorts of knowledge are mixed; he yearns to tackle one set of variables at a time and wants to keep his levels of analysis clearly separate. Translation and amalgamation processes have been fairly well developed in many fields—the businessman translates economic principles and combines them with a knowledge of psychological and cultural factors in the immediate situation; the engineer and cook are other translators and amalgamators.[5]

The practitioner often must act even when he knows that his information is incomplete. Where the pure scientist is apt to say "let's wait till we have more knowledge," the practitioner will say "let's go ahead and make the best use of the knowledge we have." These are different orientations that imply different conceptions of what usable knowledge is. Thus, Richard Meier's scheme of planning a society's progress is based on an assessment of knowledge very different from that underlying the schemes in Part I of this book, "Concerning Frameworks." There analytic congruences and conceptual purity were given first priority. In contrast, here we are given a version of things that seem to work. This is a kind of pragmatism, where one tries things out, is alert to indications of effectiveness, and accepts a variety of feedback for the purpose of changing one's approach. Eclecticism and flexibility are hallmarks. The scientific purist is apt to look down on such efforts as "mere" technology—cookbook science. The applied scientist, however, has different priorities. He is a doer, he is *in* the world, not a creator of theories *about* the world.

There are old debates among sociologists about the kind of social involvement that a sociologist should have. From Max Weber comes the admonition that sociology must try to be "value-free"; yet Max Weber's life is an illustration of the idea that a scientist can, apart from his scholarly work, actively attempt to influence society. One need not renounce the role of active citizen while being an active student of social processes. Yet, wrote Weber, one's *scholarly* pursuits should be separate and geared to the world of dispassionate objectivity. The debate continues. Indeed, there has probably been increasing polarization with respect to this issue. Conflict occurs in science, too, between those who stress the need for refining scientific techniques and those who call for the immediate assumption by scientists of their responsibility to society. All of this implies that there are significant links between knowledge usage and knowledge development. On the intellectual level, the debate centers on accusations that postures concerning social involvement are inherent in supposedly pure theoretical formulations. For instance, the structure-functionalists, with their interest in social systems and, therefore, social order, are allegedly supporting the *existing* order. The conflict theorists presumably are more concerned with the socially exploited and deprived, who see social structures and stability as social constraints that limit freedom. Or, in a view considered less charitable, the conflict theorists are part of a movement to help *create* the view that social structures are constraints and, therefore, intolerable.[6]

It is my view that the work of building frameworks and models requires a considerable degree of noninvolvement in the ongoing society. But building theories also includes work on the concrete level, and this usually includes active participation in social affairs. "Participation" can take the form of social engineering, social prediction, or policy-making. Sociologists participate far less in these matters than, say, economists. This is due at least partly to the relatively underdeveloped state of the field of sociology. Most work on the concrete level is geared to harnessing knowledge for tackling specific, concrete problems. This procedure involves the application of existing knowledge. It also involves developing knowledge about the harnessing process—the process of translating abstract knowledge into concrete usable form—and amalgamating knowledge assembled from different intellectual perspectives and, therefore, "stored" under different systems of intellectual "housekeeping."[7] Work at the concrete level is not centrally concerned with the process of developing systemic knowledge of the kind that is found in any one of the separate housekeeping units.

Finally, whereas the pure analytical scientist tries to study the world without influencing it, the applied scientist must be increasingly aware that he does influence the concrete world. For example, when game theory was being developed, it was thought to place far more importance on rationality than actually existed in the field of economics. This criticism may have been valid at the time. Now, however, business firms increasingly use game theory, including the type of rationality that game theory utilizes. It is as though "when the facts don't fit the theory, the *facts* change."[8] This situation raises great problems in the creation of analytic theory from which generalizations can be made. But it is often a fact-of-life that cannot be ignored.

MACROSCALE CONCRETENESS

The selections by Karl Deutsch and Bertram Gross set forth methods for developing a coherent body of data about society's ongoing state of affairs. Richard Meier's essay is also methodological, but his focus is on transforming traditional societies into modern societies. The selections by Reinhard Bendix, Seymour Lipset, and Harvey Cox are focused on specific concrete problems— the selection by Bendix on social classes in relation to various political processes, the selection by Lipset on values in relation to democracy, and the selection by Cox on bureaucracy in relation to work.

Karl Deutsch's suggestions for developing "data programs," which he offers in his selection, "The Theoretical Basis of Data Programs," are addressed to the problem of getting comparative sociology effectively under way. Comparative data should be made available on a relatively large scale so that modern data-handling techniques can be effectively used to test ideas. This would simplify the comparison of societies, which would be a significant step toward developing truly generalized sociological knowledge.

Bertram Gross' discussion of economic accounting on a national level in "The State of the Nation" gives an overview that a noneconomist can follow. His treatment goes beyond a narrowly conceived economic focus. Gross provides a method of social-system accounting that has not been fully explored by sociologists and that appears to have considerable potential for measuring the social pulse. Its objective is not merely to summarize the existing state of affairs, but to offer help in planning the future.

In "Open Systems for Growth and Development," Richard Meier summarizes a number of previous theories dealing with the use of knowledge in social planning. These are the "achievement-motivation" theory, social conflict theories, and the theory of the existence of an image of a desired future and the possibility of achieving that image. The assessment of these theories forms the underpinning of his own "information theory of development," which emphasizes information and knowledge as fundamental ingredients of societal structure. Information is regarded as a commodity that can be "created, transmitted, stored, accumulated, bought . . . lost" and handled quantitatively. His is a cybernetic theory that uses the production, flow, and management of knowledge as its principal ingredients. In terms of traditional disciplines, it is highly eclectic—physical and social sciences intertwine and rarely is one discipline allowed to stand very long as the focus on any one problem. The problems tend to be defined concretely; for example, the theory might be addressed to the question: "how does a country become modernized?" This concrete posture helps to define "real" issues in the world, to which the analytic scientist sometimes seems to be oblivious. Yet as the cybernetic approach becomes systematized, it too is apt to become increasingly analytic. This development is foreshadowed in some of the propositions that Meier offers.

Reinhard Bendix's essay, "Class Relations in an Age of Contract," deals with the quest of the poor for full-scale citizenship, especially as it evolved among the working classes in England during the eighteenth century. Although Bendix describes specific events, he is concerned with spelling out general principles rather than merely describing historical phenomena. He suggests that a thorough analysis of the data points to two processes essential to the attainment of full-scale citizenship: democratization and industrialization. Scholars have often assumed that these were fused. But Bendix calls attention to the modern "national community [where] the reciprocity of rights and duties is gradually extended and redefined." This reciprocal process does not, as Marx thought, depend only on economic and related social forces. It also depends on the "international position of the country," and on ideals about what "the proper distribution in the national community ought to be, and [on] the give and take of the political struggle." The theory is highly inductive. The general principles are processes that can be found in historical events. Their generality consists in the fact that they depict fundamental problems and socially developed answers that appear to be applicable to many countries. In Bendix's book from which the excerpt was taken, the basic problem considered is how to bring about a reasonable degree of participation by the total citizenry as countries become modern. This approach to theory is in the spirit of Max Weber. By thorough immersion in a great deal of historical material, the scholar may attempt to extract and describe the fundamental movements in societies. He is not satisfied with describing unique occurrences. Instead, he looks for comparable features in different social contexts, thus adding generalizing power to the description. The kinds of theoretical concepts that emerge—such as Weber's concept of bureaucratic organization—have proved to be very fruitful as guides to research. It is too early to tell whether Bendix's conception of the expansion of political participation will have an equally fruitful impact in the study of modernization processes.

The selection by Seymour Lipset on "Values and Democratic Stability" cites Britain, the United States, Germany, France, and Sweden to illustrate the different social conditions under which democracy can thrive. The analytic tools he uses are the value dichotomy of elitism-equilitarianism, and Parsons' pattern variables: universalism-particularism, diffuseness-specificity, and achievement-ascription. Lipset suggests that democracy can become stabilized under different circumstances, that is, that it can exist in different combinations of value patterns, as the values are incorporated in major social patterns, especially in the political and economic structures. Here, theory is used to clarify the morphology of one concrete phenomenon, democracy, as it occurs at different times and in different places. The fact that democracy is shown to have diverse structural characteristics when it occurs in various contexts illustrates the concretist use of theory, which takes into account the convergence of different forces impinging on the particular features that are being explained.

"The Bureaucratic Organization of Work," taken from Harvey Cox's *Secular City*, is about complex social organizations. The message is twofold. First, it states that we should discard our fear of the tribalism of our present world and our longing for an earlier society (that probably never existed) where the individual reigned supreme, where organizations did not exist, where man was free, self-reliant and virtuous. Second, it states that we should recognize that despite their shortcomings, organizations are "increasingly the basic integrating principle of our society" and that they have highly valuable features—flexibility, orientation toward the future, secularization, and limited claim on members—that can be utilized to make fundamental contributions to human welfare. But to accomplish these valued ends, people must become increasingly willing to participate in the fight for control and responsible use of organizations. From an unsentimental point of view, claims Cox, the organization is not inherently good or evil. Its impact can be manipulated. Cox's words were written before the appearance of the New Left movements that have, indeed, tried to wield influence on major organizations in many countries. As a piece of theoretical sociology, Cox's view enables us to take a given concrete social pattern such as the modern bureaucratic organization, and look outward, to see its divergent influences on the world around it. This is an obvious corollary to another concretist perspective, the study of convergence, which deals with the ways various social forces impinge on a particular social pattern or set of persons.

MICROSCALE CONCRETENESS

The sections by Geoffrey Vickers and James Ridgeway deal with the practical application of sociological knowledge. Vickers, speaking from personal experience as a designer and administrator of organizations, considers some problems that are "common to the regulation of all kinds of organization." Ridgeway, speaking as a critical observer of the social scene, gives an example of a new breed of social problem-solving firm. Milton Yinger and Peter Blau are concerned with certain conceptual distinctions which, in their respective views, need to be made as one tries to develop theory for the microsociological level. Both are *micro*sociological, since they focus on the individual in relation to the group; both are *sociological* (as opposed to psychological), since they distinguish the structure of the group from the characteristics of the persons (Yinger is more explicitly concerned with this matter than is Blau). The selections from both are classified as concretist theory because, in addition to offering theoretical formulations, they deal with the process of discovering theory. Yinger discusses problems in the measuring process, and linguistic confusions in sociology; Blau illustrates the act of reformulation of theory as new evidence becomes available. Along different lines, Edward Spicer and Alvin Gouldner both offer explanations of specific events that have occurred historically. Their explanations are theoretical because they evoke principles that have applicability to additional situations.

Geoffrey Vickers' "Criteria of Success of Social Organizations" illustrates that organizations may be involved in a great deal of flux and adaptive behavior—"optimizing-balancing"—while their form may persist. This situation is characterized by diversity and lack of adequate guidelines; multivalued choices are common and "all men of action hate it"—"the shadow of insecurity is never far away." A dilemma exists, not only because of the internal complexity of the large modern organization, but because of the fact that in a modern society, any organization has to adapt to a social environment that intrudes into it in complex ways. Finally, and most important, Vickers assumes that there are minimal, irreducible features within any system that limit its flexibility. Below the minimal level, the system will not survive. Thus, a "shortage of food, at a critical point, robs a creature of the energy to seek even the food it could get and starts a vicious circle which involves the whole complex system in dissolution." Vickers' examples are largely considered from the point of view of management of industrial firms. However, his discussion has pertinence for nonindustrial organizations and for people at all levels of organizations, not merely for administrators.

The selection "Social Problem-Solvers" by James Ridgeway describes how an aggressive young consulting firm is using mathematical modeling and, especially, computer simulation and human-player game-playing to analyze and to offer resolutions for a variety of complicated social problems. According to Ridgeway's description of these firms, there is excitement in the air. Important problems are being tackled; there is considerable confidence in the firm's work; "it could become big business." In relation to theory, the methods help to harness knowledge from very diverse sources. Computer simulation and human-player game-playing are particularly suited to the pragmatic eclecticism needed to deal with specific, concrete problems. The emphasis here is on the process of molding abstract knowledge to make it useful for doing work in the concrete world. It is conceivable that the same method could be used to manufacture rather systematic theories. The overview by Ridgeway is necessarily very brief. Probably the best exposure to the "real thing" is to be a participant in a game-playing situation. Indeed, sociologists are increasingly incorporating such participation into introductory courses.[9]

Milton Yinger, in his selection, "Individual Facts and Group Facts," discusses some very common areas of confusion. He notes that group characteristics are often thought to be merely aggregated personal characteristics. Whereas, "to be a peasant in a society where 80 percent of one's fellows share the same status is one thing; to be a peasant in a middle-class society is something else." Yinger considers a variety of factors that show the links as well as the disparities between personal and group characteristics. Another major point is his insistence that the scholar resist the temptation to explain the total range of facts by his particular model. For example, one must resist the tendency to think that behavior *is* the expression of personality, or that behavior *is* culture. Personality structure is deduced from ongoing behavior, and so are various other conceptually defined patterns.   Related to this fact is Yinger's emphasis on illustration of the idea that there is no "one-to-one relationship between social, cultural, and personality facts."   This points up the inherent abstractness and arbitrariness of theory, as well as the necessary limitations of any one type of theory as one looks at on-going behavior from a concretist point of view.

Peter Blau's selection, "Social Integration, Social Rank, and Processes of Interaction," focuses on one particular set of conceptual distinctions as it explains the process of gathering data about informal work groups: the differences between a member's *integration* in a group (his acceptance by others, his security in the group) and his *rank* in a group (his standing and his competitive advantage in the group).   Methodologically, the two points rest, respectively, on how frequently others originate interaction with the person, and how frequently the person originates activities for others.   Blau lets the reader in on a process of evolving theory.   He starts with a disparity between the findings of one study and those of a follow-up study done some years later.   Instead of dismissing one or both sets of findings as the products of methodological mistakes, Blau explores new explanations that fit both sets of findings.   This kind of reassessment is part of the scientific process.   It is sometimes dismissed as *post hoc* reasoning because, after all, the new categories were not incorporated into the original research design.   In contrast with Blau's article, and despite acknowledgment of the possibility of serendipitous, unanticipated findings in any ongoing research, the typically ritualistic way of writing research reports usually leaves out a frank assessment of one's own previous explanations.[10]

The anthropologist Edward Spicer, in his selection, "Social Structure and the Acculturation Process," emphasizes the idea that in studying cultures that are in contact with one another, serious attention should be paid to the patterns that evolve in the immediate social situation of acculturation.   Spicer speaks of fusion and syncretism.   He also speaks of traits from one culture being interpreted differently in other cultures, and of these cultural traits being affected by the social relationships in which they are transmitted.   It must be recognized that any concrete activity, any specific phenomenon that is studied, is made up of diverse forces that have converged and produced a new pattern.   This syncretism is an essential feature of concreteness.   It is well illustrated in Spicer's article.

Alvin Gouldner, in his selection, "Interpersonal Strains and Homosexuality," suggests that homosexuality among upper-class males in classical Greece solved certain fundamental problems.   Men of that era were expected to be highly competitive.   In that situation, friendship became a very ambivalent thing. Competitiveness interfered with friendship.   Yet competitiveness also created a need for allies and for the kind of support that comes from some sort of intimacy.   It was an age when extended kinship was declining and the family provided little intimacy.   Women were considered so inferior to men that they served a negligible function as intellectual and emotional intimates.   Homosexuality among males of the upper classes appears to have solved this "crisis of intimacy."   It provided emotional intimacy among persons who valued each other's social standing.   However, homosexuality was not a perfect solution, since it promoted such new problems as jealousies among men for favored youths, and new pressures toward competitiveness.

Gouldner's essay is an example of a structural explanation of a concrete phenomenon. To formulate such an explanation, one begins with a particular existing pattern (a culture complex, or social behavior that is relatively institutionalized) and judges it in terms of its contribution to solving problems that exist by virtue of strains in the existing social order. That is, the pattern is assessed in terms of its consequences for other existing patterns. But the explanation of the pattern is not conceived merely in terms of its contribution toward solving problems. The explanation takes into account any further impact that the pattern has on other patterns. The pattern that has served as a solution to problems resulting from strains in the social order frequently creates new strains. To the extent that one has a clear idea of the nature of the structures that exist and the nature of the interdependence among them, one can assess where and how great the strains are; for new patterns, one can predict where strains will appear. The new strains are, in a sense, the price that is paid for adopting the particular pattern, or solution. Sociologists are not very far along in developing calculations to specify such social prices. Another typical feature of the structural method of explanation is that hypothetical alternatives are explored: If a different solution to the problem were utilized, what would be the impact on the structures? This is part of specifying the social price of a particular course of action.

Ideally, structural explanations would be carried out with far greater precision. Rules of combination and rules of transformation of social structures would be developed. These would be applicable to the world of concrete social reality, enabling predictions to be made. Structural explanations differ from completely descriptive explanations in that they tend to sidestep the fortuitous and accidental occurrence. Structuralists search for order amid the flux, for calculable relationships among the components of the concrete world. The conviction is that the modesty of our ability to explain and predict is not due to the absence of order, but to the inadequacy of the existing conceptual tools. Here is the challenge.

Notes

1. Karl Mannheim, *Man and Society in an Age of Reconstruction*, New York: Harcourt, Brace & World, 1940, p. 50.
2. Alvin Gouldner, *Enter Plato*, New York: Basic Books, 1966, p. 294.
3. See, for example, Don K. Price, *The Scientific Estate*, Cambridge, Mass.: Belknap Press of Harvard University, 1968.
4. For a review of such research, see Paul F. Lazarsfeld *et al.*, eds., *The Uses of Sociology*, New York: Basic Books, 1967.
5. The cook's main science mentor is the nutritionist. In organizations that are science-oriented, such as hospitals and schools, one often finds ignorance of the translation process, presumably because it is not purely scientific. Such organizations sometimes place nutritionists in charge of kitchens—with well-known results!

6. The conflict point of view has much in common with the progressive ethos in which, according to Oscar Gross, "man—the individual . . . is virtuous. . . . But interest groups are self-seeking, and parties corrupt. . . . Direct democracy, if feasible, would be best. . . ." Cited from Oscar Gross, "The Literature of American Government," *Commentary*, June 1966, p. 70.

7. For a more complete sociological analysis of knowledge translation, see Fred E. Katz, "The Third Culture," in Milton Albrecht (ed.) *Studies in Sociology*, State University of New York, Buffalo Studies, December 1967.

8. From a lecture by D. M. Winch at McMaster University, Hamilton, Ontario, February 28, 1968.

9. See, for example, William A. Gamson, *SIMSOC*, New York: Free Press, 1969.

10. For a rather complete break with the ritualistic way of reporting research, see James D. Watson, *The Double Helix*, New York: New American Library, 1968. For an informal report on research in sociology, see Phillip E. Hammond, ed., *Sociologists at Work*, New York: Basic Books, 1964.

Macroscale Concreteness

24. The Theoretical Basis of Data Programs
Karl W. Deutsch

. . . What is the nature of data that we can most hopefully expect to use for [the] dialogue between data and theories? Four kinds seem in the forefront at the moment. The first are *aggregative data*, the kind of data which in the first approximation one can get out of libraries and statistical offices. These are census statistics, economic and trade statistics, price statistics, budget data, and voting data. All these are public and, to some extent, the task of gathering these data has already been done by governmental or private institutions for purposes of their own. The task of the scholar then is first to find out something of the bias in the selection, the probable error margins, the inaccuracies, and the possibility of supplementing these data; but the main intellectual effort has then to be spent upon the analysis of the data which are already gathered. Many of the nineteenth-century political and social theories in the grand manner were built up with the help of such data, such as Werner Sombart's hypothesis of the declining importance of foreign trade with industrial development and economic growth, a thesis which now seems to be confirmed long after Sombart's time.[1]

The second type are *sample survey data* which have given us a whole world of new evidence and, in addition, a major tool for closing the gaps in the aggregative data.[2] Sample surveys are divided into the polling techniques of asking a very

From Richard L. Merritt and Stein Rokkan (eds.), *Comparing Nations: The Use of Quantitative Data in Cross-National Research* (New Haven, Conn., 1966), pp. 41–54, by permission of Yale University Press. Copyright © 1966 by Yale University.

few questions of very many people, and the depth surveys where very few people are asked many questions in series of interviews which may stretch over fifteen hours.[3]

The third type of data stem from *content analysis*, as discussed above [in Merritt and Rokkan (eds.), *Comparing Nations: The Use of Quantitative Data in Cross-National Research*].

Finally there are the *cultural data* which cultural anthropologists or the perceptive literary scholar can uncover. The configurations of symbols, the configurations of cultures are examples, and so are the psychiatrist's evidence, the anthropologist's evidence, the evidence of the student of literature.

Several other needs are apparent. One is the need for the systematic correlation of these data. We do not even know, for instance, how well the Adorno F-scale correlates with the Minnesota Personality Inventory. We suffer from the curse of enforced originality which makes it a crime for a graduate student to replicate somebody else's experiment and forces the unhappy man to think up a new wrinkle on every experiment. I wish we could get an interuniversity agreement that we expect everybody who earns a degree to do two things: first, to replicate honestly one experiment in social science and then, if he must, invent a new one. If physicists and chemists had not replicated each other's experiments, they would still be in the age of alchemy.

Just as we do not have replication, we do not have intercorrelation among different tests. There is, for instance, very little correlation between what appears in government statistics and what is found in sample surveys, although such work is now being begun. For a sample of Turkish voters, for example, the researcher usually takes the government's statistics as a yardstick for knowing whether his sample was correctly drawn. It may be that the sample was right in the first place and the government statistics were wrong. But we will not know when a particular country's official statistics are inaccurate, deliberately or not, until we have sampled about 50 countries and compared these sample data with the aggregative data in the statistical yearbooks.

We need to know more than we do now about the relationship between the few questions answered on mass surveys and the many questions answered on depth interviews. For instance, we have some questions asked about anti-Semitism in Germany on mass surveys, and some attempts to make depth studies of anti-Semites; we also have similar materials for the United States. But I have not seen a systematic attempt to correlate the number of percentage of "off-the-cuff" anti-Semitic answers given on a quick survey with deep-seated anti-Semitic attitudes as revealed in a depth interview. The same, of course, is true of all ethnic and race prejudices and discrimination. It is conceivable that people who give superficially a prejudiced answer on a survey may only be conformists, and less than half of them may actually have deep-seated racial prejudices. Although the political and social implications are very large, we do not yet know very much about these processes.[4]

Similarly we do not know what the correlation is between attitudes given by opinion surveys and attitudes revealed in content analysis. If we knew for ten countries, which had both surveys and mass media, whether and to what extent a frequency of achievement aspiration or achievement needs revealed in depth interviews among this elite, then we could make at least some guesses for ten other countries where we have only content analysis but no surveys.

And we do not know yet what the correlation is between a cultural pattern—for instance, of a Weberian "Protestant spirit" or an African *negritude*—and particular, measurable traits emerging in content analyses. It may turn out, for instance, that there is no discoverable difference between the distribution of symbols in the communication of Leopold Senghor of Senegal, who is an exponent of cultural *negritude*, and those of the average educated French radical.

STATISTICAL TECHNIQUES AND DISTRIBUTIONS

One of the easiest things to be done—it can be done without machines, but must have loving care—is to get the rank order distribution of several variables. This already will begin to give us, oddly enough, a style of thought and some political implications. We may think of the 100 or more nations of the world as a fascinating multitude. If we rank order them by population, however, it turns out that more than one half of mankind lives under four governments. Eventually we shall have two tables (see Table 1) for each rank order profile. The first table should be for all the units for which we have data. The second table should be for a standardized ensemble of units, including, let us say, all countries in the United Nations as well as those which have been proposed seriously for membership and would be in the United Nations had not some other member nation vetoed their membership. This would bring in for statistical purposes West Germany, the East German regime, North and South Korea, mainland China, and possibly others. A universe of 133 countries with effectively operating governments would enable us to eliminate from consideration many of the small units which clutter up the statistics and distort the median and average values of the distribution. As Table 1 suggests, we cut greatly the median and average values for many series by inflating the number of units from 133 to 218.

Using a standardized set of units has operational importance. If we can make world leaders and social scientists aware of the fact that, for example, half of the world's population is in four countries, then they may realize that international agreements among perhaps eight or ten of the most populous countries will go far toward adequate coverage for atomic test bans or for international economic cooperation or for getting rid of a great deal of slavery and of racial peonage or race discrimination.

Often the political, social, and educational tasks of the world become different in definition once you think of them; the same is true of intracountry variations. In the days when Britain wanted to point out that India could not be independent, it was a favorite device of language surveys to say that India had 212 languages and dialects. On closer inspection it turns out that almost 200 of these are lesser known dialects on the Tibet-Burma border, with little or no political and economic significance, and that something like 80 or 90 per cent of the Indian people are covered by fourteen languages. Fourteen languages are still a handful, but they are a good deal fewer than two hundred. Now we are getting statement after statement that an African country has twenty or thirty native languages or dialects. Upon investigation of frequency distributions it usually turns out that bilingualism is often present. Considerations of this sort shed light upon such important problems as the extent to which elementary education should be offered in the mother tongue rather than an alien language.

Table 1   World Population (1961)

		UNIVERSE OF 218 COUNTRIES		STANDARDIZED LIST OF 133 COUNTRIES	
Rank	Country	Population (in Millions)	As Per Cent of Total	Population (in Millions)	As Per Cent of Total
1	China (M)	694	22.7%	694	22.8%
2	India	442	14.4	442	14.5
3	U.S.S.R.	218	7.1	218	7.2
4	U.S.	184	6.0	184	6.1
			50.2%		50.6%
	Remaining countries	1521	49.8	1503	49.4
	Total	3059	100.0%	3041	100.0%
	Mean	13.9		22.9	
	Median	1.6		5.5	

Source: Bruce M. Russett *et al.*, *World Handbook of Political and Social Indicators* (New Haven, Yale University Press, 1964), pp. 18–21; and data in the files of the Yale Political Data Program.

To be more precise, we would like to know what the actual mathematical shape of such rank order curves are, or rather what mathematical model will fit which curve most closely—the Zipf distribution, for example, the Yule distribution, or other.[5] If we can find a mathematical distribution which fits set of phenomena fairly closely, we can perhaps interpolate some rough estimates of the figures for the countries for which we have no data. Alternatively, we can check whether particular countries are genuine deviants, or whether they have unusually imaginative statisticians, or whether the figure given happened to be just a misprint.

Finally, just as we should have one record or profile for all units as well as for the standardized universe of 133 countries, we also need a cumulative summation. This could be obtained for each variable by first ranking the countries in order of the variable, but then computing for each such rank order profile how many of the world's population are at or above each point as we go down the range of that particular variable. This is essentially the same as correlating each variable with population. The same procedure could then be followed for the cumulative percentages of the total amount of the specific variable covered by that particular rank order profile. Thus, in ranking countries in order of the ratio of foreign trade to Gross National Product, one computation should show how many per cent of the world's people live in countries whose foreign trade is at least, say, 35 per cent of their GNP, and another computation should show how many per cent of world exports are represented by this class of countries. A good mathematical and/or graphic method for presenting such relationships ought to be feasible and would tell us a great deal.[6]

Another way of looking at the distributions would be to get the geographic distribution of transactions both between countries and within countries. This would immediately permit us to test certain hypotheses. For instance, it is Myrdal's hypothesis that the national state is a major instrument for reducing intracountry inequalities, whereas it is the theory of Lenin that an empire is precisely the opposite, an engine for exacerbating and increasing intracountry differences between exploiting and exploited areas. It ought not to be too difficult, as we get enough data on intracountry variations, to find out whether on the whole most countries in the world now correspond more to Myrdal's model or to Lenin's model, or which model fits which countries best.

We could also find out more about the distribution of variables over time. We suspect that, at least between 1900 and 1960, intercountry differences have been increasing. We may find out, therefore, in many different ways, what an "alien," or alienated, political relationship is—that is, a relationship where variations, on the whole, seem to follow the regularities observed in international life; and what a national and integrative political community is, a community where the distribution of variables follows more regularly the patterns observed in modern advanced national states. This would give us a statistical definition of alienated communities or of deeply or fundamentally divided communities.

We could get other distributions. For instance, Alker and Russett have done very important and helpful work comparing systematically available techniques for the measurement of inequality used by certain statisticians—the Gini index, the Schutz coefficient, and others.[7] It ought to be one of the services of the Yale Political Data Program to provide what might be called "translation tables" between the precise measurements of the social scientist who has to keep his value commitment in the background (or who must, though he has values, be willing to make his evidence available to anyone, including those whose value commitments are different from his own) and the language of action, the language that the legislator or the public servant might understand, for instance, about the inequality of land tenure, or the inequality of legislative and electoral apportionment between districts.

Here again we can interpolate. If we know, for instance, the income shares for nine countries and distribute these among the different deciles of income from top to bottom, we can draw a Lorenz curve for each of these countries. In a Lorenz curve we measure vertically the per cent of incomes and horizontally the per cent of population. If every per cent of population received exactly the same per cent of income, the resulting plot would be a straight line at forty-five degrees. If in fact, the poor get a smaller share and the rich a larger one, the Lorenz curve will look more or less curved; the greater the inequality, the steeper the curvature of the resulting "boomerang." Even if we have only ten, or four, or three points—if really out of luck, only one or two—we could still fit a Lorenz curve to the few points we have, knowing that there could be a flattening in the middle indicating that the curve was wrong by a definite but moderate amount.

We could therefore arrive at estimates of inequality and, in addition, comparisons of the estimates of inequality between many different countries. In one country we will be told how much land the top one per cent of landholders own, and in the second country we will get the figure for the top five per cent; in the third country, for the top two-and-one-half per cent. By drawing Lorenz curves for all these countries we can arrive at estimated values, knowing that they carry error margins of some size; nevertheless, we make what previously were incomparable figures a great deal more comparable than they were before.

We can then go on from distribution functions to paired correlations. We can ask, first of all, if the overall correlations are significant or not. We can then ask for two quite different but related things which should be given in a standard manner: one number saying how *accidental* the correlation is, and a second number saying how strong it is. This is particularly important with small numbers. If you toss a coin twice and it comes up heads twice, the strength of the relationship, in a certain sense, is one hundred per cent; that is to say, if you assume that the coin is loaded in the direction of heads and it came up heads twice, you predict a very strong load. But since you have actually made only two tosses of the coin, the statistical significance of what you did is fairly low, and you may be dealing in fact with a perfectly true coin.

Quite often these two descriptions of correlations are confused. Some studies give the significance level of the findings but do not indicate for how many per cent of the observed variation the findings actually account. It is quite possible to have a factor which is based on so many cases that it is significant almost beyond peradventure of a doubt. Only once in a thousand times would you get such a factor by chance; nevertheless, this factor may account for no more than ten per cent—or even for only two per cent—of the observed variation in the outcome. This is quite different from another factor which is significant only at the five or ten per cent level but which, if it exists at all, would explain thirty or forty per cent of the outcome. We do not as yet have a highly satisfactory standardized system of notation for reporting such data.

We may find that the correlation between two variables is nonlinear and is different for different parts of the range of one of them. As numbers increase, the slope of the regression may change sharply. Thus, if one of the two correlated variables is income, it may be that among the poor, correlation is very weak; among the rich, it is very strong; and somewhere in the middle, it is about even. There may be many paired variables where the correlation varies over parts of the range. In fact, there may be thresholds, there may be step functions, so that eventually we will want to know a great deal about these pairs.

In the *World Handbook of Political and Social Indicators* alone, with its 75 variables, 2,775 pairs can be generated. Clearly, not all pairs will be of interest. A computer can be programmed to pick out only those pairs with statistical significance at the five or ten per cent level. We might even ask the computer to rank the correlations by statistical significance and also by the strength of relationships; we might then extract all those correlations that are high on both counts and go through them a second time, to see which correlations are predicted by what theories. We will therefore eventually match the correlations against propositional inventories such as the series proposed by Harold Lasswell. If in the near future we can prepare a punch card for every numbered proposition in *Power and Society*[8] as well as a number or card for every proposition in Paul Lazarsfeld's voting studies,[9] then eventually we shall find which correlations are predictable by means of what theories, models, and data. This is possible only in the future because it will involve working out matching criteria for testing verbal predictions by quantitative data. Eventually we shall be able to build some three-way correlations as, for instance, of literacy and income with political stability. Clearly, however, we cannot grind out all possible triplets on a computer; the number becomes too high. But we shall find possibly a few dozen which are of particular interest.

So far I have spoken only of deterministic statistics; I have treated all these figures as given. We might eventually want to know something more about probability distributions. If we use the full range of variance, we begin to take in the deviant cases; we shall be able to make more full use of standard deviations and of extreme values that occur more rarely in the same distribution. We shall therefore find out what the distribution of phenomena is. Eventually we can induce theorists to pay more attention to the following paradox: If an outcome depends on the presence of several actions or stages, or on many repeated trials, then this overall outcome may be improbable, even though every component condition, action, or stage is highly probable in and by itself. It may be dangerous, therefore, to concentrate only on the central tendencies of each statistic (assuming that the statistics include all the factors we are interested in), even if they are all distributed in well-peaked standard distributions. Thus, if it would take seven mutually independent elements to produce an outcome, and each element had a 90 per cent probability of being present at the average number, then the resulting likelihood of the outcome would be .9 to the seventh power, which is less than one half. The matter can be put conversely. If each of the component conditions or stages has a probability distribution such that it could produce a relatively rare outcome, or take an extreme once in, say, ten, or a hundred, or a thousand times, then the likelihood that at least one of these rare outcomes will occur in at least one of the component conditions or stages will increase with the number of components, or with the number of repeated trials, in the system, with which we are concerned.

Let me repeat: if many conditions or factors are needed for an outcome, even a very high probability of every component still yields a relatively low probability for the final outcome. This is, I would say, a mathematically crude statistical formulation of Carl Friedrich's suggestion to expect in politics the unexpected. More sophisticated work on "extreme values" in statistics has been done by the mathematician E. J. Gumbel.[10] With many different factors, all of which have strongly marked central tendencies, we must expect with reasonably high probability that at least one of the factors present in every concrete situation will have a deviant value rather than a central one.

We will need time series. Here I would suggest that we develop a standard way of describing all time series, by trying to compress every time series into at least four standard components. The first component would be the trend, which is an average trend usually over time. Second is the variance distribution around the trend, and, in the third place, there is a cyclical component. Very often there are fluctuations and it is often possible to model these fluctuations as a simple wave motion or a combination of two or more wave motions. Think, for instance, of economic growth, which is a clear trend but which is modified by regional variance as well as by a business cycle fluctuation with a fairly marked periodicity in certain times of history. And finally, the fourth component is the stochastic component, which is a random process superimposed on the whole series.

If we could get a standard system of notations for these four components, it would give us a more sophisticated model than the nineteenth-century scientists had, who only tried to find either trends or cycles and felt terribly bold if they combined the two. We could then get alternative models for contingencies and for the overall output. What is the general pattern that we find at a particular time and place? What are the deviant cases to be expected? We have some such models. Keynes' model emphasized savings and investment. Anatol Rapoport tried to divide many international conflicts into fights which could be modeled on Richardsonian equations, games which could be modeled on rational decisions according to von Neumann and Morgenstern, and debates which would involve mind or attitude changes and which could be modeled on the theories of students of semantics and communication and persuasion processes.[11] In my own work, I have tried to develop simple flow models for national assimilation, differentiation, and social mobilization. These are all highly simplified models, trying to provide, nevertheless, an overall picture of some particular process with predictions of the quality, direction, and, if possible, the speed and size of some output function. When we have such models and others, we will need computer programs that can be shared for dealing with them.

One of the dangers of the sociology of social science arises at this point. As every cobbler resents the competition of factory-made shoes, so too every hand-loom weaver dislikes power looms, and almost every historian resents the idea that a social scientist should pick up his book, find a fact in it, and use if for a social science theory. The historian feels that he is being degraded to the level of an instrument. Similarly the man who has done the actual interviewing resents the coder who simplifies the subtleties of the interviews; the coders are slightly jealous of the people who write up the findings of the survey because the coders think they know much more about the details of these findings; and the person who has written the survey resents the man who is trying to compare ten surveys, because how can a man who tries to compare ten surveys understand the infinite subtleties of every one of them? By the same token, the man who runs a computer program for making rank order profiles will try every six months to change it a little. He will also try to develop the program in such a way as to fit only his unique IBM 709 Model DZ, so that it will take about three days and $700 to adapt it to the next IBM 709 with another subscript; and many of his colleagues elsewhere will do likewise. This seems to be part of intellectual work; partly it may be human playfulness; and it also seems to promise making almost every programmer indispensable.

Despite these ubiquitous tendencies toward fencing in every little plot of knowledge, we must try to make such knowledge much more freely and impersonally transferable if the computer age is to reach its full potential in the fields of social science. We need to work out nationally or internationally a certain set of minimum basic routines for people who want to use computers for matrix analysis, for simulation, for rank order profiles, for latent structure analysis, for correlations.

Eventually the day will come when computers will be used for pattern combination, for initiating new techniques of analysis in social science, so that we can use the computer not as a substitute for the scholar but as a partner—as a partner not only for the drudgery but even as a partner in the work of imagination and discovery.

To accomplish all this, perhaps we should follow the example of the United States Air Force in World War II. It waged a permanent war against the designers who would have so endlessly improved fighter planes that they would never have gone into production. The Air Force said that, after all, their pilots needed planes and not drawings; and so they froze the P-38 fighter at a certain moment saying, "Now, let's get this show on the road!" Only after a period of production did they again permit design changes. We ought to agree that every three or five years we would change the basic computer routines, but the demands of dissemination militate against the demands of constant computer improvement.

* * *

Notes

1. Werner Sombart, *Die Deutsche Volkswirtschaft im neunzehnten Jahrhundert* (3d ed. Berlin, Bondi, 1913).
2. By now, in turn, the census offices have learned the art of using the sample survey. The United States census office is using samples for certain figures and the Indian statistical office uses a 25,000 family sample for many important points. Quite often private sample surveys can be used to ask questions that governments for political reasons do not wish to ask. The Indian government, for instance, does not ask questions about caste since officially it is already unimportant; as caste does make a difference in the practice of politics, we must depend on private surveys to get this information.
3. E.g., in Robert E. Lane, *Political Ideology* (New York, Free Press, 1962).

4. A fascinating theory by Merton says it depends mainly on what is defined as conforming behavior at the time and place where the survey is made, but we do not know figures or have any numbers on this. See Robert K. Merton, *Social Theory and Social Structure* (Glencoe, Ill., Free Press, 1957).

5. For a recent discussion of some other politically relevant aspects of the Zipf distribution and its close fit to certain communication data, see Richard L. Merritt, "Distance and Interaction Among Political Communities," in *General Systems Yearbook*, 9 (1964), 255–63.

6. A beginning has been made in Russett *et al.*, *World Handbook of Political and Social Indicators*, by stating for each of 75 variables the percentage of the relevant world population covered by the table, and then presenting the quartiles of the "table population" alongside the rank order profile.

7. See Chap. 16 in [*Comparing Nations: The Use of Quantitative Data in Cross-National Research*].

8. Harold D. Lasswell and Abraham Kaplan, *Power and Society: A Framework for Political Inquiry* (New Haven, Yale University Press, 1950).

9. Paul F. Lazarsfeld *et al.*, *The People's Choice: How the Voter Makes Up His Mind in a Presidential Campaign* (2d ed. New York, Columbia University Press, 1948); Bernard R. Berelson *et al.*, *Voting: A Study of Opinion Formation in a Presidential Campaign* (Chicago, University of Chicago Press, 1954).

10. Emil J. Gumbel, *Statistics of Extremes* (New York, Columbia University Press, 1960).

11. Rapoport, *Fights, Games, and Debates* [Ann Arbor, University of Michigan Press, 1961].

25 . The State of the Nation: Social System Accounting . Bertram M. Gross

NATIONAL ECONOMIC ACCOUNTING

National economic accounting is one of the great social inventions of the modern world. Its origins go back to the *Political Arithmatick* of William Petty (1623–1687), an English physician, and to the *tableau économique* of François Quesnay (1694–1774), the French physiocrat. Quesnay saw the preparation of economic tables as an aid in the strengthening of agriculture. He and his followers were greatly influenced by the rise of business accounting in the great trading companies and by the historic work of Colbert (1619–1683) in developing accounting methods for governments.

The idea of preparing tables to give a statistical view of the total output and income of a nation was further developed by the so-called "classical" economists.

From Raymond A. Bauer (ed.), *The Social Indicators* (Cambridge, Mass., 1966), pp. 162–171, by permission of the American Academy of Arts and Sciences.

It received its greatest impetus from the Cambridge school under Alfred Marshall (1842–1924) and, somewhat later, under John Maynard Keynes (1883–1946), two of the great line of British economists.

The great surge in national economic analysis took place—at an accelerating rate—during the three periods of the Great Depression, World War II, and the period of postwar reconstruction and expansion. During each of these periods, national economic accounts were seen as an instrument of national economic planning. In the United States and England, however, the sophistication of national economic accounting went far beyond its immediate practical usefulness. Indeed, economists who favored more national planning busied themselves in developing new accounting concepts that could be used when the opportune time came. In the Soviet Union under Stalin, conversely, where a limited form of national economic accounting was in daily use, the creative development of new accounting tools was often discouraged.

CONTENT OF ECONOMIC ACCOUNTING

The essence of national economic accounting is that it provides a way of looking at the total sum of a country's economic activity in at least two ways:

1. The total output of goods and services (GNP) by types of expenditures and products.

2. The distribution of national income by sectors of origin and types of income.

Each of these separate "accounts" adds up to a total for the entire nation. Through a few additions and subtractions each may be adjusted to equal any of the other totals. Thus, GNP can be converted to national income by subtracting capital consumption allowances (which gives net national product), indirect business taxes, business transfer payments, and current surplus of government enterprises, and by adding government subsidies.

More important, each account provides a significant cross section of the "economic system." Their use facilitates many kinds of analysis, prediction, and control that would otherwise be impossible. They also tie in with other basic sets of economic statistics and analyses.

Thus, the GNP, through the net export item, is related to a nation's international balance of payments. The national income by sectors of origin ties in with data on employment in divisions of production. With some slight adjustments a government's budget can be fitted into the GNP by types of expenditures, while its revenue calculations can be based on estimates of the national income by types of income (see Table 1).

Many forward steps are constantly being made in national economic accounting—both in developing ever more refined concepts and in collecting information to fit the new concepts. One basic area of improvement is in the collection of price data and the development of indices that make possible the expression of quantity information in terms of "stable" (that is, theoretically stabilized) monetary units. Perhaps the greatest area of progress is in the field of input-output

Table 1   Major National Economic Accounts

GNP BY TYPES OF		DISTRIBUTION OF NATIONAL INCOME BY	
Expenditures	*Products*	*Sectors of Origin*	*Types of Income*
Personal consumption	Durable goods (exc. construction)	Agriculture, forests, fisheries	Compensation of employees
Gross private domestic investment	Construction goods	Mining Manufacture	Business and professional
Government	Nondurable goods	Construction	Income of farm proprietors
Net exports of goods and services	Services	Transportation and communication	Rental income of persons
		Electricity, gas, water	Net interest
		Trade	
		Finance	
		Government	
		Other services	

analysis, as developed by Wassily Leontief,[1] Henry Lee Professor of Economics at Harvard University, and a host of his followers in many countries.   The input-output matrix provides a useful way of detecting inconsistencies or bottlenecks in any national program for the expansion of investment or production.

ITS DOUBLE ROLE

National economic accounting plays two increasingly important roles in public affairs, one analytical and the other social.

The first role—technical analysis—provides the following:

1. A method of ordering vast quantities of information on monetary aspects of economic phenomena.
2. A doorway through which one can enter and explore a vast domain of social phenomena, including those that are but imperfectly reflected in economic terms.
3. Some indication of possible interrelations among various policies and programs.
4. A language for the expression of many important objectives and aspects of performance.
5. An impetus to fact-orientation by policy makers and the collection of desirable data.

The second role—although intimately associated with the first—is a social one. In this sense, national economic accounting provides

1. A dramatic way of expressing objectives, one that capitalizes on modern-day "number magic."[2]
2. Stimulus to the formulation of objectives by providing professional legitimation of various desires and aspirations.
3. A unifying language for a professional elite of trained economists.
4. Opportunities for economists to win limited access to central points of power, thereby often bringing into the public service people with a greater variety of social backgrounds and with a dedication to the possibility of more rational efforts at decision making.

These factors help explain the widespread use of national economic data by political leaders (including some who do not understand them) as well as the frequent propensity of some economists and statisticians to use such data without indicating the tremendous margins of error that often exist.

LARGE MARGINS OF ERROR

As pointed out by Oskar Morgenstern in *The Accuracy of Economic Observations*,[3] there are three principal sources of error in national income statistics: (1) inadequate basic data, (2) the fitting of the data to the concepts, and (3) the use of interpolation and imputation to fill gaps. The weighted margin of error for such estimates has been estimated as ranging from 10 per cent to 20 per cent. Yet, most of the collection agencies do not make—or else refuse to release—estimates of margins of error. The behavior of economists and statisticians in exaggerating the quality of national income data would in itself be a revealing subject of social—even statistical—research.

In his attack on the accuracy of economic statistics, Morgenstern analyzes the many reasons for error in economic statistics. One of the most pervasive sources stems from the fact that

economic statistics are not, as a rule, the result of designed experiment. . . . In general, economic statistics are merely by-products or results of business and government activities and have to be taken as such, even though they may not have been selected and designed for the analyst's purpose. Therefore, they often measure, describe, or simply record something that is not exactly the phenomenon in which the economist would be interested. They are often dependent on legal rather than economic definitions of process.[4]

Morgenstern also points out that in the physical sciences "it is customary to report data together with their carefully determined errors of observation. . . . In the social sciences such habits have not been developed. . . ."[5] His conclusion is that most economic statistics should not be stated in the manner in which they are commonly reported. It is, therefore, essential "to insist that economic statistics be only published together with an estimate of their error."[6]

In presenting his viewpoint, of course, Morgenstern is thinking of the analytical, not the social, role of the data. For purposes of achieving important social goals, economists often feel it essential to use highly inaccurate data. This use is particularly justified as a way of educating people on national income concepts and developing the demand for better data. Thus, in contrast to the "Morgenstern doctrine" of "truth in packaging," we find the "Malenbaum doctrine," as proclaimed in a discussion of India's national income statistics, that "lack of precision is not a sufficient explanation for the failure to use them."[7]

THE "NEW PHILISTINISM" IN ACCURATE ECONOMIC DATA

Yet, as against the dangers flowing from errors in economic statistics, I must also point out, as no less dangerous, the bias resulting from accurate economic statistics. Greater accuracy may easily bring with it greater irrelevance. For example, the most accurate part of a company's balance sheet is its statement of cash on hand. To focus on this alone would be a ridiculous way of analyzing a company's financial position. The balance sheet, as a whole, does not reflect the assets that the company enjoys in the form of its clients' good will and the support of its cooperating organizations. These "intangible" factors, however, cannot be dealt with as quantitatively as the estimated value of inventories and receivables. Hence, they tend to be ignored by executives who are hypnotized by the quantitative data in the balance sheet. (To repeat what has been said before, the fact that a variable can be quantified—by present techniques—may be illusory or deceptive.)

Similarly, the highly quantitative economic data in today's economic survey documents tend to detract attention from ideas that cannot be so readily expressed in quantitative terms. When a statistical indicator has been established— whether it is for gross national product or a cost of living index—it tends to take on a lifelike character of its own. Attention is inevitably directed to the small changes that take place from time to time in the selected indicator while other important and relevant aspects of the situation are neglected. Economic statistics, as a whole, emphasize the monetary value of goods and services. By so doing, they tend to discriminate against nonmonetary values and against public services for which costs invariably serve as surrogates of output value. Because figures on health and life expectancy are not directly incorporated in national economic accounts, progress in these areas may be seriously ignored, either in formulating goals or in evaluating performance. Let us suppose that during a given period of time the incidence of disease in a certain country will decline sharply and life expectancy will rise. During the same period the growth in gross national product will be less than that provided for in the plan. In this case the regular economic statistics will reveal a "shortfall." In other words, the larger aggregation of quantitative data will draw attention away from other indicators. Similarly, the size of this shortfall will not change one iota, moreover, if during the same period the public sector, with no increase in expenditures, succeeds in providing a larger quantity of essential services in education, health, and related fields.

In short, national economic accounting has promoted a "new Philistinism"— an approach to life based on the principle of using monetary units as the common denominator of all that is important in human life. The "new Philistinism" shows up in different forms:

1. The cost-benefit analysts who recognize no benefits (or dis-benefits) that cannot be expressed in dollars and cents.
2. The econometricians still operating on the ludicrous premise that there is, or should be, a "single-valued, objective welfare function" by which one could judge alternative courses of action.
3. The pathetic effort in the United States to debate policies for the "Great Society" and the "quality of life" on the basis of concepts developed decades ago to fight depression and provide minimum material sustenance for the population.

Statisticians have too little interest in removing bias of this kind. True, in the early days, statisticians were vitally interested in the kinds of data to be collected. More recently, however, their major concern has been on "technical matters of 'how' quite independent of content and purpose."[8]

This bias can be overcome only by persistent efforts to develop broader models that include many more variables than those thus far used by economists.

TRENDS TOWARD BROADENING

Among the many efforts to introduce technical refinements into national economic accounting, there are certain avenues of proposed improvement that go beyond economics. While they point to certain extensions of economic accounting, they at the same time raise questions that can be dealt with adequately only by some form of social accounting.

First of all, national accounting deals mainly with current performance— measured in terms of output, income, or current investment. Unlike corporate accounting, it does not present a balance sheet showing a nation's accumulated assets and liabilities. Various efforts, however, have been made to develop systems of national capital accounting. One of the pioneering efforts in this field is the work led by Raymond Goldsmith on a national balance sheet for the United States.[9] Technically, one of the great difficulties in this field is how to calculate annual depreciation on natural resources and government property. In fact, one may seriously question whether such calculations are worth the effort. A much greater problem—not previously tackled—is that of including manpower resources. Economists are generally agreed that manpower and human skills are the most important of all resources. Yet, these cannot be readily incorporated in monetary accounts.

Second, national economic accounting gives but an extremely small glimpse of the structure of an economy. Although Leontief's pioneering book in input-output analysis was titled *The Structure of the American Economy*, his matrix shows only the current interchange of output among sectors. Other conceptual techniques are needed to reveal economic structure in terms of the assets and size of organizations, and the power relations among them. Therefore, any serious effort in this direction must necessarily go in the direction of dealing with the social structure as a whole.

Third, within the area of current economic performance, some of the most fundamental concepts of national economic accounting are being stretched far beyond their traditional limits. The biggest stretch has come in the area of investment, long calculated entirely in terms of hard goods. John Kendrick in *Productivity Trends in the United States*[10] has proposed an extension of this concept to cover two forms of "hidden investment": (1) investment in persons, including education and health expenditures that are traditionally classified as consumption outlays; and (2) intangible investment by business and government in research and development, training, and improved methods. Theodore Schultz in "Investment in Human Capital"[11] has insisted on attention to five categories of "human investment": (1) health facilities and services; (2) on-the-job training; (3) formally organized education; (4) study programs; and (5) migration to adjust to changing job opportunities. In another article, "Capital Formation by Education,"[12] Schultz estimates for the United States that from 1900 to 1956 the annual investment in organized education alone rose from one-tenth to one-third of all investments in physical assets. This proposed extension may lead one day not far off to major changes in the structure of national economic accounts. It may even strengthen the case for "asset accounting" in human terms. At the same time, it may reach inevitably into areas of analysis far wider than economics that cannot be dealt with readily in monetary terms alone. Conceivably, still another "stretch" may be imminent in the concepts relating to output. One of the weakest points in present-day output accounting is the lack of sufficient attention to quality.

Thus, as economists have long pointed out, there is an "upward bias" in the price indices for almost every category of expenditure. For commodities, it exists because quality changes and the introduction of new products cannot be integrated adequately into the price data. For services, it exists because, by and large, the value of services is assumed not to increase, although Richard Ruggles, in "The U.S. National Accounts and Their Development,"[13] presents strong evidence that it does. Peter Wiles, after developing a similar line of thinking in considerable detail in *The Political Economy of Communism*, finds in it "a disagreeably large revolution in statistical theory. Its consequences, if correct, will reverberate very widely, since it demonstrates that nearly all existing output and cost of living indices are wrong. The latter rise much too rapidly, and the former much too slowly." Wiles maintains that all data on national output should be adjusted to take into consideration changes in utility resulting from quality changes or innovation. Recognizing that any such adjustments may mean the use of guesswork instead of accurate information, he takes his stand by favoring imprecise answers to the right questions, as opposed to precise answers to the wrong questions.[14]

It is likely that the collectors and analysts of national economic data will move slowly and cautiously in this direction.   But in so doing they will be deserting the area of data on directly observable transactions in monetary terms. From this, it is not a far cry to dealing more directly and openly with the nonmonetary indicators of human satisfaction.

The measurement of the quality and quantity of nonmarketed output becomes particularly difficult in the growing area of nonmarketed government services. In national economic accounting, the volume of this service output is calculated by the monetary cost of input.   This may easily result in a serious underevaluation of output in the public sector.   Various ways of adjusting such output figures upward could be devised.   For example, when expenditures for education remain stable while the number of students, curriculum hours, and graduates rises, the expenditure figures could be adjusted upward to give a better monetary representation of the total educational output.   Yet, it might make more sense, instead of relying entirely on adjustments in monetary measures, to use some form of nonmonetary account that would deal directly with various social measures of educational output.

In general, the effort to squeeze all relevant information on action under national planning into an improved system of economic accounts would be tortuous.   It would seem much more fruitful to build a broader system of national social accounts that, while not limited to calculations in monetary aggregates, would nonetheless include—and capitalize on—the basic concepts of national economic accounting.   This would make it possible to deal more systematically with information that goes beyond the data in the economic accounts, and help to explain the whys and wherefores of economic performance.

* * *

Notes

1. The classic work in this field, *The Structure of the American Economy 1919–1939* (New York: Oxford University Press, 2nd ed., 1953).
2. The nature of modern "number magic" is discussed in "The Clarity-Vagueness Balance," in Bertram Gross, *The Managing of Organizations* (New York: Free Press of Glencoe, Inc., 1964), 2 vols., pp. 494–501.
3. Princeton, N.J.: Princeton University Press, 1963, rev. ed., pp. 242–282.
4. *Ibid.*, pp. 13–14.
5. *Ibid.*, p. 8.
6. *Ibid.*, pp. 304–305.
7. Wilfred Malenbaum, *Prospects for Indian Development* (New York: Free Press of Glencoe, Inc., 1962), pp. 199.
8. Albert D. Biderman, in Chapter 2 of [*Social Indicators*].
9. Raymond W. Goldsmith, Robert E. Lipsey, and Morris Mendelson, *Studies in the National Balance Sheet of the United States* (Princeton, N.J.: Princeton University Press, for the National Bureau of Economic Research, 1963), 2 vols.   Another step in the direction of a

national balance sheet is "flow of funds accounting," which tries to summarize all financial transactions and thereby provides a link between income and asset accounts.   This work, still in its early stages, was pioneered by Morris Copeland in *A Study of Money Flows in the United States* (New York: National Bureau of Economic Research, 1952).

10. Princeton, N.J.: Princeton University Press, 1961, pp. 104–110.
11. *American Economic Review, LI* (March 1961), 1–17.
12. *Journal of Political Economy, 68* (1960), 571–583.
13. *American Economic Review, XL* (March 1959), 94.
14. Cambridge, Mass.: Harvard University Press, 1962, pp. 246–247.

26. Open Systems for Growth and Development . Richard L. Meier

When monetary returns are obscure, the dual-society* concept can be fitted very readily to the tasks of decision and action.   Politicians and administrators have already been sensitized to the differences between modern and traditional approaches to problems and can confirm from personal experience the value of many of the prescriptions that may be inferred from the existence of the dual society. The concept is nevertheless a simplification of the real world and may sometimes mislead in the course of the search for suitable policies.   Still more frequently, it has little relevance to many significant issues that arise.   Therefore it is worthwhile to consider several complementary conceptualizations of growth and development which make it possible to render more than one judgment of a proposed line of action for a nation.

A reconsideration of the other well-known concepts underlying economic and social growth has been undertaken recently by Hagen in his book *On the Theory of Social Change*.   He has endeavored to probe more deeply into the behavioral sciences in order to identify the processes of growth after accepting the conclusion

---

* Dual-society refers, roughly, to traditional and modern social practices.   Meier defines dual-society on p. 44 of *Developmental Planning* as a condition where ". . . two coherent views of social organization prevail in the same population and many among the inhabitants are put into the position of having to live within both and find appropriate compromises." (Ed.)

that knowledge about resources, technologies, and organizations must grow if the socioeconomic system is to develop. Essentially, his interest is in the manner in which knowledge is used to promote growth.

Hagen is concerned, for example, with the reasons for the stability of the traditional society. Why are the outlooks and the behavioral patterns transmitted from one generation to the next with remarkably little change? Under many circumstances, we now know, it is quite normal for the younger generation to rebel and reject the social roles and some of the values of the parents, but this reaction seldom ever occurs in the traditional agrarian society. The latter has shown a strong tendency to breed true and replicate itself generation after generation.

Traditional society, as Hagen depicts it, is an ultrastable system where, each time a deviation from the norm is detected, a force (as often unconsciously directed as conscious) is set into motion to restore the original conditions. Unconscious forces are at work mostly at the level of child training and cultural indoctrination (the "little tradition"). A conscious force is the use of authority by an elite which is regulated by a great historically oriented tradition. Thus the mass of peasants and artisans are kept in line by the principles of behavior transmitted from parents to children, but the exceptions are dealt with by intervention of the military leaders, the priests, and the nobility, who comprise that part of the elite which is granted authority. (Hagen does not give the frequency of exceptions, but one would judge from the instances cited that they might range from 3 to 10 per cent, and of these many more among males than females.) Such a strong interdependence between the elite and the masses has been established that the support of the elite falls off, and its ability to fulfill traditional obligations is constrained, if obedience to tradition by the peasants declines. On the other hand, temporary surpluses produced by the masses are properly (according to the "great tradition") consumed by the elite in feuds, affairs of honor, quests for power, or ostentatious display. Knowledge can accumulate in such a strongly interdependent system, particularly when the elite is intent upon restoring a prior state of affluence that had been interrupted by a catastrophe, but the rewards obtained from the possession of knowledge are meager. The traditional agrarian society uses the family enterprise and the chronicles of the royal courts for the preservation of information. These are rather inefficient institutions for the purpose, so it is not surprising that many productive concepts need to be rediscovered repeatedly.

Change most often comes to traditional societies in catastrophic form: invasions, epidemics, earthquakes, floods, famines, etc. Large portions of the elite may be lost, and significant fractions of the rural population may disappear with them, but regrowth occurs—usually by incorporating invading or subject tribal elements—so that the economic base and the social structure are restored to the same dimensions and outline. Reconstruction and some new growth may continue for a generation or even more, but the profiteers join the gentry and invest in land, and the surpluses are thereafter consumed. A traditional agrarian society is thus brought into being again, although it is somewhat modified by the new cultures assimilated during the regrowth phase.

Despite their ultrastability, traditional societies are passing. Hagen emphasized the effects of innovations, which are now coming in larger numbers than can be accommodated by the restoring forces that are present, as the triggers of change. The upbringing of children has been disturbed, the frequency of youthful rebelliousness is increasing, and there are at least a few ways of making a living within the society while still rejecting its traditions. Thus innovations can persist, and may reinforce each other.

Whereas in former times traditional societies responded to challenge by *retreatism*, a move toward fantasy, or a rigid *ritualism*, depending upon the degree of shock, nowadays they more frequently undertake an innovational or reformist tack. Innovations, when adopted, represent shortcuts to accepted ends within the existing social framework, but reforms require an overhauling of the institutional structure, including forms of government, religion, education, and etiquette, in an attempt to modernize the society.

When Hagen's recapitulation of classical theory is fitted to case studies, which range from (1) modern Burma, (2) twentieth-century Colombia, (3) nineteenth-century Japan, (4) fifteenth- to eighteenth-century Britain, to (5) contemporary Sioux Indians living on a reservation, it is seen that there are many loose ends and indeterminate factors. None of these instances of development (or lack of it) was *planned* or even guided in the direction of a goal, so that one gets the feeling that random elements are dominant.[1]

A much more explicit behavioral explanation of development is to be found in McClelland's book, *The Achieving Society*. It starts from the measurement of human motives and behavioral characteristics. Motives, he has argued, can be gauged by reviewing the spontaneous thoughts and by analyzing the resultant freely produced visual and verbal images. The interests that seem to be guiding the transitions from one image to the next can be standardized to some extent by asking people to write out their impressions of specific pictures. From the flow of ideas produced it was discovered that at least three motivational themes can be identified: (1) a need for achievement, (2) a need for affiliation, and (3) a need for power.

A scale can be constructed by counting the number of ideas related to a given theme that are produced in the spontaneous response. This scale can be connected to other scales based upon the public imagery employed in the society that is available for analysis—the art, poetry, drama, street ballads, popular novels, sermons, etc. In brief, McClelland found that nAchievement (the index measuring the prevalence of the achievement motive) was a predictor of development, that nAffiliation was negatively correlated with development, and that nPower seems to be irrelevant.[2]

These studies (which have been carried out on a wide variety of societies, contemporary and historical) suggest that a society-wide enhancement of nAchievement is a necessary but not sufficient cause of economic and cultural development. People must feel that the struggle to reach personally set goals is more important than pleasing members of the family or friends in the community; they must also feel it to be more important than controlling the behavior of others.

When an increasing number of persons in the population accept these value orientations, it becomes possible to promote development.

McClelland's most spectacular success in illustrating the significance of the relation of nAchievement to development was obtained in quantitative studies which explain the golden age of Athens in classical times. He and his collaborators also worked out methods for comparing many different contemporary cultures by analyzing the content of the readings presented to elementary school children in 1925 and 1950. After considering 65 to 70 different discriminations, it was discovered that many of the attitudinal requirements for economic development, previously hypothesized as necessary by sociologists and economists, were not connected with growth; but it was found that achievement motivation images (e.g., hard work is a means to an end, action is more important than interaction, large long-range goals are to be preferred over others) and "other-directed" indicators (demanding cooperation of others, being aware of the signals that call for conforming to styles set by peers, rapid borrowing of good ideas, etc.) alone seemed to exist *before* a society began to develop rapidly. A shift from tradition-directed behavior to a dependence upon public opinion has a much greater likelihood of producing conditions conducive to rapid growth.

How is the achievement motive enhanced in a society? Most commonly, the idea of achievement is encouraged through the educational system. Chances to travel and make comparisons need to be greatly improved because many people discover goals worth working toward in this manner. Opportunities to improve social status through effort must be provided also. Once change has begun there is likely to be a wave of religious reform which takes hold and reinforces a *protestant ethic*, a pattern of beliefs founded upon achievement.

Other-direction—the second key to growth—can be strongly increased by mixing up the new immigrants to cities with the established urbanites while they are at work and when they are purchasing household goods. Watching how other people respond to social situations is a rather obvious means of resolving one's own doubts about how to behave.

The affiliation motive can be suitably reduced by setting up national interests as superior to family and community, by giving responsibilities to youngsters at an earlier age, and by inducing a sensitivity to public opinion. Attempts to reduce the rate of population growth should also be influential. However, McClelland points out that low nAffiliation indices combined with high nPower tend to lead to dictatorship and an authoritarian form of society. He did not suggest in his own study how the nPower could be affected by reforms of social institutions, but this objective has been the focus of attention of a considerable group of social psychologists, so there is no scarcity of suggestions. What is lacking, however, is an effective procedure for intervention in child raising, so this authoritarian hazard of development promotion can only be noted in passing. Recommendations for action in the typical situations cannot be formulated at this time.

Studies of the behavioral policies prerequisite for development are still sketchy and incomplete. In any society, some individuals are high in nAchievement, regardless of the strength of tradition. This cluster can be encouraged to propagate and diffuse; normally, the middle classes embrace it first. Then, if political circumstances do not interfere and the natural resources situation is not too adverse, an accumulation of skills and capital should result. *Thus these isolated reservoirs of nAchievement should be considered a special resource which needs to be discovered, assayed, and exploited for growth purposes.* The policies intended to affect motives and attitudes when redirecting society should enable it to expend governmental effort with greater assurance of desired results. Each instance, however, deserves closer study because the *n*Achievement score is an even grosser concept than the economists' per capita–income index, and it is therefore more susceptible to misuse when guiding the programs and plans of a society.

THE IMAGE AND THE PLAN

McClelland's discovery of achievement motivation as a force for producing growth and development is only a beginning. Also necessary is (1) an image of a more desirable future, (2) at least one course of action that enables the society to achieve it, and (3) hierarchical ordering and structure. Miller, Galanter, and Pribram, in their collaborative book *Plans and the Structure of Behavior*, have borrowed some terminology from Boulding and have designated the first of these the *Image* and the second the *Plan*. The third characteristic represents an insight into the requirements for organization of higher order. Their study explores the relation between the Image and the Plan at the level of individual behavior. Their mode of thinking is quite appropriate also for the behavior of groups, institutions, and nations.

The Image they consider actually embodies the sum of the knowledge that a person has accumulated. All the past experience affects directly or indirectly the view of the future, much of it in the form of preferences about what should not *recur* in the future. The Image is a mosaic of facts that are ordered and arranged by values. The Image is organized by concepts into a set of hierarchical levels, but the strata are frequently disturbed and sometimes interleaved. The concepts are not entirely consistent and unambiguous. This is mainly because the housekeeping in the Image is always running behind the accumulation of experience, so that some facts have not yet been put into their proper places. The Image is made up of a series of memories of environments containing both physical and social elements, and each of the environments is made up of a series of typical situations. The latter may be further subdivided into messages and impressions that are both sent and received (transactions). Messages carry imagery that fits into hierarchical arrangement even more neatly. Their structure will be analyzed later in this chapter.

The Plan is the process which controls the order of a sequence of operations to be performed. If the Plan is to be feasible, the respective operations must already be part of the Image. However, an outline for a course of action, with details unspecified under some of the headings, can still be a Plan because during the latter stages of execution one may choose any of several operations on the basis of opportunism. The Plan can be outlined because it also is hierarchically organized, the levels being programs, projects, and lesser units of behavior. The sequencing of programs in the Plan is usually termed *strategy*, that of the subsidiary projects within a program is called *tactics*, while the execution of the minor elements will be referred to here as *actions*.

Miller, Galanter, and Pribram identify the building blocks of action as a cybernetic loop as shown in Figure 1. They then demonstrate how this elementary unit can be assembled into hierarchical structures such that the next highest level in the hierarchy will have the same kind of loop but may process different inputs.

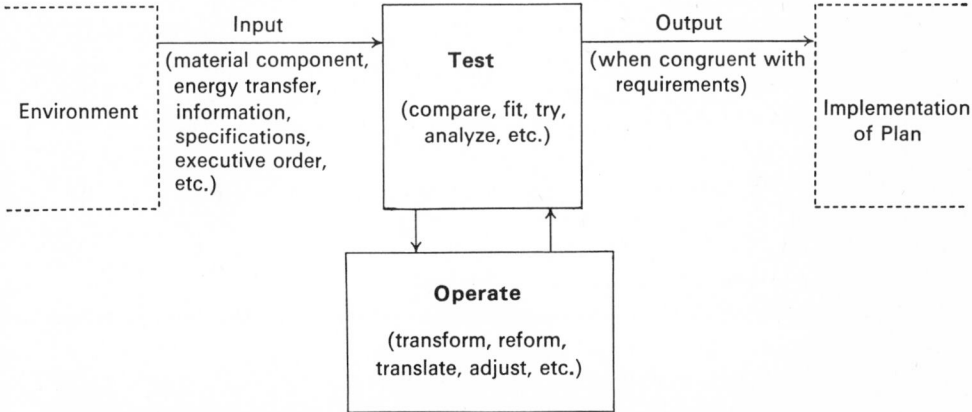

Figure 1. **Requirements for organized action. This diagram is an elaboration of the model of Miller, Galanter, and Pribram. An input from the environment is tested for suitability for standard actions, accepted tactics, and the strategy agreed upon earlier. If it does not fit, it is operated upon and modified. It is then retested. This recycling may be repeated several times until a satisfactory output is found or the attempt is abandoned. This element can be made a component of a hierarchy.**

Thus the Plan consists of tests and operations, the tests being part of the Image that is desired for the future. The more complex the Image, the more multitudinous and exacting are the tests. Similarly, the operations that go into the Plan need to be more precise.

These authors are highly conscious of the fact that the scope of individual Plans is limited by the capacities of a human being, in the same manner that the plans of a society are limited by its history and its resources. The constraints they identify are under such headings as (1) source of the Plan (borrowed, adapted, or invented), (2) time span (also called horizon), (3) internal consistency (has it been "debugged"?[3]), (4) interchangeability of parts (flexibility), (5) speed of construction, (6) information retrieval, and (7) the "stop orders" (which determine when a given Plan is obsolete and another should take its place). These constraints have equivalents in the plans drawn up for societies. This analysis directed them to the essential subprocesses of communication that underlie the Plan—remembering, speaking, searching, etc. Communication is even more fundamental to the preparation of national plans.

Finally, there is the question of the construction of Plans. These authors ask themselves, "Where do personal Plans come from?" They answer their own question by noting that Plans are usually made up of old Plans that have been assembled in a new way. They are very much aware of the fact that the goal-directed problem-solving computer programs have been built up in the same manner. But this is not enough. There must be a plan for Plans (what the philosophers would call a *metaplan*) which contains rules that do not always work but still apply much more often than chance would permit (the proper name for such a rule is *heuristic*). They recognize that Newell, Simon, and Shaw's "General Problem Solver" program for a large computer serves as a generator of programs by using heuristics which have worked well in the past even if not universally. Heuristics could find proofs to many theorems in *Principia Mathematica*, or find many good moves when playing a chess master, but are not universally successful. Presumably there are other heuristics, less well known to ordinary problem solvers, which need to be added to the General Problem Solver before it can handle the remaining problems with the computing resources at hand. The metaplan, therefore, suggests tentative Plans, which must be tested by the information at hand for appropriateness to the problem.

A book on developmental planning must be just such a metaplan. It must start from insights derived from observing successes and failures. It should concentrate upon heuristics that would apply to open societies because that is the only kind of society that will draw extensively from such experience. It ought to produce suggestions for constructing explicit national plans at the level of strategy and incorporate some of the tactics and actions that seem to be required if the key programs are to succeed.

It should be pointed out at once, however, that at least one grave deficiency can be found in the modeling of Plans after computer programs. When a conflict develops within the program, or between programs that are being run simultaneously, the computer stops, and a debugging operation begins. Living systems, such as individuals or societies, cannot afford to cease operations in that manner. They must find ways of resolving conflicts before the breakdown occurs. Successful plans foresee conflicts and avoid them or, if the conflicts already exist, find ways of bridging over the difficulties.

In Chapter 1 [of *Developmental Planning*] it was demonstrated quite clearly that countries fortunate enough to have rich reserves of natural resources are also subject to internal conflicts. Less fortunate countries have inherited historic feuds which are no less troublesome. It is evident that growth has been forestalled by such conflicts. Surprisingly, until now no social scientist aside from Boulding has analyzed conflict in a systematic way, so we may draw upon Boulding's observations.[4] Because of the paucity of prior work, a brief review of the basic considerations of the dynamics of conflict, and their effects upon growth, is needed before the growth process itself is elucidated.

CONFLICT SYSTEMS

Conflict between individuals and between organizations is extremely expensive. If one adds up the losses from family feuds and communal struggles, the waste due to bureaucratic wrangling, the inefficiencies due to cutthroat competition, the strikes and slowdowns of organized labor that protest injustice on the part of employers, the cost of the military budget, and the destruction of war, it will be seen that vast sums are dissipated in conflict and preparations for conflict. In most parts of the world this inability to prevent the threat of conflict uses up a quarter to a half of the income potential.

In order to understand conflict, the typical environment in which it occurs must be described: Take a territory of some sort with natural boundaries imposed by history; this territory is occupied by organizations of various sizes which are loosely coordinated into a society. Some organizations are being formed, others are dying, but most are in a steady state with fluctuating fortunes. Boundaries of the total system may also expand or contract, thus changing the interaction between the organizations and the area occupied by each. Of particular concern is what happens under conditions of growth.

Organizations that grow within a given social environment cause increased conflict. The basic reasons are readily apparent. Growth brings with it increased flows in and out; and therefore increased demands for channel capacity in transport and communications; it may also introduce potentials for action in a new domain. If the space for maneuver was almost fully occupied before the growth occurred, a contest develops wherever two or more organizations seek to grow into the same space. A similar situation is encountered when expanded transport and communications flows are required to support a larger-size organization, but competing organizations make demands upon the same capacity in order to meet their own needs. How shall the limited capacity be divided? Finally, growth may bring an organization to a level where it operates no longer within a community or region but in the nation, and there it comes into contact with a new circle of competitors and must battle with the giants for its place in the sun.

In the course of development the organizations within a society have a broad range of growth rates. Some expand much more rapidly than the society itself (these are one set of troublemakers), others at about the same rate, others at a slow rate; quite a few are not growing at all (another set of troublemakers), and some are visibly declining in size and capability. Organizations with exceedingly rapid growth contribute most heavily to the development process, but they also may trigger off conflicts which tear the whole social system apart. On the other side of the spectrum, the shrinking organizations tend to evade or postpone conflict until they are cornered and forced to face a threatened take-over by an aggressor organization, often a potential predator type that would extract the liquid assets and leave the shell. Occasionally all the remaining assets are wasted in conflict. Nevertheless, declining organizations contribute little to the level of conflict encountered during general social and economic development.

A typical conflict arising from growth has to do with the fixing of boundaries and the possession of territory. A static organization almost always has stable boundaries, or limits, to its activity, which are well recognized by the members of the organization. It is challenged by an upstart, with no recognizable tradition behind it, which wants some territory or share of the market presently under the control of the static organization. In its comparatively long history a static organization has developed a series of alarms graduated to meet the scale of the perceived threat. Alarms are set off which impel the organization to mobilize its liquid resources, which may be manpower reserves, mutual-help obligations owed to it by other organizations in the vicinity, or cash. The simple objective is to repel the invaders, obliterate the sources of their power, and secure the traditional boundaries. This model fits closely the behavior of city-states in ancient history.

Recall that many kinds of organizations exist in society. Some, such as ethnic communities, occupy territory. The picture described above would apply very well to ethnic communities in a crowded metropolis. Business firms are drawn into similar conflicts for a part of the market. Government agencies fight their battle for a proper share of the budget and for authority to act; nevertheless, the conflict can be analyzed in an analogous fashion. Voluntary organizations often get involved in vicious conflicts while trying to obtain "their share of the private donations and public charities." Thus there is always a "conflict field" similar to land upon which the battles are fought. Organizational resources are converted into leverages (power and influence) which operate on that field. Victory implies undisputed control of the field in question. Defeat implies not only a loss of control, but also a loss of viability, which could result in the disappearance of the organizational entity.

If growth and development are the prime objective of the whole society, action to diminish the cost of conflict will be taken at the national level. All wasteful destruction of valued resources on the part of the respective organizations must be curbed. Rules are therefore laid down for the resolution of conflicts before they get out of hand. Society is willing to invest in police systems, one for each well-known field of conflict, in order to make sure that its rules are obeyed. Conflict resulting from aggressive and rapacious behavior can then be deterred. A regulated competitive system results, with concepts of justice, propriety, and fair play determining the relations between organizations.

A strong tendency exists for the rules designed to prevent conflicts to yield a system which moves rapidly toward equilibrium, a condition of nongrowth. A growing society must bias its rules in favor of growing organizations. Vigorous organizations are to be deterred only when several neighbors feel threatened, and are likely to form a coalition to fight back even if it means going outside the law. Both capitalist and socialist societies have provided such biases in favor of the growing units in the modern sector of the society. It is often done through forbearance to prosecute for small offenses. In the field of conflict represented by the market, preference is shown through the choice of excise taxes, tariffs, subsidies, and incentive payments.

Another procedure for preventing destructive conflict and maintaining civil order is the development of a modern system of corporate law.   Then the injured parties have access to the courts in order to reestablish control over lost "territory."   In effect, a new field for conflict is created which uses the services of well-trained advocates as contestants.   Property is not destroyed, lives are not lost, but still a significant fraction of the time and effort available to a society is spent in the creation and maintenance of a system of law.   (Usually in the range 1 to 3 percent of the productive activity is committed to these purposes in human society, not counting education and indoctrination in the schools.)   Some fights are thereby reduced to debates.

Many expensive conflicts continue outside of the law.   They include feuds, destructive competition between firms, political clashes in the course of seeking popular support, and struggles between ethnic communities.   Their cost may be reduced through identifying the common sources of conflicts, the kinds of gains and losses incurred, and the mechanisms of the spread of the conflict that tend to involve more organizations than those originally concerned.   For the settlement of such conflicts a series of peacemakers or mediators must be supported who go into a conflict situation and attempt to get the parties to give up fighting and find some compromise which is acceptable for the moment.   The compromise might easily also become a convenient precedent for settlement in the future.   Certainly any society attempting to minimize the cost of lawless conflict, as a component of its development program, would make plans of this sort.

Some kinds of conflicts are more significant than others, and it is possible to sort them out by the frequency of appearance and the damage that results.   Collisions between two rapidly growing organizations are more common than would be expected on the basis of random interactions between organizations because rapidly growing organizations tend to be concentrated in the same vicinity, they are often neighbors, and they see roughly the same opportunities at the same time. Growing organizations tend to have several options for action open to them. Therefore it is relatively easy for them to bargain *quid pro quo*; both organizations can find a way of getting much of what they want by giving up a little.   Problems of conflict between rapidly expanding organizations in a growing society are matters of concern for the government, but they are not likely to build up to such a scale that the bases for overall growth are destroyed.

Static organizations have a more jaundiced attitude toward conflict; they have been sparring with their neighbors over some time and therefore have arrived at a fairly accurate appraisal of relative power.   Static organizations bordering on other static organizations have the most stable boundaries.   Occasionally they do get thrown into mortal combat with each other, where only one can win.   This means that the immediate social and economic environment has become less favorable and only one organization can survive where two or more existed before. These circumstances are common in depressed regions or markets, or when sources of support are dwindling.   Such battles affect the rates of growth and development very little.

In the typical dual society—the modern-traditional dichotomy—conflict is polarized around the new versus the old. The challenges stimulate the modern organizations far more than the traditional. The modern have a much larger body of experience to search for bringing new tactics and new resources to the attention of the decision makers than has the typical traditional organization. Nevertheless, the history of war suggests that many traditional organizations grasp the significance of innovations in a conflict situation when at any other time the potentials would have been ignored. The traditional units adopt the innovations in the emergency, one innovation leads to another, and the unit starts undergoing rapid modernization. More often, however, chaos results, owing to the "retreatism" of traditional organizations, which proceeds at an even more rapid rate than the advance of the modern agencies in the same field. Individuals without their organizations, or with impotent ones, feel a normlessness, or *anomie*. Some of the major costs of growth and development in a society are borne by members of organizations which fight modernism and lose. Special welfare organizations, such as the Salvation Army and the settlement houses, may need to be created in the cities which recruit these displaced individuals into the low-skilled services for the modern sector of the society.

Until this point in the analysis, conflict has been regarded as destructive of resources, but it has a constructive contribution as well. Just as in biological societies, the rank of an organization among its peers is determined by its apparent ability to damage competitors and not be damaged by them. Its capability is judged in the course of sparring for superiority. Both the contestants and observers arrive at similar conclusions, but the contestant's information about relative strength is far more explicit and more likely to affect its decision making. Once the rank, or pecking order, as it is called in a flock of birds, has been clearly established in a population of organizations or individuals, the amount of conflict diminishes to a relatively low but not insignificant level. Some conflictful interaction is apparently necessary to expedite the gradual changes in relationships due to accident, maturation, and aging. The continuous friction keeps the individual organizations alert, and it requires a repeated search of the environment for resources that may be useful for self-defense.

IMAGES AND ORGANIZATION

It is time to put together the subassemblies of argument that have thus far been introduced. The procedure employed for unraveling the principles for planning over the next decade or two has involved a consideration of the factors that hinder growth and development. It was seen that the presence of natural resources is less necessary than in the past, while the settling of disputes before they become destructive is more necessary than ever. The presence of an achievement-oriented, other-directed contingent in the society seems to be needed, and it must have in addition a modern, organized Image of the future which serves as a goal. The image of the sovereign nation, capable of interacting as an entity with other nations and attracting the loyalty of its citizens, has been introduced. Actually, if the parties in power within a nation are attempting to foster development, they must grant highest priority to the growth of a great variety of groups, circles, departments, bureaus, companies, and institutions in the modern sector. The degree of interaction of these components must increase.

A company or institution may be regarded as a special kind of machine which uses men as replaceable parts, but these social machines are so marvelous they do not yet have adequate analogues in the mechanical world. One unusual property they have is that they are self-constructing; they were started when one or more of the "parts" went forth and recruited others to carry out complementary and co-ordinated behaviors. These companies are to a high degree also self-repairing systems; when damage is sustained, they will readjust the relations between the parts in order to maintain as much output as possible under conditions of stress. When conditions in the national environment become more favorable, the output of most of the various organized units should expand at a greater rate than their recruitment of participating individuals. When such a marked advance in productivity per head can be discerned, it is highly probable that development is proceeding rapidly.

An astonishing property of the majority of the new human organizations which need to be propagated is that they are primarily concerned with intangibles. Even the attention paid to the output by consumers is rarely associated with the necessities of life, but deals with side issues. For example, food has always been prepared from certain natural materials by time-tested recipes, but in order to preserve food and reduce spoilage, a food processor must come into being. This new processor must standardize the shape, texture, and taste of the product, package it, and put a printed label on the package. Most of the organizational activity concentrates on these aspects. Success for a food processor depends much more upon his taking cognizance of these qualities of the output than the price differential he is able to maintain.

Another example of the importance of the external qualities of the product can be drawn from the institutions providing for living accommodations and shelter. Many buildings have been raised in the traditional society, either by those who wished to live in them or by craftsmen who were acquainted with traditional materials and forms. However, development implies that architectural and engineering firms would come into existence which pay special attention to structure and configuration. Individualized appearances are superimposed upon buildings to signify their unique uses. These intangible elements, the patterns that may be either unique or standard, are recognized by a portion of the population coming into contact with them; they stimulate predictable behavior on the part of the population that identifies them. Such intangibles are most often transmitted by means of speech and writing, although quite a few may have visual form alone, or primarily affect the senses of odor and touch.

These particular intangibles will be called *images* because they are tiny fragments of what Miller, Galanter, and Pribram—also Boulding some years before them—have called the Image. By successive stages of clarification, their qualities will be made so explicit that the images can be counted and the size of the repertoire of images assembled by individuals or institutions can be measured. The size of the inventory of different images recognizable within a society will be shown to be an indicator of its social and cultural wealth.   It is probably a more significant index than the accumulation of livestock or property, which have been used to measure wealth in the economic sense.   The variety of images available to a social unit reflect its capabilities for responding to its social and physical environment.   They indicate the degree to which it has become organized.

Images are all-important in the creation of new organizations.   The natural history of any social unit from the time before it was conceived to the time it expires can be explained in terms of the images that are readily recognized by its members and its clients.   Image sharing is the basis for the coherence of the organization.   The following brief description of the evolution of a well-organized modern social unit illustrates the manner in which images function.

Long before any social organization can come into being there must exist in the milieu some unfulfilled service or collective need.   How can such an idea of need arise ?   Primarily from making comparisons, often between himself and strangers, an individual is stimulated to imagine a new state of affairs—different from anything he ever observed or experienced before—that ought to be distinctly preferable to the present.   This concept may be the consequence of dissatisfaction, or even envy of some other person, but it is also invention.   An immediate outcome of invention is a reconstruction of the inventor's Image.   He feels he knows a future that could well exist.   If the idea can be communicated to other people, the inventor must describe it in terms of images he already shares with them.   If they are able to transmit the idea to others in an essentially accurate form, the reconstructed Image is likely to survive for a while in the population as a hypothetical ideal.

Imagine, for example, that the reconstructed Image allows for the possible prevention of a well-known disease.   Sometime later (the amount of time may range from seconds to decades) the discrepancy between what is observed to exist and what is contained in the Image about a possible future is evaluated morally. The gap is felt to be unnecessary.   Then the actions of individuals that maintain the present state of affairs suddenly appear stupid, evil, reactionary, primitive, etc.   These moral judgments are rendered by reformers.   They call attention to the value differences between the standard traditional Image and the new one. They assert loudly that the gap is scandalous and that society should reform itself. Many people take delight in scandals; they recognize the possible validity in the arguments but do nothing about the inconsistency themselves.   They do not have the motivation to right wrongs or achieve a new state of affairs.   The reform is discussed abstractly, as a matter of public morals and justice, which is someone else's responsibility.

However, some persons may see this gap, the inconsistency in the mosaic that makes up the Image, as an opportunity.   They survey the situation to discover whether the necessary resources can be assembled, a staff can be hired and trained, and the means for closing the gap in at least one locale can be produced.   Thus a new social unit is created.   Unsuccessful promoters of new organizations lose their time and capital and disappear from the scene. Successful units, however, accumulate over time.

Achievement of the objective creates a valuable outcome in the social milieu. At least a part of this value can be measured in monetary terms—dollars, pounds, yen, etc. In a market system much of the value is returned to the organization, which then pays the participants and yields a profit to the promoter. Whatever remains stays with the part of the public that has benefited. In a bureaucracy the successful promoters are paid off in prestige if they create a new activity or service for the institution. Thus a fragmentary image of what the future could be has been converted into an image whose meaning is being experienced in the present.

As promotion expands and is imitated, an increasing proportion of the public shares in the experience and in the benefits. In the example of disease prevention, they have taken their immunization shots, or decontaminated their water, and thus have taken effective action to prevent the contraction of the disease. Ultimately people will come to depend upon the absence of the disease and improve the organization of their production system, educational system, and other institutions wherever they were affected.

As soon as a novel image is introduced in this manner, and a working organization has appeared to propagate it, inefficiencies become obvious to persons with calculating minds. These managerial types find shortcuts and make minor inventions which "improve the art" and reduce the cost of the service provided by the unit. New subsidiary images are created in the process. Thus the degree of organization is enhanced; the unit may become indefinitely viable. Again in the case of disease prevention, the small inventions that become minor images may be clinical test routines or procedures for treatment. Managers who seek these improvements are found in public health services and in hospital staffs.

Thus an image acts as a social propellant. It triggers specific actions on the part of many people. It gets modified in meaning by the accumulation of experience, and, as it is increasingly employed in communication, it may become fuzzy and indefinite at the fringes, but it stands distinct from all other images in the mosaic. The added images are the intangibles that pull a society out of the rut of tradition. They represent something of great value to individuals and organizations—valuable enough to stimulate effort.

INNOVATION AND THE FLOW OF INFORMATION

Emphasis thus far has been placed upon images—their origins, role, function, and identification. These intangibles in social process have been singled out and made discrete. Now attention must be paid to the transmission of images, or communication.

A communications system is constructed to transmit *messages*. Whatever else may flow over a communications channel, and is not understood, should be regarded as noise. Messages contain *terms* that are understandable to both sender and receiver(s). As noted before, a term may be a word or a group of words representing an image. A term may also be a pattern incorporated into a picture. Terms are built up from *symbols*, which have no meaning (i.e., concrete referents) of their own but can be manipulated readily for tests and operations (as in Figure 1) carried out by the receiver. This hierarchy is completed by noting that symbols can be defined as a *set of stimulus patterns* for an organism. The transmission of any member of that set conveys the symbol, and a pattern of symbols similarly conveys a term, while an assembly of terms is needed to convey a concept. This mode of organization of communications has resulted from the scarcity of human time that could be allotted to social endeavors. Pictorial channels have been left open for the fuzzier and less explicit images, but language has become a medium for precise communication. A good language is one that reflects the degree of imprecision in the minds of the senders and receivers regarding the concepts in a message and at the same time permits exact statements. Mathematical notations are extensions of language with some of these constraints removed.

Now, reconsider briefly the flow of communication required for invention, the adoption of invention, the production of a new product, and the development of expanding uses for the new product. Whenever the message content has recognizable value to the receiver, it will be called *information*; information flow in this context first occurs when some messages interact with a felt need. If the messages were novel, or the need was new, a new concept might well result. Such a concept, if it is to be manipulated with ease, must be represented by a new image. This is an invention. Inventions, it must be noted, are preceded by flows of information, and the speeding up of invention requires increased communication.

Still larger flows of information are required for comparing the invention with alternative means for achieving the same ends. If an entrepreneur makes an energetic search for satisfactory alternatives and fails, he is then encouraged to innovate. An innovation extracts social value from an image. An innovator must switch to the role of sender and persuade suppliers, workers, wholesalers, retailers, sources of credit, and customers to accept the implications of this innovation. He sets off a wave of communication much larger than what is needed to maintain the less useful alternatives. An invention, therefore, is an image that acts as a trigger.

Information that has been distributed in a society by these processes is likely to be useful in carrying out tasks that are assigned at a later date. Learning is involved. The third or fourth occasion that the innovation is used should take observably less time to implement. As that task is repeated, the time to completion will be shortened until fatigue or some other limit becomes significant. After many such experiences with innovation and the acquistion of information, most people "learn how to learn," so that most novel situations are handled with dispatch. The people carrying out instructions have come to trust their sources of information, and so are not held back by doubt and suspicion. They make fewer errors in interpreting the messages they receive. Any information acquired relating to innovations and changes in the society should then result in more output in less time. *In general, the greater the innovation rate and the associated flow of information, the greater is the rate of social improvement.* This relationship holds until fatigue, or confusion, sets in and effective responses are inhibited.

This argument can be stated in the inverse: An increase in economic efficiency requires at least a shift in the flow of information in the economic system. People must know more in order to manipulate the factors of production and obtain greater output. More often than not, the extra messages needed to acquire the knowledge are added to the regular transmission so that, in sum, an increase in information flow is to be anticipated.

The inverse argument can also be put in sociological terms. In the course of social development a great many important new organizational roles are created outside of the family. If these organizational roles are to be filled, people must learn to carry out explicit tasks. The more information a person has at his disposal, the more likely he is to perform these tasks competently. By so doing he would meet the expectations of others and obtain their approval.

If a person wishes to gain prestige, a society usually offers several routes by which he can move into such roles. In a developing society it appears that information, either in the form of educational preparation or knowledge obtained by other means, has become a principal means for getting and holding prestigeful positions. The other methods, which include conspicuous consumption, landownership, saintliness, and prowess in battle, require less information and are less effective during a period of growth.

A parallel argument connecting information flow to cultural development starts with a body of cultural traits. For each of these traits there will almost certainly be found at least one word or term in the vocabulary of the society. Development implies that the range of these traits (which include rituals, symbols, styles, techniques, and types of artifacts) must be increased and the number of ways they are combined must increase even more. Communication is required for the diffusion of these traits through the society so that most persons have a wider range at their disposal. For the word "traits" the word "images" can be substituted to give a still more general cultural proposition.

Administrative systems are also capable of development. Their progress depends upon the creation of large institutions. New activities, such as central government, integrated transport service, electric power production, water supply, medical service, military defense, and municipal administration, require larger and more intricate organizations than existed before. Before these bureaucracies can function and provide their designated services, they need quite large numbers of educated persons to fill the respective positions. They also need modern media of communication, such as a postal service, a telephone system, news publications, and banking services. Thus administrative development demands an accelerated buildup of communications through the educational system, as well as a set of public carriers with very much enlarged capacities.

A close connection between political development and enhanced communications has already been introduced in Chapter 2 [of *Developmental Planning*]. Politicians who wish to retain the backing of their supporters will employ every new medium of communication as a means of making contact with potential supporters. As soon as a new medium, such as television, has become available, the successful politician is the one who rebuilds his party organization around the special advantages offered by the new medium. A two-way communication system results, with appeals, promises, and informing statements flowing from the political leader to the public, and the concerns, fears, petitions, and suggestions being transmitted by the public to the politicians. The superior, or dominant, political organization over the long run is the one that has perfected this communications circuit so that large amounts of information flow in both directions.

Review for a moment the concepts that exist in each of the social sciences as encapsulated in the preceding paragraphs. They suggest that development cannot be achieved over the long run without very substantial increases in communications flow and large-scale accumulations of knowledge, both in people's heads and in collections of books and files. If people improve their economic productivity, advance their social status, enrich their culture, organize themselves for large tasks, and make their political action more sensitive, they cannot avoid placing more emphasis upon the quantity of messages that is received and sent. The respective systems—economic, social, cultural, administrative, and political —require it.

Outside of these systems, the psychology of the individual in the developing society must be considered. He has aspirations of some sort for the future. Some individuals particularly value freedom of choice in the marketplace; they would naturally work specifically to increase their money income. For most individuals, however, the urge to acquire a higher income is regarded only as a means to some other end. Very frequently, for example, the end is family security. For some others the extra product would go toward the creation of an effective nation that could command the respect of other nations and no longer be dominated by outsiders. Some individuals belong to oppressed minorities, and they aspire to gain higher social status and to occupy professional roles hitherto denied them. Still others yearn for a cultural life, rich in imagery, that will offer continual opportunities to experience new aesthetic creations. Having more money does not automatically assure one of achieving such aspirations, but wealth greatly increases one's chances.

To realize his aspirations, the individual must be alert to opportunities. He becomes interested in education because it guides his progress. He is also interested in the news because it brings information about possible opportunities. But the ordinary individual in the society remains a poor judge of what he needs to know. The student of the development process will be able to infer from comparisons of several societies in various stages of development what the curriculum should be, approximately how much effort should be expended in purveying the news, and what kinds of content would be the most informative.

Because the history and the aspirations are different for each country, it is not feasible to lay out an explicit plan for information-gathering systems. Differences in attitude toward information and concerning means for its distribution are among the major reasons why nations remain separate: they do not see any identity of aspirations and approach. Otherwise nations might easily federate and amalgamate in their efforts toward development. There is, however, a central core of information and procedures which is expected to be common to all nations and which embraces more than just science, technology, and world affairs. Therefore this study will concentrate upon a typical scheme for communicating the known body of needed information while being mindful that there is a unique component within each society as well which must be dealt with in the actual planning.

Thus far, information has been treated as a commodity which could be created, transmitted, stored, accumulated, bought, and lost. All this implies that information is something which can be handled quantitatively, and that there must be some sort of physical unit, similar to *tons* or *ergs*, by which to measure it. It is therefore proper at this point to consider carefully the logical foundations for relating information to growth, which should lead to the most relevant procedures for measurement.

THE PROPERTIES OF INFORMATION SYSTEMS

Underlying the foregoing judgments concerning the properties of communication and information are some basic principles connecting social change with the state of information. They cannot be proved in any scientific or philosophic sense of the word, but they can be shown to be logically consistent as well as representative of the true state of affairs. These principles, extricated from their immediate context, may be stated as propositions.

PROPOSITION ONE: SOCIAL CONTROL REQUIRES PRIOR KNOWLEDGE

Increasing control of a situation by human organization requires information useful for a short-range forecast of the future as well as knowledge of new opportunities for preventing threatened losses.

An executive group, charged with directing an organization, must know trends in the social, physical, and political environment before it can act in a reasonable manner. It must ask questions and collect data before reaching a decision. The questions executives pose to assistants and to the people around them cause the latter to generate many more questions. With this aggregate information, the opportunities for controlling a situation will be either equal to or greater than the ability without it. Almost always, then, any attempt to control the environment should be preceded by the collection of more facts than were already on hand.

PROPOSITION TWO: ECONOMIC GROWTH IS PRECEDED BY THE ACQUISITION OF NEW INFORMATION

Each increment of new economic growth and social organization requires prior infusion and diffusion of new information into the economic system.

Before steady growth can be recorded in any sector of the economy there must be a surge in the marketing of a line of products and services. Expanded use must be preceded by new information regarding the potential value of the product or service.[5] People rarely modify their consumptive choices upon the receipt of a single message with a new image; they almost always wait until they have had many confirming signals. The expansion also requires that needed workers be trained a year or so beforehand and new production and distribution services be organized at the same time. New facilities would have been designed two to five years earlier, and investors persuaded to commit their savings to the projects. All these new activities require a level of communications far beyond the national average. It is true that there may be some offsetting loss of information about the displaced activities, but such knowledge is slow to disappear completely because the backward areas of society retain knowledge of the former activities for generations after they have been abandoned in the modern component. Thus economic growth presupposes rapid advances in public information in some sectors and only a slow erosion of tradition generally.

PROPOSITION THREE: THE PRESENT STOCK OF NATURAL RESOURCES IS AN OUTGROWTH OF ACCUMULATED KNOWLEDGE

Any addition that is made to the reserves of natural resources is obtained through the use of reconnaissance, prospecting, surveying, and assaying the opportunity provided by nature. The value, which ultimately depends upon human wants, must also be ascertained. In addition, the technology for transforming the resource into useful products must be reasonably practical.

A given ore deposit, waterfall, or fishery cannot be considered a resource until the knowledge has been acquired which allows its conversion into products whose value exceeds anticipated expenditures. An increasing body of technological knowledge leads to opportunities for substitution and interchangeability, so that on the world scene there are already substitutes available, at a not impossible cost, for all the exhaustible resources.

PROPOSITION FOUR: A DECISION SYSTEM CONSUMES INFORMATION

Many decisions make some information obsolete and useless because alternatives that were investigated are no longer possible.

A functioning decision center is fed with information. If it is to generate growth, it must have a varied diet and plenty of action. It should be noted, however, that once an irrevocable decision has been made and the consequent action taken, the decision becomes history and the bulk of the information produced to inform the decision makers becomes virtually valueless. Hence all the original information collected can be quickly buried, except possibly for an otherwise useful principle or generalization that might have been formulated along the way.

PROPOSITION FIVE: KNOWLEDGE MUST BE RENEWED

Many random factors, such as fire, accident, death, and forgetfulness, combine to reduce the body of knowledge over time, and only new observations, inventions, and concurrences can increase the stock.

Contemporary knowledge exists as the memory of individuals, much of which has been transcribed to paper, film, or magnetic tape. Knowledge is considered here as only those memories with which other observers agree as to their correctness. It includes information about the states of nature and the structure of social action. Recorded knowledge is therefore several steps behind the actual state of knowledge in the society. For example, many specialized food-processing crafts will vanish in the course of a famine; or political knowledge will disappear upon the death of a great leader and the dissolution of his circle of advisers, so the total know-how of the culture would diminish more and more over time unless some source that produces new knowledge is present. It seems likely that many more societies in the historic period have regressed over time than have progressed. The losses are more often attributable to the consequences of conflict than to any of the other causes mentioned—one of the principal reasons for giving an unusual amount of attention to the resolution of conflict elsewhere in this analysis.

PROPOSITION SIX: SCIENTIFIC FINDINGS ARE SYSTEMATIZED KNOWLEDGE

Science, both fundamental and applied, attempts to establish relationships between phenomena so that various observers can agree upon facts and relationships as being true enough to act upon. Its more important contribution is the development of theories which collect most of the facts together into several meaningful, teachable systems that save time and trouble in discerning details.

Scientists are specialists in the creation and preservation of knowledge that promises to be of value to people in general. They take great care, when reducing their observations to some published form, to employ words with precise, unambiguous meanings. Methods of observation are specified, and the relationships to prior works are almost always established. As a result much less of the scientific information is consumed in the course of institutional decision making (most of which is applied science) than of other forms of information (including judgments of motivations of people, temporary scarcities, the implications for setting certain precedents, etc.).

Behind these propositions exist two fundamental concepts—information and knowledge—which are ultimately capable of quantification. *Information* is defined as the content of a message or a signal which permits the recipient to make what he feels are better choices in subsequent behavior. The interpretation of the message may tell him (1) more about the ends or outcomes of the decisions, (2) more about the risks associated with alternatives already being considered, (3) some hints of new paths of action of which he had previously been unaware, and (4) warnings of new kinds of choices which may soon need to be made.   The transfer of information, therefore, is a property of communications of all kinds, including observations made upon features of the surroundings.   Information flows are a direct outcome of communication rates.   *Knowledge* represents stored information, remembered primarily because it is believed that sometime in the future it might be useful.   Knowledge takes the form of a series of statements which are felt to be true and pertinent to the actions of individuals, groups, institutions, and sociopolitical systems at the national and international level.   The amount of knowledge that a person has acquired about a given subject (say, international affairs) can be judged by the score he makes in a comprehensive examination on that subject.   This might be called personal knowledge, as distinguished from public knowledge which can be drawn upon by referring to an encyclopedia or a library.

In science, over the past fifteen years or so, methods have been devised for measuring the amount of potentially useful information that is contained in a message, and generalizations have been reached regarding typical human rates for absorbing information.   The same measures can be applied to the stored messages residing in files and in libraries.   The advantage of measurement is that it establishes whether or not growth in information flow and storage has occurred over time.   If it has, then one of the prerequisites for social and economic growth will have been met.   In practice, however, it will be advisable not to make extensive measurements of total information flow but to find a few simple indexes which reflect growth and decline of message flow in important sectors of the culture.   Such statistics are even more fundamental to a growth-promoting policy than most financial data that are being collected today.

INFORMATION, IMAGES, AND GROWTH

Consider a typical struggling society when it is looked at through this new lens provided by modern information principles.   What is its current state of affairs?   It is improper to invade privacy and look behind the walls of the household, but it is possible to scrutinize what transpires in public, because all significant social, political, and cultural phenomena must eventually be detectable in public transactions.   By definition, the actors in public are in a fishbowl and are fair game for systematic observation.

It will be noted that people frequently come together and exchange remarks.   They send mail to each other and make telephone calls.   Apparently these interactions have utility.   There is a pattern to these interchanges also, which changes with the time of day, the day of the week, and the season.   Each person outside of his household may engage in scores or even hundreds of such "public" transactions per day.   Often, through newspapers, radio, and television, the public world is brought into the household itself so that public transactions may occur there also.   These transactions bind households together into a much larger unit;

they comprise attempts on the part of individuals and households to explore and adjust to the external realities.   The market, the government, the job, the cultural events, and the educational system, each and all, are included in any comprehensive survey of the public communications transactions.

In a society based upon an oral tradition, the spoken interchanges provide the supports for cooperation and integration.   Even in these societies there are some accessory supports and images, such as temples, rituals, tribal emblems, and artistic forms which are not oral, but the inscriptions and signs enter into only a trivial fraction of daily activities.   The stock of knowledge in such a society resides in the memories of its respective members.   The skills of the artisans, the techniques of agriculture, the history of political and social organization, the framework for public service, all of these must be known to at least a few people who must pass their own knowledge down to the next generation by teaching. The key to the stock of knowledge in such a society lies in the language—it needs a word for almost everything that is preserved.   The capacity for rote learning and remembering of designated names of things in such a society is often phenomenal by present standards.

The use of writing, the scriptural tradition, because of the impersonal means of communication afforded by writing and ciphering, brings about a major advance in the society that adopts it.   Many more facts and ideas can be transmitted from one generation to the next, and the likelihood of loss is greatly reduced.   However, it has been the introduction of printing that has wrought the most powerful revolution in societies.   With printing, writing could be multiplied and put into many hands; it could be stored simultaneously in many different places, and so it led the way to universal literacy.   The stock of knowledge then could be built up many times over and be diffused much more widely through the population. With the flowering of science and technology, much of the knowledge rose to levels of generality and applicability which were recognizably higher than folk wisdom and the handicrafts.   Thus the basis is provided for modern society. Modernity consists of participating to a very marked extent in world culture and drawing upon the rapidly growing body of knowledge that is internationally valid.

Thousands of images are acquired at an early age in family life, but tens of thousands are learned in public life.   One learns, for example, to link thousands of names to an equal number of faces and to identify their kinship and social role. Each item in the marketplace carries with it not only impressions of its shape, design, and purpose but also the process by which it is used.   Thousands of addresses are known, and are distinguished both by location and by peculiarities of the structure at the given address.   Many thousands more images cover concepts of public behavior, customs, rituals, routines, and issues.   Thus a person may be able to recall to consciousness any of tens of thousands of images, contrast them, rank them, use them to work out tentative solutions to problems, and communicate them to others in order to gain approval and cooperation.   The same person can recognize several times more images with which he has less familiarity and confidence, and his curiosity, if nothing else, will induce him to cooperate when exposed to them in human associations so long as there is no indication of threat.

Images are the object of cultural play. Each person reassembles them in his thoughts and his dreams. Novelists are adept at presenting them with words that evoke a segment of life that presumably could have been lived. Musicians play with variations in timing and tone. Cinema directors string together visual images, backed by speech, in a persuasive fashion. Poets invent new images by making deft contrasts between old ones and put into words subtleties that had previously escaped description. All of these artistic skills are directly concerned with imagery. They fill in gaps and round out the spectrum of the possible images that can be based upon mutual experience.

The most numerous body of images by far is provided in science. Each distinct species and strain of organism represents a different image for which a verbal designation exists. There are many millions of these alone. Compositions of matter, inorganic and organic, make up another set of images, and there are millions of these, too. There are other images of relations between images, and so scientific principles come into being. Principle can be piled upon principle, so that a huge intellectual structure of images has been built up in science. Most of a scientist's training is spent becoming acquainted with the logic of this struc-ture so that he can find his way to the specific images that are of interest and trace their connections with the others. Science has gone so far, far beyond the capac-ity of the human memory that the basic strategy is to establish paths for getting around in the records, almost always in a highly specialized region, of knowing *how* to find past observations rather than remembering in detail *what* has been found. Research adds to both the number of images and the number of relation-ships that are known to exist between them.

Each of the images in the repertoire of people may be assigned a market value, an emotional value (a feature deliberately removed from scientific images in order to reduce the likelihood of costly conflict and misunderstanding), and an information value. These properties are quite convenient for persons who think like economists. For example, the more frequently an image is used in communi-cations, the less likely its use will convey anything new (and therefore informative) to the recipients; as a consequence, less information is diffused by its transmission. Hence the growth of information transmission cannot be based upon the simple repetition of messages. On the other hand, the precisely defined image used only on rare occasions results in a very high level of information transmission, provided that an appreciation of the precision exists at the point of reception. The same arguments can be made for market value (because supply is restricted) and for emotional value (because satiation is not a factor).

Thus a society has a stock of knowledge, made up of the combined repertoire of images available to its members together with the relations of the images to each other, and this stock is diffused through a population according to need and in-terest.

The stock has properties similar to those of an inventory of capital goods in economics, and the flow has properties similar to a consumption function. Yet the whole system of market transactions taken up in economic studies ordinarily makes up only a minor part of this cultural flow. Despite the preconceptions of economists, most images do *not* have explicit money prices attached to them—in fact, in many societies it is often judged to be immoral if money is charged or paid. Nevertheless, the utility of the images can be measured. This eiconic view of society and culture resembles the economic picture, with each image representing a commodity that is being exchanged, but it can be far more general.

A repertoire of images is a *living* system. In a body of images that is shared by a given society some images are being born, others are being adopted, and many are dying of neglect. Images come into being when observers agree that it is convenient to make distinctions between stimuli originally lumped under a single image. It might be said that such images have undergone fission, much as bacteria reproduce. Others, when contrasted with each other, yield a new concept whose parentage is obvious. Sometimes an instrument, or a technique of exploration—a single image—may generate a whole string of new images. All such offspring images have to be re-used occasionally, otherwise they will be lost. Even the most esoteric scientific image must be republished every half century or so if it is not to be lost. Images die largely because they are obsolete; other images have been found in their stead which convey more value.

A traditional society has a small repertoire of shared images, and most of the possible relationships between them have already been worked out. The images it has are relatively infertile and are rarely split into new ones. New images that are formed usually are balanced in number by others which disappear owing to accidents or lack of concern.

In the dual economy—after noting all the reservations introduced earlier when the term was defined—the modern sector is aware of most of the images of the traditional society within which it (the modern sector) is embedded; but it has downgraded the value of most of them and is concerned with establishing connections with images borrowed from outside the society. It discovers that a rich variety of images has been brought into existence in the modern cultures and that these are for the most part freely available; one need only take the time to study and to acquire copies of the written record.

Yet a creative effort remains. It is that of merging the traditional system with those parts of the modern that are accessible. These combinations must be tried out by experiment, and most of the experiments will end as failures. The literature and art associated with these initial attempts at synthesis are, with few exceptions, exceedingly poor. The newly created images intended to connect the old with the new are crude, clumsy, and shallow in conception during the first stages of this acculturation process. But, first in the large organizations with on-the-job teaching programs (government and industry), then later in the schools and studios, suitable compromises are eventually found and the results can be very exciting indeed. Thereafter the stock of images available to the whole society can be expanded by accelerated borrowing. The diffusion process into the traditional sector can be subdivided into easy steps which allow the ambitious youth to break out of the confines of the traditions within which he was raised and move into far more imposing edifices of images which are shared in a large part with the rest of the world. This cultural hybridization is most evident in Japan over the last two decades.

MEASURES OF GROWTH AND OPENNESS

If the accumulation of a stock of new images and their distribution through the population are highly indicative of social and cultural growth and a determinant of economic growth potential, what indexes should be uesd for the measurement of this very basic kind of growth? What implications are suggested for governmental policy?

These questions point up a deficiency in developmental planning as presently practiced. They are questions that have never been adequately approached before in publications and have never been undertaken in practice, yet they follow logically from the principles that have already been expressed.

The basic data are supplied by a lexicon—a list of words employed in a society at a given time. On the theory that a term must exist for every significant phenomenon, a lexicon should provide a fairly comprehensive list of images current in the society. If in addition a dictionary of local usage has been prepared by a team of linguists, the list would also contain idioms, phrases, and the multiple meanings of some overworked words for each dialect. It would be much more complete than a lexicon and would constitute a bench mark against which subsequent measures could be made.

Linguists in their fieldwork try to identify new usages for words that are currently being employed for human activity in public. Their ears are tuned to discovering new slang, new loan words from the outside, new word arrangements, and new intonations. A few of these word mutations are traceable to the natural drift of the language and to the flow of events within the society, but most are due to outside contacts and the importation by such routes of viable images. Some may be attributed to the strains set up in the language by earlier borrowing; people, in order to be perfectly clear in their expression, tend to modify it accordingly so as to emphasize key phrases. Thus the changes in the popular language tend to reflect very sensitively the images being added to the stock previously available to the society.

Ordinarily linguists would prepare notes on each new usage and its context each time some innovation in language is detected. Such notes, however, represent nominations for change, since poorly educated persons may make errors which are corrected as soon as the deviation is brought to their attention. Only after a new usage has been noted in a given number of independent contexts (three would be sufficient) would it be formally designated an addition to the language and be recorded in the next comprehensive dictionary. If the new usage can be traced to the appearance of a new image that is growing in significance, frequency of use, and utility, it can be expected to be introduced then into a still wider range of contexts.

Perhaps an example would be helpful to demonstrate the subsequent proliferation. Take the image of "fertilizer"; it has probably already entered the repertoire of virtually every society at one point or another. But the subsidiary concepts will enter later—superphosphate, urea, ammonium nitrate, potash assay, spreaders, and various trade names of premixed fertilizers on the international market. Each time any of these words are used they disseminate a unique image about a specialized fertilizer or its constituents and imply possible advantages that follow upon the acquisition of this knowledge. Repeated demonstrations of Western technology show that this knowledge of fertilizers itself promises eventually to produce a striking increase in agricultural production; but before this can occur there must be modifications in the practice of traditional agriculture. These improvements in agriculture can only follow arguments presented by leaders and specialists who are likely to invent a new term or two to summarize their recommendations. Increases in the yield tend to require emergency storage and transport, and these makeshifts also are likely to introduce additions to the language. In the end, scores of images would be contributed to the society merely by the introduction of synthetic fertilizer.

In a comprehensive dictionary of the terms employed in the spoken and written language of a specific society, linguistic specialists can identify quite closely the dates of appearance and the probable source of each term. When studying the language of a developing society, one expects to see the rate of appearance of new terms increasing. The source of the terms is also important. An open society will be borrowing terms from the contacting societies that provided the image. Thus the borrowing rate of loan words over time should be an indicator of openness. The borrowing process goes on most rapidly at the borders of a country and in the centers of its cities. Oppositely, the loss of an image is not so easily established in any society because usage retreats from the cities to the most isolated regions, where it may persist for centuries. The total size of the lexicon, therefore, is more difficult to measure than the rates of accretion.

The growth rate of indigenous terms, drawn from the slang and the argot of specialized groups, should rise in response to urbanization and to the diffusion of local interpretations of modern culture. The adoption of new terms with internal origins should therefore accelerate sometime after the rate of adoption of loan words had begun to increase. The ratio between these two rates—internal versus external—should be a still more sensitive index of openness. It would be interesting to compare this ratio with internal versus external intercity travel (an indicator of the growth of larger social organization), and internal versus external sources of capital.

The linguistic connections between cultural growth and economic growth follow directly from the foregoing propositions. They deserve a great deal of research similar to that on motivational factors coordinated by McClelland. This lexicographical research is vital in a newly developing country and need not be expensive. A society of amateurs made up of newspaper reporters, writers, editors, printers, policemen, social workers, teachers, and similar people will do the bulk of the work with enthusiasm. Only a small committee (drawn from among university staff, technicians, and statisticians) is then needed to supervise the accumulation of materials and rule on doubtful inclusions. True, some countries are forced to maintain a larger organization if, like Indonesia and Israel, they need to *create* a national language and produce a full range of textbooks in that language.

There are no arbitrary values for these indexes depicting growth of the repertoire of terms, or images, which can be compared across cultures. So much depends upon each country's history of colonialism, invasion, foreign aid, discovery of natural resources, and its location, that counts of new terms introduced have meaning only when viewed in the perspective of the country's own evolution.

The cross-national transfer of lexicographical terms signals the beginning of a new type of influence, or a greater depth for well-known types of influence. The influence is never unidirectional because the developed societies also pick up many novel images in their contacts with the less developed societies. The developed societies have the most to learn in the areas of plant and animal ecology, herb medicine, linguistic variations, art forms, and geography.

This complementarity in the exchange of images often can cause misunderstandings among the new nations. Most ultranationalistic elites try to guard the national language as expressed in schools, newspapers, and books against contamination. They decry the use of loan words. They also resent the interest of inquisitive, camera-carrying foreigners in the backward portions of the society, and even may legislate against foreign contacts. They thereby reduce both the openness and the growth of the society.

MORE PRECISE MEASURES OF GROWTH

There is a way of starting from the study of language and obtaining a measure of growth of communications and knowledge which can be used for comparisons *between* societies. It requires estimations of the frequency with which the respective terms in the repertoire turn up in the public communications.

The background arguments and a description of the methods to be employed for obtaining an index of cultural growth are provided in a previous book by the author, *A Communications Theory of Urban Growth*. The technique has not been applied to any countries as yet (except in outline as an academic exercise to discover its properties), nor could it be carried out with any real precision until the latter part of the 1960s. The principles upon which the proposed technique is based are quite new. An outline of the relevant elements can be presented here.

Once a reasonably complete lexicon of terms in a given society has been assembled, the public communications of the society need to be sampled. The sampling cannot follow the areal divisions of the census because the highest rate of communication is reached away from the residence. The proper unit for sampling is a metropolitan area combined with the hinterland that it dominates. The sample should be stratified according to the kinds of public communications engaged in: reading, television and films, radio and recordings, social discussions, telephone conversations, observations of the environment, etc. A sample can also be based upon measures of the time spent by the population while engaging in these various communications.

The crude index of information flow can be obtained by finding the number of times each term is being received in the society per unit of time, multiplying by $p \log p$, where p is the frequency of appearance, and summing up overall terms in the message flow. The crude index overstates the flow of potentially useful information, but equilibration forces in social institutions almost always act so as to assure that potentially useful information remains a relatively constant proportion of the total.

Estimates of the potentially useful information flow can be obtained by carrying out experiments upon typical receivers of the transmitted communications: Which of the terms employed were repetitive, unnecessary, or redundant; which were not recognized at all? It is also possible to obtain by experiment the receivers' judgment of the likelihood that the respective terms would appear in the context that they do. Then, by substituting the subjective probability of the appearance of a term into the mathematical phrase $p \log p$, a more realistic measure can be obtained of information actually transmitted. The cost of obtaining such statistics is at present quite high, but it can be reduced by careful planning of the routine accumulation of statistics (as discussed in Chapter 4 [of *Developmental Planning*]). The primary value of the statistics is for the guidance of investments in education and urban services.

One meaning that can be attached to the numbers obtained in this index is that it represents the number of *bits* of mechanical memory that would be required for storing the content of the communication after it had been translated into the most efficient possible binary code, where the units employed are *bits*. Knowing the capacity of magnetic tape, for example, it is possible to calculate how much tape would be required. However, when dealing with human memories for the frequency of terms in the repertoire within environmental contexts—a far more subtle storage device—the unit of information is called a *hubit*.

Preliminary estimates of net information flow in various societies, drawn from descriptions of public life and social interactions within them, have been calculated. Residents of the large cities of the poorest societies (Indonesia, Ethiopia, etc.) appear to transmit 100,000 to 1,000,000 hubits per capita per year. Completely modernized, urbanized, and literate societies exceed 100,000,000 per year. Recall, for purposes of comparison, that per capita incomes for these same societies range from an estimated $40 at the bottom to a measured $1,000 to $3,000 per year at the top, a ratio of at least one to twenty-five but not exceeding one to seventy-five. The corresponding ratio for information flow is much greater, being more nearly one to five hundred. This means that growth rates in the transmission of information must be greater than those exhibited for income, as well as being registered sooner in the growth process—an argument that has already been emphasized.

Some indication of the significance of these indexes of knowledge (as demonstrated by the lexicon size) and of the transmission of information is provided by reconsideration of the war-damaged countries in the process of reconstruction discussed in Chapter 1 [of *Developmental Planning*]. If samples had been taken of the vocabulary employed even at the period of greatest suffering and deprivation, there is little doubt that the range of images employed still would be many times greater than that of an underdeveloped country at the same consumption level. Gradually the communication rate climbed, organizations were recreated, and the gaps in them were filled by quick retraining of persons. In reconstruction, the knowledge that resided in the memories of men and the surviving records of their organizations were reconstituted first in concrete, steel, and glass, and later in the form of marketable goods built to specifications that had been established as suitable to the climate and the culture years before. The war-damaged countries did not have to take time to innovate or test other people's images for suitability to the environment; they needed only to recapitulate what already existed in the culture, and fit the pieces together into plans which were much more rational and laborsaving than the hodgepodge that existed before the war. During this period of exceedingly rapid economic growth, therefore, the stock of knowledge index would show a much slower rate of growth of images and only a rather ordinary growth in the flow of information index after radio and newspapers had been reestablished and television introduced. The poetry, novels, and music would be quite dull—in the main merely affirmations of what had been felt to be valuable decades earlier. Some images were lost forever in the destruction, and some others needed to be denied; as a result the working vocabulary might display some significant gaps during the reconstruction.

This slowdown in cultural growth during reconstruction disappears when increased leisure, mobility, and security permit large interchanges of population. Then many new images are borrowed, and satisfaction with one's own cultural heritage is challenged. The success of the postwar reconstruction period in Western Europe has provided a foundation for a ferment that is already detectable in the spoken languages and in the kinds of discussions underway in periodicals. The acceleration should be measurable by applying the kinds of indexes described here. Current measurements, however, could give no indication of the bloom of cultural creativity that should result when the dispersion of images across national boundaries has been digested.

Thus the argument is made here that *the image must precede the physical reality, and that, as long as the image remains, the physical reality can be quickly reconstituted.* Development, then, is fundamentally a mental task requiring first the assimilation of new images and then the reconstruction of relationships between all the images. The images may be distinguished from one another and counted, primarily because language is such a precise instrument, and the accessories to language—pictures and diagrams—can be catalogued in a manner closely resembling methods used for language. An enrichment of the culture presages the formation of social organizations which are able to translate the images into physical reality.

A RESTATEMENT IN EVOLUTIONARY SEQUENCE

Anyone who has studied *growth phenomena* in economic systems, in businesses, in service organizations such as hospitals or libraries, in learning processes, or even in biology, will quickly discern the universal applicability of the central arguments presented in the foregoing "information theory of development." There seem to be general principles of growth that apply to all living systems, but some systems are more elaborate and complex than others.   In no case, however, is the knowledge about the components of a system combined with the knowledge of the principles sufficient for one to instigate and direct growth at will.   Our understanding is presently a few steps ahead of what was available before, but in all these areas of expertise it still falls far short of what is needed for reliable control over the development process.

Growth has its origins in some system that has matured and come into equilibrium with its environment.   A seed of change is introduced and a new system grows up to displace the old because the new is better able to cope with the challenges presented by the environment.

In our typical case of social-political-economic-cultural growth, we begin with a territory with a human population living within it.   The human population has found a *modus vivendi* at its existing size by employing tools that it has known for a long time.   Thus it has achieved a kind of equilibrium within itself as well as with nature.   The seed of change, as was said before, is information about conditions outside the territory.   Some information diffuses in from the edges of the territory so that people on the borders come to accept some of the customs and techniques of peoples in neighboring territories, even if they are enemies. News about the outside world, and cultural influences emanating from foreign capitals, converge upon the decision-making centers, usually the residences of chiefs, kings, or chief ministers and their advisers.   If there has been a radical transformation in the parts of the world making contact, then the change may significantly affect the security and welfare of the more knowledgeable people, either for better or for worse, before it affects the others.   Part of the governing elite worries about whether it should or should not adopt some elements of the change.

Once such contact has been made and the seed of change has begun to swell, attention must be paid to structural details within *the system* under observation, as well as its environment.   Our instrument for observation must have four focuses: one for the assemblage of nations and territories; the second for the territory with the properties already given; the third for groups and organizations within the territory; at the fourth level we scrutinize the behavior of individual human beings that is being coordinated through the groups and organizations. Change becomes apparent at each of these levels in the course of the growth process.

The developmental stage following upon the introduction and adoption of new ideas is the formation of the dual society, as depicted in Chapter 2 [of *Devel-*

opmental Planning]. The image of the future that comes into being in the modern sector of the dual society is based upon a composite of the images of the modern nations with which its members have had direct and indirect contacts. The traditional sector senses the change, regards it as a disturbance with mixed good and bad aspects, and tries to abolish the undesirable results without having very great knowledge regarding either the immediate causes of the change or the effects of attempts to repress it.

Following this is a period of wholesale borrowing of foreign images. The languages and culture of foreign countries are learned, and as many as possible of their artifacts and styles are introduced. The latter choices are usually made by individuals and families, without much subsidy from the government. As noted earlier in this chapter, the greatest friction is between the growing modern organizations and the relatively static but powerful traditional institutions.

With the formation of the dual society comes nationalism, and ultimately the creation of the nation-state. The new state requires the invention of scores more of new images, mainly calculated to induce unity of purpose in the population and to suggest equivalence to other states in the world arena. These new images include flags and other insignia, postage stamps, uniforms, constitutions, roles of leadership, etc. Attempts are made to legitimize the new by borrowing images from tradition. Then, shortly after nationhood is achieved, an architectural style for public buildings is chosen for many of the same reasons: a history of the nation must be synthesized which befits its self-image.

The proliferation of images that occurs at this stage is to be found primarily in the political sphere because they are needed as a means of orienting loyalties. Those adopted are hybrids of various sorts, invented to reduce conflict and assist in the creation of institutions. Thereafter undisciplined acceptance of foreign images is frowned upon by those in power, the xenophobic versions of nationalism being quite extreme in their prohibition of outside images. But such attitudes are unproductive.

After the inception of the nation, when the planning begins in earnest, the natural resources and the goals of the people determine the value of the respective images. Certain international specializations must be learned in all their technical details, so that this particular nation is as likely as any other to produce innovations which are imitated by other nations. Thus, nations that plan become quite selective concerning what images shall be systematically borrowed. If organizations do not already exist for acquiring and installing a body of technical knowledge, they are created by fiat and carefully nurtured with grants and subsidies until they can operate independently. If an insufficient number of individuals had acquired the basic technical skills during the period of wholesale borrowing, the nation might have to start with selecting students for foreign study and postpone the creation of the organizations for five to ten years.

In the organizing process of developing a national institution, an extra burst of communications activity is experienced. It is exceeded in volume only by the "public information" that is later undertaken to sell the increasing quantities of the product or service.

Thus, the Image of the nation in a developed state—with all its implications for behavior—comes first.   Next—if there are no mistakes or interruptions—come the modern manufactures and associated services, such as medicine or radio broadcasting.   Finally comes the actual consumption and adjustments in the pattern of living by households and individuals.

Therefore, if a nation wishes to know how well it is doing in preparing for the succeeding decade of growth, rather than for the next few years, it would do well to sample the images that are distributed through the various agencies in the society.   Where there is growth in the variety and frequency of modern images, expansions in physical capacity are likely to follow—provided they are at all advantageous economically.

A nation has at best only partial control over the *social* communications of its citizens.   There is a strong temptation to manipulate the press, the textbooks, and public statements so that only the "right" images are transmitted.   Such procedures are not easily administered in a liberal fashion; they are either ignored (and the force of law is weakened by the winks of the officers), or they are too strictly interpreted and the growth of imagery is stunted.

The supply of images, and the behaviors associated with them, existing within a population operate as a kind of reserve for meeting emergencies and opportunities.   Maintaining a stock of images is equivalent in many respects to holding substantial inventories.   If the prerequisites for meeting an emergency require existing products and components, the challenge can be met.   A society's stock of images serves much the same purpose.   Its repertoire covers all the monetized sector, besides a large area in addition where respect and cooperation cannot be obtained with monetary payments.   The possession of a *balanced* supply of images can in fact contribute more to the creation of a flexible, adaptive, and growing society than would a plentiful supply of cash.   Indeed, the chief problem of the countries richly endowed with natural resources is to find a reasonably efficient (i.e., conflict-free) means for converting hard currency into *social* resources of this kind.

As the images are employed in an institutional framework, they assist in the making of decisions at every level.   The internal structure of the enterprises, government bureaus, schools, and other organizations that aid the short-range decision making can also make a difference in how effectively the images are used. Structure determines the *speed* with which the stock of images can be mobilized and directed to the challenge that has arisen.   For enterprise, the quicker the response, when in competition with other countries, the more likely the country is to obtain the first fruits rather than the leavings.   The institutions related to planning, however, are expected to take many more facts into account and to make the long-range decisions affecting the allocation of resources after several alternatives have been compared.   Thus, rather than quickness of response, it is the *breadth* of adequate response that is emphasized in plan-oriented organizations.

At the final stage in development (this is the one that Japan is presently entering and Italy is not far behind) the distinctions between modern and traditional begin to disappear.   The peasants have television sets and small tractors; the poorest people in the cities have unions, churches, political associations, sports clubs, and community-improvement organizations.   The social structure contains many intermediate roles which are neither modern nor traditional, but instead represent various kinds of compromises.   As growth continues, the educational requirements and technical ability demanded of persons filling the more common roles are increased.   This is another way of saying that comprehension of a larger repertoire of modern images is needed to fill the post satisfactorily.   Standards of performance are being raised.   The *quality* of the goods and services produced becomes a matter of grave importance.

Growth can continue for a long while thereafter, as the Western European and American economies have demonstrated.   Communications flow in urban areas may increase by five to fifty times beyond what it is now in these advanced countries, before human limits are reached.   The number of images that may be added to the repertoires from science and the arts appears to be close to infinity; but as the number is enlarged, human beings will need machines to sort out the images, identify those that are of particular interest, and submit them to the study groups in some convenient manner.   Therefore, image-processing machines seem to constitute a prerequisite for growth in advanced societies.   Computers are now being used for these purposes, but they are still exceedingly clumsy.

When the "information theory of development" is stated in this evolutionary form, it appears less formidable and more like common sense.   Its propositions and computations are more useful for the fine calculations needed to choose the best projects and to assess the needs of programs already under way.   This evolutionary form is more convenient, too, for understanding the strategy of development and the more specific needs for "openness."

Bibliography

Boulding, K. E.: *The Image*, The University of Michigan Press, Ann Arbor, Mich., 1957.
An elementary discourse on the properties of images and the systems that encompass them.

Hagen, E. E.: *On the Theory of Social Change*, Dorsey Press, Homewood, Ill., 1962.
A reconsideration of the major extraeconomic factors underlying economic growth.

Hoselitz, B. F.: *Sociological Aspects of Economic Growth*, The Free Press of Glencoe, New York, 1960.
Connects social change and economic development with the classical theories of demography, social structure, and organization.

Kuhn, Alfred: *The Study of Society: A Unified Approach*, The Dorsey Press and Richard D. Irwin, Inc., Homewood, Ill., 1963.
A reconstruction of economic, social, and cultural theory around the concepts of transactions and organizations.

Lewis, W. A.: *The Theory of Economic Development*, George Allen & Unwin, Ltd., London, 1955.
This book introduced and gave strongest emphasis to the importance of education, administrative institutions, and knowledge for the process of economic development in mixed economies.

Machlup, F.: *The Production and Distribution of Knowledge in the United States*, Princeton University Press, Princeton, N.J., 1962.
Concludes after wide-ranging empirical assessments that 29 percent of American GNP is expended for communication, education, research, and other knowledge processes, which grow twice as fast as the rest of the economy.

McClelland, D. C.: *The Achieving Society*, D. Van Nostrand Company, Inc., Princeton, N.J., 1961.
Isolates the "need for achievement," a psychological factor necessary for rapid development, in historic and contemporary societies, and describes how it can be measured.

McLuhan, Marshall: *The Gutenberg Galaxy*, University of Toronto Press, Toronto, Canada, 1962.
A humanistically oriented analysis of the transformation in social structure brought about by the transition from oral to printed images in the Western world, which in turn was caused by a technological transition.

Meier, Richard L.: *A Communication Theory of Urban Growth*, The M.I.T. Press, Cambridge, Mass., 1962.
Lays foundations for the identification of images and the measurement of information flow.

Miller, G. A., et al.: *Plans and the Structure of Behavior*, Holt, Rinehart and Winston, Inc., New York, 1960.
A systems theory approach to the essentials for organizing individual and social behavior.

Ornstein, Jacob: "Patterns of Language Planning in the New States," *World Politics*, vol. 17, pp. 40–49, 1964.
Lists factors determining success of second-language programs and language synthesis.

Polak, F. L.: *The Image of the Future: European Aspects*, transl. by Elise Boulding, Sythoff, Leyden, The Netherlands, 1961, 2 vols.
A humanistic and cultural assessment of the futures that have engaged European intellectuals.

Zollschan, G. K., and Walter Hirsch (eds.): *Explorations in Social Change*, Houghton Mifflin Company, Boston, 1964.
The most wide-ranging up-to-date review of the present thinking about social change, whether revolutionary, evolutionary, or induced.

Notes

1. A reconstruction of Hagen's theory using more operational forms of psychology was undertaken by John H. Kunkel in "Psychological Factors in the Analysis of Economic Development," *Journal of Social Issues*, vol. 19, pp. 67–68, 1963. His version offers a persuasive explanation but is no more useful for planning since it is concerned with the conversion of a traditional society into a transitional society, while planning can begin only after this modification is well advanced.

2. A moderately high nPower index may not be irrelevant to the existence of the nation as an independent unit, another prerequisite for development in most parts of the world, but McClelland collected his data in such a way that the connection between this motive and the development of the nation would not be revealed.

3. A term used by engineers who at one time attributed the inoperability of new equipment to the presence of "bugs"; the word was borrowed by computer programmers and has now become a part of standard nomenclature.

4. K. E. Boulding, *Conflict and Defense*, Harper & Row, Incorporated, New York, 1962. However, Boulding mixes competition with the conflict situation where adversaries are mutually aware of an incompatible Image and both are determined to have their way.

5. Economic theorists can show there is a logical possibility that this statement is not necessarily true, but the exceptions are trivial cases.

27. Class Relations in an Age of Contract
Reinhard Bendix

INDIVIDUALISTIC AUTHORITY RELATIONSHIPS

The reciprocity of social relations falls into patterns because men orient themselves toward the expectation of others and every action of "the other" limits the range of possible responses. Authority means that the few in command have a wide choice of options. Conversely, subordination means that the many who follow orders have their range of choice curtailed. But the options of the few are limited, even when the power at their command is overwhelming. One of these limits is that even the most drastic subordination leaves some choices to those who obey. Tacit noncooperation can be varied, subtle, and more important than overt protest. Subordinates make judgments, leading to degrees of cooperation or noncooperation that are important variables in every established pattern of authority.

The traditional ideology which defends the privileges of the aristocracy in the name of its responsibilities must be seen in this light. Tocqueville emphasizes the positive aspects of the social relations which correspond to this world view. However willful and evasive individual lords were, it is reasonable to assume that for a time the sense and practice of aristocratic responsibility for their inferiors were relatively high, just as the loyalty and obedience of subordinates were genuine. Indeed, without some responsibility on one side and some loyalty on the other, it would be meaningless to say that traditional authority relations were disrupted. It is best to consider the traditional pattern as partly a behavior

From Reinhard Bendix, *Nation Building and Citizenship: Studies of Our Changing Social Order* (New York, 1964), pp. 56–75, by permission of John Wiley & Sons, Inc.

pattern and partly an ideal in view of the violent conflicts which also characterize medieval society.   Ideals are essential in this connection because they affect the orientation even of those who fail to live up to them.   Traditional authority relations remain intact as long as the actions and beliefs which deviate from this pattern as well as those which sustain it do not undermine the basic reciprocity of expectations.

To say that a crisis of transition sets in when men consciously question previously accepted agreements and conventions, does not help us to distinguish this questioning from the continual adjustments of rights and obligations which occur while traditional authority relations remain "intact."   Such adjustments involve modifications of detail which turn into a questioning of basic assumptions only if they should cumulate.   Usually, the contemporary observer is barred from recognizing this distinction.   He can see a crisis (no age is without its Cassandras), but he cannot tell whether it is *the* crisis and where it will lead.   In his analysis of traditional authority relations in decline, Tocqueville observes that the masters increasingly evade their responsibility "to protect and to remunerate" but retain their customary privileges as an inalienable right.   This process extends over centuries, during which the actual rejection of responsibility is thoroughly obscured by the traditional ideology.   When does this discrepancy between the rights and responsibilities of the masters become manifest?

Ideas concerning the position of the poor do not provide the best clue in this respect.   Throughout the centuries the poor are taught the duty to labor and the virtue of being satisfied with the station to which God has called them.   Condemnation of their indolence and dissipation are a constant theme, but these failings are considered ineradicable—a token of low social rank.   Human quality and social responsibility are believed to go together.   The low station and quality of the poor also exempt them from responsibility; not much can be demanded of them.   On the other hand, high rank also means great responsibility.   Even where traditional practices are abandoned, it is easy to continue the convenient pretext that the rich and powerful treat the laboring poor as parents treat their children.   Throughout much of the nineteenth century paternalism retains its appeal; a deeply ingrained view is not readily destroyed.   It is all the more striking, therefore, that in the early phase of English industrialization the responsibility of protecting the poor against the hazards of life is rejected explicitly.   The contrast with paternalism makes this rejection of upper-class responsibility a visibly new phenomenon.

During the last half of the eighteenth century a number of clergymen, writers, and political economists begin to reject the "responsibility of the rich" as a pious fraud.   The dislocations of the industrial revolution with their cruel effects upon masses of people lead to or call for new interpretations of the cause of poverty.   Three of these interpretations are cited here.   Though closely linked one with the other, they represent more or less separable themes of English social thought when, toward the end of the eighteenth century, traditional charity and the old poor-law legislation as a means of helping the indigent become controversial issues.[1]

One approach sees the cause of poverty in the very effort to relieve distress. The poor are not inclined to exert themselves; they lack the pride, honor, and ambition of their betters. Previously this observation supported the view that the poor must be guided; now it supports the view that charity only destroys incentive and hence intensifies poverty. Indolence increases where provision is made to succour the poor; dire necessity is the most natural motive of labor, for it exerts unremitting pressure on the poor. "The slave must be compelled to work; but the freeman should be left to his own judgment and discretion."[2] Here the accent is on the supposition that the rich cannot help the poor, even if they would, and further that the lower orders must depend upon themselves. Rejection of upper-class responsibility goes hand in hand with the demand that the poor should be self-dependent.

In the second approach the pernicious efforts of charity are linked with the market theory of labor. Hunger must be permitted to do its work so that laborers are compelled to exert themselves. Otherwise they will reduce their efforts and destroy their only safeguard against starvation. Here labor is viewed as a commodity like any other, its wage being determined by the demand for this commodity rather than the need of the laborer or his ability to survive. The only relevant question is what the labor is worth to the employer. For the employer is subject to the same necessities of supply and demand as the laborer. This means in the long run that he cannot pay him more than he offers without jeopardizing his enterprise, and hence that the interests of capital and labor are identical. The market theory means that the employer cannot act irresponsibly without damaging his own interest and that the laborer has no safeguard but exertion and no guarantee against starvation.

The third approach, specifically identified with the work of Malthus, relates this market theory of labor to the theory of population. Instead of asserting a harmony of interest between rich and poor, Malthus acknowledges the inevitability of periodic and acute distress. He attributes this phenomenon to the tendency of population to increase faster than the means of subsistence, a law of nature which the upper classes are powerless to alter. Malthus states that poverty is inescapable and a necessary stimulus to labor, that charity and poor relief only increase indolence and improvidence, that the higher classes are not and cannot be responsible for the lot of the poor. But in terms of the present context he also adds an important idea. If it is a law of nature for the poor to increase their numbers beyond the available food supply, it is the responsibility of the higher classes to understand this law and instruct the lower orders accordingly. Improvidence may be a natural tendency, but it also results from ignorance and lack of moral restraint, and these failings can be combated through education.

Education, then, is the keynote of the new, entrepreneurial ideology, since employers no longer possess the all-encompassing personal authority of the aristocratic master. Much reliance is placed on such impersonal forces as economic necessity and the pressure of population on resources—much more reliance than was the case when the master exercised an entirely personal domination over his household. Even so, employers must deal with the management of men, and early in the nineteenth century complaints are heard concerning the increasing personal distance which makes such management difficult, especially on the old, paternalistic basis. With the spread of equalitarian ideas the emphasis on social rank declines; the gulf between the classes widens, as Tocqueville observes, and the personal influence of employers declines. Accordingly, reliance is placed not only on impersonal economic forces but also on the impersonal influence of ideas and education. It is in this context that free-lance propagandists such as Samuel Smiles formulate the new entrepreneurial ideology with its emphasis on the "immense amount of influence" which employers possess, if they would approach their workers "with sympathy and confidence" and "actively aid [them] in the formation of prudent habits."[3] Henceforth entrepreneurial ideologies consist of thematic combinations of the following three elements: (1) the paternalistic element, modeled after the traditional household in which personal domination of the master over his family and servants is the keynote; (2) the impersonal element, modeled after the market conception of the classical economists in which the anonymous pressure of supply and demand, of the struggle for survival, forces the workers to do the bidding of their employers; and (3) the educational element, modeled after the classroom, the psychological laboratory, or the therapeutic session in which instruction, incentives and penalties, or indirect, motivational inducements are used to discipline the workers and prompt them to intensify their efforts.

For the course of Western European industrialization we can posit a sequence leading first to a decline of the paternalistic and a rise of the impersonal element and subsequently a declining reliance on market forces and an increasing reliance on educational devices. The sequence applies most closely to the English and American development, though even here it is a rough approximation. For paternalism always includes an educational element, reliance on market forces has often been adumbrated in a paternalistic manner, and the educational dimension is compatible with an impersonal as well as a personal approach. Different cultural antecedents as well as the changing organizational structure of economic enterprises have much to do with varying emphases among managerial ideologies such as those of the United States, Germany, and Japan.[4]

The political dimension of these ideologies is of special moment, however. In an emerging nation-state which has destroyed the earlier fragmentation of public authority, agencies of the national government afford employers of labor legal protection for their rights of property. These rights are part of a broad egalitarian trend which also finds expression in the praise of frugal habits and hard work, qualities that enable every man to acquire property and status. At the impersonal level of ideological appeals this approach produces certain typical paradoxes that are of political significance.

Individualistic interpretations of the authority relationship do not remain confined to the enterprise. The idea of an impersonal market which will induce workers to offer their services and work diligently calls for policies that will facilitate the operation of that market. Moreover, recourse to ideological appeals and educational methods suggest that impersonal incentives are insufficient.

Entrepreneurs also seek to inculcate the desired habits and motives. But by encouraging the self-dependence of the workers, they run the risk that such individualism will eventuate in social and political protest rather than cooperation and compliance.

For the praise of good habits and hard work lends itself to invidious judgments of a very provocative type. The good and honest worker is a model to be followed as distinguished from the lazy and improvident one, whose deficiencies are broadcast for the benefit of all who will listen and as a warning that invites contempt and condemnation. The public manner in which these "collective attributes" are discussed makes them into a political issue. The moral division of the lower classes into diligent and improvident poor not only challenges the complacency of the idle, but also jeopardizes the self-respect of those who remain poor despite the most strenuous efforts. That self-respect is jeopardized still further when economic success is interpreted as a synonym of virtue and failure as a sign of moral turpitude. In a context of widening agitation such judgments help to make the civic position of the lower orders into a national political issue. The individualist interpretation of authority relations in industry appears from this standpoint as an effort to deny the rights of citizenship to those who are unsuccessful economically, an approach that can arouse a new sense of right on the part of the lower classes and lead to groping efforts to define the position of these classes in the national political community. Just as Tocqueville focuses attention on a transition in domestic relations, marked by a change in the terms of commands and obedience, so the following discussion will focus attention on a transition in group relations on the national level, marked by changing ideas concerning the rights and obligations of the lower classes.

LOWER-CLASS UNREST BECOMES POLITICAL: ENGLAND

When political developments are attributed to economic determinants, the changing position of the lower classes and the emergence of national citizenship appear as by-products of industrialization. This line of interpretation develops at the end of the eighteenth century. It appears plausible in the sense that the revolutions in the United States and France "reflect the rise of the bourgeoisie," while the industrial revolution in England leads to the political mobilization of an emerging industrial work force. Greatly simplified as these statements are, they refer to historical phenomena rather than general principles. Yet it is in the light of these *historical* phenomena that *all* political events were first construed as more or less direct by-products of social and economic processes.[5] Today we know that elsewhere political revolutions have occurred in the absence of an economically strong and politically articulate middle class, or perhaps because of that absence, as in Russia or Japan. Again, the political mobilization of the lower classes has occurred as a prelude to industrialization, rather than as a result of it, as, for example, in the United States. Thus, although changes in the economic and political spheres are closely related, their influences work in both directions.

Hence we get little guidance if we tacitly accept Western Europe and especially England as our model. It is true that there democratic ideas originated under circumstances in which socio-economic changes had a massive impact upon the political structure, but these ideas have spread around the world ever since in the absence of similar circumstances. National citizenship and modern industrialism have been combined with a variety of social structures; hence we should recognize democratization and industrialization as *two processes*, each distinct from the other, however intimately they have been related on occasion.

The two processes have been closely linked in England. For a long time the English development has served as a model for an understanding of economic growth in relation to political modernization—perhaps simply because England was the first country to develop a modern industry. Just for these reasons it may be well to show that even in England it is possible to distinguish the political element in the midst of economic change. We saw that prior to the eighteenth century the lower classes might try to wring concessions from the ruling powers by a "legitimist" posture mixed with violence; or that they might compensate for their exclusion from the exercise of public rights by millenarian fantasies and banditry. Different forms of lower-class protest became possible, however, after enlightened despotism and the philosophers of the Enlightenment had formulated the principle of equal rights for all men. The spread of this idea was certainly facilitated by industrialization, a fact which was recognized early:

> Of the working men, at least in the more advanced countries of Europe, it may be pronounced certain that the patriarchal or paternal system of government is one to which they will not again be subject. That question was decided, when they were taught to read, and allowed access to newspapers and political tracts; when dissenting preachers were suffered to go among them, and appeal to their faculties and feelings in opposition to the creeds professed and countenanced by their superiors; when they were brought together in numbers, to work socially under the same roof; when railways enabled them to shift from place to place, and change their patrons and employers as easily as their coats; when they were encouraged to seek a share in the government, by means of the electoral franchise.[6]

In this statement Mill describes a relatively industrialized country, and his references to dissenting preachers and the electoral franchise point to conditions that are more or less peculiar to England at this time, But he also notes several factors which have been rather generally associated with the recruitment of an industrial work force: the literacy of workers, the spread of printed matter among them, physical concentration of work, increased geographic mobility, and the depersonalization of the employment relationship. Mill's descriptive account may be considered equivalent to Mannheim's statement that "modern industrial society"—by physically and intellectually mobilizing the people— "stirs into action those classes which formerly only played a passive part in political life."[7]

Under the influence of ideas of equality this mobilization of lower-class protest comes to be oriented, broadly speaking, toward realizing full participation in the existing political community or establishing a national political community in which such participation would be possible. This consideration may be applied initially to some of the popular disturbances in early nineteenth-century England. For Marx these disturbances are similar to the sporadic rebellions in which for several centuries peasants and artisans have destroyed machines as the most immediate instruments of their oppression.[8]   Later writers have shown that this violence was directed against bankers or money-lenders as much as against machines, and that despite their obvious agitation the workers of early nineteenth-century England show a most surprising respect for property not directly connected with their distress.   By distinguishing in practice between looting and a "justified" destruction of property, the workers may be said to have engaged in "collective bargaining by riot" at a time when combinations were prohibited by law.[9]   Such evidence is compatible with the idea that the workers who engage in violence desire at the same time to demonstrate their respectability.   They are face to face with a manifest legal inequity; they are prevented from combining for peaceful collective bargaining, while combinations of employers are tolerated or even encouraged.   Hence, "collective bargaining by riot" easily accompanies the demand for civil rights which has been denied despite acceptance of formal equality before the law.[10]

Although very inarticulate at first, the appeal against legal inequities involves a new dimension of social unrest.   To get at the relative novelty of this experience we have to rely on the circumstantial evidence of the period.   In the late eighteenth and through the nineteenth centuries the civic position of the common people became a subject of national debate in Europe.   For decades elementary education and the franchise are debated in terms of whether an increase in literacy or of voting rights among the people would work as an antidote to revolutionary propaganda or as a dangerous incentive to insubordination.[11]   It is difficult to know what sentiments such debates arouse among the people themselves.   Faced with the inequity of their legal position and a public debate over their civic reliability, there is naturally much vacillation.   The people seem to alternate between insistence on ancient rights and violent uprisings against the most apparent causes of oppression; protestations of respectability and cries for bloody revolution; proposals for specific reforms and utopian schemes of bewildering variety.   But such a diversity of manifestations can have a common core in the transitional experience which Tocqueville characterizes:

> . . . there is almost always a time when men's minds fluctuate between the aristocratic notion of subjection and the democratic notion of obedience.   Obedience then loses its moral importance in the eyes of him who obeys; he no longer considers it as a species of divine obligation, and he does not yet view it under its purely human aspects; it has to him no character of sanctity or justice, and he submits to it as to a degrading but profitable condition.[12]

In England, at the political level, this ambivalence is resolved as the idea gains acceptance that the people's rights as citizens have been denied unjustly because as working people they have rights by virtue of their contribution to the nation's wealth.

There are several reasons for accepting the plausibility of this interpretation, even though it may be impossible to prove. One such reason is that legal inequity and the public debate over the people's civic unreliability represent a cumulative denial of their respectability which occurs just when industrialization and the spread of equalitarian ideas stirs "into action those classes which formerly only played a passive part in political life" (Mannheim). On occasion this denial of respectability is tantamount to a denial of the right to existence, as in this passage from Thomas Malthus, which became a notorious object of socialist attacks.

> A man who is born into a world already possessed, if he cannot get subsistence from his parents on whom he has a just demand, and if the society does not want his labour, has no claim of right to the smallest portion of food, and, in fact, has no business to be where he is. At Nature's mighty feast there is no vacant cover for him. She tells him to be gone, and will quickly execute her own orders.[13]

Extreme statements such as this or Burke's reference to the "swinish multitude" were made by intellectuals and may not have been widely known. However, haughtiness and fear were widespread in middle-class circles, and it is reasonable to expect a growing sensitivity among the people, however inarticulate, in response to this public questioning of their respectability.

Contemporary observers frequently commented on the popular reaction. These observers are often remote from working-class life, partisans in the debate concerning the "lower classes," and divided among themselves. Their biases are many, but partisanship can sensitize as well as distort understanding. In England such different observers as Thomas Carlyle, William Cobbett, Benjamin Disraeli, and Harriet Martineau comment on the feeling of injustice among the workers, on their loss of self-respect, on the personal abuse which the rulers of society heap upon them, on the Chartist movement as the common people's expression of outrage at the denial of their civil rights, and on the workers' feeling of being an "outcast order" in their own country.[14] Such a civic disaffection of the people was regarded with grave concern by prominent spokesmen in many European societies. In retrospect this concern appears justified in the sense that the position of the "people" as citizens was indeed at issue.[15]

The implicit or explicit denial of the peoples' civic respectability is countered rather naturally by an insistence on people's rights which must not be abrogated. That insistence is founded first on a sense of righteous indignation at the idea that labor which is "the Cornerstone upon which civilized society is built" is "offered less . . . than will support the family of a sober and orderly man in decency and comfort."[16] This conception of a "right to subsistence" with its traditional overtones, the idea of "labor's right to the whole product," and the belief that each able-bodied worker has a "right to labor" are the three inherent or natural rights put in opposition to the contractually acquired rights that alone are recognized by the prevailing legal system.[17] Although the theoretical elaborations of these concepts in the socialist literature do not reveal the thinking of the ordinary man, it is plausible to assume that the common theme of these theories expresses the strivings of the workingman in the nation-state.[18]

In England, lower-class protests appear to aim at establishing the citizenship of the workers.   Those who contribute to the wealth and welfare of their country have a right to be heard in its national councils and are entitled to a status that commands respect.   In England, these demands never reach the revolutionary pitch that develops rather frequently on the Continent, although occasionally violent outbursts disrupt English society as well.   If the political moderniza- tion of England for all its conflicts occurred in a relatively continuous and peace- ful manner, then one reason is perhaps that throughout much of the nineteenth century England was the leader in industrialization and overseas expansion. English workers could claim their rightful place in the political community of the leading nation of the world.[19]   Within that favorable context the national debate concerning the proper status of the lower classes is carried on in the traditional language of religion.   Certainly, English workers are greatly disillusioned with the established Church and with religious appeals which all too often are thinly disguised apologies for the established order.   Nevertheless, doctrinaire atheism is rare, and English working-class leaders often couch their demands in Biblical or quasi-Biblical language.[20]   Thus, England's prominence as a world power and a common religious background may have facilitated the civic incorporation of the workers, even though the new national balance of rights and duties was not accomplished easily.

An example from the field of industrial relations illustrates the niceties of this English transition to a modern political community.   At first glance, the legal prohibition of trade unions in the early nineteenth century looks like brute sup- pression.   "Workingmen's combinations" are said to curtail the employer's as well as the worker's formal legal rights.   However, in their survey of early trade unionism, the Webbs conclude that the inefficient organization of the police, the absence of effective public prosecution, and the inaction of the employers were responsible for the widespread occurrence of illegal combinations despite this unequivocal legal prohibition.[21]

More recently, a publication of documents on the early trade unions has re- vealed why neither employers nor government officials would resort to all the legal remedies open to them.   Apparently, the employers wished the govern- ment to institute proceedings against illegal combinations.   An opinion of the Attorney General, sent to the Home Secretary in 1804, is of special interest in this respect.   The opinion sets forth details of the great evil of combinations among workmen throughout the country, combinations said to be clearly illegal and liable to prosecution.   But if the government were to initiate the prosecution in the case under consideration, then applications for similar actions on the part of the government can be anticipated from every other trade, since "combinations exist in almost every trade in the kingdom."

> It will lead to an opinion that it is not the business of the masters of the trade who feel the injury to prosecute, but that it is the business of Government. . . . It must be admitted indeed that the offence has grown to such height and such an extent as to

make it very discouraging for any individual to institute a prosecution—as the persons whom he would prosecute would be supported at their trial and during their imprisonment by the contributions of their confederates, and his own shop would probably be deserted by his workmen. But then it is clear that it is owing to the inertness and timidity of the masters that the conspiracy has reached this height, and it may well be feared that this inertness will be rather increased than diminished by the interference of Government. . . . When they once think the punishment of such offences to be the business of Government, they will think it also the business of Government to procure the evidence, and not theirs to give it, so that the future detection and prosecution of such offences would probably be rendered more difficult. Besides . . . the impartiality of Government would be awkwardly situated, if, after undertaking a prosecution at the instance of the masters against the conspiracy of the journeymen, they were to be applied to on the part of the journeymen to prosecute the same masters for a conspiracy against their men.[22]

This opinion is instructive, even though its judiciousness cannot be considered representative.

Whatever their partiality toward the employers, the magistrates are responsible for maintaining law and order. This task is complicated time and again by the reluctance of employers to make use of the law prohibiting combinations, by their repeated attempts to induce the government to do it for them, by their tendency to connive in these combinations when it suits their purpose, and finally by their tendency to reject all responsibility for the consequences of their own actions in the belief that ultimately the government will maintain law and order and protect their interests. It is not surprising that the magistrates are often highly critical of the employers, holding that the latter act with little discretion, that they can well afford to pay higher wages, and that the complaints of the workers are justified even though their combinations are illegal. Sometimes the magistrates even act as informal mediators in disputes between employers and their workers in the interest of maintaining the peace.[23] Thus, neither the partiality of the magistrates nor the principle of a hands-off policy nor the employers' evident opportunism is tantamount to suppression, even though in practice little is done to meet the workers' complaints except on terms calculated to injure their status as self-respecting members of the community.

In this period of transition Tocqueville sees a major revolutionary threat. The master continues to expect servility, but rejects responsibility for his servants, while the latter claim equal rights and become intractable. At the societal level the English case approximates this model. Many early English entrepreneurs certainly reject all responsibility for their employees and yet expect them to obey; they reject all governmental interference with management, though they seek to charge government with responsibility for any untoward public consequences of their own acts.[24] Government officials support the entrepreneurs in many cases because they are profoundly concerned with unrest and truculence. But having said this, several reservations must be added. There are some manufacturers who acknowledge the traditional obligations of a ruling class. Among some magistrates the principle of noninterference by government is adhered to by a detached and critical attitude, even in the first decades of the nineteenth century. Finally, the demand for quality of the developing working class is cast in a more or less conservative mold in the sense that on balance it adds up to a quest for public acceptance of equal citizenship. In other words, English society proved itself capable of accommodating the lower class as an equal participant in the national political community, though even in England this development involved a prolonged struggle and the full implications of equality as we understand them today evolved only gradually.

THEORETICAL IMPLICATIONS

The preceding discussion is confined to developments in England. Industrialization can be initiated only once; after that its techniques are borrowed; no other country that has since embarked on the process can start where England started in the eighteenth century. England is the exception rather than the model. For a time England possessed a near monopoly on the most advanced techniques of industrial production, and other countries borrowed from her. For the better part of the nineteenth century England stood in the forefront in that she combined industrial with political pre-eminence. In retrospect we know that as a result of these and related conditions she possessed a national political community in which the rising "fourth estate" was eventually permitted to participate through a gradual redefinition of rights and obligations rather than as a consequence of war or revolution. But an understanding of as singular a case as this is important in the comparative study of social and political change, for indirectly it may point to what many of the other "cases" have in common.

As we compare industrial latecomers with England and democratic latecomers with France, we can ask: what happens when a country does not possess a viable political community or if the community which it possesses is so "backward" in comparison with democratically and industrially advanced countries that it must be reconstituted before the demand for "full citizenship" becomes meaningful at all? It is not a novel idea to suggest that lower-class protest may progress from a demand for full citizenship within the prevailing political community to a demand for a change of this community in order to make full citizenship possible. But although this idea is compatible with Marx's theory of an advance from machine breaking to political action, it should be noted that I emphasize the alienation from the political community rather than the alienation which results from "creative dissatisfactions," as Marx does. This shift of emphasis helps us to see together two mass movements of the nineteenth century—socialism and nationalism—in contrast to Marx who explains the first while ignoring the second. There is a very close link between socialist and nationalist agitation in that both aim in different ways at the political integration of the masses previously excluded from participation. This link is obscured by the Marxist separation of these movements and by the fact that England's pre-eminence as a world power made it unnecessary for the English lower class to demand a national political community to which it could belong in self-respect.[25]   Yet, the exceptional development of England has served social theorists for a century as the model which other countries are expected to follow.

The approach here proposed is not a mere reversal of the Marxist theory. Marx looks upon social movements of the nineteenth century as protests against psychic and material deprivations that cumulate as a result of the capitalist process; he sees in the masses a fundamental craving for creative satisfactions in a good society.   I interpret these protest movements as *political* and define their character in terms of the contrast between a premodern and a modern political community.   When this view is taken, the eighteenth century appears as a major hiatus in Western European history.   Prior to that time the masses of the people were entirely barred from the exercise of public rights; since then they have become citizens and in this sense participants in the political community.   The "age of democratic revolution" extends from that time to the present.   During this period some societies have universalized citizenship peacefully, while others have been unable to do so and have consequently suffered various types of revolutionary upheavals.   So conceived, the problem of the lower classes in a modern nation-state consists in the political process through which at the level of the national community the reciprocity of rights and duties is gradually extended and redefined.   It is quite true that this process has been affected at every turn by forces emanating from the structure of society.   But it is here maintained that the distribution and redistribution of rights and duties are not mere by-products of such forces, that they are vitally affected by the international position of the country, by conceptions of what the proper distribution in the national community ought to be, and by the give and take of the political struggle.[26]

My thesis is in keeping with Tocqueville's stress on the reciprocity of rights and obligations as the hallmark of a political community.   In Europe the rising awareness of the working class expresses above all an experience of *political alienation*, that is, a sense of not having a recognized position in the civic community or of not having a civic community in which to participate.   Because popular political participation has become possible for the first time in European history, lower-class protest against the social order relies (at least initially) on prevailing codes of behavior and hence reflects a conservative cast of mind, even where it leads to violence against persons and property.[27]   Rather than engage in a millenarian quest for a new social order, the recently politicized masses protest against their second-class citizenship, demanding the right of participation on terms of equality in the political community of the nation-state.[28]   If this is a correct assessment of the impulses and half-articulated longings characteristic of much popular agitation among lower classes in Western Europe, then we have a clue to the decline of socialism.   For the civic position of these classes is no longer a pre-eminent issue in societies in which the equality of citizenship has been institutionalized successfully.

* * *

Notes

1. The details need not concern us here.   For fuller discussion and citations see my study, *Work and Authority in Industry* (New York: John Wiley & Sons, 1956), pp. 73 ff.
2. Statement of Rev. Townsend quoted in *ibid.*, p. 74.
3. Quoted in *ibid.*, p. 112.
4. *Ibid.*, Chap. 5; Heinz Hartmann, *Authority and Organization in German Management* (Princeton: Princeton University Press, 1959), *passim*; and James G. Abegglen, *The Japanese Factory* (Glencoe: The Free Press, 1958).
5. To some extent modern social and economic theories still reflect the historical situation in which they were first developed, but a century and a half later it should be possible to guard against this bias.   See Chap. I, Sect. c, 4 above [in *Nation Building and Citizenship: Studies of Our Changing Social Order*].
6. John Stuart Mill, *Principles of Political Economy*, II, pp. 322–323.   Mill's statement is cited here as an exceptionally clear formulation of what was apparently a common topic of conversation.   See the illuminating survey of the growing consciousness of class relations by Asa Briggs, "The Language of 'Class' in Early Nineteenth Century England," in Asa Briggs and John Saville, eds., *Essays in Labour History in Memory of G. D. H. Cole* (London: Macmillan, 1960), pp. 43–73.
7. This is Karl Mannheim's definition of "fundamental democratization," which is compatible with different forms of government, not only with "democracy."   The definition is useful, however, because it highlights the emergence of a national political community in which all adults regardless of class are citizens and hence participants.   See Karl Mannheim, *Man and Society in an Age of Reconstruction* (New York: Harcourt, Brace, 1941), p. 44.
8. See Karl Marx, *Capital* (New York: Modern Library, 1936), pp. 466–478 for his survey and interpretation of such rebellions.
9. The phrase has been coined by E. J. Hobsbawm, "The Machine Breakers," *Past and Present*, I (1952), 57–70.   Evidence concerning the distinction between looting and such disturbances as the famous Luddite riots is analyzed in Frank O. Darvall, *Popular Disturbances and Public Order in Regency England* (London: Oxford University Press, 1934), pp. 314–315 and *passim*.
10. Note in this respect Marx's emphasis upon the way in which combinations of workers and employers stimulated each other and the reference in the text below to the awareness of this inequity among English magistrates.   A study of industrial and agrarian disputes in Japan suggests that much the same mechanism operates in a very different cultural setting.   See the comment that "an increasing number of tenant farmers became convinced of the need for political action, when they learned how often court verdicts, which were based on existing laws, went against them," in George O. Totten, "Labor and Agrarian Disputes in Japan Following World War I," *Economic Development and Cultural Change*, IX (October 1960), pt. II, 194.
11. Similar questions were raised with regard to universal conscription, since arms in the hands of the common people were considered a revolutionary threat.   A case study of the conscription issue and its significance for the development of class relations in Germany is Gerhard Ritter, *Staatskunst und Kriegshandwerk* (Munich: R. Oldenbourg, 1954), pp. 60–158 and *passim*.   See also the related discussion in Katherine Chorley, *Armies and the Art of Revolution* (London: Faber & Faber, 1943), pp. 87–107, 160–183.   The related debates on literacy are analyzed in detail with reference to the English experience in M. G. Jones, *The Charity School Movement* (Cambridge: Cambridge University Press, 1938), *passim*.
12. Tocqueville, *Democracy in America*, II, 194–195.
13. Thomas Malthus, *An Essay on the Principle of Population* (2nd ed.; London: J. Johnson, 1803), p. 531.   This passage was modified in the later editions of the Essay.
14. See the chapter "Rights and Mights" in Thomas Carlyle, *Chartism* (Chicago: Belford, Clarke, 1890), pp. 30–39; G. D. H. and Margaret Cole, eds., *The Opinions of William Cobbett*

(London: Cobbett, 1944), pp. 86–87, 123–124, 207, and *passim*; *Hansard's Parliamentary Debates*, Vol. XLIX (1839), cols. 246–247; and R. K. Webb, *The British Working Class Reader* (London: Allen & Unwin, 1955), p. 96 for the sources of these statements.   Also relevant here is the famous simile of the "two nations between whom there is no intercourse and no sympathy; who are as ignorant of each other's habits, thoughts and feelings, as if they were dwellers in different zones, or inhabitants of different planets, who are formed by a different breeding, are fed by a different food, are ordered by different manners, and are not governed by the same laws."   This passage occurs in Benjamin Disraeli's novel *Sybil* (Baltimore: Penguin Books, 1954), p. 73.

15. For a survey of propagandistic efforts to counteract this "civic disaffection" in England, see R. K. Webb, *op. cit.*, *passim*, and Reinhard Bendix, *Work and Authority in Industry*, pp. 60–73.

16. The quoted phrase is from a Manchester handbill of 1818 reprinted in J. L. and Barbara Hammond, *The Town Labourer* (London: Longmans, Green, 1925), pp. 306–308.   In Tocqueville's paradigm this idea may be said to fall midway between the belief in "ancient rights" that have been wrongfully abrogated and the claim that the servants themselves should be the masters.   Note also the analysis by von Stein who states that the antagonism between workers and employers "arises from the belief in the rights and worth of the individual workers, on one hand, and from the knowledge that under present conditions of machine production the wages of the worker will not be commensurate with his claims as an individual."   See Lorenz von Stein, "Der Begriff der Arbeit und die Prinzipien des Arbeitslohnes in ihrem Verhältnisse zum Sozialismus und Communismus," *Zeitschrift für die gesamte Staatswissenschaft*, III (1846), 263.

17. For a detailed exposition of these conceptions of natural rights in socialist thought and of their incompatibility with the law of property, see Anton Menger, *The Right to the Whole Produce of Labour* (London: Macmillan, 1899), *passim*.

18. Presumably, Marx's use of the labor theory of value had its great moral impact on the basis of these conceptions of "natural rights," as analyzed by Menger.

19. Engels considered the two phenomena causally linked, as in his comment to Marx that the "bourgeoisification of the English proletariat" was in a sense "quite natural in a nation that exploited the whole world."   See his letter to Marx of October 7, 1858, in Karl Marx and Friedrich Engels, *Ausgewählte Briefe* (Berlin: Dietz Verlag, 1953), pp. 131–132.   Yet, this interpretation ignores the historical legacies which prompt a "national reciprocity of rights and obligations" despite the threat of revolutionary ideas and the strains of rapid economic change.   The coincidence of England's favored position and her favorable legacies for effecting this political "incorporation" of the "fourth estate" has been discussed so far only in bits and pieces.   See J. L. Hammond, "The Industrial Revolution and Discontent," *The Economic History Review*, II (1930), 227–228; Henri de Man, *The Psychology of Socialism* (New York: Henry Holt, 1927), pp. 39–41, with regard to the role of injured self-respect in English radical protest: and Selig Perlman, *A Theory of the Labor Movement* (New York: Augustus Kelley, 1949), p. 291, who emphasizes the special significance of the franchise issue.

20. Some evidence of the relation between religious revivalism and working-class protest is discussed in my *Work and Authority in Industry*, pp. 60–73, but the issue is controversial.   In his *Social Bandits and Primitive Rebels*, pp. 126–149, Hobsbawm questions that the religious movements among workers diminished their radicalism.   In his *Churches and the Working Classes in Victorian England* (London: Routledge and Kegan Paul, 1963), K. S. Inglis assembles a mass of evidence which suggests that English workers were markedly indifferent towards religious observances throughout the nineteenth century.   But even Inglis admits (*ibid.*, 329–332) that atheism was rare among English workers (though pronounced among their fellows on the Continent), and that large numbers of working-class children attended Sunday schools.   Such an admission may well be critical, however, since the question is not whether English workers were true believers, but whether they continued to use religious ideas in their "quest for respectability."   Religious ideas are not necessarily less important when they become associated with secular concerns.   See the analysis of secularity and religion in the American context by S. M.

Lipset, *The First New Nation* (New York: Basic Books, 1963), pp. 151–159, and of the exacerbation of class-relations in the absence of a viable religious language by Guenther Roth, *The Social Democrats in Imperial Germany* (New York: The Bedminster Press, 1963), *passim*.

21. Sidney and Beatrice Webb, *The History of Trade Unionism* (New York: Longmans, Green & Co., 1926), p. 74.

22. A. Aspinall, ed., *The Early English Trade Unions, Documents from the Home Office Papers in the Public Record Office* (London: Batchworth Press, 1949), pp. 90–92.

23. For examples of these several aspects, see *ibid.*, pp. 116, 126, 168–169, 192–193, 216–219, 229, 234–235, 237–238, 242, 259–260, 272, 283, and so on.

24. On this basis even staunch ideological spokesmen for *laissez-faire* were actively engaged in the extension of governmental controls. For details see Marion Bowley, *Nassau Senior and Classical Economics* (London: Allen & Unwin, 1937), pp. 237–281; S. E. Finer, *The Life and Times of Edwin Chadwick* (London: Methuen, 1952), *passim*; J. B. Brebner, "Laissez-faire and State Intervention in 19th Century Britain," *Journal of Economic History*, VIII (Supplement 1948), 59–73.

25. See the following statement from a speech of the Chartist leader Hartwell, delivered in 1837: "It seems to me to be an anomaly that in a country where the arts and sciences have been raised to such height, chiefly by the industry, skill and labours of the artisan . . . only one adult male in seven should have a vote, that in such a country the working classes should be excluded from the pale of political life." Quoted in M. Beer, *A History of British Socialism* (London: Allen & Unwin, 1948), II, pp. 25–26. It is instructive to contrast this statement with that by the Italian nationalist leader Mazzini: "Without Country you have neither name, token, voice, nor rights. . . . Do not beguile yourselves with the hope of emancipation from unjust social conditions if you do not first conquer a Country for yourselves. . . . Do not be led away by the idea of improving your material conditions without first solving the national question. . . . Today . . . you are not the working class of Italy; you are only fractions of that class. . . . Your emancipation can have no practical beginning until a National Government [is founded]." See Joseph Mazzini, *The Duties of Men and Other Essays* (New York: E. P. Dutton, 1912), pp. 53–54.

26. This approach differs from Marxism which treats politics and government as variables dependent upon the changing organization of production, without coming to grips either with the relative autonomy of governmental actions or the continuous existence of national political communities. It also differs from the sociological approach to politics and formal institutions which construes the first as mere by-products of interactions among individuals and the second as the "outward shell" inside which these interactions provide the clue to a realistic understanding of social life. See a critical analysis of this reductionism in Wolin, *op. cit.*, Chaps. 9 and 10. An alternative approach which emphasizes the partial autonomy as well as the interdependence of government and society is contained in the work of Max Weber, as discussed above on pp. 15–17 [of *Nation Building and Citizenship: Studies of Our Changing Social Order*].

27. See in this connection Engels' expression of disgust with regard to the ingrained "respectability" of English workers and their leaders in his letter to Sorge of December 7, 1889, in *Ausgewählte Briefe*, p. 495.

28. The perspective presented above has been developed by a number of my former students. The study by Guenther Roth of "Working-Class Isolation and National Integration" in Imperial Germany was cited earlier. See also Gaston Rimlinger, "The Legitimation of Protest: A Comparative Study in Labor History," *Comparative Studies in Society and History*, II (April 1960), pp. 329–343, by the same author, "Social Security, Incentives and Controls in the U.S. and the U.S.S.R.," *loc. cit.*, IV (November 1961), pp. 104–124, and Samuel Surace, *The Status Evolution of Italian Workers, 1860–1914* (Ph.D. Dissertation, Department of Sociology, University of California, Berkeley, 1962).

28. Values and Democratic Stability
Seymour M. Lipset

Parts I and II of this study [*The First New Nation*] examined how the United States produced a particular set of "structured predispositions," which is one way of defining values, for handling strains generated by social change. These predispositions have affected the status system, the "American character," the pattern of American religion, and the development of class interests among the workers. The effort has been to demonstrate that American status concerns, "other-directedness," religious participation, church organization, labor union structure, and the like, differed from those of other nations because of our distinctive value system. Within self-imposed limitations, this has represented an effort to present an integrated view of American society. Only in the treatment of trade-union behavior did the analysis move toward an attempt also to explain behavior in other countries.

In this concluding section of the book [*The First New Nation*], I turn from a concentration on the United States to comparative analysis of a given institutional structure—the organization of democratic polities.[1] In a sense, the discussion here represents a further effort to illustrate the worth of the preceding analyses of American society by a systematic presentation of the way American institutions differ from those of other nations with varying value systems. It represents an effort to extend the type of value analysis employed in preceding chapters [of *The First New Nation*] to locate some of the sources of variation among a number of national polities, including the American. However, it should be obvious that institutions and reactions cannot be derived solely or even primarily from the basic value systems; and, as one illustration of the way in which specific legal enactments may influence the course of nations, I turn in the final chapter of this section [of *The First New Nation*] to a discussion of the processes through which the varying structure of the polity may itself affect the form and stability of the political system.

Since I have attempted elsewhere to elaborate a sociologically meaningful definition of a democratic system, I do not want to repeat these discussions here.[2] Essentially, I have urged the view that *realistically* the distinctive and most valuable element of democracy in complex societies is the formation of a political elite in the competitive struggle for the votes of a mainly passive electorate. This definition is premised on the common assumption that democracy means a system in which those outside of the formal authority structure are able significantly to influence the basic direction of policy. If the citizenry as a whole are to have access to decisions, there must be a meaningful competitive struggle within the political elite which leads factions within this elite to look for generalized as well as specific support. But the political elite can be leaders *and representatives* only if there are mechanisms within the culture which foster the kinds of personal motivations that lead men to perceive and strongly support their interests within a political system which has relatively well-defined rules. Mechanisms that undermine the democratic rules or which inhibit institutionalized conflict are destructive of democracy, in that they restrict the general population's access to, or power over, key societal decisions. Hence it is necessary to look for factors which, on the one hand, sustain the separation of the political system from the excesses inherent in the populist assumptions of democracy—the belief that the majority will is always sovereign—*and*, on the other, encourage participation in organizations that conflict with one another and with state agencies concerning the direction of public policy on all major issues.

Earlier I argued that the effects of American values on the American labor movement could best be specified by comparing that movement with those in countries at relatively similar levels of development. The same argument applies to any attempt systematically to examine the way in which a nation's values affect its polity.

VALUE PATTERNS AND A DEMOCRATIC POLITY

To compare national value systems, we must be able to classify them and distinguish among them. Talcott Parsons has provided a useful tool for this purpose in his concept of "pattern variables." These were originally developed by Parsons as an extension of the classic distinction by Ferdinand Tönnies between "community" and "society"—between those systems which emphasized *Gemeinschaft* (primary, small, traditional, integrated) values, and those which stressed *Gesellschaft* (impersonal, secondary, large, socially differentiated) values.[3] The pattern variables to be used in the following analysis are achievement–ascription, universalism–particularism, and specificity–diffuseness. According to the achievement–ascription distinction, a society's value system may emphasize individual ability or performance or it may emphasize ascribed or inherited qualities (such as race or high birth) in judging individuals and placing them in various roles. According to the universalism–particularism distinction, it may emphasize that all people shall be treated according to the same standard (*e.g.*, equality before the law), or that individuals shall be treated differently according to their personal qualities or their particular membership in a class or group. Specificity–diffuseness refers to the difference between treating individuals in terms of the specific positions which they happen to occupy, rather than diffusely as individual members of the collectivity.[4]

The pattern variables provide us with a much more sensitive way of classifying values than the older polar concepts of sociology, such as the folk–urban, mechanical–organic, primary–secondary, or *Gemeinschaft–Gesellschaft*, etc. For instance, they make it possible for us to establish differences in value structures between two nations that are at the same end of the *Gemeinschaft–Gesellschaft* continuum, or are at similar levels of economic development or social complexity. They are also useful for describing differences within a society. Thus the family is inherently ascriptive and particularistic while the market is universalistic and achievement oriented—the weaker the kinship ties in a given society, the greater the national emphasis on achievement is likely to be.

The manner in which any set of values is introduced will obviously affect the way the values are incorporated into a nation's institutions. In France, for instance, where the values of universalism, achievement, and specificity were introduced primarily through a political revolution, we would expect to find them most prominent in the political institutions; in Germany, where they have been introduced primarily through industrialization, we would expect to find them most prominent in its economic institutions. The American example suggests that for democratic values to become legitimate in a post-revolutionary polity the norms of universalism, achievement, and specificity must be introduced into its economic institutions as well. This fosters rapid economic development, and encourages the underprivileged to believe that they as individuals may personally improve their status.[5]

I shall add the equalitarian–elitist distinction to the pattern variables just outlined. According to this, a society's values may stress that all persons must be given respect simply because they are human beings, or it may stress the general superiority of those who hold positions of power and privilege. In an equalitarian society, the differences between low status and high status people are not stressed in social relationships and do not convey to the high status person a general claim to social deference. In contrast, in an elitist society, those who hold high positions in any structure, whether it be in business, in intellectual activities, or in government, are thought to deserve, and are actually given, general respect and deference.[6] All ascriptively oriented societies are necessarily also elitist in this use of the term. On the other hand, achievement orientation and egalitarianism are not necessarily highly correlated, since a stress on achievement is not incompatible with giving generalized deference to all who have achieved their elite positions. To a considerable degree societies which are in the process of changing from an emphasis on ascription to one on achievement seem disposed, as we shall see later, to retain their elitist orientations and institutions when contrasted with societies in which ascriptive values have never had a preeminent role.

In actual fact, *no society is ever fully explicable by these analytic concepts, nor does the theory even contemplate the possible existence of such a society.*[7] Every society incorporates some aspect of each polarity. We may, however, differentiate among social structures by the extent to which they emphasize one or another of these polarities.[8] It should be added that classifications of the relative emphases among nations with respect to certain value polarities do not imply that such values are either prescriptive or descriptive of actual behavior. Rather, they are intended to provide base lines for comparative analysis.

I have chosen to discuss the United States, Great Britain, Canada, Australia, France, and Germany to illustrate the relationship between values and the stability of democratic political systems.[9] These nations are all relatively industrialized, all have capitalist or mixed economies, and the religious traditions of all can be traced back to the same Hebraic-Christian source. They all have democratic political systems. Yet they differ in one important respect: the United States, Britain, Canada, and Australia have stable polities, while France and Germany have (or have had) unstable ones. The prime empirical focus in this chapter is on the four most populous countries; the two overseas dominions of the British Crown are contrasted with the United States and Britain in the next chapter [of *The First New Nation*].

THE UNITED STATES AND GREAT BRITAIN

Though the United States and Great Britain are both urbanized, industrialized, and stable politically, they are integrated around different values and class relations. Tocqueville's *Democracy in America* and Bagehot's *The English Constitution* accurately specified these different organizing principles. According to Tocqueville, American democratic society was equalitarian and competitive (achievement oriented); according to Bagehot, Britain was deferential (elitist) and ascriptive. As both Tocqueville and Bagehot indicated, a society in which the historic ties of traditional legitimacy had been forcibly broken could sustain a stable democratic polity only if it emphasized equality and if it contained strong, independent, and competitive institutions. Conversely, if the privileged classes persisted and continued to expect ascriptive (aristocratic) and elitist rights, a society could have a stable democratic system only if the lower classes accepted the status system. These differences will be explored in more detail subsequently. Suffice it to say now that a stable democracy can result from different combinations of pattern variables.

The United States, more than any other modern non-Communist industrial nation, emphasizes achievement, equalitarianism, universalism, and specificity.[10] These four tend to be mutually supportive. This does not mean that other stable combinations are not possible or that the "American" combination does not exhibit tensions. From the perspective of the polity, however, this combination of variables does encourage stable democracy. The upper classes can accept improvements in the status and power of the lower strata *without feeling morally offended*. Since all men and groups are expected to try to improve their position *vis à vis* others, success by a previously deprived group is not resented as deeply as in countries whose values stress the moral worth of ascription.[11] Similarly, the emphasis on equalitarianism, universalism, and specificity means that men can expect—and within limits do receive—fair treatment according to the merits of the case or their ability.   Lower-class individuals and groups which desire to change their social position *need not be revolutionary*; consequently their political goals and methods are relatively moderate.   There is little class consciousness on their part, since this consciousness is in part an adaptation to the behavior of the upper class in those societies characterized by ascription, elitism, particularism, and diffuseness.   The latter values imply that men will be treated by others and will treat each other diffusely in terms of class status. American values support interaction with an individual in terms of his role as worker in one situation, as suburban dweller in another, as a member of the American Legion in a third, and so forth.

The above comments are, of course, an oversimplification.   In fact, American society does display ascriptive, elitist, particularistic, and diffuse culture traits. These are not completely dysfunctional, as will be shown.   They do create frictions (see the analyses of McCarthyism as a reaction to "status-panic"),[12] but in general, with the exception of race and ethnic relations, these have not affected the basic stability of the polity.

The American South, which has stressed ascriptive-elitist-particularistic-diffuse values in race relations and to some extent in its total social system, has constituted a major source of instability in the American polity.   It was retained in the nation only by force, and down to the present it does not have a stable, democratic polity.   To the extent that its citizens have felt the pull of the dominant value system, the South has always found it difficult to build an integrated regional social order on its own terms.[13]

Britain has come to accept the values of achievement in its economic and educational system, and to some extent in its political system, but retains a substantial degree of elitism (the assumption that those who hold high position be given generalized deference) and ascription (that those born to high place should retain it).[14]   Tocqueville described the British class system as an "open aristocracy," which can be entered by achievement but which confers on new entrants many of the diffuse perquisites of rank enjoyed by those whose membership stems from their social background.[15]   Thus Britain differs from the United States in having, in terms of pattern variables, a strong emphasis on ascriptive, elitist, particularistic, and diffuse values.

In the nineteenth century the British business classes challenged the traditional pre-industrial value integration.[16]   But the British upper class (in contrast to most Continental aristocracies) did not strongly resist the claims of the new business classes, and later those of the workers, to take part in politics.   For reasons to be discussed later, when pressure for political participation developed within these classes in Britain, it was members of already enfranchised classes who took the leadership in reform movements.   If communication between the different strata in Britain had been blocked by jealously guarded privileges—as it had been in France—conflicts over the suffrage might have become more divisive. As Robert Michels once pointed out, the presence of upper-class leaders in a working-class party serves to reduce conservatives' hostility toward it.   To the extent that the social system permits a "left" party to recruit leaders fom the existing elite, it is easier for this party to become an accepted part of the polity.   It is worth noting that, unlike the British Labour Party, the Germany socialists have recruited few, if any, leaders from the old upper classes.

Thus the *economy* and *polity* in Britain have been characterized by achievement, elitism, universalism, and diffuseness.   The *social class* system, however, retains many elements of ascription, elitism, particularism, and diffuseness.   The traditional upper classes and their institutions—the public schools, the ancient universities, and the titled aristocracy—remain at the summit of the social structure.[17]   At the same time, achievers in job and school are not barred from securing diffuse elite status, and the lower classes feel that the political institutions operate for their benefit.   Like the liberal bourgeoisie before them, the British workers have never seriously developed the objective of eliminating the old privileged classes, either socially or economically.[18]   Having been allowed into the political club almost as soon as British labor developed organizations of its own, working-class leaders have supported the rules of the parliamentary game. Unlike many early continental socialist parties, they were willing, while a small minority party, to cooperate with one of the older parties.   And currently they remain the only socialist party whose policies "sustain" the legitimacy of aristocracy; their leaders, like other members of the Establishment, willingly accept aristocratic titles and other honors from the Crown.[19]

The deference shown to the system by the leaders and the rank and file of the labor movement is not simply a reaction to the strength of the status system.   The British upper class has long shown a high level of sophistication in handling the admission of new strata to the "club."   Thus in 1923, as Labour was about to form its first government, the *Sunday Times* printed a manifesto by Richard Haldane (Viscount of Cloan) urging that the two old parties give Labour a fair chance at government:

We have to recognize that a great change is in progress.   Labour has attained to commanding power and to a new status.   There is no need for alarm.   All may go well if as a nation we keep in mind the necessity of the satisfaction of two new demands—that for recognition of the title to equality, and for more knowledge and its systematic application to industry and to the rest of life. . . . The result of the General Election may prove a blessing to us if it has awakened us to our neglect of something momentous which has been slowly emerging for years past. . . . Three quarters of a century since, the old Whigs, wise in their limited way, refused to meet the Chartist movement merely with a blank refusal.   Thereby they earned our gratitude.   For while most of the nations of Europe were plunged into revolution as a result of turning deaf ears to their violent progressives, we were saved, and remained in comparative quiet. . . . We had spoken with the enemy in the gate, and he had turned out to be of the same flesh and blood as ourselves. . . .[20]

Edward Shils, in *The Torment of Secrecy*, seeks to account for the great emphasis on publicity concerning political matters in the United States, *e.g.*, congressional investigations, as contrasted with the stress on privacy and secrecy in Britain. His explanation hinges on the fact that Britain is still a deferential society as compared with the United States:

> The United States has been committed to the principle of publicity since its origin. The atmosphere of distrust of aristocracy and of pretensions to aristocracy in which the American Republic spent its formative years has persisted in many forms. Repugnance for governmental secretiveness was an offspring of the distrust of aristocracy.
>
> In the United States, the political elite could never claim the immunities and privileges of the rulers of an aristocratic society. . . .
>
> American culture is a populistic culture. As such, it seeks publicity as a good in itself. Extremely suspicious of anything which smacks of "holding back," it appreciates publicity, not merely as a curb on the arrogance of rulers but as a condition in which the members of society are brought into a maximum of contact with each other.
>
> . . . Great Britain is a modern, large-scale society with a politicized population, a tradition of institutionalized pluralism, a system of representative institutions and great freedom of enquiry, discussion, and reporting. . . . British political life is strikingly quiet and confined. Modern publicity is hemmed about by a generally well-respected privacy. . . .
>
> Although democratic and pluralistic, British society is not populist. Great Britain is a hierarchical country. Even when it is distrusted, the Government, instead of being looked down upon, as it often is in the United States, is, as such, the object of deference because the Government is still diffused with the symbolism of a monarchical and aristocratic society. The British Government, of course, is no longer aristocratic . . . [But it] enjoys the deference which is aroused in the breast of Englishmen by the symbols of hierarchy which find their highest expression in the Monarchy. . . .
>
> The acceptance of hierarchy in British society permits the Government to retain its secrets, with little challenge or resentment. . . . The deferential attitude of the working and middle classes is matched by the uncommunicativeness of the upper-middle classes and of those who govern. . . . The traditional sense of the privacy of executive deliberations characteristic of the ruling classes of Great Britain has imposed itself on the rest of the society and has established a barrier beyond which publicity may not justifiably penetrate.[21]

The protection from populist criticism which an elitist system gives to all who possess the diffuse status of "leaders" extends not only to the political and intellectual elites but to school teachers and the school system as well. A study of the comparative position of teachers in England and America points this out well:

> Conservative, Labour, and Liberal parties alike have consistently held to the view that the content of education and methods of instruction are not matters for popular debate and decision, but should be left in the hands of teachers themselves and of other professional educators. This being so, individuals or groups seeking to "use" the schools for their own purposes are confronted, not by the hastily constructed defenses of the teacher or of a single school or school board, as in America, but by the massive disregard of experienced politicians and administrators. This willing delegation of educational issues to educators is possible because the latter form a coherent and predictable element in the authority structure that moulds society. . . .
>
> The relation between the school and the family also differs in the two countries.

In America, for the most part, the parents hand over their child to the school system, but maintain a continuous scrutiny over progress. In England, "interference" by the parents in the school is resisted both by teachers and by educational administrators. Parents' associations and parent-teacher associations are becoming increasingly common, but they limit their activities to social functions and to meetings at which school policy is explained but not debated.[22]

Ralph Turner also shows how variations in the basic values of the two societies impinge on their educational systems. American education reflects the norms of *contest mobility*, "a system in which elite status is the prize in an open contest and is taken by the aspirants' own efforts. . . . Since the 'prize' of successful upward mobility is not in the hands of the established elite to give out, the latter are not in a position to determine who shall attain it and who shall not." Conversely, British education reflects the norms of *sponsored mobility*, in which "elite recruits are chosen by the established elite or their agents, and elite status is *given* on the basis of some criterion of supposed merit and cannot be *taken* by any amount of effort or strategy. Upward mobility is like entry into a private club, where each candidate must be 'sponsored' by one or more of the members."

The American system, with its emphasis on the common school and opportunities for further education at every level, encourages all to advance themselves through their own efforts. "Every individual is encouraged to think of himself as competing for an elite position, so that in preparation he cultivates loyalty to the system and conventional attitudes."[23] Conversely, the British system has always selected the minority who will go ahead in the educational system at a relatively early age. Those not selected, the large bulk of the population, are taught to "regard themselves as relatively incompetent to manage society. . . . The earlier that selection of the elite recruits can be made, the sooner the masses can be taught to accept their inferiority and to make 'realistic' rather than phantasy plans."[24] Those selected for the elite, on the other hand, are removed from competition and admitted to a school, either public or grammar, in which there is great emphasis on absorbing the elite's aesthetic culture, manners, and sense of paternalism toward the non-elite. Unlike the situation in America, where in the absence of a sense of a special elite culture the masses retain their right and ability to determine taste, English society operates on the assumption that only the elite may determine what is high or low quality.[25]

In his discussion of the sources of stability of English democracy, Harry Eckstein observes that authority patterns vary among the classes—authoritarian relations increase as one moves down the social ladder. Within the British elite, he suggests, social relations

> tend to be quite surprisingly democratic, or at least consultative and comradely; here . . . we might note the ubiquity of committees at every conceivable level in the higher civil service, the unusual use of staff committees in the military services, and the easy relations among officers of all ranks in military regiments, especially in elitist regiments like the Guards . . . , while behavior among pupils [in upper-class public schools] is modeled to a remarkable extent on the political system.
>
> [Conversely, where hierarchical relations are involved, as] between members of

the Administrative Class [of the Civil Service] and their underlings, officers and their men, managers and their help, relations are highly non-consultative and certainly not comradely. . . .[26]

The United States and Great Britain differ, of course, not only in these patterns, but in the extent to which the same value orientations dominate the key status, economic, and political subsystems of the society. Presumably, Eckstein would relate the stability of American populist democracy to the fact that there are egalitarian social relations within all levels. American society has more homogeneity of values than the British. On the other hand, the particular distribution of different value orientations in Britain would also seem to be congruent with the stability of an industrialized democracy, since it legitimates open participation by all groups in the economy and polity, while the diffuse elitism rewards all with a claim to high position.

FRANCE AND GERMANY

The values of France and Germany—our politically unstable cases—resemble those of the United States and Britain in many respects. France, through her Great Revolution of 1789, sought to adopt the same syndrome of values which the United States developed: achievement, equalitarianism, universalism, specificity. The Declaration of the Rights of Man, like the Declaration of Independence, proclaims doctrines subsumed by these concepts. Germany has resembled Britain in that the pressures stemming from economic change and the rise of new social groupings in the nineteenth century did not result in a political revolution which proclaimed a new value ethos. Rather, Germany seemingly sought to modify existing institutions and to create diverse value patterns in different hierarchical subsystems in ways very similar to those which developed in Britain. The French failure stems from the fact that, in contrast to America, the forces of the Revolution were not strong enough to sustain value consensus among the key social groupings; in Germany the new combinations of values, though powerful, were basically incompatible with the requirements for a stable *non-authoritarian* political system.

French society is difficult to classify in terms of basic values. Its internal political tensions flow in large measure from the fact that major social groupings adhere to largely incompatible values. The French sociologist François Bourricaud has pointed this out:

It is . . . difficult to seize upon and isolate the unconscious or semiconscious motivations [basic values] which give French institutions their tone and their specific color. They are more apparent in some groups than in others. Certain themes of French culture are more clearly discernible, more sharply outlined, among the bourgeois than among the workers. All research of this nature begins by determining what social groups are culturally dominant. America, for example, has developed a culture of the middle classes. But in France a group can be culturally dominant in one area and not at all present in another. . . . For example, the tradition of the noble life continues without doubt to be very influential in French society even though the nobility as a social group does not amount to much. . . . In brief, cultural themes are very far from being unified even within the society, both by reason of the diversity of the groups which make up this society and the diversity of activities by which this culture is expressed.[27]

These internal cleavages result from the fact that the French Revolution succeeded in eliminating neither the old set of ascriptive-particularistic values nor some of their key institutional supports, particularly the Church. A large part of the French bourgeoisie, whose status and economic objectives sustained the Revolution, never completely rejected the traditional value system.[28] And, as François Goguel points out, this traditional value system was directly hostile to democracy:

> A pessimistic idea of human nature—an idea of Catholic origin, and directly opposed to the optimism of J. J. Rousseau—is at the basis of this conviction; man, being naturally evil, must have teachers, or guides, to direct him toward good. These guides are the traditional institutions, the social authorities. The first is the authority of monarchy, temporally the highest, and then the First Families, predestined by birth and wealth to a leading role. Finally, above all, there is the Catholic Church, charged with shaping conscience and soul and conditioning them toward the social order and eternal salvation. These theocratic ideas, expounded by Bonald at the time of the Restoration, survived much longer than one would have thought possible. . . .[29]

France has maintained particularistic values in commerce and industry more than any other industrial nation. The economic policies of many French small businessmen emphasize the maintenance of the family fortune and status. They refuse to take economic risks or to enter into serious competition with one another.[30] The politics of the petty bourgeoisie has stressed the stability of existing business, even though this has limited the economy's potential for expansion.[31] French employers, particularly in small plants, have expected particularistic loyalties from their employees.[32] All through its history, French industry has attempted to deny representation rights to trade unions, and when forced to grant them has undermined these concessions as soon as possible. To permit the unions rights of representation—and thereby to acknowledge universalistic norms—has been seen as morally offensive. The behavior of the French businessman is, of course, more complicated than this brief analysis suggests, since a capitalist system inevitably dictates a considerable degree of universalism.[33] As François Bourricaud has pointed out: "Between the 'bourgeois' money criterion and more aristocratic criteria—antiquity of family and connection—the bourgeois hesitates. This ambiguity explains in part, perhaps, why his relations with the workers have been so difficult."[34]

The French working class, on the other hand, has supported in ideology, if not always in action, the revolutionary values of achievement, equalitarianism, universalism. However, it has been faced with a situation in which individual and collective mobility are morally disapproved of by the more privileged orders—although, of course, as in other industrial societies, considerable individual mobility does occur.[35] French workers' efforts to improve their lot through collective action are bitterly resisted by the bourgeoisie, and the emphasis on local particularism inhibits the unions' efforts to form strong nation-wide organizations.[36] There is perhaps no more impressive evidence of the deep moral hostility of many French employers towards unions than the systematic effort to demolish all union rights during the period of the "phony" war, from September 1939 to May 1940. Seemingly both employers and their political representatives in the government put "teaching the workers and unions a lesson" ahead of national unity and, in the last analysis, national survival.[37]

The effort to sustain traditionalist norms within a growing economy has inhibited the creation of a democratic parliamentary system based on achievement and universalism. Every French republic has sought to institutionalize these values, and has given the lower classes equal rights of access to government. In most other countries such rights and norms have led to the tempering of aggressive ideologies in the lower classes; in France it has led to an intensification of these ideologies.

Thus the most disruptive element in French culture has been the cleavage between pre-industrial values, supported by the upper classes and the church, which have continued to affect the economic sector, and the legitimacy of the Revolution, which has formally dominated the political structure. The ascriptive, elitist, and particularistic aspects of French values facilitated the emergence of politics along class lines, while the emphasis on equalitarianism, universalism, and achievement has led the less privileged strata to sharply resent their position. Tocqueville pointed to this problem in an exaggerated form when he suggested: "To conceive of men remaining forever unequal upon a single point, yet equal on all others, is impossible; they must come in the end to be equal upon all."[38]

The retention of pre-industrial values within French capitalism did not mean, of course, that all of French industry adhered to them. Within large-scale industry as within government, the corollaries of bureaucratization and rationalization emerged: stable definition of rights and duties, systematic universalistic ordering of authority relationships, publicity of decisions, the appearance of personnel experts or specialists in labor relations as a consequence of the division of labor. And though one generally expects workers to be more radical in large-scale industry than in small, in those sections of France where industry was large and bureaucratic—in general the North—the business classes demonstrated a greater willingness to accept trade unions as a legitimate and permanent part of the industrial system; there, syndicalism and Communism were weakest. Before 1914, the Socialists were strongest in the areas of the country with large industry, while the anarcho-syndicalists had their greatest strength in those parts of the nation where the particularistic values of small business were dominant. These differences were paralleled between the two great wars by the variations in support of the Socialists and Communists. The Communists, in general, took over the centers of syndicalist strength, though since World War II they have become the party of the French industrial workers almost everywhere.

The picture of a relatively stagnant France with "stalemate" politics, a reluctance to take advantage of economic opportunities, and a low birthrate, which was accurate enough before World War II, has changed drastically since then. The European economic miracle—great and rapid economic growth and a sharp increase in the consumption of mass-produced items—has affected France as much as any country. The net reproduction birth rate, which stood below 100 (the rate at which a population reproduces itself) all during the inter-war years, has hovered around 125 since 1946.[39] A number of observers of the French scene have argued that "the combination of 'new men and new attitudes' inherited from the war period has made French society much less different from the societies of other industrial nations."

> In the civil service, in business, in professional organizations, even in the military forces, new groups of "technocrats" appear—men who specialize in the management of a highly industrialized and bureaucratic society, men who earn high incomes without necessarily owning much capital. . . .
> Within the business world, a kind of managerial revolution has led to a new conception of profits, in which management and ownership are less tightly fused and in which the firm's power counts more than the owner's fortune.[40]

The emergence of a "modern" France would seem to be negated by the continued strength of the Communists as a party and union movement (CGT) among the industrial workers, and the highly unstable political system. It may be argued, however, that the current instabilities of the political system now reflect the tensions of rapid change superimposed on a polity whose political leadership has a traditional bent toward uncompromising rhetoric. The Communists have retained most of the working-class electoral following which they secured in the late 1930's and the 1940's. They have not gained new votes, and they have lost a large proportion of their party and trade-union membership. But if the majority of French workers still vote Communist, various opinion surveys suggest a relatively low level of class alienation among the workers. On the "right," the principal version of anti-democratic extremism—the Poujadist movement—secured almost all of its backing from the declining middle-class strata, often in regions that were being economically impoverished. That is, those who found their relative or absolute economic and social position worsening as a result of changes in French society were attracted to a politics that was "against the system." The tensions over the Algerian War similarly involved efforts to resist inherent "modernizing" tendencies. In a real sense, the Gaullist fifth republic is engaged in an effort to bring France's polity and values into line with the changing reality of its class and economic structures. But political and organizational loyalties do not disappear quickly, and consequently the political system, in which conflicts over these values are acted out, seems much more resistant to change than are other institutions.

The way in which historic tensions are maintained may be seen most clearly by examining the sources of the perpetuation of value differences between those white-collar workers who are employed in the bureaucracy of industry and those employed by government. In France, it has not been possible to speak of the "white-collar worker" as such; rather, there are the sharply differing backgrounds of the *employé* (private employee) and the *fonctionnaire* (civil servant).   As the French sociologist Michel Crozier has described the situation in his country:

> We meet two opposite types of participation and integration in society; one type which can be described as paternalistic and which is present among traditional white-collar workers (bank employees, insurance employees, and those employed in industry), and an egalitarian type, present in the world of the lower civil servants. . . . The same basic psychological situation has produced two role types, and with these two roles, two different concepts of society, two sets of religious attitudes, two approaches to politics.   These differences have tended to decline since the second World War, but there are still two different worlds which are determined in one case by channels of social mobility through the lay and anti-clerical sector of the society, and in the other through paternalistic and even confessional methods of entrance.[41]

These two non-manual strata are recruited from different sectors of French society.   Private industry tends to secure its employees from the graduates of the Catholic schools, often on the basis of personal recommendations, and "many private firms examine carefully the family origins . . . of prospective employees." The Civil Service is recruited almost exclusively from state schools whose faculties are overwhelmingly on the political left.   Its recruitment procedures and operation emphasize rigorous selection criteria and formal academic achievement. These differences in the recruitment and membership deeply affect French trade-union political life, since the Catholic trade-union federation (CFTC) and the liberal Catholic party (the MRP) have their principal base of support in the white-collar workers employed in private industry, while the socialist-influenced union federation, *Force Ouvrier* (FO), and the socialist party (SFIO), have their strongest supporters among the lower echelons of civil service workers.

> The political consequences of these differences are known; the inability of the parties of the Center, of the Third Force, to overcome their differences and to form any permanent unity.   These differences support, and are in turn nourished by, the opposition of the socialist FO and the Catholic CFTC unions, a conflict based in the last analysis on the essential incompatibility between the religious mentality of the old Federation of White-Collar workers, the base of the CFTC, and the lay mentality of the federations of Civil Servants in the FO.[42]

Thus France remains unstable politically.   It may currently be in the final process of cultural "modernization," but historic institutional commitments still prevent the emergence of a fully modern domestic politics, one in which the basic internal issues revolve around an interest struggle for the division of national income within a welfare state.   Rather, issues concerning the legitimacy of various institutions, the role of the religious and secular school, and the structure of authority still divide the nation.   Historically, the resistance of the French ascriptive and particularistic "right" to accepting changes in power relations within industry, to legitimating (i.e., morally accepting) unions, was in large measure responsible for the fact that the French workers, though possessors of the suffrage before workers elsewhere in Europe, remain alienated from the polity.[43]   Conversely, to the extent that the workers have supported extremist tendencies, anarcho-syndicalism and Communism, the conservative strata have been enabled to feel morally sustained in their refusal to share power. To break through this vicious cycle of extremism and counter-extremism is not an easy task, even though the cleavages in basic values may be ending.

The difficulties of the German polity stem from sources which are, in one sense, the obverse of the French. Where France has encouraged political participation by the lower classes but denied them rights in industry, the German system has given the working class rights and protection within industry while limiting their access to the polity. Until 1918 at least, the German aristocratic classes success-fully maintained ascriptive and particularistic values in the non-economic areas of life, while encouraging achievement and universalism, but not equalitarianism, in the economic order. That is, the old upper classes permitted, and sometimes even encouraged, the working class to improve its economic position through social legislation and trade unions. They were not willing, however, to accede to achievement criteria in the status and political orders. Individuals were still judged and rejected according to their social origins. This meant that, as is usual in an ascriptively oriented status system, political movements emerged based on distinct status or class lines which were buttressed by the class organizations in industry. However, these political groupings could never gain a secure foothold in the political system.

Concretely, the Prussian aristocracy and the Wilhelmine monarchy, while sympathetic to the objectives of the unions in industry, first attempted to suppress the Socialists as a party between 1878 and 1891, and then refused to accept a democratic electoral system in Prussia, the chief state of the Reich, up to the over-throw of the monarchy in 1918. This refusal to allow the workers' political representatives a share in political power forced the Socialist movement to main-tain a revolutionary ideological posture which was at complete variance with its social position and aspirations. The workers' movement did not want to destroy the state, but rather to be admitted to it. In southern Germany, where ascriptive status lines were much less rigid than in Prussia, and where the conservative classes admitted the workers' political movements into the body politic, the Socialist parties quickly developed a moderate, reformist, and pragmatic ideology. In these states, the revisionist doctrines of Eduard Bernstein had their earliest and strongest advocates; in some, the Social-Democrats supported cooperation with non-socialist parties, thereby reducing the emphasis on class warfare.[44] In Weimar Germany, the Social Democratic Party developed into a moderate organ-ization, and, until the outbreak of the Great Depression and the rise of Nazism, absorbed most of the old socialist and Communist electoral strength.

Many conservative groups, particularly those which had been involved in the status system of the old empire—for example, the landed aristocracy, the teachers, the professional officers, and much of the civil service—never accepted the Weimar Republic and its universalistic norms.[45] The middle classes wavered between embracing a political system which incorporated the universalistic values that they had long supported and reacting against the challenge to the privileges and the deferential norms they retained as part of the socially privileged. The support which both the old and new middle classes gave to Nazism in the early 1930's has been linked by many observers to the strong German emphasis on ascription and elitism. Faced with a dire economic threat to their status, the middle classes turned to the Nazis, who promised a national socialism which would restore prosperity and preserve the values of the *Ständestaat* (strong respect for hierarchical rankings).

In discussing the pattern variables, I have assumed that the industrial economic order requires a greater application of universalistic, specific, and achievement criteria than do the political and social orders. Employers must deal with workers in terms of these values, and workers, in turn, are constrained to secure a stable, universalistic definition of their rights in industry. The demand for universalistic treatment in the factory is a prime demand of workers in modern society. The demand for universalistic treatment in the political sphere occurs often as part of the struggle in the economic order. On the other hand, the middle and upper classes tend to be more oriented toward maintaining their privileged position in terms of status rather than in economic terms—that is, toward enforcing the norms inherent in elitism. Hence, a working class which has made gains in the economic order will be relatively satisfied, while a middle and upper class which feels threatened in its position of status will react aggressively. It may be contended that in Weimar Germany the majority of the workers were relatively moderate politically because they had secured access to the economic and political orders, while traditional conservative groupings and the middle classes were disposed to accept militant politics in a crisis because their value orientations of elitism and ascription led them to perceive such gains on the part of the workers as a threat to their over-all status position and to their sense of "the way things ought to be."

Harry Eckstein argues that the instability of the Weimar Republic was a result of the strains between the authoritarian norms which characterized all non-governmental institutions and the democratic patterns of the political system:

> The German governmental pattern was . . . one-sidedly democratic, at any rate if we confine analysis to the level of parliamentary representation and decision-making. . . . On the other hand, social life, including life in parties and political interest groups, was highly authoritarian. . . . Not only were society and polity to some degree incongruent; they existed in unprecedented contradiction with one another. . . .
>
> This unalleviated democracy (pure proportional representation, strong detailed bill of rights) was superimposed upon a society pervaded by authoritarian relationships and obsessed with authoritarianism. . . . German family life, German schools, and German business firms were all exceedingly authoritarian. German families were dominated, more often than not, by tyrannical husbands and fathers, German schools by tyrannical teachers, German firms by tyrannical bosses.[46]

Eckstein does not contend that the Germans as individuals always preferred authoritarian politics. Rather, he points to the fact that from the first universal suffrage elections in Imperial Germany down to 1928, liberal, center, and socialist parties secured between 80 and 90 per cent of the vote, and that anti-democratic pre-Nazi parties were always in a small minority. He seems to suggest that a more authoritarian kind of "democratic" regime, such as that of Imperial Germany, would have provided a "proper base" for a stable regime. It might be argued, in line with the reasoning behind both my own and Eckstein's analyses, that Germany could have best evolved into a stable constitutional democracy through the gradual growth of a system which retained elitist and monarchical forms and strong executive power in the hands of a powerful Chancellor. The symbolic retention of legitimate power in the hands of a Kaiser conceivably might have preserved the allegiance of the middle and upper classes to a democratic political system.

Arguments such as these are impossible to prove, but it may be suggested that the political history of Sweden illustrates "what might have been" in Germany. In many ways, pre-World War I Swedish social structure resembled that of Germany. The Swedish privileged classes strongly resisted universal suffrage, and adult suffrage was adopted only in 1909 for the lower house and in 1921 for the upper one.[47] Swedish social life contained many of the same authoritarian patterns that characterized Germany's, and Sweden instinctively looked to Germany for intellectual and cultural leadership. But Sweden was both small and geographically isolated from European wars; it escaped the tensions resulting from the overthrow of a monarchy after military defeat. Its radical Socialist party became moderate and its extreme conservatives and upper class came to accept the right of the workers to participate in, and ultimately to dominate, the polity. But even today, the values of the Swedish status system contain strong elements of ascription, elitism, particularism, and diffuseness.

Much of the elitist quality of Swedish life has gradually declined under the impact of thirty years of Socialist government. Successful political rule by this party, many of whose leaders began life as workers, has undoubtedly weakened the value orientations which sustained elitism. Yet Swedish politics remain highly particularistic. For example, Swedish telephone books still list individuals alphabetically *within* occupational groups. So to look up a Swede in the phone book, you must know his occupation. He is still a doctor, printer, or carpenter before he is a person.

To a considerable extent the egalitarian changes reflect conscious policies of the governing Socialists. Thus the Swedish educational system has been changing, from one similar to that of Britain and other parts of Europe with their class-stratified divisions of secondary schools—modern, technical, and grammar—to "single-type comprehensive schools, into which all the existing schools are to be incorporated. . . . The eventual aim is a 9 year school, with differentiation beginning in a very mild form in the 6th year, and only taking shape in 3 different 9th classes [at age 16] (preparation for higher education; general finishing class with mainly theoretical bent; and preparatory vocational training with some theoretical courses)."[48]

C. A. R. Crosland, who sees class values in his own England as little changed in spite of the great structural reforms introduced by the Labour government of 1945–1951, twenty years of full employment, and the welfare state, has pointed to at least one of the major conditions required for a political impact on class values in a democracy:

> Political power can also have an influence on class attitudes, but in a democracy only, I think, *if one party remains in office for a long time. . . .*
>
> Thus in Britain, before the war, when Conservative Governments seemed the natural thing, collective feelings of superiority and inferiority were intensified by the belief that political power was an additional, semi-permanent attribute of a class which already appeared to possess all the other attributes of a ruling class. Conversely in Sweden, the fact that a Socialist Government now seems the natural order of things has a profound effect in weakening collective class feelings, since at least the attribute of political power is differently located from the other attributes of the "upper class."
>
> It creates, in other words, a definite "scatter," and prevents a concentration of "top-class attributes". . . . Thus political power counterbalances the influence of other class determinants, and hence diminishes the likelihood of strong, coagulated class feelings. But this will occur only if the period of one-party rule is sufficiently prolonged to cause a definite adjustment in psychological attitudes.[49]

Evidence secured in a Swedish survey study confirms the thesis that long tenure in office by a workers' party may modify the traditional assumptions concerning the inter-relationship of different indicators of high position. Those interviewed were asked, "Which class do you think is the most influential in our society today?" The responses indicate that Swedes who perceive their status as "working class" are most likely to believe that their class is the most influential one than self-defined "middle-class" individuals believe is the case with the middle class. And to explain this phenomenon of consensus across class lines concerning the greater power of the working class, Torgny Segerstedt comments: "Perhaps I ought to remind you that we have had a Labour government in office in Sweden for more than 20 years."[50]

To return to Germany briefly, major changes in its value system, which weaken ascriptive values, appear to have been developing since the end of the last war. Two of the major bulwarks of ascriptive and particularistic values in the society no longer exist or have been weakened: the army and the Prussian aristocracy. The major regions of Germany previously dominated by these values (most of old Prussia) are now in Russia, Poland, or Communist East Germany. What is now West Germany is largely composed of areas which even before World War I were willing to admit the working class into the political club. In addition, the upheavals of Nazism and World War II have upset the old German class structure and have reduced the significance of ascriptive elements.[51]

Yet ascriptive, elitist values are far from dead in West Germany. ,To some extent, the society still emphasizes social origins as a determinant of status, and men are still reacted to in terms of status position—professors, engineers, industrialists, and others are members of an elite. While workers are part of the body politic and not outside it, they have not secured an end to a diffuse emphasis on class. The continued significance of elitist values has been pointed up in a recent study of the German entrepreneurial class. Heinz Hartmann suggests that this stratum has laid claim to diffuse respect: "[M]anagement does not claim elite status with respect to a specific task, area, or group but rather in relation to the total society."[52]   In effect, the German *Unternehmer* (entrepreneurs) have laid explicit claim to the deference and authority once received by now decimated classes:

> Management's drive toward ascendancy quite frequently is justified by reference to the death or incapacitation of previous elite groups.   When Winschuh, for instance, addressed a conference of Young *Unternehmer* in 1950, he pointed out that "due to the destruction of old elites, the importance of the *Unternehmer* for the formation of a new elite group has increased."   He reminded his audience of the "mass annihilation and expatriation of the Elbian feudatory" and called the attention of his listeners to "the decimation of numerous families of officers and civil service officials." . . . All of this led up to the finding that "society needs more authority in leadership, more determination and speed in administration" than it enjoys at the time and that the *Unternehmer* were willing and able to provide all of this.[53]

The West German system is probably moving toward the British or the Swedish model.   There is also much more authoritarianism—or perhaps, more accurately, executive power—in Bonn than there was in Weimar.   Chancellor Adenauer has played a role much more comparable to that of Bismarck in the Imperial system than to any of the Weimar chancellors, and elections have been fought to a considerable degree as contests for the Chancellorship.[54]   Whether Germany will actually maintain itself as a stable democracy, only time will tell.   Particularly crucial will be the resolution of the challenge to the values of the privileged classes when the working-class-based Social Democrats actually move toward national office.[55]

* * *

Notes

1. I have dealt with such problems in preceding publications.   Thus *Political Man: The Social Bases of Politics* (Garden City, N.Y.: Doubleday, 1960) is addressed to an analysis of the relationship between stages or degrees of economic development and political systems, and to the effect of varying types of legitimacy on the intensity of conflict within political systems.   *Union Democracy*, with Martin Trow and James Coleman (Glencoe, Ill.: The Free Press, 1956) and *Agrarian Socialism* (Berkeley: University of California Press, 1950) dealt with the ways in which variation in the number and type of secondary organizations mediate between the population and the government and thus affect the conditions for democracy or dictatorship.
2. See *Political Man*, pp. 21–41 and 45–48; and my Introduction to a new paperback edition of Robert Michels, *Political Parties* (New York: Collier Books, 1962), pp. 15–39, especially pp. 33–38.
3. Ferdinand Tönnies, *Community and Society, Gemeinschaft und Gesellschaft* (East Lansing: Michigan State University Press, 1957).   A somewhat more complex specification of the component elements of these two concepts may be found in Charles P. Loomis, *Social Systems: Essays on Their Persistence and Change* (Princeton, N.J.: Van Nostrand, 1961), especially pp. 57–63.   The pattern variables may also be seen as derived from Max Weber's types of social action, especially the traditional and the instrumentally rational.   See Max Weber, *The Theory of Social and Economic Organization* (New York: Oxford University Press, 1947), pp. 115–118.

4. Parsons has two other pattern variables which I ignore here, largely for reasons of parsimony: affectivity–affective neutrality, and the instrumental–consummatory distinction. A third set—self-orientation–collectivity-orientation—is discussed briefly toward the end of Chapter 7 [of *The First New Nation*]. For a detailed presentation of the pattern variables, see Talcott Parsons, *The Social System* (Glencoe, Ill.: The Free Press, 1951), pp. 58–67. Parsons' most recent elaboration of the relationship of pattern variable analysis to other elements in his conceptual framework is "Pattern Variables Revisited," *American Sociological Review*, 25 (1960), pp. 467–483; see also his article, "The Point of View of the Author," in Max Black, ed., *The Social Theories of Talcott Parsons* (Englewood Cliffs, N.J.: Prentice-Hall, 1961), pp. 319–320, 329–336.

5. Karl W. Deutsch, S. A. Burrell, R. A. Kann, M. Lee, Jr., M. Lichterman, R. E. Lindgren, F. L. Loewenheim, R. W. Van Wagenen, *Political Community and the North Atlantic Area* (Princeton, N.J.: Princeton University Press, 1957).

6. Although all four polarity distinctions are important to the analysis of the political system, ascription–achievement and universalism–particularism seem more important than the other two. As Parsons has suggested, these are the variables which have the most reference to the total social system, rather than to subparts or to the motivation of individuals. "They are concerned . . . with the type of value-norms which enter into the structure of the social system." Combinations of these pairs are also most useful to help account for "structural differentiation and variability of social systems." See Parsons, *The Social System*, p. 106. The other two pairs, specificity–diffuseness and equalitarianism–elitism, are to a considerable degree dependent on the particular combinations of the first two.

7. As Parsons has put it: "In a very broad way the differentiations between types of social systems do correspond to this order of cultural value pattern differentiation, but *only* in a very broad way. Actual social structures are not value-pattern types, but *resultants* of the integration of value-patterns with the other components of the system." *Ibid.*, p. 112. (Emphases in the original.) Gabriel Almond has criticized the utility of pattern-variable analysis for the study of comparative politics on the grounds that it results in exaggerations of the differences among political systems, particularly between Western and non-Western and primitive ones. He argues that "all political systems—the developed Western ones as well as the less-developed non-Western ones—are transitional systems in which cultural change is taking place." Thus they both include elements of each polarity of the pattern variables in many of their institutions. See Gabriel Almond, "Introduction: A Functional Approach to Comparative Politics," in Gabriel Almond and James S. Coleman, eds., *The Politics of Developing Areas* (Princeton, N.J.: Princeton University Press, 1960), pp. 20–25. This criticism is useful if it is considered as a warning against reifying these concepts, or tending to exaggerate the integrated character of societies, whether large or small. However, there is no reason why use of the pattern variables for analytic purposes need fall into these errors, and Parsons himself repeatedly stresses that systems and structures are never wholly one.

A detailed criticism of Parsons' analysis of politics, which, however, does not touch on the concepts dealt with here may be found in Andrew Hacker, "Sociology and Ideology," in Max Black, ed., *The Social Theories of Talcott Parsons* (Englewood Cliffs, N.J.: Prentice-Hall, 1961) pp. 289–310.

8. It is important to note also that the pattern variables can be and have been used to distinguish among and within different orders of social systems or structures. Thus we may characterize total epochs (feudalism compared to capitalism), whole nations (the United States compared to Britain), subsystems within nations that logically may operate with different combinations of the variables (the state, or industry), subsystems within nations that logically must follow a specific set of pattern variables (the family), and subsystems within which there is conflict between different pattern variables (*e.g.*, the French business system, to be discussed later).

9. There have been other efforts at using the pattern variables for political analysis. For the most part, however, they do so in the context of specifying differences between Western and agrarian societies and hence posit ideal types of integrated *Gemeinschaft* and *Gesellschaft*

cultures. A paper which does attempt to use the variables to analyze contemporary differences is William Evan, "Social Structure, Trade Unionism, and Consumer Cooperation," *Industrial and Labor Relations Review*, 10 (1957), pp. 440–447.

10. For a discussion of the American value system, see Robin Williams, *American Society* (New York: Alfred A. Knopf, 1951), pp. 372–442; see also Talcott Parsons and Winston White, "The Link Between Character and Society," in S. M. Lipset and Leo Lowenthal, eds., *Culture and Social Character* (New York: The Free Press, 1961), pp. 98–103; on values and the political system see William Mitchell, *The American Polity* (New York: The Free Press, 1963). I devote less space here to elaborating on American values than on those of the other nations, since I have already dealt with them in detail in the earlier chapters of this book [*The First New Nation*].

11. Like all comparative generalizations, this is a relative rather than an absolute statement. It is obvious that in the United States, as in other countries, those with higher status dislike any challenge to their privileged positions, and resist and resent new claimants. The common resistance to the claims for status equality of upwardly mobile ethnic groups such as the Jews, the Irish, and the Italians illustrates this. Status resentments against rising groups have been a frequent source of social tension all through American history.

12. Daniel Bell, ed., *The Radical Right* (Garden City, N.Y.: Doubleday, 1963).

13. See the essays in Charles Sellers, ed., *The Southerner as American* (Chapel Hill: University of North Carolina Press, 1960), for interesting insights on the difficulties faced by Southern whites both before and after the Civil War in resolving the conflicts generated within the society and within the individuals by the sharply varying dictates of alternative value systems.

14. The general concept of elitism explicitly affects the training given to prospective members of the British upper class. Thus a description of the English public schools (private in the American sense) reports that "learning and the getting-fit are represented as part of the 'training for leadership' which many public-schoolmasters see as their social role. . . . It infects the whole set-up with a certain smugness and a certain frightening *elite* concept. The word 'breeding' is often on their lips. . . . Many of these boys go around looking for people to lead: they actually say at the University interviews that they feel they have been trained to lead . . ." John Vaizey, "The Public Schools," in Hugh Thomas, ed., *The Establishment* (New York: Clarkson Potter, 1959), pp. 28–29.

"What does the middle-class Briton mean when he says that Eton or some obscure public school in the Midlands will develop his son's character? . . . I would say that he includes in character such traits as willingness to take responsibility, loyalty to the class concept of the nation's interests, readiness to lead, which implies, of course, a belief that he is fit to lead and that people are willing to be led. . . ." Drew Middleton, *The British* (London: Pan Books, 1958), pp. 230–231.

The role of the public schools as a means of training an elitist upper class which took into itself the best of the *arrivistes* was an explicit objective of the reforms of the public school system initiated by Thomas Arnold in the 1830's. He strongly admired aristocracy, saw respect for it at the heart of England's security and freedom, and wanted to make certain that it would not be corrupted. As he saw it, public school boys were "destined to become the new masters, the epitome of all the new tendencies, annexed and made subservient to the old aristocratic order of things. 'You should feel,' he said in addresssing the boys of the Sixth Form, 'like officers in the Army or Navy.' Officers! This comparison has been applied ever since to the public school men of England." G. J. Renier, *The English: Are They Human?* (New York: Roy Publishers, 1952), p. 249 and pp. 229–270; see also Asa Briggs, *Victorian People* (Chicago: University of Chicago Press, 1954), pp. 150–177; and Denis Brogan, *The English People* (New York: Alfred A. Knopf, 1943), pp. 18–56.

15. Writing in Thomas Arnold's day in 1833, Tocqueville pointed out that what distinguished the English aristocracy "from all others is the ease with which it has opened its ranks. . . . [W]ith great riches, anybody could hope to enter into the ranks of the aristocracy. . . . The reason why the French nobles were the butt of all hatreds, was not chiefly that only nobles had the right to everything, but because nobody could become a noble. . . . The English aristocracy

in feelings and prejudices resembles all the aristocracies of the world, but it is not in the least founded on birth, that inaccessible thing, but on wealth that everyone can acquire, and this one difference makes it stand, while the others succumb. . . .

"[O]ne can clearly see in England where the aristocracy begins, but it is impossible to say where it ends. It could be compared to the Rhine whose source is to be found on the peak of a high mountain, but which divides into a thousand little streams and, in a manner of speaking, disappears before it reaches the sea. The difference between England and France in this manner turns on the examination of a single word in each language. 'Gentleman' and 'gentilhomme' evidently have the same derivation but 'gentleman' in England is applied to every well-educated man whatever his birth, while in France *gentilhomme* applies only to a noble by birth. . . . This grammatical observation is more illuminating than many long arguments. . . .

"[I]f you speak to a member of the middle classes; you will find he hates some aristocrats but not the aristocracy. . . .

"The whole of English society is still clearly on an aristocratic footing, and has contracted habits that only a violent revolution or the slow and continual action of new laws can destroy. . . ." Alexis de Tocqueville, *Journeys to England and Ireland* (New Haven, Conn.: Yale University Press, 1958), pp. 59–60, 67, 70–71.

Similarly, the great French student of English history, Elie Halévy, described the English upper class as "an aristocracy in which no rank was a closed caste, an aristocracy in which the inferior regarded the superior not with envy but respect. It was not impossible to climb into a superior class and those who respected those above them were respected in turn by those below. . . ." *History of the English People in the Nineteenth Century* (London: Ernest Benn Ltd., 1961), Vol. IV, p. 345. See also Vol. I, pp. 221–222.

For a recent discussion stressing the same point, see Anthony Sampson, *Anatomy of Britain* (New York: Harper & Bros., 1962), especially pp. 3–30.

16. For a detailed analysis of the way in which the values regulating class relations gradually changed with the rise of industry, see Reinhard Bendix, *Work and Authority in Industry* (New York: John Wiley, 1956), pp. 100–116.

17. See C. A. R. Crosland, *The Future of Socialism* (London: Jonathan Cape, 1956), pp. 232–237; Raymond Williams, *The Long Revolution* (New York: Columbia University Press, 1961), pp. 318–321; Sampson, *Anatomy of Britain*, pp. 160–217.

18. Writing in the early 1860's, before Bagehot laid down his thesis that the stability of the British polity rested on the strength of deferential ties, Taine predicted that these social relations would maintain the class structure even under conditions of universal suffrage: "[B]eneath the institutions and charters, the bill of rights and the official almanacs, there are the ideas, the habits and customs and character of the people and the classes; there are the respective positions of the classes, their reciprocal feelings—in short a complex of deep and branching invisible roots beneath the visible trunk and foliage. . . . We admire the stability of British government; but this stability is the final product, the fine flower at the extremity of an infinite number of living fibres firmly planted in the soil of the entire country. . . .

"For the grip of tradition, sentiment and instinct is tenacious. There is no stronger attachment than—attachment. . . . Even at the time of the rotten boroughs Parliament was representative of the people's will, as it is today although the number of people having a vote is rather small. And it will still be so in ten years' time, if the Reform Bill extends the suffrage. In my view changes in the law relating to the suffrage do no more than perfect the system in detail, without affecting fundamentals. The important thing remains the same, public assent. And, enfranchised or not, the labourer and the 'shopkeeper' agrees in wanting a man of the upper classes at the helm." On the other hand, Taine felt that "attachment" to leaders or representatives was absent in his native France; democracy could not work well there because France was characterized by "egalitarian envy," while at the same time it lacked the educated mass base which made possible "an intelligent democracy" in the United States. Hippolyte Taine, *Notes on England* (Fair Lawn, N.J.: Essential Books, 1958), pp. 162, 164–165.

19. Clement Attlee, speaking as leader of the Labour Party in the House of Commons on July 9, 1952, opposed sweeping economies in royal expenditures on the following grounds: "it is a

great mistake to make government too dull.   That, I think, was the fault of the German Repub-
lic after the first World War.   They were very drab and dull," Cited in Edward Shils and
Michael Young, "The Meaning of the Coronation," in S. M. Lipset and Neil Smelser, eds.,
Sociology: The Progress of a Decade (Englewood Cliffs, N.J.: Prentice-Hall, 1961), p. 221.

"In 1957, three people in five throughout the country were still keeping souvenirs from the
1953 Coronation; and three in ten claimed to have a picture of a royal person in their house."
Tom Harrison, *Britain Revisited* (London: Victor Gollancz, 1961), p. 232.

George Orwell suggested that elitist sentiments are strong among British workers as well.
"Even in socialist literature it is common to find contemptuous references to slum-dwellers. . . .
There is also, probably, more disposition to accept class distinctions as permanent, and even to
accept the upper classes as natural leaders, than survives in most countries. . . . The word 'Sir'
is much used in England, and the man of obviously upper-class appearance can usually get more
than his fair share of deference from commissionaires, ticket-collectors, policemen, and the
like.   It is this aspect of English life that seems most shocking to visitors from America and the
Dominions."   *The English People* (London: Collins, 1947), p. 29.

The British journalist Jenny Nasmyth has pointed out that "most Labour M.P.s who can
afford it, and many who cannot, send their children to the traditional [public] schools of the
governing classes.   They do this, perhaps, not primarily because they are snobs, but because,
having themselves assumed the obligations of governing, they have an easy conscience (so easy
that they seem blind to the inconsistencies between their political principles and their private
lives) about partaking in the privileges of the governing classes."   "Dons and Gadflies,"
The Twentieth Century, 162 (1957), p. 386.

20. Quoted in Kingsley Martin, *The Crown and the Establishment* (London: Hutchinson, 1962),
p. 88.

21. Edward A. Shils, *The Torment of Secrecy* (Glencoe, Ill.: The Free Press, 1956), pp. 37-51.
This book deserves recognition as at least a minor classic of sociological analysis of a social
problem; and yet curiously is not well known.   There are few other books I know of which are
as illuminating concerning the interrelationships of American society and polity.   The earlier
article by Shils and Michael Young on the monarchy is also well worth reading in the context
of problems raised in this chapter.   "The Meaning of the Coronation," *op. cit.*, pp. 220-233.
See also H. H. Hyman, "England and America: Climates of Tolerance and Intolerance," in
Daniel Bell, ed., *The Radical Right*, pp. 227-258.

Other articles and books which present interesting case materials on significant differences
between various aspects of British and American society are: Stephen Richardson, "Organizational Contrasts on British and American Ships," *Administration Science Quarterly*, 1 (1956),
pp. 189-207; L. C. B. Gower and Leolin Price, "The Profession and Practice of Law in England
and America," *Modern Law Review*, 20 (1957), pp. 317-346; Roy Lewis and Rosemary Stewart,
The Managers: A New Examination of the English, German, and American Executive (New
York: Mentor Books, 1961); P. S. Florence, *The Logic of British and American Industry* (Chapel
Hill: The University of North Carolina Press, 1953); E. Lipson, *Reflections on Britain and the
United States—Mainly Economic* (London: The Pall Mall Press, 1959), see especially Chapter 1,
"The American and British Way of Life"; C. A. R. Crosland, *The Future of Socialism*, pp. 238-
257 and *passim*; and George Baron and Asher Tropp, "Teachers in England and America," in
A. H. Halsey, Jean Floud, and C. A. Anderson, eds., *Education, Economy, and Society* (New
York: The Free Press, 1961), pp. 545-557.

22. Baron and Tropp, "Teachers in England and America," *op. cit.*, p. 548.

23. Ralph Turner, "Modes of Social Ascent through Education: Sponsored and Contest Mobility," in Halsey, Floud, and Anderson, *Education, Economy, and Society*, pp. 122, 125.
(Emphasis in original.)   For a discussion of the elitist assumptions and consequences of the
English school system by a Labour Party leader who is much impressed by the egalitarian aspects of the American educational system, see Crosland, *The Future of Socialism*, pp. 258-277
and *passim*; see also Sampson, *Anatomy of Britain*, pp. 174-194.

24. Turner, "Modes of Social Ascent . . .," *op. cit.*, p. 126.   One of the key differences between
England and the United States that has been noted as most clearly reflecting the contrast be-

tween an egalitarian society with a "common school" and an elitist society with a highly class segregated system of education is accent variations. As C. A. R. Crosland has put it: "[P]art of the reason why these differences [between classes in England] make so strong an impact is that they are associated with, and exaggerated by, the most supremely unmistakeable of all symbols of social standing—differences of accent and vocabulary. In no other country is it possible in the same way to assess a person's social standing the moment he opens his mouth . . . ," *The Future of Socialism,* pp. 177–178.

And in a recent report on English life, the founder of Mass Observation (an organization which has studied mass behavior through systematic observation techniques since 1937), writing about working-class life, comments that in spite of all the other major changes that have occurred since they began their observations: "No voice changes can be detected between 1937 and 1960. Radio, television and other outside impacts oriented to a more standard English appear to have had little or no effect. A tiny minority have consciously altered their voices. But elocution and speech training are still not important here. An English master at one of the big local schools . . . gave his considered opinion that if anything the standard of speaking of what he called 'King's English' had gone *down.*" Harrison, *Britain Revisited,* p. 32. (Emphasis in original.)

25. For an analysis of the way in which the variations in the status of elites, diffuse or specific, affect the position of intellectuals in England and America, see my *Political Man,* pp. 326–328. A. G. Nicholas has argued that although intellectuals do not have high status *within* the elite in England, the intellectual there receives more overt respect from the population as a whole than does his compeer in America because the former "has been in some degree sheltered by his very position in what Bagehot called a 'deferential' society. Not *very* deferential to him, perhaps; less deferential than to the landowner, the administrator, the soldier, the clergyman, or the lawyer, over all of whom the protective gabardine of the appellation 'gentleman' has fallen more inclusively, with fewer ends sticking out. Nevertheless the [English] intellectual has shared in it too. . . ." "Intellectuals and Politics in the U.S.A.," *Occidente,* 10 (1954), p. 47; see also Gertrude Himmelfarb, "American Democracy and European Critics," *The Twentieth Century,* 151 (1952), pp. 320–327.

A clear indication of the differences in the values of those in charge of English elite education and those of comparably placed Americans may be seen in the criticism of the views of the former president of the highest status American university, Harvard, by the Master of the Manchester Grammar School: "When Professor Conant demands 'a common core of general education which will unite in one cultural pattern the future carpenter, factory workers, bishop, lawyer, doctor, sales-manager, professor and garage mechanic,' he is simply asking for the impossible. The demand for such a common culture rests either on an altogether over-optimistic belief in the educability of the majority that is certainly not justified by experience or on a willingness to surrender the highest standards of taste and judgment to the incessant demands of mediocrity." Cited from E. James, *Education for Leadership,* in Michael Young, *The Rise of the Meritocracy* (New York: Random House, 1959), p. 40.

26. Harry Eckstein, *A Theory of Stable Democracy* (Princeton, N.J.: Monograph No. 10. Center for International Studies, Princeton University, 1961), pp. 15–16.

27. François Bourricaud, "France," in Arnold M. Rose, ed., *The Institutions of Advanced Societies* (Minneapolis: University of Minnesota Press, 1958), pp. 500–501.

28. Tocqueville has argued that fear of social revolution led the bourgeoisie to return to Catholicism. As he put it: "The Revolution of 1792, when striking the upper classes, had cured them of their irreligiousness; it had taught them, if not the truth, at least the social usefulness of belief. . . . The Revolution of 1848 had just done on a small scale for our tradesmen what that of 1792 had done for the nobility. . . . The clergy had facilitated this conversion by [giving] . . . to long established interests, the guarantees of its traditions, its customs and its hierarchy." *The Recollections of Alexis de Tocqueville* (London: The Harvill Press, 1948), p. 120.

29. François Goguel, "The Idea of Democracy and the Political Institutions," in Saul K. Padover, *French Institutions, Values and Politics* (Stanford, Calif.: Stanford University Press, 1954), pp. 12–13.

30. See the articles by John E. Sawyer, "Strains in the Social Structure of Modern France," and by David S. Landes, "French Business and the Businessman: A Social and Cultural Analysis," in Edward M. Earle, ed., *Modern France* (Princeton, N.J.: Princeton University Press, 1951), pp. 293–312; 334–353. See also Roy Lewis and Rosemary Stewart, *The Managers*, pp. 182–187. For a discussion of similar attitudes and consequences in Italy, see Maurice F. Neufeld, *Italy: School for Awakening Countries* (Ithaca: N.Y. State School of Industrial and Labor Relations, 1961), pp. 36 and *passim*.

31. Raymond Aron, who differs from most analysts of the French scene in arguing that there has been a rapid rate of growth in the total French economy in most of this century, agrees, however, that "the usual idea that France is still the nation of small business is, then, not false. . . . It is quite likely that in many sectors there are still large numbers of firms which are too small and more or less unproductive. Sometimes these marginal enterprises are protected rather than opposed by the larger ones, which thus ensure extra profits by maintaining prices at levels desired by the former.

"This relative slowness in concentration is attended by the survival of precapitalistic legal entities. . . .

"The French seem to attach importance to independence and at times to prefer it to higher income. Resistance [to incorporation into larger units] . . . expresses a characteristic of the national psychology just as it is a result of a policy adopted by governments under pressure from the electorate or grouped interests." *France: Steadfast and Changing* (Cambridge, Mass.: Harvard University Press, 1960), pp. 60–62.

32. In discussing the French businessman, Roy Lewis and Rosemary Stewart have pointed out these tendencies in detail: "The businessman is paternalistic and autocratic, treating his employees as '*mes enfants*,' as much a part of his '*maison*' as his own children and domestics. In an age of rapid technological change, this has led not only to discontent among the children, but also to a failure to modernize. . . .

"Their labor relations are also prejudiced, and even French big business lacks 'industrial-relations sense.' In France, the dogged anti-labor attitude of the businessman has ended not only with businesses paying for social welfare out of their own pockets directly, but also with an irreconcilably bitter anticapitalist feeling among the workers, who vote Communist often for that reason and no other." *The Managers*, pp. 186–187.

33. See Aron, *France: Steadfast and Changing*, pp. 45–77.

34. Bourricaud, "France," *op. cit.*, p. 478.

35. There is some evidence and opinion to sustain the belief that successfully mobile French are more likely to hide this fact than would be true for comparable individuals in other countries. See S. M. Lipset and R. Bendix, *Social Mobility in Industrial Society* (Berkeley: University of California Press, 1959), pp. 19, 82–83.

36. Val Lorwin, *The French Labor Movement* (Cambridge, Mass.: Harvard University Press, 1954), pp. 36–37.

37. See Herbert Luethy, *The State of France* (London: Secker and Warburg, 1955), p. 87; Val Lorwin, *The French Labor Movement*, pp. 87–88; Henry W. Ehrmann, *French Labor, From Popular Front to Liberation* (New York: Oxford University Press, 1947), pp. 169–232.

38. Alexis de Tocqueville, *Democracy in America* (New York: Vintage Books, 1956), Vol. I, p. 55. (Equality in this sense does not mean equality of condition, but rather universalistic treatment in all sectors.)

39. Charles P. Kindleberger, "The Postwar Resurgence of the French Economy," in Stanley Hoffman, Charles P. Kindleberger, Laurence Wylie, Jesse R. Pitts, Jean-Baptiste Duroselle, and François Goguel, *In Search of France* (Cambridge, Mass.: Harvard University Press, 1963), p. 133.

40. Stanley Hoffman, "Paradoxes of the French Political Community," in Hoffman, *et al.*, *In Search of France*, p. 61.

41. Michel Crozier, "Classes sans conscience ou préfiguration de la société sans classes," *European Journal of Sociology*, 1 (1960), pp. 244–245.

42. *Loc. cit.*

43. It should also be noted that this alienation cannot be explained primarily by low wages. "In comparison with European wages, they are not low. Higher than in Italy or Holland, certainly not as high as in Sweden or Switzerland, a little lower than in Great Britain, they have been somewhat better in buying power than in Germany and are still at least equal in that respect." Raymond Aron, *France: Steadfast and Changing*, p. 49.

44. Peter Gay, *The Dilemma of Democratic Socialism: Eduard Bernstein's Challenge to Marx* (New York: Columbia University Press, 1952), pp. 254–255 and *passim*. See also Arthur Rosenberg, *The Birth of the German Republic* (New York: Oxford University Press, 1931), pp. 48 ff.

45. "From 1920 onwards the history of the Weimar Republic was only a rearguard action against the revitalized social forces on which the German state structure had been built under Bismarck: Army, *Junkers*, big industrialists, and the higher strata of the Civil Service." J. P. Mayer, *Max Weber and German Politics* (London: Faber and Faber, 1956), p. 64.

46. Eckstein, *A Theory of Stable Democracy*, pp. 17–18.

47. Dankwart Rustow, *The Politics of Compromise* (Princeton, N.J.: Princeton University Press, 1955), pp. 65–85; Douglas Verney, *Parliamentary Reform in Sweden* (New York: Oxford University Press, 1957), pp. 159–173, 202–214.

48. Perry Anderson, "Sweden," *New Left Review*, No. 7 (1961), pp. 6–7. For other objective factors which have served to reduce hierarchical differentiation and class tension in Sweden, see the second part of Anderson's article, *New Left Review*, No. 9 (1961), pp. 34–35.

49. Crosland, *The Future of Socialism*, pp. 181–182. (Emphasis mine.)

50. Torgny Segerstedt, "An Investigation of Class-Consciousness among Office Employees and Workers in Swedish Factories," *Transactions of the Second World Congress of Sociology* (London: International Sociological Association, 1954), Vol. II, pp. 300–301, 305.

51. There are relatively few men of aristocratic or Junker origin in the various elites of contemporary Germany as contrasted with Weimar or Imperial times. "In the German Federal Republic, the . . . barriers of class have become greatly simplified, compared to the past. . . . In terms of social origins, all elites are now predominantly middle-class, with the exception only of the SPD [Social Democrats] and trade union leaders. The aristocracy has largely disappeared. . . . For the average of . . . twelve elites, 70 per cent are of middle-class background, while only 8 per cent bear aristocratic names and 10 per cent indicate some working-class background. . . ." Karl W. Deutsch and Lewis J. Edinger, *Germany Rejoins the Powers* (Stanford, Calif.: Stanford University Press, 1959), p. 125; see also p. 139.

52. Heinz Hartmann, *Authority and Organization in German Management* (Princeton, N.J.: Princeton University Press, 1949), p. 11.

53. *Ibid.*, p. 242.

54. See Eckstein, *A Theory of Stable Democracy*, p. 37.

55. Contemporary West Germany, of course, continues to differ from Britain and Sweden, which retain deferential elements in their status system, by not being a monarchy. This, as I have tried to demonstrate in *Political Man* (pp. 78–79), is not an unimportant difference. To create legitimacy is much more difficult than to transfer the symbolic legitimacy of the older political system to a new one, as is done in monarchical democracies. I will discuss some of the sharp differences between the Bonn Republic and its predecessors in Chapter 9 [of *The First New Nation*]. It should be stressed, however, that a variety of public opinion polls and studies of elite opinion indicate that attachment to democratic values is extremely fragile in Germany. For detailed summaries and discussion of such data, see Deutsch and Edinger, *Germany Rejoins the Powers*.

29 . The Bureaucratic Organization of Work
Harvey Cox

The secularization of work has produced the organization, and with it something called the "Organization Man." Already he has become the business equivalent of the supposedly faceless urbanite we discussed in Chapter 2 [of *The Secular City*]. He has replaced the fat capitalist as the perennial villain of the steady glut of "social criticism" that flows from American presses. The "Orgman's" identifying symbols are as predictable as the arrows of Saint Anthony in a medieval fresco. In his beat classic *Naked Lunch*, William Burroughs portrays him: "Young, good looking, crew-cut, Ivy League, advertising executive type . . . the white teeth, the Florida tan, the two hundred dollar sharkskin suit, the button-down Brooks Brothers shirt. . . ."[1] From ladies' club rostrums, beatnik pads, and suburban pulpits there pours a flood of fulminations against gray flannel suits and attaché cases.

The irony is that the very people who buy these books and listen so avidly to these tirades *are* the organization. Beat poets, back-to-the-soil romantics, angry young (affluent) playwrights, sociologists with academic tenure or well-uphol-stered berths in foundations all depend on an organized society to deliver their mail, collect their garbage, and market their epithets. What is the real meaning of this noisy outburst against the organization, this orgy of ritual self-laceration?

To begin to answer this question, we must first realize that the organization is here to stay. There is simply no other way to run a world brimming with three billion people in the midst of an industrial epoch. Unless a nuclear war returns us to a culture of hunting and gathering tribes, our world will be increasingly organized as the decades go by. If we choose to live responsibly in the world, then we must face the issue of how we can harness organizational power for authentic human purposes.

We are right in refusing to allow organizations to identify persons completely with the functions they perform. As individuals we do well to develop a degree of "technological asceticism," a discipline that will prevent our becoming captives of our gadgets. But we should never make the mistake of identifying this personal stance with the wishful thinking that hankers after Walden Pond. As David Bazelon says in *The Paper Economy*, "The problem of the individual should not be confused with the problem of the corporate system, because we have already made our commitment to the latter."[2] This same confusion, however, lies at the root of much of today's antiorganization thinking. It is the modern

Reprinted with permission of The Macmillan Company from *The Secular City* by Harvey Cox. © by Harvey Cox 1965. Reprinted also by permission of SCM Press Ltd.

equivalent of the equally mistaken idea that social problems can be solved only by converting individuals one by one. The truth is that our freedom in the age of organization is a question of the responsible control and exercise of power— vast, towering, unprecedented power. Freedom in such a society is really a kind of power over power. The advent of the organizational age means that the mechanism of political democracy, which in the past three centuries has been applied to the state, must now be extended to the ponderous economic structures and service bureaucracies that have developed in the past decades. The sore point is *not* that these massive bureaucratic empires exist, but that we have not yet learned how to control them for the common welfare. We persist in living by stale ideologies deriving from a bygone age.

The problem is not that we do not know enough about man in society. Modern mass-persuasion techniques, "human engineering" in industrial manage- ment, psychotherapy, motivational research, brainwashing through group dynam- ics, all demonstrate that we have already acquired an awesome grasp of what makes homo sapiens tick. The question is one not of knowledge but of power. The fact is that the massive organizations of our society are not yet answerable to the population. We have developed a network of private governments whose rulers praise the virtues of competition while they in fact administer the flow of production, distribution, and services. We have a kind of "voluntary totalitar- ianism" by which we delegate vast segments of our society's decision making to managers who perpetrate the fib that we are still making these decisions ourselves, through consumption choices and shareholding. But everyone knows that stock voting is hardly more than a ritual. Corporations are run not by the so-called owners (the shareholders) but by the managers. My "consumer vote" is equally fictitious. The principle of "price leadership" is an established fact. Recipients of welfare services have no role in controlling these services. This produces a donor-client relationship that is tyrannical and almost inevitably seethes with hostility.

For years the keenest observers of our economic system, from Thorstein Veblen to John Kenneth Galbraith, have demonstrated that our cherished image of market competition has precious little to do with the way our economy really functions. If we would humanize the organizational world, we must begin by demythologizing our sacred economic theologies. We must not be deceived by the frumpery of our socio-economic house of mirrors; we must find out where the power really lies. Only then can the mechanism be understood, altered, and steered in the direction of human community. The unvarnished fact is that our system is already a planned and administered system. The only remaining ques- tions are: By whom is it planned? for whom is it administered? and how well is it being done? The answer to all these questions is the organization. Let us then turn to an unsentimental look at what an organization really is.

As one aspect of secularization, the organization principle derives in part from the impact of the biblical faith on Western culture. This point is well argued by the German sociologist Dietrich von Oppen.[3] He insists that in order to under- stand the "organization" we should compare it to the "order," the integrative principle it has replaced in Western society. The difference is crucial. The order had a traditional, ethnic, or sacral basis. The medieval guild, the Gothic tribe, the Greek polis, the primitive clan are examples of orders. An order encompasses all or most of the facets of social existence. It relates a person to a mythical past, a total way of life, a secure identity. It corresponds roughly to certain aspects of what we have designated as tribal and town society. In contrast to the order, the organization is flexible, future-oriented, secularized, and limited in its scope. Although its predecessors appeared long ago, only in the secular epoch has it become the characteristic principle of social integration. In contradiction to its bucolic critics' claims, the organization offers many more possibilities for choice and creativity than were available in the age of the sacral order. Let us examine the four marks of the organization.

1. The organization is *flexible*. It is consciously constructed to accomplish specific purposes. Whether its purpose is to build automobiles or to teach people how to dance, the organization as such makes no claim to ultimate origin or significance. It can be reorganized, merged, or disbanded if circumstances demand it. It must constantly change its practices to meet changing conditions. If it does develop a kind of tradition, the tradition plays a secondary and not a determinative role.

2. The organization is *future-oriented*. It is formed to achieve certain particular ends. An order views the present in terms of the past. An organization remolds and utilizes past experience to solve future problems. A prince assumes the throne solely because his father was king. An executive is selected because somebody thinks he can tackle the problems of the future. Of course family connections and nepotism continue to play a role, but when they do, it is because of a malfunctioning of the organization principle and is not an expression of its real genius.

3. The organization is *secularized*. It rejects inherited rituals that are preserved from criticism by religious taboos and makes use, instead, of technical procedures which must be constantly criticized and refined. The members of an organization submit to no blood oaths or ritual initiation. When remnants of these practices do appear today, they are obviously phony frosting on a functional cake; they are frills. They do not define the relationships within the organization the way, for example, the oath of the serf did in binding him to his feudal lord. People move from one organization to another and belong to many at the same time without violating the principle that holds them together.

4. The organization makes only a *limited claim on its members*. It is interested only in that aspect of the individual's life by which he makes a contribution to the organization's purposes. Its power is relative and not absolute. In the medieval guilds, for example, legal, economic, political, social, and religious goals were all mixed together. The authority of the leaders in a modern labor union or professional association is limited, again with obvious and anachronistic exceptions, to the activities that relate to the specific purposes of the organization.

Where the organization principle obtains, the members are assumed to be free and responsible persons with other, more definitive relationships. Only the fanatic defines his existence in terms of his membership in an organization. It serves one purpose among many and he expects it to stay in its place. In return, the organization helps the person achieve some desired end, but does not seek to endow him with a total identity or life meaning. The organization world confronts him with the "terrible freedom" to choose his own associations and his own life-style. If he chooses to abdicate that freedom to someone else, he should not blame his misery on someone else. The possibility for freedom-in-responsibility is there to a degree that was impossible within the tight and sacrally ordered culture.

Von Oppen believes the organization principle entered Western history with the Christian Gospel. The Gospel posed a demand for *personal* decision, if necessary at the expense of family, religious, or ethnic relationships. The new community of the church made a decisive break with all preceding traditional orders. It radically relativized national and racial groupings and produced a wholly new kind of integrative principle. It was a community based on free choice and not on blood ties or ethnic consanguinity. The first Christians shared a life that violated previous religious and racial taboos ("There is no longer Jew nor Greek"). They lived not to cherish a sacred tradition but to prepare for an imminent future. Here, then, the seeds of the organization principle were planted in the soil of Western history.

Admittedly the tender shoot did not always prosper in the next two thousand years. During the era of Constantine (really only now coming to a close), the organization principle was frequently buried under "established" churches, the so-called conversion of entire Visigothic tribes, the mistaken notion of "Western Christendom," the Reformers' acceptance of *Landeskirchen* and *Volkskirchen*, and the mixture of Christianity with Americanism or the Southern way of life. During the sixteenth and seventeenth centuries, the organization principle flourished briefly among the early Baptist, Quaker, and Free churches. These were radical, often socially utopian free associations whose members frequently took an active part in political movements. Most of these people, however, were either hounded into submission or expelled to America where they founded their own—unfortunately often theocratically ordered—states. Only in the past century have all the conditions been present for a flowering of the organization principle. Is it already going to seed? Christians have a special responsibility here. In a sense they started the whole thing. They preached about a Man who called not clans but persons, and who called them not *out of* but *into* the world. Freedom of association and disciplined world affirmation began with the response to this call; the principle of organization is the twentieth-century outcome. It is hardly cricket now for Christians to back down and call the whole thing a mistake.

Of course today's colossal organizations never completely fit the description of the organization principle just outlined. Today's organizations still atrophy and lose their flexibility. They obey Parkinson's Law and multiply functionaries when their function has vanished. They cook up spurious traditions or seek to inject an *ersatz* "family spirit" through the company house organ. Most seriously, however, they extend officious tentacles into the lives of organization members at points where the organization has no legitimate business. But when the organization does any of these things, it does so in contradiction to the anonymous, functional thrust of the organization principle itself. At all of these trespass points we have every right to blow the whistle on the organization—not because it is an organization but because it is trying to be something else.

Organization is increasingly the basic integrating principle of our society. In order to live in society we have to live organizationally. Now the question is how to do so responsibly. Many believe it cannot be done. Our street-corner prattle reveals a fatalistic resignation about the possibility of authentic personal responsibility in the organization age ("You can't beat City Hall"). The cynicism comes from diverse quarters. There is a curious similarity between the beat advocates of disaffiliation and the conformist junior executives: both have decided not to fight the system. The beat chooses monasticism; the conformist prefers adjustment. Between the two there rages a symbiotic love–hate dependence. In a culture in which thrift, ambition, and hard work are psychologically bound up with deferred pleasures and sexual repression, the beats supply a convenient *alter ego* on which the junior executives can project their incompletely sublimated sexual fantasies and their resentment of the organization. The beats gleefully perform their assigned social function. They are the well-fed court jesters of modern society. But they know how long their leash is and they instinctively bark within its limits. The beat poet and the young man with attaché case agree with each other wholeheartedly on one thing: the political power struggle in America is a dirty, disgusting business. The two occasionally lay aside their dissimilar life-styles long enough to clasp hands tenderly and sing imprecatory anthems against the crooked politician.

Meanwhile the organization rolls on, deepening and extending its influence. Within, however, a titanic struggle is now going on, the outcome of which will shape the countenance of America and of the world for decades to come. It is a duel to the death between the rising new technically educated class and the old class of zealous business barons. The prize in this contest is nothing short of control of the organization itself. Bazelon describes the conflict as a "rather quiet and mostly polite revolt of the Intellectuals," the people who are trained to work with concepts and whose mental skill replaces "property" as the way to produce income. These are the people who are today in fact carrying off a revolutionary seizure of power. They are attempting to take over the organization from its present controllers, the classic, hard-hitting, inner-directed managers whose forte was administrative command rather than cerebral competence. These men liked to be called "Boss." They were tough, resilient, and lived by a fairly simple free-enterprise ideology. The intellectuals want, quite simply, to be less managed by these corporate chieftains. They want to push the managerial revolution, the "organizational principle," even further. They have no interest in "marrying" the company like an old-style martinet manager, barking into six phones at once and dying in harness. They have a different style. But one should not be deceived by their soft-sell unpretentiousness. They hold the high card in today's technically systematized organization—they know how to run it.

They represent in effect the elite that is moving us from town to technopolis, but the chances that they will usher in paradise appear highly dubious. Like every revolutionary class before them, they have their own vested interests. Unlike preceding revolutionary elites, many of them seem interested in capturing the centers of power not to change things but precisely to keep things as they are. Many have simply been bought off, justifying the nastiest slams the beats can voice. Others, to revert to Marxist rhetoric once more, either have lost or never had any "class consciousness." They do not grasp what is going on in their own history or what role their own group is playing. If and when this kind of new elite gains mastery over the organization, there is no assurance whatever that they will use it more responsibly than their predecessors. Too many in the new elite either lack the willingness to use power or have no clear vision toward the realization of which power could be used.

We asked earlier about the peculiar psychological need our culture feels to stick pins in organization-man dolls. Now the answer becomes clearer. It is a residual element of tribalism, a fetish whereby the organization people purify themselves and stay in the organization without assuming responsibility for the battle now raging inside. It is a ritual by which they deny the distasteful reality, settle for a pseudo-protest, and thus abdicate the controls to others. It is a dodge.

But even if we wanted to exercise power in the organization, to what ends should such power be directed?

Here there is room for discussion, but certainly among these ends are (1) simply to produce the wherewithal for a world free of hunger, disease, and misery and (2) to extend the range of democratic decision making as widely as possible. Full production and democratic control should be the characteristics of an economic system. On both counts our system today is failing. It no longer does what it is intended to do—produce *and* distribute. Our society could produce enough to demonstrate to the world that industrial abundance does not require totalitarian politics. We are caught in the contradiction between the old free-enterprise ideology and the scientific-administrative actuality.

Our social vision must be revolutionary. The difference between us and the Communists is not that they favor a world revolution and we do not. Rather, we must espouse a different *kind* of revolution, a revolution that makes the fruits of the earth available to all people without depriving them of the benefits of political and cultural freedom. We must be *more* revolutionary than the Communists and we must carry through the revolution first in the United States if it is to convince anyone anywhere else. "It is required," as David Bazelon says, "that the most conservative nation in the world devote its great power to leading a world social revolution—beginning at home."

Our task in the age of organization is the recognition and responsible use of power. The frequent question, "How can I preserve my own individual values in a giant organization?" may be falsely put. From the biblical perspective, the first question is never "How can I save my own soul, skin, values, or personality?" Man is summoned to be concerned, first of all, for his neighbor. In the age of organization he can only do this by getting into the fray, by losing a little skin from his own nose, perhaps even a spiritual value here and there, in the tough but epochal battle for the control of the organization. But as he does leap in, perhaps at the risk of his own life, he may discover that, even in the age of organization, precisely he who loses his life gains it.

* * *

Notes

1. William Burroughs, *Naked Lunch* (New York: Grove Press, 1962).
2. David Bazelon, *The Paper Economy* (New York: Random House, 1963).
3. Dietrich von Oppen, *Die Personale Zeitalter* (Stuttgart: Verlagsgemeinschaft Burkharathaus und Kreuz-Verlag GMBH, 1960).

Microscale Concreteness

30 . Criteria of Success of Social Organizations . **Sir Geoffrey Vickers**

A sharp distinction is sometimes drawn between business management and public administration.   I believe that this distinction is much less fundamental than is often supposed; that its importance is growing less; and that it needs to diminish even further, if a mixed economy is to be viable.   I shall try to define the factors which are common to the regulation of all kinds of organization and thus to determine what difference, if any, there is in principle between the 'economic' decisions of business and the 'political' decisions of government and public service.

I spent half my life as a corporation lawyer, designing organizations to fit a multitude of different needs and conditions; and the other half, as an administrator, helping to manage a variety of such undertakings.   The differences of which I was conscious as a lawyer had little relation to the problems which concerned me as an administrator.   Varied as these were, their variety was much the same, whatever the nature of the organization and whatever the object of its activities.   Clearly there is much in common in the management of, say, a government department, a public corporation, a private manufacturing enterprise, a law firm, a professional body, a publicly administered hospital and a private charity. What is it?

Chapter 5 of *Towards a Sociology of Management* by Sir Geoffrey Vickers, © 1967 by Geoffrey Vickers, Basic Books, Inc., Publishers, New York.   Reprinted also by permission of Chapman & Hall Ltd.

The most obvious common characteristic of all these organizations is that they are all 'open systems'.   They maintain a form more enduring than their constituents by constantly drawing from and returning to the world around them materials, money and men.   This is most obvious in a manufacturing industry as it converts raw materials into finished products and scrap (consuming many other materials in the process); but it is equally true of a newspaper or a city government or a charity.   The visible activity consists in streams of materials, money and men, flowing inwards and outwards at varying rates through invisible but enduring channels.

The proverb has it that we never step twice into the same river.   It is equally true that we never go to work twice in the same undertaking.   It is also equally false; for these words 'river' and 'undertaking' do not denote unchanging substances, but continuing forms.   The language of business and administration is full of such words.   Capital, revenue, profit and loss; stock, throughput, turnover, plant; staff, wastage, work-load, capacity; all these and a hundred others refer to relations and aspects of relations between inflows and outflows, distinguished by administrators in the complex process which it is their job to regulate.   Some of these words define the state of a balance at a point in time, like the balance in a bank account or the water level in a reservoir.   Others define a rate of flow, such as the output from a production line or the volume of water over a dam, in some unit of time.   Yet others define the relation between two rates of flow, as do profit and loss.   All are descriptive of relationships.

There is nothing unusual in this.   The familiar forms of language conceal from us the extent to which the objects of our attention are not 'things' but relations extended in time.   I stress this, because the most essential common characteristic of the administrator's job in any organization is that he has to regulate a process extended in time.

The relations to which these words refer need not be constant; usually they are not. A bank balance is a bank balance, however much it fluctuates and whether it is black or red.   It can even continue to exist at zero, so long as the account remains open.   We have no difficulty in recognizing continuity through change, as well as time, provided the streams to which the relation refers continue to flow or are regarded as still capable of flowing.

On the other hand, organizations, like organisms and other open systems survive only so long as they keep their constituent variables within critical limits. Shortage of money, beyond a critical point, creates a self-exciting disturbance of relationships which overflows suddenly across all the activities of an undertaking, probably with irreversible effects; just as shortage of food, at a critical point, robs a creature of the energy to seek even the food it could get and starts a vicious circle which involves the whole complex system in dissolution.

Organizations, unlike organisms, have usually no built-in programme to govern their future growth and it is not normally the task of their regulators either to hold them constant or to follow a prearranged development.   But it is their task to keep the constituent flows sufficiently in phase to enable the system to *survive*.   Whether and how far they are also permitted or expected to generate the resources for future growth is a variable, marking one of the major distinctions[1] between organizations of different types.

Thus the management of every organization involves what I will call a balancing function of great complexity. A large number of inflows and outflows have to be kept at levels and within mutually related limits which are necessary to survival. These are relations so like those which enable an animal to go on generating the energy needed for survival that I will call them metabolic relations.

These relations, however, can also be seen in another way. They meet the needs of other systems; they thus serve a social function. They would not long continue unless they continued to be valued by the other parties to the relationship. Thus no organization—or so I shall suggest—can be described in terms of balancing alone. It is concerned also to fulfil the functions by which it lives; for these are conditions of its continuance. Some of these are also among its own *purposes*, in that their performance is regarded as a measure of success by the organization itself. Management is concerned to realize all these relations, in so far as it can. Their demands are multiple and partly conflicting and cannot all be fully realized with the resources available, so long as aspiration exceeds current possibilities of achievement—as our present culture insists that it always should. So management, in addition to its balancing function, has the task of realising what it judges to be the best combination of these functions which it can achieve within the resources available to it; or at least a combination good enough to satisfy its standards of success. It has thus what I will call an 'optimizing' function, though this would more exactly be called a 'satisficing' function, to borrow a verb usefully coined by Professor Herbert Simon. I will refer to the combined administrative task as 'optimizing-balancing.'

The combination and the conflict of balancing and optimizing is best seen in an organization such as a local authority, which has multiple, specific responsibilities imposed on it by law. In each of its functional fields, education, health, welfare, housing, highways, police and so on, it is responsible for maintaining some relation or group of relations within the standards regarded as acceptable by itself, the users and others concerned. Such relations may be qualitative, like the acceptability of the education provided, no less than quantitative, like the relation between the number of places in the schools and the number of children to be accommodated. At the same time, it must keep the total demand of this and all its other services within its total resources of men, money and materials, not to speak of those no less critical and less expansible resources, skill, time and attention. These resources are themselves not a datum but to some extent a function of policy.

The settlement of a budget by such a body involves the comparison of what seem to be disparate values. The process by which their relative priorities are decided and constantly changed is part of the political process. This process is not confined to organs of central and local government. The governing bodies of professions often have to compare proposals which cannot be referred to any one criterion, yet which conflict with each other or compete for limited resources—for example, proposals involving the protection of its members, its professional education, the public interest and its public image. Charitable foundations have to compare applications for grants for diverse purposes, all within their objects. Public corporations are often set by statute multiple tasks, which cannot be resolved into one. Thus the multi-valued choice[2] is a commonplace of corporate, as of individual life.

Everyone knows from personal experience that the control of an individual life, at least in our culture, involves the process I have called 'optimizing-balancing'— the regulation through time of a host of relationships, not all fully attainable, often sharply conflicting, so as to realize an acceptable combination of them with the resources available. The decisions which give effect to this regulative process are what I mean by multi-valued choices. Politics involves the making of multi-valued choices in the area where they have to be collectively made. Later ages wonder, as other cultures may wonder now, how anyone in a highly developed society like our own can cherish the belief that undertakings operating for profit in a market can escape the embarrassing value judgments inherent in the multi-valued choice.

This belief rests on two assumptions, both of which are even less true today than they used to be. One is the assumption that managing a business can be *fully* described as managing an investment and that therefore *all* the criteria which determine success in business management can be reduced to or derived from those which determine success in managing an investment. The other—a necessary corollary—is that companies operating for profit in a market can leave the multi-valued choosing to the individual buyers, to whom it rightly belongs. The market will convert their manifold priorities into signals which will guide the profit-seeking entrepreneur on the course best calculated to satisfy them, as well as himself—or will eliminate him in favour of rivals who can read the signals better.

Few people today accept these assumptions in the unqualified form which was acceptable to their grandfathers but even fewer, I think, realise how far they have been eroded or how far their residual truth is itself a cultural artifact, subject to cultural change.

They have been eroded by changes in economic conditions. In the free market of classical economics buyers and sellers were so numerous that price was a function of the market, independent of any individual operator. Such markets barely exist today in any important field, whether in goods or services, in foreign exchange or in labour which is only uneasily regarded as a market at all.

These assumptions have also been eroded by political changes. In an ever wider field—for instance, in the land and property market—the preferences and values expressed by individual buyers and sellers represent so small a fraction of the social valuing and preferring which is involved that the missing element is increasingly expressed either by public regulation of the market or by the entry of government, central or local, as buyers or sellers, using market mechanisms to express political choice. An increasing volume of individual needs can be satisfied only by political choice—for example, the need for viable roads, as distinct from automobiles, for viable towns, as distinct from houses. The social costs and values of all activities, public and private, demand entry into a calculus far beyond that of the market. Political choice, which is simply the multi-valued choice of a collectivity, rather than of an individual, takes over increasingly from market choice, as individual choice becomes over-charged with social implications; and thus displaces the market as a calculus of value, even whilst retaining it as a distributive mechanism.

The assumption that business success should be measured solely by the criteria applicable to managing an investment derived its validity—and still derives such validity as it has—from the fact that it was and to some extent still is incorporated in the mores of society. In so far as it is no longer so accepted, the reason is that society has developed wider and different expectations of business; and in consequence, business management, itself an integral part of that society, has responded by accepting these expectations and partly incorporating them in its own standards of success.

And this is just what we should expect, from any just appreciation of the psychosocial nature of societies. If we boggle at the idea in business, whilst we accept it in every other field, it is because the imposing structure of economics conceals from our notice the inadequate model of man adopted by the early economists—inadequate even in their day in its exclusion of his social nature but doubly inadequate today with the change both of market conditions and of social expectations.

This is, in my experience, a fact of common observation. Anyone who has sat on the board of a business corporation will recall the variety of items which come before it. They concern its relations with its staff and employees, its customers and its suppliers, its bankers and its rival colleagues in the trade, with local government, central government and several different public opinions. Although all these are considered for their bearing on the profitable continuance of the business, yet in every field discussion reveals other autonomous standards of expectation entertained not only by others but by the directors themselves about themselves and their undertaking. Their aim is not merely to survive and to grow but to attain and improve on those standards which, in every one of those fields, they have somehow come to regard as standards of success.

There is, indeed, a difference in degree between undertakings operating through the market and those which more directly formulate political choices. To this extent policy decisions in business are usually easier than those on more political bodies. Where growth, as well as survival, is culturally regarded as a major standard of success, metabolic criteria are more pervasive, at least up to whatever level is currently regarded as 'success'. I have already dissented from the idea that in this or any other field success means 'maximizing', rather than 'satisficing'.

Yet I think it well to insist on the ubiquity of the multi-valued choice, in business as elsewhere, because of the dangerous and increasing pressures to mask or ignore it.

It is often masked by concentration on problems of survival. Competitive enterprises are not necessarily less secure than others, nor do they necessarily feel so. (It has been my experience that successful competitive enterprises worry less about money than do most public monopolies, for the simple reason that they often feel rich, whilst public monopolies are carefully guarded from such dangerous euphoria.) Yet the metabolic relations of business undertakings are often more directly a function of their own policy and hence occupy more of their attention. And since they must survive by their own efforts in a necessarily uncertain future, the shadow of insecurity is never far away.

The multi-valued choice is also masked—in all undertakings but most easily in business undertakings—by the fact that all men of action hate it. It involves seeing a situation in more than one way, a conceptual feat difficult in itself and one which also vastly complicates the task of regulation. It is hard enough to keep the manifold variables involved in survival and growth in line with their governing relations. When to these multiple and often conflicting criteria are added functional criteria, requiring judgments which cannot be derived from financial estimates (though of course these must limit them) life for the administrator becomes even harder. Even in government, balancing budgets, realizing surplusses, improving 'efficiency', are often mistaken for standards, rather than mere conditions of success. In business, the traditional authority so to regard them reinforces a powerful natural inclination.

Yet the industrial policy maker shares many of the troubles of his more 'political' counterpart and there is every reason why he should. I once participated in the debate on an industrial board concerned to decide how high to set its target for export, in response to government emphasis that this should be given priority on national grounds. No one doubted that exports could be increased—at a price. Everyone knew, on the other hand, that every increase in export sales at that time would correspondingly reduce home sales, which were several times more profitable and would make it even harder than it then was to keep home delivery dates short enough to retain the business. It would have been easier, safer and more profitable to leave exports as they were; yet no one suggested this course. The struggle for survival was not at the time so fierce as to mask, in the minds of the directors, the other expectations which society had of them; nor would it have done so in the minds of shareholders, consumers or any other of the parties concerned, if they could have been parties to the discussion and the decision.

In fact, one need not look outside the range of metabolic criteria to find the endemic, multi-valued choice. At what point, for example, should stock levels be fixed, so as to secure work against the likelihood of interruption, without locking up more capital than need be? Rival answers appeal to the same metabolic criterion (we may call it maximizing 'profit' or 'worth' or what you will) but no known calculus can derive an answer without weighting dangers and probabilities in a way which we cannot specify and do not understand. Or to take a clearer example, how much of a year's profit should be distributed to shareholders and how much retained in the business? This familiar exercise involves not only the same unspecifiable calculations but also the assessment of conventional standards which are as much a part of the social mores as any other governor of behaviour and are equally a product of the process which they help to direct.

I invite you, therefore, to mute the distinction which we are accustomed to draw between 'political' and commercial policy; to accept the multi-valued choice as endemic in all collective, as in all individual regulation; and to disbelieve every attempt to reduce it, in theory or in practice, to logical deduction from a single criterion.

So far, I have argued this in terms of examples drawn from 'top-level' decision making; but if it is true, it should apply at all levels; and so it does. The girl in charge of a typing pool has to manage a bundle of relationships as disparate in their way and on their scale as those of the managing director. She has to handle a varying work load with a varying staff, in a manner sufficiently acceptable to her various clients (whose expectations and tolerances differ). She has to maintain the morale and the technical standards of her team, satisfy her own standards and keep the demands on herself within her own capacity and standard of acceptability. Each of these different dimensions has along it some point beyond which deviance will beget self-exciting confusion in the sub-system she has to manage. Within these limits her capacities and standards of regulation define the state at which she shall maintain the sub-system for which she is responsible. Her role contains in miniature the whole profile of management.

This also we should expect. Chester Barnard[3] first compared the relation of a corporation with its management team to the relation of the body with the brain and central nervous system. This is a sub-system not separate from the body but part of it, drawing its energy from the body's metabolic processes, dependent on the body for its continued existence; yet none the less regulative of the organism as a whole and capable of directing it on courses sustained through time; courses, incidentally, which may stress, jeopardize, even defeat its own self-maintenance. Since he wrote, communication engineers have designed regulative mechanisms as parts of larger systems, such as space craft and automatic factories, which make his model familiar from another angle.

An organization, like an organism, is a hierarchy of systems. Each is able to act as a whole only because its subordinate systems are so organized as to hang together—as the typing pool continues to function only because the woman in charge knows how to keep it together, even at the cost of staving off demands it cannot safely try to meet. Whatever be the level to which we happen to direct our attention, be it a plant in a large complex, a department of the plant or an office of the administration, we can assume a set of relations internal to it which keep it together and which are separate from and sometimes in conflict with the set of relations which links it inseparably with other sub-systems and with the larger configurations of which it forms part. It is a necessary function of management at any level to remember that many of the relations internal to it are external when viewed from the level of some sub-system on which it depends, a sub-system which has its own stabilities to guard and its own standards of success. These subordinate standards deserve close attention and unceasing

respect.   For the organization functions as a whole only in so far as its subordinate sub-systems function as wholes.   It is no less dependent on them than they
on it.

Thus the entire structure is a tissue of mutual expectations systematically organized in mutually supportive sub-systems, governed by standards which are partly
self-generated and constantly self-changed.   And it is itself linked to the society
within which it functions not merely by the mutual expectations of organization
and society but by the interlocking and multiple roles of every one of its members,
from top to bottom, especially those who form part of the management team.

I am sure that many of you remain convinced that for a business enterprise,
survival and growth are the necessary and sufficient criteria of success.   True,
these are pursued today within limitations more rigorous than existed a few
decades ago.   Public regulation, public opinion, organized labour and full employment impose on the operator requirements more exacting than his father
knew; but the basic condition (you may say) remains unchanged.   The operator
pursues a unitary standard of success, namely survival and growth, well recognized and accepted by the whole business community, even though he pursues it
within the limitations of multiple conditions.   Taking this view, you will find me
perverse in promoting these conditions to the status of rival standards of success.
All other types of organization (you may concede) from governments to charities,
exist to perform functions, sometimes multiple and conflicting functions and their
success must be judged by themselves and others by reference to such standards
of performance as may seem reasonable; but business is happily exempt from such
a multi-valuational quagmire.

If you take this view, I cannot prove you wrong; and I must defer most of my
further persuasion to a further talk (ch. 6 [of *Towards a Sociology of Management*]).   But because survival and growth hold so dominant a place in the
evaluation of business success, I will explore them a little further to show that they
are neither so unitary nor so precise as they are sometimes supposed to be.

The least questionable status that can be assigned to survival is simply this.
Few organizations aspire only to survive—except, perhaps, at moments when their
dissolution seems too imminent to leave room for other thoughts.   None, on the
other hand, can do anything else, unless they do survive.   Survival, then, is a
universal *condition*, but only occasionally a *standard* (or criterion) of success.

This claim is over-simplified, because it implies that survival and non-survival
are 'on-or-off', mutually exclusive states, like life and death, which can be pred-
icated of some clearly definable 'thing' called 'the organization'.   The actual
position is more complex.   Since an organization consists of many overlapping
systems, the interest of the regarding mind determines which of them shall be
regarded as critical and what degree of discontinuity shall be regarded as 'non-
survival'.

For this purpose the legal criterion of liquidation is almost irrelevant.   Liquidation incidental to reconstruction may leave unchanged all the significant relations of investors, managers, workers and staff.   Conversely, a discontinuity

which displaces them all may yet preserve formal continuity of incorporation—and a useful balance of losses, carried over for the benefit of the new owner's tax liability.

Consider *what* survival is threatened by the prospect of three diverse events—liquidation through insolvency; nationalization by compulsory acquisition of assets; and a take-over bid. The first is, potentially, the most radical, since it threatens the continuity of relations deemed critical by investors, managers, employees and creditors alike. But even in this case, the optimum path to 'survival'—more exactly, to preserving as much as possible of what they value most—may differ sharply for each group.

The second involves a dichotomy of a revealing kind. The company is threatened with the loss of its business but not of its capital. Even the business, lost to the company, will be virtually undisturbed. It will continue as a going concern within a larger system. Management may go with the business, retaining continuity of employment through change of employer or may stay with an employer whose business will be new. The investors will retain the substance of an investment which has wholly changed its form. In so complex a metamorphosis it is especially clear that what 'survives' and what does not depends on the position and the value structure of the regarding mind.

The third example illustrates in a different way the difference between legal and sociological realities. In form, the take-over bid invites no more than a voluntary transaction between buyers and sellers of shares. It has no direct effect on management, business or employees. It involves the board only to the extent that their advice will influence the potential sellers and is thus of importance to the potential buyers. In fact, of course, the directors are involved not only or chiefly as disinterested counsellors. Their past policy may be by implication criticised, their future is shadowed by doubt. Whether they will continue in office and if so with what colleagues, under what direct or indirect influence or curtailment of discretion, all this and more is at risk. Of all the relations which matter to them none may survive the change. Nor is the threat purely a personal one. The policies with which they have identified themselves may have become so much a part of the undertaking's character that others beside themselves regard the survival of the business as at stake.

Already several systems have emerged, each of which may be separately threatened. The shareholder's eye and the director's eye select for attention different aspects of the undertaking's activity and group them differently with others which are of concern to them. And each of them may view the company as an investment or a business activity or a social entity or in all these ways and will find different variables critical to each view.

These complexities do not exhaust the manifold systematic views which other eyes may select. Only one of my three examples is likely to threaten the survival of those systematic relations on which almost all the employees depend—the metabolic relations by which work done elicits money earned; the functional relations by which the same activities provide the doer with status, security, support and the opportunity to exercise skill. These sub-systems, however, are constantly threatened by changes which seem far less radical when viewed from the board-room. A minor change in production method may eliminate the whole of one or many such sub-systems, depreciating skills, altering relations and eliminating jobs. These are not less serious or less complex threats to those whom they affect than the threats to the board-room implicit in the take-over bid.

Survival is indeed no simple, unitary, on-or-off concept, to be transferred without qualification from the biological to the business world—even when its biological meaning is understood. In fact, the mythology of capitalism is haunted by evolutionary concepts which biologists outgrew decades ago.

It is still an honoured, if not a well-explored assumption of many business men that survival is not only a condition but an ultimate criterion of success; that every judgment can and should in the last analysis be justifiable as the choice of a best path to that unitary, metabolic goal, enhanced capacity to survive. This makes little sense in terms of evolutionary biology and much less in terms of modern capitalism. Evolution is concerned not with individuals but with species. It produces by elimination not necessarily the fittest but the fit enough—hence its infinite variety. It produces these types step by (usually) irreversible step—hence its 'wastefulness' and 'inefficiency' when judged by the standards to which our culture attaches value. It throws little, if any light on the behaviour even of species during the period, often reckoned in tens of millennia, during which they are disappearing—a state which no doubt includes all but a tiny and unidentifiable fraction of the organizations around us today. Great as has been the contribution of evolutionary theory to human thought, its influence on the mythology of capitalism must surely be reckoned on the debit side.

Leaving aside these more ambitious and illusory claims, the preservation of *some* set of relationships through time and change remains a condition, though not a criterion of success. I have stressed the manifold variety of relations which may be identified with survival not to diminish its importance but to stress its variety and its relativity.

When we turn to the other familiar yardstick, growth, we find the same variety and the same relativity; but the picture is even harder to compress into a small compass, so I will simplify it in terms of what seem to me to be the three main patterns, in terms of which it may be understood.

Consider, first, the relation of the manager to the system which it is his job to regulate. If his capacity is fully taxed, he will welcome any growth which will make his task easier—for example, by increasing the resources available to him in his 'optimizing-balancing' function or by reducing the demands on it—and he will correspondingly avoid growth in any dimension which would have the opposite effect. If on the other hand he is conscious of unused capacities in himself, he will try to expand his job to the limit of his powers. This tendency is commonly called power-seeking or empire-building. The terms are correct but I avoid them because they carry a pejorative sense which I wish to exclude. Our gratitude, as well as our hate, is chiefly due to power-seekers and empire-builders. The growth of economic, as of political empires is usually due to the initiative of the builders, rather than to any particularly favourable features of their resources or their circumstances.

This pattern is powerfully affected by another, our cultural attitude to growth. Here, in our present time and place, the main feature is the sharp difference between our attitudes to growth in the public and the private sector. Briefly, growth in the public sector still tends to be suspect and resented, even in fields of obvious and urgent need, whilst growth in the private sector still tends to be accepted and approved, or at least tolerated, even where the activity is widely regarded as futile or dangerous. This cultural pressure strongly modifies the attitudes, as well as the tasks of regulators in the two sectors.

A third pattern, not identical with the second, further affects the other two. This is the institutional pattern by which the resources for growth are generated. The main distinction falls between undertakings which recover their costs from users, members, supporters or subscribers and those which recover them from public revenues by acts of political choice. Private enterprises, charities and many public utilities fall on one side of the line, though the last are usually limited in their facilities for raising or accumulating capital. The rest of government enterprise falls on the other side. Bodies in which membership is in fact unavoidable for those concerned, as in many professional organizations and trade unions provide a curious intermediate case.

Thus the attitude of any manager towards growth as a criterion of success is mainly determined by the interaction of three factors—his own situation in relation to the current regulative state of his organization; the expectations entertained of him by the culture (which to some extent he doubtless shares); and the resources for growth which are available to him.

An unique course of history explains the present patterns in the second and third fields. Briefly, two successful achievements have bred their own reversals. One curbed the irresponsible exercise of political power and harnessed it to the private sector. The other built, within the private sector organs of economic power irresponsible to political control. The huge dichotomy is painfully healing; political power reluctantly accepts economic responsibilities, as economic power reluctantly accepts political responsibilities, each fortified in its reluctance by the cultural values developed in its previous phase.

Against this background, consider very briefly some of the variables in which growth may be seen by different eyes as a criterion of success.

Investors in profit-making enterprises—but not in other enterprises—rate the success of their investment in terms of increasing profitability and increasing net worth. Managers of profit-making enterprises, however, watch the growth of other indices also. (The old-fashioned entrepreneur, managing a business financed with his own money, did not have to distinguish between the elements of financial and entrepreneurial success; but his usually separate descendants, the investor and the professional manager, have inherited different parts of his estate.) The manager regards as a criterion of success growth in any variable, physical or financial, which enlarges the system he has to regulate (if he is under-stressed) or makes its regulation easier (if he is over-stressed). Changes in the structure of business have added increased value to growth in some of these dimensions. For example, the industrial manager is interested in the growth of those physical variables, notably turnover, which are associated with the economies of mass production; and all managers are interested in the growth of those variables—a wider set—which enable a business to carry a heavier load of overhead expenses and thus of expensive management skills and management aids (for example, computers).

On the other hand, mass production methods and a rising proportion of indirect expenses make businesses more vulnerable to any shortfall in demand below their planned capacity; and this is reinforced by a cultural valuation, dating from the 1930's, that under-employment of resources, especially of human resources need not and should not be tolerated. A system so set, is bound, if it succeeds, to run constantly into the troubles bred of scarce resources and to seek relief in physical growth, each step in which will raise the level not only of what can be used but of what must be used and will thus further speed the process.

This in turn speeds the concern of industry with the expansion and creation of markets. Competing industrialists found out long ago that they had far more to gain from expanding their total market than from competing with each other for shares in a static one. (It is rare for any business undertaking to prosper in a shrinking market or to fail to prosper in one which is expanding.) Hence the growing concentration of industry on the promotion of demand, which early economists could simply assume.

Government fans the flame for another reason. Standards of human expectation rise not only in those fields where desire can be satisfied by purchase across a counter but also in areas which must be defined by the political process, provided by the public sector and paid for at the public expense—in education, health, sanitation, public order, roads, transport and so on. And with a growing population, it costs ever more even to maintain these services at levels minimally acceptable by the standards of the past. Clearly, an ever larger slice of the gross national product is needed to satisfy these demands. But a powerful cultural valuation resists the growth of organization in this sector, however urgently desired its products and however obvious and resented its shortcomings, and still more fiercely resists increases in the proportion of the national wealth devoted to it. Since another conventional valuation precludes governments from manipulating preferences with the freedom used by operators in the private sector, the growth of the gross national product largely limits the rate of growth in the public services.

These are among the tendencies which have combined to create in Western cultures a self-exciting economic system of the kind we know. One of its effects is to give a central place to growth in the culture's value system and to draw this sharp and curious distinction between its valuation in the private and the public sectors—or, more exactly, between the sector which operates through the market (even though it is in no real sense *regulated* by market forces) and the sector which does not. The manager operating in the sector where growth is favourably valued will often find this valuation attached uncritically to growth in variables (especially technological variables) for no better reason than its association with the generally benign view of growth, just as he may find fields in which stability is, for no better reason, equated with stagnation—a powerful example of the power of words to pre-judge issues to which they are applied.

I am not concerned here to criticize these evaluations, still less to criticize them for being evaluations. I am concerned only to point out that they *are* evaluations, judgments made within the framework of a specific culture, themselves disclosures of that culture's setting and influences in its change. Like survival, growth is measured along many dimensions, valued from many standpoints and often adopted as a yardstick for reasons justified only by history or even superficial analogy. Such valuations, their differences and their conflicts are products of our culture, facts but also artifacts, perhaps the highest, certainly the most basic of our mental and social creations, permitting and demanding conscious, as well as unconscious change.

The significance of these conclusions, however, depends on a much closer understanding of the process by which standards of success in the minds of administrators are set and changed by the social process of which they are part. . . .

Notes

1. I have traced the varieties of organization along this variable in *The Art of Judgment* (ch. 11). (1965) London: Chapman and Hall, and New York: Basic Books, Inc.
2. I have developed this further in a paper, 'The Multi-valued Choice,' in *Communication, Concepts and Perspectives* (edited by Lee Thayer). (1966) Washington D.C.: Spartan Books Inc.
3. Barnard, Chester J., *The Functions of the Executive*. (1938) Cambridge, Mass.: Harvard University Press.

31 . Social Problem-Solvers . **James Ridgeway**

Abt Associates, Inc., of Cambridge, Mass., uses technology in attempting to solve complex social and economic problems. This is a relatively new sort of work, and to judge by Abt's success, it could become big business.

Two years ago Clark Abt, 37, quit his job as manager of Raytheon's Advanced Systems Department and went into business for himself. At Raytheon, Abt had tried his hand at applying technology to arms control research, but the government wasn't much interested and all in all the work was disheartening. Abt was intrigued with the possibilities of using technology in dealing with such problems as transportation and education, and since there was no opportunity for him to do this at Raytheon he took a gamble and started a research and consulting firm. To begin with he had two employees, and one small contract to help Educational Services, Inc. devise educational games for children. He soon got another small contract from the Pentagon which wanted Abt to do research in counter-insurgency.

These were meager enough beginnings. By the end of 1966, however, Abt Associates had gross sales of $560,000 and expect this year to reach $1 million. The staff grew from three people to 30, and Abt moved the office from a tiny clutch of rooms atop a machine shop on a back alley to a large new building. His business has shifted from the military to planning and the design of educational curricula for civilian government agencies and private industry. Most of this involves using techniques of mathematical modeling, computer simulation or human-player gaming.

Abt, who is both an engineer and political scientist with degrees from MIT and Johns Hopkins, does not care to be too closely linked with the fad in games. Nonetheless, the company uses games extensively, and its first major success came from designing several counterinsurgency games for the Pentagon's Advanced Research Projects Agency. The first of these was called Agile-Coin (Coin stands for counterinsurgency) and it sought to simulate some of the main aspects of the terror-phase of internal revolutionary conflict in a Southeast Asian setting.

Gaming gets pretty complicated, and the introduction to Agile-Coin helps explain what Abt set out to do: "If the problems of counterinsurgency could be described in terms of a small number of variables, like most physical processes, mathematical analysis could soon solve them. If the state of social science knowledge were comparable to that of physical sciences, in which most important variables and relationships can be defined quantitatively, direct mathematical analysis would possibly be more attractive than simulation.

"The situation now is that we must deal as best we can with a complex problem that has not been described in quantitative form. Simulation is one way of moving from the qualitative to quantitative, and from subjective impressions to objective analysis, theory building, experiment, theory correction, prediction and control. And that is the final objective of our applied research—control of insurgencies."

In Agile-Coin, actors represent insurgents, government forces and villagers. The insurgents and government forces are meant to knock each other off, at the same time gaining the loyalty of as many villagers as possible. For their part, the villagers try to keep losses down, stop the conflict as soon as possible and end on the winning side. In playing the game the actors can be spread around in different rooms, or, in an outside version, they use tents. In approaching a village in the game, the insurgent player is accompanied by Control; by flashing cards back and forth at the village player, the insurgent either is ambushed or admitted to the village. Once in the village, the insurgent can make deals, arrange an ambush, impress villagers into his service, or if he likes, assassinate the government's representative. All of this is accomplished by flashing cards and recording movements with Control.

Although Agile-Coin was constructed as a research tool to find out more about terror, the military were excited by its educational possibilities, and used the game in teaching officers about counterinsurgency at the special forces school at Fort Benning, Georgia.

Abt made two other games about counterinsurgency. One was called Politica or Counter-Conspiracy. It is a simulation of internal national conflict in a Latin American setting. The players find out what can happen in a "pre-revolutionary" conflict—whether it results in democratic change, revolution or reaction. The third game, and perhaps the most popular of all, is Urb-Coin. It resembles Agile-Coin, but in an urban setting. Now, the government and the insurgents, often disguised as members of the population, wrestle back and forth for control of the city. The actors representing the people get white "chips," those from the government and insurgents have blue and red chips. The chips are worn around the player's neck in a "chiplace," (an Abt word). In addition, the belligerents get weapons chips and bomb cards they can show if they want to blow up something. Cheating is to be expected, but this can be embarrassing. Once, a Pentagon officer who had been invited to play Urb-Coin got so carried away with his role as a secret agent, that he hid his weapons chips in his shoes. He was disgraced when an Abt employee pinned the officer against the wall and pulled off his shoes. Urb-Coin is used in training military police at Ford Gordon, Georgia. A version of the game, called Raid, proved to be useful in catching the attention of youngsters in the Boston slums. Raid is about a protection racket in the slums. The youngsters choose sides, some playing members of the protection gang; others are cops who fight the gang: and the rest are slum dwellers whose main object is to avoid paying money to the gang and stay alive.

Abt is matter of fact about the games. In part he sees them as tools for social science research. On the other hand, games have had some success in schools, involving youngsters in learning and getting them to see different sides of a problem. From the standpoint of Abt's business, games serve as both a promotional device and an interesting way of putting across research. For example, instead of presenting a bank with a thick report telling it what to do about a training program, Abt gives the management a game which he helps them play. This way they learn to see some of the assets and liabilities of various kinds of training programs. They can pick and choose as they wish from a "menu" of strategies provided by Abt.

Abt has collected a diverse staff of people around him. Most are in their twenties. "The cost effectiveness of people in their middle twenties is unbeatable," Abt says. The staff has capabilities in mathematics, physics, systems engineering, computer programming, industrial management, economics, political science, sociology, anthropology, psychology, linguistics, history and fine arts.

The employees sell as well as manage. Part of the idea in running the company is to hire unusual people other firms wouldn't take and turn them into efficient managers. Average salaries are $12,000 and profit is made very much a part of the "reward system." "The more you produce the more you get" was the way it was described to me. Abt holds out the possibility of a salary increase every six months and gives year-end bonuses. The company's stock is held by the employees.

In pricing the work, Abt figures out the total man-months involved in a project, adds on cost and a fee of from 10 to 15 per cent. In managing the research projects, he uses a computer to determine how many hours should be spent by each employee on the various projects each week.

The company now is engaged in a wide range of jobs, very few of them for the military. Last year Abt Associates designed an education system cost effectiveness model for the Office of Education. Now it is helping the National Science Foundation develop a way to measure the production of knowledge. The Foreign Policy Association has hired the company to make a game that shows the different foreign policy strategies that were available in dealing with the Korean war. Abt hopes professional actors will play this game on educational television; other games are to be serialized in trade magazines. The company is helping the First National City Bank with a curriculum for a new college the bank wants to open. It is designing curricula for Creative Playthings, CBS's educational subsidiary. And, for the first time, the company will make games purely for entertainment—games, Abt says, "a middle-class intellectual would like his kids to play."

A GAME FOR TRANSPORTATION

Abt does its selling in an offhand sort of way. Last year it demonstrated Agile-Coin, the popular counterinsurgency game, for 35 employees in the government, and this eventually led to a $50,000 contract from the new Transportation Department for a game to help explain some of the complicated economic and political interests that influence development of a new transportation policy for the Northeast corridor (Boston to Washington, D.C.).

The Abt people still are taking the kinks out of this game, but as Richard H. Rosen, the senior operations analyst at Abt described it to me, the game works something like this: Eighty different actors, representing different economic and political interests play for two days at simulating the economy and politics of the Northeast corridor. The objective of each actors is to come up with a plan that will benefit his interests. Nine rooms are required for play, three of them for negotiating.

Control has representatives in each room and they try to keep the game moving along. Thirty economic actors represent various business interests, such as the New York textile industry, the Providence jewelers, Connecticut and Massachusetts tool makers, etc. The communications industry actor is made to resemble the late Henry Luce. The economic actors lead off in the game, as they might in the "real world," by placing orders for raw materials and specifying how the goods are to be shipped.   As the economic actors go through the motions of buying, manufacturing and shipping goods in the Northeast corridor, the data are run through a computer, and begin to show the transportation system bogging down.   Each round of the game lasts about 40 minutes but with the help of the computer, the 40 minutes simulate a year's time (the game repesents what happens between 1960 and 1980).

The economic actors become more and more frustrated as the computer shows them losing increasing amounts of money due to late or lost shipments.   The businessmen actors look around for politicians to fix things up.   Now the political actors, who have been sitting on the sidelines, begin to play.   They represent all sorts of elected officials—senators, congressmen, mayors, heads of state legislatures—as well as representatives from political pressure groups, trade associations, conservation societies, state and local planning agencies.   There is even a team of actors representing federal bureaucrats who squabble over who gets to do what.

Everyone is equipped with a scenario of his role, telling him how he would be acting in the "real world"; otherwise, the play is free, and as Rosen says, "the actors can negotiate, lie, steal, cheat, anything so long as it's in concert with their objective, which is to make a transportation plan that satisfies their own needs."

SENATORS WILL SIMULATE THEMSELVES

After five or six rounds of wheeling-dealing, the federal government calls a conference and presents a plan, which in the test plays was hooted down.   More conferences follow, with state and local governments and other interested parties presenting different plans.   The haggling drags on; under the game rules, a new plan must be agreed upon by the end of the first day of play.   Rosen points out that in the "real world," one way to get political agreement is to wear down the participants.   Thus, in the transportation game, the actors have to continue playing into the wee hours of the morning until they agree on a plan.   This, says Rosen, "is a real simulation of reality."   During the second day of the game, a computer is used to break down the general plan into details, and then it simulates the new system.   The players watch to see how well it works.

The transportation game can be broken down to deal with regional problems. In one test play involving the states of Connecticut and Rhode Island, actors hammered out an interstate transportation plan.   Basically the problem was how to get workers in Providence to jobs in Hartford.   The participants agreed to build a high-speed rapid transit system from Hartford to Providence as well as a fast highway between the two cities.   These measures would facilitate transportation of both people and goods.   In addition, it was agreed that Connecticut should enlarge the Hartford airfield into an international airport, and a high-speed subway should be run from the center of town out to the airport. (The subway could interconnect with rapid transit systems coming up from New York

and down from Boston.)   To pay for much of this, Connecticut decided to float
a bond issue.   This was feasible, because the actors representing United Aircraft,
based in Hartford, agreed to buy the bonds which offered a good yield.   In
addition, United, which makes aircraft engines as well as the high-speed railway
equipment, stood to profit from the increased business.   Rhode Island got some
federal money to develop the Providence harbor, and more important, Connecticut promised not to develop the harbors of New London and New Haven, which
might have competed with Providence.   Thus Connecticut traded Rhode Island
the rights to build a major seaport in exchange for a big air center.

Abt plans to run the final play of this game within the next couple of months,
and the company hopes to heighten the reality by getting senators and congressmen and industrialists to represent themselves.

In the future, Abt would very much like to have the company open a new kind of
school which he calls the "Free School."   The children could start attending
when they were three or four and would be free to pursue at their own pace subjects that attracted them.   Abt is interested in getting children to teach one another and they would have a chance to do so at his school.   Some of Abt's
educational ideas may be put into practice in a somewhat different setting fairly
soon.   The company is discussing with the Office of Economic Opportunity the
possibility of running a Job Corps camp in a large city.   As Abt conceives this
project, the corpsmen would remain in the community, living in refurbished
tenements or houses.   The youngsters would do much of the teaching in the
camp, and would control its operation.

In using technology to solve social problems, Abt Associates, and companies
like it, raise some unanswered questions.   One is that this kind of enterprise can
very well result in removing decision-making even further from the people, by
taking it out of the hands of government bureaucrats and placing it in the hands
of a new kind of intellectual elite able to raise and solve political and economic
issues.   Abt tries to keep clear of this situation by insisting that his clients ask
the questions they want answered; Abt won't ask the questions for them.   But
what happens when a client has a dubious political aim it wants put across?   For
example, the purpose of the Agile-Coin research was to provide the client, the
Pentagon, with knowledge to control "insurgencies" in foreign countries.   Abt
says the company is "apolitical," but this is hardly so; its politics seem to be
defined by the interests of its clients, whether they are in the government or big
business.   Will technology result in making people's lives more free, or is it to
serve a small group of managers in their manipulation of society?   It will be
interesting to see how this group of intellectual businessmen deal with this question.

32 . Individual Facts and Group Facts
J. Milton Yinger

. . . One aspect of the tendency to blur levels of analysis is the fact that an important term may be used to refer to different systems of variables.   Careful attention to context may permit one to make necessary translations; but often this is not possible or is not done.   Since this problem will be dealt with at several points in the chapters [of *Toward a Field Theory of Behavior: Personality and Social Structure*] that follow, I shall only illustrate it here by reference to a term to be explored carefully later.

Anomie, in Durkheim's formulation of the term,[1] was applied to a social situation in which there was low normative agreement *among* individuals.   It cannot be measured or even conceptualized, as he defined it, except with reference to a group.   To speak of an anomic individual would be meaningless.   Strictly speaking, the term refers to the lack of cultural integration, the lack of consensus on norms.   Anomie does not imply some particular individual tendency (an equivalent normative confusion within the person, for example); a wide range of different individual patterns can be found among the members of a group that is anomic.   Nor does the term imply some particular pattern of social relationships.

Anomie is a cultural, a normative term.   The patterns of human interrelations that may occur within a group which is anomic are numerous; they are not implicit in the fact of anomie.   There may be conflict, or movements toward cultural reintegration, or the imposition of norms by those who are powerful.   To use the same term, as is sometimes done, to refer to a state of social structure, of culture, and of individuals is to imply a one-to-one relationship among the social, cultural, and personality facts.   Such usage obscures the basic research questions: What *are* the patterns of social relationships that develop under conditions of low cultural consensus (anomie)?   What *are* the various individual responses (which in turn become causes) to anomie?

This is not to imply that a cultural situation is a poor clue to probable individual and social structural facts.   To know that individuals are living in an environment that is anomic is to have valuable information about their possible personality development and behavior, as Durkheim showed in his study of suicide.   But Durkheim did not confuse the fact of an anomic cultural situation with individual facts.   Only a tiny fraction of those living in highly anomic situations commit suicide.   Others respond in different ways, perhaps destructive of individual and group values or perhaps creative.

Why do many terms refer to both individual and group levels without adequate discrimination between them?   The confusion arises in part because certain group and individual facts are found together empirically so often that one term seems to cover the complex of events in which they are embedded.   An individual's perceived obligations often do have a close association with the culturally defined role.   Anomie and individual normative confusion occur frequently together.   Even when we are concerned with purely psychological or sociological questions, we must study behavior, from which alone we can *infer* the inner structure of the person or the patterns of the sociocultural system.   It is scarcely surprising that we should sometimes confuse our inferences with the behavior from which they were derived.

The lack of precision in the vocabulary of studies of human behavior is related also to the pattern of academic training.   Most students of human behavior have been trained in only one of the disciplines concerned with the topic.   Few are willing to depart far from home territory—from the colleague group, the sources of prestige or promotion, the main reference group.   In our home territory we find the continuing work being guided by the same models we have learned to use. Under such conditions, we are proud of and are rewarded in proportion to the "purity" of our research model.   Yet insofar as we are interested in behavior, we are tempted to extend the reach of that model to cover all levels of influence. Our terms often reflect this tendency to explain the total range of facts by a partial theory.

The confusion of social and individual facts also rests partly on the measuring process.   Group facts are often averages or ranges that derive from summation or aggregation of individual measures.   To say that the average height of a group of men is 5 feet 10 inches tells nothing about any one individual, yet the group fact has been derived from a series of individual measures.   To discover that schizophrenics come in larger proportion from highly mobile urban areas, measured in averages, is not to say that the specific individuals who become schizophrenic experience high mobility.   It is now generally recognized as an "ecological error" to assume that the average measure of a heterogeneous area can be used to explain individual experiences therein.   Not all persons in an area of high delinquency become delinquent; not all persons in an area of high anomie experience normlessness.   Our vocabularies should be subtle enough to reflect the differences in levels of analysis to which we are referring at a particular time.[2]

Psychologically oriented persons sometimes assert that an aggregated fact has no importance in its own right, since it is derived from a series of individual facts. A moment's reflection will reveal, I believe, the error in this point of view.   We readily speak of a "peasant society" or a "middle-class society" to refer to situations where large majorities can be identified as peasants or middle class.   That is, the group designation is based on aggregated individual facts; but it is not confused with them.   To be a peasant in a society where 80 per cent of one's fellows share the same status is one thing: to be a peasant in a middle-class society is

INDIVIDUAL FACTS AND GROUP FACTS . 487

something else.   The proportion, which is a group fact, is of great importance in determining the meaning of the various individual facts, as can be recognized by comparing the implications of middle-class status in an "underdeveloped" country with its implications in a highly industrialized country.

Lazarsfeld and Menzel have distinguished between the kind of aggregative group property illustrated above, which they term analytical, and another group dimension derived from individual measures which is more readily recognized as a group characteristic.   The appearance of "stars" in sociometric choices, for example, is based not only on individual selections but also on their patterning. Lazarsfeld and Menzel call this a structural property of groups.   It is based on a relationship among the individual facts and thus cannot reside in them separately.[3]

There are in addition, of course, "integral" or "global" group properties that are not derived from facts about individuals.   The use of money as a medium of exchange and the presence of written rules are examples.[4]

The characteristics of individuals can also be classified in various ways. Cattell and Eysenck have sought to isolate "traits" by extensive factor analysis, a procedure that runs the risk of drawing an excessively sharp line between the individual and his situation, but is not inherently reductionist.   Lazarsfeld and Menzel have noted that some individual characteristics imply relationships with others.   They distinguish absolute properties, which can be obtained without further knowledge of relationships to others (income, age), relational properties (one's sociometric score), comparative properties (sibling order), and contextual properties (residence in a racially mixed neighborhood).[5]

The distinction between individual and group properties is sometimes overlooked because of an assumed parallel relationship between them.   Social class status, for example, may be referred to as a "sociological variable."   But as a measure of an individual's comparative level of income, education, and prestige, it is in fact an individual property.   The average status level of his neighborhood is a group property.   And the two measures may differ widely.   Lack of parallelism is clearly illustrated by a hung jury—a group made indecisive by the very fact that its individual members are decisive and unwilling to yield their positions.[6]

In his examination of the mathematical study of small groups, Coleman has noted that many such studies are in fact concerned with individual behavior. "These experiments develop generalizations about the behavior of an individual under certain social conditions, leaving unexamined the behavior of the social system which constitutes these conditions."[7]   Neither the analytic sciences of the individual and the group nor a behavioral science that studies their relationships can develop until their separate properties are clearly specified.

Some of those most inclined to interdisciplinary work are liable to the temptation to develop an interlevel terminology that blurs rather than integrates.   In an excellent chapter on roles, for example, Sargent writes:

> One reason sociologists have failed to agree upon a concept of role is that some have approached role as an objectively defined aspect of the culture pattern which can be

considered apart from the persons who actually enact or play the roles. Other sociologists include personal variables in their concept. The social psychologist, always concerned with individuals, naturally leans toward the latter type of conceptualization. His problem is to frame a concept of role which is broad enough to cover such cases as those just mentioned, yet specific enough to have meaning. Can we then define role so as to embrace cultural patterning and personal modifications, including that elusive but very important individual perceptual factor?

With these considerations in mind, I venture the following definition: *A person's role is a pattern or type of social behavior which seems situationally appropriate to him in terms of the demands and expectations of those in his group.*[8]

Although by this definition Sargent seeks "to embrace cultural patterning and personal modifications," the cultural element in the definition is lost. What an individual sees as "situationally appropriate to him" may or may not correspond to a role viewed as "an objectively defined aspect of the culture pattern." One cannot use the same term to cover these two different facts without promoting a tendency to confuse one for the other. (In Chapter 6 [of *Toward a Field Theory of Behavior: Personality and Social Structure*] I shall suggest a terminology to refer to the various levels involved in the concept of role.)

Sometimes individual facts can be used as an *index* of social facts if the operations involved are carefully specified. Selvin, for example, having no direct measure of the actual behavior of the officers in a military unit that might have been summed and averaged to arrive at a social measure of "leadership style," used the perceptions of the privates concerning their leaders' behavior.[9] Selvin was well aware that the perceptions of the privates were not the same thing as the leadership being measured; they simply comprised an index to that leadership. The only question in such usage would be "Is it a good index? Does it accurately measure what it is supposed to measure?" Although I have doubts about the value of this particular index (a problem I shall not explore here), the procedure is legitimate and often necessary. Properly used, the indexing process need not confuse different types of events. No one mistakes the rising and falling of mercury in a glass tube for the temperature changes which such variation records.

The confusion of social and individual facts rests, finally, on the kinds of units we have become accustomed to regard as "real." The boundaries of an individual can be comprehended by our senses; his reality seems self-evident. If a biochemist suggests that an individual is "nothing but" a series of interconnected cells, it is simple to emphasize that interconnectedness and to note that much which is important emerges only out of the pattern of their relationships. And, of course, the same applies to groups. Their reality lies in the relationships among individuals and cannot, therefore, rest with the individuals taken separately.[10]

Language patterns are the carriers, and in part the causes, of some of our difficulties in maintaining clarity in our view of analytic separation on one hand and empirical interaction on the other. I shall not explore here the thesis developed by Whitehead, Wittgenstein, Korzybski, and others that a philosophical picture of the world, broadly associated with Aristotle and reflected in the very structure of most European languages, distorts our perception and disrupts our logic.[11] It is now widely recognized that to say, e.g., "the rose is red" is to adopt a linguistic form that does violence to the process of observation and to nature. Less poetically but more accurately, we must note that redness is the result of the interaction of certain wave lengths and certain receptors in a particular situation: redness is field-determined. Thus we can reunite, in harmony with the natural world, what our linguistic habits have separated, which in this example is the perceiver and the perceived.

There is an opposite language problem, however, which also blocks understanding. Some terms are used as analytic constructs designed precisely to isolate some part of the empirical world, in order to study better the various combinations in which it may be found. If there is such a thing as substantial agreement among the members of a group regarding the proper ways for one of their members to behave when he occupies a given position, we need a name for that agreement. I shall call it a role. Now this is not behavior; nor is it the way the individual believes he should behave (although he may agree); it is an abstraction inferred from the words and actions of group members. It is a name for a consistent orientation to action shared by most group members. We need to conceptualize it independently in order to be able to inquire what happens when, for example, group agreement begins to fall off, or an individual who does not share the norms is confronted with expectations regarding them from others. What this means is that effective integration of a field or interlevel system requires, somewhat paradoxically, great clarity in the definition of single-level terms. I suppose saying this is to express some sympathy for the farmer in Robert Frost's poem who keeps insisting that "good fences make good neighbors." A wall, no; but a low fence, perhaps.

Notes

1. See Émile Durkheim, *Suicide*, The Free Press of Glencoe, 1951.
2. See W. S. Robinson, "Ecological Correlations and the Behavior of Individuals," *American Sociological Review*, June, 1950, pp. 351–357; Leo A. Goodman, "Ecological Regressions and Behavior of Individuals," *American Sociological Review*, December, 1953, pp. 663–664; Otis D. Duncan and Beverly Davis, "An Alternate to Ecological Correlation," *American Sociological Review*, December, 1953, pp. 665–666; John A. Clausen and Melvin Kohn, "The Ecological Approach in Social Psychiatry," *American Journal of Sociology*, September, 1954, pp. 140–151.
3. See Paul Lazarsfeld and Herbert Menzel, "On the Relation between Individual and Collective Properties," in Amatai Etzioni (ed.), *Complex Organizations*, Holt, Rinehart and Winston, Inc., 1961, pp. 422–440.
4. See *ibid*. and Hanan Selvin and Warren Hagstrom, "The Empirical Classification of Formal Groups," *American Sociological Review*, June, 1963, pp. 399–411. On the properties of groups see also Robert Merton, *Social Theory and Social Structure*, 2d ed., The Free Press of Glencoe, 1957, pp. 310–326; Raymond B. Cattell, "Types of Group Characteristics," in Harold Guetzkow (ed.), *Groups, Leadership, and Men*, Carnegie Press, 1951, pp. 16–52; Edgar F. Borgatta,

Leonard Cottrell, Jr., and Henry J. Meyer, "On the Dimensions of Group Behavior," *Sociometry*, December, 1956, pp. 223–240; and John K. Hemphill and Charles M. Westie, "The Measurement of Group Dimensions," *Journal of Psychology*, April, 1950, pp. 325–341.

5. See R. B. Cattell, *Personality: A Systematic, Theoretical, and Factual Study*, McGraw-Hill Book Company, 1950; R. B. Cattell, *Personality and Motivation Structure and Measurement of Behavior*, World Book Company, 1957; H. J. Eysenck, *The Structure of Human Personality*, John Wiley & Sons, Inc., 1953; and Lazarsfeld and Menzel [3].

6. *Ibid.*, p. 430.

7. James S. Coleman in Herbert Solomon (ed.), *Mathematical Thinking in the Measurement of Behavior*, The Free Press of Glencoe, 1960, pp. 13–14. My preference would be to substitute the term "processes" for "behavior" in the phrase "behavior of the social system."

8. S. S. Sargent in Rohrer and Sherif [John Rohrer and Muzafer Sherif (eds.), *Social Psychology at the Crossroads*, Harper & Row, Publishers, Incorporated, 1951], pp. 359–360.

9. Hanan Selvin, *The Effects of Leadership*, The Free Press of Glencoe, 1960.

10. Émile Durkheim, *The Rules of Sociological Method*, The University of Chicago Press, 1938; C. K. Warriner, "Groups are Real: A Reaffirmation," *American Sociological Review*, October, 1956, pp. 549–554.

11. See Alfred N. Whitehead, *Process and Reality*, The Macmillan Company, 1929; L. Wittgenstein, *Tractatus Logico-Philosophicus*, trans. D. F. Pears and B. F. McGuinness, Humanities Press, 1961; Alfred Korzybski, *Science and Sanity*, 2d ed., International Non-Aristotelian Library Publishing Company, 1941.

33 . Social Integration, Social Rank, and Processes of Interaction . Peter M. Blau

The relationships between patterns of social interaction and informal status observed in a recent field study of white-collar work groups in a complex organization seem to contradict some conclusions reached in an earlier study. This paper presents an attempt to reconcile these apparently conflicting findings by refining the theoretical conceptions underlying the earlier interpretation.

The systematic study of social interaction is essential for an understanding of work groups and, indeed, of all kinds of human groups. It is in the course of social interaction that group norms emerge and are enforced, that the relationships between group members become defined, and that informal status becomes differentiated along various dimensions. Processes of interaction define the social structure of work groups and the informal status of their members, and they, therefore, exert an important influence on the operations of the organization.

From *Human Organization*, Vol. 18, No. 4, Winter 1959–1960, pp. 152–157, by permission of the Society for Applied Anthropology.

Whereas systematic research on interaction processes in small groups has received increasing attention in recent years, for example, by Robert F. Bales and his associates,[1] field studies of work groups in formal organizations, in contrast to experiments with laboratory groups, have not been conspicuous in the development of this new approach. In field studies of work groups, there seems to be a hiatus between those which are concerned with social interaction but pay little attention to the quantification of empirical measures,[2] and those which provide quantitative information about *workers* but tend to ignore the patterns of interaction among them.[3] One reason for the scarcity of quantitative research on interaction in work groups is undoubtedly the fact that the methods developed for this purpose in the laboratory, such as Bales' Interaction Process Analysis,[4] although they have been used successfully outside the laboratory,[5] do not readily lend themselves to being used in investigations in formal organizations, where the disturbance created by observation procedures must be kept at a minimum. Chapple's simpler method for the quantitative study of interaction, however, can be applied to research in complex organizations without difficulty.[6] Nevertheless, its use in the empirical study of work groups has not become widespread.[7] A possible reason for this is that a conceptual confusion has plagued this method for many years.

A crucial concept in the systematic study of social interaction is that of origination of action. But this concept has been used to refer to two distinct social processes, which has resulted in much confusion, as William F. Whyte has recently pointed out.[8] Some investigators have employed the term to refer to the tendency of one individual to originate the *interaction* or social contacts between himself and others, whereas other investigators referred by it to the tendency of one individual to originate *activities* for others. This distinction can be easily illustrated. If A goes up to B and asks him, "What shall I do now?" and B tells him and A does it, then A has originated the interaction with B, but B has originated an activity for A. These are clearly two entirely different phenomena. The frequency of origination of interaction indicates the extent to which a member of a group takes the initiative in bringing about social contacts. The frequency of origination of activities for others, in contrast, indicates the degree of influence a member exercises over the rest of the group. The latter measure, but not the former, distinguishes leaders from followers. Whether the individuals who often initiate social contacts also tend to exert a disproportionate influence over the activities of others is, of course, an empirical question and not one which can be decided on logical grounds or by definition.

SOCIAL INTERACTION IN A LAW ENFORCEMENT AGENCY

In an earlier study of a federal agency of law enforcement, all interactions of a group of seventeen officials under a superior were observed and recorded for 30.5 hours, using essentially the method suggested by Chapple and Arensberg. The officials had separate desks in a large room. Whenever a social contact occurred, a tally was made, indicating who originated the interaction, and who was the recipient. (The duration of social contacts was also recorded, but here we shall deal only with frequency and not with duration.) On the average, an official had 8.3 social contacts per hour.[9]

This record of pair events furnished measures of the extent to which each official originated interaction, or social contacts, with colleagues and the extent to which he received social contacts from colleagues, as well as a variety of other indices, such as the amount of his social interaction with the outgroup—officials who were not members of his own section. The exact frequency with which an official originated activities for others could not be observed, but his informal status could be ascertained. In contrast to what Chapple and others have found in set events, various measures of social rank were not related to the frequency of originated contacts in these pair events, while all were related to the frequency of received contacts. Moreover, the extent of received social contacts, and not that of originated ones, was related to various other patterns of conduct of these officials.

Apparently, the extent to which others originated social contacts with an official was the aspect of social interaction which was most salient for his informal status in the group and which influenced his conduct most strongly. The specific findings were: First, competence was related to received contacts. Experts were more frequently contacted by colleagues than others, whether the measure of competence used is the evaluation of the supervisor, the respect of colleagues, or the extent to which others sought the advice of an official. Second, there was a direct relationship between received social contacts and amount of social interaction with the outgroup. Third, officials who received few social contacts seemed to be less apt to maintain under all conditions a detached orientation toward the members of the public with which they dealt. Fourth, there was a direct relationship between received contacts and the tendency to take the initiative in the discussions at official section meetings. Finally, the observer had the impression (without having a quantitative measure to validate it) that officials who received many contacts were more prone than those who received few to assume a dominant role in the interaction in colleague groups and to make suggestions which others followed.

The following interpretation was suggested for these findings: Competence as a law enforcement officer was highly valued in this organization. Experts were looked up to and respected, and this made them particularly attractive associates in the eyes of their colleagues. These officials originated social contacts with experts disproportionately often not only to ask their advice but also to seek their companionship, since associating with a prestigeful person is more desirable than with one who is not respected. (The original study showed that there were also alternative ways of becoming attractive to colleagues.[10])

By approaching a colleague often in the course of voluntary social interaction, the other members of the group give concrete expression of their positive feelings of attraction toward him. The frequency of received social contacts, therefore, furnishes a group member with social evidence of the degree of his acceptance by and his significance for his colleagues. It is in the process of receiving such behavioristic evidence of his social worth in the course of daily interaction that an individual becomes and remains integrated in his work group. The extent to which others originate social contacts with a person signifies how much social support he receives from colleagues and how integrated he is in his work group, and it strongly affects his feelings of security in the work situation. The greater insecurity of the official whose company is rarely sought by colleagues, as compared with the highly integrated official, tends to interfere with his ability to establish friendly relations with outsiders and to remain calm even in the face of excitable clients. Peer group support facilitates social intercourse beyond the boundaries of the ingroup.

It was further suggested—and this will have to be qualified, as we shall see—that a person whose status among colleagues is secure will find it easy to make suggestions in interaction with them, whereas an insecure status will discourage an individual from making suggestions and incline him to follow the suggestions of others lest his opposition further worsen his position in the group. This implies that differences in received contacts and integration give rise to differences in social rank and influence. If insecure group members are predisposed to follow the suggestions of the more secure ones, the former will become subordinate to the latter. These considerations would explain why officials who received relatively many contacts from colleagues tended to assume a dominant role in group situations, that is, in the discussions at section meetings and in the interactions of smaller subgroups.

SOCIAL INTERACTION IN A WELFARE AGENCY: A REPLICATION

A recent study of a public welfare agency in a large city provided an opportunity for replicating this investigation of social interaction among public officials in a somewhat different context. The interaction in four work groups, which shared a common room, each containing five or six caseworkers under a supervisor, was observed for 24.3 hours, using the same procedure as in the earlier study. The average number of contacts per hour was 10.3.

In this agency, it was possible to validate the use of received social contacts as an index of the individual's integration in his peer group. If the amount of contacts received from colleagues is actually indicative of an integrated position among them, it must be associated with being accepted by colleagues, that is, being the object of their positive sentiments. A sociometric index of such acceptance is whether or not a person is called by his first name by other members of his work group, according to the statements of the others. Table 1 shows that there was a direct relationship between the frequency of contacts received from colleagues and being called by one's first name by colleagues, a finding which serves to validate received contacts as a measure of integration.

In contrast to the law enforcement agency, however, expertness as a caseworker was not related to frequency of received contacts in the welfare agency. Not the supervisor's evaluation of the competence of a worker, nor the respect he enjoyed among his colleagues, nor the extent to which they consulted him when they had a problem—none of these indications of expertness was related to the extent to which others originated social interaction with a caseworker.

Table 1. Received Ingroup Contacts and Being Called by First Name by Members of the Ingroup

BEING CALLED BY FIRST NAME BY MEMBERS OF THE INGROUP	NUMBER OF CONTACTS RECEIVED FROM INGROUP PER HOUR	
	Four or More	*Under Four*
Yes	8	4
No	2	6
Total	10	10

Some of the other findings duplicate those obtained in the earlier study, but some do not. Thus, in the welfare agency, just as in the other agency, the frequency of contacts received from members of the ingroup was directly related to the amount of social interaction with the outgroup, that is, with persons who

Table 2. Received Ingroup Contacts and Total Outgroup Contacts*

TOTAL NUMBER OF CONTACTS WITH OUTGROUP PER HOUR	NUMBER OF CONTACTS RECEIVED FROM INGROUP PER HOUR	
	Four or More	*Under Four*
0.9 or more	8	5
0.8 or less	3	6
Total	11	11

* If caseworkers are divided, not on the basis of an absolute number, as in this table, but on the basis of the unit medians, the relationship becomes more pronounced; two-thirds of the 12 workers who received many contacts from the ingroup, in contrast to only two-tenths of the 10 who received few, had a disproportionately large number of contacts with the outgroup.

were not members of one's own work group, as Table 2 shows. Similarly, received contacts were in both organizations directly associated with detachment toward clients. Most caseworkers were observed as they interviewed several clients, and the observer classified their attitude toward clients in these interviews as positive, negative, or neither. The data presented in Table 3 indicate that workers who received many contacts from colleagues throughout the day were more apt than others to remain quite impersonal, expressing neither positive nor negative feelings, in their interviews with clients.   The fact that a worker reports that he rarely or never, rather than sometimes or often, worries about his cases after working hours, as another index of detachment, was also directly related to the frequency of received contacts.

Table 3.   Received Ingroup Contacts and Approach to Clients

APPROACH TO CLIENTS	NUMBER OF CONTACTS RECEIVED FROM INGROUP PER HOUR	
	Four or More	Under Four
Detached	9	3
Not detached	2	6
Total*	11	9

* Differences between tables in the distribution of the total row are due to the fact that not all pieces of information are available for all respondents.

Caseworkers in the welfare agency who received relatively many contacts from colleagues, however, were not more apt than others to participate in the discussions at official section meetings.   On the contrary, the recipients of frequent contacts were slightly less prone to participate in these discussions.   Moreover, an impressionistic classification of caseworkers on the basis of the amount of influence they seemed to exert in relation to colleagues revealed no relationship to received contacts.   Both of these findings contradict those obtained in the earlier study.   A comparison of the findings from the two studies is schematically presented in Table 4.

Table 4.   Correlates of Received Ingroup Contacts in Two Studies

	FEDERAL AGENCY	WELFARE AGENCY
1. Social rank as expert (three measures)	Yes	No
2. Extent of interaction with outsiders	Yes	Yes
3. Detachment toward clients	Yes	Yes
4. Participation in discussion at meetings	Yes	No
5. Assuming a dominant role with colleagues	Yes	No

RECONCEPTUALIZATION

Such contradictory findings might be simply dismissed as due to methodological error or statistical chance, particularly since they are based on relatively few cases in only two organizations.   But if we want to learn from our mistakes, we must take the findings seriously and re-examine the theoretical assumptions and conceptions on the basis of which some generalizations were advanced which are apparently not valid. Which concepts must be refined, which assumptions must be discarded, and how do the generalizations suggested have to be refined to account for the new evidence?

Conceptually, the earlier study failed to make explicit and to clarify the analytical distinction between various dimensions of informal status in work groups, notably that between social integration and social rank among colleagues. Specifically, the earlier interpretation implicitly assumed that the same social and psychological processes which lead toward acceptance and integration in the work group also give rise to superior rank. It was suggested that the group member who is attractive to others and often drawn by them into social interaction becomes not only integrated among his peers but ultimately also achieves a superordinate position over them. In other words, it was assumed that feeling secure enough to make suggestions freely is a sufficient condition for achieving a position of influence over colleagues, and hence that received social contacts produce differences in social rank. This proposition is contradicted by the second study, where it was found that received contacts and hierarchical informal status were not related.

Both the individual's integration in a group and his informal rank or hierarchical status are here conceived as resulting from the sentiments of the other group members toward him as they find expression in their interaction with him. Social integration refers to the individual's full acceptance by others which is manifest in their tendencies freely to associate with him in friendly social intercourse. Social rank refers to the respect and deference the individual commands among others which is manifest in their tendencies to follow his directives and suggestions. This distinction is related to the one between originating interaction and originating activity for others which was made at the beginning of this paper. The most direct measure of integration is the frequency with which others originate interaction with a person, provided that social interaction is voluntary and relatively free of conflict, and the most direct measure of rank is the frequency with which a person originates activities for others, although problems of observation often require the use of other indices. Social integration is not a scalar status, to use Barnard's term,[11] but social rank, of course, is. All the members of a group, or none of them, might be highly integrated, that is, fully accepted by one another, whereas the respect and deference which elevates the rank of some members subordinates others. An integrated position in a work group, since it implies social support, makes an individual more secure. But it does not give him a competitive advantage over other group members; only his relative rank does that.

A crucial difference between the work groups in the two organizations under examination was that the individual's integration and his informal rank were closely related in the one agency but not in the other. The experts who were highly respected and often consulted were generally also the better integrated officials in the federal agency of law enforcement, but this was not the case in the public welfare agency. The frequency of received social contacts, although it is an index of integration and not of rank, differentiated officials in terms of rank as well as integration in the federal agency, because these two factors were closely related there. As a result, the distinctive consequences of integration could not be separated from those of rank, and some misleading inferences were drawn. The findings from the welfare agency, where rank and integration were not correlated, make it possible to distinguish between the consequences of these two aspects of informal position.

Social conduct with the outgroup appears to be influenced by integration in the ingroup, whereas social conduct which places a person into competition with other members of his own work group is more apt to be governed by rank. Social integration and the peer group support it implies reduce feelings of anxiety and insecurity in the work situation. Whether an official feels free to establish relationships with others beyond the boundaries of his immediate co-workers, or whether he has enough self-control to keep his temper regardless of how excited clients become, depends on his feelings of security. Hence, such conduct would be expected to be influenced by the individual's integration in his work group. This is, indeed, the case; received ingroup contacts, as an index of integration, were directly related to the frequency of outgroup contacts and to detachment toward clients in both organizations. But feelings of security are not sufficient to produce success in competition with other members of the ingroup. Social conduct which involves competition between the members of a group, therefore, is influenced by rank and not by integration. Participation in the discussions at section meetings, where the members of the group compete for impressing the supervisor and one another, exemplifies such rivalry. Consequently, participation in those discussions was related to received contacts only in the federal agency where received contacts were associated with rank, and not in the welfare agency, where received contacts were only indicative of integration and not of rank. This interpretation implies that rank should also be related to participation at section meetings in the welfare agency. The data support this inference; five of the six workers who were highly respected by all others in their own work group participated much in the discussions at the meetings, in contrast to only five of the thirteen less respected workers.[12]

A question which still has to be answered is why received social contacts were associated with social rank in the federal agency. A major reason for this was that consultations among colleagues, although they occurred in both organizations, were more significant and prevalent in the federal than in the welfare agency. Such consultations involve patterns of social interaction in which the processes of social integration and of differentiation of status, which are otherwise distinct, become more or less fused. To clarify this point, it is necessary to analyze these two processes.

SOCIAL INTEGRATION AND SOCIAL DIFFERENTIATION

The accepting interaction of others with a member produces his integration in the group, and the deferential interaction of others with a member produces his superior rank.   An important difference is that rank becomes differentiated in unilateral social processes, whereas integration arises in reciprocal ones.   Ego's deference which helps to *raise* alter's social rank simultaneously *lowers* his own, but ego's acceptance which contributes to alter's integration does not impede but often improves his own.   Friendly acceptance invites, and, indeed, depends on, a corresponding accepting attitude of the other, whereas there is no such mutuality in deference.   Both the process of integration and the process of differentiation involve an exchange of social utilities,[13] but the nature of the exchange is quite different.

In order to become integrated in a group, an individual must motivate the other members freely to associate with him.   Unless they find him attractive, they will not be inclined to seek his company.   The newcomer, therefore, has strong incentives to try to make a good impression by displaying his attractive qualities and concealing any qualities which would make him unattractive in the particular group.   But his attempts to present an exceptionally impressive front will make him appear unapproachable and involve him, in effect, in competition with the others for maximum popularity in the group.   Although feeling attracted to him, the others will also feel threatened by his attractiveness, and this will put them on the defensive and prevent them from acting on their feelings of attraction and from approaching him to draw him into friendly social intercourse. To overcome these obstacles to becoming integrated, the newcomer must prove that he is easily approachable and that he wants to be accepted by the others and not to compete with them.   The form this usually takes is self-depreciation. Completely reversing his earlier strategy of attempting to impress others with his outstanding qualities, the individual now flaunts his weaknesses by talking about experiences which reveal him as blundering, foolish, or generally non-threatening.   Such modesty is disarming, because it demonstrates that the individual does not try to exploit his attractiveness to achieve superior standing in the group but only seeks to win full acceptance.   It obviates the need for defensiveness and consequently induces the others to accept the newcomer as one of them.   To maintain his integration, the individual exchanges his accepting attitude of others for their acceptance; the exchange is reciprocal.[14]

In order to achieve superior rank in a group, an individual must motivate the other members to respect his suggestions and defer to his wishes.   In the competition for relative standing in the group, each member has an incentive to withhold respect and deference from the others as much as possible.   These defensive tactics in the competition for maximum respect produce a potential impasse, just as those in the competition for maximum popularity do, but the method of breakthrough is different.   While an individual achieves integration by surrendering any claim to superior standing, a person achieves superordinate status by making a claim for deference which cannot be denied by others.   This requires that a person have resources which enable him to furnish important services to others. For example, his competence makes it possible for him to help others in their work.   By rendering services to others, an individual establishes social obligations.   These obligations constrain the others not to oppose his suggestions but to follow them, that is, to become subordinate to him. Their deference to him is not simply a concomitant of their respect for his ability but the result of the obligations which his ability has permitted him to establish. It is this exchange of instrumental services for deference which gives rise to differentiation of social rank in a group.

Let us now return to the question of why received contacts were related to social rank in the federal agency. In a consultation, where A asks B for advice, A originates the social interaction with B, and A also pays his respect to B by acknowledging B's superior competence implicitly in asking for his advice. Moreover, by accepting the advice, A lets his behavior be influenced by B's directives, and if the consultation is part of a recurrent pattern, he incurs obligations which will constrain him to follow B's suggestions in other situations.[15] The exchange which occurs in consultations gives rise to differentiations of status; it makes the informal rank of the consultants, who are also the recipients of the social contacts, superordinate to that of the questioners.

If all the social interactions under observation were consultations, therefore, received contacts would be indicative of superior rank. Of course, this is hardly a plausible assumption. A variety of other task-oriented social contacts occur in work groups, and a large proportion of the social interaction in most work groups, if not in all, are sociable rather than instrumental; this certainly was the case in both organizations studied. However, a larger proportion of the observed interactions in the federal agency than of those in the welfare agency were consultations (although no quantitative measure of the exact difference is available). This may well be one reason why received contacts were associated with social rank in the former agency but not in the latter. But this technical factor alone cannot answer the more basic substantive question of why social integration and social rank were related in the federal agency but not in the welfare agency.

Most federal agents were strongly identified with their work and highly valued expertness as a law enforcement officer. On the basis of this orientation, expertness became a characteristic which made an official generally attractive as an associate among his colleagues. In contrast, the thorough knowledge of procedures required for expertness in the public welfare agency was negatively valued by many workers, who considered a concern with procedures detrimental to good casework service. As a result of these conflicting values, expertness commanded only limited respect and did not make a worker a particularly attractive associate for most colleagues. In short, the respect commanded by technical competence had a halo effect which gave experts prestige and made them generally attractive in the federal agency, but not in the welfare agency. Moreover, turnover was lower and cohesiveness was higher in the federal group than in any of the groups of caseworkers. Long-established relations in the cohesive group discouraged the experts in the federal agency from exploiting their superior standing by making too great demands for deference. But in the welfare agency, experts often made such demands of newer workers, for example, by asking them to bring something for them. Social distance between those of superior and inferior rank seemed to be greater in the latter than in the former organization.

In the welfare agency, then, experts were neither particularly attractive nor easily approachable.   Workers went to experts for technical advice when they had problems with procedures, and they paid for the advice they got with deference, but they usually found other workers most attractive and thus did not tend to select experts as sociable companions.   The process of differentiation of informal rank and the process of integration remained distinct in this situation.   In the federal agency, on the other hand, experts were found to be particularly attractive and they remained relatively easily approachable.   Officials often went to the same persons for advice with whom they also engaged most often in sociable interaction.   Hence, the process of differentiation and the process of integration became somewhat fused in this organization.

CONCLUSIONS

Social scientists have often emphasized that social differentiation occurs along several dimensions.   Max Weber's distinction between social status, economic class, and political power is the most famous case in point.[16]   Although economic and political institutions do not have exact counterparts in small groups, other dimensions of social status can be distinguished there, too.   Much research on small groups, however, fails to make such distinctions.   Laboratory studies often introduce experimental variations in the feeling of being accepted by others and implicitly assume that they are dealing with differences in hierarchical rank. Field studies tend to contrast isolates and leaders in work groups, ignoring that these concepts refer to social position along two different dimensions.

To be sure, there are some exceptions.   Thus, Bales and Slater distinguish an instrumental and a socio-emotional dimension of leadership.[17]   The distinction made in this paper between social rank and social integration also refers to an instrumental and a sociable dimension of informal status in face-to-face groups, but there is an important difference between the two dichotomies.   Bales and Slater examine two aspects of *relative* standing in the group, whereas the concept of social integration is defined as a non-hierarchical dimension of informal position, in contrast to social rank, which is, of course, a hierarchical dimension of status.   To be sure, there are differences in integration in most groups; some members are more fully accepted than others.   And, occasionally, there may be little or no differentiation of rank in a group; equality reigns and no member commands the deference of others.   In principle, however, integration does not refer to relative standing in the group, while rank does, because acceptance is not an intrinsically scarce resource in small groups, but deference is.   To express feelings of acceptance toward some new members does not require withdrawal of acceptance from some of those who have already been integrated, but to manifest deference to a new leader inevitably involves withdrawing deference from the former leader, since by following the directives of one person, the group members, at least implicitly, refrain from following those of another.   Moreover, the acceptance of others is won and secured by being accepting of them and their normative standards, and this reciprocity exerts an equilibrating force on social integration.   To achieve a superordinate rank, in contrast, requires that a person command the deference of others *without* reciprocating by manifesting deference to them.

The sentiments of the members of a group toward one of them as they find expression in their interaction with him define his informal status.   An individual is considered to be integrated in a group if most others fully accept him and express their acceptance by often drawing him into sociable interaction.   An individual is considered to have superior rank in a group if he commands the respect and deference of most others and this manifests itself in the influence he exerts over their activities.   The frequency with which others originate sociable interaction with an individual is the most direct measure of his integration.   (On the assumption that the majority of social interaction in most work groups is sociable or has sociable elements, the total frequency of received contacts may be taken as an indication of integration.)   The frequency with which an individual originates activities for others is the most direct measure of his rank.

Differences in informal rank arise in social processes in which instrumental services are exchanged for deference.   The person who renders services to others —for example, by helping them with their work—establishes social obligations which constrain them to defer to his wishes.   Social integration, on the other hand, is the result of reciprocal social processes in which competitive advantages are ostentatiously relinquished in exchange for social acceptance.   After proving himself to be an attractive associate, the newcomer must demonstrate his accepting attitude of the group by modestly refusing to compete with the others for maximum popularity and by strictly conforming with group standards before he will be accepted by the other members as one of them.

The conceptual distinction between these two dimensions of informal status helps to clarify apparent contradictions in the findings of two studies on work groups in bureaucratic organizations.   The frequency of social contacts received from colleagues was related to more aspects of social conduct in the one organization than in the other.   The reason for this was that informal rank and social integration, as indicated by received contacts, were related in the first organization, but these two factors were not related in the second organization.   In the first agency, therefore, the influences of social rank as well as those of social integration on conduct were reflected in the correlations with received contacts. The data from the second agency, where this was not the case, make it possible to distinguish between these two kinds of social influence.   Patterns of conduct that depend on feelings of security but that do not involve competition among the members of the ingroup are influenced by the individual's integration among colleagues, because the social support inherent in an integrated position reduces feelings of anxiety and insecurity in the work situation.   Conduct which places an individual into competition with the rest of his own work group, however, is influenced by social rank and not by integration, because only rank gives a person a competitive advantage over other members of his own group.

Notes

1. A number of studies on small groups, many of which use the method developed by Bales, are collected in A. Paul Hare *et al.*, *Small Groups*, Knopf, New York, 1955.
2. See, for example, William F. Whyte, *Human Relations in the Restaurant Industry*, McGraw-Hill, New York, 1948.
3. See, for example, Daniel Katz and Robert L. Kahn, "Recent Findings in Human Relations Research in Industry," in Guy E. Swanson *et al.*, *Readings in Social Psychology*, Holt, New York, 1952.
4. Robert F. Bales, *Interaction Process Analysis*, Addison-Wesley, Cambridge, Mass., 1950.
5. See, for example, Fred L. Strodtbeck, "Husband-Wife Interaction over Revealed Differences," *American Sociological Review*, XVI (1951), 141–145; and William A. Caudill, *The Psychiatric Hospital as a Small Society*, Harvard University Press, Cambridge, Mass., 1958.
6. E. D. Chapple, with the collaboration of Conrad M. Arensberg, "Measuring Human Relations," *Genetic Psychology Monographs*, XX (1940), 3–146.
7. For an early application of this method in the study of industrial work groups, see A. B. Horsfall and Conrad M. Arensberg, "Teamwork and Productivity in a Shoe Factory," *Human Organization*, VIII, No. 1 (Winter, 1949), 13–25.
8. William F. Whyte, *Man and Organization: Three Problems in Human Relations in Industry*, Richard D. Irwin, Homewood, Ill., 1959, pp. 49–53.
9. See Peter M. Blau, *The Dynamics of Bureaucracy*, University of Chicago Press, Chicago, Ill., 1955, pp. 117–130, 138–139.
10. *Ibid.*, pp. 119–122.
11. Chester I. Barnard, "Function and Pathology of Status Systems in Formal Organizations," in William F. Whyte (ed.), *Industry and Society*, McGraw-Hill, New York, 1946, pp. 47–52.
12. The sociometric index of respect is based on answers to the question of who the three best caseworkers in the section are.
13. See George C. Homans, "Social Behavior as Exchange," *American Journal of Sociology*, LXIII (1958), 597–606.
14. A more detailed analysis of the tentative theory of social integration adumbrated here is presented in a forthcoming article.
15. See Blau, *op. cit.*, pp. 105–110.
16. H. H. Gerth and C. Wright Mills (eds.), *From Max Weber:Essays in Sociology*, Oxford University Press, New York, 1946, pp. 180–195.
17. Robert F. Bales and Philip E. Slater, "Role Differentiation in Small, Decision Making Groups," in Talcott Parsons and Robert F. Bales, *Family, Socialization and Interaction Process*, The Free Press, Glencoe, Ill., 1955, pp. 259–299.

34 . Social Structure and the Acculturation Process: Social Structure and Cultural Process in Yaqui Religious Acculturation
Edward H. Spicer

The theme of this paper is that the social structure of contact situations is an important determinant of the cultural change which goes on when two societies with differing cultures come into contact.   This proposition is certainly not new or revolutionary, but it often seems neglected.   If it is taken seriously, it does not permit one to advocate such generalizations as, for example, that under contact conditions material culture changes more readily than other aspects of culture, that core values (whatever they may be) are the most resistant elements to change, or even that traits from one culture which are incompatible with traits in another are resisted by participants in the latter.   It promotes abandonment of this type of generalization simply because it requires any general statement about sequences of change in acculturation to include some reference to the structure of cultural transmission.   It directs attention to the nature of the social relations through which contact is maintained and suggests that they have a determinable influence on the character of the innovations offered, on the acceptance and diffusion of these, and on the modification of the innovations which takes place.   The view implied is not that social structure is the major determinant.   It is rather that no instance of acculturation can be adequately described so long as the social structure of contacts is omitted, and hence that no change sequence can be explained without some consideration of the nature of the social structure.

I wish to illustrate the proposition by consideration of some cultural changes among Yaqui Indians of northwestern Mexico.   In the examples presented I shall try to show how the social structure of contact communities influenced changes in such cultural innovations as ritual artifacts, ritual behavior, and ritual beliefs.   The present paper does not present comparative data which would help

Reproduced by permission of the American Anthropological Association from the *American Anthropologist*: Vol. 60 (1958), pp. 433–441.   NOTE: The paper by Spicer was part of a symposium at the annual meetings of the American Anthropological Association at Santa Monica, California, December 1956.   The presentation ... grew out of an Interuniversity Summer Seminar on Differential Culture Change sponsored by the Social Science Research Council at the University of New Mexico, 1956.   Other participants were Edward Bruner (Yale), Helen Codere (Vassar), David French (Reed), E. Z. Vogt (Harvard) and Ronald Kurtz (recorder, New Mexico).—W.G. [Ed., *American Anthropologist*].

to illuminate the nature of the relationship between social structure and processes of cultural change. . . .

The innovations with which we are concerned are some of those introduced to the Yaquis through Jesuit missionaries in the years between 1617 and 1767. During that period of a century and a half, a large number of beliefs and rituals of Roman Catholicism were taught and demonstrated to Yaquis as part of the Spanish program for bringing civilization to the Indians of northwestern New Spain. It appears, moreover, that the overwhelmingly greater part of those introduced were accepted—the major occasions for ceremony in the Christian calendar, baptism, the cross and the sign of the cross, sacred dramas and dances, prayers, and so forth—including scores of different trait complexes. It is difficult to name any trait from the list of Christian innovations that was clearly rejected, unless we could so classify the act of confession and the concept of Hell; these came closest to being wholly rejected, but there were times when confession was accepted, and an idea of Hell as the origin place of irreverent ceremonial clowns is well established in Yaqui mythology (for inventories of borrowed elements, see Beals 1945: 107–118, 165–189; Spicer 1954: 114–174).

But to say that acceptance of Christian beliefs and rituals was general is not to tell the whole story. The acceptance may be characterized further as involving a very large number of replacements of the forms of native Yaqui religion by the introduced forms. Little beyond a few ritual dance complexes escaped this pervasive replacement. However, the borrowed forms were not simply accepted with the meanings explained or demonstrated by the Jesuits; in general it may be said that they were invested with a combination of the meanings of the replaced Yaqui forms and some of the Christian meanings, the old meanings in most instances predominating. Thus the general process that took place was a fusion of new forms with old and new meanings. This process affected the whole religious system and resulted in its transformation. Moreover, it was a type of adjustment of divergent traditions which extended to the political and economic systems, and in lesser degree to the kinship system. This is a process of contact change resulting in what Herskovits and others have termed syncretism (Herskovits 1948: 553–55).

It would be possible to illustrate the nature of the changes by choosing any one of dozens of elements in the Yaqui religious system. Whether we begin with one of the church sodalities, the conception of Jesus, the Mass for the Dead, godparent customs, the concept of grace, the drama of the Passion, All Souls ritual, or almost any of the traits or trait complexes of Yaqui religion, we find evidence of the pervasive process of fusion. For the sake of brevity we may confine ourselves in this paper to consideration of a single example—that of the relatively simple trait of the cross. However, because there are at least three distinct classes of Yaqui crosses, we shall consider only a single class.

THE PROCESS OF FUSION

Of the three kinds of crosses important in Yaqui ritual, one consists of rough pieces of mesquite wood, fitted together in the form of a cross, with the vertical member approximately three times as long as the horizontal. This is employed in five different spatial contexts (Spicer 1954: 139–154).

It is found embedded in houseyards. Every Yaqui houseyard has one such cross, usually to the east and some thirty paces from the house; it may be from three or four to six or seven feet high. The houseyard cross is a center of family rituals and of ceremonial sodality activities centering in the household.

A second context is that of the churchyard. The town church and also its counterpart, the temporary field altar, are characterized by crosses similar to those in the houseyards, though sometimes much larger. Their role in ceremony is similar to that of the houseyard cross, but with the church as point of reference.

A third context is that of the Way of the Cross, a ceremonial roadway extending for several hundred yards through a Yaqui town surrounding the church. The Way of the Cross figures in the dramatization of the Passion of Christ and is marked by fourteen rough crosses at regular intervals, representing primarily the Stations of the Cross.

A fourth context is that of individual graves in the cemetery in the churchyard. These crosses, in contrast to the others mentioned, may be permanently decorated with coats of paint, usually blue. They are the centers of regular monthly and annual family rituals in the cemetery.

The fifth context is that of the interior of the church. One of the standard pieces of altar equipment in every Yaqui church is a rough cross of varying size embedded in a section of mesquite. This is employed at various times on the church altar as one of the "santos." On the Day of the Finding of the Holy Cross in May, an occasion in the Catholic calendar, it is a central object of devotion.

Considering the location as part of the form of this kind of cross, it is clear that three of the five variants were direct Jesuit introductions. The churchyard, the grave, and the Way crosses—all located in relation to the Jesuit innovation of the church itself—are certainly to be so classed. The Holy Cross of the church altar equipment is also probably to be included among these, although it remains doubtful whether all of its ritual contexts were sanctioned by the Jesuits. The houseyard cross, on the other hand, was definitely an extension of the Jesuit introduction to a social context not defined by Jesuit teachings. The five variants, viewed in terms of form alone, thus include primary innovations from Spanish culture and secondary innovations growing out of these. That all probably involved replacements in the Yaqui ritual system is irrelevant to our analysis here.

Viewed with reference to meanings, the unworked cross presents no such relatively simple picture of a Jesuit introduction with extensions of context. In the first place, the most commonly employed names for these variants include both Spanish and Yaqui terms, the latter with associations which ramify deeply into non-Christian derived aspects of belief. The borrowed term *kus*—an adaptation of the Spanish *cruz* to the Yaqui phonetic system which does not permit initial consonant clusters—is employed for all the variants, but associated in each instance with Yaqui terms. Thus the houseyard and churchyard crosses are called *tebatpo kus*, loosely translated "patio cross," which as we shall see in our consideration of meanings constitutes a linkage with the concept of "sacred or sung-over ground," widespread in north Mexican aboriginal religious concept and most fully preserved in modern Tarahumara ceremonialism (Bennett and Zingg 1935: 286). Similarly, the combined Yaqui-Spanish term for the cross of the Way—*bo'ota kus*—also links this variant with a concept of ritual procession stemming from aboriginal ceremonialism.

Full consideration of the meanings of the unworked cross would take much space, but we may for purposes of illustration here confine ourselves to two of the focal meanings. Greatly simplified, these might be summarized as follows:

1. A female supernatural—*Itom Ae*, or Our Mother—who is the mother of all Yaquis and hence also the mother of Jesus, who was a Yaqui (Spicer 1954: 115–116).
2. A magical symbol which wards off danger and misfortune.

These two meanings are very closely related and lead at different times to the treatment of a cross as either a person or a thing. This is most clearly seen in the periodic dressing of the Holy Cross of the altar in skirts, necklaces, and other feminine wear, occasions which alternate with treatment of the cross as a piece of furniture. It is also apparent in the use of an alternative term to kus—Itom Ae, Our Mother—most frequently applied to the houseyard and the altar crosses. Full analysis in terms of meanings also shows intricate linkages of houseyard, churchyard, and grave crosses through the concept not only of the female supernatural, Our Mother, but also through the concept of the "sacred patio," or ground which has been removed temporarily from profane associations through being sung over and danced upon.

The various meanings of the unworked cross are developed to some extent in mythology. One myth which most clearly illustrates Yaqui thinking is the one in which it is told that Mary—Our Mother—turned herself into the tree which was made into the cross on which Jesus was crucified, so that he was held protectively in her arms during his last agony. In the myth it is clear that the cross is a loving female, associated with flowers and trees of the wild area outside the towns, whose protective powers triumph over any misfortune. These associations with bush, or *monte*, are explicit in the ritual of Holy Cross Day in May.

Enough has been said to illustrate the combination of forms and meanings in this one instance of a Jesuit introduction. Data bearing on the point have been published by Beals and other students of Cahita culture. What has been shown in the case of the one class of cross is demonstrable for scores of other ritual acts, ritual objects, and beliefs which have made up the Yaqui religious system since early contacts with the missionaries.

THE SOCIAL STRUCTURE OF CONTACT

The Yaqui communities in which this kind of syncretism took place were formed under the guidance of Jesuit missionaries as part of the general program of directed change undertaken by the Spanish government in northwestern New Spain. These communities took shape rapidly—in a period of five or six years—

immediately following the entrance of the Jesuits into Yaqui territory, that is, between 1617 and about 1625 (Decorme 1941: 326–32). Once established, these communities persisted for more than one hundred years under peaceful conditions. They differed in fundamental structural features from those formed among the Tarahumaras (Dunne 1948: passim) and the Upper Pimas in the same general region, despite the fact that the latter were also directed by Jesuits. The Yaqui communities were basically similar to those of the Mayos and the Opatas, except for some important demographic features which influenced cultural change differently in the latter (Bannon 1955: 128–39).

The primary innovators in the Yaqui communities were the Jesuits. They came to the Yaquis with high prestige as a result of their activities among Cahita-speaking people to the south. Both the agricultural and religious practices which they had introduced there were well known and highly regarded by Yaquis. They came at Yaqui invitation, after the Yaquis had defeated the Spanish soldiers and driven them out of the territory. At Yaqui stipulation, they came unescorted by soldiers and established themselves without any Spanish aides. During the hundred years of which we speak, the Jesuit missionaries—for the first years only three but later one or two for each of the eight towns—were the only Spaniards in residence. A few Spanish ecclesiastical and military officials visited the missions periodically, but encomiendas were not established, mines were not opened in or near the Yaqui country, and contacts with Spanish culture were therefore channeled almost exclusively through the missionaries.

The immediate result of the entry of the first two Spanish priests in 1617 was the nominal conversion to Christianity of all 30,000 Yaquis (Pérez de Ribas 1645). Like the Mayos, and in contrast to the Tarahumaras, the Yaquis accepted baptism on a mass basis and began immediately to cooperate with the Jesuits in a program of centralizing their eighty rancherías. Eight churches were built, together with their accompanying agricultural establishments, and these eight centers rapidly became the nuclei of large settlements. Within a half dozen years the new churches had become focal centers of towns of approximately 3000 inhabitants. It was in these newly concentrated settlements that the work of the Jesuits proceeded peacefully for the next hundred years. Some of the population remained outside the towns and offered passive resistance, but the overwhelming majority, without any direct application of force, accepted the mission community regime.

Although the communities were new creations in the sense that settlement patterns had been profoundly altered and the organizational framework of the Spanish town had been accepted, they were nevertheless communities in which the old leadership was still present. In contrast with central Mexico, there was no political decapitation. The successful military resistance to the Spaniards had stimulated a tribal unity and pride. As the Spanish form of town organization was adopted, the titles were assumed by men who had had responsibility during the previous military crisis. Without any Spanish military support closer than a hundred and fifty miles, the Jesuits built their influence on accommodation to the strong Yaqui leadership.

The role of the missionary in each of the eight towns was that of teacher and preacher. Under the rules of the Order, none was allowed to assume his duties without a knowledge of the native language. Each began to work immediately at perfecting his knowledge of Yaqui through a program of translation of prayers, the training of catechists or assistants in the church rituals, and of foremen of the herds and the agricultural establishment. The missionaries appointed large rosters of administrators for the sodalities introduced to carry out the dramatization of the Christian mythology. Administration of civil and ceremonial affairs in communities of 3000 or more required much indirect supervision. Each missionary was a prestigeful, influential, and active participant at the hub of affairs in the community, but he was working at only one level in what quickly became a highly integrated organization of Yaquis. The pre-Spanish extended families and ceremonial societies continued to function, and their members were free to interpret the meanings of the new words, concepts, and rituals which the Jesuits introduced. Moreover, the missionaries were generally inclined to preach new meanings for native ceremonies rather than to attempt to suppress them.

During the first hundred and twenty years, the Jesuits had a free hand in developing the Yaqui communities in accordance with their concept of slowly evolving transitional socioeconomic units in the Spanish Empire. Tribute was never exacted through the town organizations, nor was any effort made to impose individual land distribution. The Jesuits themselves required that Yaquis contribute the agricultural surplus, which grew rapidly under missionary tutelage, to furthering the missionary program to the north, but this was apparently accepted wholeheartedly by the Yaquis as part of the mission regime. Spanish civil authority rested lightly on the Yaqui towns until after the discovery of silver in the Mayo territory toward the end of the 1600's. A generation later, the full impact of the conflict in Spanish culture between civil and ecclesiastical authority began to be felt by Yaquis: in 1740, rebellion resulted and the Jesuit regime was disrupted. However, this was after nearly a century and a quarter of integration of cultural traditions in the mission communities. After a brief interval of suppression, the new developments even increased the autonomy of the Yaqui communities. The pattern of accommodation which had become so well established continued for another hundred and fifty years.

SOCIAL STRUCTURE AND CULTURAL PROCESS

The process of change which we have here called fusion or syncretism involves extensive modification of some features of innovations widely accepted by members of a society maintaining certain kinds of social relationships with members of another society which offers the innovations. The results of this process consist in a recombination of forms and meanings, giving the modified innovations a culture content quite different from the elements originally offered. In the Yaqui case, this involved primarily great differences in meanings and lesser differences in forms. At the same time, although this part of the analysis was not developed here, the modified innovations assumed functions which were identical with neither the partially replaced elements in Yaqui culture nor the elements offered as they had functioned in Spanish culture.

The conditions under which this fusion took place may be analyzed, in part, in terms of the structure of social relations that linked the members of the different societies. That set of conditions will be analyzed here as one determinant of the fusional type of process. We may think of what took place in Yaqui communities after the arrival of the Jesuits as a process in a system of communications. The Jesuits were attempting to communicate to the members of the Yaqui communities a large number of ritual artifacts, ritual behaviors, and ritual ideas. The effective communication of these depended on the nature of social relations maintained between Jesuits and Yaquis.

The innovations which the Jesuits offered were selected from the inventory of Spanish culture elements as a result of the interests of the missionaries as a speciality group in Spanish society. Their success in communicating with the Yaquis rested solidly on the role which they assumed in the Yaqui communities. In the first place, they had immense prestige as possessors of new ritual techniques and as dispensers of what Yaquis regarded as desirable food-producing resources such as cattle and hoes. But this prestige was merely a basis from which the missionaries worked. Equally if not more important in their successful communication of innovations was the position each missionary held as the organizer of a new community. This grew out of the plan for "reducing" settlements from many and often scattered rancherías to a few towns centered around churches, in which the missionary was the dominant authority.

The rapid growth of the eight towns under missionary direction, without application of military force, suggests not only the great prestige of the Jesuits among the Yaquis, but also the considerable restructuring of Yaqui community life. Under such conditions of rapid reorganization of local groups, the missionaries moved into strategic places for influencing change. Moreover, from the very beginning, with a knowledge of the Cahita language gained in activities to the south, the Jesuits enjoyed not only prestige and key social roles but also proficiency in the Yaquis' own means of communication.

The innovations, such as the cross, with which the Jesuits were concerned diffused through the newly forming communities along at least three lines: (1) to Yaquis, called by the missionaries *temastianes*, whom they selected for intensive instruction in Christian doctrine; (2) to Yaqui officials of the town organization who did not undergo intensive indoctrination, but who accepted the missionaries' authority in carrying out ceremonial and political functions; and (3) to the 3000 or so inhabitants of each town who attended church ceremonies and listened to the preaching of the missionary and the temastianes. In addition, the Jesuits instituted a system of indoctrinating children in mass groups which they collected at the church periodically, with the help of *fiscales* (Yaqui: *pihkanya' uchim*), church officials appointed by the missionary or his appointees. In this way, the missionaries and the temastianes assumed some of the enculturation functions of kin and other groups in Yaqui society.

The effectiveness of the communication of innovations along these various lines differed greatly. The temastianes maintained close and repeated contacts with the missionaries and may be assumed to have approached most closely to the missionaries' own understanding of the ritual innovations, but they still maintained residence in their kin groups and had to adjust their new knowledge to the ways of thought in such groups. The village officials had direct, but less close and less frequent contact with the missionaries in connection with their duties as organizers and leaders of ceremonials enjoined by the missionary, but the bulk of their interactions were in their kin and other groups and with one another. The general population of a town had only sporadic contacts with the missionaries except for attendance at Mass and other formal rituals.   Thus, as the innovations diffused through the established communication lines, there was abundant opportunity for attaching old meanings to new forms and for misinterpreting what was taught by the missionary.

This modification went on in settlements which were isolated from any Spanish communities that might have served as demonstrations and from any intensive contact with other Spaniards.   The community life went through a short period of reorganization, but there is nothing to indicate that there was any important disruption or breakdown in social relations.   Community life continued to be directed by old leaders whom the missionaries appointed to office or allowed the people to select.   The social relations in the towns were thus such that old patterns of behavior and old ways of thought continued as the cultural matrix of the innovations.   It would seem that there were conditions favoring a high degree of modification of the innovated forms.

Viewed in this way, the social structure of the contacts appears to be an important determinant of the process of fusion.   The wide acceptance of forms of Christian ritual and the extensive modification of their meanings both seem in large part explicable by reference to the social roles of the missionaries in the seventeenth-century Yaqui communities.   However, a complete explanation of the nature of the fusion would depend on further analysis of the situation in terms of the configuration of the Yaqui religious system at the entry of the Jesuits as compared with the configuration of the Catholic religious system.   Unfortunately, the data for such an analysis are far less satisfactory than are those which contribute to an understanding of the relationship between the social structure of contact and the nature of the cultural change.

References Cited

Bannon, John Francis, S. J. 1955.   The Mission frontier in Sonora 1620–1687.   United States Catholic Historical Society, Monograph Series XXVI.   New York.

Beals, Ralph L. 1945.   The contemporary culture of the Cahita Indians.   Bureau of American Ethnology Bulletin 142, Washington D.C.

Bennett, Wendell C. and Robert M. Zingg 1955.   The Tarahumara, an Indian tribe of Northern Mexico.   Chicago, University of Chicago Press.

Decorme, Gerard, S. J. 1941. La Obra de los Jesuitas Mexicanos Durante la Epoca Colonial 1572–1776. Vol. II, Las Misiones. Mexico, José Porrua e Hijos.

Dunne, Peter Masten, S. J. 1948. Early Jesuit missions in Tarahumara. Berkeley and Los Angeles, University of California Press.

Herskovits, Melville J. 1948. Man and his works. New York, Alfred Knopf.

Pérez de Ribas, Andrés 1645. Historia de los Triomphos de Nuestra Santa Fee entre gentes las mas Barbaras y Fieras del Nuevo Orbe. Madrid, A. de Paredes. (Microfilm)

Spicer, Edward H. 1954. Potam, a Yaqui village in Sonora. American Anthropological Association Memoir No. 77.

35 . Interpersonal Strains and Homosexuality
Alvin W. Gouldner

We might begin an effort, such as that following, to relate the contest system to Greek homosexuality by remembering Hector's soliloquy at the beginning of the twenty-second book of the *Iliad*, where he debates with himself the advisability of accepting Priam's plea to withdraw and fight behind the walls of Troy.   He considers the shame of such a retreat, counterbalancing to it the glory of an open fight with Achilles; then vacillating further, he entertains the possibility of stripping himself of his armor and entreating Achilles to accept terms in which Troy would return Helen and give the Achaeans half the city's treasure.

Hector decides against this course, however, for Achilles might "take no pity upon me nor respect my position, but kill me naked so, as if I were a woman. . . . There is no way any more from a tree or a rock to talk to him gently whispering like a young man and a young girl, in the way a young man and a young maiden whisper together."[1]   In effect, Hector's momentary fantasy is to approach Achilles as if he were a girl.   While it would be too long a leap to allow this to suggest that Greek homosexuality may, in general, be motivated by an underlying fear of aggression and express a quest for security by sexual surrender to the aggressive competitor, it is noteworthy that the contest between Achilles and Hector, the very paradigm of contest for Greek culture, did elicit this incipiently homosexual response.

Such a linking of the contest system with homosexuality may have something to recommend it, but it would lead into some of the more dubious depths of

From *Enter Plato* by Alvin W. Gouldner, © 1965 by Basic Books, Inc., Publishers, New York. Reprinted by permission of Basic Books and Routledge & Kegan Paul Ltd.

Freudian psychodynamics. I propose to bypass this here, linking homosexuality and the contest system through their interconnections with the friendship, system.

The competitive striving and envious sentiments fostered by the contest system could not help but profoundly affect the quality of interpersonal relations. In particular, friendships would seem of necessity to have been strained; as Aeschylus observes, "In few men is it part of nature to respect a friend's prosperity without begrudging him. . . ."[2] Aristotle reports it was "commonly said" that successful and happy men "have no need of friends," and he quotes Euripides' *Orestes* to that effect: "When Fortune smiles on us, what need of Friends?"

In what I think to be one of the most discerning analyses of the dilemmas of friendship ever written, Aristotle notes that men "cease to be friends" when they "drift apart in respect of virtue or vice or wealth or anything else. . . ."[3] If this is true, he asks, then how is it possible for friends truly to wish each other the greatest good? If they get their wish, "they will no longer have them for friends."[4] It would seem then that, if differential success impairs friendship, men must be somewhat ambivalent about wishing their friends well; they therefore cannot wholeheartedly feel the very sentiments deemed appropriate to friends. Because it induces men to seek relative superiority and fosters envy, the contest system inhibits men from feeling the sentiments incumbent upon friends and thereby undermines their relationship.

While friendly sociability is being thus impaired, the need for friends is, however, being heightened: there develops an endemic crisis of intimacy. As the extended kinship system continues to decline it became proverbial that "a man needs friends as well as relatives." There is a growing need for relationships in which a mutual revelation of selves might be made safely and in which feelings of lonely isolation could be overcome; there is, as well, a need for friends with whom one might enter into coalitions even if only temporarily in the contest for fame. Yet the competitiveness, envy, and distrust intrinsic to the contest system make this difficult. Indeed, so deep is mutual distrust that there is for a period an almost pathological fear of being poisoned.[5] As a result of these mutually contradictory forces the orientation toward friendship becomes profoundly ambivalent; on the one hand it is extolled and idealized as the most ennobling and gratifying of relationships, while on the other a pervasive and continual distrust of friendship is expressed. Friendship, like all else, is seen as evanescent and unreliable.

Although there are many forces that doubtless contribute to the development of homosexuality in Greece, homosexuality is probably also reinforced by this crisis of intimacy. Specifically, homosexuality may be seen as enabling Greek men to resolve their ambivalent orientation to men and to establish close relationships with some of them. The homosexual relation provides a basis for trust and security which, by allying interpersonal social needs with sensual or sublimated sexuality, can overcome the avoidance side of the ambivalence toward friends.

The use of homosexuality as a way of coping with the crisis of intimacy is also probably heightened by the decline of alternative forms of personal involvement. One of these, the dissolution of the extended kinship system, means a loosening of the individual's bonds with the family of orientation into which he was born. At the same time, however, these weakened involvements are not counterbalanced by deep attachment to the family of procreation. The low regard in which women are held in the classical period, as well as the seclusion of wives in segregated household quarters, reduces their contact with men; it makes them ignorant of the public affairs in which their husbands are often deeply involved and, to that degree, a less interesting and attractive companion than men.

In short, both the family of orientation and the family of procreation provide men with few opportunities for gratifying and secure personal friendships. These alternatives curtailed, the Greek male—who can, unlike his wife, move freely outside the home—is constrained to seek close personal relations with nonkinsmen, whether male or female. In this connection, the emergence of the *hetairai*, or courtesans, is no less relevant than the spread of pederasty: relationships with *hetairai* serve a similar function of relieving the crisis of intimacy, for men can, and do, talk to them.

The ability of the *hetairai* to function in this manner is, however, limited precisely because they are women. Although obvious, it must be stressed that the crisis of intimacy is most intense in relations among males, for it is the males who are competing most aggressively with one another. And it is only from other men that a man can obtain full validation of his public performance.

If, as we suggest, Greek pederasty is in part a response to the crisis of intimacy occasioned by distrust and envy, then pederasty must be most common among the males most deeply involved in the contest system, and thus most common among the upper classes or aristocracy. This, in fact, appears to be the case. In particular, the section of the aristocracy that affects the Spartan manner, the *Lakōnizontes* (or Spartan sympathizers), view pederasty as a Spartan and hence noble tradition.

Homosexuality, like other forms of sexuality, provides an apt occasion for the development of intimate communication, permitting mutual revelation and validation of the selves involved. The suggestion, then, is that Greek pederasty serves to satisfy a desire for personal closeness in a situation in which self-validation and intimate communication in the context of heterosexual relations is restricted and where friendship among males is undermined by distrust and envy.

If the need for a confidant who could provide validation of a man's public performance and self is one of the underlying motives for Greek pederasty, then we would expect that male slaves would not be preferred as lovers, and this, too, seems to have been the case. It is more difficult to communicate intimately about the self to another who is much lower in status; it is, also, more difficult for the very low to provide those higher with convincing validations of the self.

The same status considerations that inhibit the male slave from serving as an intimate also blocks Greek women from performing a similar role. Women's low status impairs the use of heterosexual relations for intimate and validating self-revelation, reinforcing the pattern of peer homosexuality among males. It is notable that while Greek homosexuality excludes the male slave, Greek hetero-sexuality includes the female slave. Inasmuch as intimate communication is not conventionally defined as important to heterosexual relations—except perhaps with *hetairai*—low or slave status need not disqualify a woman as a bedmate.

The ideal conception of homosexual relations held by the Greek upper classes stresses that they should occur between a somewhat older and a younger man, the former presumably serving as a model for the latter who, in turn, is supposed to admire, emulate, and learn from the elder with a view to earning his approval. (Doubtless this ideal of homosexuality is fulfilled in reality about as often as our own romantic conceptions of heterosexuality, if that much.) Even in its ideal form, however, the preferred homosexual relation is not seen as one between equals but stresses a well-defined system of superiority and dependence. This establishes an interpersonal context from which all hint of mutual competition has been eradicated, walling the relationship off from the usual stresses of the contest system. It thus provides a context in which the older male could receive a trustworthy validation of his superiority—one all the more valuable to the ex-tent that the younger is attractive and sought by others—while the younger man is able to be closer to men of higher rank and eminence who might sponsor his career, achieving public visibility greater than his youth might otherwise allow.

In one way, the prevalence of homosexuality is a cementing force in the male community, diminishing—as does the isolation of women from public life—the likelihood that their already tense relations will be further imperiled by competition for women. Yet there seems little doubt that homosexuality also heightens other tensions among males and exacerbates the strains of public life. First, there is bound to be competition among the older males for "fair and noble" youths. This would be difficult to isolate from their other forms of competition, which would now be intensified by feelings of sexual jealousy. Secondly, since public fame is a factor in making an older man attractive as a lover, the desire for sexual success would further motivate and exacerbate competitive efforts in the public arena. Third and finally, it is not socially inconsequential that pederasty at its worst could also be expensive; the eel-smooth, bright-cloaked, gold-ring-leted boys sometimes require costly presents. If the relationship between an older and younger man lends itself to exploitation, it is not always easy to say who is exploiting whom.

Even under conditions where homosexuality is endorsed by the upper classes and institutionalized, the homosexual relation seems to have been precarious and strained, lacking as it does a stabilizing involvement in the kinship system and the binding constraints of children, marriage, and dowry. In *Phaedrus*, Plato remarks that the lover is "always fancying that everyone is leagued against him. Wherefore also he debars his beloved from society; he will not have you intimate with the wealthy, lest they should exceed him in wealth, or with men of education, lest they should be his superiors in understanding; and he is equally afraid of anybody's influence who has any other advantage over himself. If he can per-suade you to break with them, you are left without a friend in the world. . . ."[6]

Socrates sums it up, quoting the verse, "As wolves love lambs so lovers love their loves."[7]

Homosexuality often exerts a disruptive effect upon the public life of the *polis* because of these strains, particularly its proneness to sexual jealousies, and because it is especially common among the upper classes most implicated in the contest system.   An example of this is the assassination of Hipparchus, the brother of Hippias, who, according to Thucydides, succeeded his father Pisistratus as tyrant of Athens.   Their government, says Thucydides, "was not grievous to the multitude, or in any way odious in practice; and these tyrants cultivated wisdom and virtue as much as any. . . ."[8]   Yet Hipparchus was assassinated by two lovers, Aristogiton and Harmodius: "Harmodius was then in the flower of youthful beauty, and Aristogiton, a citizen in the middle rank of life, was his lover and possessed him."[9]   Harmodius was solicited, without success, by Hipparchus, who, being rejected, insulted him publicly in return, thus exasperating Aristogiton on two counts.   In revenge the lovers slew Hipparchus, thereby inducing his brother to take alarm for his own safety and to make his regime more fearful and oppressive.   Rather than stressing the manner in which their homosexual love strengthened Harmodius and Aristogiton in a patriotic resolve to strike a blow against tyranny, as do Plato and the *Lakōnizontes*, Thucydides is quite clear that the affair was motivated by personal jealousy and the strains involved in homosexual love: "[O]ffended love first led Harmodius and Aristogiton to conspire . . .";[10] their daring action was "undertaken in consequence of a love affair."[11]

Notes

1. Here I think the point is more clearly seen with Lattimore's modern translation than with Lang's.   *Iliad of Homer* (Chicago: University of Chicago Press, 1962), p. 438.   I am indebted to my colleague Professor William Sale for calling this passage and its possible significance to my attention.   For Sale's discussion of the heroic value system, see his "Achilles and Heroic Values," 2, no. 3 (Autumn 1963), *Arion*, 86–100.
2. *Agamemnon* i. 60. 832–833.
3. Aristotle, trans. J. A. K. Thomson, *The [Nicomachean] Ethics of Aristotle* (London: Penguin Books, 1956), p. 241.
4. *Ibid.*
5. Ehrenberg, *op. cit.*, p. 198.   It seems that women, in particular, were suspected of being poisoners.
6. *Phaedrus.*   232C.
7. *Phaedrus.*   241C.
8. Thucydides.   400.
9. Thucydides.   400.
10. Thucydides.   402.
11. Thucydides.   400.

Postscript

This book is an attempt to promote sociological theorizing. I have tried to accomplish this by illustrating some of the range of present-day theory in sociology while, at the same time, trying to avoid some of the sourses of impotence that stand in the way of the would-be theorist. Impotence can manifest itself by too worshipful an attitude toward existing theories and the intellectual heroes of the past. As Michael Simmons puts it in the following poem, man must overthrow the Lord in order to achieve his image. In sciences the overthrow of the Lord, and his prophets, must occur rather frequently. However, impotence can also manifest itself in the opposite pattern, in excessive hostility toward the intellectual heritage. Here one danger is that one remains too ignorant of the contribution of others and is thereby doomed to repeat many of their accomplishments, as well as their follies. Another danger is inherent in the psychological price of perversity. Some degree of antagonism toward others may well serve as a catalyst for developing new theories. But doubtless there is a point where perversity becomes a full-time activity, where creative theorizing is extinguished. The heated debates between proponents of this or that school often reflect this impotence of perversity. In Michael Simmons' words, there is madness in the practical world; one's sanity is maintained if one accepts "the dialectic of the Lord" that includes both the need for irreverent overthrow of othodoxy and recognition of the fact that total wisdom "surpasseth man" while, at the same time, knowing that many languages—many approaches toward wisdom—are available.

The Lord's Dialectic*

When the Lord formed man of the dust of the ground,
and breathed into his nostrils the breath of life, He
neglected to tell man that he must
overthrow the Lord fully to achieve his image.

And in this neglection the Lord, in his wisdom,
created the sin of omission.

And unto this neglection was soon joined another sin,
that of commission, for soon it came to pass
that the whole earth was of one language,
and of one speech.
And those known as man, having intuited partially,
but not cognized fully, the cunning of reason,
aspired to build them a city and a tower
whose top might reach unto heaven.

And the Lord, upon viewing this subversive activity, went
down among man and, in His wisdom, confounded their
language and scattered them upon the face of the earth.

* From *The Undergraduate and the Lord*, an unpublished poem by Michael Simmons, Jr.
Published, here, by permission of the author.

And thus the Lord, in the glory of His praxis,
created the sin of omission, and also created He
the sin of commission, and then increased He the
glory and the magnitude of His creations,
by cleaving them one unto the other.

Thus, through the praxis of the Lord,
was created the sin of omission,
and was created the sin of commission,
which are known, when cleaved one upon the other,
as the Lord's dialectic.

And thus it was, through His praxis,
the Lord created His dialectic,
which is the burden of man.   And whose total
understanding surpasseth man, who is scattered
upon the face of the earth, but whose partial
cognition may be found among those who aspire to build them
a city and a tower,
whose top may reach unto heaven.

And thus it is in nations
whose language is liberal and humane,
and in whose practice is centered madness,
the many have learned that their sanity is maintained
in the acceptance of the dialectic of the Lord.
And the many aspire to be fruitful
and to have dominion over every living thing
that moveth upon the earth. . . .

This book has attempted, above all, to promote the view that the task of the theorist is to produce theories.   At the present time different kinds of theorizing are practiced by sociologists.   This offers opportunity for creative participation to persons of widely differing interests and talents.

The book also attempted to display the perspective and some of the resources available to the structural sociologist.   The concrete world may appear as harmonious, symphonic music or as discordant, irritant noise.   As Lévi-Strauss might put it, both cases contain themes and patterns whose orderliness can be discovered if we bring to it an empirically informed and intellectually daring sensitivity.   The Lord's "sin of commission"—the multiplicity of human expression—that gives rise to so much diversity can be disentangled.

SUGGESTED READINGS

Blau, Peter M.   *Exchange and Power in Social Life*.   New York: Wiley, 1964.
An effort to develop a theory of exchange processes that will cover a wide range of social phenomena.   Blau is aware that large-scale social phenomena have "emergent" characteristics that cannot be derived from the characteristics of

small-scale, person-to-person interactions. Yet the scheme is more successful in explaining small-scale phenomena than it is in explaining large-scale phenomena.

Buckley, Walter (ed.). *Modern Systems Research for the Behavioral Scientist.* Chicago: Aldine, 1968.
This book contains a rather broad series of papers using cybernetic models. Cybernetics and general system theory need considerable "shaking down" before cogent sociological theories emerge. These papers provide a refreshing relief from the overembeddedness of sociological theory in applied topics such as delinquency, race relations, and family stability. Several of the papers embrace the serious play with models that is a prerequisite to building theory.

Eisenstadt, Shmuel N. *The Political Systems of Empires.* New York: Free Press, 1963.
Combines broad, in-depth study of certain historical phenomena with recent structuralists' concern with highlighting a few significant variables; a combination of Weberian, theory-focused historical scholarship with Parsonian emphasis on social systems. Macroscopic sociology.

Etzioni, Amitai. *The Active Society.* New York: Free Press, 1968.
A review and synthesis of major recent intellectual trends. Conflict theory, structure-functional theory, cybernetics, and several other themes are clearly described and put to use in a model of society that combines effort to achieve analytic and predictive power with possibility of human control over the social destiny.

Gross, Llewellyn. *Symposium on Sociological Theory.* Evanston, Ill.: Row, Peterson, 1959.
Based on a movement in sociology and philosophy to analyze the internal and epistemological characteristics of social theory. The bridge between this type of work and the process of theorizing, which the present text emphasizes, has not yet been created.

Homans, George C. *The Human Group.* New York: Harcourt, Brace & World, 1951.
A fine model of groups as social systems. The method involves a reworking of several existing empirical studies. This is a favorite procedure of many theorists; data-gathering is often shunned as a time-consuming and laborious chore. The opposite extreme is a belief in the tangible reality that supposedly adheres to interviewing, data-sorting, computer-programming, and so forth. The model is formulated in qualitative form. Microscopic sociology.

Katz, Fred E. *Autonomy and Organization: The Limits of Social Control.* New York: Random House, 1968.
The main theme is that autonomy is a necessary component of most, if not all,

social relationships.   Autonomy tends to be incorporated into stable, structural arrangements.   Its location, scope, and function can be understood.   In
the operation of social systems, autonomy constitutes limits to control over
behavior.   Conversely, autonomy constitutes built-in indeterminance.   But
this indeterminance tends to have clearly defined limits.   For instance, members of organizations typically have areas of behavior in which they can exercise discretion.   Typically, also, there are rather clear stipulations of how far
the discretion may go—there are limits to their autonomy.   Structured
autonomy, then, is determinate indeterminance within social systems.

Leach, Edmund R.   *Rethinking Anthropology*.   London: Athelone Press, 1968;
especially Chap. 1.
Advocates the need to develop *generalizations* in contrast to comparisons:
". . . comparison is a matter of butterfly collecting—of classification, of
arrangement of things according to their types and subtypes . . . Instead of
butterfly collecting let us have inspired guesswork . . . But if you are going to
start guessing, you need to know *how* to guess. . . ."   To come up with guesses
that are apt to be generalizations one should think "of the organizational ideas
that are present in any society as constituting a mathematical pattern."   Leach
attacks functionalists on two grounds: (1) Their overemphasis on the relation
of parts to a whole.   He wants it replaced by focus on "the principles of
operation of partial systems."   This is somewhat similar to Merton's advocacy
of middle-range theories; see comments on Merton.   (2) Their overemphasis
on the *context* of phenomena, which makes it very difficult to develop
generalizations.
   Leach is an anthropologist of the Lévi-Strauss vein; his ideas are worth the
attention of sociologists.   For example, our concern with typologies sometimes comes close to butterfly collecting.

Lenski, Gerhard.   *Power and Privilege*.   New York: McGraw-Hill, 1966.
Presents a typology of societies based on technological development and
correlated forms of social stratification.   Strictly *social* variables—status
ranking, structuring of power, and so forth—are used in a model of social
evolution.   Macroscopic sociology.

Lévi-Strauss, Claude.   "The Story of Asdiwal," in Edmund R. Leach (ed.),
The Structural Study of Myth and Totemism.   London: Tavistock Publications,
1967.
A good example of Lévi-Strauss's structural sociology in this analysis of a
particular myth.   The thesis is that this myth contains, in highly intermingled
and blended form, a variety of "structural" themes that relate to fundamental
dilemmas of life in the society.   The dilemmas typically involve binary opposition—dialectics—that relate to such areas of life as economics, geography,
social relations, and cosmology, of which the members of the society are
aware.   In its concrete form, a myth is a symphonic piece.   To understand it
the sociologist must disentangle the themes and relate them to the various

frameworks that exist in the minds of members of the society. The frameworks, in turn, concern themselves with certain major spheres of social existence.

————*The Scope of Anthropology.* London: Jonathan Cape, 1967.
A brief view of Lévi-Strauss's conception of social structure. It is far less technical and difficult than his *Structural Sociology* (New York: Basic Books, 1963) or *The Savage Mind* (University of Chicago Press, 1966).

Levy, Marion J., Jr. *The Structure of Society.* Princeton, N.J.: Princeton University Press, 1966.
The work represents very precisely formulated and fully worked-out schemes of the social structure of societies. Heavy use of Parsons' functional scheme, but determined adherence to sociological (as opposed to psychological) features of social systems. Probably the most complete *sociological* framework in existence.

Merton, Robert K. *Social Theory and Social Structure.* Enlarged ed. New York: Free Press, 1968.
This book has a twofold claim to being a sociological masterpiece. (1) It advances a "middle-range" brand of theorizing that combines serious attention to empirical evidence with speculative formulation of explanatory models. However, one of the unanticipated consequences of promoting middle-range theorizing is that disciples of this approach have shunned large-("grand-")scale social phenomena in favor of small-scale phenomena. It is as though physicists were to regard the structure of planetary systems to be more "grand" in scale than the structure of subatomic particles; conceptually each is equally "grand," and equally "middle," even though, concretely, the phenomena take place on very different scales. Among sociologists, middle-range theorizing has tended to lead to concern with social-psychological problems, since these phenomena are, concretely, smaller than many other social phenomena. (2) In an age when sociologists are routinely accused of taking atrocious liberties with the English language, Merton's writings stand as beacons of light. Among theorists he comes close to enjoying a monopoly in the use of excellent English.

Nadel, Siegfried F. *Theory of Social Structure.* Glencoe: Free Press, 1957.
A structure-functional approach to sociology. There is attention to morphology and to delineating structures in ways that can be presented in visual models. Nadel does not actually present many visual models of social relationships, but his mode of thinking lends itself well to developing visual models. Roles are major units in Nadel's scheme.

Needham, Rodney. *Structure and Sentiment: A Test Case in Social Anthropology.* Chicago: University of Chicago Press, 1960.
This book concerns the subject of a heated intellectual debate between George Homans and David Schneider, on the one hand, and Lévi-Strauss on the

other. By itself, the book constitutes a fine statement of the difference between "sociologistic" social structure and "psychological-reductionistic" social structure.

Parsons, Talcott. *The Structure of Social Action*. New York: Free Press, 1968. Originally published in 1937 by McGraw-Hill.

———, and Edward Shils (eds.). *Toward a General Theory of Action*. New York: Harper Torchbook, 1962.

———, Robert F. Bales, and Edward Shils. *Working Papers in the Theory of Action*. Glencoe: Free Press, 1953.
Parsons's work remains the most impactful orientation in contemporary sociology. It contains few precisely stated theorems that can be proved or disproved. But it provides a many-faceted way of systematically looking at social phenomena.

Smelser, Neil J. *Theory of Collective Behavior*. New York: Free Press, 1963.
Social-structural approach applied to processes of change. Develops a model for looking at sequences of behavior that have traditionally been treated social-psychologically.

Sorokin, Pitirim A. *Contemporary Sociological Theories*. New York: Harper & Row, 1928.

———. *Sociological Theories of Today*. New York: Harper & Row, 1966.
A scholar of great depth and versatility. An excellent survey of "schools" of sociology.

Stinchcombe, Arthur L. *Constructing Social Theories*. New York: Harcourt, Brace & World, 1968.
This book exudes enthusiasm for actually doing work with theory; it is a good compendium for the present book. It displays theory-formulation processes around specific conceptual and concrete problems, especially Part Three. Its focus is on devising theory eclectically, to provide explanations of concrete occurrences.

Yearbooks of the Society for General Systems Research.
See comments on cybernetics under Buckley.

Index

Acculturation, 366, 503–511

Achievement-motivation, 388–390, 396, 424, 442

Action flow, 9

Actor, 11

Adaptive function, 19–20

Analytic theory, 3–4; societal analysis, 91–94; structure, 8

Authority relations. *See* Class

Autonomy, 46–47, 61, 519–520; bureaucratic, 38–39, 240, 311, 314, 326–327; Indian, 59; Islamic, 55; Japanese, 50; and modernization, 60–61; religious, 43

Birth control, 227

Boundaries of systems, 36, 156–157, 169, 191–205; maintenance, 33, 46–48

Boundary process, 21–23

Caste. *See* Stratification

Change, social, 6–7, 32–33, 162–164, 169–170, 172–173, 177, 180–182, 190, 231–245, 336–337, 341–343, 503–510; in capitalistic democracies, 181–184; Chinese, 52–53; and comparative statics, 268–270; and conflict, 393–396; economic, *see* Industrial society; in empires, 39–41; institutionalization of, 49–50; Islamic, 54–55; Japanese, 28; measuring, 410–418; models of, 156, 166, 188; predicting, 388–389; promoting, 389–418; in traditional societies, 387–388

Citizenship, 363, 424–431, 439–451

Class, 221–222; relations, 420–431

Classifications, 75–77. *See also* Totemism

Clique analysis, 323–325

Coercion, 221, 345; model of society, 187–191

Cognitive dissonance, 159, 329–345

Collectivities, 15–16, 183; collectivist approach, 167

Communication, 399–410, 412–414

Community, 169

Comparative statics. *See* Keynesian model

Competition. *See* Conflict

Computers, 375–377, 392. *See also* Simulation

Concepts, 105; conceptual structure of primitive, 71–72

Concreteness, 3, 359–367; macroscale, 362–364; microscale, 364–367

Conflict, 221, 392–396, 464–466; and homosexuality, 511–515; interorganizational, 159; management, 310–327; model of society, 156, 187–191, 361; staff-line, 314

Consensus, 221; and control, 178–179; defined, 178; formation, 179–180; model of society, 156, 187–191

Conservative, 157, 220–222; religious, 44, 51

Cybernetics, 156, 158, 165–167, 210–211, 243, 248–262, 362–363, 519

Data, 308, 359, 363; accuracy in, 381–383; analysis, 369–377

Demand flow patterns, 142

Democracy, 179–181, 363, 465–466; democratization, 181, 425–431; stratification in, 104, 222–229; and value systems, 435–459; and want conversion, 146–149

Determinism, in Keynesian model, 268; and morphogenesis, 251

Differentiation, 34, 36, 50, 139, 145, 164–165, 172, 311–327; political, 199–200

Discontinuity within nature, 78

Distributive justice, theory of, 330–333

Dual-society, 386

Eclecticism, 3–4, 360–361

Economic, analysis and simulation, 277–309; decisions, 467–479; growth, 403–404; models, 159, 249–250; national accounting, 378–385; statistics, 381–385; theory, 12–13. *See also* Keynesian model

Education, 422–423, 441–442

Elites, 222–229, 464–465; decision-making, 173–176; Japanese, 58; political, 435–451; religious, 43–44, 52; in traditional society, 387

Empires, 33–44

Entropy, 158, 211–213, 263–266

Environment and organizational change, 231–245

Equilibrium, in Keynesian model, 267–276; of social system, 188; systems and cybernetics, 248–249

Evolution, 78, 252–255; environmental, 231–245; of systems, 217

Exchange, 82–83, 518; informational, 242; social, 159–160, 345–357; system, 231–232

Explanations, reassessment of, 490–502

Family, 47, 86; Chinese, 52–53; Japanese, 30, 57

Feedback, 9, 249–262

Feudalism, Japanese, 56

Frameworks, 3–9, 155; macroscale, 5–8; microscale, 8–9

Functional imperatives, 16–18

Religion, in empires, 41–45; Islamic, 53–54; Japanese, 28–29, 56; Protestantism, 61–64

Research and development, 310–327, 479, 484

Role, xi, 11, 125–129; of theorist, x, 518

Sanction, 12–13, 33

Science, 405–406, 408; primitive, 69–71, 75–76

Secularization, 460–466

Simulation, computers, 278, 359, 365, 480–484; of economic development, 159, 277–309; game playing, 265, 480–484

Social action, 9; and change, 503–510; class, *see* Stratification; control, 403; participation, 360–361, 363; planning, 277–278, 291, 308, 358–362, 379–382, 388–418, 479–484; positions, 8, *see also* Status; problems, xi, 359–361, 365, 479–484; structure, 90, 125, 139, 521–522

Socialism, 430–431

Society, 11, 18, 221; dual, 395–396, 409–410, 415–416; traditional, 387–388, 409–410

Sociobernetics, 167–184

Sociometric structure, 310–327, 490–501

Status, 490–501; consistency-inconsistency, 159, 329–345; Protestant orientation to, 63; symbols, 38; system, *see* Stratification

Stochastic model, 218–219, 266

Stratification, 103–105, 420–431, 520; Chinese, 52; Indian castes, 59–60; in industrial society, 222–229; Islamic, 55; Japanese, 56–57; primitive castes, 85; in role relationships, 131–137. *See also* Status; Elites

Structural sociology, xi–xii, 5, 8, 32, 367; criticism of, 8, 32, 80–81, 361; and social change, 6, 48

Suicide, 336

Surveys, 369–371

Syncretism, 503–511

Systems, 6, 169, 198; analysis, 17–18; closed, 193–196, 214–215, 231–234; deviation-amplifying, 248–262; economic, 14–16, 18–20, 23–24, 277–309, 379–385; intra-extra societal, 200–205; open, 194–197, 215, 231–234, 236, 468; political, 191–205; social, 11–12, 15–16, 90–91

Systems theory, 6, 156–157, 206–220, 519

Technology, 242, 479–484, 520

Tension management, 17

Theory, doing, x–xi, 116–121, 496–501, 522

Time series, 376

Totalitarianism, 181, 224–225; and want conversion, 146

Totemism, 71–75, 82, 84–88

Training, of theorists, x, 4–5

Utility, 20

Values, 6, 46, 188, 363; cultural, 28–29; economic, 21; and goal attainment, 27–28; multivalued, 469–473; and the polity, 435–459; value system maintenance, 16–17

Voluntarism, 165–167

Want conversion, 9, 138–151

Yaqui, 503–510